D0789177

The Borderers

The Cornell Wordsworth

General Editor: Stephen Parrish
Associate Editor: Mark L. Reed
Assistant Editor: James A. Butler

The Salisbury Plain Poems, edited by Stephen Gill
The Borderers, edited by Robert Osborn
The Ruined Cottage and *The Pedlar*, edited by James Butler
The Prelude, 1798–1799, edited by Stephen Parrish
Home at Grasmere, edited by Beth Darlington
Benjamin the Waggoner, edited by Paul F. Betz

CENTER FOR
SCHOLARLY EDITIONS
AN APPROVED EDITION
MODERN LANGUAGE
ASSOCIATION OF AMERICA

The Borderers

by William Wordsworth

Edited by

ROBERT OSBORN

CORNELL UNIVERSITY PRESS

ITHACA AND LONDON

THIS BOOK HAS BEEN PUBLISHED WITH THE AID OF A GRANT FROM THE HULL MEMORIAL PUBLICATION FUND OF CORNELL UNIVERSITY.

THE PREPARATION OF THIS VOLUME WAS MADE POSSIBLE IN PART BY A GRANT TO THE EDITORS FROM THE PROGRAM FOR EDITIONS, THE NATIONAL ENDOWMENT FOR THE HUMANITIES, AN INDEPENDENT FEDERAL AGENCY.

First published 1982 by Cornell University Press.
Published in the United Kingdom by Cornell University Press Ltd.,
Ely House, 37 Dover Street, London W1X 4HQ.
Second printing, 1982.

Printed in the United States of America

Library of Congress Cataloging in Publication Data

Wordsworth, William, 1770–1850.
The borderers.

(The Cornell Wordsworth)
I. Osborn, Robert. II. Title.
PR5870.A1 1980 822′.7 80-11212
ISBN 0-8014-1283-8

The paper in this book is acid-free, and meets the guidelines for permanence and durability of the Committee on Production Guidelines for Book Longevity of the Council on Library Resources.

The Cornell Wordsworth

The individual volumes of the Cornell Wordsworth series, some devoted to long poems, some to collections of shorter poems, have two common aims. The first is to bring the early Wordsworth into view. Wordsworth's practice of leaving his poems unpublished for years after their completion, and his lifelong habit of revision—Ernest de Selincourt called it "obsessive"—have obscured the original, often the best, versions of his work. These original versions are here presented in the form of clean, continuous "reading texts" from which all layers of later revision have been stripped away. The second aim of the series is to provide, for the first time, a complete and accurate record of variant readings, from Wordsworth's earliest drafts down to the final lifetime or first posthumous publication. The most important manuscripts are shown in full transcription; on pages facing the transcriptions of the most complex and interesting of these manuscripts, photographs of the manuscript pages are also provided. Besides the transcriptions and the photographs, on which draft revisions may be seen, and an *apparatus criticus* in which printed variants are collected, a third device for the study of revisions is adopted: when two versions of a work match sufficiently well, they are arrayed on facing pages so that the steps by which one was converted into the other become visible.

Volumes in the series are unnumbered, but upon publication their titles are inserted into the list of volumes in print in the order in which the works were written. A more detailed introduction to the series may be found in the first volume published, *The Salisbury Plain Poems*, edited by Stephen Gill.

S. M. Parrish

Ithaca, New York

Contents

Preface

William Wordsworth's play *The Borderers*, a tragedy in five acts, was composed in 1796 and 1797 and remained in fair-copy manuscript form for "more than a generation of years."[1] In its early version it was entitled simply *A Tragedy*.[2] It was eventually named *The Borderers* and published, after much revision in 1841 and 1842, in *Poems, Chiefly of Early and Late Years* (1842). The early version is now for the first time published as a complete text, and the late version is set facing it so that the two versions, separated by more than forty years, may be compared.

The Borderers was Wordsworth's first major work, and stands at the threshold of the "great decade" (1797–1807). In the course of its composition in 1796 and 1797 he achieved the beginnings of a breakthrough to the blank-verse style and the dominant themes that characterize the outstanding long poems that followed it—*The Ruined Cottage* (1797–98), *The Pedlar* (1798–1802), and the two-part *Prelude* (1798–99), all now available in the Cornell Wordsworth series. The play is colored by the combination of Gothicism and sentimentality that typify his earlier *Salisbury Plain* poems (1793–96) and is stylistically uneven; hence it does not consistently attain the depth of insight and power of the very finest work that it anticipates. Yet *The Borderers* deserves greater recognition as a literary achievement than it has been given. It is to be hoped that the publication of the complete early version, its prefatory essay, and the manuscript drafts that precede that version will not only contribute to an understanding of Wordsworth's development as a poet but increase appreciation of *The Borderers* in its own right, as one of the neglected masterpieces of the English Romantic movement, in the "closet drama" genre of Byron's *Manfred* and Shelley's *Prometheus Unbound*.

In addition to reading texts of the early and late versions of the play, this edition presents complete transcriptions of the Rough Notebook, which contains the earliest drafts (MS. 1), together with transcriptions of the manuscript text of the early version with its prefatory essay and its later revisions (MS. 2) and the later manuscript (MS. 3) in which Wordsworth carried out the

[1] *LY*, III, 1387.

[2] The play is referred to simply as a "play" or a "tragedy" throughout the extant early correspondence, except for a single letter of 1797 known only from Christopher Wordsworth's brief report of it in *Memoirs of William Wordsworth* (2 vols.; London, 1851).

bulk of his revision for publication. For ready comparison, the transcriptions of MSS. 2 and 3 are presented on facing pages, followed by specimen photographs of MS. 2. An *apparatus* to MS. 2 provides cross-references to MS. 2A, a brief manuscript contemporary with the revision work in MS. 2. An *apparatus* to MS. 3 records further revision incorporated in the fair copy sent to the printers (MS. 4) and in the surviving proof sheets, and gives cross-references to further additions to MS. 3 in MS. 3A, separately transcribed. The variants in the printed text up to 1850 are included as a brief *apparatus* to the reading text of the late version, and variants in a second manuscript text of the prefatory essay are given as an *apparatus* to the transcription of the main manuscript. Transcripts and *apparati* taken together therefore provide the scholar with access to every stage in *The Borderers*' textual history.

The Appendixes present two poems connected with *The Borderers*, both previously published by Ernest de Selincourt in the Appendix of Juvenilia to the first volume of his *Poetical Works of William Wordsworth* (1940). The first of these poems, titled by de Selincourt *Fragment of a "Gothic" Tale*, is extant in Wordsworth's manuscripts only in extremely rough draft form, and the text presented by de Selincourt is essentially of editorial reconstruction. The Appendix to this edition presents a new and more accurately constructed text of the *Gothic Tale*, followed by transcriptions of the extant drafts of that poem, facing photographs of the manuscript. The other text presented is that of the *Argument for Suicide*, a brief blank-verse meditation touching on psychological preoccupations similar to those found in *The Borderers*.

The first scholar to publish materials connected with the early version of *The Borderers* was, of course, Ernest de Selincourt, who reproduced "The Hitherto Unpublished Preface to Wordsworth's *The Borderers*" in *Nineteenth Century* in 1926,[3] and included readings from the early version in the *apparatus* and notes to the first volume of his *Poetical Works*. Among the living, my greatest benefactors in the preparation of this edition are Jonathan Wordsworth, Marijane Osborn, Mark Reed, James Butler, and Stephen Parrish. Jonathan Wordsworth radically deepened my appreciation of Wordsworth, encouraged my interest in working on *The Borderers*, and has been my keenest, most percipient and long-suffering critic at all stages in my study of the play. Equal gratitude is due to Marijane Osborn, who turned aside from *Beowulf* to provide tireless skilled assistance and scholarly advice. The contributions of James Butler, Mark Reed, and Stephen Parrish became such that they are essentially co-editors of this volume. Their accuracy in correcting readings, their skill at reshaping matters of presentation, and their determination in carrying this project through have been as unflagging as their hospitality and advice have been generous.

[3] Pp. 723–741; see also his *Oxford Lectures on Poetry* (Oxford, 1934), pp. 157–179.

My thanks are also due to Worcester College, Oxford, to the Bodleian Library, to Cornell University, and especially to the Trustees of Dove Cottage. I am indebted to Cornell University Press for permission to incorporate in my introduction material from my essay "Meaningful Obscurity: The Antecedents and Character of Rivers," in *Bicentenary Wordsworth Studies*, edited by Jonathan Wordsworth (Ithaca, 1970). John West, in Grasmere, helpfully provided a number of the photographs. I am grateful to other friends who have supplied information and encouragement at various times, particularly to Adrienne Atkinson, Paul Betz, Tess Coslett, Beth Darlington, Kristine Dugas, Marta Emmitt, the late John Finch, Stephen Gill, Carol Landon, Joseph Kishel, Robert Woof, and the late Lionel Trilling. And finally, I am grateful to many students at Columbia and Lancaster universities whose engagement with Wordsworth has been a continuing assurance that the presentation of new texts of his early work is an entirely worthwhile task.

ROBERT OSBORN

Lancaster University
Lancashire

Abbreviations

ASP	*Adventures on Salisbury Plain*, in *The Salisbury Plain Poems of William Wordsworth*, ed. Stephen Gill (Ithaca, 1975).
BNYPL	*Bulletin of the New York Public Library.*
Chronology: EY	Mark L. Reed, *Wordsworth: The Chronology of the Early Years, 1770–1799* (Cambridge Mass., 1967).
Chronology: MY	Mark L. Reed, *Wordsworth: The Chronology of the Middle Years, 1800–1815* (Cambridge, Mass., 1975).
DC MS.	Dove Cottage manuscript.
DCP	Dove Cottage miscellaneous manuscript, unnumbered.
DW	Dorothy Wordsworth.
EV	The completed early version of *The Borderers* (citations by act, scene, and line number).
EY	*Letters of William and Dorothy Wordsworth: The Early Years, 1787–1805*, ed. Ernest de Selincourt (2d ed.; rev. Chester L. Shaver, Oxford, 1967).
GT	*Gothic Tale*, fragment, constructed reading text.
JC	John Carter, Wordsworth's secretary at Rydal Mount.
LV	The completed late version of *The Borderers*, published in *Poems, Chiefly of Early and Late Years* (citations by line number).
LY	*Letters of William and Dorothy Wordsworth: The Later Years, 1821–1850*, ed. Ernest de Selincourt (3 vols.; Oxford, 1939).
MH	Mary Hutchinson, later Mary Wordsworth.
M of H	Jonathan Wordsworth, *The Music of Humanity* (London, 1969).
Moorman	Mary Moorman, *William Wordsworth: A Biography* (2 vols.; Oxford, 1957, 1965).
MS. 1	The Rough Notebook for *The Borderers*, DC MS. 12.
MS. 2	The early version of *The Borderers*, with late revisions, in DC MS. 23.
MS. 2A	Drafts drawn up in revision of *The Borderers* in DC MS. 151/8, formerly Verse 102 (7).
MS. 3	The late version of *The Borderers* in DC MS. 148, formerly Verse 16.
MS. 3A	Drafts drawn up in revision of *The Borderers* in DC MS. 151/3, formerly Verse 102(2).
MS. 4	The late version of *The Borderers* in DC MS 149, formerly Verse 17 (except for the final leaf).
MS. 4a	The final leaf of DC MS. 149.
MW	Mary Wordsworth.
PELY	William Wordsworth, *Poems, Chiefly of Early and Late Years* (London, 1842).
Prelude	*The Prelude*, ed. Ernest de Selincourt, rev. Helen Darbishire (2d ed.; Oxford, 1959). References are to the 1805 text.

Prose	*The Prose Works of William Wordsworth*, ed. W. J. B. Owen and J. W. Smyser (3 vols.; Oxford, 1974).
PW	*The Poetical Works of William Wordsworth*, ed. Ernest de Selincourt and Helen Darbishire (5 vols.; Oxford, 1940–49; rev. 1952–59).
RC	*The Ruined Cottage*, from "*The Ruined Cottage*" *and* "*The Pedlar*" *by William Wordsworth*, ed. James Butler (Ithaca, 1979). References are to the MS. B text unless otherwise stated.
SH	Sara Hutchinson.
SPP	*The Salisbury Plain Poems of William Wordsworth*, ed. Stephen Gill (Ithaca, 1975).
STC	Samuel Taylor Coleridge.
STCL	*Collected Letters of Samuel Taylor Coleridge*, ed. Earl Leslie Griggs (6 vols.; Oxford, 1956–71).
WW	William Wordsworth.

A Note on Literary References and Cross-references

Quotations from Wordsworth's poems are whenever possible accompanied by line references to published texts. *PW* references are identified by volume and line numbers. Cross-references to reading texts from the Rough Notebook give short title (e.g., Churchyard Scene) and line number, and references to transcriptions of *The Borderers* manuscripts give leaf and line numbers. References to the early version of *The Borderers* are distinguished from references to the late version by being given as act, scene, and line (e.g., II.iii.208–211), whereas the latter is numbered continuously and referred to by line only (e.g., ll. 1297–1299). The early version is used as the standard text, and characters are normally referred to by their EV names; readers confused by name changes should refer to Table 1, page 8.

Quotations and citations from Shakespeare's plays are from the standard *Oxford Shakespeare*, edited by W. J. Craig (reset edition, 1943); those from Milton's poems are from Helen Darbishire's edition of *The Poems of John Milton* (Oxford, 1961). Some of the Shakespearean and Miltonic echoes recorded in the notes have previously been noted by de Selincourt (*PW*, I), and many Shakespearean echoes have been noted in Charles J. Smith, "The Effect of Shakespeare's Influence on Wordsworth's *The Borderers*," *Studies in Philology*, 50 (1953), 625–639. For the sake of brevity, the observations of these and other previous annotators have not normally been specifically acknowledged. Other main secondary sources for annotation are B. Sprague Allen, "Analogues of Wordsworth's *The Borderers*," *PMLA*, 38 (1923), 267–277; Margaret Cooke, "Schiller's *Robbers* in England," *Modern Language Review*, 11 (1916), 156–175; Emile Legouis, *The Early Life of William Wordsworth*, trans. J. W. Matthews (New York, 1918), pp. 269–278; Marijane Osborn, "Wordsworth's *Borderers* and the Landscape of Penrith," *Transactions of the Cumberland and Westmorland Antiquarian and Archaeological Society*, n.s. 76 (1976), 144–158; and H. F. Watson, "Historical Detail in *The Borderers*," *Modern Language Notes*, 52 (1937), 577–579.

The Borderers

Introduction

I

In 1843 Wordsworth recollected that *The Borderers* "was composed at Race Down in Dorset:re during the latter part of the year [17]95 & in the course of the following year."[1] But he dated the play one year too early. The earliest recorded reference to the play is a fragment from October 24, 1796, quoted in Christopher Wordsworth's *Memoirs of William Wordsworth* (2 vols.; London, 1851), in which Dorothy reported that William was "now ardent in the composition of a tragedy" (*EY*, p. 172). Four months later, in a letter postmarked February 27, 1797, Wordsworth brought his friend Francis Wrangham up to date after nearly a year's silence with the news that he had "been employed lately in writing a tragedy the first draught of which is nearly finished" (*EY*, p. 177). "Nearly finished" was the phrase that recurred in Dorothy's letter to her brother Richard of May 28, this time in the context of Wordsworth's "good hopes" of getting his tragedy shown to Sheridan (*EY*, p. 186). In the first week of June 1797, Coleridge arrived at Racedown, and "the first thing that was read after he came was William's new poem *The Ruined Cottage* with which he was much delighted; and after tea he repeated to us two acts and a half of his tragedy *Osorio*. The next morning William read his tragedy *The Borderers* . . ." (*EY*, p. 189). These letters establish that the bulk of the composition of *The Borderers* took place between the autumn of 1796 and the spring of 1797, when Wordsworth turned to his "new" poem, *The Ruined Cottage*. Within this period MS. 1 of *The Borderers*, the Rough Notebook (DC MS. 12) containing drafts for the play, must have been drawn up.[2]

Wordsworth's "good hopes" for showing his play to Sheridan rested with Coleridge, who was writing his own tragedy at Sheridan's invitation; shortly after Coleridge had taken up the invitation, at the end of March 1797, Wordsworth paid him a visit (*STCL*, I, 304, 318, 319). By June *The Borderers* was complete enough for the first of several readings that took place through the summer and autumn of 1797. Lamb complained (in 1800) that he saw little of

[1] From the Fenwick note (see Appendix III, below). This is also the date given in *PELY*.

[2] See *Chronology: EY*, pp. 329–330, which summarizes most of the evidence reviewed here.

the play while visiting Stowey in the second week of July 1797,[3] but on July 17 Coleridge invited Thomas Poole to a reading "under the Trees" (*STCL*, I, 332) (which Mark Reed suggests took place on July 23), followed by a dinner for fourteen people (*Chronology: EY*, p. 203). Charles Lloyd heard part of the play about September 10–14, and informed Southey that he was staying on in the hope of hearing "the remaining acts" (*STCL*, I, 345, n.3). The plan was, nonetheless, that *Osorio* should be finished and receive Sheridan's verdict before his attention was drawn to *The Borderers*. Southey's report on September 22 that "Coleridge [had] written a tragedy . . . Wordsworth [a] great part of a tragedy" probably reflects the precedence given to *Osorio*, for by this date *Osorio* was within three weeks of being sent off.[4] But perhaps Southey's report also reflects the fact that the text of *The Borderers* had remained slightly rough, if readable, throughout the summer—only "nearly finished" in terms of readiness for submission to theatrical managements, to use Dorothy's earlier phrase. When Sheridan's response to *Osorio* was delayed, Coleridge "procured for Wordsworth's Tragedy an Introduction to Harris, the Manager of Covent-garden," who promised to "read it attentively and give his answer immediately—and if he accept it, to put it in preparation without an hour's delay" (*STCL*, I, 358). As a preliminary, the play was shown first to Thomas Knight, "one of the principal Actors of Covent Garden," for advice on theatrical production, and it was to him the play went on November 20, 1797, "finished," as Dorothy reported (*EY*, p. 195). This letter provides the outside terminal date for the composition of *The Borderers*.

In 1842 Wordsworth recalled that *The Borderers* had at first been written as a closet drama, "without any view to its exhibition upon the stage" (*PELY*, p. 405), and in the Fenwick note of 1843 he explained that it had been "curtailed" at Knight's suggestion before submission to Harris. Dorothy described the circumstances in a letter dated December 8, 1797:

My dear Kitt—

You will be not a little surprized to hear that I am in London. William has been induced to come up to alter his play for the stage at the suggestion of one of the principal Actors of Covent Garden to whom he transmitted it. We have been in town more than

---

[3] E. W. Marrs, Jr., ed., *The Letters of Charles and Mary Anne Lamb* (Ithaca and London, 1975), I, 220.

[4] Kenneth Curry, ed., *New Letters of Robert Southey* (2 vols; New York and London, 1965), I, 148–149. What Southey saw is uncertain. It is possible that he visited Alfoxden between September 6 and 14 or between September 18 and 22, but more probably he met Wordsworth and perhaps Coleridge in Bristol on September 21 or 22. Southey's letter apart, the evidence of the 1797 letters supports Wordsworth's 1843 recollection of the relative dates of *The Borderers* and *Osorio*: "Much about the same time, but a little after, Coleridge was employed in writing his Trajedy" (Fenwick note, Appendix III, below).

a week, he has finished it, and it is presented to the Manager and we wait his decision which is expected in the course of a few days.[5]

Harris reviewed the curtailed text with exemplary dispatch. On December 13 Wordsworth reported to Joseph Cottle that "Mr. Harris [had] pronounced it impossible that [*The Borderers*] should succeed in the representation" (*EY*, p. 196). According to Elizabeth Threlkeld, "the metaphysical obscurity of one character, was the great reason of its rejection" (*EY*, p. 197, n. 1). (*Osorio* was also rejected on grounds of "obscurity"—in this case, "of the last three acts"—about December 1; see *STCL*, I, 358.) Wordsworth justifiably attributed his failure "to the deprav'd State of the Stage at present," and was "undetermin'd" whether to wait for a change in theatrical taste "or publish it . . . immediately" (*EY*, p. 197, n. 1).

Three months later, around March 13, 1798, Coleridge wrote at Wordsworth's request to Cottle, asking what he would pay for "our two Tragedies—with small prefaces containing an analysis of our principal characters," with a view to raising funds for the projected visit to Germany (*STCL*, I, 399–400). The idea of including "small prefaces" of character analysis was almost certainly suggested by the fact that Wordsworth's essay on the character of Rivers had already been composed, probably in the late spring or summer of 1797. In 1843 Wordsworth recollected that he "wrote a short essay" "while" he was composing the play (Fenwick note; see Appendix III, below), and internal evidence indicates that though the essay postdates composition of the bulk of the play, it predates composition of III.iv (see below, pp. 15–16). Jonathan Wordsworth has argued convincingly that the essay's close connection with themes of *Lines Left on a Seat in a Yew-Tree* indicates a date contemporary with *Lines* (*M of H*, p. 66). The *Lines* were largely composed about April 1797, but the appearance of the word "imagination" in the final paragraph led Jonathan Wordsworth to speculate that this paragraph may have been a late insertion in 1798 (*M of H*, p. 206n). But another appearance of this word in Wordsworth's writing is in the essay. Stephen Parrish has pointed to parallels between the last paragraph of *Lines* and both *Osorio* and Coleridge's letters of roughly that date, and suggested that Coleridge himself may have drafted the paragraph in the summer of 1797 (see *The Art of the Lyrical Ballads* [Cambridge, Mass., 1973], pp. 66–70). At any rate, Cottle seems to have disliked the financial terms of the proposal, and plans for publishing the two plays were swiftly abandoned (*STCL*, I, 401–403).

---

[5] *EY*, p. 195. It has generally been assumed that the text submitted to Knight had already been "altered and shortened" for the stage (see Moorman, I, 310–311, 345, and 350; see also *Chronology*: *EY*, p. 330), but there is no substantial evidence to suggest this; rather it seems likely that Knight's advice was sought before the curtailing.

The letters show some confusion about the number and state of the manuscripts of *The Borderers* that Wordsworth left behind him when he visited Germany in September 1798. To Thomas Poole he sent a text in a "sad incorrect state," advising him that if his apprentice, Ward, were to make a copy, he must "use his best eyes and his best sagacity in decyphering it" (*EY*, p. 231). He arranged to have a copy sent to his brother Christopher, who read it with his tutor in Cambridge.[6] Inquiring about this copy on February 3, 1799, Dorothy expressed concern: "if it were lost, the work would be irrecoverably gone" (*EY*, p. 246). Whether or not she was overstating the case, it appears that on his return to England in the spring of 1799, Wordsworth was eager to have a new copy of the play drawn up, and that it was this new copy that Coleridge referred to in a letter to Daniel Stuart of July 15, 1800, as the "one perfect Copy" of the play (*STCL*, I, 603). The copy drawn up in 1799 was in fact DC MS. 23, the vellum-bound notebook that contains MS. 2 of *The Borderers*, the one extant text of the early version of the completed play.[7]

In the summer of 1800 Coleridge attempted to revive the idea of stage production, and even persuaded Sheridan himself to write to Wordsworth "requesting him to write a Tragedy for Drury Lane" (*STCL*, I, 646). But though Wordsworth probably did once again allow the play to be considered for the theater, he "would not submit to having one syllable altered, [and said] that if in its present form it was not fit for the stage, he would try the experiment whether it was adopted for the closet" (G. B. Greenough; see *Chronology: MY*, pp. 72n–73n). In a letter of September 22, 1800, Coleridge observed that *The Borderers* was "not likely to emigrate from Grasmere" (*STCL*, I, 624), and it was indeed not until the tragedy had lain "ambushed for more than a generation of years" (*LY*, III, 1387) that Wordsworth eventually decided to revise it for publication in *Poems, Chiefly of Early and Late Years* (1842). In 1837 he had used the "Action is transitory" passage (III.v.60–65) as the first five lines of a new motto for the revised *White Doe of Rylstone*, noting only that he had recited them "more than thirty years since" to William Hazlitt, who had

[6] See references and discussion in *Chronology: EY*, p. 254n, where Reed attempts to unravel some of the mystery surrounding the arrangements Wordsworth made for *The Borderers* before leaving for Germany.

[7] For a description of DC MS. 23, see below, p. 446. The date of the manuscript is discussed in *Chronology: EY*, p. 330. Letters in *STCL*, I, 547, and *EY*, p. 277, indicate that a promised fair copy had not been drawn up by Christmas 1799, but probably refer to an additional fair copy that Dorothy planned, either to fulfill an old promise to Thomas Poole (*STCL*, I, 415) or to give to Coleridge, who may already have been reviving the Sheridan scheme mentioned below. If these letters do refer to DC MS. 23, then it would have to date from Mary Hutchinson's visit to Dove Cottage, February–April 1800, rather than from the summer of 1799 at Sockburn. There is, of course, a possibility that DC MS. 23 incorporates revisions that postdate Wordsworth's return from Germany in 1799, but the evidence indicates that at this point Wordsworth showed great obstinacy in refusing to be "diverted by any thing from the prosecution of his Great Work" (*STCL*, I, 646), or to alter "one syllable" of what had consumed so much "time . . . thought . . . and genius" (*STCL*, I, 402) in 1796–97.

misquoted them in *The Spirit of the Age* (London, 1825; see *PW*, III, 548–549). In *PELY* he noted that the lines "would not have been used elsewhere, if I had foreseen the time when I might be induced to publish this Tragedy" (see below, p. 71). Wordsworth did not start work on revising *The Borderers* for *PELY* until after March 1841 (*LY*, III, 1072), and the dates of the postmarks on MS. 2A indicate that the bulk of revision took place between December 1841 and May 1842, when Wordsworth was in London adding further revisions at the proof stage and considering the inclusion of the essay. MS. 3 and its revision in particular bear witness to the tremendous industry that Wordsworth and Mary must have put into revising *The Borderers* in the first two months of 1842.

II

Evidence of the manner in which *The Borderers* took shape in the latter part of 1796 and the first months of the following year is to be found in DC MS. 12, the Rough Notebook containing the MS. 1 drafts for the play.[8] Of the 124 leaves that the notebook originally contained, all but 32 have been cut out, including the whole of the last two-thirds of the notebook. Apart from two historical extracts from Elizabethan records and a bibliography on Druids that suggest prior use as a commonplace book, its extant pages are wholly taken up with drafts for *The Borderers*, including rough notes on both front and back inside covers. These entries are clearly only a small sample of the work done in drafting the play, whether on the pages later cut from the notebook during copying or in other manuscripts now lost. Some of the deductions based on examination of the extant entries and their relation to the finished text of the early version are bound to be speculative, given the size of the sample. Yet enough entries have survived to give a fair indication of the manner in which Wordsworth set about the business of composing his tragedy.

Two distinct phases of composition are represented in the notebook, conveniently signaled by a change in the names allotted to the hero and villain of the piece. In the earlier phase, they are Ferdinand and Danby, respectively; in the later phase, they are Mortimer and Rivers, the names retained in the early version of the play (see Table 1). The entries of the earlier phase reveal Wordsworth at work on a plot whose Gothic and sentimental themes echo those of his *Adventures on Salisbury Plain* (1795–96) and *Fragment of a Gothic Tale* (1796). Those belonging to the later phase show him starting to develop the psychological interaction between hero and villain on which the credibility of the plot ultimately depends. The completed drama, the EV *Borderers*, brings into prominence the philosophy and psychology that frame the play's action—just as, later, the completed *Ruined Cottage* was to highlight the context within

---

[8] For a full description of the contents of DC MS. 12, see below, pp. 299–301.

Table 1. Name changes in *The Borderers*

Ur-Borderers (MS. 1, early entries)	Early version (MS. 2, base text)	Late version (MS. 2, revisions; MSS. 2A, 3, 3A, 4; *PELY*)
Ferdinand	Mortimer	Annandale (MS. 2A), Marmaduke
Danby	Rivers	Oswald
Herbert	Herbert	Herbert
Matilda	Matilda	Idonia (MS. 3), Idonea (MSS. 3A, 4; *PELY*)
Peasant, Cottager, Robert	Robert	Eldred
Margaret	Margaret	Eleanor
Peasant	Two Woodmen	A Forester
Old Pilgrim*	Old Pilgrim	Old Pilgrim

Note: In addition, lines spoken by one member of the band of borderers in the early version are occasionally spoken by another in the late version, and one member, Norwood, appears only in the early version.

* In the prose synopsis for Act III in MS. 1, the Pilgrim is revealed as Herbert's long-lost wife. In the Churchyard Scene, the Pilgrim is a disconsolate wanderer, probably male. In the early and late versions, he is Herbert's former traveling companion.

which the tale of Margaret's suffering is told and heard. The earlier of the two phases of drafting in the Rough Notebook is concerned primarily with the tale of *The Borderers*, rather than its context. I shall call this tale the *Ur-Borderers*, and the phase represented by the earlier entries in the Rough Notebook the *Ur-Borderers* phase.

Before the *Ur-Borderers*' tale is summarized, it will be useful to review more closely the nature of the materials for the *Ur-Borderers* in DC MS. 12, on which that summary will be based. They consist of a prose synopsis for "3rd Act," the surviving fragment of a synopsis of the final act, and draft and fair-copy texts of parts of five scenes for the play. The synopses are probably the earliest surviving entries for the play, and may be the remains of an act-by-act series covering more or less the whole of the *Ur-Borderers* plot, dictated to Dorothy in sequence. They were entered near the front of the notebook, ahead of all other surviving entries for the *Ur-Borderers*. The plot is crudely outlined, as if the scenes into which it is to be divided are just coming into focus. Dorothy has gone back to insert additional details for the opening of Act III, and the synopsis for the final act breaks off with an exclamation point at the moment of climactic confrontation: "Ferdinands reason which had been disordered restored by the sight of Danby!"[9] The impression given is of materials dictated

[9] Rough Notebook, 18^r^. The synopses are included in the reading texts of earliest entries in MS. 1, below. The tragedy outlined may have been in four or five acts.

close to the outset of Wordworth's work on his tragedy, while he was establishing a rough narrative frame.

It is not possible to arrange with certainty the entries for the five scenes for the *Ur-Borderers* in an overall order of composition. They are, in dramatic sequence: Prose Fragment for Act I, Churchyard Scene for Act III, and what is roughly a sequence of scenes—Margaret and Peasant Scene, Edge of a Heath Scene, and Matilda at the Cottage Door Scene—for the equivalent of Act V of the EV play. Though the order of composition is doubtful, the entry of the Margaret and Peasant Scene probably postdates the entry of the Edge of a Heath Scene, and both the names and the positioning indicate that the Matilda at the Cottage Door Scene is later than either of the other two. None of these entries appears to be a first draft. There are several redraftings of parts of the Edge of a Heath Scene, using the EV name Robert in place of the Cottager of the original entry; Robert is also the name used in the Matilda at the Cottage Door Scene, which must therefore postdate both the Margaret and Peasant Scene (which uses Peasant) and the original entry for the Edge of a Heath Scene. There are inconsistencies between the synopsis for Act III and the Churchyard Scene, and between the Margaret and Peasant Scene and the Edge of a Heath Scene: Wordsworth's concept of the detailed plot of his play, like the names allotted to Margaret's husband—Peasant, Cottager, Robert—seems to have been variable throughout the *Ur-Borderers* phase. Nevertheless, it is possible to use these scenes in conjunction with the synopses to reconstruct the broad outlines of the plot that Wordsworth had in mind during the *Ur-Borderers* phase.

One further entry in the notebook sheds considerable light on the plot of the *Ur-Borderers*, though this entry postdates the name changes from Ferdinand and Danby to Mortimer and Rivers: a roughly noted synopsis for the first part of Act II on leaf 18^r draws on setting and incidents in Wordsworth's *Fragment of a Gothic Tale*. It is safe to assume that elements in the *Gothic Tale* retained in this synopsis or carried right through to the finished EV play were already included in Wordsworth's concept of his plot during the *Ur-Borderers* phase.

The tale told by the *Ur-Borderers* is Gothic and sentimental, set in the age of the Crusades. It relates the action and suffering of three principal characters: Ferdinand, the naive hero; the blind and aged Herbert, his victim; and Matilda, Herbert's daughter and guide. Less directly involved in the action is Danby, the Iago-like confidant who deceives Ferdinand into believing Herbert to be guilty of some terrible crime against nature—perhaps the murder of his wife, or the exploitation of Matilda's filial piety—and so sets the plot in motion. In the synopsis for Act III Ferdinand is "enraged" at learning that Matilda has been reunited with her mother and that they are seeking Herbert for a reunion of husband and wife; Ferdinand's rage must imply that the discovery of this family trio is at odds with what Danby has "invented." In the

Edge of a Heath Scene, Ferdinand confesses that he "did not think [Herbert] had a living child"; presumably Wordsworth had already at this point included among Danby's inventions the idea that Herbert was masquerading as Matilda's father. Danby is also known to Matilda as "a friend." When Matilda separates from her father, who is weary after crossing a heath (establishing Herbert's weariness appears to be the primary function of the Prose Fragment), to go on an errand, Ferdinand seizes the opportunity to offer to guide Herbert from the inn where he is staying to a nearby convent. The details of errand, inn, and convent were inserted by Dorothy Wordsworth between the lines of her original entry for the synopsis of Act III. This, then, was how the tragedy was to be set up in Act I.

Act II was to have as its centerpiece a stormy night scene at a ruined castle, closely modeled on events in the *Gothic Tale:* Ferdinand has led Herbert to the castle, where the old man takes shelter in a dungeon. Ferdinand, stirred up to murder him, is disturbed by the serenity of a single star and interrupted by a mysterious band of smugglers. He is presumably accompanied by Danby up to this point; but when they separate, Ferdinand eventually abandons Herbert to the mercies of the savage heath rather than murder him outright. I infer that the plot demanded Danby's presence at the castle from the earliest stage so that incidents from the *Gothic Tale* might be presented in dialogue form. That the original plot already included the abandonment of Herbert without Danby's knowledge may be deduced from the synopses and scenes for the rest of the play.

Act III was to open with a return to Matilda. In the synopsis, Matilda learns of her father's departure for the convent, and then comes to a churchyard where she "meets a pilgrim whom she discovers to be her mother"—a device reminiscent of the use of coincidence to reunite husband with (dying) wife in *Adventures on Salisbury Plain.* The Churchyard Scene deviates from the synopsis. Here the disconsolate Old Pilgrim whom Matilda meets is male, though his sex becomes a little ambiguous when he faints toward the end of the scene (see headnote below, p. 45). Both the synopsis and the Churchyard Scene then have Matilda, with the Pilgrim, hastening to rejoin Herbert. The synopsis continues: they are to be met by Danby, who then encounters Ferdinand. Thinking that the latter has by now killed Herbert, Danby reveals his deceit "to drive Ferdinand to despair." Ferdinand returns to the heath "to see if Herbert may yet be saved."

The last part of the story, for which there are no act divisions, must be pieced together from the Margaret and Peasant, Edge of a Heath, and Matilda at the Cottage Door scenes and the fragment of a further synopsis. Two new characters are introduced, the cottagers Margaret and her husband (identified variously as Peasant, Cottager, and Robert), who live on the edge of the heath and, like the cottagers in *Adventures on Salisbury Plain*, act as chorus to the denouement:

And while his silence, looks, and voice they scan,
And trembling hands, they cried, "He is the man!"
[*ASP*, ll.805–806]

The cxtant scenes establish that the opening of this section has brought Matilda to the cottage, and that Herbert, who was found by Robert on the heath but left there to die, now lies in the cottage, dead. The Margaret and Peasant Scene reports that Ferdinand has been seen on the heath, and is deranged. This scene and the Edge of a Heath Scene may well reflect alternative schemes to dramatize events leading up to the denouement (see headnote below, p. 46), for in the latter scene Ferdinand learns that the Cottager has found Herbert, and the Cottager, suspecting him of involvement in Herbert's death, leads him to the cottage. The final scene takes place at the cottage, where Matilda at first refuses to meet the suspect. Later in the scene there was perhaps to be an altercation between Robert and the deranged Ferdinand (see V.iii.182–208), since in the synopsis "Matilda rushes in to prevent it," Danby arrives, and Ferdinand's reason is restored for a final confrontation with his deceiver.

This outline of the *Ur-Borderers* plot reconstructs what must have been more or less Wordsworth's starting point for the tragedy: the development of a story. The number of scenes that he went on to compose during the *Ur-Borderers* phase is a matter for conjecture. Wordsworth's conception altered as he wrote, and there is no reason to suppose that the play was ever completed in its *Ur-Borderers* form—with the attempted murder interrupted by smugglers rather than, as in the EV *Borderers*, by Mortimer's own band of virtuous border outlaws (borrowed from Schiller's *Robbers*),[10] and with Danby's role as compressed as it appears in this outline. Nevertheless, there is every reason to suppose that the drafting at the *Ur-Borderers* phase was a good deal more substantial than the fragments of five scenes that have survived in the notebook.

Working the play out from its starting point in the prose synopses, Wordsworth may well havc drafted substantial parts of it in prose, some of which he then turned into verse. The two instances of this procedure of which there is direct proof in the Rough Notebook are the Prose Fragment and the Edge of a Heath Scene. In the latter, the original entry opens with the prose of Ferdinand's soliloquy, and then breaks into verse with the appearance of the Cottager. Later, but still in the *Ur-Borderers* phase, Wordsworth used the blank pages nearer the front of the notebook to rework the soliloquy as verse. The soliloquy was not included in the EV *Borderers*. In the case of the Prose Fragment, reference to the early version discloses echoes from these seven lines of

[10] The brief intrusion of the Beggarwoman "with two or three of her companions" at II. iii.243–246 of the EV is perhaps a vestigial trace of the smugglers of the revised plot sketch on 18^r of the Rough Notebook, who derive directly from the "mysterious men" of the *GT*. Schiller's *Robbers* appears to have become a direct source for *The Borderers* only in the later stages of composition, possibly as a result of Wordsworth's visit to Coleridge in March.

prose scattered through twenty-five lines of verse in which Matilda and Herbert converse on their way to the inn shortly after their first entrance in the play. Since the Prose Fragment was entered on the page following the end of the synopses, and appears to be a fair copy that may have continued for six more leaves (stubs 20–25), one is tempted to speculate that it is a remnant from the very beginning of the opening scene of the *Ur-Borderers*, which we may therefore conjecture began with the introduction of Herbert and Matilda.

Further evidence that substantial parts of the play were originally composed in prose is found in the survival of prose in the text of the EV *Borderers*; the prose of II.iii.87–133 and II.iii.254–291 was eventually rendered into verse in MS. 2A in 1841. The fact that these passages contain close echoes of the *Gothic Tale* supports the case for including them among the materials composed during the *Ur-Borderers* phase. Act IV, Scene iii, of the EV *Borderers* is also largely in prose, and the case for attributing its composition to the *Ur-Borderers* period is equally strong. As I have observed in my summary of the probable outline for the *Ur-Borderers*, the Margaret and Peasant and Edge of a Heath scenes clearly imply a preceding scene that has established Matilda's arrival at the cottage and Robert's encounter with the dying Herbert. Act IV, Scene iii, serves precisely that function, and must surely have been drafted before the end of the *Ur-Borderers* phase, perhaps to await the intended reworking in verse that it did not, in the end, receive.

The surviving entries in the notebook, then, represent only a portion of the scenes that were drafted in some form during the *Ur-Borderers* phase. Some of this work was carried forward into the EV text of *The Borderers* with comparatively little revision. The prose of II.iii.87–133 and II.iii.254–291 and the prose of IV.iii are recognizably work of the *Ur-Borderers* phase only because they were not later turned into verse; and among the drafts extant in the Rough Notebook, the texts of the Edge of a Heath and the Matilda at the Cottage Door scenes are notably close to the text that derives from them in the EV *Borderers* (V.ii and the opening of V.iii). The same is true of the relationship between the actual text of parts of the Margaret and Peasant Scene and V.i, though in this case the dramatic function of the scene has been radically altered by the transferral of the Peasant's report on Ferdinand's derangement to two Woodmen reporting to Rivers (the Peasant wants to prove Ferdinand "guilty of a damning crime" to minimize his own risk of being suspected; whereas in the EV *Borderers* Rivers specifically wants to protect Mortimer from arrest, preferring "A shadow of myself, made by myself"). On the whole, it seems likely that a great deal of the text of the final part of the play in its EV form (IV.iii to the end) is fairly closely derivative from *Ur-Borderers* drafts, which, in the Rough Notebook, are literally cut off in their earliest *Ur-Borderers* form halfway through the Edge of a Heath Scene. But the same is not true of the extant drafts for the preceding acts. Not a single line from the Churchyard

Scene survives in the EV *Borderers*. The equivalent scene has been moved back from its *Ur-Borderers* position in Act III after the abandonment of Herbert on the heath to a position in Act II, before the attempted murder at Mounteagle Castle, and the disconsolate Old Pilgrim of the Churchyard Scene has become a far more stalwart figure—a former traveling companion of Herbert's who knew Matilda as a toddler. Similarly, as I have said, the seven lines of prose comprising the Prose Fragment for Act I are scattered as echoes over twenty-five lines of the EV verse text for I.i. What other *Ur-Borderers* material may be similarly embedded in the text of the first three acts of the EV *Borderers* we can only guess.

On realizing the scope of the likely *Ur-Borderers* drafts, we may be tempted to link the *Ur-Borderers* with the phrase "first draught" in the letter to Wrangham of February 27, 1797: "I have been employed lately in writing a tragedy the first draught of which is nearly finished." This linkage, however, is not warranted by the evidence we have reviewed. That evidence establishes that drafting was extensive in the *Ur-Borderers* phase, but the extant entries in the Rough Notebook suggest a half-completed jigsaw puzzle. The entries are in a variety of states (synopses; the fragment of a scene in prose; a fair copy in verse and prose; drafts that turn prose into verse) and they include inconsistencies and unresolved questions, such as whether "Act 3^{d}" shall open at the churchyard or at the inn, whether the Pilgrim is to be Matilda's mother or an old man who has lost his son, how and whether both the Margaret and Peasant Scene and the Edge of a Heath Scene will be fitted into the play. There is no reason to suppose that the *Ur-Borderers* amounted to more than such a jigsaw puzzle. More important, there are no extant early drafts of scenes including Danby. In the synopses, Danby is the Iago: he stands back from the action and the suffering of his victims, Ferdinand, Herbert, and Matilda, but he is no less a central character than they. From its inception, the play required the development of Danby's role. The *Ur-Borderers* demonstrably possessed, in outline form, a complete plot, but it is highly unlikely that it ever amounted to a complete play, or to the "nearly finished" first draft of a complete play.

What the sample of Wordsworth's work on *The Borderers* in the Rough Notebook strongly suggests—and it is only a sample—is that his work on the story of the consequences of Ferdinand's deception by Danby preceded his work on the way in which that deception was achieved. It was with "Drafts for the Deception," as I have titled them, that he filled the blank spaces left between *Ur-Borderers* entries when he began a new series of drafts for *The Borderers* using the names Mortimer and Rivers. The "Drafts for the Deception" occupy 38^{v}–42^{v} (see 38^{v}n). Their positioning suggests that at this stage Wordsworth was continuing to work roughly toward the front of the notebook, filling in empty spaces left from earlier drafting, as he had done with the Ferdinand and Robert drafts and the Matilda at the Cottage Door Scene, and as he did with the *Gothic Tale* entries in DC MS. 2. The later extant entries are nearly all for Act I, though the draft for what became I.ii, the scene at the inn where Herbert decides to accept Mortimer and Rivers's offer to guide him to the convent, also contains lines that appear in II.i of the finished play (the scene in which they leave the inn together). We see here an indication of the expansion that was necessary to develop the opening interaction between Mortimer and Rivers to the point it reaches in the EV *Borderers*. The structure within which Wordsworth was working in the Rough Notebook draft for the scene at the inn implies that Rivers develops his plot in a single scene, and that he and Mortimer then guide Herbert from the inn:

Postulated draft structure

Scene A (a road)	(a)	Matilda and Herbert introduced, exit.
	(b)	Rivers convinces Mortimer of Herbert's guilt, suggests waylaying him.
Scene B (the inn)	(a)	Matilda and Herbert part.
	(b)	Rivers and Mortimer enter, leave with Herbert.

The structure that the opening of the play achieves in the EV *Borderers* greatly expands this action. The deception proceeds in waves.

EV Borderers structure

I.i (a road)	(a)	Mortimer and Rivers's preliminary discussion of Herbert.
	(b)	Matilda and Herbert pass.
	(c)	Mortimer and Rivers—further hints of Herbert's guilt.
I.ii (the inn)	(a)	Matilda and Herbert part.
	(b)	Mortimer and Rivers propose departure with Herbert.
I.iii (a wood)	(a)	Mortimer and Rivers—further hints.
	(b)	They hear Beggarwoman's false story, which confirms Mortimer's worst fears.
II.i (the inn)	(a)	Rivers persuades Mortimer to take Herbert to the ruined castle.
	(b)	Herbert joins them; they leave with him.

This expansion is under way in the Rough Notebook, which includes a draft of the encounter with the Beggarwoman (I.iii).

The elaboration of the plot of the *Ur-Borderers* postdates, rather than coincides with, the changing of names to Mortimer and Rivers. The roughly noted synopsis for the beginning of Act II evidently predates the introduction of Mortimer's band, since it refers to the mysterious intervention of a group of smugglers who have overheard the conversation between Mortimer and Rivers at Mounteagle Castle. The draft for I.i.197–225 does, however, establish that Mortimer is playing a philanthropic role in the border wars ("Six plundered families" have come for succor to his "tent"), and that Rivers is a companion at arms. The later stages of composition, in which Wordsworth built up the role of the borderers and greatly expanded the intervals between the main dramatic events (delaying Herbert's abandonment on the heath until Act III, Scene iii) are hardly represented at all in the Rough Notebook, whose extant pages contain no drafts for the philosophical speeches that so dominate the action of the finished play, or for Rivers's great autobiographical confession in Act IV, Scene ii. The fact that the later drafts in the notebook are predominantly concerned with the first act does suggest, however, that the key to the transformation of the *Ur-Borderers* lay in Wordsworth's turning his attention to the origins of the action he had sketched at the *Ur-Borderers* stage. The effect, ultimately, was a fundamental shift from the *Ur-Borderers*' emphasis on the spectacle of action and suffering (particularly on the spectacle of derangement linked with guilt) toward emphasis on the philosophic basis of action and suffering. This redirection greatly enlarged the intellectual scope of the play. It was accompanied by the elevation of Rivers from his Danby role as the deceiver who triggers the action to the role of initiator in a special kind of perception, the central experienced commentator on the main psychological and philosophical themes in *The Borderers*.

Wordsworth's preoccupation with Rivers in the late stages of composition is reflected in the writing of "a short essay illustrative of that constitution & those tendencies of human nature which make the apparently *motiveless* actions of bad men intelligible to careful observers" (Fenwick note; see Appendix III, below), which prefaces the early version. The essay must have been composed after the play had been largely completed, since it is obviously an apology for an already created character. But in 1843 Wordsworth recalled that he wrote the essay "while" he was composing the play, and the relation between the discussion of "superstition" in the essay and one scene in *The Borderers* suggests that the early version as we know it may not have been entirely complete at the time of the writing of the essay. That scene is III.iv, in which members of the band discuss Rivers's motives. They attribute his action to a "superstition" that he never demonstrates in the course of the play, and which in fact conflicts with the preeminence he claims for the fully independent mind. Far from paying allegiance to "spirits, and the sun in heaven" (III.iv.32), such a mind acknowledges in nature only the formative power of "mighty objects" that "impress their forms / To build up this our intellectual being" (IV.ii.134–

135). The "intellectual being" is superior to all created things—

> I seemed a being who had passed alone
> Beyond the visible barriers of the world
> And travelled into things to come.
> [IV.ii.143–145]

and it owes allegiance only to itself ("Is its own origin of ill and end," as Byron's Manfred was later to express the concept). The discrepancy between Rivers's demonstrated views and those advanced by the band is, I think, most easily explained if III.iv is seen as a postscript to the main composition of the play, illustrative, along with the essay, of Wordsworth's obsession with the need to justify the "metaphysical obscurity" of one of the characters, to which, indeed, the managers of Covent Garden were shortly to make objection.

One further scene, IV.i, in which Robert discovers Herbert vainly trying to scale the rocks, is also likely to postdate the rest of the play. Though less obviously so than III.iv, this scene is again extraneous to the main action, with which it slightly conflicts: it presents us with an image of Robert sympathetically assisting Herbert off the stage, rather than fearfully abandoning him. The sudden appearance of the word "stage" in the directions for the scene provides the explanation. The only elaborate stage directions in the play occur in this short scene:

> a ridge of rocks rises at the bottom of the stage . . . HERBERT enters in the depth of the stage . . . he crosses the stage . . . . He sinks down in a corner of the stage. Enter ROBERT at another part of the stage . . . Draws him gently off the stage.

The scene is uniquely redolent of scenic and sound effects (bell, wind, groans) and unusual in providing many instructions for dramatic gestures. The obvious conclusion to be drawn is that the scene was added very late in the composition of the play, with a view to stage performance.

In revising *The Borderers* for publication in 1841–42, Wordsworth changed the names of his characters (see Table 1) and introduced various minor plot changes. Earliest were the omission of the feigned placing of a sleeping potion in Herbert's drink in II.iii (a change made while the prose of the early version was being reworked into verse) and the omission of all reference to the captain's daughter to whom Rivers is betrothed, and who goes mad upon learning of her father's death, in IV.ii.79–89 of the early version. Changes introduced in the opening of the play also required some reordering of the discussion among the band in III.iv: Wordsworth decided in 1841–42 to open the play with a preliminary discussion between two members of the band, Wallace and Lacy, who express disquiet that their leader is so close to Oswald, before introducing Marmaduke in conversation with his servant Wilfred, and for this purpose some lines were transferred from III.iv of the early version. The most significant changes were introduced in V.iii, the final scene of the play. In the late version, Marmaduke's confession is immediately authenticated by the production of the letter signed by Herbert in II.i, at which Idonea faints and is carried out. Oswald then enters immediately and delivers one short speech before Marmaduke forgives him and utters a passionate harangue expressing the hope that Oswald, like himself, will dedicate the rest of his life to remorse.

The late version thus tones down the spectacle of derangement and guilt that precedes Rivers's entry in the early version, in which it takes some time for Matilda to grasp what has happened, and in which a frantic Matilda and then an equally frantic Mortimer take turns pulling the hapless Robert around the stage. The ironic exchange in which Rivers catechizes Mortimer before the "I forgive thee" speech is completely omitted in the late version, and that speech is greatly expanded to introduce the new theme of remorse. This theme continues to the end of the play, stressed by the absence of such distractions as Matilda's reentry and the entry of the friars in the early version, and by the reworking of the speech in which Marmaduke resigns his captainship of the band and condemns himself to lifelong exile on the heath in search of "expiation."

III

The Borderers is set in the period of the barons' wars; the reference in II.iii. 330–334 to Henry III's dissolution of the "Barons' League" implies that the action takes place shortly after the Battle of Evesham, August 1265. This period provides an absence of established government (Fenwick note, Appendix III) and a mediaeval background of Crusades, convents, hermits, and baronial tyranny. A certain historical verisimilitude is provided by the names of the major characters—Mortimer, Matilda, Herbert, and Rivers—and by the two barons in the background, Clifford and St. Clair (V.iii.192). The historical Sir Roger de Mortimer (1231?–1282) was the barons' leader against Henry, though he was associated with the Welsh marches rather than the Scottish border. Possibly Wordsworth's choice was influenced by Michael Drayton's historical poems *Matilda the Faire and Chaste* (1594) and the *Mortimeriados* (1596), later titled *The Barons' Warres*. The name Herbert was not politically important until the late sixteenth century, but Wordsworth certainly chose it for its seventh-century religious associations: St. Herbert of Derwentwater, a friend of St. Cuthbert mentioned in Bede's *Historia Ecclesiastica*, IV, Chapter 29, lived on "St. Herbert's Island," Derwentwater (see *PW*, IV, Inscription XV, pp. 206–208, composed in 1800). The name Rivers may have been taken from Shakespeare's *Richard III*, or suggested by the historical Peter de Rivaulx (pronounced "Rivers" in the north of England), who was a friend of Henry III, or by a later historical Rivers connected with border events (see *Elegy III, Written amongst the Ruins of Pontefract Castle*, in John Bell's *Classical Arrangement of Fugitive Poetry* [14 vols.; London, 1789–93], IX [1789], 22). As David Erdman has pointed out, the rechristening of Rivers as Oswald in 1841 links the villain of *The Borderers* with the English Jacobin colonel John Oswald, a protégé of Brissot who was active in the French Revolution in the early 1790s. The recollections of Oswald published by Henry Redhead Yorke in *Letters from France in 1802* (London, 1804) present Oswald as an eccentric advocate of the "independent intellect," a man who had traveled extensively outside of Europe, who attacked democracy on much the same grounds as Rivers does in *The Borderers*, and who was once reprimanded by Thomas Paine for his "most voracious appetite for blood."[11] The historical Clifford family kept Brougham Castle, just outside Penrith, and Wordsworth's decision to degrade Sir Roger de Clifford from his status as hero at the Battle of Evesham to that of lecher was perhaps suggested by the tradition that a later Sir Roger built the house on the Penrith–Appleby road known as Julian's Bower for his mistress (see Wordsworth's note to his sonnet *Hart's-Horn Tree, Near Penrith* [*PW*, III, 535]). The St. Clair family belonged to Rosslyn, near Edinburgh, and the Rydal Mount sale catalogue of books auctioned after Wordsworth's death lists a presentation copy of the privately printed *Genealogie of the Sainte-claires of Rosslyn* (1834), which suggests some special connection with that family. De Selincourt notes that Wordsworth's choice of names was "partly guided by local history": in Joseph Nicolson and Richard Burn, *History and Antiquities of the Counties of Westmorland and Cumberland* (2 vols.; London, 1777), "Mortimer and Marmaduke, Matilda, Idonea and Clifford are names that constantly recur in records of the twelfth and thirteenth centuries" (*PW*, I, 344).

Place-name references establish a fairly unspecific borderland setting (Liddersdale, Tweed and Esk, Cheviot Beacon), but Marijane Osborn has shown in "Wordsworth's *Borderers* and the Landscape of Penrith," *Transactions of the Cumberland and Westmorland Antiquarian and Archaeological Society*, n.s.76 (1976), 144–158, that details in Wordsworth's landscape derive largely from the Penrith area, where his grandparents, the Cooksons, lived. The main literary sources influencing Wordsworth's treatment of that landscape seem not to have included one obvious possibility: though Wordsworth admitted to having read George Ridpath's *The Border History* (London, 1776), he said in the Fenwick note (see Appendix III) that he "found there nothing to [his] purpose." But he did make use of William Gilpin's *Observations . . . on Cumberland, and Westmoreland* (2 vols.; London, 1786), William Hutchinson's *An Excursion to*

[11] I am indebted to David Erdman for information about this character. Erdman first pointed out the connection between John Oswald and Wordsworth's villain in "Wordsworth as Heartsworth; or, Was Regicide the Prophetic Ground of Those 'Moral Questions'?" in *The Evidence of the Imagination*, ed. Donald H. Reiman et al. (New York, 1978), pp. 12–41.

the Lakes in Westmoreland and Cumberland (London, 1776), Thomas West's *Guide to the Lakes in Cumberland, Westmorland, and Lancashire* (London, 1778), and James Clarke's *Survey of the Lakes of Cumberland, Westmorland, and Lancashire* (London, 1787). Clarke's work appears to have been the single most useful background source, especially for its description of the Penrith area at the beginning of Book I, for the references to banditti and borderers throughout the Introduction, and for the Appendix on border history.

IV

The earliest antecedents of *The Borderers* in Wordsworth's own work are two fragments that he entered in DC MS. 2 in 1788 or thereabouts. One belongs to the eighteenth-century Gothic-descriptive genre:

> Now gleam'd the Moon; on a high rock he view'd
> A Castle perch'd—on either side a wood
> Wav'd solemn to the hollow wind.—It seem'd
> Like some grim Eagle on a naked rock
> Clapping its wings and wailing to the storm.[12]

The other fragment belongs to the genre of sentimental realism, as its reference to Thomas Gray's *Journal* indicates.

A Tale

"God bless you," said a voice to me in a tone so pathetic that my heart melted at the sound, "God bless you, and may he that maketh his Sun to rise on the evil and on the good, and sendeth rain on the just and on the unjust, may he give you as much happiness in this world as I trust he will give me in the next."

It was at the very Village and I was passing by the very churchyard from which on a Sunday noon about twenty years ago the congregation were issuing when Gray returned from his visit to the vale of Elysium.

My astonishment at being thus unusually accosted did not prevent [me] from observing that the object which addressed me was surrounded by a group of eight or ten Villagers. The voice proceeded from a woman somewhat above the midd[l]e size.

Her dress, if you ex[c]ept a black [hat], which bore no other marks than that of being drench'd in rain, tied by a dark green ribband which knotted under chin, was not much more warm or becoming than that of such of those numerous wretches, the poor, the lame, and the blind, who have no fire but the light of a Window seen at a distance and whose candle is the little g[?lowworm]. Her eyes were large and blue, and from the wrinkles of her face, which from their fineness seemed rather the wrinkles of Sorrow than of Years, it was easy to see they had been much acquainted with weeping; yet had not perpetual tears been able to extinguish a certain wild brightness which

[12] The text given here is that of the latest readings on 86^r; punctuation has been added or emended.

at the first view might have been mistaken for the wildness of great joy. But it was far different: it too plainly indicated she was not in her true and perfect mind.[13]

The two fragments nicely reflect the two aspects of eighteenth-century literary tradition out of which *The Borderers* chiefly grew. They are also specific sources. The description of a castle in a storm was incorporated in the roughly drafted *Fragment of a Gothic Tale* entered in DC MS. 2 in mid-1796, and later became part of the setting for Mortimer's attempt to murder Herbert at Mounteagle Castle; while numerous close echoes indicate that *A Tale* was a main source for the Churchyard Scene, which, though finally omitted from the completed early version, clearly defines the ethic of Herbert and Matilda, as well as exploring the conjunction of blessedness, blessing, dislocation, and madness in ways that are touched on elsewhere in *The Borderers*, and lead directly to *The Ruined Cottage*.

It is possible to exaggerate the importance of Wordsworth's earliest fragments as source materials for his later work, for as Jonathan Wordsworth remarks of the widows in the poetry (*M of H*, pp. 4–5), Wordsworth was apt to employ "stock situation[s]" of which he "simply varied the details to suit his preoccupation of the moment." By the time they entered *The Borderers*, the images of castle and demented woman had been overlaid with themes of the psychology of guilt and sorrow developed in *Salisbury Plain* (1793), *Adventures on Salisbury Plain* (1795–96), and *The Convict* (1795–96); with themes that reflected the influence of Shakespeare and Godwin, in whose writing Wordsworth found models for both the moral situations and the characters developed in his own tragedy; and with themes that first emerged clearly either in the *Fragment of a Gothic Tale* (perhaps particularly influenced by Joseph Fawcett's *Art of War*) or during the actual composition of *The Borderers* itself. Yet the two fragments of c. 1788 not only represent starting points for the development of themes and motifs employed in the play; they are also emblematic of the two extremes in the human condition which *The Borderers* explores as tragic forms of isolation. The first fragment offers a vision of man placed in a Gothic solitude that enhances his individual dignity, and is an emblem of the heroic ideal to which Rivers promises to lead Mortimer:

Solitude!
The eagle lives in solitude—
[III.v.53–54]

Such grandeur is in the world of *The Borderers* to be achieved only through the loss of innocence and integrity. The second fragment describes a condition of

[13] The text is that of the latest readings, with punctuation added or emended, and missing letters, canceled and conjectural readings, and omitted words supplied in square brackets. In most respects my text agrees with that in *Prose*, I, 7–8. See *Chronology: EY*, p. 313, where the reference to Gray's journal of his tour of the lakes is identified.

suffering for which the only consolation can be the religious one sought by Herbert when he blesses his daughter:

> when I think of man
> I bless her with sad spirit; when of God,
> I bless her in the fulness of my joy!
> [III.iii.113–115]

In the world of *The Borderers*, which is a world deprived of hospitality as of miracles ("There was no food, no drink, no grass, no shade . . ." [IV.ii.24]), such a consolation must eventually fail in the face of an unrelieved pain that "has the nature of infinity" (III.v.65).

The immediate origins of *The Borderers* lie in Wordsworth's preoccupation with criminal psychology in 1795–96, which is reflected in his *Fragment of a Gothic Tale*. The *Gothic Tale* is an experimental horror poem in which Wordsworth describes the psychological impact of Gothic surroundings on a young man intent on murdering a blind old sailor for his money. The setting for the poem may be traced to the descriptions in William Gilpin's *Observations* (1786), and to the supernatural "Strange forms" in "black damp dungeon[s]" and natural "tall and sable . . . firs" bowing their "grim black forehead[s]" menacingly in the night wind in Wordsworth's *Vale of Esthwaite* (c. 1786–1788) (*PW*, I, ll. 39–42, 211–218). But *The Vale of Esthwaite* belongs to the eighteenth-century tradition that celebrated "the pleasures of imagination" in natural and supernatural scenes that were primarily features of an inner landscape—

> forms of Fear that float
> Wild on the shipwreck of the thought,
> While fancy in a Demon's form
> Rides through the clouds and swells the storm . . .
> [*PW*, I, 546–549]

—whereas the "black Appearance" that was "never sent to live / Amid the weakness of a mortal heart" in the *Gothic Tale* (ll. 172–175) is wholly explicable in rational terms, and so belongs to the tradition of Ann Radcliffe's popular *Romance of the Forest* (1791):

> And gone he left the stripling light of soul,
> Nor doubting but the hand that vault had shown
> Was earthly, 'mid lamp-smothering vapours foul,
> So fashioned to his eye by sparkles thrown
> On the thick air from fire-detaining wood
> Or flint whose sound the wind had made its own.
> [*GT*, ll. 181–186]

Mrs. Radcliffe's apparitions are designed to satisfy her audience's desire for spectral sensationalism without offending their rationalist sensibilities. Wordsworth's concern is to demonstrate the psychological susceptibility of his protagonist. The psychological theory behind the poem reflects, of course, the general prevalence of David Hartley's theory of the association of ideas. But the specific source that provided a model for the poem was probably the description of murder in Joseph Fawcett's antiwar poem, *The Art of War* (London, 1795):

It is a deed,
Which when determin'd by a tempted wretch,
All his dire fund of fortitude in ill
He must call forth to do, and wind his heart
As high as it will stretch. His choice of time
He fixes on the hour when all the world
Is dead; when with the colour of his act
Darkness accords; and every eye is clos'd.
*Between his purpose and his dreadful stroke
Wild is the space within him: **to the scene
Of his dark act, with a light-falling foot,
Ghost-like he glides; and fancifully fears
Lest strange and wondrous voices wake the world
And babble of his business.

**Julius Caesar*
***Macbeth*
[*The Art of War*, ll. 1017–1030; footnotes Fawcett's]

In the *Gothic Tale* Wordsworth gives Fawcett's generalized description a particular context. The wild scenery and "mysterious men" drawn from the various Gothic sources discussed above become the means by which the murderer's heart is wound "as high as it will stretch":

For as they came the precipice's ridge
[Lessons of death] [at every step] had given,
And at the crossing of the pendent bridge
With impulse horrible his heart had striven;
And now with black regret he cursed agen
The fragment which the winds had idly riven,
But chief that place and those mysterious men
There seen did for his bloody purpose plead,
Of every human fear disburthening the deed.
[*GT*, ll. 145–153]

But the stripling's sense that the wild scene is sympathetic to his scheme—his feeling that "with the colour of his act / Darkness accords" (Fawcett)—is purely subjective; and when he attempts to throttle the old man, a second series of episodes dispels his sense of union with his surroundings and replaces it with equally subjective superstitious fears. One of the episodes in this second sequence reappears in *The Borderers*:

At length he rose, by irksome thought impelled,
And, looking up in restless walk, on high
Above the dungeon's roof a star beheld,

Whose sparkling lustre through [the] crevice shed
Sent to his fluttering heart a momentary dread.
[*GT*, ll. 194–198]

Mortimer I cast my eyes upwards, and through a crevice in the roof I beheld a star twinkling over my head, and by the living God, I could not do it— [*The Borderers*, II.iii.289–291]

The interruption is peculiarly Wordsworthian, and like many of the scenic details in *The Borderers* may have had a partially autobiographical origin. In *The Prelude* (I, 318–324) Wordsworth describes his bird-snaring exploits in a passage reminiscent of the *Gothic Tale*, and in later conversation with Thomas De Quincey he observed:

. . . if, under any circumstances, the attention is energetically braced up to an act of steady observation, or of steady expectation, then, if this intense condition of vigilance should suddenly relax, at that moment any beautiful, any impressive visual object, or collection of objects, falling upon the eye, is carried to the heart with a power not known under other circumstances. Just now . . . at the very instant when the organs of attention were all at once relaxing from their tension, the bright star hanging in the air above those outlines of massy blackness fell suddenly upon my eye, and penetrated my capacity of apprehension with a pathos and a sense of the infinite, that would not have arrested me under other circumstances. ["Lake Reminiscences, From 1807 to 1830 by the English Opium-Eater . . . ," *Tait's Edinburgh Magazine*, 6 (1839), 94][14]

Whether or not the star that halts the stripling is based on Wordsworth's personal experience, it is clearly used to provide a dramatic instance of fears like those that had beset Fawcett's murderer:

Of heaven and earth he feels himself accurst.
With wildest superstition seiz'd, he dreads
That preternat'ral Providence will point
Its finger at his guilt.
[*The Art of War*, ll. 1034–1037]

The "black Appearance," the single star sighted above the dungeon's roof, and the sight of the calmly sinking moon "leading the storm's remains along th'horizon's brink" (*GT*, l. 207) arouse in the stripling, rationalize as he may, an overwhelming terror "Lest strange and wondrous voices wake the world / And babble of his business" (Fawcett). Finally, there is a "painful outcry strange" (*GT*, l. 216), which reduces the stripling to a state of paralysis and wakes up the old man.

For *The Borderers* Wordsworth replaced the stripling's greed with a more honorable motive for murder. Mortimer, the "stripling" of the play, is convinced that Herbert has committed crimes "beyond the reach of thought" (II.iii.60), and he attempts to murder the saintly, blind old man in order to

[14] Quoted and discussed by Arthur Beatty, *William Wordsworth: His Doctrine and Art in Their Historical Relations* (2d. ed.; Madison, Wis., 1927), pp. 161–162.

fulfill what he regards as his sacred duty to destroy "this enormous culprit" (II.iii.394). He thus approaches the murder in a spirit akin to that with which Othello approaches the murder of Desdemona. Othello is on the one hand determined that Desdemona "must die, else she'll betray more men,"[15] and on the other appalled by the staunchness with which she maintains the appearance of innocence:

> O perjur'd woman! thou dost stone my heart,
> And mak'st me call what I intend to do
> A murder, which I thought a sacrifice.
> [*Othello*, V.ii.63–65][16]

In *The Borderers* it is because the sight of a star makes Mortimer call what he intends to do a murder, which he thought a sacrifice, that he fails to kill Herbert at Mounteagle Castle.

V

In the *Gothic Tale* Wordsworth contrasts the mode in which the stripling responds to the wildness of the night with the sentimental response of his blind companion, the sailor. For the stripling, each new incident "did for his bloody purpose plead, / Of every human fear disburthening the deed" (ll. 152–153). For the sailor, on the other hand, the youth's protection almost rekindled human hope in a mind "devoted to the grave" (l. 209), creating a filial bond between himself and his guide which he was loath to lose, and which he pathetically offered to cement by adopting the stripling as his heir. The blind sailor of the *Gothic Tale* is obviously Herbert's antecedent, and both embrace the ethic of "sentimental morality"[17] that Wordsworth had previously preached in *Adventures on Salisbury Plain* (and *The Convict*):

> Much need have ye that time more closely draw
> The bond of nature, all unkindness cease,
> And that among so few there still be peace:
> Else can ye hope but with such num'rous foes
> Your pains shall ever with your years increase.
> [*ASP*, ll. 660–664]

---

[15] *Othello*, V.ii.6. Also borrowed from *Othello* is the sexual horror that preys on Mortimer's mind; see I.i.249–266, I.iii.171–183, II.i.117–122, II.iii.215–282, III.ii.43–66, and III.v. 111–180. In the last of these scenes Wordsworth rather clumsily attempts to imitate the dramatic tension in the dialogues in which Othello and Desdemona misunderstand each other's allusions.

[16] In the *GT*, also, there is a shift of perception: the stripling first views his action as a heroic assertion of self in a supportively wild scene, but after seeing the star and the calm sky he returns from the courtyard a mere murderer, as the verb makes clear: "So back he slunk . . ." (l. 208).

[17] See O. J. Campbell and P. Mueschke, "Guilt and Sorrow: A Study in the Genesis of Wordsworth's Aesthetic" and "*The Borderers* as a Document in the History of Wordsworth's Aesthetic Development," *Modern Philology*, 23 (1926), 293–306 and 465–482. The latter article is marred by the authors' somewhat melodramatic view of the part played by Annette Vallon in creating Wordsworth's supposed "moral crisis" in the years 1793–1797.

But unlike the sailor, Herbert possesses a child of his own; and his response to Mortimer's protection in Act II is made in a semireligious mode that reflects the kind of strength he draws from the "bond of nature" between himself and his daughter.

The Churchyard Scene in the *Ur-Borderers* provides a study in the failure of the "bond of nature." Like Herbert, the Old Pilgrim of this scene visited the Holy Land and returned to find himself isolated with his child and condemned to a perpetual pilgrimage. But whereas Matilda was for Herbert "a raven sent to [him] in the wilderness" and the comforter of his despair, the Old Pilgrim's child was infected and finally killed by his father's alienation from the world that had rejected him; the Old Pilgrim's misfortunes have reduced him to a position where his heart "answers not any purposes of being." The "functions of a man" have become similarly deranged, so that his laughter is like Robert's "freaks of merriment" in *The Ruined Cottage* (see ll. 213–241).[18] The only solution to his misery, and the final object of his pilgrimage, is death.

Matilda and the Old Peasant first respond to the Pilgrim's account of his alienation with a sentimental consolation—

> At length thou shalt be quiet and lie still;
> Sorrow shall seek at morn and shall not find thee.
> [Churchyard Scene, ll. 61–62][19]

then by proposing to create new "bond[s] of nature" by uniting two "void" hearts. (One is reminded of the blind sailor's wish to adopt the stripling as a son [*GT*, ll. 127–130] and the union forged between Herbert, the Old Pilgrim, and the infant Matilda during Herbert's wanderings—"we joined our tales of wretchedness together" [II.ii.18]—the kind of alliance Wordsworth first presented in *Salisbury Plain.*) Matilda's final response is a triumphant assertion of the unfailing powers of "the common offices of love":

> Yes, trust me, pilgrim: long as thy red blood
> Is warm, this old man knows, there is a power
> Even in the common offices of love
> And friendly ministration, to revive
> Nature within thee, bid thee smile again
> With those that smile, and weep with them that weep.
> [Churchyard Scene, ll. 95–100]

The contrast between the Old Pilgrim's death wish and Herbert's humble and joyful acceptance of his poverty with Matilda establishes both Herbert's

---

[18] The Churchyard Scene would appear to be the first poetry in which Wordsworth systematically employed the symbols of relationship and alienation used with such delicacy throughout *The Ruined Cottage* (discussed in *M of H*, pp. 102–120).

[19] Compare Armytage's "sentimental" consolation in *RC*, MS. D, l. 512: "She sleeps in the calm earth, and peace is here."

faith in "the common offices of love" and the terms in which that faith is maintained. In this last respect, Wordsworth goes further than he had in his earlier poetry toward proposing the terms on which reconciliation with the natural world can occur. Later, in *Tintern Abbey*, he was to reaffirm that "Nature never did betray / The heart that loved her," not because his former relationship is unchanged, but because it is subsumed in a more mature religious relationship with the guardian of his heart and "moral being." Similarly, in *The Borderers* Herbert's unshaken faith in the "bond of nature" depends on the fact that with the loss of his eyes the bond has been renewed in religious terms, Matilda functioning for Herbert as "nature's priest," and Herbert for Matilda as a religious as well as secular father (a pairing that foreshadows the present and projected relationship between William and Dorothy in *Tintern Abbey*). Herbert differs from the earlier advocates of the "bond of nature" in *Adventures on Salisbury Plain*, *The Convict*, and the *Gothic Tale*. He has renounced the world, and shares with the Old Pilgrim the mystical sanctity of a man whose "life is hidden with God"[20] but without having lost his "true and perfect mind." Herbert's language is pervaded with biblical references and biblical rhythms: his vocabulary, his age, his blindness, and his humility all identify him as a holy man, and strengthen his association with Herbert of Derwentwater. On returning to a home that no longer recognizes his secular claim to his baronetcy, he has become a perpetual pilgrim. Implicit is a parallel with Christ: "The foxes have holes, and the birds of the air have nests, but the Son of Man hath not where to lay his head" (Matthew 8:20). Yet the gospel that Herbert preaches is not Christianity but a natural religion derived from biblical myth and realized in his relationship with Matilda:

I heard a voice
Such as by Cherith on Elijah called;
It said, "I will be with thee." A little boy,
A Shepherd's lad, ere yet my trance was gone,
Hailed us, as if he had been sent from heaven,
And said with tears that he would be our guide;
I had a better guide—that innocent babe
Who to this hour hath saved me from all evil,
From cold, from death, from penury and hunger.
Therefore I bless her: when I think of man
I bless her with sad spirit; when of God,
I bless her in the fulness of my joy!
[III.iii.104–115]

---

[20] This is the phrase Wordsworth applies to idiots in his defense of *The Idiot Boy* in the letter to John Wilson (*EY*, p. 357). The mystical sanctity of the Old Pilgrim is linked with his idiocy, and is established in the opening lines of the Churchyard Scene.

As secular saints, Herbert and Matilda are of course modeled on their counterparts in *King Lear*. Matilda is, like Cordelia, her father's one prop in a desolate old age, and she ministers to him in the same saintlike manner. Herbert is like Gloucester in his blindness, but all of his most important characteristics—his devotion to his daughter, his age, his feebleness, and his holiness—are qualities of the reformed Lear. Both the language of the play and the use of the heath as the dramatic setting for Herbert's ordeal establish the importance of *King Lear* as a model for *The Borderers*. Nor is this importance limited to simple correspondences in character, language, and setting. For *The Borderers*, like *Lear*, is a tragedy concerned with testing the effectiveness of myths on which one may base one's life. In his portrayal of Herbert and Matilda, Wordsworth has combined the sentimental and religious motifs of his earlier poetry with those of *King Lear* to present the ultimate failure of "the common offices of love" to sustain either the saintly blind old man or his daughter in a friendless world in which man is "betrayed" and nature unsympathetic to his sufferings. When Herbert begs to know if anyone is about, Mortimer answers him sternly:

Not a soul!
Here is a tree, ragged and bent and bare,
Which turns its goatsbeard flakes of pea-green moss
From the stern breathing of the rough sea wind—
We have no other company, my friend!
[III.iii.36–40][21]

Matilda's sustaining principles are her faith in the regenerative bond between man and nature, faith in "the common offices of love," and obedience to her father's command to "bless all mankind" (V.iii.61). In an exchange with Herbert which echoes her attempt to rally the despairing Pilgrim in the discarded Churchyard Scene, she rallies her father by attributing his gloom to a literal lack of perception:

Matilda:
. . . you hear the woods
Resound with music; could you see the sun,
And look upon the pleasant face of Nature—

Herbert:
I understand thee: I should be as chearful
As if we two were twins; two songsters bred
In the same nest, my spring-time one with thine.
[I.i.117–122]

---

[21] Mary Moorman remarks that "Nature in *The Borderers* is always a 'benevolent' influence" (Moorman, I, 306), and quotes this passage as an instance. But the tree is emblematic of, not sympathetic to, Herbert's suffering. See Peter L. Thorslev, Jr., "Wordsworth's *Borderers* and the Romantic Villain-Hero," *Studies in Romanticism*, V (1966), 84–103.

The passage echoes, in undomesticated form, Lear's resolution that he and Cordelia will sit and "sing like birds i' the cage" (*Lear*, V.iii.9). In *Lear*, of course, it is the old man whom the gods eventually mock by hanging his poor fool, the "raven sent to him in the wilderness." In *The Borderers*, it is the daughter who survives to witness the failure of their shared semimystical ideal of "sentimental morality." In soliloquy in Act II, Rivers had described such idealists as "fools of feeling":

> . . . mere birds of winter
> That haunt some barren island of the north,
> Where if a famishing man stretch forth his hand
> They think it is to feed them.—
> [II.i.5–8]

The point is sharply brought home when the pious image of the biblical raven is bleakly realized in the ministrations of the "solitary crow" that Matilda disturbs at her father's corpse (V.ii.64–73).

VI

In his capacity as a deceiver, Rivers derives most obviously from Iago, even to the sexual revulsion that underlies his warning to Mortimer that "The world is poisoned at the heart" (II.iii.344). Descendants of Iago who may also have been an influence on the villain of *The Borderers* are Francis and Spiegelberg in Schiller's *Robbers* and the cunning Gines in William Godwin's *Things as They Are: or the Adventures of Caleb Williams* (3 vols.; London, 1794). Either independently or through *Caleb Williams*, Schiller's *Robbers*, translated by A. F. Tytler in 1792, is the obvious source behind Mortimer's philanthropic leadership of a band of borderers among whom there is one Judas figure. But in dominating by philosophic rhetoric rather than by cunning, Rivers appears to derive from the eighteenth-century romance tradition of rationalist philosopher-villains, specifically, as Emile Legouis noted, from the Marquis de Montalt in Ann Radcliffe's *Romance of the Forest* (1791):

> "There are, I repeat it," said the Marquis, "people of minds so weak, as to shrink from acts they have been accustomed to hold wrong, however advantageous. *They never suffer themselves to be guided by circumstances, but fix for life upon a certain standard, from which they will, on no account, depart.* Self-preservation is the great law of nature; when a reptile hurts us, or an animal of prey threatens us, we think no farther but endeavour to annihilate it. When my life, or what may be essential to my life, requires the sacrifice of another, or even if some passion, wholly unconquerable, requires it, I should be a mad-man to hesitate."[22]

---

[22] Quoted by Legouis in *The Early Life of William Wordsworth*, trans. J. W. Matthews (New York, 1918), p. 272; his italics.

Legouis rightly remarked that Mrs. Radcliffe's chief virtue for the literary historian is that she is "our best source of information on what the reader of the moment considered a faithful representation of a criminal."[23] He observed that the character of the Marquis "faintly foreshadows" that of Rivers:

> They are alike in their contempt for every sort of "prejudice," that is to say, in ordinary language, for all the feelings which go to make up human nature. They admit no settled moral law, and claim the right of deciding for themselves, without any intermediary, what they ought to do. Both of them justify murder as a sign and proof of the moral independence of the murderer.[24]

"Faintly foreshadows" is clearly an understatement. In addition to the similarity between the words of the Marquis and Rivers's praise of the "independent intellect" to which Legouis draws attention, the parallel that the Marquis draws between killing men and killing reptiles, with its appeal to the concept of "natural law," is used twice by Rivers (II.iii.231–234 and III.v.92–105), and Rivers's scorn at the concepts of justice, remorse, and dishonor echoes the Marquis's attitude (V.iii.252–255).

The archetype behind both the Marquis and Rivers is doubtless the Satan of *Paradise Lost.* The "independence" to which Rivers aspires, and which he seeks to create in Mortimer, is analogous to that proclaimed by Satan:

> Receive thy new Possessor: One who brings,
> A mind not to be chang'd by Place or Time.
> The mind is its own place, and in it self
> Can make a Heav'n of Hell, a Hell of Heav'n.
> [*Paradise Lost*, I, 252–255]

Like Satan, Rivers asserts the inviolability of his new-found autonomy; and like Satan, who "trusted to have equal'd the most High, / If he oppos'd" (*Paradise Lost*, I, 40–41), Rivers demands a shadow of himself as proof of his independent power. The knowledge that Rivers offers is the knowledge of lost innocence—

> What if you have bid
> Eternal farewell to unmingled joy
> And the light dancing of the thoughtless heart—
> [III.v.66–68]

—in place of which he promises that satanic magnificence which links "pleasure with greatness" (IV.ii.207–209). But most important, Rivers is, like Satan, a deceiver-initiator committed to bringing about the reenactment of his own fall. The ambivalence of Rivers's function as hypocritical Machiavel and his function as sincere initiator reflects the paradox implicit in the act of satanic appropriation: while the act of precipitating the "fall" is deliberately

[23] Legouis, *Early Life of William Wordsworth*, p. 271.
[24] Ibid., p. 272.

destructive and achieved through deception, it is also an initiation into that state which pride compels both Satan in *Paradise Lost* and Rivers in *The Borderers* to regard in all sincerity as their most precious, unique possession—the state of the "fallen" and therefore "independent" consciousness. The theme of satanic appropriation recurs throughout Rivers's speeches, being reflected, for instance, in his reference to the "chain of adamant" with which he has bound Mortimer to him, and in his use of the term "cleave" (ritualistically repeated twice) to describe an unholy sacrament that mocks Mortimer's earlier dream of marriage to Matilda.

But Rivers's relationship to Satan does not dominate the play. Neither Rivers's nor Mortimer's "fall" is original, nor is Rivers the only satanic character in the play (behind the present action looms Clifford). Rivers's promise of intellectual independence is not an invitation to desert the Garden of Eden but an attempt to escape the consequence of Adam's fall:

> Remorse,
> It cannot live with thought, think on, think on,
> And it will die.—
> [III.v.81–83]

In common with the radicals of the 1790s, Rivers hopes to become "The Man to come parted as by a gulph, / From him who had been" (*Prelude*, XI, 59–60):

> The genuine and wholesome state of mind is, to be unloosed from shackles, and to expand every fibre of its frame according to the independent and individual impressions of truth upon that mind. How great would be the progress of intellectual improvement, if men were unfettered by the prejudices of education, unseduced by the influence of a corrupt state of society, and accustomed to yield without fear to the guidance of truth, however unexplored might be the regions and unexpected the conclusions to which she conducted us? [William Godwin, *Enquiry Concerning Political Justice*, II, 195]

Enid Welsford[25] rightly finds in this passage a specific source for the language in which Rivers congratulates Mortimer for supposedly murdering Herbert:

> You have taught mankind to seek the measure of justice
> By diving for it into their own bosoms.
> To day you have thrown off a tyranny
> That lives but by the torpid acquiescence
> Of our emasculated souls, the tyranny
> Of moralists and saints and lawgivers.
> You have obeyed the only law that wisdom
> Can ever recognize: the immediate law
> Flashed from the light of circumstances
> Upon an independent intellect.
> [III.v.24–33]

---

[25] *Salisbury Plain: A Study in the Development of Wordsworth's Mind and Art* (Oxford, 1966), p. 146.

But though Rivers's language derives from *Political Justice*, he is fundamentally lacking in Godwinian benevolence. Implicit in Wordsworth's characterization of Rivers is the denial that the intellect can ever be truly independent. The philosophy that promises "to abstract the hopes of man / Out of his feelings" offers only a "Tempting region . . . Where passions [have] the privilege to work, / And never hear the sound of their own names" (*Prelude*, X, 808–814). Neither *The Borderers* nor Book X of *The Prelude*, in which Wordsworth recounts his temporary alignment with Rivers's philosophy, can be regarded as totally repudiating the thought of the radical movement of the 1790s characterized by *Political Justice*. Society's need for salvation is made abundantly clear in both *The Borderers* and Book X of *The Prelude*. And in both, as throughout his so-called great decade, Wordsworth upholds the tenets of the new morality advanced by Godwin, his attack on "just" punishment, and his ideals of selflessness, humanity, and sincerity. Wordsworth, in describing the period of his own radical rationalist speculations, portrayed himself as having been "betray'd"

> By present objects, and by reasoning false
> From the beginning, inasmuch as drawn
> Out of a heart which had been turn'd aside
> From nature by external accidents . . .
> [*Prelude*, X, 884–887]

But he insisted as much on "what then I learn'd, or think I learn'd, of truth" as he did on "errors into which I was betray'd." Yet the primacy that Wordsworth gives to emotion in shaping men's actions and intellectual convictions makes the Godwinian concept of salvation through intellectual independence absurd: not only does "passion in a state of solemn and omnipotent vehemence always [appear] coolness to him in whom it domineers" (*Caleb Williams*, III, 283–284), but passion always domineers: "Such a mind cannot but discover some truths, but he is unable to profit by them and in his hands they become instruments of evil" (essay on Rivers, p. 65, below).

If the influence of *Political Justice* on the formulation of Rivers's character has been overstressed by commentators, that of *Caleb Williams* has been oddly neglected. In the development of Rivers's role as initiator, Godwin's novel is of the first importance. The imperious tragic villain of the novel, Falkland, is presented as the victim of the psychological circumstances that drove him to commit murder. The secret of his guilt creates a complex, mutually destructive intimacy between himself and his secretary, Caleb Williams, which culminates in Caleb's realization, in the dramatic courtroom scene at the end of the novel, that he has become his master's shadow. Each comes to the courtroom prepared to confront the other in an act of final self-justifying repudiation, yet each remains to confess his own guilt and to bless his tormentor. Falkland in so doing regains something of his original innocence, and Caleb Williams assumes the full burden of his master's guilt:

> "I have told a plain and unadulterated tale. I came hither to curse, but I remain to bless. I came to accuse, but am compelled to applaud. I proclaim to all the world that Mr. Falkland is a man worthy of affection and kindness, and that I am myself the worst of villains! . . . In thus acting I have been a murderer, a cool, deliberate, unfeeling murderer." [*Caleb Williams*, III, 296]

The mutually destructive relationship that was presented in *Caleb Williams* as the tragic consequence of Falkland's past reappears in *The Borderers* as Rivers's deliberate objective. What Rivers seeks in Mortimer is precisely what Falkland found so reluctantly in Caleb Williams, a "son" who will be set apart from

> the world's presumptuous judges
> Who damn where they can neither see nor feel,
> In the hard-hearted pride of ignorance.
> [III.v.39–41]

In the final courtroom scene of *Caleb Williams* Falkland throws himself into Caleb's arms; in *The Borderers* an equivalent confession of kinship is anticipated in IV.ii.186–189, and achieved in the pledge given by Mortimer in the final scene:

> *Rivers* We are then friends—
> *Mortimer* I am the friend of all men.
> *Rivers* Of me especially—
> *Mortimer* Why, yes!
> *Rivers* A pledge—
> *Mortimer* Here is my hand . . .
> [V.iii.227–229]

Concealed in Rivers's confession is even, perhaps, the distant hope of achieving a new innocence like that which Falkland gains unexpectedly at the close of the novel. The attainment of such forgiveness is the motive hinted at when "One of the Band" asks:

> What if he mean to offer up our Captain,
> An expiation, and a sacrifice
> To those infernal fiends?
> [III.iv.38–40]

The infernal fiend to whom Rivers shows himself to be bound is a psychological fiend, the conditioning imposed upon him by his own past. And it is from the guilt arising from that bondage that Mortimer delivers him:

> There are men
> Who with bare hand would have plucked out thy heart
> And flung it to the dogs.—But I forgive thee.
> [V.iii.247–249]

It is perhaps significant that it is only after these words have been spoken that Rivers wholly disengages himself from his "shadow" and dispassionately describes the instrument of his expiation as "A fool and Coward blended to my wish."

VII

In the notes to the 1842 text, Wordsworth emphasized his concern with psychological truth, particularly "in respect to the two leading Persons of the Drama":

> The study of human nature suggests this awful truth, that, as in the trials to which life subjects us, sin and crime are apt to start from their very opposite qualities, so are there no limits to the hardening of the heart, and the perversion of the understanding to which they may carry their slaves. During my long residence in France, while the Revolution was rapidly advancing to its extreme of wickedness, I had frequent opportunities of being an eye-witness of this process, and it was while that knowledge was fresh upon my memory, that the Tragedy of "The Borderers" was composed. [*PELY*, p. 405; see Appendix III, below].

The passage, as well as inviting speculation as to possible life models for Rivers, highlights Wordsworth's concern with what in the 1843 Fenwick note he termed "transition in character." The term is one that Mortimer uses of himself, and is italicized in the early version:

> there is something
> Which looks like a *transition* in my soul . . .
> [II.i.91–92]

"Transition in character" is in *The Borderers* inextricably linked with the experience of betrayal. Looking back on the sequence of experiences that led to his marooning of the sea captain, Rivers speaks of himself as having been "deserted / By man and nature" (IV.ii.17–18); and his definitive "crime" was to harden his heart to impose the same desertion on his imagined persecutor. For Mortimer, the transition begins with the breakdown of his own sense of identity in the face of Herbert's supposed betrayal of the sanctity of fatherhood:

> The firm foundation of my life appears
> To sink from under me. This business, Rivers,
> Will be my ruin.——
> [I.iii.181–183]

By the middle of Act II Mortimer's mind has been, in Rivers's phrase, "upturned," and he is suffering from Hamlet's disease—deep shock in the face of the apparent disjunction between appearance and reality. The "fearful ordeal" to which his hardened heart leads him to subject Herbert mirrors his own experience of alienation from the star that appeared as the eye of

God (II.iii.205) but was merely "a twinkling atom" (III.ii.78). As Herbert's physical guide, he betrays the old man who has betrayed him as a moral guide, and the ordeal takes the form of exposure to what Mortimer now perceives as the true nature of nature.

The context within which Mortimer undergoes the "transition in character" that leads him to abandon Herbert on the heath is an artificial one. Through Rivers's agency he is betrayed "By man and nature," as Rivers himself was betrayed by the captain's crew. The chain of circumstance is strengthened by two other betrayals in the background: Clifford's betrayal of the crazed maid who now haunts the churchyard in the descriptions of I.iii.5–22 and II.i.13–31, and the unjust imprisonment that lies behind Robert's failure to succor Herbert. Rivers's famous lines on action and suffering go further in suggesting that any action is in some sense a crime against nature, awakening us to guilty self-consciousness and dooming us to pass on to the other definitive attribute of the human condition, which is the experience of suffering:

> Action is transitory, a step, a blow—
> The motion of a muscle—this way or that—
> 'Tis done—and in the after vacancy
> We wonder at ourselves like men betray'd.
> Suffering is permanent, obscure and dark,
> And has the nature of infinity.
> [III.v.60–65]

He who has been betrayed into "crime" becomes in his turn the betrayer. The sense of guilt that drives such a betrayer becomes the dominant theme in the last act of *The Borderers*. Thus Robert, guilty of having failed to stay beside the dying Herbert, seeks to exculpate himself by pointing his finger at Mortimer: "A wicked man should answer for his crimes" (V.iii.7). Matilda, herself troubled by her failure to come to her father's aid, nevertheless remains staunch to his precepts at first, and refuses to respond to Robert's plea that she confront the "murderer" (V.iii.1–17). But when Mortimer enters, driven by his continuing obsession with justice and the desire for punishment, he is more successful in seducing her:

> Matilda, at this moment
> I feel a most unusual fondness for thee.
> Thou must be wise as I am, thou must know
> What human nature is, decoyed, betrayed—
> I have the proofs.
> [V.iii.56–60]

His language is that of *Paradise Lost*: with "unusual fondness" he proffers the apple, "Thou must be wise as I am." Adam's failing was to be "fondly overcome with Femal charm" (*Paradise Lost*, IX, 999). Here the seduction is reversed, but equally effective:

> Oh! miserable father!
> Thou did'st command to bless all mankind,
> Nor to this moment have I ever wished
> Evil to any living thing—but hear me,
> Hear me, ye Heavens! (*kneeling*) may vengeance haunt the fiend
> For this most cruel murder—let him live
> And move in terror of the elements . . .
> [V.iii.60–66]

With her curse, Matilda satisfies Mortimer's lust for a judgment, and in so doing rejects the creative alternative to the cry for justice—the ethic of blessing "all mankind" taught her by her father. Matilda's fall, like that of Mortimer when he abandoned Herbert with no hope of rescue save by miracle, is marked by a degeneration into superstition—a sure indication of the "distance and distaste" (*Paradise Lost*, IX, 9) that now separate her from the "natural religion" she embraced during her father's lifetime.

Superstition is presented in the play as the first step on the path to insanity, that final refuge of unrelieved suffering. When the "firm foundations" of life have been betrayed, the mind counters its sense of isolation and helplessness by turning to "seek for sympathies / In dim relations to imagined beings" (III.iv.36–37). Thus in II.iii Mortimer, like Lear in the storm, superstitiously projects his own moral outrage onto nature, and in the last act both Robert and Matilda invoke supernatural intervention to identify and punish the "murderer." But nature in *The Borderers* is insensitive to human appeal. What the outer world provides for the mind to project upon appears to be controlled by chance. To Rivers, a victim of his own projections, the universe in which we act and suffer is one

> Where the least things controul the greatest, where
> The faintest breath that breathes can move a world—
> [III.v.84–85]

In the face of this realization the alienation of the protagonist deepens, and the mind turns inward again—whether, as in the case of Rivers, to find "within" "A salient spring of energy, a fire / Of inextinguishable thought" (IV.ii.118–120) with which to defy "suffering," or, as in the case of the crazed woman in the churchyard or the captain's daughter (omitted in the late version), to descend into "a fearful world of [its] own making / . . . cut off from the society / Of every rational thing" [IV.ii.87–89]. The implication is that suffering and guilt alike—both of which are experienced as betrayal—lead to psychosis, as the mind once more projects its demons:

> *Mortimer*
> There is something
> That must be cleared away . . . That staff
> Which bars the road before me there.—'Tis there,
> 'Tis there breast-high and will not let me pass—
> [V.iii.197–200]

The Beggarwoman, herself already "haunted" by her part in the deception, envies Mortimer the condition on the edge of which she trembles:

> He is crazed,
> Poor Gentleman! and *I* have wrought this evil.
> The little children from the cottages
> Will be his friends—he will be blessed and pitied.
> —What will become of me?—
> [V.iii.213–217]

Mortimer himself, envisioning Matilda as reduced, like the sea captain's daughter, to "her father's skeleton," sees death as the preferable alternative.

The spectacle of Mortimer's degeneration into madness is brought to an abrupt halt in the early version by the arrival of his tormentor, who proceeds to catechize him to see if he has now finally been purged of the legacy of faith in traditional morality, guilt, and punishment. In the late version, Wordsworth toned down Mortimer's (now Marmaduke's) derangement, and omitted the catechism entirely. Marmaduke's confession to Idonea places less emphasis on his guilt than on the fiendishness of the deceit wrought on him (2225–2236), and his speech to Oswald commends remorse as the link of "sympathy" that should now bind betrayer and betrayed in "an incommunicable rivalship" (2260–2279). Marmaduke's piety, hardly ruffled by the band's prompt murder of Oswald (a "rash deed" that produces Marmaduke's reproof and his resignation of the captainship), continues into the final speech, in which Marmaduke describes his "penitence" and his hope that his search for "expiation" will lead to the time when finally "anger is appeased / In Heaven, and Mercy gives me leave to die" (2320–2321).

Readers who compare the early version of the final scene with the late version may find the latter, if somewhat priggish, a good deal smoother than the former, in which Mortimer's confusion abruptly ceases on the arrival of his apparent "master," the arrival of the band is equally abrupt, and the stage is inexplicably flooded with friars before Mortimer's final speech. There is in this scene a degree of crude melodrama that is unmatched elsewhere in the play; and the final exchanges, from Rivers's entry onward, are cryptic in the extreme. Yet the degeneration and derangement of Matilda and Mortimer bring home the nightmare of guilt and suffering that has haunted Mortimer since he "thought [he] saw a skeleton of Matilda" in the image of the crazed woman walking "round and round" in the graveyard (II.i.29–31), and feared that "This business, Rivers, / Will be my ruin." It is a theatrical demonstration of the tragic cycle of action and suffering from which Herbert's doctrine of "natural religion" has failed to protect either himself or his daughter (the spectacle of the old man crawling toward the sound of a bell blown by the wind reinforces the impression of how completely we may be "deserted / By man and nature"), which a belief like Mortimer's naive faith in "justice" fails to ameliorate, and to which Rivers still, on his entry, appears to have the most powerful answer.

In *Adventures on Salisbury Plain* and in *The Convict* Wordsworth had expressed an entirely Godwinian horror at the vicious round of betrayal, crime, guilt, and punishment perpetuated, as Godwin had argued, by the self-righteous quest for justice in an unjust society. The protagonist of *Adventures on Salisbury Plain* embraced death, "Not without pleasure" (l. 812), as a relief from "a burden not to be sustain'd" (l. 800). Yet the society that calls such an end "justice" is wholly sick:

> They left him hung on high in iron case,
> And dissolute men, unthinking and untaught,
> Planted their festive booths beneath his face;
> And to that spot, which idle thousands sought,
> Women and children were by fathers brought . . .
> [*ASP*, ll. 820–824]

In *The Convict* Wordsworth had been as appalled by the criminal's soul-destroying obsession with his guilt as he was by the conditions in which he languished. But whereas rehabilitation programs might provide a solution to the sufferings of the Convict, the disease of man's condition as presented in *The Borderers* has a new depth, and a new universality, which Godwin's "benevolence" cannot hope to reach: "The world is poisoned at the heart" (II.iii.344). The theme of alienation between man and nature first appears to be given its full weight in Wordsworth's composition of *The Borderers*, which is dominated by a landscape to which he was to return for one of the "spots of time" in the *Prelude*—the landscape of Stainmore, above Penrith:

> I left the spot
> And, reascending the bare Common, saw
> A naked Pool that lay beneath the hills,
> The Beacon on the summit, and more near,
> A Girl who bore a Pitcher on her head
> And seem'd with difficult steps to force her way
> Against the blowing wind.
> [*Prelude*, XI, 302–308]

Rivers's claim is to have freed himself from the bond of nature, conceived of both as sociopsychological and cosmological, and to have been reborn as what in *Prelude* X Wordsworth calls "the Man to come":

> I seemed a being who had passed alone
> Beyond the visible barriers of the world
> And travelled into things to come.
> [IV.ii.143–145]

His superior power is dramatically demonstrated when his final entry instantly calms Mortimer's "foolish freaks," and the sardonic catechism begins.

But there is an undercurrent of irony in the evenness with which Mortimer holds his ground in his cryptic responses to his apparent master. The sting comes at the end:

> There are men
> Who with bare hand would have plucked out thy heart
> And flung it to the dogs.—But I forgive thee.
> [V.iii.247–249]

Even if "forgiveness" is at one level, as I have suggested, what Rivers seeks, and confirms for him that Mortimer is "a fool and Coward" and in some sense his slave (though whether he sought a slave or a companion was ambiguous), the way in which Mortimer allows the threat "There are men . . ." to hang in the air before he delivers forgiveness as his blow indicates mastery rather than slavery.

This speech marks Mortimer's final transition in character. The questions raised concerning Mortimer in the final scene are both psychological and moral: how far has Mortimer fallen for Rivers's "repetition compulsion" solution to the tragedy of the action/suffering cycle, and what other way remains for him to find through this tragic maze, in which innocent and guilty alike are so ensnared? These questions remain held in brilliant dramatic poise until the final lines of the play. There Mortimer, like his mentor, undertakes a "lonely wandering"; and like Rivers, he recognizes that individuated man is characterized by "intensity of thought," which enables him to recognize the absolute distinction between the inner world of mental activity and the outer world of the serenely atomic star. But to Mortimer it is "mere" intensity. He thus reverses Rivers's value system and reaches toward the venerable Armytage of *The Ruined Cottage*, the wise old man who sees both our suffering (the tear in an old man's eye) and our "restless thoughts" as "the weakness of humanity."

The Borderers anticipates *The Ruined Cottage* in presenting a shattered idyll (the strength of the father-daughter relationship that is Mortimer's inspiration) as a kind of fall from grace, despite the innocence of the characters whose myth fails to protect them from that fall. The point is more subtly made in *The Ruined Cottage* when Margaret experiences her tears as unnatural ("And I could never die") and the cottage door is stained by the dye markings of the passing sheep. Reconciliation in *The Ruined Cottage* is a matter less of philosophy than of an experiential dynamic: the relief the reader experiences, within the tale, in the eventual end to unrelievable suffering, and Margaret's achievement, in her final days, of a "stillness" as relatively permanent as the "enormous elms" outside her door; the relief experienced, more mystically, outside the tale, in Armytage's memory of the weeds and spear-grass "silver'd o'er" in a still image of tranquillity, and in the gentle juxtaposition of linnet and elm as the once-halted travelers move out of the frame. The final lines of *The Borderers* do not invoke, as Armytage perhaps does, the doctrine of the "One Life" that Wordsworth was about to develop in his new association with Coleridge. But Mortimer does in the final lines of the early version propose a route toward the healing of the opposition between man and nature through an openness to suffering that will eventually be redeemed through the experience of "forgetfulness." The burden Mortimer takes on is that of experiencing total exposure to the "nature of nature," and thereby the nature of man's condition *in* nature, which he had imposed on Herbert as an "ordeal." Wordsworth's achievement in *The Borderers* is thus to develop as the emblem with which the tragedy closes, as well as in the descriptive style he achieves in the play's finest verse, the orientation toward a philosophy of total acceptance of the world that is, the world wherein "we find our happiness, or not at all" (*Prelude*, X, 728). This is the characteristic strength of the poetry of the "great decade"—the strength that, in Arnold's words, makes it appear that he has "no style," that nature has taken the pen from his hand to write with her "own bare, sheer, penetrating power." The rhetoric is a little self-conscious, the situation is Gothic, but the strength is there:

> I will go forth a wanderer on the earth,
> A shadowy thing, and as I wander on
> No human ear shall ever hear my voice,
> No human dwelling ever give me food
> Or sleep or rest, and all the uncertain way
> Shall be as darkness to me, as a waste
> Unnamed by man! and I will wander on
> Living by mere intensity of thought,
> A thing by pain and thought compelled to live,
> Yet loathing life, till heaven in mercy strike me
> With blank forgetfulness—that I may die.
> [V.iii.264–275]

Editorial Procedure

Like other volumes in this series, this edition provides two kinds of texts: (1) "reading texts," from which all complexities have been stripped away, and (2) transcriptions of manuscripts, in some cases accompanied by photographic reproductions on facing pages. The two kinds of text demand two kinds of editorial procedure. The presentation of transcriptions of MSS. 2 and 3 in parallel on facing pages displays the complexity of the process of revision that the play underwent in those two manuscripts and complements the presentation of the early and late versions of *The Borderers* in parallel reading texts.

Reading texts in this volume are derived from early notebooks used for drafting, from a fair-copy notebook of 1799 not used for rough work until 1841, and from the printed page. The nature of the materials calls for some variations in editorial practice in preparing reading texts from these sources. The printed text of 1842 has been reproduced in its original form, but with nine emendations noted in the *apparatus criticus*. The early version that it faces reproduces the fair-copy readings in MS. 2 as they stood in 1799, but with the format for speaker identification and stage directions restyled to match the conventions adopted for the text of 1842. The speaker-identification and stage-direction format is more simply standardized for the reading texts of the *Ur-Borderers* materials. With the exception of the editorially constructed reading text of the *Gothic Tale* in Appendix I, which demanded the procedures described there, these reading texts are based on the underlying or fair-copy entries in the manuscripts, incorporating only immediate emendations made in the course of the original entry, such as the copyist's correction of mis-writings. Original capitals and variations in spelling have been preserved, but misspellings have been silently corrected and ampersands and abbreviations expanded. Punctuation in the manuscripts is incomplete and inconsistent; it has been editorially modified and supplemented, but sparingly. Brackets are used to indicate gaps, conjectural readings, and illegible words in the manner illustrated below. In the reading texts *only*, brackets are also used, rarely, to enclose readings supplied by the editor; in such cases, the basis of the reading is explained in a note, except in the case of missing speaker identifications, which are supplied in square brackets without additional annotation. Further particulars of special tactics adopted for individual reading texts are given in the headnotes to each text.

The editorial procedure adopted in the presentation of transcriptions is more complicated. Here the aim is to show with reasonable typographic accuracy everything in the manuscript that could be helpful to a study of the poem's growth and development. Even false starts and corrected letters can sometimes reveal the writer's intention, and they are here recorded, though reinforced letters and random marks are normally not. Passages in Wordsworth's hand are printed in roman type; those in the hands of his amanuenses appear in italics, with footnotes identifying the copyist, though identification of hands must sometimes be conjectural, especially in the case of scattered words or parts of words. Revisions are shown in type of reduced size, and an effort has been made to show deletion marks, spacing, and other such physical features so that they resemble those of the manuscript itself, though some minor adjustments have been made in the interest of clarity; in transcriptions that face photographs, doubled-back lines are shown approximately as they appear in the manuscript. In the numbering of leaves, stubs and leaves now missing from original gatherings are counted, but leaves pasted to the endpapers are not. Reading texts are accompanied by line numbers in the margin, and these numbers appear again in the transcriptions, either in the margins, line by line, or within brackets at the head of the page, as a roughly corresponding range.

The following symbol is used in reading texts only:

[evidence]	Reading supplied by the editor.

The following symbols are used in both reading texts and transcriptions:

[ ]	Gap or blank in the manuscript.
[?peace]	Conjectural reading.
[?]	Illegible word.

The following symbols are used in transcriptions; the first three also appear in the *apparatus criticus*:

d} has}	An overwriting: original reading, "has," converted to "had" by writing "d" upon the "s."
{s {	A short addition, sometimes only a mark of punctuation.
[—?—?—]	Deleted and illegible word or words.
that more	Word or words written over an erasure: original reading is uncertain. Notes record conjectural readings.
{peace {press	Word written over an erasure: original reading, "press," is still legible or partly legible.

Reading Texts

Earliest Work from MS. 1, the Rough Notebook, 1796–97

The reading texts presented here are based on fragments found in the Rough Notebook:

Fragments of a Prose Synopsis. These may well be the surviving fragments of a series of synopses covering more or less the whole play, drafted at the outset of composition (see Introduction, pp. 8–9). The names of hero and villain are Ferdinand and Danby respectively. The outline of Act III indicates that Wordsworth had in mind a discovery akin to the coincidence through which the protagonist is reunited with his (dying) wife in *Adventures on Salisbury Plain.* The remnant of an outline for the final act suggests events not unlike those that comprise Act V, Scene iii, of the finished early version, but which emphasize the hero's derangement and dramatic recovery on reencountering his betrayer.

Prose Fragment. This fragment reveals two people in conversation about the crossing of a heath. Reference to the early version discloses echoes from these seven lines of prose scattered through twenty-five lines of verse in which Matilda and Herbert converse on the road shortly after their first entry (I.i.77–102). It is tempting to speculate that at this stage, Wordsworth intended to open his play with the introduction of Herbert and Matilda, overheard perhaps by Ferdinand and Danby, on their way to the inn (see Introduction, pp. 11–12).

Churchyard Scene. This scene again indicates the distance between the style and content of some of Wordsworth's early drafts and those of the early version, in which its remote equivalent is Matilda's encounter with a foster figure, her father's former traveling companion, in Act II, Scene ii. The scene is headed "Act 3ᵈ," and should be compared with the synopsis for Act III. In the synopsis, the Pilgrim whom Matilda meets at the churchyard is revealed as her mother. Here the Pilgrim is male, and has lost a son. Toward the end of the scene, however, the Pilgrim faints and "her" appears in the manuscript rather than "his" and "him." We may probably assume that Wordsworth was working from a draft that was closer to the plot of the synopsis. Many details in the scene echo Wordsworth's earlier description of an encounter with a deranged old woman in *A Tale* (c. 1787), which is quoted in full in the Introduction (see above, pp. 19–20). A stylistic and thematic model may have been "The Blessings of a Shepherd's Life," an extract from *3 Henry VI*, II.v.21–54, in Vicesimus Knox's *Elegant Extracts, or Useful and Entertaining Pieces of Poetry* (Dublin, 1789), page 431 (see Zera Fink, *The Early Wordsworthian Milieu* [Oxford, 1958], p. 127).

Margaret and Peasant Scene. The primary function of this scene is to provide a preliminary description of Ferdinand's derangement. The description that the Peasant offers to Margaret was transferred, in the early version, to two Woodmen, who offer a similar description to Rivers in Act V, Scene i. In the form in which it has been entered in the notebook, the scene is designed to run on into the following Edge of a Heath Scene. The reference to an "inquest" (l. 5), however, appears to presuppose a scene in which Herbert's body has been brought into the cottage, whereas in the Edge of a Heath Scene this event is established by reportage and Ferdinand's state of mind is presented dramatically. These two scenes, then, may have originally provided alternative means of setting up the denouement; that they are alternative in origin is also suggested by the difference in the names Peasant (this scene) and Cottager (Edge of a Heath Scene) used to identify Margaret's husband.

Edge of a Heath Scene. The copying of this scene into the notebook clearly predates the Margaret and Peasant Scene's run-on ending, since it stands as a separate scene. Ferdinand's opening prose soliloquy has no equivalent in the early version, but following it, the verse of the exchange between Ferdinand and the Cottager anticipates V.ii.1–60. The entry breaks off in mid-scene, and only stubs of the remainder of the scene survive. They indicate that the entry continued, but as the stubs continue for 134 pages, right to the end of the notebook, it is not clear how much more of the rest of the play the notebook originally contained. Working back through the notebook on leaves that are still extant, however, Wordsworth redrafted Ferdinand's soliloquy in verse, and also parts of the rest of what was to become Act V, Scene ii, now using the name Robert in place of Cottager. The existence of these drafts strongly suggests that the original entry for the Edge of a Heath Scene contained the whole scene. The reader may wish to supplement the broken-off earliest text of the Edge of a Heath Scene by referring to the Ferdinand and Robert drafts in the transcription of MS. 1, leaves 50^r–50^v (Draft A), 51^r–51^v (Draft B), and 49^v (a further fragment connected with Draft B).

Matilda at the Cottage Door Scene. Its position in the notebook, before the Ferdinand and Robert drafts, and its use of the name Robert both indicate that this scene in this form is later than the Edge of a Heath Scene, and suggest that it is, like the Ferdinand and Robert drafts, a redrafting of materials cut out of the notebook a few leaves beyond where the original entry for the Edge of a Heath Scene breaks off. The text is followed fairly closely in the early version, in which this fragment corresponds to the opening section of the final scene, V.iii.1–18.

The reading texts presented here are based on the earliest states of the entries concerned, as corrected in the process of composition or transcription. In footnotes, certain substantive revisions are recorded. They include all completed revisions introduced by Dorothy Wordsworth and all of William Wordsworth's completed revisions for the Churchyard Scene which represent his final intentions before he abandoned this scene.

[Fragments of a Prose Synopsis]

Third Act

Matilda having executed her commission comes to a church yard—meets a pilgrim whom she discovers to be her mother. Her joy at the thought of meeting her father. Danby meets Matilda and her mother to whom as a friend she relates her good fortune; soon after parting with her in this way he meets with Ferdinand, understands from him that he has put Herbert to death, then informs him that he had discovered Matilda with her mother. Ferdinand enraged. Danby, to drive Ferdinand to despair, informs him that he had invented these things. Ferdinand resolves to go back to see if Herbert may yet be saved.

[Final Act]

. . . [Ma]tilda rushes in to prevent it; at which time Danby comes up, who had suspected what Ferdinand had done to Herbert, intending to murder him himself if he had found him. Ferdinand's reason, which had been disordered, restored by the sight of Danby!

[Prose Fragment]

[*Matilda*] . . . if the nights had been warmer [?it ?would] have been better to have made a bed of the dry heath, and wrapping ourselves up in our cloaks have laid us down on the ground together, and thus divided our journey by a necessary repose.

[*Herbert*] Indeed, it was too much for me.

Third Act The opening was revised to read: "Matilda, having heard at the inn where she had left her father that he was gone to the convent where they had slept, proceeds after him; goes on, comes to a church yard . . ."

[Churchyard Scene]

Act Third

Scene: *a Churchyard*
Peasants having just entombed a body

Peasant That droning pipe heard from the wood below
Proclaims some pilgrim nigh.
Old Peasant Of all that pass
I never till this afternoon beheld
One on whose brow Affliction's hand had left
So little of earthly: wrinkles that might seem
Wrinkles of sorrow rather than of years
Had traced his temples with religious touch;
Acquainted though his eyes appear with weeping
Nor tears nor sorrow have subdued their lustre.
Bright lights break out at times about their orbs
That speak the wildness of great joy: perhaps
He is not in his true and perfect mind.
He begged an alms, and lingering at my door
Talked much of those who at Jerusalem
Die in the Lord, and from that very moment
—And as he spoke he smiled with extreme joy—
Are born to paradise and the ten thousand.
And sure he is a man beloved of heaven,
For at the word a long slant evening beam
Such as in shower time dart between the hills
Shot from between two clouds upon his face.
I took it as a sign from him who hung
The bow in heaven, we are not all to sleep,
But we shall all be changed.——
For afterwards, in milder mood, he talked
Of man, and of man's heart, and things below,
And human sufferings, chief of those that toil
After their friends are in the world of rest;
Till the wild joy that lighted up his tears,

21–22 Between these two lines an additional line, "And added to his smile a fearful glory," was inserted.

Grown dim like dying lamps or suns that set,
Gave one bright glance and seemed to pass for ever.
But he approaches—'tis the very same.

(Enter Pilgrim)

[*Pilgrim*] I come not, Brothers, to disturb your rites;
If Misery, as we're told, may give a claim
On heaven, my prayers will sure be acceptable.

Old Peasant Thanks, holy Pilgrim, but the rites are finished.

Pilgrim Hah! 'tis an infant's grave. I once had infants—
(A pause. Pilgrim's eyes fixed on the grave)

Old Peasant Then are they happy if the grave—

Pilgrim The grave
May at the call of Nature—one by one—
Receive the infant fruits of fondest love,
And after a few throbs the heart be still.
But Death has shapes *so* terrible—(*A pause*) and yet
Heaven in his kindness surely took thee from me—
For it was at a time when fear had just
Blanched my young hair and shattered my poor brain.
We wandered much together through deep woods
And trackless wastes.— Yes, yes, 'twas well, (*firmly*) '*twas* well.
The very shewolf of the woods had been
[ ] a nurse less terrible than I:
For he would mock at times, with innocent mirth,
My lifted hands, and seem to tear his hair,
Making a plaything of my bursting heart;
At times my poor dear boy [ ] he would stare,
And roll his infant eyes in wildest motion,
As if my face reflecting, till I feared
—He saw, poor boy, no human face but mine—
(*Hurried*)
To nurse him, holy saints, in ideotcy.
(*Faints*)

Matilda Run, run for Water from the spring! Oh God,
How did [his] eyes shrink back into [his] head;
—Ye saw the blackness pass across [his] face!
At length thou shalt be quiet and lie still;
Sorrow shall seek at morn and shall not find thee.
Where are they? Are they coming?— Crowd not so,
Let the air breathe upon [him].

59, 60, 64 The manuscript reads "her" rather than "[his]" and "[him]"; see Introduction, p. 10.

(*After a pause, Pilgrim recovering*)
[*Pilgrim*] My good friends,
Spare, spare your needless pains that would undo
That spellwork—for I feel I am myself.
Old Peasant That cot below the waterfall, whose smoke
Curls from beneath the elms, is mine: two moons
Have lit our sheepwalks since I eat my meal
In solitude; since my son took the cross,
Thoughts that awhile could soften pangs of parting
Have lost their influence, and my heart is void.
That cot shall be your home, there shall you dwell,
And be to me in all things as a son.
Pilgrim Alas, you do not know me; for sometimes
I am disturbed in mind.
Old Peasant A holy man:
We know you are heaven-favoured; freshest grass
Shall strew your chamber, and a candlestick
And crucifix with picture of the virgin
Stand at the right hand of your humble bed,
And you shall feed my sheep, and the long day
Their quiet shall be yours—
Pilgrim Yes, honest swain,
Give me a crook the simple flock to guide,
The lost ones to recall—Ah, teach me first,
If not to bring back all I've loved, at least
To rescue my poor thoughts, which now and ever
Bleed helplessly in Memory's piercing thorns.
—A shepherd, I? I, who have seen the lamb
Run from its milk to sport amid its fellows,
Have seen it spring to meet its mother's call,
Have seen, and had no pleasure at the sight?
No! No! [ ] A heart like mine
Answers not any purposes of being,
And never will its uses be restored.
Matilda Yes, trust me, pilgrim: long as thy red blood
Is warm, this old man knows, there is a power
Even in the common offices of love
And friendly ministration, to revive
Nature within thee, bid thee smile again
With those that smile, and weep with them that weep.

73 Revised to read "shall you go"
88 A stage direction, "smilin[g]," was inserted after "A shepherd I?"
92 Revised to read: "No! No! [ ] my heart"

Pilgrim Look in my face. I have not yet forgotten
All functions of a man, I weep and laugh:
But with no fond endearing unison
Of social smiles and sympathetic tears—
No, 'tis in dreadful contrariety
To all mankind, as now I laugh that thou
Givest Physic, damsel, to the senseless dead.
Matilda But be persuaded—
Old Peasant Do go home with me.
Henceforth the seat beneath the elms is yours,
And yours the corner chair when winds blow sharp
Through the bare thorns. The sound of the farm gate,
At evening, when you enter from the fields,
Closing behind you, shall be dear and welcome;
The dog that barks at you shall be chastized,
And my son's little-ones shall reverence you,
And run with joy to lift the latch and meet you;
And she their little sister, had she not
Slept in that grave, should have been taught to love you.
Pilgrim I am perplexed, and cannot think it true
That thus thou speak'st to me; and where I am
I know not, nor if this be the same air,
And the same sun, and we are fellow beings,
Or all is changed. I am indeed perplexed,
And poor, old. I understand thee not,
And know not what it is that works within me—
Matilda Rest with this good old man a little while,
An[d] soon shall he restore thee to thyself;
Thy looks are changed already—
Pilgrim 'Tis most true.
I never have been so beguiled before.
But it is past—and I am once again
The thing I was.—
Old Peasant With patience you have run
The race of duty—you have visited
The sepulcre, and now you ought to rest.
Pilgrim No, good old man, it cannot, cannot be.
A few days' journey, and my feet shall reach
My infant home, the dwelling of my fathers;
That *human* pilgrimage performed—and then—
(*A long pause*)

---

135 my] overwritten "these"

Yet, old man, I will thank thee—and my ear,
Though it be dull and cold, shall vibrate long
As if it heard thy voice; and I will pray
That he whose sun shines on the evil and good,
Who sends his rain upon the just and unjust,
That he will love to look upon thy sheepwalks,
And chiefly be the shepherd of thyself
And family, and i' this thorny scene.

Old Peasant Farewell.

(*Exeunt Peasants.*
Manent Matilda and Pilgrim)

Matilda (*aside*) With best success, even to my Father's wish
Thus far have I returned, my errand sped.
And yet from such a service one short hour
I fain would spare for this sweet Pilgrim's sake,
For I do feel in his sad story's spite
My heart has yet some chearfulness behind
Which it would gladly lend him.

Pilgrim Know you, maiden,
How far 'tis called to Rhudland?

Matilda Thitherward
My journey lies, and fellowship in travel
May be endured when grief would otherwise
Covet to be alone—a few leagues hence
My Father waits for me: the good old man
Will clasp my hand and weep to hear you talk,
And he will bid me listen.

Pilgrim Oh—the grief
On which the heart that owns it dare not look
Doth ask no sympathy. But stay a moment,
I have a little business yet. That done,
And we will on together.

(*Pilgrim approaching the grave, which he regards stedfastly for some time*)

No! The grave
Contains not all that perish, though the dead
Be sacred, and with darkness ought to dwell.

---

160 The line was revised to read "And evermore at every piteous word / Will bid me listen."
166 Beneath this line a horizontal rule was drawn across the page in the manuscript.

[Margaret and Peasant Scene]

Scene: *Margaret and Peasant*

Margaret In what you say, though strange, I do not see
Sufficient cause therein to justify
Your quick return, and interpose delay
In this affair. You must not hesitate:
The inquest must be taken. Never fear,
His daughter will protect you.
Peasant It may be,
Bethink thee so, that I shall soon be summoned
Elsewhere to give particular account
Of all that has befallen me at this time.
Caution is needful—therefore hear me further.
Margaret You said a sudden turning of the road
Down in the neighbouring dingle to your eye
Did first present him—
Peasant And at such short distance
That I could mark him well, myself unseen.
He leaned upon the bridge that spans the glen
And down into the bottom cast his eye,
That fastened there as it would check the current;
And so he stood for several minutes' space.
The[n] starting up, it seemed from intimation
Of things to me invisible, he look'd
All about him with an eye of fear
As if it wished to miss the thing it sought.
Margaret But did he utter nothing that explained
The cause of these appearances?
Peasant Anon
He smote his breast, the motion of his eye
Settled upon the ground.
I heard these words, the whole of what he spoke:
"The dust doth move and eddy at my feet."
This was most strange, the air being dead and still.
Margaret 'Tis some poor wretch of a disordered fancy.
Peasant So at first I thought,
And meant to pass him there forthwith, unwilling

To meddle with a business that might lead
To dangerous issues.
Margaret Then you mark[ed] him further?
[*Peasant*] That instant he spread out his arms, as 'twere
To save himself from falling, and as far
As judgement may be made from such impression,
As I till then ne'er saw on human face,
And such convulsive starts of joints and limbs
As never seized before on mortal frame.
I do believe some horrible phantom then
Did pass before him, such as God will not
Permit to visit any but a man
Who has been guilty of a damning crime.
Margaret Alas poor man—
Peasant Dear wife, [?once] it is known,
As soon it will be, that I was the man
Last seen with him who perished yesternight,
Until the real murderer is found out
I never shall be safe. I do believe
This stranger has some business with the cause
Of this my errand, and am now returned
To plan with thee what it were best to do.
But see him coming—I will watch further.

---

41 WW altered "horrible" to "terrible."
45 The uncertain word was overwritten "when."

[Edge of a Heath Scene]

Scene: the edge of a heath
Enter Ferdinand, his hair loose and dress disordered
his looks betraying extreme horror

How many hours have I wandered night and day through every corner of this dreary heath.— My eyes have been strained, my voice has called incessantly, but in vain.— I shall never be able to travel half a mile in the darkness of the night again. Not a bush or solitary tree did I meet but my heart leaped. This morning the huntsmen were abroad upon the moor. I halloed after them but they took no notice of me.— There was something most horrible in the cry of those dogs.— I think I shall hear it till the hour of my death.— The night was not cold; I have yet some hope; what a fever have I about my heart—I could drink up whole rivers.— Whither shall I betake me now?—(*Casting his eyes about*) Ha! here is one from whom something may be learnt. (*Enter Cottager*)

Have you seen,
In any corner of this savage heath,
A poor, forsaken, famished, blind old man?
Cottager I heard—
Ferdinand Heard! Then I live again! You heard?
Where? When you heard him? Had you any food?
Was any dwelling nigh? He called you to him?
Cottager The search of a stray heifer yesternight
While yet the moon was up had led me far
Into the wildest part of this wild h[e]ath,
When, hearing as I thought a sudden voice,
I stopped and listened, not without such fear
Upon me as the time and place might breed.
I looked, but neither could I hear or see
Aught living, only silent as the ground
The cotter's shaggy ponies pastured near,
And geese were heard afar to send a dreary cry.
So, thinking that my fancy had deceived me,

16 Revised by DW to read ". . . You heard him, where?"
27 Emended by DW to "And geese from far sent forth a dreary cry"

I turned away when straight a second sound,
A human voice distinct, smote on my ear.
Thus guided, distant a few steps I found
A poor old man, and such as you describe.
Ferdinand And was he very feeble? Of all men,
The best and kindest. How shall I repay thee?
My good Angel! But how looked he? Lead me to him,
That I may ask forgiveness. What said he?
Quick, did he speak of me?
Cottager He only spoke
[ ] of a dear dear daughter
Who, so he feared, would never see him more,
And of a stranger to him, one by whom
He had been sore misused. But you are troubled,
Perhaps you are his Son?
Ferdinand No Son, Heaven knows
I did not think he had a living child.
But when he was recovered?
Cottager He was torn,
His head was bruised, and there was blood about him—
Ferdinand That was no work of mine!
Cottager Nor mine, God knows.
Ferdinand But had he strength to walk? I could have borne him
A thousand miles.
Cottager I am in poverty,
And I have felt the cruel gripe of power,
And know how busy is Suspicion's eye:
I did not wish his blood upon my head.
My wife and children came into my mind,
And though it smote me—more than tongue can speak—
I left him.
Ferdinand Left him! Oh, monster, what, to perish left him?
There is no heart in man! Infirm and blind,
Of all forsaken—what, could nothing move thee?
What damning Fiend has poisoned thee in th' ear?
Oh, monster, monster, there are three of us!
In the flames prepared for me I shall not be alone,
But we shall howl together. Where, where was [?it]?

35–38 Appears to be prose only partially converted into verse (see transcription).
60 DW, in incomplete revision, moved "in the flames" to the end of the line above; WW later emended the lines (see transcription).

Let us to the spot, and with the speed o' the wind.
I've heard that men have lain whole weeks entranced,
And to all outward seeming dead,
And life yet in them; if there is a spark,
I'll find it!

(*Dragging him along*)

Cottager 'Tis needless, spare your violence—his daughter

[Matilda at the Cottage Door Scene]

Matilda at the cottage door, her cheek upon her hand in stupid grief.

[*Robert*] Your Father, whom last night I chanced to find
In those wild tracts which I am used to range
[   ] from a wilful hand
Has met unkindness; so indeed he told me,
And, you remember, such was my report.
From what has just befallen me I have cause
To fear he has been murdered.
Matilda   He is dead:
Why comest thou to me with a tale like this?
I thought thou'dst other business.
Robert   It is fit
That a bad man should answer for his crimes.
Matilda Thou see'st me what I am—
Robert   It was most heinous,
And doth call out for vengeance!
Matilda   Do not add,
I prithee, to the harm thou'st done already,
But back upon thy errand—
Robert   Maid, hereafter
Thou'lt thank me for this service.
I met a man, who from the plainest proofs
Of interfering heaven I have no doubt
Laid hands upon your father—fit it were
You should prepare to meet him; he is coming.
(*Matilda continues silent, taking no notice of this*)
                    The wounds were slight,
But there are ways to end a man that leave
Small trace of their effect—
                    He did insist
To be conducted to you—I suppose
That he may straight proclaim himself, and so

22–31 WW appears to have been working from a draft containing only Robert's lines and emphasizing Matilda's continuing silence, and it is not precisely clear whether Matilda's responses were composed in the course of the original entry or added in revision (see transcription).

Find all the ease he can expect on earth:
The heavens have mercy on him!
(*Matilda still silent*)
I remember
I spied a mark upon your father's throat—
Matilda How! how!
[*Robert*] But see him yonder, guided by my wife.
What must be done?
(*Matilda looking that way*)
Robert Your purpose—
Speak—
[*Matilda*] Help me to my father—I have nothing
To do with him.

Essay Prefaced to the Early Version (1797)

The text is based on the fair copy of the essay prefaced to *The Borderers*, MS. 2; where this copy is deficient, the text in DC MS. 27 has been drawn upon (see transcription of the essay, below). Spelling and capitals of the fair-copy text have been preserved, but obvious copyist's errors have been mended, and corrections made in the course of transcription have been incorporated. Punctuation has been sparingly modernized, apostrophes have occasionally been supplied, and ampersands are expanded. The presence of identical paragraphing in the manuscripts from the point where Dorothy Wordsworth took over the copying of DC MS. 27 has been taken as evidence that the whole essay was intended to be paragraphed (see headnote to transcription), and paragraph breaks have therefore been introduced in the first part of the essay, and that fact recorded in the notes.

Line numbers have been provided as a key to the footnotes, but as a reminder that these numbers are not in step with the lines as set in the transcription, they are printed in italic.

[On the Character of Rivers]

Let us suppose a young Man of great intellectual powers, yet without any solid principles of genuine benevolence. His master passions are pride and the love of distinction. He has deeply imbibed a spirit of enterprize in a tumultuous age. He goes into the world and is betrayed into a great crime.

That influence on which all his happiness is built immediately deserts him. His talents are robbed of their weight; his exertions are unavailing, and he quits the world in disgust, with strong misanthropic feelings. In his retirement, he is impelled to examine the reasonableness of established opinions and the force of his mind exhausts itself in constant efforts to separate the elements of virtue and vice. It is his pleasure and his consolation to hunt out whatever is bad in actions usually esteemed virtuous and to detect the good in actions which the universal sense of mankind teaches us to reprobate. While the general exertion of his intellect seduces him from the remembrance of his own crime, the particular conclusions to which he is led have a tendency to reconcile him to himself. His feelings are interested in making him a moral sceptic and as his scepticism increases he is raised in his own esteem.

After this process has been continued some time his natural energy and restlessness impel him again into the world. In this state, pressed by the recollection of his guilt, he seeks relief from two sources, action

---

1 Moorman, I, 304, suggests that the opening of the essay is "self-descriptive," but compare the early history of Falkland in *Caleb Williams*, whose upbringing promoted pride without sufficient "genuine benevolence," Godwin's criterion for moral worth in his *Enquiry Concerning Political Justice* (1793), the second edition of which WW read on its publication in 1796 (*EY*, p. 170). Compare *Lines left upon a Seat in a Yew-Tree* (and see *M of H*, p. 66, and the discussion above, p. 5):

In youth, by genius nurs'd,
And big with lofty views, he to the world
Went forth, pure in his heart, against the taint
Of dissolute tongues, 'gainst jealousy, and hate,
And scorn, against all enemies prepared,
All but neglect: and so, his spirit damped
At once, with rash disdain he turned away,
And with the food of pride sustained his soul
In solitude.

[*Lyrical Ballads* (1798), 13–21]

5 No paragraph break in MSS.

6–19 Compare Rivers's account of the psychological consequences of his crime, IV.ii.75–164.

19 No paragraph break in MSS.

and meditation. Of actions those are most attractive which best exhibit his own powers, partly from the original pride of his character and still more because the loss of Authority and influence which followed upon his crime was the first circumstance which impressed him with the magnitude of that crime and brought along with it those tormenting sensations by which he is assailed. The recovery of his original importance and the exhibition of his own powers are therefore in his mind almost identified with the extinction of those painful feelings which attend the recollection of his guilt.

Perhaps there is no cause which has greater weight in preventing the return of bad men to virtue than that good actions being for the most part in their nature silent and regularly progressive, they do not present those sudden results which can afford a sufficient stimulus to a troubled mind. In processes of vice the effects are more frequently immediate, palpable and extensive. Power is much more easily manifested in destroying than in creating. A child, Rousseau has observed, will tear in pieces fifty toys before he will think of making one.

From these causes assisted by disgust and misanthropic feeling, the character we are now contemplating will have a strong tendency to vice. His energies are most impressively manifest in works of devastation. He is the Orlando of Ariosto, the Cardenio of Cervantes, who lays waste the groves that should shelter him. He has rebelled against

---

26–27 Here the text of MS. 2 contains a haplographical error, and the missing portion of the sentence is supplied from DC MS. 27.

31 No paragraph break in MSS.

38–39 Compare Jean-Jacques Rousseau, *Emilius and Sophia: or, a New System of Education*, trans. "by the translator of Eloisa" (4 vols.; London, 1767):

> A child will often put things into disorder, will break every thing it comes near, will grasp a sparrow, as it would a stone, and kill it, without knowing what it is doing. And why? . . . Whether it makes or marrs, it is all one to a child, provided the situation of things be changed; as every change necessarily implies action. If it seem to have a propensity to destroy things, it is not from a vicious principle; but because the action, necessary to make or compose any thing, is tedious and slow, whereas that of spoiling and breaking things to pieces, being quicker, agrees better with its natural alertness and vivacity. [I, 77–78]

39 No paragraph break in MSS.

43 Compare *Orlando Furioso*, XXIII, 131–135. Though Cardenio, like Orlando, is described as attacking the local shepherds, he does not lay waste the groves in which he hides. WW probably had in mind Don Quixote's discussion of models he should draw on when abandoning himself in lovesick madness, which occurs immediately after Don Quixote has encountered the deranged Cardenio in the Sierra Morena:

> Very well, quoth *Sancho*; but pray, Sir, what is it that you mean to do in this Fag-end of the World? Have I not already told thee, answer'd *Don Quixote*, that I intend to copy *Amadis* in his Madness, Despair, and Fury? At the same time I will imitate the valiant *Orlando Furioso's* Extravagance, when he ran mad, after he had found the unhappy Tokens of the fair *Angelica's* dishonourable Commerce with *Medor* at the

the world and the laws of the world and he regards them as tyrannical masters; convinced that he is right in some of his conclusions, he nourishes a contempt for mankind the more dangerous because he has been led to it by reflexion. Being in the habit of considering the world as a body which is in some sort at war with him, he has a feeling borrowed from that habit which gives an additional zest to his hatred of those members of society whom he hates and to his contempt of those whom he despises. Add to this, that a mind fond of nourishing sentiments of contempt will be prone to the admission of those feelings which are considered under any uncommon bond of relation (as must be the case with a man who has quarrelled with the world): the feelings will mutually strengthen each other.

In this morbid state of mind he cannot exist without occupation, he requires constant provocatives, all his pleasures are prospective, he is perpetually ch[a]sing a phantom, he commits new crimes to drive away the memory of the past. But the lenitives of his pain are twofold: meditation as well as action. Accordingly, his reason is almost exclusively employed in justifying his past enormities and in enabling him to commit new ones. He is perpetually imposing upon himself; he has a sophism for every crime. The *mild* effusions of thought, the milk of human reason, are unknown to him. His imagination is powerful, being strengthened by the habit of picturing possible forms of society where his crimes would be no longer crimes, and he would enjoy that

---

Fountain: at which time in his frantick Despair, he tore up Trees by the Roots, troubled the Waters of the clear Fountains, slew the Shepherds, destroy'd their Flocks, fir'd their Huts, demolish'd Houses, drove their Horses before him, and committed a hundred thousand other Extravagancies worthy to be recorded in the eternal Register of Fame. [Miguel de Cervantes, *The History of the Renowned Don Quixote de la Mancha*, trans. Peter Motteux (4th ed., revised by John Ozell, 4 vols.; London, 1719), I, 259–260]

54 Compare "common offices of love," Churchyard Scene, l. 97, and discussion of it above, pp. 24–28. Common bonds of relation foster "established opinions" (Essay, l. 10, above). The misanthrope admits feelings based on "uncommon bonds," that is, the experience of "a heart which had been turn'd aside / From nature" (*Prelude*, X, 886–887). Thus the experience of alienation is self-reinforcing, and rather than fostering genuine independence of mind, leads to a redefinition of morality in uniquely subjective self-serving terms. Owen and Smyser note a parallel with the discussion of "unwarranted antitheses" in the second of WW's *Essays upon Epitaphs* (1809–10).

56 No paragraph break in MSS.

59 DC MS. 27 reads "chusing," though it is possible that the copyist misread an open "a" in the (postulated) holograph. In MS. 2, the vowel has been erased, leaving a hole. "Chasing" is the more likely intended word, though "chusing a phantom" is an appropriate description of one suffering from "repetition compulsion."

61–64 Owen and Smyser note the comparison of WW's discussion in *Essay on Morals* (1798), published in *Prose*, I, 103–104: "when we have been unworthily employed . . . we are all activity & keenness; then it is that we repair to systems of morality for arguments in defence of ourselves; & sure enough are we to find them . . . lifeless words, & abstract propositions, will not be destitute of power to lay asleep the spirit of self-accusation & exclude the uneasiness of repentance."

estimation to which from his intellectual attainments he deems himself entitled. The nicer shades of manners he disregards, but whenever upon looking back upon past ages, or in surveying the practices of different countries in the age in which he lives, he finds such contrarieties as seem to affect the principles of *morals*, he exults over his discovery and applies it to his heart as the dearest of his consolations. Such a mind cannot but discover some truths, but he is unable to profit by them and in his hands they become instruments of evil.

He presses truth and falshood into the same service. He looks at society through an optical glass of a peculiar tint: something of the forms of objects he takes from objects, but their colour is exclusively what he gives them, it is one, and it is his own. Having indulged a habit, dangerous in a man who has fallen, of dallying with moral calculations, he becomes an empiric—and a daring and unfeeling empiric. He disguises from himself his own malignity by assuming the character of a speculator in morals and one who has the hardihood to realize his speculations.

It will easily be perceived that to such a mind those enterprizes which are the most extraordinary will in time appear the most inviting. His appetite from being exhausted becomes unnatural. Accordingly, he will struggle so [ ] to characterize and to exalt actions little and contemptible in themselves by a forced greatness of *manner* and will chequer and degrade enterprizes great in their atrocity by grotesque littleness of manner and fantastic obliquities. He is like a worn out voluptuary—he finds his temptation in strangeness. He is unable to suppress a low hankering after the *double entendre* in vice, yet his thirst after the extraordinary buoys him up, and supported by a habit of constant reflexion he frequently breaks out into what has the appearance of greatness; and in sudden emergencies when he is called upon by surprize and thrown out of the path of his regular habits, or when dormant associations are awakened tracing the revolutions through which his character has passed, in painting his former self he really *is* great.

---

88 Both MSS. contain the lacuna "so [ ] to," but the passage makes sense if "so" is omitted. The lacuna may be the result of an incomplete cancellation mark in WW's postulated holograph.

92–100 The syntax here is somewhat involved, but it appears that WW intends to classify two kinds of situation in which such a villain rises to greatness: (1) when he is "thrown out of the path of his regular habits" by a crisis; (2) when his powers of association have been awakened and remind him of the "revolutions through which his character has passed," so that he becomes preoccupied with autobiography. These two kinds of "greatness" correspond to the two moments in the play at which Rivers rises to the occasion most strikingly: in II.iii.326–429, when his plot has been endangered by the unexpected arrival of Lacy and Wallace, and he responds by delivering a fine "set" speech in praise of the concept of sacrificial justice (a concept that he privately despises); and in IV.ii. where he recounts his past history to Mortimer.

Benefits conferred on a man like this will be the seeds of a worse feeling than ingratitude. They will give birth to positive hatred. Let him be deprived of power, though by means which he despises, and he will never forgive. It will scarcely be denied that such a mind by very slight external motives may be led to the commission of the greatest enormities. Let its malignant feelings be fixed on a particular object and the rest follows of itself.

Having shaken off the obligations of religion and morality in a dark and tempestuous age, it is probable that such a character will be infected with a tinge of superstition. The period in which he lives teems with great events which he feels he cannot controul. That influence which his pride makes him unwilling to allow to his fellow-men he has no reluctance to ascribe to invisible agents: his pride impels him to superstition and shapes out the nature of his belief: his creed is his own: it is made and not adopted.

A character like this, or some of its features at least, I have attempted to delineate in the following drama. I have introduced him deliberately prosecuting the destruction of an amiable young man by the most atrocious means and with a pertinacity as it should seem not to be accounted for but on the supposition of the most malignant injuries. No such injuries, however, appear to have been sustained. What are then his motives? First it must be observed that to make the nonexistence of a common motive itself a motive to action is a practice which we are never so prone to attribute exclusively to madmen as when we forget ourselves. Our love of the marvellous is not confined to external things. There is no object on which it settles with more delight than on our own minds. This habit is in the very essence of the habit which we are delineating.

But there are particles of that poisonous mineral of which Iago speaks gnawing his inwards; his malevolent feelings are excited and he hates the more deeply because he feels he ought not to hate.

---

110 See III.iv.19–40. But in the play, Rivers appears to be strikingly without superstition, in contrast with Mortimer, Robert, and the Beggarwoman: see above, pp. 15–16. WW is perhaps seeking additional grounds for defending Rivers's credibility here; compare the use of "superstition" to define and defend the character of the "retired" sea captain in the prose apology added to *The Thorn* in the second edition of *Lyrical Ballads* (1800).

129–131 Cf. Iago:

> For that I do suspect the lusty Moor
> Hath leap'd into my seat; the thought whereof
> Doth like a poisonous mineral gnaw my inwards;
> And nothing can or shall content my soul
> Till I am even'd with him . . .
>
> [*Othello*, II.i.307–311]

We all know that the dissatisfaction accompanying the first impulses towards a criminal action where the mind is familiar with guilt acts as a stimulus to proceed in that action. Uneasiness must be driven away by fresh uneasiness; obstinacy, waywardness and wilful blindness are alternatives resorted to, till there is an universal insurrection of every depraved feeling of the heart.

Besides, in a course of criminal conduct every fresh step that we make appears a justification of the one that preceded it; it seems to bring back again the moment of liberty and choice; it banishes the idea of repentance and seems to set remorse at defiance. Every time we plan a fresh accumulation of our guilt we have restored to us something like that original state of mind, that perturbed pleasure, which first made the crime attractive.

If after these general remarks [I am asked] what are Rivers's motives to the atrocity detailed in the drama?— I answer they are founded chiefly in the very constitution of his character; in his pride which borders even upon madness, in his restless disposition, in his disturbed mind, in his superstition, in irresistible propensities to embody in practical experiments his worst and most extravagant speculations, in his thoughts and in his feelings, in his general habits and his particular impulses, in his perverted reason justifying his perverted instincts. The general moral intended to be impressed by the delineation of such a character is obvious: it is to shew the dangerous use which may be made of reason when a man has committed a great crime.

There is a kind of superstition which makes us shudder when we find moral sentiments to which we attach a sacred importance applied to vicious purposes. In real life this is done every day and we do not feel the disgust. The difference is here. In works of imagination we see the motive and the end. In real life we rarely see either the one or the other, and when the distress comes it prevents us from attending to the cause. This superstition of which I have spoken is not without its use, yet it appears to be one great source of our vices; it is our constant engine in seducing each other. We are lulled asleep by its agency and betrayed before we know that an attempt is made to betray us.

I have endeavoured to shake this prejudice persuaded that in so doing I was well employed. It has been a further object with me to shew that from abuses interwoven with the texture of society a bad man

---

145 A gap was originally left in both MSS. "I am asked" was added in pencil in DC MS. 27 in 1841–42.

157–166 For a discussion of this "difficult paragraph," see *Prose*, I, 85.

may be furnished with sophisms in support of his crimes which it would be difficult to answer.

One word more upon the subject of motives. In private life what is more common than when we hear of law-suits prosecuted to the utter ruin of the parties, and the most deadly feuds in families, to find them attributed to trifling and apparently inadequate sources? But when our malignant passions operate, the original causes which called them forth are soon supplanted, yet when we account for the effect we forget the immediate impulse and the whole is attributed to the force from which the first motion was received. The vessel keeps sailing on, and we attribute her progress in the voyage to the ropes which first towed her out of harbour.

To this must be added that we are too apt to apply our own moral sentiments as a measure of the conduct of others. We insensibly suppose that a criminal action assumes the same form to the agent as to ourselves. We forget that his feelings and his reason are equally busy in contracting its dimensions and pleading for its necessity.

Parallel Texts of the Early Version (1797–99) and the Late Version (1842)

The reading text of the early version (on the left-hand pages) is based on the 1799 fair-copy readings of DC MS. 23, which is reproduced also below as MS. 2. The spelling and capitals of the fair-copy text have been preserved, but a few obvious copyist's errors have been mended, and corrections made by the copyist in the course of transcription have been incorporated, as have the few minor revisions made in 1799 (cited in the notes). Uncertain readings are shown with question marks in brackets, and empty brackets enclose spaces left in the text in 1799. Punctuation has been sparingly modified; apostrophes have been supplied where necessary and ampersands expanded. In the stage directions and speaker identifications, conventions established in the printed version of 1842 have been followed, and a *dramatis personae* has been constructed to match that of 1842. The 1842 text, in *Poems, Chiefly of Early and Late Years*, is reproduced as the late version (on the right-hand pages), emended in eleven cases by reference to the manuscripts and to later printed editions. These emendations are noted in the *apparatus criticus*, as are variant readings introduced in the three later lifetime London editions of the play, identified as follows:

1845 *Poems* (1845; reissued 1847, 1849)
1846 *Poetical Works* (7 vols., 1846; reissued 1849)
1849 *Poetical Works* (6 vols., 1849–50)

The early version is numbered by act, scene, and line; the late version is numbered continuously and its line numbers correspond to those of de Selincourt's text in *PW*, I. Bracketed line numbers in the right-hand margin of the early version key it to the late text. Beneath the early version are critical and interpretive notes, most of which apply equally to the late version.

[DRAMATIS PERSONAE.

MORTIMER.	Of the Band of Borderers.	Host.
RIVERS.		Two Woodmen.
WALLACE.		Robert, a Cottager.
LACY.		Peasant, Pilgrims, &c.
LENNOX.		
NORWOOD.		MATILDA.
HERBERT.		Female Beggar.
WILFRED, Servant to MORTIMER.		MARGARET, Wife to ROBERT.

SCENE, *Borders of England and Scotland.*
TIME, *the reign of Henry III.*]

DRAMATIS PERSONÆ.

MARMADUKE. OSWALD. WALLACE. LACY. LENNOX.	Of the Band of Borderers.	Host. Forester. ELDRED, a Peasant. Peasant, Pilgrims, &c. IDONEA.
HERBERT.		Female Beggar.
WILFRED, Servant to MARMADUKE.		ELEANOR, Wife to ELDRED.

SCENE, *Borders of England and Scotland.*
TIME, *the Reign of Henry III.*

READERS already acquainted with my Poems will recognise, in the following composition, some eight or ten lines, which I have not scrupled to retain in the places where they originally stood. It is proper however to add, that they would not have been used elsewhere, if I had foreseen the time when I might be induced to publish this Tragedy.

February 28,
1842.

A TRAGEDY

On human actions reason though you can,
It may be reason, but it is not man;
His principle of action once explore,
That instant 'tis his principle no more.
Pope.——

[Scene I] ACT I

SCENE, *Road in a Wood.*——

MORTIMER — WILFRED.

WILFRED

Be cautious, my dear Master!

The epigraph is from Pope's *Moral Essays, Epistle I* (to Cobham), "Of the Knowledge and Characters of Men," ll. 23–28. For the first word, MS. 2 incorrectly reads "Of"; the epigraph as quoted in DC MS. 27 correctly reads "On" (see p. 444, below).

THE BORDERERS:

A Tragedy.

ACT I.

SCENE, *road in a Wood.*

WALLACE *and* LACY.

LACY.

The Troop will be impatient; let us hie
Back to our post, and strip the Scottish Foray
Of their rich Spoil, ere they recross the Border.
—Pity that our young Chief will have no part
In this good service.

WALLACE.

Rather let us grieve
That, in the undertaking which has caused
His absence, he hath sought, whate'er his aim,
Companionship with One of crooked ways,
From whose perverted soul can come no good
To our confiding, open-hearted, Leader.

LACY.

True; and, remembering how the Band have proved
That Oswald finds small favour in our sight,
Well may we wonder he has gained such power
Over our much-loved Captain.

WALLACE.

I have heard
Of some dark deed to which in early life
His passion drove him—then a Voyager
Upon the midland Sea. You knew his bearing
In Palestine?

LACY.

Where he despised alike
Mahommedan and Christian. But enough;
Let us begone—the Band may else be foiled. [*Exeunt.*

Enter MARMADUKE *and* WILFRED.

WILFRED.

Be cautious, my dear Master!

MORTIMER (*smiling*)

I perceive [21]
That fear is like a cloak which old men huddle
Around their love, as 'twere to keep it warm.

WILFRED

Nay, but my heart is sad
To part with you.—This Rivers—

MORTIMER

What of him?

WILFRED

You know that you have saved his life—

MORTIMER

I know it. [27]

WILFRED

And that he hates you! (*seeing* MORTIMER *displeased*)
Pardon me, perhaps
That word was hasty.

MORTIMER

Fie! no more of this.

WILFRED

Dear Master! Gratitude's a heavy burthen [30]
To a proud soul.—Nobody loves this Rivers;
Yourself you do not love him.

MORTIMER

I do more,
I honor him.

WILFRED

O, Sir!

MORTIMER

Peace, my good Wilfred.
Repair to Liddersdale, and tell the Band [41]
I shall be with them in two days, at farthest.

---

13 Liddersdale, also referred to as Liddisdale (see I.iii.145) was the dale named from the Liddle River, which marked the boundary between Cumberland and Scotland. The dale was an outlaw stronghold throughout the period of the border troubles.

MARMADUKE.

I perceive
That fear is like a cloak which old men huddle
About their love, as if to keep it warm.

WILFRED.

Nay, but I grieve that we should part. This Stranger,
For such he is——

MARMADUKE.

Your busy fancies, Wilfred,
Might tempt me to a smile; but what of him?

WILFRED.

You know that you have saved his life.

MARMADUKE.

I know it.

WILFRED.

And that he hates you!—Pardon me, perhaps
That word was hasty.

MARMADUKE.

Fy! no more of it.

WILFRED.

Dear Master! gratitude's a heavy burden
To a proud Soul.—Nobody loves this Oswald—
Yourself, you do not love him.

MARMADUKE.

I do more,
I honour him. Strong feelings to his heart
Are natural; and from no one can be learnt
More of man's thoughts and ways than his experience
Has given him power to teach: and then for courage
And enterprise—what perils hath he shunned?
What obstacles hath he failed to overcome?
Answer these questions, from our common knowledge,
And be at rest.

WILFRED.

Oh, Sir!

MARMADUKE.

Peace, my good Wilfred;
Repair to Liddesdale, and tell the Band
I shall be with them in two days, at farthest.

WILFRED

Farewell! and Heaven preserve you—

[*Exit* WILFRED.

Enter RIVERS (*with a bunch of plants in his hand*).

RIVERS

This wood is rich in plants and curious simples. [44]

MORTIMER (*looking at those in* RIVERS' *hand*)

The wild rose, and the poppy, and the night-shade—
Which is your favourite, Rivers?

RIVERS

That which, while it is
Strong to destroy, is also strong to heal.

[*Looking forward, as to a distance.*

Not yet in sight! We'll saunter here a while;
They cannot mount this hill unseen by us.

MORTIMER (*a letter in his hand*)

It is no common thing when men like you [50]
Perform these little services, and therefore
I feel myself much bounden to you, Rivers.
'Tis a strange letter, this.—You saw her write it?

RIVERS

And saw the tears with which she blotted it.

MORTIMER

And nothing less would satisfy him?

RIVERS

No less. [55]
For that another in his child's affection
Should hold a place, as if 'twere robbery,
He seemed to quarrel with the very thought.
Besides, I know not what strange prejudice
Seems rooted in his heart: this band of ours, [60]
Which you've collected for the noblest ends,
Here on the savage confines of the Tweed
To guard the innocent, he calls us outlaws,
And for yourself, in plain terms he asserts
This garb was taken up that Indolence [65]
Might want no cover, and rapaciousness
Be better fed.

---

23 Mortimer had used Rivers as a go-between while asking for Matilda's hand in marriage (much as Othello used Iago).

WILFRED.

May He whose eye is over all protect you! [*Exit.*

Enter OSWALD (*a bunch of plants in his hand*).

OSWALD.

This wood is rich in plants and curious simples.

MARMADUKE (*looking at them*).

The wild rose, and the poppy, and the nightshade:
Which is your favorite, Oswald?

OSWALD.

That which, while it is
Strong to destroy, is also strong to heal—

[*Looking forward.*

Not yet in sight!—We'll saunter here awhile;
They cannot mount the hill, by us unseen.

MARMADUKE (*a letter in his hand*).

It is no common thing when one like you
Performs these delicate services, and therefore
I feel myself much bounden to you, Oswald;
'Tis a strange letter this!—You saw her write it?

OSWALD.

And saw the tears with which she blotted it.

MARMADUKE.

And nothing less would satisfy him?

OSWALD.

No less;
For that another in his Child's affection
Should hold a place, as if 'twere robbery,
He seemed to quarrel with the very thought.
Besides, I know not what strange prejudice
Is rooted in his mind; this Band of ours,
Which you've collected for the noblest ends,
Along thc confines of the Esk and Tweed
To guard the Innocent—he calls us "Outlaws;"
And, for yourself, in plain terms he asserts
This garb was taken up that indolence
Might want no cover, and rapacity
Be better fed.

MORTIMER

Never may I own
The heart which cannot feel for one so helpless.

RIVERS

Thou knowest me for a man not easily moved, [69]
But death! it stirs my very soul to think
Of what I witness'd.

MORTIMER

Well! to day the truth
Shall end her wrongs.

RIVERS

But if the blind man's tale
Should yet be true?

MORTIMER

Would it were possible!
Did not the soldier tell thee that himself,
And others who survived the wreck, beheld [75]
The Baron Herbert perish in the waves
Upon the coast of Cyprus?

RIVERS

True, he did so;
And something of the kind—though where, I know not—
It seemed that I had heard before: and verily
The tale of this his quondam Barony
Is cunningly devised, and on the back [80]
Of his forlorn appearance could not fail
To make the proud and vain his tributaries
And stir the pulse of lazy charity.
The seignories of Herbert are in Cornwall;
We, neighbours of the Esk and Tweed: 'tis much [85]
The wily vagrant——

MORTIMER

Nay, be gentle with him;
Though I have never seen his face, methinks
There cannot be a time when I shall cease
To love him.—I remember, when a Boy [89]

---

43 When Matilda is confronted with the "truth" that Herbert is not her father but an impostor, then she will be free to marry Mortimer.

MARMADUKE.

Ne'er may I own the heart
That cannot feel for one, helpless as he is.

OSWALD.

Thou know'st me for a Man not easily moved,
Yet was I grievously provoked to think
Of what I witnessed.

MARMADUKE.

This day will suffice
To end her wrongs.

OSWALD.

But if the blind Man's tale
Should *yet* be true?

MARMADUKE.

Would it were possible!
Did not the Soldier tell thee that himself,
And others who survived the wreck, beheld
The Baron Herbert perish in the waves
Upon the coast of Cyprus?

OSWALD.

Yes, even so,
And I had heard the like before: in sooth
The tale of this his quondam Barony
Is cunningly devised; and, on the back
Of his forlorn appearance, could not fail
To make the proud and vain his tributaries,
And stir the pulse of lazy charity.
The seignories of Herbert are in Devon;
We, neighbours of the Esk and Tweed: 'tis much
The Arch-impostor——

MARMADUKE.

Treat him gently, Oswald;
Though I have never seen his face, methinks,
There cannot come a day when I shall cease
To love him. I remember, when a Boy

Of six years' growth or younger, by the thorn
Which starts from the old church-yard wall of Lorton,
It was my joy to sit and hear Matilda
Repeat her father's terrible adventures
Till all the band of play-mates wept together,
And that was the beginning of my love.
And afterwards, when we conversed together
This old man's image still was present: chiefly
When I had been most happy.

RIVERS

Whence this paleness?
Two travellers!

MORTIMER (*points*)

The woman is Matilda.

RIVERS

And leading Herbert.

MORTIMER

We must let them pass—
This thicket will conceal us.

[*They retire.*

Enter MATILDA (*leading* HERBERT *blind*).

MATILDA

Dear Father, you sigh deeply; ever since
We left the willow shade, by the brook side,
Your natural breathing has been troubled.

HERBERT

Nay,
'Tis not so bad with me, and yet I know not,
Our last night's march——

MATILDA

Plague on that dismal heath!
In spite of all the larks that cheered our path

63–64 The famous tree in the old churchyard at Lorton is actually a yew; see Wordsworth's *Yew-Trees*, *PW*, II, 209, and Wordsworth's comment on a similar confusion between thorn and sycamore in his Fenwick note to *Suggested by a View from an Eminence in Inglewood Forest*, quoted in *PW*, III, 534.

65–68 Cf. Othello's description of his wooing of Desdemona, *Othello*, I.iii.128–168.

75–109 The opening of *Samson Agonistes* appears to be at the back of Wordsworth's mind throughout this episode, with slight verbal echoes, notably at l. 107. Herbert's depression is also reminiscent of the blind sailor's despair in *Gothic Tale*.

Of scarcely seven years' growth, beneath the Elm
That casts its shade over our village school,
'Twas my delight to sit and hear Idonea
Repeat her Father's terrible adventures,
Till all the band of play-mates wept together;
And that was the beginning of my love.
And, through all converse of our later years,
An image of this old Man still was present,
When I had been most happy. Pardon me
If this be idly spoken.

OSWALD.

See, they come,
Two Travellers!

MARMADUKE (*points*).

The female is Idonea.

OSWALD.

And leading Herbert.

MARMADUKE.

We must let them pass—
This thicket will conceal us. [*They step aside.*

Enter IDONEA, *leading* HERBERT *blind.*

IDONEA.

Dear Father, you sigh deeply; ever since
We left the willow shade by the brook-side,
Your natural breathing has been troubled.

HERBERT.

Nay,
You are too fearful; yet must I confess,
Our march of yesterday had better suited
A firmer step than mine.

IDONEA.

That dismal Moor—
In spite of all the larks that cheered our path,

100 female] woman *1845–*

I ne'er shall love it more. How chearfully
You paced along while the dim moonlight cloud
Mocked me with many a strange fantastic shape.
I thought the convent never would appear,
It seemed to move away from us; and yet,
That you are thus the fault is mine: for truly,
The air was warm, no dew was on the grass,
And midway on the heath, ere the night fell, [117]
I spied a little hut built with green sods—
A miniature it was: and, as it seemed,
Some shepherd's boy had raised it, half in sport
To cheat the lazy time and half to screen him
From rain and the bleak wind—in that small hut
We might have made a bed of the dry heath
And lying down together rested safely
Wrapped in our cloaks, and with recruited strength [124]
Have hailed the morning sun. But cheerly, Father!
That staff of yours, I could almost have heart
To fling't away from you; you make no use
Of me, or of my strength; come, let me feel
That you do press upon me. There.—Indeed, [129]
You are quite exhausted.—Here is a green bank,
Let us repose a little. [*He sits down.*

HERBERT (*after some time*)

You are silent.
That is a silence which I know, Matilda!

MATILDA

Wherefore thus reproach me?
When I behold the ruins of that face, [135]
Those eye-balls dark—dark beyond hope of light,

81–83 William Gilpin, in *Observations . . .* [*on*] *the High-lands of Scotland* (2 vols.; London, 1789), II, 9, warns the landscape artist to "avoid all shapes of animals, or other objects, into which clouds are sometimes apt to form themselves. I have seen a good picture spoiled from having the clouds formed in the shape of a swan. From this mischief Shakespear may guard us." Gilpin then quotes *Antony and Cleopatra*, IV.xii.2–7:

> Sometimes you see a cloud, that's dragonish;
> A vapor sometimes like a bear, or lion;
> A tow'red citadel, a pendent rock;
> A forked mountain; or blue promontory
> With trees upon't, that nod, and mock the eye
> With empty air.

85–97 Cf. the prose fragment for Act I, p. 48 above.

I never can forgive it: but how steadily
You paced along, when the bewildering moonlight
Mocked me with many a strange fantastic shape!—
I thought the Convent never would appear;
It seemed to move away from us: and yet,
That you are thus the fault is mine; for the air
Was soft and warm, no dew lay on the grass,
And midway on the waste ere night had fallen
I spied a Covert walled and roofed with sods—
A miniature; belike some Shepherd-boy,
Who might have found a nothing-doing hour
Heavier than work, raised it: within that hut
We might have made a kindly bed of heath,
And thankfully there rested side by side
Wrapped in our cloaks, and, with recruited strength,
Have hailed the morning sun. But cheerily, Father,—
That staff of yours, I could almost have heart
To fling't away from you: you make no use
Of me, or of my strength;—come, let me feel
That you do press upon me. There—indeed
You are quite exhausted. Let us rest awhile
On this green bank. [*He sits down.*

HERBERT (*after some time*).

Idonea, you are silent,
And I divine the cause.

IDONEA.

Do not reproach me:
I pondered patiently your wish and will
When I gave way to your request; and now,
When I behold the ruins of that face,
Those eyeballs dark—dark beyond hope of light,

And think that they were blasted for my sake,
The name of Mortimer is blown away;
Father, I would not change this proud delight
For the best hopes of love.

HERBERT

Nay, be composed:
Few minutes gone a faintness overspread [141]
My frame, and I bethought me of two things
I ne'er had heart to separate—my grave,
And thee, my child!

MATILDA

Believe me, Sir,
'Tis weariness that breeds these gloomy fancies, [145]
And you mistake the cause: you hear the woods
Resound with music; could you see the sun,
And look upon the pleasant face of Nature—

HERBERT

I understand thee: I should be as chearful
As if we two were twins; two songsters bred [150]
In the same nest, my spring-time one with thine.
Well, be it so—you have indulged me, child!
In many an old man's humour. Sitting here
I feel myself recovered. The bequest
Of thy kind patroness, which to receive [156]
We have thus far adventured, will suffice
To save thee from the extreme of penury.
But when thy father must lie down and die,
How wilt thou stand alone?

MATILDA (*earnestly*)

Is he not strong? [160]
Is he not valiant?

HERBERT

[

]

120–122 Cf. "We two alone will sing like birds i' the cage" (*King Lear*, V.iii.9) and the union of youth and age in the "Matthew" poems, *The Two April Mornings* and *The Fountain*.

131–132 The gap perhaps reflects the "sad incorrect state" of the manuscript from which Mary Hutchinson copied the text of the play (see Introduction, p. 6. Space was left for a line and two half lines.

And think that they were blasted for my sake,
The name of Marmaduke is blown away:
Father, I would not change that sacred feeling
For all this world can give.

HERBERT.

Nay, be composed:
Few minutes gone a faintness overspread
My frame, and I bethought me of two things
I ne'er had heart to separate—my grave,
And thee, my Child!

IDONEA.

Believe me, honored Sire!
'Tis weariness that breeds these gloomy fancies,
And you mistake the cause: you hear the woods
Resound with music, could you see the sun,
And look upon the pleasant face of Nature——

HERBERT.

I comprehend thee—I should be as cheerful
As if we two were twins; two songsters bred
In the same nest, my spring-time one with thine.
My fancies, fancies if they be, are such
As come, dear Child! from a far deeper source
Than bodily weariness. While here we sit
I feel my strength returning.—The bequest
Of thy kind Patroness, which to receive
We have thus far adventured, will suffice
To save thee from the extreme of penury;
But when thy Father must lie down and die,
How wilt thou stand alone?

IDONEA.

Is he not strong?
Is he not valiant?

HERBERT.

Am I then so soon
Forgotten? have my warnings passed so quickly
Out of thy mind! My dear, my only, Child;
Thou wouldst be leaning on a broken reed—
This Marmaduke——

---

144 honored] honoured *1845–*

MATILDA

O could you hear his voice— [165]
Alas! you do not know him. He is one
(I guess not what bad tongue has wronged him with you),
All gentleness and love. His face bespeaks
A deep and simple meekness; and that soul,
Which with the motion of a glorious act [170]
Flashes a terror-mingled look of sweetness,
Is, after conflict, silent as the ocean
By a miraculous finger stilled at once. [173]

HERBERT

Unhappy woman!

MATILDA

Nay, it was my duty
Thus much to speak.
But think not, think not, father, I forget
The history of that lamentable night
When, Antioch blazing to her topmost towers, [178]
You rushed into the murderous flames, returned
Blind as the grave, but, as you oft have told me,
You clasped your infant daughter to your heart.

HERBERT

Thy mother too—scarce had I gained the door—
I caught her voice, she threw herself upon me,
I felt thy infant brother in her arms,
She saw my blasted face—a tide of soldiers [185]
That instant rushed between us, and I heard
Her last death-shriek, distinct among a thousand.

133–141 The description of Mortimer evokes a Christlike figure and concludes with a specific allusion to Christ's calming of the storm on the Sea of Galilee (Matthew 8:26–27).

143–177 The conversation between Herbert and Matilda echoes the recapitulation of previous events in Prospero's conversation with Miranda in *The Tempest*, I.ii.

144–155 De Selincourt suggests that the phrase "topmost towers" is an echo from Marlowe's *Dr. Faustus*: "And burnt the topless towers of Ilium" (Scene 18). Information on the siege of Antioch may have come from Thomas Fuller's *Historie of the Holy Warre* (4th ed.; Cambridge, 1651), which he used almost verbatim at some points in the *Ecclesiastical Sonnets*. The siege mentioned in *The Borderers* would seem to involve a fusion of two separate accounts in Fuller, that of the great siege that ended in June 3, 1098, when "the Christians issuing in, and exasperated with the length of the siege, so remembred what they had suffered, that they forgot what they had to do, killing promiscuously Christian citizens with Turks" (p. 26), and that of the loss of the city to the Mameluke prince in 1268: "The citie of Joppa he took and burned; and then wonne Antioch, slaying therein twenty thousand, and carrying away captive an hundred thousand Christians" (p. 214). The whole dialogue of ll. 145–155 is reminiscent of Vergil's description of Aeneas losing his wife while escaping from burning Troy.

IDONEA.

O could you hear his voice:
Alas! you do not know him. He is one
(I wot not what ill tongue has wronged him with you)
All gentleness and love. His face bespeaks
A deep and simple meekness: and that Soul,
Which with the motion of a virtuous act
Flashes a look of terror upon guilt,
Is, after conflict, quiet as the ocean,
By a miraculous finger, stilled at once.

HERBERT.

Unhappy Woman!

IDONEA.

Nay, it was my duty
Thus much to speak; but think not I forget—
Dear Father! how *could* I forget and live—
You and the story of that doleful night
When, Antioch blazing to her topmost towers,
You rushed into the murderous flames, returned
Blind as the grave, but, as you oft have told me,
Clasping your infant Daughter to your heart.

HERBERT.

Thy Mother too!—scarce had I gained the door,
I caught her voice; she threw herself upon me,
I felt thy infant brother in her arms;
She saw my blasted face—a tide of soldiers
That instant rushed between us, and I heard
Her last death-shriek, distinct among a thousand.

MATILDA

Nay, father, stop not, let me hear it all:
'Twill do me good.

HERBERT

Dear daughter, dearest love—
For my old age it doth remain with thee
To make it what thou wilt.—Thou hast been told
That when, on our return from Palestine,
I found that my domains had been usurped,
I took thee in my arms, and we began
Our wanderings together. Providence
At length conducted us to Rossland. There
Our melancholy story moved a stranger
To take thee to her home; and for myself,
Soon after, the good abbot of Saint Cuthbert's
Supplied my helplessness with food and raiment,
And, as thou knowest, gave me that little cottage
Where now I dwell.—For many years I bore
Thy absence, 'till old age and fresh infirmities,
Now six months gone, exacted thy return.
I did not think that during that long absence
My child, forgetful of the name of Herbert,
Had given her love to a base freebooter
Who here, upon the borders of the Tweed,
Doth prey alike on two distracted countries,
Traitor to both.

MATILDA

Oh could you hear his voice!
I will not call on heaven to vouch for me,
But let this kiss speak what is in my heart.

Enter a Peasant.

PEASANT

Good morrow to you, lady!
I guess that you are strangers; if you need
One better skill'd—

---

167 The "good abbot of St. Cuthbert's" who gave Herbert a cottage is possibly connected not with the geographical location of a particular abbey but rather with the saint himself, an association picked up from James Clarke's *Survey of the Lakes* . . . (London, 1787), p. 84, where Clarke mistakenly asserts that St. Cuthbert gave St. Herbert his hermitage on Derwentwater.

173–178 Herbert's unsympathetic view of Mortimer's band as mere outlaws echoes that expressed throughout eighteenth-century histories and guidebooks; but see II.iii.330–334n.

IDONEA.

Nay, Father, stop not; let me hear it all.

HERBERT.

Dear Daughter! precious relic of that time—
For my old age, it doth remain with thee
To make it what thou wilt. Thou hast been told,
That when, on our return from Palestine,
I found how my domains had been usurped,
I took thee in my arms, and we began
Our wanderings together. Providence
At length conducted us to Rossland,—there,
Our melancholy story moved a Stranger
To take thee to her home—and for myself,
Soon after, the good Abbot of St. Cuthbert's
Supplied my helplessness with food and raiment,
And, as thou know'st, gave me that humble Cot
Where now we dwell.—For many years I bore
Thy absence, till old age and fresh infirmities
Exacted thy return, and our reunion.
I did not think that, during that long absence,
My Child, forgetful of the name of Herbert,
Had given her love to a wild Freebooter,
Who here, upon the borders of the Tweed,
Doth prey alike on two distracted Countries,
Traitor to both.

IDONEA.

Oh, could you hear his voice!
I will not call on Heaven to vouch for me,
But let this kiss speak what is in my heart.

Enter a Peasant.

PEASANT.

Good morrow, Strangers! If you want a Guide,
Let me have leave to serve you!

MATILDA

The sight of inn or cottage
Would be most welcome to us.

PEASANT

Yon white hawthorn gained, [216]
You will look down into a dell, and there
[Will] see an ash from which a sign-board hangs;
The house is hidden by the shade.—Old man,
You seem worn out with travel—shall I support you? [220]

HERBERT

I thank you, but our resting-place so near
'Twere wrong to trouble you—

PEASANT

God speed you both!
You cannot miss the place. [*Exit* Peasant.

HERBERT

Matilda, we must part!

MATILDA

Part!

HERBERT

Be not alarmed—
'Tis but for a few days—a thought has struck me. [224]

MATILDA

That I should leave you at the inn, and thence
Proceed alone? It shall be so; I feel
You are quite exhausted—
[*Exit* HERBERT *supported by* MATILDA.

Re-enter MORTIMER *and* RIVERS.

MORTIMER

This instant will we stop him—a father, too!

RIVERS

Nay, Mortimer, I prithee be not hasty,
For sometimes, in despite of my conviction,
He tempted me to think the story true; [230]

---

186 MS. 2 reads "We," an apparent error corrected in pencil to "Will."

197–225 The Rough Notebook, 26^{r} to 27^{v}, contains an earlier draft of these lines; earlier than the draft equivalent to ll. 197–225 are the Rough Notebook drafts for the deception, 38^{v}, 40^{r}–42^{v}, which reveal that at that stage Wordsworth intended Mortimer to have reached a state of conviction that he does not reach in the early version until I.iii.157 (see 42^{v}).

IDONEA.

My Companion
Hath need of rest; the sight of Hut or Hostel
Would be most welcome.

PEASANT.

Yon white hawthorn gained,
You will look down into a dell, and there
Will see an ash from which a sign-board hangs;
The house is hidden by the shade. Old Man,
You seem worn out with travel—shall I support you?

HERBERT.

I thank you; but, a resting-place so near,
'Twere wrong to trouble you.

PEASANT.

God speed you both.
[*Exit* Peasant.

HERBERT.

Idonea, we must part. Be not alarmed—
'Tis but for a few days—a thought has struck me.

IDONEA.

That I should leave you at this house, and thence
Proceed alone. It shall be so; for strength
Would fail you ere our journey's end be reached.
[*Exit* HERBERT *supported by* IDONEA.

Re-enter MARMADUKE *and* OSWALD.

MARMADUKE.

This instant will we stop him——

OSWALD.

Be not hasty,
For, sometimes, in despite of my conviction,
He tempted me to think the Story true;

'Tis plain he loves the girl, and what he said
That savoured of aversion to thy name
Appeared the genuine colour of his soul,
Anxiety lest any harm should reach her
After his death.

MORTIMER

I have been much deceived. [235]

RIVERS

But sure, he loves the girl; and never love
Could find delight to nurse itself so strangely,
And thus to plague her with *inventions*! Death!
There must be truth in this—

MORTIMER

False! False as hell—
Truth in the story! Had the thing been true
He must have felt it then, known what it was, [240]
And thus to prey upon her heart had been
A tenfold cruelty—

RIVERS

What strange pleasures
Do we poor mortals cater for ourselves!
To see him thus provoke her tenderness
With tales of symptoms and infirmities—and yet
I'd wager on his life for twenty years. [246]

MORTIMER

We will not waste an hour in such a cause.

RIVERS

Why, this is noble! shake her off at once.

MORTIMER

Matilda has a heart.—It is her virtues
Of which he makes his instruments.—A man
Who has so practiced on the world's cold sense [250]
May well deceive his child—what, leave her thus,
A prey to such a traitor? —No—no—no—
'Tis but a word, and then—

RIVERS

There must be something
More than we see, or whence this strange aversion?
Mortimer! I suspect unworthy tales [255]
Have reached his ear—you have had enemies.

'Tis plain he loves the Maid, and what he said
That savoured of aversion to thy name
Appeared the genuine colour of his soul—
Anxiety lest mischief should befal her
After his death.

MARMADUKE.

I have been much deceived.

OSWALD.

But sure he loves the Maiden, and never love
Could find delight to nurse itself so strangely,
Thus to torment her with *inventions!*—death—
There must be truth in this.

MARMADUKE.

Truth in his story!
He must have felt it then, known what it was,
And in such wise to rack her gentle heart
Had been a tenfold cruelty.

OSWALD.

Strange pleasures
Do we poor mortals cater for ourselves!
To see him thus provoke her tenderness
With tales of weakness and infirmity!
I'd wager on his life for twenty years.

MARMADUKE.

We will not waste an hour in such a cause.

OSWALD.

Why, this is noble! shake her off at once.

MARMADUKE.

Her virtues are his instruments.—A Man
Who has so practised on the world's cold sense,
May well deceive his Child—what! leave her thus,
A prey to a deceiver?—no—no—no—
'Tis but a word and then——

OSWALD.

Something is here
More than we see, or whence this strong aversion?
Marmaduke! I suspect unworthy tales
Have reached his ear—you have had enemies.

---

239 this.] *the period is missing from some copies of 1842*

MORTIMER

Away! I tell thee they are his own coinage.

RIVERS

But wherefore should his love exclude a rival?
To one so helpless, it should seem the safeguard
Of such a man as thee should be most welcome.
I do not like this—

MORTIMER

Like it! for my part—

RIVERS

But there is something here—

MORTIMER

What hast thou seen?

RIVERS

No, no, there is no mystery in this;
As you have said, he coins himself the slander [262]
With which he taints her ear.—For a plain reason:
He dreads the presence of a virtuous man
Like you, he knows your eye would search his heart,
Your justice stamp upon his evil deeds [266]
The punishment they merit.—All is plain:
It cannot be—

MORTIMER

What cannot be?

RIVERS

Yet that a father
Should torture thus the heart of his own child—

MORTIMER

Nay, you abuse my friendship!

RIVERS

Heaven forbid! [271]
There was a trifling circumstance; indeed,
Though at the time it struck me, I believe
I never should have thought of it again
But for the scene which we just now have witnessed. [275]

MORTIMER

What do you mean?

RIVERS

In truth, I think I saw—
'Twas at a distance and he was disguised—

MARMADUKE.

Enemies!—of his own coinage.

OSWALD.

That may be,
But wherefore slight protection such as you
Have power to yield? Perhaps he looks elsewhere.—
I am perplexed.

MARMADUKE.

What hast thou heard or seen?

OSWALD.

No—no—the thing stands clear of mystery;
(As you have said) he coins himself the slander
With which he taints her ear;—for a plain reason;
He dreads the presence of a virtuous man
Like you; he knows your eye would search his heart,
Your justice stamp upon his evil deeds
The punishment they merit. All is plain:
It cannot be——

MARMADUKE.

What cannot be?

OSWALD.

Yet that a Father
Should in his love admit no rivalship,
And torture thus the heart of his own Child——

MARMADUKE.

Nay, you abuse my friendship!

OSWALD.

Heaven forbid!—
There was a circumstance, trifling indeed—
It struck me at the time—yet I believe
I never should have thought of it again
But for the scene which we by chance have witnessed.

MARMADUKE.

What is your meaning?

OSWALD.

Two days gone I saw,
Though at a distance and he was disguised,

---

259 Perhaps] perhaps *1845*, *1849*

Hovering round Herbert's door, a man whose figure
Resembled much that cold voluptuary
The villain Clifford.—He hates you, and he knows [280]
Where he can stab you deepest.

MORTIMER

Clifford never
Would stoop to hover round a blind man's door—
It could not be—

RIVERS

And yet I now remember
That when your praise was warm upon my tongue, [284]
And I began to tell how you had rescued
A maiden from the ruffian violence
Of this same Clifford, Herbert grew impatient
And would not hear me—

MORTIMER

No, it cannot be—
I dare not trust myself with such a thought— [289]
Yet whence this strong aversion? You are a man
Not used to rash conjectures—

RIVERS

If you deem it [291]
A thing worth further notice, it befits us
To deal with caution, we must sift him artfully.

[*Exeunt* Mortimer *and* Rivers.

[Scene 2] Scene *changes to the door of an inn.*

Herbert, Matilda *and* Host.

HERBERT (*seated*)

As I am dear to you, remember, child,
This last request—

MATILDA

You know me, Sir! Farewell! [295]

HERBERT

And are you going, then? Come, come, Matilda,
We must not part—I have measured many a league
When these old limbs had need of rest.—No, no,
I will not play the sluggard.

The Rough Notebook contains a draft for the whole of Scene 2, beginning 34^v–36^v and continuing 33^v–34^r. The text is close to that of the early version.

Hovering round Herbert's door, a man whose figure
Resembled much that cold voluptuary,
The villain, Clifford. He hates you, and he knows
Where he can stab you deepest.

MARMADUKE.

Clifford never
Would stoop to skulk about a Cottage door—
It could not be.

OSWALD.

And yet I now remember,
That, when your praise was warm upon my tongue,
And the blind Man was told how you had rescued
A maiden from the ruffian violence
Of this same Clifford, he became impatient
And would not hear me.

MARMADUKE.

No—it cannot be—
I dare not trust myself with such a thought—
Yet whence this strange aversion? You are a man
Not used to rash conjectures——

OSWALD.

If you deem it
A thing worth further notice, we must act
With caution, sift the matter artfully.
[*Exeunt* MARMADUKE *and* OSWALD.

SCENE, *the door of the Hostel.*

HERBERT, IDONEA, *and* Host.

HERBERT (*seated*).

As I am dear to you, remember, Child!
This last request.

IDONEA.

You know me, Sire; farewell!

HERBERT.

And are you going then? Come, come, Idonea,
We must not part,—I have measured many a league
When these old limbs had need of rest,—and now
I will not play the sluggard.

MATILDA

Nay, sit down.

[*Turning to the* Host.

Good Host, such 'tendance as you would expect
From your own children, if yourself were sick,
Let this old man find at your hands—poor [ ],
We soon shall meet again.—If thou neglect thy charge
Then ill befal thee!
The little fool is loth to stay behind.
Sir Host! by all the love you bear to courtesy,
Take care of him—and feed the truant well.

HOST

Fear not, I will obey you; but one so young,
And one so fair, in truth it is a pity
That you should travel unattended, Lady!
I have a palfrey and a groom. The lad
Shall squire you— (*To* HERBERT) would it not be better, Sir?—
And for less fee than I would let him run
For any lady I have seen this twelvemonth.

MATILDA

You know, Sir, I have been too long your guard
Not to have learnt to laugh at foolish fears.
Why, if a wolf should leap from out a thicket
A look of mine would send him scouring back,
Unless I differ from the thing I am
When you are by my side.

HERBERT

Matilda! Wolves
Are not the enemies that move my fears.

MATILDA

No more of this.—Three days at farthest
Will bring me back to you.—Farewell! farewell!

[*Exit* MATILDA.

HOST

'Tis never drought with us—St. Mary and her pilgrims,
Thanks to them! are a stream of comfort to us:

---

9 The dog's name, Tray, was added to fill the blank, probably in 1841. Tray was also the name used in the Rough Notebook draft for the scene.

25 "To scour" meant "to run with great eagerness and swiftness; to scamper" (Johnson).

31 The pilgrims are perhaps on their way to St. Mary's, Carlisle.

IDONEA.

Nay, sit down.

[*Turning to* Host.

Good Host, such tendance as you would expect
From your own Children, if yourself were sick,
Let this old Man find at your hands; poor Leader,

[*Looking at the Dog.*

We soon shall meet again. If thou neglect
This charge of thine, then ill befal thee!—Look,
The little fool is loth to stay behind.
Sir Host! by all the love you bear to courtesy,
Take care of him, and feed the truant well.

HOST.

Fear not, I will obey you;—but One so young,
And One so fair, it goes against my heart
That you should travel unattended, Lady!—
I have a palfrey and a groom: the lad
Shall squire you, (would it not be better, Sir?)
And for less fee than I would let him run
For any lady I have seen this twelvemonth.

IDONEA.

You know, Sir, I have been too long your guard
Not to have learnt to laugh at little fears.
Why, if a wolf should leap from out a thicket,
A look of mine would send him scouring back,
Unless I differ from the thing I am
When you are by my side.

HERBERT.

Idonea, wolves
Are not the enemies that move my fears.

IDONEA.

No more, I pray, of this. Three days at farthest
Will bring me back—protect him, Saints—farewell!

[*Exit* IDONEA.

HOST.

'Tis never drought with us—St. Cuthbert and his Pilgrims,
Thanks to them, are to us a stream of comfort:

Pity the maiden did not wait a little;
She could not, Sir, have failed of company.

HERBERT

Now she is gone I fain would call her back again.

HOST (*calling* MATILDA)

Hola!

HERBERT

No, no, the business must be done.
But what is all this noise? (*A noise heard*)

HOST

The villagers
Are flocking in.—A wedding festival, [331]
That's all—

Enter MORTIMER *and* RIVERS.

(*To them*) God save you, Sirs!

RIVERS

Ha! as I live, the Baron Herbert.

HOST

For Heaven's sake!
—Mercy, Sir, I did not know your Lordship—

RIVERS

So far into your journey! on my life,
You are a lusty traveller.—But how fare you? [335]

HERBERT

Well as an old man can expect.—And you, Sir?

RIVERS

I do not see Matilda.

HERBERT

The good creature
Is gone before, to spare my weariness. [338]
But what has brought you hither?

RIVERS

A little business
That will be soon dispatched.

HERBERT

There was a letter
Which we entrusted to you?

RIVERS

Be at peace.
You'll hear no more of him——

Pity the Maiden did not wait a while;
She could not, Sir, have failed of company.

HERBERT.

Now she is gone, I fain would call her back.

HOST (*calling*).

Holla!

HERBERT.

No, no, the business must be done.—
What means this riotous noise?

HOST.

The villagers
Are flocking in—a wedding festival—
That's all—God save you, Sir.

Enter OSWALD.

OSWALD.

Ha! as I live,
The Baron Herbert.

HOST.

Mercy, the Baron Herbert!

OSWALD.

So far into your journey! on my life,
You are a lusty Traveller. But how fare you?

HERBERT.

Well as the wreck I am permits. And you, Sir?

OSWALD.

I do not see Idonea.

HERBERT.

Dutiful Girl,
She is gone before, to spare my weariness.
But what has brought you hither?

OSWALD.

A slight affair,
That will be soon despatched.

HERBERT.

Did Marmaduke
Receive that letter?

OSWALD.

Be at peace.—The tie
Is broken, you will hear no more of *him*.

HERBERT

Well, this is comfort.
That noise! would I had gone with her as far
As the Lord Clifford's mansion: I have heard [345]
That in his milder moods he has express'd
Compassion for me—he has great influence
With Henry, our good King. I might have restored them,
Perhaps he would have heard my suit—no matter,
I do not like the man. (*Noise again*) This noise, alas!
I shall have neither sleep nor rest—the convent
Will give me quiet lodging—you have a boy, good Host,
And he must lead me back.

RIVERS

This is most lucky, [354]
Our journey lies that way; my friend and I
Will be your guides.

HERBERT

Alas! I creep so slowly,
A wearisome companion!

RIVERS

Never fear,
We'll not complain of that.

HERBERT

My limbs are stiff, [359]
I must repose. You cannot wait an hour?

RIVERS

O certainly! come, let me lead you in,
And while you rest yourself, my friend and I
Will stroll into the wood.

[RIVERS *conducts* HERBERT *into the house. Various* villagers *croud in.* RIVERS *returns to* MORTIMER, *and they go out together. More* villagers, *and among them a* rustic musician.

HERBERT.

This is true comfort, thanks a thousand times!—
That noise!—would I had gone with her as far
As the Lord Clifford's Castle: I have heard
That, in his milder moods, he has expressed
Compassion for me. His influence is great
With Henry, our good King;—the Baron might
Have heard my suit, and urged my plea at Court.
No matter—he's a dangerous Man.—That noise!—
'Tis too disorderly for sleep or rest.
Idonea would have fears for me,—the Convent
Will give me quiet lodging. You have a boy, good Host,
And he must lead me back.

OSWALD.

You are most lucky;
I have been waiting in the wood hard by
For a companion—here he comes; our journey
[*Enter* MARMADUKE.
Lies on your way; accept us as your Guides.

HERBERT.

Alas! I creep so slowly.

OSWALD.

Never fear;
We'll not complain of that.

HERBERT.

My limbs are stiff
And need repose. Could you but wait an hour?

OSWALD.

Most willingly!—Come, let me lead you in,
And, while you take your rest, think not of us;
We'll stroll into the wood; lean on my arm.
[*Conducts* HERBERT *into the house. Exit* MARMADUKE.

Enter Villagers.

OSWALD (*to himself coming out of the Hostel*).

I have prepared a most apt Instrument—
The Vagrant must, no doubt, be loitering somewhere
About this ground; she hath a tongue well skilled,
By mingling natural matter of her own
With all the daring fictions I have taught her,
To win belief, such as my plot requires. [*Exit* OSWALD.

Enter more Villagers, *a* Musician *among them.*

HOST (*to him*)

Into the court, my friend! and perch yourself
Aloft upon the elm-tree. Pretty maids!
Garlands, and flowers, and cakes, and merry thoughts
Are here to send the sun into the west.——

[Scene 3] SCENE *changes to the wood adjoining the Inn,*
MORTIMER *and* RIVERS *entering.*

MORTIMER

I would fain hope that we deceive ourselves:
When I beheld him sitting there, alone,
It struck upon my heart—I know not how.

RIVERS

Let us dismiss the business from our thoughts;
To day will clear up all.—You marked a cottage,
That ragged dwelling close beneath a rock
By the brook side; it is the abode of one,
A maid, who fell a prey to the Lord Clifford,
And he grew weary of her, but alas!
What she had seen and suffered—the poor wretch,
It turned her brain—and now she lives alone,
Nor moves her hands to any needful work.
She eats the food which every day the peasants
Bring to her hut, and so the wretch has lived

5–22 Perhaps the cottage is connected with Julian's bower; see above, p. 18. The description of the maid places her in an eighteenth-century tradition of mad maidens; compare Cowper's "Crazed Kate" in *The Task* (I, 534–566). This and other sources for the motif are identified by Jonathan Wordsworth in *M of H*, pp. 60–62.

10–23 Cf. *A Ballad* (*PW*, I, 265–266):

She saw—and wept—her father frown'd,
Her heart began to break;
And oft the live-long day she sat
And word would never speak . . .

Reflected once in Mary's face
The village saw a mind more fair;
Now every charm was all o'erhung
By woe and black despair.

And oft she roam'd at dark midnight
Among the silent graves;
Or sat on steep Winander's rock
To hear the weltering waves.

Cf. also *Dirge* (*PW*, I, 269):

By frequent feet the grass around
His grave shall all be worn away.

HOST (*to them*).

Into the court, my Friend, and perch yourself
Aloft upon the elm-tree. Pretty Maids,
Garlands and flowers, and cakes and merry thoughts,
Are here, to send the sun into the west
More speedily than you belike would wish.

SCENE *changes to the Wood adjoining the Hostel—*
MARMADUKE *and* OSWALD *entering.*

MARMADUKE.

I would fain hope that we deceive ourselves:
When first I saw him sitting there, alone,
It struck upon my heart I know not how.

OSWALD.

To-day will clear up all.—You marked a Cottage,
That ragged Dwelling, close beneath a rock
By the brook-side: it is the abode of One,
A Maiden innocent till ensnared by Clifford,
Who soon grew weary of her; but, alas!
What she had seen and suffered turned her brain.
Cast off by her Betrayer, she dwells alone,
Nor moves her hands to any needful work:
She eats her food which every day the peasants
Bring to her hut; and so the Wretch has lived

Ten years; and no one ever heard her voice.
But every night at the first stroke of twelve
She quits her house, and in the neighbouring church-yard
Upon the self same spot, in rain or storm,
She paces out the hour 'twixt twelve and one,
She paces round and round, still round and round,
And in the church-yard sod her feet have worn
A hollow ring; they say it is knee-deep——
Ha! what is here?

[*A female* BEGGAR *rises up, rubbing her eyes as if waking from sleep—a child in her arms.*

BEGGAR

Oh! Gentlemen, I thank you;
I've had the saddest dream that ever troubled
The heart of living creature.—My poor babe
Was crying, as I thought, crying for bread
When I had none to give him, whereupon
I put a slip of foxglove in his hand
Which pleased him so that he was hushed at once;
When into one of those same spotted bells
A Bee came darting, which the child with joy
Imprisoned there, and held it to his ear—
And suddenly grew black as he would die.

---

16 The clock here, and in II.i.27–28, is an anachronism; see also II.iii.90n.

23 Rivers's use of the Beggarwoman is equivalent to Iago's use of the handkerchief as a piece of false circumstantial evidence.

24–42 The Beggarwoman's two dreams are placed in a setting derived from *An Evening Walk* (1793), ll. 242–278. But whereas the natural objects that quiet the children in *An Evening Walk* are friendly, in *The Borderers* they turn out to be treacherous and vicious. The bee from which one expects sweetness and receives a sting and the carnivorous dog are both traditional figures; Paul Christian records their traditional meanings in *The History and Practice of Magic* (1870), trans. James Kirkup and Julian Shaw (2 vols.; New York, 1952), II, 378, 381. On the bee that poisons the pleased child in the ear compare *Hamlet*, IV.v.89–90:

> Feeds on his wonder, keeps himself in clouds,
> And wants not buzzers to infect his ear . . .

On the dog compare the spectral hunt of the hounds in the Edge of a Heath Scene (ll. 5–8), tradition familiar in the folklore of northern England, thought to portend death.

25–29 Cf. *An Evening Walk* (1793), ll. 257–260:

> I see her now, deny'd to lay her head,
> On cold blue nights, in hut or straw-built shed;
> Turn to a silent smile their sleepy cry,
> By pointing to a shooting star on high.

Ten years; and no one ever heard her voice;
But every night at the first stroke of twelve
She quits her house, and, in the neighbouring Churchyard
Upon the self-same spot, in rain or storm,
She paces out the hour 'twixt twelve and one—
She paces round and round an Infant's grave,
And in the churchyard sod her feet have worn
A hollow ring; they say it is knee-deep——
Ha! what is here?

[*A female* Beggar *rises up, rubbing her eyes as if in sleep—*
a Child in her arms.

BEGGAR.

Oh! Gentlemen, I thank you;
I've had the saddest dream that ever troubled
The heart of living creature.—My poor Babe
Was crying, as I thought, crying for bread
When I had none to give him; whereupon,
I put a slip of foxglove in his hand,
Which pleased him so, that he was hushed at once:
When, into one of those same spotted bells
A bee came darting, which the Child with joy
Imprisoned there, and held it to his ear,
And suddenly grew black, as he would die.

---

396 Ha!] Ah! *1845*, *1849*

MORTIMER (*to* RIVERS)

We have no time for this.
(*To the* Beggar) My babbling gossip,
Here's what will comfort you. [*Gives her money.*

BEGGAR (*to* MORTIMER)

The Saints reward you
For this good work.—Well Sirs, this passed away;
And afterwards I fancied a strange dog
Trotting alone, along a beaten road,
Came to the child as by my side he slept
And fondling licked his face, then on a sudden
Snapped fierce to make a morsel of his head.
But here he is! (*Kissing the child*) It must have been a dream.

RIVERS

When next inclined to sleep, take my advice
And put your head, good Woman! under cover.

BEGGAR

Oh Sir! you would not talk thus if you knew
What life is this of ours, how sleep will master
The weary-worn.—You gentlefolks have got
Warm chambers to your wish—I'd rather be
A Stone than what I am—but two nights gone
The darkness overtook me, wind and rain
Beat hard upon my head—and yet I saw
A glow-worm through the covert of the furze
Shine [   ] as if nothing ailed the sky
At which I half-accused the God in heaven—
You must forgive me, Sirs——

RIVERS

Well, well—today
Has made amends.

49–55 Compare the following lines from "The road extended o'er a heath," a fragment related to the *Salisbury Plain* poems entered in DC MS. 2, a reading text of which is given in *SPP*, p. 289:

I saw safe sheltered by the viewless furze
The tiny glowworm, lowliest child of earth,
From his green lodge with undiminished light
Shine through the rain, and strange comparison
Of Envy linked with pity touched my heart
And such reproach of heavenly ordonnance
As shall not need forgiveness.

These lines date from about the same time as the *Gothic Tale*; see *Chronology: EY*, pp. 344–345.

53 The blank was filled in 1841 with "calmly."

MARMADUKE.

We have no time for this, my babbling Gossip;
Here's what will comfort you. [*Gives her money.*

BEGGAR.

The Saints reward you
For this good deed!—Well, Sirs, this passed away;
And afterwards I fancied, a strange dog,
Trotting alone along the beaten road,
Came to my child as by my side he slept
And, fondling, licked his face, then on a sudden
Snapped fierce to make a morsel of his head:
But here he is, (*kissing the Child*) it must have been a dream.

OSWALD.

When next inclined to sleep, take my advice,
And put your head, good Woman, under cover.

BEGGAR.

Oh, sir, you would not talk thus, if you knew
What life is this of ours, how sleep will master
The weary-worn.—You gentlefolk have got
Warm chambers to your wish. I'd rather be
A stone than what I am.—But two nights gone,
The darkness overtook me—wind and rain
Beat hard upon my head—and yet I saw
A glow-worm, through the covert of the furze,
Shine calmly as if nothing ailed the sky:
At which I half accused the God in Heaven.—
You must forgive me.

OSWALD.

Ay, and if you think
The Fairies are to blame, and you should chide
Your favourite saint—no matter—this good day
Has made amends.

BEGGAR

Thanks to you—but oh! Sir! [431]
How would you like to travel on whole hours
As I have done, my eyes upon the ground,
Expecting still, I knew not how, to find
A piece of money glittering through the dust. [435]

MORTIMER

This woman is a prater.—Pray, good Lady,
Do you tell fortunes?

BEGGAR

Oh! Sir! you are like the rest.
This little one—it cuts me to the heart—
Well! they might turn a beggar from their door,
But there are mothers who can see the babe [440]
Here at my breast and ask me where I bought it:
This they can do and look upon my face.
—But you, Sir, should be kinder.

MORTIMER

Come here ye fathers,
And learn of this poor wretch.

BEGGAR

Aye, Sir, there's nobody that feels for us. [445]
Why now—but yesterday I overtook
A blind old grey-beard and accosted him—
I'th'name of all the saints and by the mass
He should have used me better! Charity!
If you can melt a rock he is your man. [450]
But I'll be even with him—here again
Have I been waiting for him.

RIVERS

Well! but softly,
Who is it that has wronged you?

57–58 Cf. *The Old Cumberland Beggar* (1800), ll. 45–47:

On the ground
His eyes are turn'd, and, as he moves along,
They move along the ground.

77–90 In the Rough Notebook draft for these lines the Beggarwoman herself drops the name of Herbert, and at the end of her speech is questioned: "Well but softly / Who is it that has wrongd you?" (18v).

BEGGAR.

Thanks to you both; but, O Sir!
How would you like to travel on whole hours
As I have done, my eyes upon the ground,
Expecting still, I knew not how, to find
A piece of money glittering through the dust.

MARMADUKE.

This woman is a prater. Pray, good Lady!
Do you tell fortunes?

BEGGAR.

Oh Sir, you are like the rest.
This Little-one—it cuts me to the heart—
Well! they might turn a beggar from their doors,
But there are Mothers who can see the Babe
Here at my breast, and ask me where I bought it:
This they can do, and look upon my face—
But you, Sir, should be kinder.

MARMADUKE.

Come hither, Fathers,
And learn what nature is from this poor Wretch!

BEGGAR.

Ay, Sir, there's nobody that feels for us.
Why now—but yesterday I overtook
A blind old Greybeard and accosted him,
I'th' name of all the Saints, and by the Mass
He should have used me better!—Charity!
If you can melt a rock, he is your man;
But I'll be even with him—here again
Have I been waiting for him.

OSWALD.

Well, but softly,
Who is it that hath wronged you?

---

431 Sir!] sir! *1842*, *1845* Sir! *(MSS. 3 and 4)*, *1846–*

BEGGAR

Mark you me:
I'll point him out—a maiden is his guide,
Lovely as any rose, a little dog
Tied by a woolen cord moves on before
With look as sad as he were dumb, the cur.
I owe him no ill will, but in good sooth
He does his master credit.

MORTIMER

As I live,
'Tis Herbert and no other!

BEGGAR

Aye, gentlemen, it is a feast to see him:
Lank as a ghost and tall—his shoulders bent
And his beard white with age—yet evermore,
As if he were the only saint on earth
He turns his face to heaven.

RIVERS

But why so violent
Against this poor old gentleman?

BEGGAR

I'll tell you:
He has the very hardest heart on earth.
I had as lief turn to the friars' school
And knock for entrance in mid-holiday.

MORTIMER

But to your story.

BEGGAR

As I was saying, Sir,
Well—he has often used me like a dog,
But yesterday was worse than all—at last,
And after trudging many a weary mile,
I overtook him, Sirs, my boy and I.
'Twas on the middle of the heath, and so

---

86 Cf. *The Discharged Soldier* (reading text in *Bicentenary Wordsworth Studies*, ed. Jonathan Wordsworth [Ithaca, 1970], pp. 433–437), ll. 41–43:

He was in stature tall,
A foot above man's common measure tall,
And lank, and upright.

94 The "holiday" would be a holy day, when the friars are fasting or praying.

BEGGAR.

Mark you me;
I'll point him out;—a Maiden is his guide,
Lovely as Spring's first rose; a little dog,
Tied by a woollen cord, moves on before
With look as sad as he were dumb; the cur,
I owe him no ill will, but in good sooth
He does his Master credit.

MARMADUKE.

As I live,
'Tis Herbert and no other!

BEGGAR.

'Tis a feast to see him,
Lank as a ghost and tall, his shoulders bent,
And long beard white with age—yet evermore,
As if he were the only Saint on earth,
He turns his face to heaven.

OSWALD.

But why so violent
Against this venerable Man?

BEGGAR.

I'll tell you:
He has the very hardest heart on earth;
I had as lief turn to the Friar's school
And knock for entrance, in mid holiday.

MARMADUKE.

But to your story.

BEGGAR.

I was saying, Sir—
Well!—he has often spurned me like a toad,
But yesterday was worse than all;—at last
I overtook him, Sirs, my Babe and I,

I begged a little aid for charity,
But he was snappish as a cottage cur.
Well then, says I—I'll out with it, at which [475]
I cast a look upon the girl and felt
As if my heart would burst, and so I left him.

RIVERS

I think, good woman! you are the very person
Whom, but some few days past, I saw in [?]
At Herbert's door.

BEGGAR

Aye, and if truth were known [480]
I have good business there.

RIVERS

I met you at the threshold, and it seemed
That he was angry.

BEGGAR

Angry! well he might;
And long as I can stir I'll dog him—yesterday
To serve me so, and knowing that he owes
The best of all he has to me and mine. [485]
But 'tis all over now.—That good old Lady
Has left a power of riches, and I say it,
If there's a lawyer in the land, the rogue
Shall give me half.

RIVERS

I fear, good woman!
You have been insolent—

BEGGAR

Aye, Sir, and there's a Lord—
I spied him sculking in his peasant's dress. [491]

RIVERS

How say you? In disguise?

MORTIMER

What's your business
With Herbert or his daughter?

---

107 The original place name was obliterated by the overwriting of "Eskdale" in 1841.
115 "The" was revised to "That" in 1799.
115–156 The Rough Notebook contains drafts for these lines, 31^{r}–33^{r}.
119–121 There is no reference to the "lord" in the Rough Notebook drafts.

And begged a little aid for charity:
But he was snappish as a cottage cur.
Well then, says I—I'll out with it; at which
I cast a look upon the Girl, and felt
As if my heart would burst; and so I left him.

OSWALD.

I think, good Woman, you are the very person
Whom, but some few days past, I saw in Eskdale,
At Herbert's door.

BEGGAR.

Ay; and if truth were known
I have good business there.

OSWALD.

I met you at the threshold,
And he seemed angry.

BEGGAR.

Angry! well he might;
And long as I can stir I'll dog him.—Yesterday,
To serve me so, and knowing that he owes
The best of all he has to me and mine.
But 'tis all over now.—That good old Lady
Has left a power of riches; and I say it,
If there's a lawyer in the land, the knave
Shall give me half.

OSWALD.

What's this?—I fear, good Woman,
You have been insolent.

BEGGAR.

And there's the Baron,
I spied him skulking in his peasant's dress.

OSWALD.

How say you? in disguise?—

MARMADUKE.

But what's your business
With Herbert or his Daughter?

BEGGAR

Daughter! truly!—
But how's the day? I fear, my little boy,
We've overslept ourselves. Sirs, have you seen him?
[*Offers to go.*

MORTIMER

I must have more of this—you shall not stir
An inch till I am answered. Know you aught
That doth concern this Herbert?

BEGGAR

You are angry,
And will misuse me, Sir!

MORTIMER

No trifling, woman!

RIVERS

You are as safe as in a sanctuary:
Speak.

MORTIMER

Speak.

BEGGAR

He is a most hard-hearted man.

MORTIMER

Your life is at my mercy.

BEGGAR

Do not harm me,
And I will tell you all—you know not, Sir,
What strong temptations press upon the poor—

RIVERS

Speak out!

BEGGAR

Oh! Sir! I've been a wicked woman—

MORTIMER

Nay, speak out, speak out—

BEGGAR

He flattered me and said
What harvest it would bring us both, and so
I parted with the child.

BEGGAR.

Daughter! truly—
But how's the day?—I fear, my little Boy,
We've overslept ourselves.—Sirs, have you seen him?
[*Offers to go.*

MARMADUKE.

I must have more of this;— you shall not stir
An inch, till I am answered. Know you aught
That doth concern this Herbert?

BEGGAR.

You are provoked,
And will misuse me, Sir!

MARMADUKE.

No trifling, Woman!—

OSWALD.

You are as safe as in a sanctuary;
Speak.

MARMADUKE.

Speak!

BEGGAR.

He is a most hard-hearted Man.

MARMADUKE.

Your life is at my mercy.

BEGGAR.

Do not harm me,
And I will tell you all!—You know not, Sir,
What strong temptations press upon the Poor.

OSWALD.

Speak out.

BEGGAR.

Oh Sir, I've been a wicked Woman.

OSWALD.

Nay, but speak out!

BEGGAR.

He flattered me, and said
What harvest it would bring us both; and so,
I parted with the Child.

MORTIMER

With whom you parted?

BEGGAR

Matilda, as he calls her, but the girl
Is mine.

MORTIMER

Yours! Woman! are you Herbert's wife? [510]

BEGGAR

Wife, Sir! his wife! not I; my husband, Sir,
Was of Kirkoswald—many a snowy winter
We've weathered out together.—Aye, poor Gilfrid!
He has been two years in his grave.

MORTIMER

Enough! [514]

RIVERS

We've solved the riddle—hellish miscreant!

MORTIMER

Do you, good dame, repair to Liddisdale
And wait for my return; I'll meet you there.
You shall have justice.—Herbert is gone by,
But leave the rest to me.

RIVERS

A lucky woman!
Depart and think that you have done good service.

MORTIMER (*to himself*)

Eternal praises to the power that saved her! [519]

RIVERS (*gives the* Beggar *money*)

Here's for your little boy—and when you christen him
I'll be his God-father.

BEGGAR

Oh Sir, you are merry with me.
In grange or farm this hundred scarcely owns
A dog that does not know me.—These good people,
For love of God I must not pass their doors.
But I will be back with my best speed; for you— [525]
God bless and thank you, masters! [*Exit* Beggar.

145 MH revised "repair good dame" to "good dame, repair" in 1799. In the Rough Notebook draft (32^{v}) Wordsworth seems to have had special difficulty in determining an appropriate meeting place for Mortimer and the Beggar. The base text gives Ravensburgh, and the alternatives considered are Delavale, Emildon, and Liddisdale on 32^{v}, as well as Merley on 33^{r}.

MARMADUKE.

With whom you parted?

BEGGAR.

Idonea, as he calls her; but the Girl
Is mine.

MARMADUKE.

Yours, Woman! are you Herbert's wife?

BEGGAR.

Wife, Sir! his wife—not I; my husband, Sir,
Was of Kirkoswald—many a snowy winter
We've weathered out together. My poor Gilfred!
He has been two years in his grave.

MARMADUKE.

Enough.

OSWALD.

We've solved the riddle—Miscreant!

MARMADUKE.

Do you,
Good Dame, repair to Liddesdale and wait
For my return; be sure you shall have justice.

OSWALD.

A lucky woman!—go, you have done good service.
[*Aside.*

MARMADUKE (*to himself*).

Eternal praises on the power that saved her!—

OSWALD (*gives her money*).

Here's for your little Boy—and when you christen him
I'll be his Godfather.

BEGGAR.

Oh Sir, you are merry with me.
In grange or farm this Hundred scarcely owns
A dog that does not know me.—These good Folks,
For love of God, I must not pass their doors;
But I'll be back with my best speed: for you—
God bless and thank you both, my gentle Masters.
[*Exit* Beggar.

---

508 With whom you parted?] Parted with whom? *1849*
520 Boy] boy *1845–*

MORTIMER (*after some time*)

Sinking, sinking,
And feel that I am sinking—would this body
Were quietly given back unto the earth
From whence the burthen came.

RIVERS (*aside*)

Pierced to the heart!

MORTIMER (*to himself*)

The cruel viper!—oh thou poor Matilda,
Now I *do* love thee.

RIVERS

Faith! I am thunderstruck.

MORTIMER

Where is she? hola! [*Calling the* Beggar. *She returns.*
(*Looking at her stedfastly in the face*)
You are Matilda's mother?
Nay, be not terrified—it does me good
To look upon you.

RIVERS (*interposing*)

In a peasant's dress
You saw, who was it?

BEGGAR

Nay, I dare not speak—
He is a man—if it should come to his ears
I never shall be heard of more.

RIVERS

Lord Clifford—

BEGGAR

What can I do? Believe me, gentle Sirs!
I love her, though I dare not call her daughter.

RIVERS

Lord Clifford! did you see him talk with Herbert?

BEGGAR

Yes, to my sorrow—under the great beech
At Herbert's door, and when he stood by the side

158–160 These lines also appear in the Rough Notebook drafts for the deception, 41^{v}–42^{r}; Mortimer returns to the same imagery on 42^{v}.

160 MH revised "it" to "the burthen" in 1799.

161–162 Cf. "Excellent wretch! Perdition catch my soul / But I do love thee!" (*Othello*, III.iii.90–91).

MARMADUKE (*to himself*).

The cruel Viper!—Poor devoted Maid,
Now I *do* love thee.

OSWALD.

I am thunderstruck.

MARMADUKE.

Where is she—holla!

[*Calling to the* Beggar, *who returns; he looks at her stedfastly.*

You are Idonea's Mother?—
Nay, be not terrified—it does me good
To look upon you.

OSWALD (*interrupting*).

In a peasant's dress
You saw, who was it?

BEGGAR.

Nay, I dare not speak;
He is a man, if it should come to his ears
I never shall be heard of more.

OSWALD.

Lord Clifford?

BEGGAR.

What can I do? believe me, gentle Sirs,
I love her, though I dare not call her daughter.

OSWALD.

Lord Clifford—did you see him talk with Herbert?

BEGGAR.

Yes, to my sorrow—under the great oak
At Herbert's door—and when he stood beside

Of the blind man, he looked at the poor girl
With such a look—it makes me tremble, Sir, [541]
To think of it——

RIVERS

Enough! you may depart.

MORTIMER (*to himself*)

Father! To God himself we cannot give
An holier name, and under such a mask
To lead a spirit spotless as the blessed [545]
To that abhorred den of brutal vice!
The firm foundation of my life appears
To sink from under me. This business, Rivers,
Will be my ruin.——

ACT II

[Scene 1] *A Chamber in the Inn*—Rivers *alone, rising from a Table, as if he had been writing.*

RIVERS

They chose him for their chief!—I had a gnawing
More of contempt than hatred!— Shame on me,
'Twas a dull spark—a most unnatural [?fire].
—It died the moment the air breathed upon it. [557]
—These fools of feeling are mere birds of winter
That haunt some barren island of the north,
Where if a famishing man stretch forth his hand
They think it is to feed them.—I have left him [561]

181–183 Cf. the base text of the drafts for the deception in the Rough Notebook (42^v).

Two plot sketches in the Rough Notebook include events related to those that occur in Act II. The early plot sketch for Act III (14^v) includes an early equivalent to II.ii. The revised synopsis for the second act (18^r) indicates that Wordsworth had the eventual shape of Act II firmly in mind by the time he made that entry, though the equivalent of II.ii is sketched out as "Matilda and old Soldier."

1–2 Compare Spiegelberg's hostility to Karl Moor in Schiller's play *The Robbers* (which Wordsworth probably read in the translation by A. F. Tytler [London, 1792]) and Iago's envy of Cassio after Cassio's promotion in *Othello*. Similar tensions are present among the thieves who waylay and then adopt Caleb Williams (vol. III, chap. 1, and following): the villainous Gines resents the naive generosity of the chivalrous Mr. Raymond. In this episode of *Caleb Williams* Godwin's source may well be Schiller.

3 The original reading was obscured by overwriting in 1841.

5–8 These lines combine two recurrent motifs, that of the bird-loving saint on an island (St. Cuthbert, friend of St. Herbert of Derwentwater, and often linked with Herbert in the play) and that of the famishing man (see especially III.v.165–167, IV.ii.63, and V.iii.255). The image of the famishing man hoping, like Elijah, for sustenance from the skies first appears in Wordsworth's poetry in the description of the freezing farmer, *Descriptive Sketches* (1793), ll. 400–408; see II.iii.124–126 and III.iii.104–113.

The blind Man—at the silent Girl he looked
With such a look—it makes me tremble, Sir,
To think of it.

OSWALD.

Enough! you may depart.

MARMADUKE (*to himself*).

Father!—to God himself we cannot give
A holier name; and, under such a mask,
To lead a Spirit, spotless as the blessed,
To that abhorrèd den of brutish vice!—
Oswald, the firm foundation of my life
Is going from under me; these strange discoveries—
Looked at from every point of fear or hope,
Duty, or love—involve, I feel, my ruin.

END OF FIRST ACT.

ACT II.

SCENE, *A Chamber in the Hostel*—OSWALD *alone, rising from a Table on which he had been writing.*

OSWALD.

They chose *him* for their Chief!—what covert part
He, in the preference, modest Youth, might take,
I neither know nor care. The insult bred
More of contempt than hatred; both are flown;
That either e'er existed is my shame:
'Twas a dull spark—a most unnatural fire
That died the moment the air breathed upon it.
—These fools of feeling are mere birds of winter
That haunt some barren island of the north,
Where, if a famishing man stretch forth his hand,
They think it is to feed them. I have left him

To solitary meditation; now
For a few swelling phrases, and a flash
Of truth enough to dazzle and to blind,
And he is mine for ever.

Enter MORTIMER.

MORTIMER

These ten years she has moved her lips all day [566]
And never speaks.

RIVERS

Who is it?

MORTIMER

I have seen her.
Just now I have been standing at her door.

RIVERS

Oh! the poor tenant of that ragged cottage,
She whom the villain Clifford drove to madness.

MORTIMER

I met a peasant near the spot, he told me [570]
These ten years she had sat all day alone
Within those empty walls.

RIVERS

Yes—I have seen her.
Chancing to pass this way some six months gone,
At midnight I betook me to the church-yard
(I do not think I ever told you of it),
'Twas a calm night as I remember well,
The moon shone clear; the air was still—so still [575]
The trees were silent as the graves beneath them.
The church-clock from within the steeple tower
Tick'd audibly—a full half hour did I
Prolong my watch; I saw her pacing round
Upon the self same spot, still round and round,
Her lips for ever moving.

10–11 See III.v.30–33.
28–29 Cf. *GT*, l. 50: "A full half hour the youth prolonged his watch."
29–31 Cf. the narrator's description of Martha Ray in *The Thorn* (1798).

To solitary meditation;—now
For a few swelling phrases, and a flash
Of truth, enough to dazzle and to blind,
And he is mine for ever—here he comes.

Enter MARMADUKE.

MARMADUKE.

These ten years she has moved her lips all day
And never speaks!

OSWALD.

Who is it?

MARMADUKE.

I have seen her.

OSWALD.

Oh! the poor tenant of that ragged homestead,
Her whom the Monster, Clifford, drove to madness.

MARMADUKE.

I met a peasant near the spot; he told me,
These ten years she had sate all day alone
Within those empty walls.

OSWALD.

I too have seen her;
Chancing to pass this way some six months gone,
At midnight, I betook me to the Churchyard:
The moon shone clear, the air was still, so still
The trees were silent as the graves beneath them.
Long did I watch, and saw her pacing round
Upon the self-same spot, still round and round,
Her lips for ever moving.

MORTIMER

Poor Matilda:
Oh Rivers! when I looked upon that woman
I thought I saw a skeleton of Matilda. [581]

RIVERS

But the old man?

MORTIMER

There is no earthly law
That measures crimes like his.

RIVERS

Would she were present!
Matilda, fit it were that we should hear
What she can urge in his defence—she loves him— [590]

MORTIMER

Yes, loves him—'tis a truth that multiplies
His guilt a thousand fold.

RIVERS

'Tis most perplexing:
What must be done?

MORTIMER

We will conduct her hither;
These walls shall witness it—from first to last [594]
He shall reveal himself—his punishment
Shall be before her face.

RIVERS

The thought is grand,
And worthy the occasion—but bethink you,
Is it not possible that some may think
It is unseemly in a man like you
To take the life of one so helpless?

MORTIMER

Oh,
Would he were older! would he were more weak,
A thousand times more helpless; verily
I do not think the tale will be believed
Till I have shed his blood.

33 In IV.ii.79–89 the captain's daughter is similarly described as "her father's skeleton." The sense is a figural usage, now obsolete: "A mere outline; a thing having a bare, meagre, unattractive character" (*OED*).

41–43 See note to I.i.197–225.

51–54 See the Fenwick Note, Appendix III, and III.v.24–33 and 95–107.

MARMADUKE.

At her door
Rooted I stood; for, looking at the woman,
I thought I saw the skeleton of Idonea.

OSWALD.

But the pretended Father——

MARMADUKE.

Earthly law
Measures not crimes like his.

OSWALD.

We rank not, happily,
With those who take the spirit of their rule
From that soft class of devotees who feel
Reverence for life so deeply, that they spare
The verminous brood, and cherish what they spare
While feeding on their bodies. Would that Idonea
Were present, to the end that we might hear
What she can urge in his defence; she loves him.

MARMADUKE.

Yes, loves him; 'tis a truth that multiplies
His guilt a thousand-fold.

OSWALD.

'Tis most perplexing:
What must be done?

MARMADUKE.

We will conduct her hither;
These walls shall witness it—from first to last
He shall reveal himself.

RIVERS

Happy are we
Who live in these disputed tracts that own [596]
No law but what each man makes for himself.
Here justice has indeed a field of triumph!

MORTIMER

Let us be gone and bring her hither; here [599]
Shall he be stretched—and after—come what will.

RIVERS

That thought escaped me.—This is an act of justice,
And where's the triumph if the delegate
Must fall in the execution of his office?
Yours is no common life! Self-stationed here,
Upon these savage confines we have seen you [606]
Stand like an isthmus 'twixt two stormy seas
That checked their fury at your bidding—
'Mid the deep holds of Solway's mossy waste
Your single virtue has transformed a band
Of fierce barbarians into ministers [611]
Of beauty and of order.—The old man
Blesses their steps, the fatherless retires
For shelter to their banners. But it is
In darkness and in tempest that we seek [616]
The majesty of the Almighty.—Yes,
Benevolence that has not heart to use
The wholesome ministry of pain and evil [619]
Is powerless and contemptible: as yet
Your virtues, the spontaneous growth of instinct,
From vigorous souls can claim but little praise.
To day you will assume a character
More awful and sublime—remember this,
And think hereafter——

60–78 Rivers's praise of Mortimer echoes Matilda's in evoking an image of Christ stilling the tempest (see note to I.i.133–141). But Rivers praises in a Satanic spirit of flattery. His description of Mortimer's role in the lawless borderlands recalls the fallen angels' discussion of their role in Hell in *Paradise Lost*, II; particular echoes can be heard in Rivers's description of Mortimer as "self-stationed" and in his instructions that Mortimer should imitate the dark majesty of the Almighty (see *Paradise Lost*, V, 859–866, and II, 263–286). More generally, here as elsewhere Rivers echoes the language and philosophy with which Karl Moor (Charles de Moor in the translation that Wordsworth probably read) apostrophizes the band in Schiller's *Robbers*: "—Who could e'er have thought that we were destined to serve as instruments in the Almighty's hand, and minister to his justice? Our fate's mysterious clue is now unravelling. This day the invisible arm of a superior Power gives dignity to our vocation.—Adore his Majesty, who honours you this day as agents in his hands to execute his wondrous purposes!—employs you as his angels to execute his stern decrees, and pour the vials of his wrath.—" (Tytler translation, p. 178).

OSWALD.

Happy are we,
Who live in these disputed tracts, that own
No law but what each man makes for himself;
Here justice has indeed a field of triumph.

MARMADUKE.

Let us begone and bring her hither;—here
The truth shall be laid open, his guilt proved
Before her face. The rest be left to me.

OSWALD.

You will be firm: but though we well may trust
The issue to the justice of the cause,
Caution must not be flung aside; remember,
Yours is no common life. Self-stationed here,
Upon these savage confines, we have seen you
Stand like an isthmus 'twixt two stormy seas
That oft have checked their fury at your bidding.
'Mid the deep holds of Solway's mossy waste,
Your single virtue has transformed a Band
Of fierce barbarians into Ministers
Of peace and order. Aged men with tears
Have blessed their steps, the fatherless retire
For shelter to their banners. But it is,
As you must needs have deeply felt, it is
In darkness and in tempest that we seek
The majesty of Him who rules the world.
Benevolence, that has not heart to use
The wholesome ministry of pain and evil,
Becomes at last weak and contemptible.
Your generous qualities have won due praise,
But vigorous Spirits look for something more
Than Youth's spontaneous products; and to-day
You will not disappoint them; and hereafter——

MORTIMER

Talk not of hereafter,
This act has virtue for a thousand lives.

RIVERS

But 'tis an act of reason, and bethink you,
Should any rashness—

MORTIMER

Hark'ee Rivers,
You are a man—and if compassion's milk
Be known unto you, you will love this woman [628]
Even as I do, but I should loathe the light
If I could think one weak or partial feeling—

RIVERS

You quite mistake me—

MORTIMER

If I ever knew
My heart, and naked saw the man within me,
'Tis at this moment.—Rivers! I have loved [633]
To be the friend and father of the helpless,
A comforter of sorrow—there is something
Which looks like a *transition* in my soul, [636]
And yet it is not.—Let us lead him in.

RIVERS

A moment's pause.—To benefit their fellows
Great souls must stoop.—Let us survey the case
Just as it is—the deed is done—performed
Here where we stand—a tribe of vulgar wretches [642]
Rush in—the villains seize us—

MORTIMER

Seize!

RIVERS

The eye
Of vulgar men knows not the majesty
With which the mind can clothe the shapes of things:
They look but through the spectacles of forms,
And from success alone they judge of actions.

MORTIMER

Fear not, the cloud will soon disperse—but stay,
Thou wilt relate the story—farewell—

MARMADUKE.

You are wasting words; hear me then, once for all:
You are a Man—and therefore, if compassion,
Which to our kind is natural as life,
Be known unto you, you will love this Woman,
Even as I do; but I should loathe the light,
If I could think one weak or partial feeling——

OSWALD.

You will forgive me——

MARMADUKE.

If I ever knew
My heart, could penetrate its inmost core,
'Tis at this moment.—Oswald, I have loved
To be the friend and father of the oppressed,
A comforter of sorrow;—there is something
Which looks like a transition in my soul,
And yet it is not.—Let us lead him hither.

OSWALD.

Stoop for a moment; 'tis an act of justice;
And where's the triumph if the delegate
Must fall in the execution of his office?
The deed is done—if you will have it so—
Here where we stand—that tribe of vulgar wretches
(You saw them gathering for the festival)
Rush in—the villains seize us——

MARMADUKE.

Seize!

OSWALD.

Yes, they—
Men who are little given to sift and weigh—
Would wreak on us the passion of the moment.

MARMADUKE.

The cloud will soon disperse—farewell—but stay,
Thou wilt relate the story.

RIVERS

Am I then
Of such light value?

MORTIMER

I had many hopes
That were most dear to me.—I mention it
That I may live in thee.

RIVERS

What, after I am dishonored?

MORTIMER

I would preserve thee; how may it be done? [652]

RIVERS

By shewing that you calculate, and look
Beyond the present object of the sense—
A few leagues hence we shall have open field, [655]
And tread on ground as free as the first earth
Which nature gave to man. Before we enter
The barren heath, just half way to the convent
We pass the beetling rock from which there hangs
A ruined castle; you have heard of it,
It is a noted spot where Clifford oft
Has held most hellish orgies, with the gloom [660]
And very superstition of the place
Seasoning his lusts. The savage debauchee
Would there perhaps have gathered the first fruits
Of this foul monster's guilt.

Enter Host *conducting* HERBERT.

HOST

The Baron Herbert
Attends your pleasure.

RIVERS (*to the* Host)

We are ready—
(*to* HERBERT) Sir! [665]
I hope you are refreshed.—I have just written
A notice for your daughter that she may know
What is become of you—you'll sit down and sign it;
'Twill glad her heart to see her father's signature

[*Gives him a letter which was lying upon the table.*

---

118 MH revised "horrid" to "hellish," probably in 1799.

OSWALD.

Am I neither
To bear a part in this Man's punishment,
Nor be its witness?

MARMADUKE.

I had many hopes
That were most dear to me, and some will bear
To be transferred to thee.

OSWALD.

When I'm dishonored!

MARMADUKE.

I would preserve thee. How may this be done?

OSWALD.

By showing that you look beyond the instant.
A few leagues hence we shall have open ground,
And nowhere upon earth is place so fit
To look upon the deed. Before we enter
The barren Moor, hangs from a beetling rock
The shattered Castle in which Clifford oft
Has held infernal orgies—with the gloom,
And very superstition of the place,
Seasoning his wickedness. The Debauchee
Would there perhaps have gathered the first fruits
Of this mock Father's guilt.

Enter Host *conducting* HERBERT.

HOST.

The Baron Herbert
Attends your pleasure.

OSWALD (*to* Host).

We are ready—
(*to* HERBERT) Sir!
I hope you are refreshed.—I have just written
A notice for your Daughter, that she may know
What is become of you.—You'll sit down and sign it;
'Twill glad her heart to see her Father's signature.

[*Gives the letter he had written.*

---

669 Father's] father's *1845–*

HERBERT

Thanks for your care. [*He sits down and writes.*

[*Exit* Host.

RIVERS (*aside to* MORTIMER)

Perhaps it would be useful [670]
That you too should subscribe your name.

[MORTIMER *looks over* HERBERT, *then writes—examines the letter eagerly.*

MORTIMER

It shall not be:
I cannot leave this paper. [*He puts it up in great agitation.*

RIVERS (*aside*)

The Blockhead! Come.

[MORTIMER *goes towards* HERBERT *and supports him—* MORTIMER *trembles much and beckons* RIVERS *to take his place.*

MORTIMER (*as he leaves* HERBERT)

There is a palsy in his limbs—he shakes. [673]

[*Exeunt* RIVERS *and* HERBERT *together*—MORTIMER *follows.*

[Scene 2] SCENE *changes to a Wood—A group of* Pilgrims *and* MATILDA *amongst them.*

FIRST PILGRIM

A grove of darker and more lofty shade
I never saw.

SECOND PILGRIM

The music of the Birds [675]
Drops deadened from a roof so thick with leaves.

AN OLD PILGRIM (*to* MATILDA)

It made my heart leap up with joy.

In the Rough Notebook synopsis (14^v) the equivalent of the "Old Pilgrim" in Scene 2 reveals herself as Matilda's mother (compare the chance encounter between the Soldier and his dying wife in *Adventures on Salisbury Plain*, 694ff.). In the Rough Notebook Churchyard Scene the figure has been recast as a male Old Pilgrim who has lost his child and is not in his "true and perfect mind," but whom Matilda feels might be cured by meeting with Herbert. In the revised sketch for Act II (Rough Notebook, 18^r), the pilgrim is described as an "old Soldier." In recasting the Old Pilgrim yet again as a lively (and sane) old man who had known Matilda and Herbert at the time of his dispossession, Wordsworth returns to a figure who conveys the promise of renewed life for Herbert (literally, who brings news of his restored title), but without the crude melodrama of the original synopsis.

1 Cf. the groves ascending to Paradise in *Paradise Lost*, IV, especially l. 138: "Insuperable highth of loftiest shade."

HERBERT.

Thanks for your care. [*Sits down and writes. Exit* Host.

OSWALD (*aside to* MARMADUKE).

Perhaps it would be useful
That you too should subscribe your name.

[MARMADUKE *overlooks* HERBERT — *then writes* — *examines the letter eagerly.*

MARMADUKE.

I cannot leave this paper. [*He puts it up, agitated.*

OSWALD (*aside*).

Dastard! Come.

[MARMADUKE *goes towards* HERBERT *and supports him*— MARMADUKE *tremblingly beckons* Oswald *to take his place.*

MARMADUKE (*as he quits* HERBERT).

There is a palsy in his limbs—he shakes.

[*Exeunt* OSWALD *and* HERBERT—MARMADUKE *following.*

SCENE *changes to a Wood—a Group of* Pilgrims *and* IDONEA *with them.*

FIRST PILGRIM.

A grove of darker and more lofty shade
I never saw.

SECOND PILGRIM.

The music of the birds
Drops deadened from a roof so thick with leaves.

AN OLD PILGRIM.

This news! It made my heart leap up with joy.

---

677 It] it *1849*

MATILDA

This news,
I scarcely can believe it.

THIRD PILGRIM

Myself I heard
The sheriff read in open court a letter
Which purported it was the Royal pleasure
The Baron Herbert who, as was supposed,
Had taken refuge in this neighbourhood
Should be forthwith restored.

PILGRIM

The hearing, Lady,
It filled my eyes with tears. When I returned
From Palestine, and brought with me a heart
Though rich in heavenly, poor in earthly comfort,
I met your Father, then a wandering outcast.
He had a guide, a Shepherd's boy; his heart
Was grieved that one so young should pass his youth
In such sad service, and he parted from him.
We joined our tales of wretchedness together
And begged our daily bread from door to door.
I talk familiarly to you, sweet Lady,
For once you loved me.

MATILDA

You shall back with me
And see your friend again. The good old man,
'Twill glad his heart to greet you.

OLD PILGRIM

It seems but yesterday.
—That cavern—does he ever talk of it?

---

6 The reading of the letter in open court may come from some special antiquarian knowledge of Wordsworth's, or from a confusion with the Court Leet, where the verdict of juries was returned to the steward in writing to be read at the following session.

7–10 After the dissolution of the Barons' League (see note to II.iii.330–334), Henry III restored the lands of many who had been deprived of their estates during the troubles.

10a/b The Old Pilgrim is identified in the MS. simply as "Pil:"

24 Despite the fact that Wordsworth makes no effort to connect the cavern with the landscape of the play, it has an equivalent in the vicinity of Penrith: the Giant's Caves on the Eamont, probably at one time a hermitage, are about two miles from Brougham Castle. The equivalent in the Churchyard Scene is the child's grave.

24–48 The anecdote anticipates Herbert's maxim that "there's a providence for them who walk / In helplessness when innocence is with them" (II.iii.70–71).

IDONEA.

I scarcely can believe it.

OLD PILGRIM.

Myself, I heard
The Sheriff read, in open Court, a letter
Which purported it was the royal pleasure
The Baron Herbert, who, as was supposed,
Had taken refuge in this neighbourhood,
Should be forthwith restored. The hearing, Lady,
Filled my dim eyes with tears.—When I returned
From Palestine, and brought with me a heart,
Though rich in heavenly, poor in earthly, comfort,
I met your Father, then a wandering Outcast:
He had a Guide, a Shepherd's boy; but grieved
He was that One so young should pass his youth
In such sad service; and he parted with him.
We joined our tales of wretchedness together,
And begged our daily bread from door to door.
I talk familiarly to you, sweet Lady!
For once you loved me.

IDONEA.

You shall back with me
And see your Friend again. The good old Man
Will be rejoiced to greet you.

OLD PILGRIM.

It seems but yesterday

No doubt you've heard the tale a thousand times.
It was a dreary afternoon—and we
Were worn with travel, when a storm o'ertook us
In a deep wood remote from any town.
A cave that opened to the road presented
A friendly shelter, and we entered in. [700]

MATILDA

And I was with you.

OLD PILGRIM

If indeed 'twas you—
But you were then a tottering little one.
We sate us down. The sky grew dark and darker.
I struck my flint, and built up a small fire
With rotten boughs and leaves such as the winds [705]
Of many winters in the cave had piled.
Meanwhile the storm fell heavy on the woods.
Our little fire sent forth a cheering warmth
And we were comforted, and talked of comfort.
But 'twas an angry night, and o'er our heads [710]
The thunder rolled in peals that would have made
A sleeping man uneasy in his bed.
Oh Lady! you have need to love your father.
His countenance, methinks I see it now,
When after a broad flash that filled the cave
He said to me that he had seen his child [716]
—A face—and a confused gleam of human flesh,
And it was you, dear Lady.

MATILDA

Heaven be praised
That I have lived to be a comfort to him!
Let us be gone, it is not two leagues hence,
And we shall greet him with these happy tidings.
This is a day of thankfulness and joy.——

[*Exeunt* MATILDA *and* Pilgrims.

43–48 Cf. the female vagrant's pleasure in viewing the "breaking smiles" of her children "thro' the dusk" (*An Evening Walk*, l. 274), and her use of lightning as a natural "torch" (l. 298). In the *Gothic Tale* a "sulphurous bolt of terror" briefly causes the blind old sailor to see (ll. 93–96).

That a fierce storm o'ertook us, worn with travel,
In a deep wood remote from any town.
A cave that opened to the road presented
A friendly shelter, and we entered in.

IDONEA.

And I was with you?

OLD PILGRIM.

If indeed 'twas you—
But you were then a tottering Little-one—
We sate us down. The sky grew dark and darker:
I struck my flint, and built up a small fire
With rotten boughs and leaves, such as the winds
Of many autumns in the cave had piled.
Meanwhile the storm fell heavy on the woods;
Our little fire sent forth a cheering warmth
And we were comforted, and talked of comfort;
But 'twas an angry night, and o'er our heads
The thunder rolled in peals that would have made
A sleeping man uneasy in his bed.
O Lady, you have need to love your Father.
His voice—methinks I hear it now, his voice
When, after a broad flash that filled the cave,
He said to me, that he had seen his Child,
A face (no cherub's face more beautiful)
Revealed by lustre brought with it from Heaven;
And it was you, dear Lady!

IDONEA.

God be praised,
That I have been his comforter till now!
And will be so through every change of fortune
And every sacrifice his peace requires.—
Let us be gone with speed, that he may hear
These joyful tidings from no lips but mine.
[*Exeunt* IDONEA *and* Pilgrims.]

---

718 Heaven] heaven *1849*

[Scene 3] SCENE—*The area of a ruined castle—on one side the entrance of a dungeon*—MORTIMER *and* RIVERS *pacing backwards and forwards*—

MORTIMER

'Tis a wild night.

RIVERS

I'd give my cloak and bonnet
For sight of a warm fire.

MORTIMER

The wind blows keen;
My hands are numb.

RIVERS (*blowing his fingers*)

Hu! hu! 'tis nipping cold.
I long for news of our brave comrades; Lacy
Would drive those Scottish rovers to their dens
If once they blew a horn this side the Tweed.
He is a stripling of great promise.

MORTIMER

I think I see a second range of towers;
This castle has another area—come,
Let us examine it.

RIVERS

In truth, 'tis cold;
I hope Matilda is well housed.—The horseman

The setting and many of the incidents leading up to Mortimer's attempted murder and its failure are closely derived from the *Gothic Tale*, and the psychology of guilt is probably based directly on Joseph Fawcett's *Art of War* (London, 1795); see Introduction, p. 22. In the Rough Notebook the revised synopsis (18^r) describes the intervention of "banditti" such as those mentioned in William Gilpin's *Observations . . . [on] . . . Cumberland, and Westmoreland* (2 vols.; London, 1786), a source for the *Gothic Tale* (see Appendix I). Here these figures have been replaced by a band of borderers who, like the band in Schiller's *Robbers*, see themselves as instruments of the divine will.

7 The term "stripling" is frequently used in the *Gothic Tale* to describe the young protagonist.

8–9 Cf. *GT*, ll. 73–77.

11–14 Cf. *GT*, ll. 118–121. The horseman in *The Borderers* may be supernatural. Such a figure is common in the folklore of Northern Europe, where his appearance presages a transition, sometimes the death of a witness or a relative. In *An Evening Walk* such a figure precedes a "gorgeous show / Of horsemen shadows winding to and fro" (ll. 183–184:

> A desperate form appears, that spurs his steed,
> Along the midway cliffs with violent speed;
> Unhurt pursues his lengthen'd flight, while all
> Attend, at every stretch, his headlong fall.
> [ll. 179–182]

In his note on this appearance, 1793, Wordsworth draws attention to James Clarke's *Survey of the Lakes . . .* (London, 1787), in which a similar "Wild Hunt" is recorded, "accompanied with vouchers of its veracity that may amuse the reader."

SCENE, *the Area of a half-ruined Castle—on one side the entrance to a dungeon—*OSWALD *and* MARMADUKE *pacing backwards and forwards.*

MARMADUKE.

'Tis a wild night.

OSWALD.

I'd give my cloak and bonnet
For sight of a warm fire.

MARMADUKE.

The wind blows keen;
My hands are numb.

OSWALD.

Ha! ha! 'tis nipping cold.
[*Blowing his fingers.*
I long for news of our brave Comrades; Lacy
Would drive those Scottish Rovers to their dens
If once they blew a horn this side the Tweed.

MARMADUKE.

I think I see a second range of Towers;
This Castle has another Area—come,
Let us examine it.

OSWALD.

'Tis a bitter night;
I hope Idonea is well housed. That horseman,

---

732 Castle] castle *1845–*

Who passed us at full speed while the dark wood
Roared in the tempest was within an ace [736]
Of sending the old fellow to his grave.—
That would have been a vile mischance.

MORTIMER

It would.

RIVERS

Justice would have been most cruelly defrauded.

MORTIMER

Most cruelly——

RIVERS

Did I not mention to you
That as we mounted up the open steep
I saw a distant fire in the north-east?
I took it for the blaze of Cheviot Beacon;
With proper speed our quarters may be gained [743]
Early tomorrow evening.

[*Looks restlessly towards the mouth of the dungeon.*

MORTIMER

When I conducted him across that plank
Hung o'er the torrent, did you hear him bless me
When he had gained the other side? I think
You could not hear—you were behind—'twas windy,
And the foam beat the rocks with deafening noise.
Those words were most delicious to me.

RIVERS

A feast
For twenty years.—How was it?

MORTIMER

And you think
This is the fittest place?

RIVERS (*aside*)

Zounds! he's turning soft.

---

15 MH inserted "a vile" in 1799.

19 James Clarke prefaces his *Survey of the Lakes* with a chart giving coordinates for the principal views from Penrith Beacon; on this chart Cheviot Beacon lies to the northeast.

23–28 Cf. *GT*, ll. 10–16.

Who at full speed swept by us where the wood
Roared in the tempest, was within an ace
Of sending to his grave our precious Charge:
That would have been a vile mischance.

MARMADUKE.

It would.

OSWALD.

Justice had been most cruelly defrauded.

MARMADUKE.

Most cruelly.

OSWALD.

As up the steep we clomb,
I saw a distant fire in the north-east;
I took it for the blaze of Cheviot Beacon:
With proper speed our quarters may be gained
To-morrow evening.

[*Looks restlessly towards the mouth of the dungeon.*

MARMADUKE.

When, upon the plank,
I had led him o'er the torrent, his voice blessed me:
You could not hear, for the foam beat the rocks
With deafening noise,—the benediction fell
Back on himself; but changed into a curse.

OSWALD.

As well indeed it might.

MARMADUKE.

And this you deem
The fittest place?

OSWALD (*aside*).

He is growing pitiful.

---

745 o'er] 'cross *1845–*

MORTIMER (*listening*)

What an odd moaning that is!

RIVERS

Mighty odd [751]
The wind should pipe a little while we stand
Cooling our heels in this way—I'll begin
And count the stars.

MORTIMER (*still listening*)

You are sure that dog of his
Could not come after us—he must have perished— [755]
The torrent would have dashed an oak to splinters—
You said you did not like his looks—that he
Would trouble us; if he were here again
I swear the sight of him would quail me more
Than twenty armies.

RIVERS

How?

MORTIMER

The old blind man [760]
Wept when you told him the mischance, and hung
Listening above the precipice.

RIVERS

In faith,
He has a tender heart!

MORTIMER

You should not, Rivers,
Have hurled the innocent animal from the precipice,
You should not—there was no occasion for it—
[RIVERS *offers to go down into the dungeon.*
How now? what mean you?

RIVERS

Truly, I was going [765]
To waken the old fellow—were there not
A farm or dwelling-house within five leagues,

---

33 MH revised "[?heads]" to "heels" in 1799.

34–38, 43–45 The dog is mentioned as the old sailor's companion in the *Gothic Tale*, but is not present when the stripling attempts the murder.

MARMADUKE (*listening*).

What an odd moaning that is!—

OSWALD.

Mighty odd
The wind should pipe a little, while we stand
Cooling our heels in this way!—I'll begin
And count the stars.

MARMADUKE (*still listening*).

That dog of his, you are sure,
Could not come after us—he *must* have perished;
The torrent would have dashed an oak to splinters.
You said you did not like his looks—that he
Would trouble us; if he were here again,
I swear the sight of him would quail me more
Than twenty armies.

OSWALD.

How?

MARMADUKE.

The old blind Man,
When you had told him the mischance, was troubled
Even to the shedding of some natural tears
Into the torrent over which he hung,
Listening in vain.

OSWALD.

He has a tender heart!

[OSWALD *offers to go down into the dungeon.*

MARMADUKE.

How now, what mean you?

OSWALD.

Truly, I was going
To waken our stray Baron. Were there not
A farm or dwelling-house within five leagues,

We should deserve to wear a cap and bells
Three good round years for playing the fool here
In such a night as this.

MORTIMER

Stop!

RIVERS

Perhaps [770]
You'd better like we should descend together
And lie down by his side, what say you to it?
Three of us—we should keep each other warm;
I'll answer for it that our four-legged friend
Shall not disturb us, further I'll not engage. [775]
Come, come, for heaven's sake.

MORTIMER

These drowsy shiverings,
This mortal stupor which is creeping over me,
What do they mean? Is not the depth
Of this man's crimes beyond the reach of thought? [781]
And yet in plumbing the abyss of vengeance
Something I strike upon which turns my thoughts
Back on myself—I think again—my breast
Concenters all the terrors of the universe,
I look at him and tremble like a child— [786]

RIVERS

Is it possible?

MORTIMER

One thing you noticed not:
Just as we left the glen a clap of thunder
Burst on the mountains with hell-rousing force.
"This is the time," said he, "when guilt may shudder; [790]
But there's a providence for them who walk
In helplessness when innocence is with them."

49–51 Cf. "This cold night will turn us all to fools and madmen" (*King Lear*, III.iv.77).
67–69 Cf. *GT*, ll. 91–94.
69–71 Cf. *King Lear*, III.ii.49–60:

Let the great gods,
That keep this dreadful pother o'er our heads,
Find out their enemies now. Tremble, thou wretch,
That hast within thee undivulged crimes,
Unwhipp'd of justice . . .
. . . I am a man
More sinn'd against than sinning.

We should deserve to wear a cap and bells,
Three good round years, for playing the fool here
In such a night as this.

MARMADUKE.

Stop, stop.

OSWALD.

Perhaps,
You'd better like we should descend together,
And lie down by his side—what say you to it?
Three of us—we should keep each other warm:
I'll answer for it that our four-legged friend
Shall not disturb us; further I'll not engage;
Come, come, for manhood's sake!

MARMADUKE.

These drowsy shiverings,
This mortal stupor which is creeping over me,
What do they mean? were this my single body
Opposed to armies, not a nerve would tremble:
Why do I tremble now?—Is not the depth
Of this Man's crimes beyond the reach of thought?
And yet, in plumbing the abyss for judgment,
Something I strike upon which turns my mind
Back on herself, I think, again—my breast
Concentres all the terrors of the Universe:
I look at him and tremble like a child.

OSWALD.

Is it possible?

MARMADUKE.

One thing you noticed not:
Just as we left the glen a clap of thunder
Burst on the mountains with hell-rousing force.
This is a time, said he, when guilt may shudder;
But there's a Providence for them who walk
In helplessness, when innocence is with them.

At this infernal blasphemy I thought
The spirit of vengeance seemed to ride the air;
[ ] I listened but
The echoes of the thunder died away
Along the distant hills.

RIVERS

What then! Great souls
Look to the world within—I mark'd you then;
Why are you not the man you were that moment?

[*He draws* MORTIMER *near the dungeon.*

MORTIMER

You say he was asleep—look at this arm
And tell me if 'tis fit for such a work.

[RIVERS *draws him near.* MORTIMER *leans upon him.*

MORTIMER

Rivers! Rivers!

RIVERS

This is some sudden seizure.

MORTIMER

A most strange faintness—will you hunt me [?]
A draught of water?

RIVERS

Nay, to see you thus
Moves me beyond my bearing; I will try
To gain the torrent's brink—

[*Exit* RIVERS.

MORTIMER (*after a pause*)

It seems an age of life
Since that man left me.—No, I am not lost.

[HERBERT *is seen at the mouth of the Dungeon.*

---

73 Cf. "heaven's cherubin, hors'd / Upon the sightless couriers of the air," *Macbeth*, I.vii.22–23.

74 The gap was later filled with "Yet nothing came."

74–76 Cf. *GT*, ll. 202–207.

82 The original reading was obliterated by the overwriting of the word "out" in 1841.

At this audacious blasphemy, I thought
The spirit of vengeance seemed to ride the air.

OSWALD.

Why are you not the man you were that moment?
[*He draws* MARMADUKE *to the dungeon.*

MARMADUKE.

You say he was asleep,—look at this arm,
And tell me if 'tis fit for such a work.
Oswald, Oswald! [*Leans upon* OSWALD.

OSWALD.

This is some sudden seizure!

MARMADUKE.

A most strange faintness,—will you hunt me out
A draught of water?

OSWALD.

Nay, to see you thus
Moves me beyond my bearing.—I will try
To gain the torrent's brink. [*Exit* OSWALD.

MARMADUKE (*after a pause*).

It seems an age
Since that Man left me.—No, I am not lost.

HERBERT

Give me your hand—where are you, my friends?

MORTIMER

This is lucky—I wanted company.

HERBERT

How goes the night?

MORTIMER

'Tis hard to say—we are not within the sound of any clock.

HERBERT

I do not hear the voice of my friend, Rivers. [807]

MORTIMER

We were thirsty—he is gone to seek for a draught of water—'tis a chearless beverage.

HERBERT

How good it was in you to stay behind! I was beginning to be afraid when I heard no answer.

MORTIMER

Why, yes, this is a place to make one fearful without knowing why.

HERBERT

Well, any shelter was a comfort, bewildered as we were, and such a storm bursting over our heads; and in a night like this to lend your cloaks to make bed for me.—It was so kind—my poor girl will weep when she hears of it—

MORTIMER

This daughter of yours is very dear to you.

HERBERT

Oh Sir! (*laying his hand upon him*) but you are young; forty years must roll over your head ere you can know how much a father may love his child.

87–133 The prose in which this exchange is written and its close verbal and situational echoes of the *Gothic Tale* suggest that these lines were drafted at an early stage in composition and little altered; see Introduction, p. 12.

90 As *The Borderers* is ostensibly set in the thirteenth century, it is hardly surprising that they are "not within the sound of any clock." Wordsworth, however, commonly measures distance from civilization in terms of the distance from church clocks, as in the "No spade for leagues . . ." fragment related to the *Salisbury Plain* poems, a reading text of which is given in *SPP*, pp. 290–292:

> Nor sound save her own steps she seemed to hear
> For ten long miles: from the Minster tower,
> The distant clock tolled out the morning's second hour.

97–100 In the *Gothic Tale* the stripling conducts the old sailor down into a dungeon in order to shelter him from the thunderstorm.

102–114 Compare the blind sailor's growing attachment to the stripling in *GT*, ll. 115–135.

HERBERT (*at the mouth of the dungeon*).
Give me your hand; where are you, Friends? and tell me
How goes the night.

MARMADUKE.
'Tis hard to measure time,
In such a weary night, and such a place.

HERBERT.
I do not hear the voice of my friend Oswald.

MARMADUKE.
A minute past, he went to fetch a draught
Of water from the torrent. 'Tis, you'll say,
A cheerless beverage.

HERBERT.
How good it was in you
To stay behind!—Hearing at first no answer,
I was alarmed.

MARMADUKE.
No wonder; this is a place
That well may put some fears into *your* heart.

HERBERT.
Why so? a roofless rock had been a comfort,
Storm-beaten and bewildered as we were;
And in a night like this, to lend your cloaks
To make a bed for me!—My Girl will weep
When she is told of it.

MARMADUKE.
This Daughter of yours
Is very dear to you.

HERBERT.
Oh! but you are young;
Over your head twice twenty years must roll,
With all their natural weight of sorrow and pain,
Ere can be known to you how much a Father
May love his Child.

MORTIMER (*aside*)

I thank you, old man, for this.

HERBERT

I am a poor and useless man—with a kind hand you have protected me this evening—I have no return to make but my prayers—may the God of Heaven bless your old age with such a daughter.—When I was an outcast, even as you see me—a miserable outcast—but I am going to talk fondly.

MORTIMER

Oh let me have it by all means, 'tis pleasant to me to hear you.

HERBERT

You will forgive me but my heart runs over—when my poor dog perished in the waters what a piercing cry you sent after him! I have loved you ever since. (*Starts*) Where are we?

MORTIMER

Oh! there is no danger.—'Tis a cold night.

HERBERT

'Twas a foolish question—but I never shall forget the shuddering that seized you when you led me over the torrent; but for you there had not been a hair betwixt my death and me.

MORTIMER

But when you were an outcast?—The heavens are just—piety like yours could not go unrewarded. The little orphan would be of service to you, I suppose?

HERBERT

I turned away from the dwellings of my Fathers when I was remembered only by those who had trampled me underfoot—I bore her in my arms—her looks won pity from the world—when I had none to help me she brought me food, she was a raven sent to me in the wilderness.—Have I not cause to love her?

MORTIMER

Oh! yes!

---

117 Cf. *GT*, ll. 116–117.

125–126 See 1 Kings 17:4–6, where the ravens feed Elijah in the desert, and see above, II.i.5–8n.

MARMADUKE.

Thank you, old Man, for this! [*Aside.*

HERBERT.

Fallen am I, and worn out, a useless Man;
Kindly have you protected me to-night,
And no return have I to make but prayers;
May you in age be blest with such a daughter!—
When from the Holy Land I had returned
Sightless, and from my Heritage was driven,
A wretched Outcast—but this strain of thought
Would lead me to talk fondly.

MARMADUKE.

Do not fear;
Your words are precious to my ears; go on.

HERBERT.

You will forgive me, but my heart runs over.
When my old Leader slipped into the flood
And perished, what a piercing outcry you
Sent after him. I have loved you ever since.
You start—where are we?

MARMADUKE.

Oh, there is no danger;
The cold blast struck me.

HERBERT.

'Twas a foolish question.

MARMADUKE.

But when you were an Outcast?—Heaven is just;
Your piety would not miss its due reward;
The little Orphan then would be your succour,
And do good service, though she knew it not.

HERBERT.

I turned me from the dwellings of my Fathers,
Where none but those who trampled on my rights
Seemed to remember me. To the wide world
I bore her, in my arms; her looks won pity;
She was my Raven in the wilderness,
And brought me food. Have I not cause to love her?

MARMADUKE.

Yes.

829 Heritage] heritage *1845–*

HERBERT

More than ever parent loved a child? [849]

MORTIMER

Yes! yes!

HERBERT

Merciful God! thou hast poured out the phials of thy wrath upon my head—but I will not murmur—blasted as I am thou hast left me both ears to hear the voice of my daughter and arms to fold her to my heart—I will adore thee and tremble!

Enter RIVERS *with water in a hunting horn.*

RIVERS (*aside*)

Herbert! Perdition! (*To* MORTIMER, *presenting the horn*)
Well, here it is—
A charming beverage to carouse upon
This bitter night.

HERBERT

Ha! Rivers! ten bright crosses [857]
I would have given not many minutes gone
To have heard your voice.

RIVERS

My good friend, I am sorry
Your rest has been disturbed.—And yet that place,
When the tempestuous wind first drove us thither, [861]
Felt warm as a wren's nest.—My good old brother
You had better step in again beneath the covert,
The storm is gathering.

[*He leads* HERBERT *to the entrance of the dungeon.*

(*To* MORTIMER) He has restored you then?
No doubt you have been nobly entertained?
But soft, how comes he here? The night-mare, conscience,
Has driven him out of harbour?

MORTIMER

I believe [867]
You have guessed right.

RIVERS (*walks about with satisfaction*)

(*Turning back to* MORTIMER *and looking at* HERBERT)

We must cure these wanderings;
I know a sovereign remedy—at times

---

130 Cf. Revelations 16:1 "And I heard a great voice out of the temple saying to the seven angels, Go your ways, and pour out the vials of the wrath of God upon the earth"; compare also the quotation from Schiller's *Robbers*, above, II.i.60–78n.

HERBERT.

More than ever Parent loved a Child?

MARMADUKE.

Yes, yes.

HERBERT.

I will not murmur, merciful God!
I will not murmur; blasted as I have been,
Thou hast left me ears to hear my Daughter's voice,
And arms to fold her to my heart. Submissively
Thee I adore, and find my rest in faith.

Enter OSWALD.

OSWALD.

Herbert!—confusion! (*aside.*) Here it is, my Friend,
[*Presents the Horn.*
A charming beverage for you to carouse,
This bitter night.

HERBERT.

Ha! Oswald! ten bright crosses
I would have given, not many minutes gone,
To have heard your voice.

OSWALD.

Your couch, I fear, good Baron,
Has been but comfortless; and yet that place,
When the tempestuous wind first drove us hither,
Felt warm as a wren's nest. You'd better turn
And under covert rest till break of day,
Or till the storm abate.
(*To* MARMADUKE *aside*). He has restored you.
No doubt you have been nobly entertained?
But soft!—how came he forth? The Night-mare Conscience
Has driven him out of harbour?

MARMADUKE.

I believe
You have guessed right.

The tooth-ache twinges me, and luckily
I have a phial.

MORTIMER

Poison! Poison!

RIVERS

Think you
I would defraud that sword of yours so vilely?
Humanity's the word with me—I wish
That since all hope of penitence is vain
The little time which he has left should be
A time of peace.

MORTIMER

Hold! hold! it is a thought
Conceived in hell.

RIVERS

Hell! say you? Poor old man!
While he is human, like ourselves, all night
Must those cold arches drip on his grey head!
His blood is thin, his bones can ill sustain
The rigours of a night like this.—'Tis mercy,
'Tis very mercy. [*He bursts away from* MORTIMER *and stops, suddenly rummaging his pockets.*
Plague, I have mislaid it!
It matters not—the main end will be answered.
(*To himself*) 'Tis an odd thought—I like the color of it;
To have an old man drugged that he may kill him.
[*Goes up to* HERBERT *and presents the horn gaily.*
Here is some cool refreshment—you will pledge us
If it were only for a traveller's pleasure
To tell by your fire side what hearty cheer
You met with at the castle.

HERBERT

You are gay,
And you are wise—I think for a short while
I could be merry too. [*He drinks.*
[MORTIMER, *who had approached, turns from him.*

RIVERS (*following* MORTIMER)

A gentle dose!
That will compose him to a child-like sleep:
There is no justice when we do not feel
For man as man.

HERBERT

The trees begin to murmur,
The big drops scatter round us. Come, my friends,
And let us house together.
[RIVERS *conducts him into the dungeon.*

RIVERS (*returns.*)

I must deal plainly with you; had I not
Esteemed you worthy to conduct this business [870]
To its most just conclusion, do you think
I would so long have struggled with my nature
And smothered all that's man in me? away!
[*Looking towards the dungeon.*
He is the property of him who best
Can feel his crimes—I have resigned a privilege: [875]
It now becomes my duty to resume it.

MORTIMER

Touch but a finger—

RIVERS

What then must be done?

MORTIMER

Which way soe'er I turn me I am curst.

RIVERS

Now on my soul I grieve for you. The misery
Of doubt is insupportable. Pity the facts [880]
Did not admit of stronger evidence. Twelve neighbours,
Plain honest men, might set us right. Their verdict
Would fortify your spirit—end this weakness—

MORTIMER

I am weak.—There is my hell.

RIVERS

True, when he said
How his old heart would leap to hear her steps, [886]
You thought his voice the echo of Matilda's.

MORTIMER

And never heard a sound so terrible.

RIVERS

Perchance you think so now?

193–194 The echo of Matilda's voice appears to "plead like angels trumpet-tongu'd against / The deep damnation" of Herbert's "taking-off" (*Macbeth*, I.vii.19–20).

HERBERT.

The trees renew their murmur:
Come, let us house together.

[OSWALD *conducts him to the dungeon.*

OSWALD (*returns*).

Had I not
Esteemed you worthy to conduct the affair
To its most fit conclusion, do you think
I would so long have struggled with my Nature,
And smothered all that's man in me?—away!—

[*Looking towards the dungeon.*

This Man's the property of him who best
Can feel his crimes. I have resigned a privilege;
It now becomes my duty to resume it.

MARMADUKE.

Touch not a finger——

OSWALD.

What then must be done?

MARMADUKE.

Which way soe'er I turn, I am perplexed.

OSWALD.

Now, on my life, I grieve for you. The misery
Of doubt is insupportable. Pity, the facts
Did not admit of stronger evidence;
Twelve honest men, plain men, would set us right;
Their verdict would abolish these weak scruples.

MARMADUKE.

Weak! I am weak—there does my torment lie,
Feeding itself.

OSWALD.

Verily, when he said
How his old heart would leap to hear her steps,
You thought his voice the echo of Idonea's.

MARMADUKE.

And never heard a sound so terrible.

OSWALD.

Perchance you think so now?

---

874 Man's] Man 's *1842* man 's *1845–* Man's *(MS. 4)*

MORTIMER

I cannot do it.
Twice did I spring to grasp his withered throat,
When such a sudden weakness fell upon me
I could have dropped asleep upon his breast.

RIVERS

Justice! Is there not thunder in the word?
Shall it be law to stab the petty robber
Who aims at one poor life, and shall *this* monster—
But you are fallen!—

MORTIMER

Fallen indeed!
Murder! asleep! blind! old! alone! betray'd!
Drugg'd and in darkness! Here to strike the blow,
Visible only to the eye of God! [*Flings away his sword.*
Away! away!

RIVERS

Nay, I have done with you.
Let's lead him to the convent.—He shall live,
And she shall love him. With unquestioned title
He shall be seated in his Barony,
And we two bless ourselves for his good deeds.
I now perceive we do mistake our masters,
And most despise the men who best can teach us.
Henceforth it shall be said that bad men only
Are brave—Clifford is brave, and that old man
Is brave.
[*Taking up* MORTIMER's *sword and giving it him.*
He would have led his daughter hither,
Into this dungeon, to this house of victims.

MORTIMER (*advancing to the dungeon*)

It must be ended.

RIVERS

For heaven's sake do not rouze him;
He will deny it to the last. He lies
Within the vault—a spear's length to the left.
[MORTIMER *descends into the dungeon.*

---

205 See II.iii.289–291.

MARMADUKE.

I cannot do it:
Twice did I spring to grasp his withered throat,
When such a sudden weakness fell upon me,
I could have dropped asleep upon his breast.

OSWALD.

Justice—is there not thunder in the word?
Shall it be law to stab the petty robber
Who aims but at our purse; and shall this Parricide—
Worse is he far, far worse (if foul dishonour
Be worse than death) to that confiding Creature
Whom he to more than filial love and duty
Hath falsely trained—shall he fulfil his purpose?
But you are fallen.

MARMADUKE.

Fallen should I be indeed—
Murder—perhaps asleep, blind, old, alone,
Betrayed, in darkness! Here to strike the blow—
Away! away!—— [*Flings away his sword.*

OSWALD.

Nay, I have done with you:
We'll lead him to the Convent. He shall live,
And she shall love him. With unquestioned title
He shall be seated in his Barony,
And we too chant the praise of his good deeds.
I now perceive we do mistake our masters,
And most despise the men who best can teach us:
Henceforth it shall be said that bad men only
Are brave; Clifford is brave; and that old Man
Is brave.
[*Taking* MARMADUKE'S *sword and giving it to him.*
To Clifford's arms he would have led
His Victim—haply to this desolate house.

MARMADUKE.

(*advancing to the dungeon*).
It must be ended!—

OSWALD.

Softly; do not rouse him;
He will deny it to the last. He lies
Within the Vault, a spear's length to the left.
[MARMADUKE *descends to the dungeon.*

RIVERS (*alone*)

The villains rose in mutiny to destroy me.
I could have quelled the cowards—but this stripling
Must needs step in, and save my life—the look
With which he gave the boon—I see it now— [920]
What if he did the deed in love—so be it,
I hate him not—now I begin to love him.
For this old venerable grey-beard—faith,
'Tis his own fault if he hath got a face
Which doth play tricks with them that look upon it:
'Twas he that put it in my thought—his countenance— [925]
His step, his figure.—Murder! what, of whom?
Of whom—or what? we kill a toad, a newt,
A rat—I do believe if they who first
Baptised the deed had called it murder, we
Had quaked to think of it. How many fools
Would laugh if I should say this youth may live
To thank me for this service! I have learned
That things will work to ends the slaves of the world [936]
Do never dream of. I *have* been what he,
This boy when he comes forth with his bloody hands,
Might envy, and am now—but he shall know
What I am now.

[*Goes and listens at the dungeon.*

Praying or parleying? Tut, [940]
Is he not eyeless? he has been half dead
These fifteen years—

Enter the female Beggar *with two or three of her companions.*

226–230 The Rough Notebook contains, inside the front cover, the note: "Having once meditated upon doing it / The deed will thenceforward be justified."

228 MH revised "do" to "doth" in 1799.

230–235 See the passage from Ann Radcliffe's *Romance of the Forest* quoted in the Introduction, p. 28, and compare Francis Moor in *The Robbers* (p. 137): "'Tis but a step—an easy one—a little murder!—None but a driveller would leave his work imperfect—or idly look on till time should finish it.—"

237–238 Cf. "There's a divinity that shapes our ends" (*Hamlet*, V.ii.10).

243–253 The "mysterious men" of the *GT* (l. 151) and the "smugglers" of the revised synopsis for Act II in the Rough Notebook (18^r) are antecedents of the beggars who threaten to interrupt Rivers's scheme, but their interruption is minimal. The two plot functions of this episode appear to be, first, to establish Rivers's dominance (especially 245–246, where something like the interaction between Macbeth and the witches is inverted—Rivers threatens to cast a spell on the beggars) and second, to establish for the audience an awareness that the beggarwoman's indictment of Herbert in I.iii was trumped up.

OSWALD (*alone*).

The Villains rose in mutiny to destroy me;
I could have quelled the Cowards, but this Stripling
Must needs step in, and save my life. The look
With which he gave the boon—I see it now!
The same that tempted me to loathe the gift.—
For this old venerable Grey-beard—faith
'Tis his own fault if he hath got a face
Which doth play tricks with them that look on it:
'Twas this that put it in my thoughts—that countenance—
His staff—his figure—Murder!—what, of whom?
We kill a worn-out horse, and who but women
Sigh at the deed? Hew down a withered tree,
And none look grave but dotards. He may live
To thank me for this service. Rainbow arches,
Highways of dreaming passion, have too long,
Young as he is, diverted wish and hope
From the unpretending ground we mortals tread;—
Then shatter the delusion, break it up
And set him free. What follows? I have learned
That things will work to ends the slaves o' the world
Do never dream of. I *have* been what he—
This Boy—when he comes forth with bloody hands—
Might envy, and am now,—but he shall know
What I am now— [*Goes and listens at the dungeon.*
Praying or parleying?—tut!
Is he not eyeless? He has been half-dead
These fifteen years——

Enter female Beggar *with two or three of her Companions.*

RIVERS (*turning round abruptly*)
Ha! speak, what art thou?
(*Recognizes her*) Heavens, my good friend!
(*To her companions*)
Begone, ye slaves! or I will raise a whirlwind
And send you dancing to the clouds like leaves. [945]
[*They retire affrighted.*

BEGGAR

Indeed we meant no harm—we lodge sometimes
In this deserted castle—I repent me—
[RIVERS *goes towards the dungeon and listens; he returns to the* Beggar.

RIVERS

Thou hast a little helpless babe. Depart.

BEGGAR

I do repent me, Sir, I fear the curses [951]
Of that Blind man.—'Twas not your money, Sir—

RIVERS

Depart.

BEGGAR (*going*)
There is some wicked deed in hand—
Would I could find the old man or his daughter! [954]
[*Exit* Beggar.

MORTIMER *re-enters from the dungeon.*

RIVERS

Well! 'tis all over then—don't you laugh at your foolish fears? you have done it cleverly—sent him into the other world without a groan; never trouble your head about burying him—we'll shove him into a corner.—In the torrent hard by there is water enough to wash all the blood in the universe. (*Examining him*) Death! I don't see a stain about you. That was dexterously managed indeed. (*Looks at his sword*) Zounds!—did you strangle him?

MORTIMER

What made you come down and lay your hand upon my shoulder? when I spoke to you, why did not you answer? you were afraid of waking him I suppose.—He must have been in a deep sleep, for I whispered to him twice.—There are damned echoes in that place—

---

257 Cf. "Will all great Neptune's ocean wash this blood / Clean from my hand?" (*Macbeth*, II.ii.61–62).

261–263 The intervention of the "black Appearance" in the *GT* (ll. 159–178) is replaced here by Rivers's imagined presence. Compare Macbeth's "Who's there? what, ho!" when he fears he has been interrupted during Duncan's murder (*Macbeth*, II.ii.9).

OSWALD (*turning abruptly*).
Ha! speak—what Thing art thou?
(*Recognises her*). Heavens! my good Friend! [*To her.*

BEGGAR.
Forgive me, gracious Sir!—

OSWALD (*to her companions*).
Begone, ye Slaves, or I will raise a whirlwind
And send ye dancing to the clouds, like leaves.
[*They retire affrighted.*

BEGGAR.
Indeed we meant no harm; we lodge sometimes
In this deserted Castle—*I repent me.*
[OSWALD *goes to the dungeon—listens—returns to the* Beggar.

OSWALD.
Woman, thou hast a helpless Infant—keep
Thy secret for its sake, or verily
That wretched life of thine shall be the forfeit.

BEGGAR.
I *do* repent me, Sir; I fear the curse
Of that blind Man. 'Twas not your money, Sir——

OSWALD.
Begone!

BEGGAR (*going*).
There is some wicked deed in hand: [*Aside.*
Would I could find the old Man and his Daughter.
[*Exit* Beggar.

MARMADUKE *re-enters from the dungeon.*

OSWALD.
It is all over then;—your foolish fears
Are hushed to sleep, by your own act and deed,
Made quiet as he is.

MARMADUKE.
Why came you down?
And when I felt your hand upon my arm
And spake to you, why did you give no answer?
Feared you to waken him? he must have been
In a deep sleep. I whispered to him thrice.
There are the strangest echoes in that place!

RIVERS

Tut! let them gabble to all eternity! 'Twas an excellent method.—You would have the grasp of a dæmon.—You are sure you finished him?

MORTIMER

Scarcely had I found the place where he was lying when I felt as if there were a string round my wrist and the blind man's dog pulling at it—

RIVERS

Well! but after? Let me have it.

MORTIMER

There was something in his face the very counterpart of Matilda.

RIVERS

Let that alone—never will my life afford me such another opportunity—why did not you allow me a share in your triumph.—Oh how I envy you—

MORTIMER

Her very looks smiling in sleep—

RIVERS

Hell! have you been playing the coward?

MORTIMER

'Twas only for a single moment—but it sent me to my prayers.

RIVERS

Plague! is he alive?

MORTIMER

Alive! who alive?

RIVERS

Herbert! the *Baron* Herbert! since you will have it, he who will be the Baron Herbert when Matilda is Clifford's Harlot.—Is *he* living?

MORTIMER

The blind man lying in that dungeon is alive. [978]

268–270 Cf. the *Vale of Esthwaite* (*PW*, I, 276, ll. 264–267):

With arms in horror spread around
I mov'd— a form unseen I found
Twist round my hand an icy chain
And drag me to the spot again.

272 Cf. "Had he not resembled / My father as he slept I had done't" (*Macbeth*, II.ii.14–15).

OSWALD.

Tut! let them gabble till the day of doom.

MARMADUKE.

Scarcely, by groping, had I reached the Spot,
When round my wrist I felt a cord drawn tight,
As if the blind Man's dog were pulling at it.

OSWALD.

But after that?

MARMADUKE.

The features of Idonea
Lurked in his face——

OSWALD.

Psha! Never to these eyes
Will retribution show itself again
With aspect so inviting. Why forbid me
To share your triumph?

MARMADUKE.

Yes, her very look,
Smiling in sleep——

OSWALD.

A pretty feat of Fancy!

MARMADUKE.

Though but a glimpse, it sent me to my prayers.

OSWALD.

Is he alive?

MARMADUKE.

What mean you? who alive?

OSWALD.

Herbert! since you will have it, Baron Herbert;
He who will gain his Seignory when Idonea
Hath become Clifford's harlot—is *he* living?

MARMADUKE.

The old Man in that dungeon *is* alive.

RIVERS

Then curse me, if ever in camp or field I obey an order of yours again—I will proclaim you, and before the whole body—they shall hear it all.—You a protector of humanity! an avenger of innocence!

MORTIMER

'Twas dark, dark as hell—yet I saw him—I tell thee I saw him, his face towards me—the very looks of Matilda sent there by some fiend to baffle me.—It put me to my prayers—I cast my eyes upwards, and through a crevice in the roof I beheld a star twinkling over my head, and by the living God, I could not do it—

[*Sinks against the scene exhausted.*

RIVERS (*after some time*)

Now may I perish if this be not joy to me.
A meaner spirit would be overwhelmed.
(*Turns to him*) My dear Mortimer,
Those words were rashly spoken—I would recall them: [993]
I feel my error.—Shedding human blood,
It is a serious thing—

MORTIMER

Not I alone—
Thou, too, art deep in guilt.

RIVERS

We have indeed [996]
Been most presumptuous.—There is guilt in this,
Else could so strong a mind have ever known
These strange infirmities? 'Tis plain that heaven
Has marked out this foul wretch as one whose crimes
Must never come before a mortal judgement seat [1001]
Or be chastized by mortal instruments—

289–291 Heaven has peeped through the blanket of the dark and cried, "Hold, hold!" (cf. *Macbeth*, I.v.54–55, and *Othello*, V.ii.63–65). In the *Gothic Tale* the star was noticed only after the stripling had already left the dungeon (ll. 194–198). See Introduction, p. 23.

304 The echo from *Julius Caesar* (II.i.63–66), expanded in Joseph Fawcett's *Art of War* (see Introduction, p. 22), aptly sums up Mortimer's confusions throughout the attempted murder:

Between the acting of a dreadful thing
And the first motion, all the interim is
Like a phantasma, or a hideous dream:
The genius and the mortal instruments
Are then in council; and the state of man,
Like to a little kingdom, suffers then
The nature of an insurrection.

OSWALD.

Henceforth, then, will I never in camp or field
Obey you more. Your weakness, to the Band,
Shall be proclaimed: brave Men, they all shall hear it.
You a protector of humanity!
Avenger you of outraged innocence!

MARMADUKE.

'Twas dark—dark as the grave; yet did I see,
Saw him—his face turned toward me; and I tell thee
Idonea's filial countenance was there
To baffle me—it put me to my prayers.
Upwards I cast my eyes, and, through a crevice,
Beheld a star twinkling above my head,
And, by the living God, I could not do it.
[*Sinks exhausted.*

OSWALD (*to himself*).

Now may I perish if this turn do more
Than make me change my course.
(*To* MARMADUKE). Dear Marmaduke,
My words were rashly spoken; I recal them:
I feel my error; shedding human blood
Is a most serious thing.

MARMADUKE.

Not I alone,
Thou too art deep in guilt.

OSWALD.

We have indeed
Been most presumptuous. There *is* guilt in this,
Else could so strong a mind have ever known
These trepidations? Plain it is that Heaven
Has marked out this foul Wretch as one whose crimes
Must never come before a mortal judgment-seat,
Or be chastised by mortal instruments.

MORTIMER

A thought that's worth a thousand worlds! 'Tis past,
And I am saved from tortures
To which the agonies of hell are mercy.
[*Goes towards the dungeon.*

RIVERS

Nay, whither now?

MORTIMER

It must be—I must see
That face of his again—I must behold it—
'Twere joy enough to end me.
(RIVERS *appears downcast*) Nay, what ails you?

RIVERS

I am dejected
To think I ever caused you so much pain.

MORTIMER

Fie! 'tis all over now, and we are safe. [1005]

RIVERS

(*As if to himself—yet speaking aloud*)
It must come to his ears at last, how stifle it?
[*Turning to him.*
Give me your sword—nay, here are stones and fragments
The least of which would beat out a man's brains
—That wall, if you should drive your head against it—
No! this is not a place to hear it:
It should be told you pinioned to your bed, [1011]
Or on some vast and solitary plain
Blown to you from a trumpet.

MORTIMER

What monster you have brooding in your breast
I know not. This I know: I have no fear
And cannot fear. [*The sound of a bugle horn is heard.*
That horn again! 'tis some one of our troop. [1016]
What do they here? Listen!

RIVERS

Dogg'd then like thieves.

319–321 Cf. *Macbeth*, IV.iii.193–195: "But I have words / That would be howl'd out in the desert air, / Where hearing should not latch them."

MARMADUKE.

A thought that's worth a thousand worlds!
[*Goes towards the dungeon.*

OSWALD.

I grieve
That, in my zeal, I have caused you so much pain.

MARMADUKE.

Think not of that! 'tis over—we are safe.

OSWALD.

(*as if to himself yet speaking aloud*).
The truth is hideous, but how stifle it?
[*Turning to* MARMADUKE.
Give me your sword—nay, here are stones and fragments,
The least of which would beat out a man's brains;
Or you might drive your head against that wall.
No! this is not the place to hear the tale:
It should be told you pinioned in your bed,
Or on some vast and solitary plain
Blown to you from a trumpet.

MARMADUKE.

Why talk thus?
Whate'er the monster brooding in your breast
I care not: fear I have none, and cannot fear——
[*The sound of a horn is heard.*
That horn again—'Tis some one of our Troop;
What do they here? Listen!

OSWALD.

What! dogged like thieves!

Enter LACY *and* WALLACE.

LACY

Ha! you are found at last—

RIVERS (*looking at* WALLACE)

That wily grey-beard—
I'd rather see my father's ghost.

LACY (*to* MORTIMER)

My Captain,
We come by order of the band. Belike
You have not heard that Henry has at last
Dissolved the Baron's League and sent abroad
His sheriffs with fit force to reinstate
The genuine owners of such Lands and Baronies
As in these long commotions have been seized.
His power is this way tending. It befits us
To stand upon our guard, and with our swords
Defend the innocent.

MORTIMER

Lacy! we look
But at the surfaces of things, we hear
Of towns in flames, fields ravaged, young and old
Driven out in flocks to want and nakedness,
Then grasp our swords and rush upon a cure
That flatters us, because it asks not thought.
The deeper malady is better hid—
The world is poisoned at the heart.

LACY

What mean you?

WALLACE

(*Whose eye has been fixed suspiciously upon* RIVERS)
Aye, what is it you mean?

330–334 These lines, a garbled reference to events after the battle of Evesham, are the only ones in the play that could be thought to refer to the year 1265 in particular, though Wordsworth seems to prefer to remain vague. Notice that Wordsworth regards Henry III's side as the right one, rather than Simon de Montfort's; in *The Borderers* the king seems to have an almost Shakespearian function of restoring the interrupted order of the universe. Wordsworth's borderers, like Robin Hood's men, are merely doing as well as they can by that order, defending "the innocent" until the king's justice is reestablished in the land.

343–344 Cf. *King Lear* (III.iv.8), "Where the greater malady is fix'd," and *Caleb Williams*, III, 302.

Enter WALLACE *and* LACY, &c.

LACY.

You are found at last, thanks to the vagrant Troop
For not misleading us.

OSWALD (*looking at* WALLACE).

That subtle Grey-beard—
I'd rather see my father's ghost.

LACY (*to* MARMADUKE).

My Captain,
We come by order of the Band. Belike
You have not heard that Henry has at last
Dissolved the Baron's League, and sent abroad
His Sheriffs with fit force to reinstate
The genuine owners of such Lands and Baronies
As, in these long commotions, have been seized.
His Power is this way tending. It befits us
To stand upon our guard, and with our swords
Defend the innocent.

MARMADUKE.

Lacy! we look
But at the surfaces of things; we hear
Of towns in flames, fields ravaged, young and old
Driven out in troops to want and nakedness;
Then grasp our swords and rush upon a cure
That flatters us, because it asks not thought:
The deeper malady is better hid;
The world is poisoned at the heart.

LACY.

What mean you?

WALLACE

(*whose eye has been fixed suspiciously upon* OSWALD).
Ay, what is it you mean?

MORTIMER

Hark'ee, my Friends—
(*With an appearance of relaxed gaiety*)
Were there a man who, being weak and helpless
And most forlorn, should bribe a mother pressed
By penury to yield him up her daughter,
A little infant, and instruct the babe
Prattling upon his knee to call him Father—

LACY

Why, if his heart be tender, that offence
I could forgive him.

MORTIMER (*going on in the same way*)

And should he make the child
An instrument of falshood; should he teach it
To stretch its little arms, and dim the light
Of infant innocence with piteous looks
Of misery that was not—

LACY

Faith, 'tis hard,
But in a world—

MORTIMER

Ay, ay—
(*Assuming a serious tone*) This self same man,
Even while he printed kisses on the cheek
Of this poor babe, and taught its innocent mouth
To lisp the name of father, could he look
To the unnatural harvest of that time
When he should give her up, a woman grown,
To him who bid the highest in the market
Of foul pollution—

LACY

Hell itself
Contains not such a monster.

MORTIMER

For this purpose
Should he resolve to taint her soul by means
Which bathe my limbs in sweat to think of them,

MARMADUKE.

Harkee, my Friends;—

[*Appearing gay.*

Were there a Man who, being weak and helpless
And most forlorn, should bribe a Mother, pressed
By penury, to yield him up her Daughter,
A little Infant, and instruct the Babe,
Prattling upon his knee, to call him Father——

LACY.

Why, if his heart be tender, that offence
I could forgive him.

MARMADUKE (*going on*).

And should he make the Child
An instrument of falsehood, should he teach her
To stretch her arms, and dim the gladsome light
Of infant playfulness with piteous looks
Of misery that was not——

LACY.

Troth, 'tis hard—
But in a world like ours——

MARMADUKE
(*changing his tone*).

This self-same Man—
Even while he printed kisses on the cheek
Of this poor Babe, and taught its innocent tongue
To lisp the name of Father—could he look
To the unnatural harvest of that time
When he should give her up, a Woman grown,
To him who bid the highest in the market
Of foul pollution——

LACY.

The whole visible world
Contains not such a Monster!

MARMADUKE.

For this purpose
Should he resolve to taint her Soul by means
Which bathe the limbs in sweat to think of them;

Should he by tales which would draw tears from iron
Work on her nature and so turn compassion
And gratitude to ministers of treason,
And make the spotless spirit of filial love
Prime mover in a plot to damn his victim
Both soul and body—

WALLACE

'Tis too horrible.
Rivers, what say you to it?

LACY

Hew him down
And fling him to the ravens.

MORTIMER

But his aspect:
It is so meek, his countenance so venerable.

WALLACE

(*with an appearance of mistrust*)
But how, what say you, Captain?

LACY (*at the same moment*)

Stab him then,
Before the altar.

MORTIMER

What if he be sick,
Tottering upon the very verge of nature,
And old, and blind—

LACY

Blind, say you!

RIVERS (*coming forward*)

Are we men,
Or own we baby spirits? Genuine courage
Is not an accidental quality,
A thing dependent for its casual birth
On opposition and impediment.
Wisdom, if justice speak the word, beats down
The Giant's strength, and at the voice of Justice

---

368 Compare the way in which Milton's Orpheus "drew Iron tears down *Pluto's* cheek" (*Il Penseroso*, l. 107).

379 Cf. *King Lear*, II.iv.149: "Nature in you stands on the very verge."

380–401 Rivers's set speech on justice may be modeled on Portia's speech on mercy in *The Merchant of Venice*, IV.i.184–205.

Should he, by tales which would draw tears from iron,
Work on her nature, and so turn compassion
And gratitude to ministers of vice,
And make the spotless spirit of filial love
Prime mover in a plot to damn his Victim
Both soul and body——

WALLACE.

'Tis too horrible;
Oswald, what say you to it?

LACY.

Hew him down,
And fling him to the ravens.

MARMADUKE.

But his aspect
It is so meek, his countenance so venerable.

WALLACE

(*with an appearance of mistrust*).

But how, what say you, Oswald?

LACY

(*at the same moment*).

Stab him, were it
Before the Altar.

MARMADUKE.

What, if he were sick,
Tottering upon the very verge of life,
And old, and blind——

LACY.

Blind, say you?

OSWALD

(*coming forward*).

Are we Men,
Or own we baby Spirits? Genuine courage
Is not an accidental quality,
A thing dependent for its casual birth
On opposition and impediment.
Wisdom, if Justice speak the word, beats down
The giant's strength; and, at the voice of Justice,

Spares not the worm.—The Giant and the worm,
She weighs them in one scale. The wiles of Women
And craft of age, seducing reason first
Made weakness a protection, and obscured
The moral shapes of things. His tender cries
And helpless innocence, do they protect
The infant lamb? and shall the infirmities
Which have enabled this enormous culprit
To perpetrate his crimes serve as a sanctuary
To cover him from punishment? Fie—Justice,
Admitting no resistance, binds alike
The feeble and the strong.—She wants not here
Her bonds and chains which make the Mighty feeble.
—We recognize in this old man a victim
Prepared already for the sacrifice—

LACY

By Heavens! his words are reason—

RIVERS

Yes, my friends,
His countenance *is* meek and venerable,
And by the mass, to see him at his prayers—
I am of flesh and blood, and may I perish
When my heart does not ache to think of it!
Poor victim! Not a virtue under heaven
But what was made an engine to ensnare thee,
But yet I trust, Matilda, thou art safe—

LACY

Matilda!

WALLACE

How! what! your Matilda?

MORTIMER

Know you Clifford?

LACY

Clifford! who ever heard of this wild castle
And doth not know him?

---

406 Cf. "Mine [my bones] ache to think on't" (*Hamlet*, V.i.99).

Spares not the worm. The giant and the worm—
She weighs them in one scale. The wiles of woman,
And craft of age, seducing reason, first
Made weakness a protection, and obscured
The moral shapes of things. His tender cries
And helpless innocence—do they protect
The infant lamb? and shall the infirmities,
Which have enabled this enormous Culprit
To perpetrate his crimes, serve as a Sanctuary
To cover him from punishment? Shame!—Justice,
Admitting no resistance, bends alike
The feeble and the strong. She needs not here
Her bonds and chains, which make the mighty feeble.
—We recognise in this old Man a victim
Prepared already for the sacrifice.

LACY.

By heaven, his words are reason!

OSWALD.

Yes, my Friends,
His countenance is meek and venerable;
And, by the Mass, to see him at his prayers!—
I am of flesh and blood, and may I perish
When my heart does not ache to think of it!—
Poor Victim! not a virtue under heaven
But what was made an engine to ensnare thee;
But yet I trust, Idonea, thou art safe.

LACY.

Idonea!

WALLACE.

How! what? your Idonea? [*To* MARMADUKE.

MARMADUKE.

Mine;
But now no longer mine. You know Lord Clifford;
He is the Man to whom the Maiden—pure
As beautiful, and gentle and benign,
And in her ample heart loving even me—
Was to be yielded up.

1104 pure] pure, *1842* pure *(MSS. 3 and 4)*, *1845–*

WALLACE

I have lived little short of seventy years,
And by the head of my own child this man
Must die. This wrinkled hand shall mat itself
In his grey hairs.

MORTIMER (*to* WALLACE)

I love the father in thee.
—You know me, friends: I have a heart to feel,
But Justice! justice—

LACY

We will have ample justice.
Who are we, friends? Do we not live on ground
Where souls are self-defended, free to grow
Like mountain Oaks, rocked by the stormy wind?
Mark the almighty wisdom which decreed
This monstrous crime should be laid open—*here*,
Where Reason has an eye that she can use
And men alone are umpires. To the camp
He shall be led, and there, the country round
All gathered to the spot, in open day
He shall be sacrificed.

RIVERS

'Tis nobly thought:
His death will be a monument to ages.

MORTIMER

Lacy,
I thank you for this hint. He shall be brought
Before the camp, and would the good and just
Of every age might there be present.—There
His crimes shall be proclaimed—and for the rest,
It shall be done as wisdom shall decide—
Meanwhile do you two hasten back and see
That all is well prepared.

WALLACE

We will obey you.

MORTIMER

Tell where you found us. At some future time
I will explain the cause.

LACY.

Now, by the head
Of my own child, this Man must die; my hand,
A worthier wanting, shall itself entwine
In his grey hairs!—

MARMADUKE (*to* LACY).

I love the Father in thee.
You know me, Friends; I have a heart to feel,
And I have felt, more than perhaps becomes me
Or duty sanctions.

LACY.

We will have ample justice.
Who are we, Friends? Do we not live on ground
Where Souls are self-defended, free to grow
Like mountain oaks rocked by the stormy wind.
Mark the Almighty Wisdom, which decreed
This monstrous crime to be laid open—*here*,
Where Reason has an eye that she can use,
And Men alone are Umpires. To the Camp
He shall be led, and there, the Country round
All gathered to the spot, in open day
Shall Nature be avenged.

OSWALD.

'Tis nobly thought;
His death will be a monument for ages.

MARMADUKE (*to* LACY).

I thank you for that hint. He shall be brought
Before the Camp, and would that best and wisest
Of every country might be present. There,
His crime shall be proclaimed; and for the rest
It shall be done as Wisdom shall decide:
Meanwhile, do you two hasten back and see
That all is well prepared.

WALLACE.

We will obey you.
(*Aside*). But softly! we must look a little nearer.

MARMADUKE.

Tell where you found us. At some future time
I will explain the cause.

END OF SECOND ACT.

ACT III

[Scene 1] SCENE, *the door of the Inn*; *a group of* Pilgrims *as before*, MATILDA *and the* Host *amongst them*.

HOST

You'll find your father, Lady, at the convent [1135]
As I have told you. He left us yesterday
With two companions: one of them, I judged,
Was his familiar friend. (*Going*) There was a letter
Of which I heard them speak—but I suppose
It was forgotten—

MATILDA (*to the* Host)

Farewell!

HOST

Gentle Pilgrims, [1140]
Saint Mary speed you on your holy errand!

[*Exeunt* MATILDA *and* Pilgrims.

[Scene 2] SCENE, *a Heath*.

RIVERS (*alone*)

Carry him to the camp! Yes, to the camp.
O Wisdom! a most wise resolve—and then
That half a word should blow it to the winds!
This last device *must* end my work—methinks [1145]
It were a pleasant pastime to construct
A scale and table of belief—as thus—
Two columns, one for passion, one for proof,
Each rising as the other falls: and, first,
Passion a unit, and against us.—Proof! [1150]
Nay, we must travel in another path
Or we're stuck fast for ever—passion, then,
Shall be a unit for us—proof, oh no,
We'll not insult her majesty by time [1154]
And place—the where, the when, the how, and all
The dull particulars whose intrusion mars
The dignity of demonstration. Well,

Scene 1 may be compared with the synopsis for Act III in the Rough Notebook (14^v): "Matilda having heard at the inn where she had left her father that he was gone to the convent where they had slept proceeds after him."

ACT III.

SCENE, *the door of the Hostel, a group of* Pilgrims *as before;*
IDONEA *and the* Host *among them.*

HOST.

Lady, you'll find your Father at the Convent
As I have told you: He left us yesterday
With two Companions; one of them, as seemed,
His most familiar Friend. (*Going*). There was a letter
Of which I heard them speak, but that I fancy
Has been forgotten.

IDONEA (*to* Host).

Farewell!

HOST

Gentle Pilgrims,
St. Cuthbert speed you on your holy errand.
[*Exeunt* IDONEA *and* Pilgrims.

SCENE, *a desolate Moor.*

OSWALD (*alone*).

Carry him to the Camp! Yes, to the Camp.
Oh, Wisdom! a most wise resolve! and then,
That half a word should blow it to the winds!
This last device must end my work.—Methinks
It were a pleasant pastime to construct
A scale and table of belief—as thus—
Two columns, one for passion, one for proof;
Each rises as the other falls: and first,
Passion a unit and *against* us—proof—
Nay, we must travel in another path,
Or we're stuck fast for ever;—passion, then,
Shall be a unit *for* us; proof—no, passion!
We'll not insult thy majesty by time,
Person, and place—the where, the when, the how,
And all particulars that dull brains require
To constitute the spiritless shape of Fact,
They bow to, calling the idol, Demonstration.

1140 Pilgrims] pilgrims *1845–*

A whipping to the moralists who preach
That misery is a sacred thing! For me, [1160]
I know no cheaper engine to degrade a man,
Nor any half so sure. This stripling's mind,
It hath been rudely shaken, and the dregs
Float on the surface—yea, the very dregs—
And in the storms and anguish of his spirit [1164]
This wretch, unutterably miserable,
Doth dream that he is happy.—We dissect
The senseless body, and why not the mind?
These are strange sights—the mind of man upturned
Is a strange spectacle.—Hem! shall I stop?
No. Thoughts and feelings will sink deep, but then [1171]
They have no shape.—Let a few minutes pass,
And something shall be done which memory
May touch when she looks back upon it.—He—

Enter MORTIMER *from behind.*

RIVERS (*turning to meet him*)

(*Earnestly*) 'Tis for my peace of mind—

MORTIMER

Why, I *believe* you, man.

RIVERS

But hear the proofs.

MORTIMER

Aye—for the proofs—prove to me when two peas
Lie snugly in a pod that then the pod [1177]
Is larger than the peas—prove this—'twere matter
Worthy the hearing.
Fool that I was to dream
It ever could be otherwise!

RIVERS

Last night [1180]
When I returned with water from the torrent
I overheard the villains.—Every word
Like red hot iron burnt into my heart.
Said one "It is agreed on.—The blind man
"Shall feign a sudden illness—and the girl, [1185]
"Who on her journey must proceed alone,
"Under pretence of violence be seized—
"She is"—continued the detested slave,
"She is right willing—A fool if she were not:

A whipping to the Moralists who preach
That misery is a sacred thing: for me,
I know no cheaper engine to degrade a man,
Nor any half so sure. This Stripling's mind
Is shaken till the dregs float on the surface;
And, in the storm and anguish of the heart,
He talks of a transition in his Soul,
And dreams that he is happy. We dissect
The senseless body, and why not the mind?—
These are strange sights—the mind of man, upturned,
Is in all natures a strange spectacle;
In some a hideous one—hem! shall I stop?
No—Thoughts and feelings will sink deep, but then
They have no substance. Pass but a few minutes,
And something shall be done which Memory
May touch, whene'er her Vassals are at work.

Enter MARMADUKE, *from behind.*

OSWALD (*turning to meet him*).

But listen, for my peace——

MARMADUKE.

Why, I *believe* you.

OSWALD.

But hear the proofs——

MARMADUKE.

Ay, prove that when two peas
Lie snugly in a pod, the pod must then
Be larger than the peas—prove this—'twere matter
Worthy the hearing. Fool was I to dream
It ever could be otherwise!

OSWALD.

Last night
When I returned with water from the brook,
I overheard the Villains—every word
Like red-hot iron burnt into my heart.
Said one, "It is agreed on. The blind Man
Shall feign a sudden illness, and the Girl,
Who on her journey must proceed alone,
Under pretence of violence, be seized.
She is," continued the detested Slave,
"She is right willing—strange if she were not!—

"They say Lord Clifford is a savage man, [1190]
"But faith! to see him in his silken tunic
"Fitting his low voice to the minstrel's harp,
"There's witchery in't. I never knew a maid
"That could withstand it. True," continued he,
"When we arrang'd the affair she wept a little [1195]
"(Not less the welcome to my Lord for that),
"And said, 'my Father, he will have it so.'"

MORTIMER

I am your hearer.

RIVERS

This much I caught, and more
That may not be retold to any ear.
The obstinate bolt of a small iron door [1200]
Detained them near the gateway. I could see,
By a small lantern which the stouter held,
That they were carrying to some inner room
Materials for a banquet. They themselves
Must share it with their master, if 'twas true,
What I distinctly heard the villains say
With damned laughter, and most foul allusion.

MORTIMER

Oh misery!

RIVERS

I knew it would disturb you,
And therefore chose this solitary heath [1209]
Here to impart the tale, of which, last night,
I strove to ease my heart when our two comrades,
Commissioned by the band, burst in upon us.

MORTIMER

Last night when I would play the murderer's part
I did believe all things were shadows, yea, [1214]
Living and dead all things were bodiless;
Till that same star summoned me back again.
Now could I laugh till my ribs ached. Oh! fool!
To let a creed built in the heart of things [1219]
Dissolve before a twinkling atom.

72–82 Compare Joseph Fawcett's two footnoted borrowings from Shakespeare in *The Art of War*, ll. 1025–1028: "*Between his purpose and his dreadful stroke / Wild is the space within him: **to the scene . . . / Ghost-like he glides" (**Julius Caesar*, II.i.63–69, and see also *Macbeth*, I.iii.137–142; ***Macbeth*, II.i.56–60).

They say, Lord Clifford is a savage man;
But, faith, to see him in his silken tunic,
Fitting his low voice to the minstrel's harp,
There's witchery in't. I never knew a maid
That could withstand it. True," continued he,
"When we arranged the affair, she wept a little
(Not less the welcome to my Lord for that)
And said, 'My Father he will have it so.' "

MARMADUKE.

I am your hearer.

OSWALD.

This I caught, and more
That may not be retold to any ear.
The obstinate bolt of a small iron door
Detained them near the gateway of the Castle.
By a dim lantern's light I saw that wreaths
Of flowers were in their hands, as if designed
For festive decoration; and they said,
With brutal laughter and most foul allusion,
That they should share the banquet with their Lord
And his new Favorite.

MARMADUKE.

Misery!—

OSWALD.

I knew
How you would be disturbed by this dire news,
And therefore chose this solitary Moor,
Here to impart the tale, of which, last night,
I strove to ease my mind, when our two Comrades,
Commissioned by the Band, burst in upon us.

MARMADUKE.

Last night, when moved to lift the avenging steel,
I did believe all things were shadows—yea,
Living or dead all things were bodiless,
Or but the mutual mockeries of body,
Till that same star summoned me back again.
Now I could laugh till my ribs ached. Oh Fool!
To let a creed, built in the heart of things,
Dissolve before a twinkling atom!—Oswald,

1197 so.'"] so'." *1845*

Philosophy! I will go forth a teacher,
And you shall see how deeply I will reason [1224]
Of laws, of qualities and substances,
Of actions, and their ends and differences.

RIVERS

You take it as it merits.

MORTIMER

One, a King,
General or Cham, Sultan or Emperor, [1229]
Strews twenty acres of good meadow ground
With carcases, in lineament and shape
And substance nothing differing from his own,
But that they cannot stand up of themselves;
Another sits in the sun and by the hour [1234]
Floats king-cups in the brook.—They are wise men,
Both are wise men.

RIVERS

Faith! I begin to think so.

MORTIMER

Now for the corner stone of my philosophy: [1240]
I would not give a denier for the man
Who could not chuck his babe beneath the chin
And send it with a fillip to its grave.

RIVERS

Nay, you leave me behind—

MORTIMER

That such a one! [1245]
So pious in demeanour! in her look

---

84 "Cham" is an obsolete form of the title "khan."

93–95 Cf. *Macbeth*, I.vii.54–59:

I have given suck, and know
How tender 'tis to love the babe that milks me:
I would, while it was smiling in my face,
Have pluck'd my nipple from his boneless gums,
And dash'd the brains out, had I so sworn as you
Have done to this.

Compare also Schusterle in *The Robbers*: "—I peep'd in, and what do you think it was? a child, a stout little rogue, that lay on the floor beneath a table, and the fire just catching it!—Poor little fellow, said I, you are starving for cold there—and so I chuck'd him into the fire!" (p. 87).

96–98 The manuscript reads "in her look," amended during late revision to "his." While it is possible that Mortimer is lamenting Matilda's corruption (the lament echoing Othello's over Desdemona), the words "pious," "saintly," and "pure" are epithets that have previously been applied to Herbert, and it is possible that "her" is a copyist's error.

I could fetch lessons out of wiser schools
Than you have entered, were it worth the pains.
Young as I am, I might go forth a teacher,
And you should see how deeply I could reason
Of love in all its shapes, beginnings, ends;
Of moral qualities in their diverse aspects;
Of actions, and their laws and tendencies.

OSWALD.

You take it as it merits——

MARMADUKE.

One a King,
General or Cham, Sultan or Emperor,
Strews twenty acres of good meadow-ground
With carcases, in lineament and shape
And substance, nothing differing from his own,
But that they cannot stand up of themselves;
Another sits i' th' sun, and by the hour
Floats kingcups in the brook—a Hero one
We call, and scorn the other as Time's spendthrift;
But have they not a world of common ground
To occupy—both fools, or wise alike,
Each in his way?

OSWALD.

Troth, I begin to think so.

MARMADUKE.

Now for the corner-stone of my philosophy:
I would not give a denier for the man
Who, on such provocation as this earth
Yields, could not chuck his babe beneath the chin,
And send it with a fillip to its grave.

OSWALD.

Nay, you leave me behind.

MARMADUKE.

That such a One,
So pious in demeanour! in his look

So saintly and so pure!—Hark'ee my friend,
I have a scheme of pleasure—on my life
There's promise in't. I'll go to the Lord Clifford's,
Plant myself full before his castle wall:
A surly mastiff kennels at the gate,
And he shall howl, and I will laugh, a medley [1250]
Most tunable.—What say you to it?

RIVERS

Faith!—
A pleasant scheme!—but first what must be done with——
How shall we wash our hands of——— eh?

MORTIMER

Oh! truly,
That mole, that weazle, that old water-rat—
Plague on my memory! I had forgot him— [1256]

RIVERS

You know we left him sitting—see him yonder.

MORTIMER

Ha, ha!

RIVERS

As you will make short work of it
I will stroll on, and take the way of the Inn—

[Scene 3] SCENE *changes to another part of the heath, at a small distance* HERBERT *is discovered, seated on a stone.*

HERBERT

A sound of laughter, too!—'tis well—I feared [1260]
The stranger had some grief which pressed upon him.
Hush! 'tis the feeble and earth-loving wind
That creeps along the bells of the crisp heath plant.
Alas! 'tis cold—I shiver in the sunshine— [1265]
My limbs are cold—I could believe the air
Portended storm—in truth, they tarry long:
What can this mean?—There is a psalm that speaks
Of the tender mercies of God, which with Matilda
I used to sing.—Listen—what foot is that
Which creeps along the grass?

8–10 Herbert probably refers to Psalm 136, for which the refrain throughout is "For his mercy endureth forever."

So saintly and so pure!———Hark'ee, my Friend,
I'll plant myself before Lord Clifford's Castle,
A surly mastiff kennels at the gate,
And he shall howl and I will laugh, a medley
Most tunable.

OSWALD.

In faith, a pleasant scheme;
But take your sword along with you, for that
Might in such neighbourhood find seemly use.—
But first, how wash our hands of this old Man?

MARMADUKE.

Oh yes, that mole, that viper in the path;
Plague on my memory, him I had forgotten.

OSWALD.

You know we left him sitting—see him yonder.

MARMADUKE.

Ha! ha!—

OSWALD.

As 'twill be but a moment's work,
I will stroll on; you follow when 'tis done.

SCENE *changes to another part of the Moor at a short distance—*
HERBERT *is discovered seated on a stone.*

HERBERT.

A sound of laughter, too!—'tis well—I feared,
The Stranger had some pitiable sorrow
Pressing upon his solitary heart.
Hush!—'tis the feeble and earth-loving wind
That creeps along the bells of the crisp heather.
Alas! 'tis cold—I shiver in the sunshine—
What can this mean? There is a psalm that speaks
Of God's parental mercies—with Idonea
I used to sing it.—Listen!— what foot is there?

Enter MORTIMER.

MORTIMER (*looks at* HERBERT)

And I have *loved* this man? and she hath loved him,
And I loved her, and she loved the Lord Clifford, [1270]
And there it ends—if this be not enough
To make mankind merry for evermore
Then plain it is as day—that eyes were made
For a wise purpose—verily to weep with! [*Looking round.*
A pretty prospect this, a master-piece [1275]
Of nature—finished with most curious skill:

(*To* HERBERT)

My antient, have you ever practiced farming?
Pray tell me what this land is worth by the acre?

HERBERT

How glad I am to hear your voice—I know not
Wherein I have offended you—last night [1280]
I found in you the kindest of protectors;
When I complained of weariness, this morning,
You took my scrip of food from off my shoulders
And threw it round your own—but for these two hours
You have only spoken to me once—when the lark
Whirred from among the fern beneath our feet— [1286]
And then you half terrified me.

MORTIMER

That's excellent!
So you bethought you of the many ways
In which a man may come to his end, whose crimes [1290]
Have roused all nature up against him—pshaw!
'Twas very idle.

HERBERT

Cast your eyes about:
For mercy's sake, is nobody in sight?
No traveller, peasant, herdsman?

18–19. Cf. *Hamlet* (II.ii.317–322): "This goodly frame, the earth, seems to me a sterile promontory; this most excellent canopy, the air, look you, this brave o'erhanging firmament, this majestical roof fretted with golden fire, why, it appears no other thing to me but a foul and pestilent congregation of vapours."

Enter MARMADUKE.

MARMADUKE (*aside—looking at* HERBERT).

And I have loved this Man! and *she* hath loved him!
And I loved her, and she loves the Lord Clifford!
And there it ends;—if this be not enough
To make mankind merry for evermore,
Then plain it is as day, that eyes were made
For a wise purpose—verily to weep with! [*Looking round.*
A pretty prospect this, a masterpiece
Of Nature, finished with most curious skill!
(*To* HERBERT). Good Baron, have you ever practised tillage?
Pray tell me what this land is worth by the acre?

HERBERT.

How glad I am to hear your voice! I know not
Wherein I have offended you;—last night
I found in you the kindest of Protectors;
This morning, when I spoke of weariness,
You from my shoulder took my scrip and threw it
About your own; but for these two hours past
Once only have you spoken, when the lark
Whirred from among the fern beneath our feet,
And I, no coward in my better days,
Was almost terrified.

MARMADUKE.

That's excellent!—
So, you bethought you of the many ways
In which a man may come to his end, whose crimes
Have roused all Nature up against him—pshaw!—

HERBERT.

For mercy's sake, is nobody in sight?
No traveller, peasant, herdsman?

MORTIMER

Not a soul!
Here is a tree, ragged and bent and bare,
Which turns its goatsbeard flakes of pea-green moss [1295]
From the stern breathing of the rough sea wind—
We have no other company, my friend!
Commend me to this place. If a man should die
And leave his body here, it were all one
As he were twenty fathom underground. [1300]

HERBERT

Where is your comrade?

MORTIMER

Do you believe
In ghosts?—the spirit of a murder'd man
Might have fine room to ramble about here,
A grand domain to squeak and gibber in.

HERBERT

Poor wretch! if thou hast any close-pent guilt
Pressing upon thy heart, and this the hour [1306]
Of visitation—

MORTIMER

No, that will not do—

HERBERT

Restore him, heaven!

MORTIMER

Oh, villain! damned villain!
She smell'd most sweet and she was fair—and now
They have snapped her from the stem.—Poh! let her lie
Besoil'd with the mire, and let the houseless snail [1311]

37–39 See Wordsworth's note to his sonnet *Hart's-Horn Tree, Near Penrith* (*PW*, III, 535): "I well remember its imposing appearance as it stood, in a decayed state, by the side of the high road . . ." William Hutchinson, in his *Excursion to the Lakes* . . . (London, 1776), described the tree thus: "On the way side [towards Penrith, midway between Whinfell Park and the Countess's Pillar], the shattered trunk of an oak, called *White Hart Tree*, is seen . . . stretching forth its withered limbs on one side, and on the other, a scanty foliage and poor remnant of life" (pp. 43–44).

47 Cf. *Hamlet*, I.i.115–116: "The graves stood tenantless and the sheeted dead / Did squeak and gibber in the Roman streets."

48–49 See V.iii.235–237, and cf. *Macbeth*, V.iii.40–45.

52 Cf. *Othello*, IV.ii.66–67: "O thou weed! / Who art so lovely fair and smell'st so sweet."

53–55 Cf. *Othello*, V.ii.13–15:

> When I have pluck'd the rose,
> I cannot give it vital growth again,
> It needs must wither: I'll smell it on the tree.

MARMADUKE.

Not a soul:
Here is a tree, raggèd and bent and bare,
That turns its goat's-beard flakes of pea-green moss
From the stern breathing of the rough sea-wind;
This have we, but no other company:
Commend me to the place. If a man should die
And leave his body here, it were all one
As he were twenty fathoms underground.

HERBERT.

Where is our common Friend?

MARMADUKE.

A ghost, methinks—
The Spirit of a murdered man, for instance—
Might have fine room to ramble about here,
A grand domain to squeak and gibber in.

HERBERT.

Lost Man! if thou have any close-pent guilt
Pressing upon thy heart, and this the hour
Of visitation——

MARMADUKE.

A bold word from *you!*

HERBERT.

Restore him, Heaven!

MARMADUKE.

The desperate Wretch!—A Flower,
Fairest of all flowers, was she once, but now
They have snapped her from the stem—Poh! let her lie
Besoiled with mire, and let the houseless snail

1294 raggèd and bent] raggèd, and bent, *1845–*

Feed on her leaves—you knew her well—ay there,
Old man! you were a very lynx, you knew
The worm was in her—

HERBERT

Mercy! Sir, what mean you?

MORTIMER

You have a daughter—

HERBERT

Oh, that she were here! [1315]
She hath an eye that sinks into all hearts,
And if I have in aught offended you
Soon would her gentle voice make peace between us.

MORTIMER

I do believe he weeps—I could weep too—
There is a vein of her voice that runs through his. [1320]
Even such a man my fancy bodied forth
From the first moment that I loved the maid
And he was still a brother in my love—
These tears—I did not think that aught was left in me
Of what I have been.—Yes, I thank thee, heaven: [1325]
One happy thought has passed across my mind.—
It may not be—I am cut off from man,
No more shall I be man, no more shall I
Have human feelings!—Now, for a little more
About your daughter.

HERBERT

Armed men
Met in the roads would bless us—little children [1331]
Rushing along in the full tide of play
Were silent as we passed them. I have heard
The boisterous carman in the miry road
Check his loud whip and hail us with mild voice,
And speak with milder voice to his poor beasts. [1336]

MORTIMER

And whither were you going?

HERBERT

Learn, young man,
To fear the virtuous, and reverence misery.

---

57 Cf. *Twelfth Night*, II. iv. 113–114: "But let concealment, like a worm i'th'bud, / Feed on her damask cheek."

Feed on her leaves. You knew her well—ay, there,
Old Man! you were a very Lynx, you knew
The worm was in her——

HERBERT.

Mercy! Sir, what mean you?

MARMADUKE.

You have a Daughter!

HERBERT.

Oh that she were here!—
She hath an eye that sinks into all hearts,
And if I have in aught offended you,
Soon would her gentle voice make peace between us.

MARMADUKE (*aside*).

I do believe he weeps—I could weep too—
There is a vein of her voice that runs through his:
Even such a Man my fancy bodied forth
From the first moment that I loved the Maid;
And for his sake I loved her more: these tears—
I did not think that aught was left in me
Of what I have been—yes, I thank thee, Heaven!
One happy thought has passed across my mind.
—It may not be—I am cut off from man;
No more shall I be man—no more shall I
Have human feelings!—(*To* HERBERT)—Now, for a little more
About your Daughter!

HERBERT.

Troops of armed men,
Met in the roads, would bless us; little children,
Rushing along in the full tide of play,
Stood silent as we passed them! I have heard
The boisterous carman, in the miry road,
Check his loud whip and hail us with mild voice,
And speak with milder voice to his poor beasts.

MARMADUKE.

And whither were you going?

HERBERT.

Learn, young Man,
To fear the virtuous, and reverence misery,
Whether too much for patience, or, like mine,
Softened till it becomes a gift of mercy.

1337 Man,] Man,— *1849*

MORTIMER

Now this is as it should be! On my soul,
I do admire you for it.

HERBERT

I am weak!
My daughter does not know how weak I am, [1342]
And, as thou seest, beneath the arch of heaven
Here do I stand alone in helplessness
With which the God of heaven has visited me!
But I had once a spirit and an arm—— [1346]

MORTIMER

Now for a word about your Barony;
I fancy when you left the Holy Land
And came to—what's your title—eh? your claims
Were little heeded?

HERBERT

Like a Mendicant
Whom no one comes to meet, I stood alone. [1351]
I murmured, but remembering him who feeds
The pelican and ostrich of the Desert,
From my own threshold I looked up to heaven,
And did not want glimmerings of quiet hope; [1355]
So from the court I passed and down the brook,
Led by its murmur, to the ancient oak
I came, and when I felt its cooling shade,
I sat me down and cannot but believe—
While in my lap I held my little babe [1360]
And clasped her to my heart—my heart that ached
More with delight than grief—I heard a voice
Such as by Cherith on Elijah called;
It said, "I will be with thee." A little boy,
A Shepherd's lad, ere yet my trance was gone, [1365]

94–95 Cf. Psalm 102: 6—"I am like a pelican of the wilderness"—and Lamentations 4: 3—"the ostriches in the wilderness."

98–101 In Macpherson's *Fingal* the meditative repose of a hero under an old tree is almost a formula; see for example the opening of Book II.

105 Cf. 1 Kings 17:3–4, where the Lord instructs Elijah: "Get thee hence, and turn thee eastward, and hide thyself by the brook Cherith, that is before Jordan. And it shall be, that thou shalt drink of the brook; and I have commanded the ravens to feed thee there." When Cherith dried up. Elijah was instructed to "get thee to Zarephath . . . and dwell there: behold, I have commanded a widow woman there to sustain thee" (8–10). Herbert has already described Matilda as his "raven" (II.iii. 124–126); the "good abbot of St. Cuthbert's" who gave him his cottage (I.i.166–169) was evidently in his eyes analogous to Elijah's widow woman.

MARMADUKE.

Now, this is as it should be!

HERBERT.

I am weak!—
My Daughter does not know how weak I am;
And, as thou see'st, under the arch of heaven
Here do I stand, alone, to helplessness,
By the good God, our common Father, doomed!—
But I had once a spirit and an arm——

MARMADUKE.

Now, for a word about your Barony:
I fancy when you left the Holy Land,
And came to—what's your title—eh? your claims
Were undisputed!

HERBERT.

Like a mendicant,
Whom no one comes to meet, I stood alone;—
I murmured—but, remembering Him who feeds
The pelican and ostrich of the desert,
From my own threshold I looked up to Heaven
And did not want glimmerings of quiet hope.
So, from the court I passed, and down the brook,
Led by its murmur, to the ancient oak
I came; and when I felt its cooling shade,
I sate me down, and cannot but believe—
While in my lap I held my little Babe
And clasped her to my heart, my heart that ached
More with delight than grief—I heard a voice
Such as by Cherith on Elijah called;
It said, "I will be with thee." A little boy,
A shepherd-lad, ere yet my trance was gone,

Hailed us, as if he had been sent from heaven,
And said with tears that he would be our guide;
I had a better guide—that innocent babe
Who to this hour hath saved me from all evil,
From cold, from death, from penury and hunger. [1370]
Therefore I bless her: when I think of man
I bless her with sad spirit; when of God, [1375]
I bless her in the fulness of my joy!

MORTIMER

Look there! he prays!
The name of daughter in his mouth, he prays!
With nerves so steady that the very flies
Sit undisturbed upon his staff—innocent!
If he were innocent—then he would tremble [1380]
And be disturbed, as I am.—It might be proved,
My eyes are weak—there is a judge above—
It dawns on me—I see the end for which
An arm invisible hath led me hither.—
He heard a voice—a shepherd's lad came
And was his guide—if once—why not again? [1395]
And in this desert? If never, then is he damned
Beyond a madman's dream!—Here will I leave him,
Here where no foot of man is found, no ear
Can hear his cries—it is a fearful ordeal!
But God is everywhere.
Here (*looking round*) cold and hunger! Pain is of the *heart*, [1399]
And what are a few throes of bodily suffering
If they can waken one pang of remorse? [*Goes up to* HERBERT.
Old man! my wrath is in a flame burnt out, [1402]
It cannot be rekindled.—Here is a sword (*draws his sword*):
Nay, I can point it to thy heart with pulse
Calm as a sleeping child—I have led thee hither
To save thy spirit from perdition——

Hailed us as if he had been sent from heaven,
And said, with tears, that he would be our guide:
I had a better guide—that innocent Babe—
Her, who hath saved me, to this hour, from harm,
From cold, from hunger, penury, and death;
To whom I owe the best of all the good
I have, or wish for, upon earth—and more
And higher far than lies within earth's bounds:
Therefore I bless her: when I think of Man,
I bless her with sad spirit,—when of God,
I bless her in the fulness of my joy!

MARMADUKE.

The name of daughter in his mouth, he prays!
With nerves so steady, that the very flies
Sit unmolested on his staff.—Innocent!—
If he were innocent—then he would tremble
And be disturbed, as I am. (*Turning aside*). I have read
In Story, what men now alive have witnessed,
How, when the People's mind was racked with doubt,
Appeal was made to the great Judge: the Accused
With naked feet walked over burning ploughshares.
Here is a Man by Nature's hand prepared
For a like trial, but more merciful.
Why else have I been led to this bleak Waste?
Bare is it, without house or track, and destitute
Of obvious shelter, as a shipless sea.
Here will I leave him—here—All-seeing God!
Such as *he* is, and sore perplexed as I am,
I will commit him to this final *Ordeal!*—
He heard a voice—a shepherd-lad came to him
And was his guide; if once, why not again,
And in this desert? If never—then the whole
Of what he says, and looks, and does, and is,
Makes up one damning falsehood. Leave him here
To cold and hunger!—Pain is of the heart,
And what are a few throes of bodily suffering
If they can waken one pang of remorse?

[*Goes up to* HERBERT.

Old Man! my wrath is as a flame burnt out,
It cannot be rekindled. Thou art here
Led by my hand to save thee from perdition;
Thou wilt have time to breathe and think———

HERBERT

Mercy!
What, *me!* would you destroy me? drink the blood
Of such a wretch as I am!

MORTIMER

That is past.

HERBERT

Oh! mercy! mercy!

MORTIMER

I will be merciful.
I know the need which all men have of mercy, [1406]
And therefore do I this—three days
Will be the limit of thy mortal course.

HERBERT

My child! my child!

MORTIMER

No more of that.
Thou wilt have many guides if thou art innocent.
Yea, from the utmost corners of the world [1410]
That woman will come o'er this heath to save thee.
[*He pauses and looks stedfastly at Herbert's staff.*
Ha! what's here! carved by her hand (*reads upon the staff*):
"I am Eyes to the blind saith the Lord,
"He that puts his trust in me shall not fail."
Yes, be it so—repent and be forgiven— [1415]
God and that staff are now thy only guides.
[*He leaves him on the heath.*

[Scene 4] SCENE, *an eminence—a Beacon on it.*

LACY, WALLACE, LENNOX, NORWOOD.

SEVERAL OF THE BAND (*confusedly*)

But patience, patience!

---

139 Cf. *Hamlet*, III.ii.415: "now could I drink hot blood."

150 Cf. Job 29:15: "I was eyes to the blind, and feet was I to the lame."

Scene 4 was probably written after the rest of *The Borderers* was largely complete; see Introduction, pp. 15–16. The setting is reminiscent of William Gilpin's description of Penrith Beacon: "In the offskip, beyond the castle, arose a hill, in shadow likewise; on the top of which there stood a lonely beacon. . . . This beacon is a monument of those tumultuous times, which preceded the union; and the only monument of the kind now remaining in these parts . . ." (*Observations . . .* [*on*] *. . . Cumberland, and Westmoreland*, II, 85). Alone among writers on the district, Wordsworth calls Penrith Beacon the Border Beacon (see *Prelude*, VI, 242).

HERBERT.

Oh, Mercy!

MARMADUKE.

I know the need that all men have of mercy,
And therefore leavc thee to a righteous judgment.

HERBERT.

My Child, my blessèd Child!

MARMADUKE.

No more of that;
Thou wilt have many guides if thou art innocent;
Yea, from the utmost corners of the earth,
That Woman will come o'er this Waste to save thee.

[*He pauses and looks at* HERBERT'S *staff.*

Ha! what is here! and carved by her own hand!

[*Reads upon the staff.*

"I am eyes to the blind, saith the Lord.
He that puts his trust in me shall not fail!"
Yes, be it so;—repent and bc forgiven—
God and that staff are now thy only guides.

[*He leaves* HERBERT *on the Moor.*

SCENE, *an eminence, a Beacon on the summit.*

LACY, WALLACE, LENNOX, &c. &c.

SEVERAL OF THE BAND (*confusedly*).

But patience!

1412 here!] here? *1845–*

ONE OF THE BAND

Curses on the Traitor!

LENNOX (*to* WALLACE)

I would have spoken out some three months gone,
But that I'd rather have a nest of vipers [1423]
Between my breast-plate and my skin than know
This Rivers was my enemy.

LACY

We have been fooled—

WALLACE (*to* LENNOX)

But for the motive?—

LENNOX

Natures such as his
Spin motives out of their own bowels, Wallace.
I learnt this when I was a Confessor.— [1429]
I know him well, there needs no other motive
Than that most strange incontinence in crime
Which haunts this Rivers.—Power is life to him,
And breath and being; where he cannot govern [1433]
He will destroy—you know he hates us all.

LACY

To have been trapped like moles! Damnation!

WALLACE

Peace!

NORWOOD

He is a guilty man—I have often heard
Dark rumours of some strange and heinous crime
Which he committed in his youth.

WALLACE (*to* LENNOX)

You knew this Rivers, as you say, in Syria?

LENNOX

I knew him there—he did despise alike
Mohammedon and Christian—

NORWOOD

I have noticed
That when the name of God is spoken of [1438]
A most strange blankness overspreads his face.

ONE OF THE BAND
(*in another part of the stage*)

Plague on your tongues! I have a dagger here
Sharp as an adder's tooth.

ONE OF THE BAND.

Curses on that Traitor, Oswald!—
Our Captain made a prey to foul device!—

LENNOX (*to* WALLACE).

His Tool, the wandering Beggar, made last night
A plain confession, such as leaves no doubt,
Knowing what otherwise we know too well,
That she revealed the truth. Stand by me now;
For rather would I have a nest of vipers
Between my breast-plate and my skin, than make
Oswald my special enemy, if you
Deny me your support.

LACY.

We have been fooled—
But for the motive?

WALLACE.

Natures such as his
Spin motives out of their own bowels, Lacy!
I learn'd this when I was a Confessor.
I know him well; there needs no other motive
Than that most strange incontinence in crime
Which haunts this Oswald. Power is life to him
And breath and being; where he cannot govern,
He will destroy.

LACY.

To have been trapped like moles!—
Yes, you are right, we need not hunt for motives:
There is no crime from which this Man would shrink;
He recks not human law; and I have noticed
That often when the name of God is uttered,
A sudden blankness overspreads his face.

1419 Tool] tool *1845–*
1436 Man] man *1845, 1849*

LENNOX (*to* NORWOOD)

Aye, there you have it.
Yet reasoner as he is, his pride has built [1440]
Some uncouth superstition of its own.

WALLACE

I do not understand you.

LENNOX

Once he headed
A band of pirates in the Norway seas,
And when the King of Denmark summoned him
To the oath of fealty, I well remember [1445]
'Twas a strange answer that he made; he said,
"I hold of spirits, and the sun in heaven."

WALLACE

He is no mad-man—

LENNOX

Wallace! restless minds,
Such minds as find amid their fellow men [1452]
No heart that loves them, none that they can love,
Will turn, perforce, and seek for sympathies
In dim relations to imagined beings.

ONE OF THE BAND

What if he mean to offer up our Captain, [1456]
An expiation, and a sacrifice
To those infernal fiends?

WALLACE

My friends, I call on you to swear, that if
The event should be as Lennox has foretold,
That heart of his shall have as many wounds [1460]
As there are daggers here.

LACY

What need of swearing!

ONE OF THE BAND

Let us away!

ANOTHER

Away!

---

36 MH wrote "sympathys."
41–44 The ceremony is reminiscent of the conspirators' actions in *Julius Caesar*.

LENNOX.

Yet, reasoner as he is, his pride has built
Some uncouth superstition of its own.

WALLACE.

I have seen traces of it.

LENNOX.

Once he headed
A band of Pirates in the Norway seas;
And when the King of Denmark summoned him
To the oath of fealty, I well remember,
'Twas a strange answer that he made; he said,
"I hold of Spirits, and the Sun in heaven."

LACY.

He is no madman.

WALLACE.

A most subtle doctor
Were that man, who could draw the line that parts
Pride and her daughter, Cruelty, from Madness,
That should be scourged, not pitied. Restless Minds,
Such Minds as find amid their fellow-men
No heart that loves them, none that they can love,
Will turn perforce and seek for sympathy
In dim relation to imagined Beings.

ONE OF THE BAND.

What if he mean to offer up our Captain
An expiation and a sacrifice
To those infernal fiends!

WALLACE.

Now, if the event
Should be as Lennox has foretold, then swear,
My Friends, his heart shall have as many wounds
As there are daggers here.

LACY.

What need of swearing!

ONE OF THE BAND.

Let us away!

ANOTHER.

Away!

A THIRD

Hark how the horns
Of those Scotch rovers echo through the vale.

LACY

Stay you behind, and when the sun is down
Light up this beacon.

ONE OF THE BAND

You shall be obeyed. [1465]
[*They go out together.*

[Scene 5] SCENE, *the Wood on the edge of the heath.*

MORTIMER (*alone*)

Deep, deep and vast, vast beyond human thought,
Yet calm—I could believe that there was here
The only quiet heart on earth.—In terror,
Remembered terror, there is love and peace. [1469]

Enter RIVERS.

RIVERS

Ha! my dear friend!

MORTIMER (*with a faint smile*)

Rivers! I am happy
To meet with you again.

RIVERS

Alone, I see.
We *may* be merry now.

MORTIMER

We may be *happy*.

RIVERS

You have done your duty.
I had hopes which now [1472]
I feel that you will justify.

MORTIMER

I had fears
Which now I feel are vain—but 'tis my wish
To be alone, and therefore we must part.

RIVERS

Nay, then—I am mistaken.—There's a weakness [1476]
About your heart—you talk of solitude—
Ask yourself if you fear a human face.
I am your friend—

A THIRD.

Hark! how the horns
Of those Scotch Rovers echo through the vale.

LACY.

Stay you behind; and when the sun is down,
Light up this beacon.

ONE OF THE BAND.

You shall be obeyed.

[*They go out together.*

SCENE, *the Wood on the edge of the Moor.*

MARMADUKE (*alone*).

Deep, deep and vast, vast beyond human thought,
Yet calm.—I could believe, that there was here
The only quiet heart on earth. In terror,
Remembered terror, there is peace and rest.

Enter OSWALD.

OSWALD.

Ha! my dear Captain.

MARMADUKE.

A later meeting, Oswald,
Would have been better timed.

OSWALD.

Alone, I see;
You have done your duty. I had hopes, which now
I feel that you will justify.

MARMADUKE.

I had fears,
From which I have freed myself—but 'tis my wish
To be alone, and therefore we must part.

OSWALD.

Nay, then—I am mistaken. There's a weakness
About you still; you talk of solitude—
I am your friend.

MORTIMER

Why says't thou this to me?

RIVERS

(*With an appearance of openness*)

Because you are my master, and have taught me
What there is not another living man [1481]
Had strength to teach. (*Altering the tone of his voice*)
Therefore I'll cleave to you
In camps and cities, in the wood and mountain,
In evil, and in solitary pain,
You still shall find that I will cleave to you.

MORTIMER

Wherefore press this on me?

RIVERS

(*resuming his former tone of openness*)

Because I feel [1484]
That I am bound to you by links of adamant.
You have taught mankind to seek the measure of justice
By diving for it into their own bosoms.
To day you have thrown off a tyranny
That lives but by the torpid acquiescence [1489]
Of our emasculated souls, the tyranny
Of moralists and saints and lawgivers.
You have obeyed the only law that wisdom
Can ever recognize: the immediate law
Flashed from the light of circumstances
Upon an independent intellect. [1496]
Henceforth new prospects ought to open on you,
Your faculties should grow with the occasion.
(*Altering the tone of his voice as before*)
I still will be your friend, will cleave to you [1499]
Through good and evil, through scorn and infamy—

MORTIMER

I would be left alone.

---

18 Cf. Genesis 2:24: "Therefore shall a man leave his father and his mother, and shall cleave unto his wife."

19 MH erased "the" before "camps" in 1799.

23 Cf. *Paradise Lost*, X, 318–319, and I, 48, "in Adamantine Chains and penal Fire." Compare also *The Robbers* (Tytler translation, p. 14): "I should be a pitiful bungler indeed, if I knew not yet how to tear a son from the heart of his father, were they link'd together with chains of iron."

MARMADUKE.

What need of this assurance
At any time? and why given now?

OSWALD.

Because
You are now in truth my Master; you have taught me
What there is not another living man
Had strength to teach;—and therefore gratitude
Is bold, and would relieve itself by praise.

MARMADUKE.

Wherefore press this on me?

OSWALD.

Because I feel
That you have shown, and by a signal instance,
How they who would be just must seek the rule
By diving for it into their own bosoms.
To-day you have thrown off a tyranny
That lives but in the torpid acquiescence
Of our emasculated souls, the tyranny
Of the world's masters, with the musty rules
By which they uphold their craft from age to age:
You have obeyed the only law that sense
Submits to recognise; the immediate law,
From the clear light of circumstances, flashed
Upon an independent Intellect.
Henceforth new prospects open on your path;
Your faculties should grow with the demand;
I still will be your friend, will cleave to you
Through good and evil, obloquy and scorn,
Oft as they dare to follow on your steps.

MARMADUKE.

I would be left alone.

RIVERS (*exultingly*)

I know your motives.
I am not of the world's presumptuous judges
Who damn where they can neither see nor feel, [1504]
In the hard-hearted pride of ignorance.
I saw the matter as it was, I knew——

MORTIMER

Wherefore this repetition?

RIVERS

It may be
That some there are, squeamish, half-thinking cowards,
Who will turn pale upon you, and call you murderer,
And you will walk in solitude among them— [1510]
A mighty evil! Bodies are like ropes:
When interwoven, stronger by mutual strength.
Thanks to our nature! 'tis not so with minds.
Join twenty tapers of unequal height,
And light them joined, and you will see the less
How 'twill burn down the taller, and they all
Shall prey upon the tallest.—Solitude! [1515]
The eagle lives in solitude—

MORTIMER

Forgive me,
If I should smile at this.

53–54 Cf. *The Robbers*, p. 28: "Curse on that peace, that would confine to earth the flight of an eagle," and p. 32: "The name of Spiegelberg shall fly from pole to pole! And you, ye cowards, ye reptiles, ye shall crawl in the dirt, while Spiegelberg shall soar to the temple of glory, with an eagle's flight!—"

OSWALD (*exultingly*).

I know your motives!
I am not of the world's presumptuous judges,
Who damn where they can neither see nor feel,
With a hard-hearted ignorance; your struggles
I witness'd, and now hail your victory.

MARMADUKE.

Spare me awhile that greeting.

OSWALD.

It may be,
That some there are, squeamish half-thinking cowards,
Who will turn pale upon you, call you murderer,
And you will walk in solitude among them.
A mighty evil for a strong-built mind!—
Join twenty tapers of unequal height
And light them joined, and you will see the less
How 'twill burn down the taller; and they all
Shall prey upon the tallest. Solitude!—
The Eagle lives in Solitude!

MARMADUKE.

Even so,
The Sparrow so on the house-top, and I,
The weakest of God's creatures, stand resolved
To abide the issue of my act, alone.

OSWALD.

Now would you? and for ever?—My young Friend,
As time advances either we become
The prey or masters of our own past deeds.
Fellowship we *must* have, willing or no;
And if good Angels fail, slack in their duty,
Substitutes, turn our faces where we may,
Are still forthcoming; some which, though they bear
Ill names, can render no ill services,
In recompense for what themselves required.
So meet extremes in this mysterious world,
And opposites thus melt into each other.

MARMADUKE.

Time, since Man first drew breath, has never moved
With such a weight upon his wings as now;
But they will soon be lightened.

RIVERS

You will perceive it.
Fortitude is the child of enterprize; [1535]
Great actions move our admiration, chiefly
Because they carry in themselves an earnest
That we can suffer greatly.

MORTIMER

Very true—

RIVERS

Action is transitory, a step, a blow—
The motion of a muscle—this way or that— [1540]
'Tis done—and in the after vacancy
We wonder at ourselves like men betray'd.
Suffering is permanent, obscure and dark,
And has the nature of infinity.

MORTIMER

I do not understand you.

RIVERS

What if you have bid
Eternal farewell to unmingled joy [1546]
And the light dancing of the thoughtless heart—
It is the passion of fools and little fit
For such a world as this. The wise abjure
All thoughts whose idle composition lives [1550]
In the entire forgetfulness of pain—
I see I have disturbed you—

MORTIMER

By no means.

RIVERS

Compassion! pity! pride can do without them,
And what if you should never know them more!
He is a puny soul who, feeling pain, [1555]
Finds ease because another feels it too.
If e'er I open out this heart of mine
It shall be for a nobler end—to teach
And not to purchase puling sympathy.
—Nay, you are pale.

66–67 Cf. *Paradise Lost*, I, 249–250: "Farewell happy Fields / Where Joy for ever dwells."

73–81 Cf. "I see, this hath a little dash'd your spirits. / Not a jot, not a jot. I' faith, I fear it has" (*Othello*, III.iii.214–215).

OSWALD.

Ay, look up—
Cast round you your mind's eye, and you will learn
Fortitude is the child of Enterprise:
Great actions move our admiration, chiefly
Because they carry in themselves an earnest
That we can suffer greatly.

MARMADUKE.

Very true.

OSWALD.

Action is transitory—a step, a blow,
The motion of a muscle—this way or that—
'Tis done, and in the after vacancy
We wonder at ourselves like men betrayed:
Suffering is permanent, obscure and dark,
And shares the nature of infinity.

MARMADUKE.

Truth—and I feel it.

OSWALD.

What! if you had bid
Eternal farewell to unmingled joy
And the light dancing of the thoughtless heart;
It is the toy of fools, and little fit
For such a world as this. The wise abjure
All thoughts whose idle composition lives
In the entire forgetfulness of pain.
—I see I have disturbed you.

MARMADUKE.

By no means.

OSWALD.

Compassion!—pity!—pride can do without them;
And what if you should never know them more!—
He is a puny soul who, feeling pain,
Finds ease because another feels it too.
If e'er I open out this heart of mine
It shall be for a nobler end—to teach
And not to purchase puling sympathy.
—Nay, you are pale.

MORTIMER

It may be so.

RIVERS

Remorse, [1560]
It cannot live with thought, think on, think on,
And it will die.—What? in this universe,
Where the least things controul the greatest, where
The faintest breath that breathes can move a world—
What, feel remorse where if a cat had sneezed, [1565]
A leaf had fallen, the thing had never been
Whose very shadow gnaws us to the vitals?

MORTIMER

Why, what is it that ails you? That a man
So used to suit his language to the time
Should thus so widely differ from himself— [1570]
It is most strange.

RIVERS

Murder! what's in the word?
I have no cases by me ready made
To fit all crimes. Carry him to the camp!
You have seen deeper—taught us that the institutes
Of nature, by a cunning usurpation [1576]
Banished from human intercourse, exist
Only in our relations to the beasts
That make the field their dwelling. If a viper
Crawl from beneath our feet, we do not ask
A licence to destroy him: our good governors, [1581]
Wise thinkers! have by forms and ceremonies
Hedged in the life of every pest and plague
That bears the shape of man, and for what purpose
But to protect themselves from extirpation? [1584]
You have burst through this flimsy superstition.

MORTIMER

He is delivered to the judge of all things——

RIVERS

Dead?

83ff. Cf. *The Robbers* (p.163), where Charles de Moor expresses a similarly determinist view: "these are but links of that eternal chain of destiny which bound me from my birth, unconscious bound me—which hung perhaps upon the humours of my nurse—my father's temperament, or my mother's blood.—"

MARMADUKE.

It may be so.

OSWALD.

Remorse—
It cannot live with thought; think on, think on,
And it will die. What! in this universe,
Where the least things controul the greatest, where
The faintest breath that breathes can move a world;
What! feel remorse, where, if a cat had sneezed,
A leaf had fallen, the thing had never been
Whose very shadow gnaws us to the vitals.

MARMADUKE.

Now, whither are you wandering? That a man
So used to suit his language to the time,
Should thus so widely differ from himself—
It is most strange.

OSWALD.

Murder!—what's in the word!—
I have no cases by me ready made
To fit all deeds. Carry him to the Camp!—
A shallow project;—you of late have seen
More deeply, taught us that the institutes
Of Nature, by a cunning usurpation
Banished from human intercourse, exist
Only in our relations to the brutes
That make the fields their dwelling. If a snake
Crawl from beneath our feet we do not ask
A license to destroy him: our good governors
Hedge in the life of every pest and plague
That bears the shape of man; and for what purpose,
But to protect themselves from extirpation?—
This flimsy barrier you have overleaped.

MARMADUKE.

My Office is fulfilled—the Man is now
Delivered to the Judge of all things.

OSWALD.

Dead!

1563 controul] control *1845–*
1564 world;] world, *1842* world; *(MSS. 3 and 4)*, *1845–*

MORTIMER

I have borne my burden to its destined end.

RIVERS

This instant we'll return to our companions. [1589]
Oh! how I long to see their faces again.

Enter MATILDA *along with the* Pilgrims.

MATILDA

What, Mortimer! (*Throws herself upon his neck*)
[*The* Pilgrims *retire.*
(*After some time*) Now thou art mine for ever—Rivers, too!
You shall relate the news to my good father,
Yourself shall tell it—it will be thrice welcome.

RIVERS

I fear I interrupt you—

MORTIMER

Oh! Matilda,
That I should ever live to see this hour—

MATILDA

Forgive me—Rivers knows it all—he knows
Each word of that unhappy letter fell [1600]
A blood-drop from my heart—

RIVERS

'Twas even so.

MORTIMER

I had much to say
Of grave and serious, of sublime and peaceful.
—Rivers, speak to her.

RIVERS

A trifle; you may soon set all things even.

MATILDA

Aye, plead for me, good Rivers! plead for me.
You are my father's friend.
(*To* MORTIMER) Alas! you know not
And never *can* you know how much he loved me. [1605]
Twice had he been to me a father, twice
Had given me breath, and was I not to be
His daughter, once his daughter—

MARMADUKE.

I have borne my burthen to its destined end.

OSWALD.

This instant we'll return to our Companions—
Oh how I long to see their faces again!

Enter IDONEA, *with* Pilgrims *who continue their journey.*

IDONEA (*after some time*).

What, Marmaduke! now thou art mine for ever.
And Oswald, too! (*To* MARMADUKE). On will we to my Father
With the glad tidings which this day hath brought;
We'll go together, and, such proof received
Of his own rights restored, his gratitude
To God above will make him feel for ours.

OSWALD.

I interrupt you?

IDONEA.

Think not so.

MARMADUKE.

Idonea,
That I should ever live to see this moment!

IDONEA.

Forgive me.—Oswald knows it all—he knows,
Each word of that unhappy letter fell
As a blood drop from my heart.

OSWALD.

'Twas even so.

MARMADUKE.

I have much to say, but for whose ear?—not thine.

IDONEA.

Ill can I bear that look—Plead for me, Oswald!
You are my Father's Friend.
(*To* MARMADUKE). Alas, you know not,
And never *can* you know, how much he loved me.
Twice had he been to me a father, twice
Had given me breath, and was I not to be
His daughter, once his daughter? could I withstand

MORTIMER

Gracious heaven!

RIVERS

'Twas virtue, 'twas a noble sacrifice.

MATILDA

Could I behold his face, could I behold
The terrible pleading of that face of his
And could I feel his arms and hear him pray
That I would not forsake him nor permit
My heart to abandon him in his old age—[*Hides her face.*

RIVERS

Indeed, she could not do it.

MORTIMER

God of justice!
She weeps, she weeps—my brain shall burn for hours [1612]
Ere I can shed a tear—

MATILDA (*rising*)

I was a woman
Shut out from every noble enterprize (*breaking off*)—
Oh! let me be forgiven!

MORTIMER

I do forgive thee—

MATILDA

But take me to your arms—this breast, alas! [1619]
It throbs, and you have a heart that does not feel it.

MORTIMER (*exultingly*)

She is innocent. [*He embraces her.*

RIVERS

Now, if I were a moralist
I should make wonderous revolutions here.
It were a quaint experiment to shew
The beauty of truth (*addressing himself to them*)—
I see I interrupt you.
I shall have business with you, Mortimer. [1625]
Follow me to the Inn.

[*Exit* RIVERS.

MATILDA

Oh, Mortimer,
This is a happy day. My father soon

His pleading face, and feel his clasping arms,
And hear his prayer that I would not forsake him
In his old age—— [*Hides her face.*

MARMADUKE.

Patience—Heaven grant me patience!—
She weeps, she weeps—*my* brain shall burn for hours
Ere *I* can shed a tear.

IDONEA.

I was a woman;
And, balancing the hopes that are the dearest
To womankind with duty to my Father,
I yielded up those precious hopes, which nought
On earth could else have wrested from me;—if erring,
Oh let me be forgiven!

MARMADUKE.

I *do* forgive thee.

IDONEA.

But take me to your arms—this breast, alas!
It throbs, and you have a heart that does not feel it.

MARMADUKE (*exultingly*).

She is innocent. [*He embraces her.*

OSWALD (*aside*).

Were I a Moralist,
I should make wondrous revolution here;
It were a quaint experiment to show
The beauty of truth— [*Addressing them.*
I see I interrupt you;
I shall have business with you, Marmaduke;
Follow me to the Hostel. [*Exit* OSWALD.

IDONEA.

Marmaduke,
This is a happy day. My Father soon

Shall sun himself before his native doors;
The lame, the hungry shall be welcome there.

MORTIMER

Now is this possible?

MATILDA

What joy for us—
No more shall he complain of wasted strength,
Of thoughts that leave him and a decaying heart.
His good works shall be balm and life to him.

MORTIMER

This is most strange—I know not what it was,
But there was something which most plainly said
That thou wert innocent.

MATILDA

How! innocent!
Oh heavens! you've been deceived.

MORTIMER

Thou art a woman
To bring damnation on the universe.

MATILDA

Already I've been punished to the height
Of my offence (*smiling affectionately*)—
I see you love me still—
The labours of my hand are still your joy.
Bethink you of that hour when on your shoulder
(*pointing to the belt on which was suspended the scrip of* HERBERT)
I hung this belt.

MORTIMER

Mercy of Heaven!
[*Sinks against the scene.*

MATILDA

What ails you?
[*Looks round in a distracted manner.*

MORTIMER

Oh! misery! the scrip which held his food!
And I forgot to give it back again—

Shall sun himself before his native doors;
The lame, the hungry, will be welcome there.
No more shall he complain of wasted strength,
Of thoughts that fail, and a decaying heart;
His good works will be balm and life to him.

MARMADUKE.

This is most strange!—I know not what it was,
But there was something which most plainly said,
That thou wert innocent.

IDONEA.

How innocent!—
Oh heavens! you've been deceived.

MARMADUKE.

Thou art a Woman,
To bring perdition on the universe.

IDONEA.

Already I've been punished to the height
Of my offence. [*Smiling affectionately.*
I see you love me still,
The labours of my hand are still your joy;
Bethink you of the hour when on your shoulder
I hung this belt.
[*Pointing to the belt on which was suspended* HERBERT's *scrip.*

MARMADUKE.

Mercy of Heaven! [*Sinks.*

IDONEA.

What ails you! [*Distractedly.*

MARMADUKE.

The scrip that held his food, and I forgot
To give it back again.

1644 again.] again? *1842* again! *1845–* again. *(MSS. 3 and 4)*

MATILDA (*returns to* MORTIMER)

How feel you now?

MORTIMER

'Tis but a shooting pang—
I know not what I said—all will be well. [1645]
'Tis a dull pain—I was disturbed to see you.

MATILDA

Oh! you can smile again.—That smile has lift in it!

MORTIMER

'Tis a bleak road across the heath at evening.
There is a cottage on its skirts—I pray you,
Rest there to night, my dearest innocent!
We shall do well—I had a thought indeed—
I will attend you to the edge of the heath,
You'll see the cottage there—for me—I have business
With my friend Rivers——

MATILDA

On the morrow early
I shall expect you.—Will you look again
As you were wont to do?—The Heavens preserve you!
[*Exeunt together.*

ACT IV

[Scene 1] SCENE, *a desolate prospect—a ridge of rocks rises at the bottom of the stage, an old chapel on the summit of one of them;—the moon behind the rocks—the night stormy—the irregular sound of a bell is heard—*HERBERT *enters in the depth of the stage much exhausted; he crosses the stage with difficulty—*

HERBERT

That bell—if I have strength—to reach it—oh!
(*Stretching out his hand*)
This wall of rocks—and the sound never nearer—

---

171 The "lift" may be a copyist's error; it was altered to "life" in 1841.
174 Cf. *Macbeth*, III.ii.45: "Be innocent of the knowledge, dearest chuck."
1 MH revised "had" to "have" in 1799.

IDONEA.

What mean your words?

MARMADUKE.

I know not what I said—all may be well.

IDONEA.

That smile hath life in it!

MARMADUKE.

This road is perilous;
I will attend you to a Hut that stands
Near the wood's edge—rest there to-night, I pray you:
For me, I have business, as you heard, with Oswald,
But will return to you by break of day.

END OF THIRD ACT.

ACT IV.

SCENE, *A desolate prospect—a ridge of rocks—a Chapel on the summit of one—Moon behind the rocks—night stormy—irregular sound of a bell—*HERBERT *enters exhausted.*

HERBERT.

That Chapel-bell in mercy seemed to guide me,
But now it mocks my steps; its fitful stroke
Can scarcely be the work of human hands.

Hear me ye men upon the cliffs that pray
To God the father of all mercy—hear me—
My child—my child—dark—dark—I faint—this wind, [1657]
This stifling wind. [*He sinks down in a corner of the stage.*

Enter ROBERT *at another part of the stage.*

ROBERT

Better this
Than have a case of dungeon walls to screen a man
From the rough visitation of the sky.
These aching fingers— [*A mourning voice is heard.*
Ha! what sound is that?
Trees creaking in the wind send forth such noises,
But all is naked here.—That tingling bell,
It half confounds a man—perchance these rocks—
Again—I never heard a sound so like
A human groan.—Ha! what is here—
Poor man! what has befallen you? speak, my friend.
Murdered! alas! speak, speak, I am your friend—
No answer: hush, poor wretch, he lifts his [hand] [1669]
And lays it to his heart. (*Kneels by him*) I pray you, speak,
In very sorrow of my heart, I pray you,
I know not what has harm'd you—hush—again,
O heaven——

HERBERT (*in a feeble voice*)

A stranger has done this to me,
And in the arms of a stranger I must die, [1672]
God be praised!—

ROBERT

Cheerly, cheerly, are you wounded?

HERBERT

I have a daughter—carry a blessing to her.
Tell her that she will never see me more.

ROBERT

Come, let me raise you up, indeed, indeed—
This is a dismal place—well—that is well—
We shall do well—I feel you are quite stout.
I was afraid—my cottage— [*Draws him gently off the stage.*

---

17 MH wrote "head," which survives in the base text of MS. 3 (1841), corrected to "hand."

Hear me, ye Men, upon the cliffs, if such
There be who pray nightly before the Altar.
Oh that I had but strength to reach the place!
My child—my child—dark—dark—I faint—this wind—
These stifling blasts—God help me!

Enter ELDRED.

ELDRED.

Better this bare rock,
Though it were tottering over a man's head,
Than a tight case of dungeon walls for shelter
From such rough dealing. [*A moaning voice is heard.*
Ha! what sound is that?
Trees creaking in the wind (but none are here)
Send forth such noises—and that weary bell!
Surely some evil Spirit abroad to-night
Is ringing it—'twould stop a Saint in prayer,
And that—what is it? never was sound so like
A human groan. Ha! what is here? Poor Man—
Murdered! alas! speak—speak, I am your friend:
No answer—hush—lost wretch, he lifts his hand
And lays it to his heart—(*Kneels to him*). I pray you speak!
What has befallen you?

HERBERT (*feebly*).

A stranger has done this,
And in the arms of a stranger I must die.

ELDRED.

Nay, think not so: come, let me raise you up:
[*Raises him.*
This is a dismal place—well—that is well—
I was too fearful—take me for your guide
And your support—my hut is not far off.
[*Draws him gently off the stage.*

[Scene 2] SCENE, *a room in the Inn.*

MORTIMER *and* RIVERS.

MORTIMER

But for Matilda, I have cause to think [1677]
That she is innocent—

RIVERS (*collecting himself*)

I shall be able
To throw some light on this part of my history
You are unacquainted with—I am a murderer.
(*Seeing his astonishment*)
Ay, just as I expected.—In my youth
I was the pleasure of all hearts—the darling [1687]
Of every tongue—as you are now—you've heard
That I embarked for Syria—on our voyage
I was convinced a foul conspiracy
Was laid against my honour, that the captain
Was the prime agent—well—we were becalmed—
The water of the vessel was exhausted— [1694]
I felt a double fever in my veins.

3–36 Rivers's account of his crime is a fusion of several sources. In *Caleb Williams*, Falkland's crime, like Rivers's, is set off by a blow that wounded his pride more than his person, and the account of his passion is similar to that of Rivers's. Rather than murder the captain directly, however, as Falkland does, Rivers abandons him on an island at sea. The principal inspiration for this abandonment may have come from current events in which Wordsworth had great personal interest. Captain Bligh, of the *Bounty* mutiny of 1789, was, like Rivers's captain, imperious of temper and hated by his crew. Before abandoning Captain Bligh at sea, Fletcher Christian, the leader of the mutiny, had likewise sustained blows, at the order of the captain whom he had thought to be his friend. Fletcher Christian had been at Hawkshead Grammar School when Wordsworth was there, and his brother Edward, who defended Fletcher at the trial, had been Wordsworth's friend at Cambridge and the family lawyer in the suit against Lord Lonsdale (see Moorman, I, 90 and 168, where Dorothy is quoted as saying that Edward Christian "knows my brother William very well"). In the *Weekly Entertainer* of 1796 there appeared an extract from a journal purportedly kept by Fletcher Christian, in which he exonerated Captain Bligh from all guilt (XXVIII, 255–256). Wordsworth was moved to write one of his rare letters to the press: "I have the best authority for saying that this publication is spurious. Your regard for truth will induce you to apprize your readers of this circumstance" (*EY*, 171). His authority, of course, was his personal knowledge that Fletcher had not been traced after leaving Tahiti in 1789 (his fate was not discovered until 1808). But the interest that moved Wordsworth to write the letter, and possibly his fears that Fletcher might have been mistaken in his belief that Bligh was personally antagonistic toward him, may have combined to inspire the confession scene of IV.ii. Zera S. Fink, pointing out that the abandonment is central to the entire action of the play, offers a possible source for the setting in *Description of a Person Left on a Desert Island* in Knox's *Elegant Extracts*, referred to in a notebook belonging to Christopher Wordsworth (*The Early Wordsworthian Milieu* [Oxford, 1958], pp. 50–52).

13 The double fever was doubtless both moral and physical. MH revised "brains" to "veins" in 1799.

SCENE, *a room in the Hostel*—MARMADUKE *and* OSWALD.

MARMADUKE.

But for Idonea!—I have cause to think
That she is innocent.

OSWALD.

Leave that thought awhile,
As one of those beliefs which in their hearts
Lovers lock up as pearls, though oft no better
Than feathers clinging to their points of passion.
This day's event has laid on me the duty
Of opening out my story; you must hear it,
And without further preface.—In my youth,
Except for that abatement which is paid
By envy as a tribute to desert,
I was the pleasure of all hearts, the darling
Of every tongue—as you are now. You've heard
That I embarked for Syria. On our voyage
Was hatched among the crew a foul Conspiracy
Against my honour, in the which our Captain
Was, I believed, prime Agent. The wind fell;
We lay becalmed week after week, until
The water of the vessel was exhausted;
I felt a double fever in my veins,

My rage suppressed itself—to a deep stillness
Did my Pride tame my pride—for many days
Beneath the burning sky on the dead sea
I brooded o'er my injuries—deserted [1699]
By man and nature—if a breeze had blown
It might have found its way into my heart
And I had been—no matter—do you mark me?

MORTIMER

Your crime? what was your crime?

RIVERS

Hear me further.
One day at noon we drifted silently
By a bare rock, narrow and white and bare. [1706]
There was no food, no drink, no grass, no shade,
No tree nor jutting eminence, nor form
Inanimate, large as the body of man,
Nor any living thing whose span of life
Might stretch beyond the measure of one moon; [1711]
To dig for water we landed there—the captain
And a small party of which myself was one.
There I reproach'd him with his treachery.
His temper was imperious, and he struck me—
A blow! I would have killed him, but my comrades
Rush'd in between us.—They all hated him—
And they insisted—I was stung to madness—
That we should leave him there, alive—we did so. [1720]

MORTIMER

And he was famished?

RIVERS

'Twas a spot—
Methinks I see it now—how in the sun
Its stony surface glittered like a shield:
It swarmed with shapes of life scarce visible;
And in that miserable place we left him— [1724]
A giant body mid a world of beings
Not one of which could give him any aid,
Living or dead.

---

18 Cf. *Prelude*, I, 1: "Oh there is blessing in this gentle breeze."
39 Cf. *Prelude*, VIII, 565–566, 572.

Yet rage suppressed itself;—to a deep stillness
Did my pride tame my pride;—for many days,
On a dead sea under a burning sky,
I brooded o'er my injuries, deserted
By man and nature;—if a breeze had blown,
It might have found its way into my heart,
And I had been—no matter—do you mark me?

MARMADUKE.

Quick—to the point—if any untold crime
Doth haunt your memory.

OSWALD.

Patience, hear me further!—
One day in silence did we drift at noon
By a bare rock, narrow, and white, and bare;
No food was there, no drink, no grass, no shade,
No tree, nor jutting eminence, nor form
Inanimate large as the body of man,
Nor any living thing whose lot of life
Might stretch beyond the measure of one moon.
To dig for water on the spot, the Captain
Landed with a small troop, myself being one:
There I reproached him with his treachery.
Imperious at all times, his temper rose;
He struck me; and that instant had I killed him,
And put an end to his insolence, but my Comrades
Rushed in between us: then did I insist
(All hated him, and I was stung to madness)
That we should leave him there, alive!—we did so.

MARMADUKE.

And he was famished?

OSWALD.

Naked was the spot;
Methinks I see it now—how in the sun
Its stony surface glittered like a shield;
And in that miserable place we left him,
Alone but for a swarm of minute creatures
Not one of which could help him while alive,
Or mourn him dead.

MORTIMER

A man by men deserted,
Not buried in the sand—not dead nor dying,
But standing, walking—stretching forth his arms:
In all things like yourselves, but in the agony [1730]
With which he called for mercy—and even so,
He was forsaken.

RIVERS

There is a power in sounds:
The groans he uttered might have stopped the boat [1733]
That bore us through the water.

MORTIMER

Rivers—Rivers,
I ought to tear you piece-meal—

RIVERS

Some scoffed at him with hellish mockery, [1736]
And laugh'd so loud it seem'd that the smooth sea
Did from some distant region echo us.

MORTIMER

We all are of one blood, our veins are filled
At the same poisonous fountain.

RIVERS

'Twas an island
But by permission of the winds and waves;
I know not how he perish'd, but the calm, [1742]
The same dead calm continued many days.

MORTIMER

But then, he was a traitor—these expedients
Are terrible.—But the fault is not ours—

RIVERS

The man was famished and he was innocent. [1748]

MORTIMER

False, false by all the fiends in hell—

RIVERS

The man
Had never wronged me.

MORTIMER

Let not the thought trouble you;
His guilt was marked—these things could never be [1751]
Were we not instruments in the hands of heaven—

MARMADUKE.

A man by men cast off,
Left without burial! nay, not dead nor dying,
But standing, walking, stretching forth his arms,
In all things like ourselves, but in the agony
With which he called for mercy; and—even so—
He was forsaken?

OSWALD.

There is a power in sounds:
The cries he uttered might have stopped the boat
That bore us through the water—

MARMADUKE.

You returned
Upon that dismal hearing—did you not?

OSWALD.

Some scoffed at him with hellish mockery,
And laughed so loud it seemed that the smooth sea
Did from some distant region echo us.

MARMADUKE.

We all are of one blood, our veins are filled
At the same poisonous fountain!

OSWALD.

'Twas an island
Only by sufferance of the winds and waves,
Which with their foam could cover it at will.
I know not how he perished; but the calm,
The same dead calm, continued many days.

MARMADUKE.

But his own crime had brought on him this doom,
His wickedness prepared it; these expedients
Are terrible, yet ours is not the fault.

OSWALD.

The man was famished, and was innocent!

MARMADUKE.

Impossible!

OSWALD.

The man had never wronged me.

MARMADUKE.

Banish the thought, crush it, and be at peace.
His guilt was marked—these things could never be
Were there not eyes that see, and for good ends,
Where ours are baffled.

RIVERS

I had been deceived.

MORTIMER

And the miserable victim was heard of no more?

RIVERS

I had been betrayed.

MORTIMER

O hell! and he found no deliverance?

RIVERS

The crew received me gladly, 'twas a plot
To rid them of a master whom they hated.
Well—we pursued our voyage—and when we landed
The tale was spread abroad—my power shrunk from me,
My plans of heroism, my lofty hopes,
All vanished—I could not support the change;
I sunk into despair. Do you attend?

MORTIMER

(*with a hurried manner, as if recovering from a fit of deep absence*)
The crew received you—

RIVERS

The unhappy man,
He had a daughter—

MORTIMER (*turning away*)

Enough, enough.

RIVERS

His only child—she did not long survive it.
She was a lovely maid—she had conjured me
At parting never to forsake her father,
To stand by him in all extremities—
The tidings reached her; from that very time
She neither saw nor heard as others do,
But in a fearful world of her own making
She lived—cut off from the society
Of every rational thing—her father's skeleton.

74–78 Cf. *Adventures on Salisbury Plain*, ll. 467–470 (*SPP*, p. 141):

And homeless near a thousand homes I stood,
And near a thousand tables pined, and wanted food.

"By grief enfeebled was I turned adrift,
Helpless as sailor cast on desart rock;

OSWALD.

I had been deceived.

MARMADUKE.

And from that hour the miserable man
No more was heard of?

OSWALD.

I had been betrayed.

MARMADUKE.

And he found no deliverance!

OSWALD.

The Crew
Gave me a hearty welcome; they had laid
The plot to rid themselves, at any cost,
Of a tyrannic Master whom they loathed.
So we pursued our voyage: when we landed,
The tale was spread abroad; my power at once
Shrunk from me; plans and schemes, and lofty hopes—
All vanished. I gave way—do you attend?

MARMADUKE.

The Crew deceived you?

1763 attend?] attend! *(MS. 4), 1842* attend? *(MS. 3), 1845–*

MORTIMER

She shall not die—no, I will have her curse
Here at my heart.

RIVERS

You do not listen to me.

MORTIMER

It is a dismal night—how the wind howls! [1765]
Go on.

RIVERS

Well, I betook me to a convent
And dozed away the time—how long I know not.
This would not do for me—I was o'erthrown
But not destroyed.

MORTIMER

The proofs, the proofs—
You ought to have seen, to have touch'd the guilt—the heavens
Have kindly dealt with me, let me be thankful.

RIVERS

You have good cause.—A fresh tide of crusaders
Drove past the place of my retreat—three nights [1772]
Did constant meditation dry my blood,
Three sleepless nights I passed in sounding on
Through words and things, a dim and perilous way;
And wheresoe'er I turned me, I beheld [1776]
A slavery, compared to which the dungeon
And clanking chain are perfect liberty.
You understand me, with an awful comfort
I saw that every possible shape of action
Might lead to good—I saw it and burst forth [1781]
Thirsting for some exploit of power and terror.
[*Marking the expression of* MORTIMER'S *countenance.*
Nay, you have had the worst.—The victory
Already was accomplished—my ferocity
Subsided like a storm that dies at once.
I felt I had been fettered by a straw,
I stood astonished at myself—my brain
Was light and giddy, and it teemed with projects
Which seemed to have no limit.

OSWALD.

Nay, command yourself.

MARMADUKE.

It is a dismal night—how the wind howls!

OSWALD.

I hid my head within a Convent, there
Lay passive as a dormouse in mid winter.
That was no life for me—I was o'erthrown,
But not destroyed.

MARMADUKE.

The proofs—you ought to have seen
The guilt—have touched it—felt it at your heart—
As I have done.

OSWALD.

A fresh tide of Crusaders
Drove by the place of my retreat: three nights
Did constant meditation dry my blood;
Three sleepless nights I passed in sounding on,
Through words and things, a dim and perilous way;
And, wheresoe'er I turned me, I beheld
A slavery compared to which the dungeon
And clanking chains are perfect liberty.
You understand me—I was comforted;
I saw that every possible shape of action
Might lead to good—I saw it and burst forth
Thirsting for some of those exploits that fill
The earth for sure redemption of lost peace.
[*Marking* MARMADUKE's *countenance.*
Nay, you have had the worst. Ferocity
Subsided in a moment, like a wind
That drops down dead out of a sky it vexed.

MORTIMER

Unhappy man!
Yet I will take thee to my heart.

RIVERS (*smiles*)

I had within me
A salient spring of energy, a fire
Of inextinguishable thought—I mounted
From action up to action with a mind [1789]
That never rested—without meat or drink
I have lived many days—my sleep was linked
To purposes of reason—my very dreams
Assumed a substance and a character.

MORTIMER

The traitor! and no meaner prey would satisfy him!

RIVERS

We drove to Syria.—Oft I left the camp
When all that multitude of hearts was still [1803]
And followed on through woods of gloomy cedar
Into deep chasms troubled by roaring streams,
Or from the top of Lebanon surveyed
The moonlight desart and the moonlight sea;
In these my lonely wanderings I perceived [1808]
What mighty objects do impress their forms
To build up this our intellectual being,
And felt if aught on earth deserved a curse,
'Twas that worst principle of ill that dooms
A thing so great to perish self-consumed. [1813]
—So much for my remorse.

MORTIMER

Oh, my poor friend!
By all that thou hast suffered doubly dear—

RIVERS

When from these forms I turned to contemplate
The opinions and the uses of the world,
I seemed a being who had passed alone [1817]
Beyond the visible barriers of the world
And travelled into things to come.

118–145 Compare the accounts of crossing the Alps and traveling down the Simplon Pass in *Prelude*, VI, 512–572.

143–145 Cf. *Adventures on Salisbury Plain*, ll. 451–452 (*SPP*, p. 140):

"Some mighty gulph of separation past,
I seemed transported to another world:—

And yet I had within me evermore
A salient spring of energy; I mounted
From action up to action with a mind
That never rested—without meat or drink
Have I lived many days—my sleep was bound
To purposes of reason—not a dream
But had a continuity and substance
That waking life had never power to give.

MARMADUKE.

O wretched Human-kind!—Until the mystery
Of all this world is solved, well may we envy
The worm, that, underneath a stone whose weight
Would crush the lion's paw with mortal anguish,
Doth lodge, and feed, and coil, and sleep, in safety.
Fell not the wrath of Heaven upon those traitors?

OSWALD.

Give not to them a thought. From Palestine
We marched to Syria: oft I left the Camp,
When all that multitude of hearts was still,
And followed on, through woods of gloomy cedar,
Into deep chasms troubled by roaring streams;
Or from the top of Lebanon surveyed
The moonlight desert, and the moonlight sea:
In these my lonely wanderings I perceived
What mighty objects do impress their forms
To elevate our intellectual being;
And felt, if aught on earth deserves a curse,
'Tis that worst principle of ill which dooms
A thing so great to perish self-consumed.
—So much for my remorse!

MARMADUKE.

Unhappy Man!

OSWALD.

When from these forms I turned to contemplate
The World's opinions and her usages,
I seemed a Being who had passed alone
Into a region of futurity,
Whose natural element was freedom—

MORTIMER

Poor wretch!
My heart aches for thee.

RIVERS

Is not shame, I said,
A mean acknowledgment of a tribunal
Blind in its essence, a most base surrender
Of our own knowledge to the world's ignorance?
I had been nourished by the sickly food
Of popular applause. I now perceived [1822]
That we are praised by men because they see in us
The image of themselves; that a great mind
Outruns its age and is pursued with obliquy
Because its movements are not understood.
I felt that to be truly the world's friend,
We must become the object of its hate.

MORTIMER

I can forgive you—but the merciless traitors!

RIVERS

Having no fear, at once I found myself
The master of the better half of wisdom.
I saw unveiled the general shapes of things,
I saw the feeble props of them that stood
And was astonished at the stupefaction
Of them who had fallen.—And now the very men,
The men to whom I owe this triumph, they
Who made me what I am, you would destroy them.
Join me in heaping blessings on their heads.

MORTIMER

(*looking up and gnashing his teeth*)
May he who made us—(*breaking off*) but I have not heard aright.
In truth, I have been strangely troubled lately.
What did you say?

RIVERS

You know wherein I differ
From common minds—and in a wiser hour
You have been proud to call me friend—one man
Was famished and ten thousand have been saved.

MARMADUKE.

Stop—
I may not, cannot, follow thee.

OSWALD.

You must.
I had been nourished by the sickly food
Of popular applause. I now perceived
That we are praised, only as men in us
Do recognise some image of themselves,
An abject counterpart of what they are,
Or the empty thing that they would wish to be.
I felt that merit has no surer test
Than obloquy; that, if we wish to serve
The world in substance, not deceive by show,
We must become obnoxious to its hate,
Or fear disguised in simulated scorn.

MARMADUKE.

I pity, can forgive, you; but those wretches—
That monstrous perfidy!

OSWALD.

Keep down your wrath.
False Shame discarded, spurious Fame despised,
Twin sisters both of Ignorance, I found
Life stretched before me smooth as some broad way
Cleared for a monarch's progress. Priests might spin
Their veil, but not for me—'twas in fit place
Among its kindred cobwebs. I had been,
And in that dream had left my native land,
One of Love's simple bondsmen—the soft chain
Was off for ever; and the men, from whom
This liberation came, you would destroy:
Join me in thanks for their blind services.

MORTIMER

It is a strange aching that—when we would curse [1845]
And cannot—

RIVERS

What! for saving a poor man perchance
From a ten years' visitation of the stone,
Or the more gentle mercies of the palsy?

MORTIMER

Thou poor old man, and I had heart for this
Because thou loved'st the infant that had fed thee,
Thy daughter—she that was the light of thy path,
The very blood that moved in thee—O! fool—
(To Rivers*)* Monster, you have betray'd me—

RIVERS

I have done
What you perhaps may live to thank me for.

MORTIMER

(*laying his hand tranquilly on his breast*)
I am content—I know that he is guiltless. [*Walks about.*
Peace—Peace—— Together we propped up his steps,
He leaned upon us both.

RIVERS

I've join'd us by a chain of adamant;
Henceforth we are fellow-labourers—to enlarge [1855]
The intellectual empire of mankind.
'Tis slavery—all is slavery, we receive
Laws, and we ask not whence those laws have come.
We need an inward sting to goad us on. [1859]
—Heavens—where's the harm of ridding an old wretch?

MORTIMER

'Twas in his face—I saw it in his face—
I've crushed the foulest crime—

RIVERS

Away with that—
More noble triumphs are prepared for you,
And nobler sympathies—of this hereafter—
That silly girl—I felt for your delusion;
The penalty be mine—yours the reward.
I would have made you equal with myself,
But that was a vain hope—you have struck home, [1867]
With a few drops of blood cut short the business;

MARMADUKE.

'Tis a strange aching that, when we would curse
And cannot.—You have betrayed me—I have done—
I am content—I know that he is guiltless—
That both are guiltless, without spot or stain,
Mutually consecrated. Poor old Man!
And I had heart for this, because thou loved'st
Her who from very infancy had been
Light to thy path, warmth to thy blood!—Together
[*Turning to* OSWALD.
We propped his steps, he leaned upon us both.

OSWALD.

Ay, we are coupled by a chain of adamant;
Let us be fellow-labourers, then, to enlarge
Man's intellectual empire. We subsist
In slavery; all is slavery; we receive
Laws, but we ask not whence those laws have come;
We need an inward sting to goad us on.

MARMADUKE.

Have you betrayed me? Speak to that.

OSWALD.

The mask,
Which for a season I have stooped to wear,
Must be cast off.—Know then that I was urged,
(For other impulse let it pass) was driven,
To seek for sympathy, because I saw
In you a mirror of my youthful self;
I would have made us equal once again,
But that was a vain hope. You have struck home,
With a few drops of blood cut short the business;

Therein for ever you must yield to me.
Enough is done to save you from the curse
Of living without knowledge that you live. [1871]
You will be taught to think—and step by step,
Led on from truth to truth, you soon will link
Pleasure with greatness, and may thus become
The most magnificent of characters.
Something you've suffered for the future hour;
'Tis his who will command it. Think of my story— [1873]
Herbert is innocent.

MORTIMER (*in a faint voice*)

That blind man—
I've spoken very lightly—if you do but
Echo my words—

RIVERS

The seed must be
Hid in the earth or there can be no harvest;
'Tis nature's law. What I have done in darkness [1877]
I will avow before the face of day:
Herbert is innocent.

MORTIMER

What fiend could prompt thee to this damning deed?
Innocent! Oh, my heart! Alive or dead,
I'll find him— [*Rushes out.*

RIVERS

Alive? ——damnation!
[*Exit* RIVERS.

[Scene 3] SCENE, *the inside of a poor cottage.*

MATILDA *and* MARGARET *seated.*

MATILDA

The storm beats hard.—A mercy to the wretches
Who have no roof to shelter their poor heads
Such nights as these.

A VOICE FROM WITHOUT

What, hola! you are merry there.

MARGARET

Oh, Heavens!

MATILDA

What means this?

---

204 MH inserted "you" with a caret in 1799.

Therein for ever you must yield to me.
But what is done will save you from the blank
Of living without knowledge that you live:
Now you are suffering—for the future day,
'Tis his who will command it.—Think of my story—
Herbert is *innocent*.

MARMADUKE (*in a faint voice, and doubtingly*).

You do but echo
My own wild words?

OSWALD.

Young Man, the seed must lie
Hid in the earth, or there can be no harvest;
'Tis Nature's law. What I have done in darkness
I will avow before the face of day.
Herbert *is* innocent.

MARMADUKE.

What fiend could prompt
This action? Innocent!—oh, breaking heart!—
Alive or dead, I'll find him. [*Exit*.

OSWALD.

Alive—perdition! [*Exit*.

SCENE, *the inside of a poor Cottage*.

ELEANOR *and* IDONEA *seated*.

IDONEA.

The storm beats hard—Mercy for poor or rich,
Whose heads are shelterless in such a night!

A VOICE WITHOUT.

Holla! to bed, good Folks, within!

ELEANOR.

O save us!

IDONEA.

What can this mean?

MARGARET

Oh, my husband!

VOICE FROM WITHOUT (*with tumult*)

In good faith,
We'll have a counting of our flocks tomorrow:
The wolf keeps festival these stormy nights.

[*Confused noises are heard that die away at a distance.*

MARGARET

Be calm, sweet Lady—'tis some wassellers
Returning from the wake—my heart beats so—
A noise at midnight does *so* frighten me—

MATILDA (*listening*)

Hush!

MARGARET

They are gone—'twas such a night as this
They dragged my husband from his bed
And cast him deep into a dungeon.—Lady,
—The place I never saw—and he was innocent,
Innocent of all crimes, and now you see
That this wretched cottage cannot save us
From cruelty and insult—

MATILDA

I have a friend;
He lives but to protect the injured. (*Listening*) There, again.

MARGARET

It is my husband's foot.—Poor Robert! Lady,
Has a kind heart, but his confinement
Has made him fearful, and he'll never be
The man he was.

MATILDA

I will retire—good night.

[MATILDA *goes into an inner room of the cottage.*

Enter ROBERT.

(*While he speaks goes and sits down in a dark part of the room.*)

ROBERT

'Tis very late.—Not yet in bed, Margaret? (*He rises up and hides a bundle*) There are stains in that frock which must be washed out—

MARGARET

What has befallen you?

ELEANOR.

Alas, for my poor husband!—
We'll have a counting of our flocks to-morrow;
The wolf keeps festival these stormy nights:
Be calm, sweet Lady, they are wassaillers
[*The voices die away in the distance.*
Returning from their Feast—my heart beats so—
A noise at midnight does *so* frighten me.

IDONEA.

Hush! [*Listening.*

ELEANOR.

They are gone. On such a night, my husband,
Dragged from his bed, was cast into a dungeon,
Where, hid from me, he counted many years,
A criminal in no one's eyes but theirs—
Not even in theirs—whose brutal violence
So dealt with him.

IDONEA.

I have a noble Friend
First among youths of knightly breeding, One
Who lives but to protect the weak or injured.
There again! [*Listening.*

ELEANOR.

'Tis my husband's foot. Good Eldred
Has a kind heart; but his imprisonment
Has made him fearful, and he'll never be
The man he was.

IDONEA.

I will retire;—good night!
[*She goes within.*

Enter ELDRED, (*hides a bundle.*)

ELDRED.

Not yet in bed, Eleanor?—there are stains in that frock which must be washed out.

ELEANOR.

What has befallen you?

1903 Eleanor?] Eleanor! *1845–*

ROBERT (*draws near*)

I have been detained to night, and you must know the cause—(*speaking low*) that is the blood of an unhappy man.

MARGARET

Oh! we are undone for ever. [1908]

ROBERT

Heaven forbid that I should lift my hand against any man. (*He pauses*) Margaret, I have shed tears to night, and it comforts me to think of it.

MARGARET

Where, where is he? [1912]

ROBERT

I have done him no harm, but (*hesitating*) Heaven will forgive me, it would not have been so once.

MARGARET

You have not *buried* any thing? you are no richer than when you left me?

ROBERT

Be at peace, I am innocent. [1917]

MARGARET (*fervently*)

Oh! God I thank thee—(*A pause in which she looks at him, her countenance mantling with pleasure*) Robert, I am happy to see you.

[*A short pause—she falls upon his neck.*

ROBERT

To night I met with an old man lying stretched upon the ground—a piteous spectacle.

MARGARET (*as if ready to run*)

Where is he? (ROBERT *looks grave*) You were not able to bring him *all* the way with you. Let us return—I am quite stout.

[ROBERT *shakes his head.*

MARGARET (*alarmed*)

But what was it that would not have been so once?

ROBERT

He did not seem to wish for life; when I had raised him up in my arms, by the light of the moon I saw the stains of blood upon my cloaths—he waved his hand, as if it were all useless, and I let him sink again to the ground.

MARGARET (*sighing deeply*)

Oh! that I had been by your side. [1929]

ELDRED.

I am belated, and you must know the cause—(*speaking low*) that is the blood of an unhappy Man.

ELEANOR.

Oh! we are undone for ever. 1908

ELDRED.

Heaven forbid that I should lift my hand against any man. Eleanor, I have shed tears to-night, and it comforts me to think of it.

ELEANOR.

Where, where is he? 1912

ELDRED.

I have done him no harm, but——it will be forgiven me; it would not have been so once.

ELEANOR.

You have not *buried* anything? You are no richer than when you left me?

ELDRED.

Be at peace; I am innocent. 1917

ELEANOR.

Then God be thanked—

[*A short pause; she falls upon his neck.*

ELDRED.

To-night I met with an old Man lying stretched upon the ground—a sad spectacle: I raised him up with a hope that we might shelter and restore him.

ELEANOR (*as if ready to run*).

Where is he? You were not able to bring him *all* the way with you; let us return, I can help you.

[ELDRED *shakes his head.*

ELDRED.

He did not seem to wish for life: as I was struggling on, by the light of the moon I saw the stains of blood upon my clothes—he waved his hand, as if it were all useless; and I let him sink again to the ground.

ELEANOR.

Oh that I had been by your side! 1929

ROBERT (*with some impatience*)

I tell you, his hands and body were cold—how could I disturb his last moments? he strove to turn from me as if he wished to compose himself to sleep.

MARGARET

But his wounds?

ROBERT

I looked at them—he had fallen—and his face was bruised—but I think his malady was cold and hunger.

MARGARET

Oh! Robert, I shall never be able to look up at this roof in dry or storm but I shall tremble.

ROBERT

It is not enough that I have been so unfortunate as to have been abroad to night till this hour; I came home, and this my comfort.

MARGARET

But did he say nothing which might have set you at ease? [1940]

ROBERT

I thought he grasped my hand while he was muttering something about his child—his daughter—what is that? (*Starting as if he heard a noise*)

MARGARET

Robert, you are a father. [1945]

ROBERT (*with a faultering voice*)

God knows what was in my heart and will not curse my son for my sake.

MARGARET

But you prayed by him? you waited the hour of his release?

ROBERT

It was far from home—the night was wasting fast; I have no friend—I am spited by the world—if I had brought him along with me and he had died in my arms.—Hush! I am sure I heard something breathing—and this chair?

MARGARET

Oh! Robert, you will die alone—you will have nobody to close your eyes—no hand to grasp your dying hands—I shall be in my grave.—A curse will attend us all—

ELDRED.

I tell you his hands and his body were cold—how could I disturb his last moments? he strove to turn from me as if he wished to settle into sleep.

ELEANOR.

But, for the stains of blood—

ELDRED.

He must have fallen, I fancy, for his head was cut; but I think his malady was cold and hunger.

ELEANOR.

Oh, Eldred, I shall never be able to look up at this roof in storm or fair but I shall tremble.

ELDRED.

Is it not enough that my ill stars have kept me abroad to-night till this hour? I come home, and this is my comfort!

ELEANOR.

But did he say nothing which might have set you at ease?

ELDRED.

I thought he grasped my hand while he was muttering something about his Child—his Daughter—(*starting as if he heard a noise*). What is that?

ELEANOR.

Eldred, you are a father.

ELDRED.

God knows what was in my heart, and will not curse my son for my sake.

ELEANOR.

But you prayed by him? you waited the hour of his release?

ELDRED.

The night was wasting fast; I have no friend; I am spited by the world—his wound terrified me—if I had brought him along with me, and he had died in my arms!——I am sure I heard something breathing—and this chair!

ELEANOR.

Oh, Eldred, you will die alone. You will have nobody to close your eyes—no hand to grasp your dying hand—I shall be in my grave. A curse will attend us all.

1948 you] You *1842*, *1846* you *(MSS. 3 and 4)*, *1845*, *1849*

ROBERT (*sternly*)

Have you forgot the bed on which you lay when I was in dungeon?

MARGARET

And you left him alive? [1959]

ROBERT

Alive! the damps of death were upon him, he could not have survived an hour.

MARGARET (*weeps*)

In the cold, cold night. [1962]

ROBERT (*in a savage manner*)

Aye, and his head was bare.—I suppose you would have had me leave my bonnet to cover him. (*Checking himself*) You will never rest till I meet with a felon's end.

MARGARET (*with feeling*)

Is there nothing to be done—cannot we go to the Convent?

ROBERT

Certainly! and say at once that I have murdered him. [1967]

MARGARET

Robert, I know that ours is the only house upon the heath—in my dreams a thousand times have I heard the cracking of your joints upon that dreadful engine. (*Affecting chearfulness*) But let us take heart—this man may be rich.—And could he be saved by our means, his gratitude—

ROBERT (*in a softer tone*)

'Tis all in vain. [1971]

MARGARET (*more eagerly*)

But let us make the attempt.—This old man may have a wife—and he may have children. Let us return to the spot; we may restore him and his eyes may yet open upon those that love him.

ROBERT

He will never open them more—even when he spoke to me, he kept them firmly sealed as if he had been blind.

MATILDA (*rushes out*)

It is, it is my father! [1978]

ROBERT

(*after his first surprize looking sternly at his wife*)

We are betrayed.

MARGARET

(*turning to* MATILDA, *who is sunk senseless on the floor*)

His daughter! God of mercy!

ELDRED.

Have you forgot your own troubles when I was in the dungeon?

ELEANOR.

And you left him alive? 1959

ELDRED.

Alive!—the damps of death were upon him—he could not have survived an hour.

ELEANOR.

In the cold, cold night. 1962

ELDRED (*in a savage tone*).

Ay, and his head was bare; I suppose you would have had me lend my bonnet to cover it.—You will never rest till I am brought to a felon's end.

ELEANOR.

Is there nothing to be done? cannot we go to the Convent?

ELDRED.

Ay, and say at once that I murdered him! 1967

ELEANOR.

Eldred, I know that ours is the only house upon the Waste; let us take heart; this Man may be rich; and could he be saved by our means, his gratitude may reward us.

ELDRED.

'Tis all in vain. 1971

ELEANOR.

But let us make the attempt. This old Man may have a wife, and he may have children—let us return to the spot; we may restore him, and his eyes may yet open upon those that love him.

ELDRED.

He will never open them more; even when he spoke to me, he kept them firmly sealed as if he had been blind.

IDONEA (*rushing out*).

It is, it is, my Father— 1978

ELDRED.

We are betrayed (*looking at* IDONEA).

ELEANOR.

His Daughter!—God have mercy! (*turning to* IDONEA.)

1978–1984 *no paragraph indentation, 1842, 1846*

MATILDA

He is dead—Oh, lift me up—carry me to the place. You are safe.—The whole world shall not harm you.

MARGARET

Robert, this Lady is his daughter.

ROBERT (*much moved*)

I'll lead her to the spot. [1983]

MATILDA

(*Springing up with wild agitation*)

Alive! you heard him breathe?—quick—quick—

[*Exeunt* MATILDA, ROBERT, *and* MARGARET.

ACT V

[Scene 1] SCENE, *a wood on the edge of the heath.*

Enter RIVERS *and two* Woodmen.

FIRST WOODMAN

He leaned upon the bridge that spans the glen [1985]
And down into the bottom cast his eye
That fastened there as it would check the current.

RIVERS

He listened too? did you not say he listened? [1988]

SECOND WOODMAN

Aye, Sir, he listened—
As if he had heard such moaning in the water
As we fear often after stormy nights.

FIRST WOODMAN

Then, as it seemed from some strange intimation
Of things to us invisible, he turned
And looked around him with an eye that shewed
As if it wished to miss the thing it sought.

RIVERS

But did he *utter* nothing which explained
The cause of these appearances?

SECOND WOODMAN

Look there!

[MORTIMER *appears crossing the stage at some distance—an expression of vacancy in his eye, which at last settles upon the ground.*

The Rough Notebook has an earlier version of Scene 1, "Scene / Margaret and Peasant."

IDONEA (*sinking down*).

Oh! lift me up and carry me to the place.
You are safe; the whole world shall not harm you.

ELEANOR.

This Lady is his Daughter.

ELDRED (*moved*).

I'll lead you to the spot.

IDONEA (*springing up*).

Alive!—you heard him breathe? quick, quick——

[*Exeunt.*

END OF FOURTH ACT.

ACT V.

SCENE, *A wood on the edge of the Waste.*

Enter OSWALD *and a* FORESTER.

FORESTER.

He leaned upon the bridge that spans the glen,
And down into the bottom cast his eye,
That fastened there, as it would check the current.

OSWALD.

He listened too; did you not say he listened?

FORESTER.

As if there came such moaning from the flood
As is heard often after stormy nights.

OSWALD.

But did he utter nothing?

FORESTER.

See him there!

MARMADUKE *appearing.*

MORTIMER

The dust doth move and eddy at my feet.

SECOND WOODMAN

This is most strange; the air is dead and still.

FIRST WOODMAN

Look there, how he spreads out his arms as 'twere
To save himself from falling! such impression
I never saw before on human face.
I do believe some terrible phantom now
Doth pass before him such as God will not
Permit to visit any but a man [1998]
Who has been guilty of a damning crime.
[MORTIMER *disappears.*

RIVERS

The game is up.

SECOND WOODMAN

If it is needful, Sir,
We will assist you to lay hands on him.

RIVERS

No, no, my friends, you may pursue your business. [2002]
'Tis a poor wretch of an unsettled fancy
Who has a trick of straying from his keepers;
We must be gentle with him, leave him to my care. [2005]
[*Exeunt* Woodmen.

(RIVERS *alone*) What, have him whipped and howling? No, no, no,
I have an eye that will take care of him,
And tame these freaks and curvetings of fancy
Into a sober fire. Henceforth I'll have him
A shadow of myself, made by myself. [2009]

[Scene 2] SCENE, *the edge of the Heath.*

Enter at opposite sides of the stage MORTIMER *and* ROBERT.
MORTIMER *raises his eyes from the ground and perceiving* ROBERT——

MORTIMER

Have you seen
In any corner of this savage heath
A feeble, helpless miserable wretch,
A poor, forsaken, *famished*, blind old man?

---

31 For curvetings, the *OED* offers "A leap of a horse . . . (often used more or less vaguely of any leaping motion)."

4 Cf. *King Lear*, III.ii.20: "A poor, infirm, weak, and despis'd old man."

MARMADUKE.

Buzz, buzz, ye black and winged freebooters;
That is no substance which ye settle on!

FORESTER.

His senses play him false; and see, his arms
Outspread, as if to save him from falling!—
Some terrible phantom I believe is now
Passing before him, such as God will not
Permit to visit any but a man
Who has been guilty of some horrid crime.

[MARMADUKE *disappears.*

OSWALD.

The game is up!—

FORESTER.

If it be needful, Sir,
I will assist you to lay hands upon him.

OSWALD.

No, no, my Friend, you may pursue your business—
'Tis a poor wretch of an unsettled mind,
Who has a trick of straying from his keepers;
We must be gentle. Leave him to my care.

[*Exit* Forester.

If his own eyes play false with him, these freaks
Of fancy shall be quickly tamed by mine;
The goal is reached. My Master shall become
A shadow of myself—made by myself.

SCENE, *the edge of the Moor.*

MARMADUKE *and* ELDRED *enter from opposite sides.*

MARMADUKE, *raising his eyes and perceiving* ELDRED.

In any corner of this savage Waste,
Have you, good Peasant, seen a blind old Man?

ROBERT

I heard—

MORTIMER

O Heavens! you heard him—

ROBERT

As you know,
The first hours of last night were rough and stormy. [2013]
I was abroad—the search of a stray heifer
While yet the moon was up had led me far
Into the wildest part of this wild heath,
When hearing, as I thought, a sudden voice,
I stopped and listened, not without such fear
Upon me as the time and place might breed,
But thinking that my fancy had deceived me, [2016]
I turned away, when streight a second sound,
A human voice distinct, smote on my ear.
Thus guided, distant a few steps I found
An aged man and such as you describe. [2020]

MORTIMER

Alive? alive? did you not say alive?

ROBERT

I said that he was living.

MORTIMER

But where? how?
You heard—he called you to him? Of all men
The best and kindest!

ROBERT

On a ridge of rocks
A lonesome Chapel stands, deserted now. [2024]
The bell remains, which no one dares remove,
And when the stormy wind blows o'er the peak
It rings as if a human hand were there
To pull the cord.—I fancy he had heard it,
And it had led him towards the precipice [2029]

21–26 Wordsworth associates the bell rung by the stormy wind with Roslin Chapel in Sonnet V of *Yarrow Revisited* (*PW*, III, 266–267), though the guidebooks suggest no such folklore associated with the chapel. The supernatural music that lures a mortal to his death is a commonplace in ballads and folktales; the sound of a church bell in folklore, on the other hand, lures the lost away from danger, fairyland, the sea, and back to humanity and life.

ELDRED.

I heard——

MARMADUKE.

You heard him, where? when heard him?

ELDRED.

As you know,
The first hours of last night were rough with storm:
I had been out in search of a stray heifer;
Returning late, I heard a moaning sound;
Then, thinking that my fancy had deceived me,
I hurried on, when straight a second moan,
A human voice distinct, struck on my ear.
So guided, distant a few steps, I found
An aged Man, and such as you describe.

MARMADUKE.

You heard!—he called you to him? Of all men
The best and kindest!—but where is he? guide me,
That I may see him.

ELDRED.

On a ridge of rocks
A lonesome Chapel stands, deserted now:
The bell is left, which no one dares remove;
And, when the stormy wind blows o'er the peak,
It rings, as if a human hand were there
To pull the cord. I guess he must have heard it;
And it had led him towards the precipice,

To climb up to the spot whence the sound came,
Poor man!

MORTIMER

And he was very feeble?

ROBERT

His head was bare—
His staff was by his side; and near the brink
Of a small pool of water he was laid, [2033]
His face close to the water. As it seemed,
He had stooped down to drink and had remained
Without the strength to rise.

MORTIMER

Well, well, he lives. [2035]
Oh God! he lives! What said he?

ROBERT

He only spake to me of a dear daughter
Who, so he feared, would never see him more, [2038]
And of a stranger to him, one by whom
He had been sore misused.—But you are troubled:
Perhaps you are his son?

MORTIMER

Heaven knows
I did not think he had a living child.
—And whither did you carry him?

ROBERT

He was torn,
His head was bruised, and there was blood about him. [2045]

MORTIMER

That was no work of mine.

ROBERT

Nor mine, God knows.

MORTIMER

But had he strength to walk? I could have borne him
A thousand miles.

ROBERT

I am in poverty
And know how busy are the tongues of men.
My heart was willing, Sir, but I am one [2050]
Whose deeds will not stand by their own light,

To climb up to the spot whence the sound came;
But he had failed through weakness. From his hand
His staff dropped, and close upon the brink
Of a small pool of water he was laid,
As if he had stooped to drink, and so remained
Without the strength to rise.

MARMADUKE.

Well, well, he lives,
And all is safe: what said he?

ELDRED.

But few words:
He only spake to me of a dear Daughter,
Who, so he feared, would never see him more;
And of a Stranger to him, One by whom
He had been sore misused; but he forgave
The wrong and the wrong-doer. You are troubled—
Perhaps you are his son?

MARMADUKE.

The All-seeing knows,
I did not think he had a living Child.—
But whither did you carry him?

ELDRED.

He was torn,
His head was bruised, and there was blood about him——

MARMADUKE.

That was no work of mine.

ELDRED.

Nor was it mine.

MARMADUKE.

But had he strength to walk? I could have borne him
A thousand miles.

ELDRED.

I am in poverty,
And know how busy are the tongues of men;
My heart was willing, Sir, but I am one
Whose good deeds will not stand by their own light;

And though it smote me more than tongue can speak—
I left him.

MORTIMER

(*looks at him for some time*)

I believe that there are beings
For unknown ends permitted to put on
The shape of man, and thou art one of them.
But human things have pressed so hard on me—

ROBERT

My wife and children came into my mind— [2058]

MORTIMER

Oh monster! monster! there are three of us,
And we shall howl together.

[*After a pause, in a feeble voice.*

I am deserted
At my worst need: my crimes have brought a judgement

(*pointing to* ROBERT)

On this innocent man—where was it? where?

[*Dragging him along.*

ROBERT

'Tis needless, spare your violence. His daughter— [2063]

MORTIMER

Aye, is there not damnation in the word?
This old man *had* a daughter.

ROBERT

To the spot
I hurried back with her—oh, save me, Sir, [2066]
From such a journey—there was a black tree,
A single tree—she thought it was her father.
Oh, Sir! I would not see that hour again
For twenty lives. The day-light dawned, and now—

MORTIMER (*as if waking from a dream*)

What damning fiend has poisoned thee i'th'ear?

ROBERT

Nay, hear my tale, 'tis fit that you should hear it. [2071]
As we approached, a solitary crow
Rose from the spot—the daughter clapped her hands

---

68 Cf. *Hamlet*, I.v.63–64 ("in the porches of mine ears did pour / The leperous distilment") and IV.v.90 ("And wants not buzzers to infect his ear").

And, though it smote me more than words can tell,
I left him.

MARMADUKE.

I believe that there are phantoms,
That in the shape of man do cross our path
On evil instigation, to make sport
Of our distress—and thou art one of them!
But things substantial have so pressed on me——

ELDRED.

My wife and children came into my mind.

MARMADUKE.

Oh Monster! Monster! there are three of us,
And we shall howl together.
[*After a pause and in a feeble voice.*
I am deserted
At my worst need, my crimes have in a net
Pointing to ELDRED] Entangled this poor man.—Where was it? where? [*Dragging him along.*

ELDRED.

'Tis needless; spare your violence. His Daughter——

MARMADUKE.

Ay, in the word a thousand scorpions lodge:
This old man *had* a Daughter.

ELDRED.

To the spot
I hurried back with her.—O save me, Sir,
From such a journey!——there was a black tree,
A single tree; she thought it was her Father.—
Oh Sir, I would not see that hour again
For twenty lives. The daylight dawned, and now—
Nay; hear my tale, 'tis fit that you should hear it—
As we approached, a solitary crow
Rose from the spot;—the Daughter clapped her hands,

2063 'Tis] Tis *1842* 'Tis (*MSS. 3 and 4*), *1845–*
2065 man] Man *(MS. 4)*, *1842* man *(MS. 3)*, *1845–*

And then I heard a shriek so terrible
[MORTIMER *shrinks back against the scene.*
The very bird quivered upon the wing,
And had an earthquake followed instantly,
It could not more have moved me.

MORTIMER

Dead, dead, dead.

ROBERT (*after a pause*)

This business, Sir, seems to concern you nearly.
I'll lead you to the maiden whom I left
With her dead Father's body at my hut
A few steps hence.

MARGARET, *who had been standing for some time at a distance, comes forward.*

MARGARET

Nay, Robert, 'tis not fit
Two wretched beings, each so miserable,
Should come together. Poor unhappy man!

ROBERT

Thou dost forget thyself—I am confirmed,
And we must see the bottom of it. (*To* MORTIMER) Sir,
I said that I would lead you to his daughter.

MORTIMER

His daughter.—Yes, lead me to his daughter.

ROBERT

Perhaps 'twere fit I should go on before
That she may be prepared.

MORTIMER

Thou hast said well.
There will be need of preparation.
[ROBERT *goes off.*

[MARGARET *makes an effort as if to check* ROBERT—*then turns to* MORTIMER.

MARGARET

Sir!
Your limbs sink under you; shall I support you?

---

83 Cf. *Troilus and Cressida*, III.iii.314–315:

My mind is troubled, like a fountain stirr'd;
And I myself see not the bottom of it.

And then I heard a shriek so terrible
[MARMADUKE *shrinks back.*
The startled bird quivered upon the wing.

MARMADUKE.

Dead, dead!—

ELDRED (*after a pause*).

A dismal matter, Sir, for me,
And seems the like for you; if 'tis your wish,
I'll lead you to his Daughter; but 'twere best
That she should be prepared; I'll go before.

MARMADUKE.

There will be need of preparation.
[ELDRED *goes off.*

ELEANOR (*enters*).

Master!
Your limbs sink under you, shall I support you?

MORTIMER (*taking hold of her arm*)
Woman! I've lent my body to the service
Which now thou tak'st upon thee.—God forbid
That thou should'st ever meet a like occasion
With such a view as mine!—

MARGARET
Oh! why have I to do with things like these?
[*Exeunt.*

[Scene 3] SCENE *changes to the door of* ROBERT's *cottage—*
MATILDA *seated at the door in stupid grief—to her enter* ROBERT.

ROBERT
Your father, Lady, from a wilful hand
Has met unkindness, so indeed he told me
And you remember such was my report;
From what has just befallen me I have cause
To fear he has been murdered.

MATILDA
He is dead.
Why comest thou to me with a tale like this?

ROBERT
A wicked man should answer for his crimes.

MATILDA
Thou see'st me, what I am—

ROBERT
It was most heinous,
And doth call out for vengeance.

MATILDA
Do not add,
I prithee, to the harm thou'st done already.

ROBERT
Hereafter you will thank me for this service.
I met a man, who, from the plainest proofs
Of interfering Heaven, I have no doubt,
Laid hands upon your Father—fit it were
You should prepare to meet him.—
But see the murderer guided by my wife.

MATILDA
Oh, help me to my father, I have nothing
To do with him—

MARMADUKE (*taking her arm*).

Woman, I've lent my body to the service
Which now thou tak'st upon thee. God forbid
That thou shouldst ever meet a like occasion
With such a purpose in thine heart as mine was.

ELEANOR.

Oh, why have I to do with things like these?

[*Exeunt.*

SCENE *changes to the door of* ELDRED'S *cottage*—IDONEA *seated*—*enter* ELDRED.

ELDRED.

Your Father, Lady, from a wilful hand
Has met unkindness; so indeed he told me,
And you remember such was my report:
From what has just befallen me I have cause
To fear the very worst.

IDONEA.

My Father is dead;
Why dost thou come to me with words like these?

ELDRED.

A wicked Man should answer for his crimes.

IDONEA.

Thou seest me what I am.

ELDRED.

It was most heinous,
And doth call out for vengeance.

IDONEA.

Do not add,
I prithee, to the harm thou'st done already.

ELDRED.

Hereafter you will thank me for this service.
Hard by, a Man I met, who, from plain proofs
Of interfering Heaven, I have no doubt,
Laid hands upon your Father. Fit it were
You should prepare to meet him.

IDONEA.

I have nothing
To do with others; help me to my Father—

ROBERT

You must speak to him.

[MATILDA *turns her head and sees* MORTIMER *who enters leaning upon* MARGARET—MATILDA *throws herself upon his neck——after some time*:

MATILDA

In joy I met thee: 'tis but a few hours—
And now we meet again.—Nay, shake not so
—In such a wilderness—

MORTIMER

To see no thing,
No, not the moon in heaven—

MATILDA

And perish so— [2107]

MORTIMER

Without a dog to howl for him—

MATILDA

Oh, think not of it,
But enter there and see him, how he sleeps
Tranquil as he had died in his own bed— [2110]

MORTIMER

Tranquil—why not?

MATILDA

Oh, Peace!

MORTIMER

He is at peace,
His body is at rest—there was a plot, [2112]
A damned plot against the soul of man:
'Tis baffled—I have baffled it.

MATILDA

Alas!
You too have need of comfort.

MORTIMER

I remember,
'Twas the first riddle that employed my fancy,
To hunt out reasons why the wisest thing
That the earth owns should never chuse to die [2120]
But some one must be near to count his groans.—
The wounded deer retires to solitude—

[*She turns and sees* MARMADUKE *leaning on* ELEANOR—*throws herself upon his neck, and after some time,*

In joy I met thee, but a few hours past;
And thus we meet again; one human stay
Is left me still in thee. Nay, shake not so.

MARMADUKE.

In such a wilderness—to see no thing,
No, not the pitying moon!

IDONEA.

And perish so.

MARMADUKE.

Without a dog to moan for him.

IDONEA.

Think not of it,
But enter there and see him how he sleeps,
Tranquil as he had died in his own bed.

MARMADUKE.

Tranquil—why not?

IDONEA.

Oh, peace!

MARMADUKE.

He is at peace;
His body is at rest: there was a plot,
A hideous plot, against the soul of man:
It took effect—and yet I baffled it,
In *some* degree.

IDONEA.

Between us stood, I thought,
A cup of consolation, filled from Heaven
For both our needs; must I, and in thy presence,
Alone partake of it?—Beloved Marmaduke!

MARMADUKE.

Give me a reason why the wisest thing
That the earth owns shall never choose to die,
But some one must be near to count his groans.
The wounded deer retires to solitude,

And dies in solitude—all things but man,
All die in solitude—an awful lesson:
There is much wisdom in it—
[MORTIMER *leaves* MATILDA *and goes towards the cottage.*
(*In going*) The fault's not mine—
If she had never lived I had not done it.

MATILDA

Alas, the thought
Of such a cruel death has overwhelmed him.

(*As* MORTIMER *enters the cottage*)

I will go too.

ROBERT

Lady, you will do well.
He has been dead and silent many hours.
If you should hear a groan or from his side
He should uplift his hand—that would be [evidence].

MARGARET

Fie, Robert, fie!

MORTIMER (*coming from the cottage*)

(*To himself*) The dead have but one face.
[*Goes up to* MATILDA.
And such a man—so mild and unoffending—
By obvious signal, to the world's protection
Solemnly dedicated—to decoy him—
[ROBERT *comes forward, listening eagerly.*

MATILDA

Oh! had you seen him living!—he had a face—
There's not a soul—

41b MH inserted "will" with a caret in 1799.

42–44 Compare *Richard III*, I.ii.55–61:

> O! gentlemen; see, see! dead Henry's wounds
> Open their congeal'd mouths and bleed afresh.
> Blush, blush, thou lump of foul deformity,
> For 'tis thy presence that exhales this blood
> From cold and empty veins, where no blood dwells:
> Thy deed, inhuman and unnatural,
> Provokes this deluge most unnatural.

The motif is a commonplace in folklore.

44 The last word was miswritten "evident."

And dies in solitude: all things but man,
All die in solitude. [*Moving towards the cottage door.*
Mysterious God,
If she had never lived I had not done it!—

IDONEA.

Alas, the thought of such a cruel death
Has overwhelmed him.—I must follow.

ELDRED.

Lady!
You will do well! (*she goes*) unjust suspicion may
Cleave to this Stranger: if, upon his entering,
The dead Man heave a groan, or from his side
Uplift his hand—that would be evidence.

ELEANOR.

Shame! Eldred, shame!

MARMADUKE (*both returning*).

The dead have but one face. (*to himself*)
And such a Man—so meek and unoffending—
Helpless and harmless as a babe: a Man,
By obvious signal to the world's protection,
Solemnly dedicated—to decoy him!—

IDONEA.

Oh, had you seen him living!—

MORTIMER

Now mark this world of ours:
A man may be a murderer and his hand
Shall tell no tales, nay, the first brook he meets
Shall wash it clean.
A man may be the father's murderer
And to the daughter the most precious thing
The world contains.—Matilda, at this moment
I feel a most unusual fondness for thee.
Thou must be wise as I am, thou must know
What human nature is, decoyed, betrayed—
I have the proofs.

MATILDA

Oh! miserable father! [2142]
Thou did'st command to bless all mankind,
Nor to this moment have I ever wished
Evil to any living thing—but hear me,
Hear me, ye Heavens! (*kneeling*) may vengeance haunt the fiend
For this most cruel murder—let him live [2147]
And move in terror of the elements—
The thunder send him on his knees to prayer
In the open streets, and let him think he sees,
If e'er he entereth the house of prayer,
The roof self-moved, unsettle o'er his head—
And let him stepping into bed at nights
Point to his wife the blood-drops on his pillow! [2154]

MORTIMER

Heaven is my witness that my heart has joined thee.

MATILDA (*leaning on* MORTIMER)

Left to the mercy of that savage man,
How could he call on his beloved child!

MORTIMER

Aye, come to me and weep. (*He kisses her*)
(*To* ROBERT) Yes, look, my friend:
The devils at such sights clap their hands. [2160]

[ROBERT *retires into the cottage alarmed.*

MATILDA

Thy limbs are torn, thy face is pale and hagard—
Hast thou pursued the monster?

52–53 Compare *Macbeth*, II.ii.68: "A little water clears us of this deed."

MARMADUKE.

I (so filled
With horror is this world) am unto thee
The thing most precious, that it now contains:
Therefore through me alone must be revealed
By whom thy Parent was destroyed, Idonea!
I have the proofs!—

IDONEA.

O miserable Father!
Thou didst command me to bless all mankind;
Nor to this moment, have I ever wished
Evil to any living thing; but hear me,
Hear me, ye Heavens!—(*kneeling*)—may vengeance haunt the fiend
For this most cruel murder: let him live
And move in terror of the elements;
The thunder send him on his knees to prayer
In the open streets, and let him think he sees,
If e'er he entereth the house of God,
The roof, self-moved, unsettling o'er his head;
And let him, when he would lie down at night,
Point to his wife the blood-drops on his pillow!

MARMADUKE.

My voice was silent, but my heart hath joined thee.

IDONEA (*leaning on* MARMADUKE).

Left to the mercy of that savage Man!
How could he call upon his Child!—O Friend!
(*Turns to* MARMADUKE.)
My faithful true and only Comforter.

MARMADUKE.

Ay, come to me and weep. (*He kisses her.*)
(*To* ELDRED) Yes, Varlet, look,
The devils at such sights do clap their hands.
[ELDRED *retires alarmed.*

IDONEA.

Thy vest is torn, thy cheek is deadly pale;
Hast thou pursued the monster?

2160 hands.] hands *1842* hands. *(MSS. 3 and 4)*, *1845–*

MORTIMER

Aye, and found him,
And he must perish.

MATILDA

Leave him to the pangs
Of his own breast.

MORTIMER

He must be put to death,
And for thy sake, for he will haunt thy bed,
Thy prayers, thy waking and thy sleeping thoughts.
—Oh, would—that thou had'st perished in the flames—

MATILDA

Art thou not here the friend of all the helpless?

MORTIMER

The feeble sought me once, and my protection
Availed against the mighty. Never more [2166]
Shall any blessings wait on deed of mine.

MATILDA

Those words, I could make mockery of them, but
Your voice is dreadful.—Oh, my only friend,
What thoughts are these? [*Taking hold of his arm.*
Here is no malady.

MORTIMER

Here is a malady (*striking his breast and forehead*)—
And here, and here—
A mortal malady.

MATILDA

Heavens!

MORTIMER

I am curst,
All nature curses me and in my heart [2175]
Thy curse is fixed.

MATILDA (*forcing a smile*)

Come, come, this desperate effort
To rid my spirit of its present sorrow,
Indeed, it is ill-judged.

MORTIMER

Look on my face.

MATILDA

Oh! when has this affliction visited thee?

MARMADUKE.

I have found him.—
Oh! would that thou hadst perished in the flames!

IDONEA.

Here art thou, then can I be desolate?—

MARMADUKE.

There was a time, when this protecting hand
Availed against the mighty; never more
Shall blessings wait upon a deed of mine.

IDONEA.

Wild words for me to hear, for me, an orphan,
Committed to thy guardianship by Heaven;
And, if thou hast forgiven me, let me hope,
In this deep sorrow, trust, that I am thine
For closer care;—here, is no malady. [*Taking his arm.*

MARMADUKE.

There, *is* a malady—
(*Striking his heart and forehead*) And here, and here,
A mortal malady.—I am accurst:
All nature curses me, and in my heart
Thy curse is fixed; the truth must be laid bare.

MORTIMER

I am the murderer of thy father.
[MATILDA *runs off into the cottage.*
(*Alone*) Three words have such a power! This mighty burden
All off at once! 'Tis done, and so done too,
That I have cased her heart in adamant.
This little scrip when first I found it here—
I sunk ten thousand fathoms into hell.
I was a coward then—but now am schooled
To firmer purposes. There doth not lie
Within the compass of a mortal thought
A deed that I would shrink from—and I can endure.
If I had done it with a mind resolved,
There had been something in the deed
To give me strength to bear the recollection,
But as it is, this scrip which would not cause
The little finger of a child to ache
Doth lie upon my bosom with a load
A mountain could not equal.

Enter MATILDA *from the cottage dragging* ROBERT.

ROBERT

Already I've been forced, an innocent man,
For many moons to make my bed with toads;
But it is come at last and I must die.

MATILDA

(*repeating* ROBERT's *former words*)
"Your father has been murdered" (*turning to* ROBERT)—
By thy hands—

ROBERT

And would you use me thus?

MARGARET

You fear too much.
He is a man too wretched far
To be your enemy.

MATILDA (*to* ROBERT)

Thou hast prevailed
Upon his gentle nature.

---

99 The line first read "I am thy father's murderer" (making l. 100 more intelligible), but appears to have been revised by DW in 1799.

105 Compare *Macbeth*, IV.ii.15: "I pray you, school yourself."

123 Compare *Macbeth*, II.iii.102–103: "The wine of life is drawn, and the mere lees / Is left . . ."

It must be told, and borne. I am the man,
(Abused, betrayed, but how it matters not)
Presumptuous above all that ever breathed,
Who, casting as I thought a guilty Person
Upon Heaven's righteous judgment, did become
An instrument of Fiends. Through me, through me,
Thy Father perished.

IDONEA.

Perished—by what mischance?

MORTIMER (*to* ROBERT, *stepping forward*)

If the dregs
Of such a life as thine be worth these tears,
Go dry them up—thou shalt not die for this.

[*Turns to* MATILDA—*presents her a letter.*

MATILDA (*reads.*)

"Be not surprized if you hear that some signal judgment has befallen the man who calls himself your father—he is now with me, as his signature will shew—suspend your judgement till you see me—
Herbert
Mortimer"

(MORTIMER *points*)

The writing yours—that signature my father's. [2193]
You have then seen my father—what of that?
It was not kind! you should have told me of it—

MORTIMER

(*his hand pointing to his heart*)

O, that that eye of thine were present here!
Now will I tell thee how I dealt with him—
Into a foaming torrent—

MATILDA

He was found,
My father, he was found upon the heath.

MORTIMER

If a man have a tongue to tell these things,
A heart that cannot suffer and a soul
That cannot fear—what has he lost? These charms,
These horrid charms of thought—

MATILDA

The convent, Mortimer—

MORTIMER

That convent was Mounteagle Castle.—Thither [2197]
I led him on that very night, resolved
That he should wait thy coming till the day
Of resurrection.—Rivers—

MATILDA

Rivers! oh!
The name has terror in it.

MARMADUKE.

Belovèd!—if I dared, so would I call thee—
Conflict must cease, and, in thy frozen heart,
The extremes of suffering meet in absolute peace.
[*He gives her a letter.*

IDONEA (*reads*).

"Be not surprised if you hear that some signal judgment has befallen the man who calls himself your father; he is now with me, as his signature will shew: abstain from conjecture till you see me.

"HERBERT.
"MARMADUKE."

The writing Oswald's; the signature my Father's:
(*Looks steadily at the paper*) And here is yours,—or do my
eyes deceive me?
You have then seen my Father?

MARMADUKE.

He has leaned
Upon this arm.

IDONEA.

You led him towards the Convent?

MARMADUKE.

That Convent was Stone-Arthur Castle. Thither
We were his guides. I on that night resolved
That he should wait thy coming till the day
Of resurrection.

IDONEA.

Miserable Woman,
Too quickly moved, too easily giving way,
I put denial on thy suit, and hence,
With the disastrous issue of last night,
Thy perturbation, and these frantic words.
Be calm, I pray thee!

MARMADUKE.

Oswald——

IDONEA.

Name him not.

2187 "Be] 'Be *1845–*
2191 "Herbert] 'Herbert *1845–*
2192 "MARMADUKE."] 'MARMADUKE.' *1845–*

Enter female Beggar.

BEGGAR

Mercy—mercy—
And he is dead! this heath, how shall I cross it?
By night, by day—never shall [I] be able [2207]
To travel half a mile alone.—Good Lady,
Forgive me—Heaven forgive me—had I thought
It would have come to this—

MATILDA

This is most strange.

BEGGAR

(*to* MATILDA *and pointing to* MORTIMER)
This innocent gentleman.—Sweet Heavens! I told him [2211]
Such tales of your dead father—God is my judge
I thought there was no harm, but that bad man,
He bribed me with his gold and looked so terrible,
Mercy, I said I know not what—oh! pity me—
I said, sweet lady! you were not his daughter. [2216]

ROBERT

Peace! woman, peace!

BEGGAR (*to* ROBERT)

I tell you, I am haunted.
Three times today I wished I were struck blind,
And then I would have prayed—and had no voice.

MATILDA

Was it my father? No, no, no, for he [2220]
Was meek, and patient, feeble, old and blind,
Helpless, and loved me dearer far than life.
—But hear me.—For one question I have a voice
That will sustain me.—Did you murder him? [2224]

MORTIMER

No, no, not murder him.—But knowest thou this?

MATILDA

That belt—the first gift of my love.
—It is the scrip that held my father's food.

MORTIMER

I led him to the middle of this heath.
I left him without food and so he died.

148 The "I" was left out by the copyist.

Enter female Beggar.

BEGGAR.

And he is dead!—that Moor—how shall I cross it?
By night, by day, never shall I be able
To travel half a mile alone.—Good Lady!
Forgive me!—Saints forgive me. Had I thought
It would have come to this!—

IDONEA.

What brings you hither? speak!

BEGGAR (*pointing to* MARMADUKE).

This innocent Gentleman. Sweet heavens! I told him
Such tales of your dead Father!—God is my judge,
I thought there was no harm: but that bad Man,
He bribed me with his gold, and looked so fierce.
Mercy! I said I know not what—oh pity me—
I said, sweet Lady, you were not his Daughter—
Pity me, I am haunted;—thrice this day
My conscience made me wish to be struck blind;
And then I would have prayed, and had no voice.

IDONEA (*to* MARMADUKE).

Was it my Father?—no, no, no, for he
Was meek and patient, feeble, old and blind,
Helpless, and loved me dearer than his life.
—But hear me. For *one* question, I have a heart
That will sustain me. Did you murder him?

MARMADUKE.

No, not by stroke of arm. But learn the process:
Proof after proof was pressed upon me; guilt
Made evident, as seemed, by blacker guilt,
Whose impious folds enwrapped even thee; and truth
And innocence, embodied in his looks,
His words and tones and gestures, did but serve
With me to aggravate his crimes, and heaped
Ruin upon the cause for which they pleaded.
Then pity crossed the path of my resolve:
Confounded, I looked up to Heaven, and cast,
Idonea! thy blind Father, on the Ordeal
Of the bleak Waste—left him—and so he died!—

[MATILDA *sinks senseless on the ground*—ROBERT, MARGARET *and the* BEGGAR *crowd round her and during the course of the following speech they bear her into the cottage.*

Why may we speak these things and do no more?
Why should a thrust of the arm have such a power [2238]
And things like these be heard in vain?
—She is not dead.—Why, if I loved this woman,
I would take care she never woke again.
—But she will wake and she will weep for me
And say no blame was mine—and so, poor fool, [2243]
Will waste her curses on another name;
And this will be when I am in my grave.
[*He walks about with a quick step.*
I'll prove it that I murdered him—I'll prove it
Before the dullest court in Christendom.

Enter ROBERT *from the cottage.*

ROBERT

Do, Sir, come in and see what may be done
To bring her to herself.—If she should die,
What will become of us?

MORTIMER

Hark'ee my friend,
That woman was to have been my wife.
(*Laughs hysterically*) Ha! ha!
(*Laying his hand on* ROBERT)
Not yet, not yet.—Thy coming is well timed.
There is a service to be done for me—
Thou must conduct me hence. The executioner
Must do the business.

ROBERT

The old man died of cold—
You are not master of the elements.
It was a bitter night—I was half-frozen.

MORTIMER (*in a commanding tone*)

Did'st hear me, man? The Baron of St. Clair
Lives in this district—lead me to his court.

ROBERT

Good Master! there was not a wound about him
That would have killed a mouse.

[IDONEA *sinks senseless;* Beggar, ELEANOR, *&c., crowd round, and bear her off.*

Why may we speak these things, and do no more;
Why should a thrust of the arm have such a power,
And words that tell these things be heard in vain?
She is not dead. Why!—if I loved this Woman,
I would take care she never woke again;
But she WILL wake, and she will weep for me,
And say, no blame was mine—and so, poor fool,
Will waste her curses on another name.

[*He walks about distractedly.*

MORTIMER

What's he to me?
[*Drags* Robert *along.*

ROBERT

Good Sir! be merciful.—If I do this,
I ne'er shall sleep in quiet.

MORTIMER

There is something
That must be cleared away—

ROBERT

How, Sir?

MORTIMER

That staff
Which bars the road before me there.—'Tis there,
'Tis there breast-high and will not let me pass—

ROBERT

Good Sir! be calm.

MORTIMER

Bestir thee—let's begone;
She will be waking soon.—Dost hear me, man?
(*Dragging him along*)
Howl, howl, poor dog! Thou'lt never find him more;
Draggled with storm and wet, howl, howl amain,
But not in my ears—I was not the death of thee.
What dost thou there, friend? Get thee out of the way,
We must not trouble it—

ROBERT

Be patient, Sir—

MORTIMER

What art thou made of, man? I would cleave a stone.

ROBERT

Good Sir! The body must be borne to Church.
This is a lonely place—but from the convent
The Holy friars will bring us needful aid.

MORTIMER

Right, fellow! Thou sayest well.
We never shall get thither—

---

203 Cf. *King Lear*, V.iii.259: "Howl, howl, howl! . . ."

BEGGAR

(*who had entered a little before from the cottage*)

He is crazed,
Poor Gentleman! and *I* have wrought this evil.
The little children from the cottages
Will be his friends—he will be blessed and pitied.
——What will become of me?—

MORTIMER (*to* ROBERT)

Take heed, good friend, that she recovers not.
Thou wilt redeem the worst of all the crimes
Thou hast to answer for—

Enter RIVERS—*he looks at* MORTIMER *unobserved by him.*

Buzz, buzz, ye fools!
That is no substance that ye settle on—
Away! away!

ROBERT (*to himself*)

—Would that some help were nigh.

RIVERS (*to himself*)

Strong to destroy—strong also to build up. [2245]

BEGGAR (*observing* RIVERS)

Look there!—oh save me from him.

[MORTIMER *and* RIVERS *mutually fasten their eyes on each other for some time.*

MORTIMER

I am a man again.

RIVERS

Nay, something more—(*Pointing to* ROBERT's *cottage*)
Dead?

MORTIMER

Quiet.

RIVERS

As his best friends could wish.
And you?

MORTIMER

Almost as quiet.

---

220 Cf. *Hamlet*, II.ii.421: "Buzz, buzz!"

224–225 Cf. *Macbeth*, I.vii.49–51: "When you durst do it then you were a man; / And, to be more than what you were, you would / Be so much more the man."

Enter OSWALD.

OSWALD (*to himself*).

Strong to o'erturn, strong also to build up.

[*To* MARMADUKE.

RIVERS (*with great pride*)

So I prophesied.
We are then friends—

MORTIMER

I am the friend of all men.

RIVERS

Of me especially—

MORTIMER

Why, yes!

RIVERS

A pledge—

MORTIMER

Here is my hand.—The hue of a pure lily,
A Lady hand—none of your crimson spots:
Not the less welcome—eh?

RIVERS

Most noble;
The starts and sallies of our last encounter— [2246]

MORTIMER

Mere foolish freaks!—

RIVERS

Bravo!— The vessel's cleared—
That pestilential weight of heaven knows what,
Those bundles packed some thousand years ago,
All plunged into the sea.

MORTIMER

Even so.

RIVERS

And you are happy?

MORTIMER

Never so happy.

RIVERS

Hum!— Stay, what's your age?

MORTIMER

Just three and twenty summers.

---

230 Cf. *Macbeth*, V.i.34: "Yet here's a spot."

The starts and sallies of our last encounter 2246
Were natural enough; but that, I trust,
Is all gone by. You have cast off the chains
That fettered your nobility of mind—
Delivered heart and head!

RIVERS

And his? (*Pointing to the cottage*)

MORTIMER

Sixty,
A few moons more or less.

RIVERS

Let us to Syria;
This is a paltry field for enterprize— [2251]

MORTIMER

Aye—what shall we do next?

RIVERS

Sickly and blind—

MORTIMER

Drugged, betrayed and starved!

RIVERS

Devils!

MORTIMER

You see I am an apt proficient—

RIVERS

Hell—

MORTIMER

Nay, here is another face hard by. [2256]
Let's in and take a peep at both together:
'Twill be a comment of your morality.

[[*Drawing*] Rivers *towards the cottage.*

RIVERS

Beyond my expectation—

MORTIMER

(*when he comes to the door stops short*)

There are men
Who with bare hand would have plucked out thy heart [2261]
And flung it to the dogs.—But I forgive thee.

[*Confused noises are heard with uproar.*

VOICES

—Hola.—There! there! Huzza!

Lacy, Lennox, Wallace, Norwood *rush in, the* Beggar *and* Wilfred *with them.*

246/247 "Drawing" is supplied from MS. 3.

Let us to Palestine;
This is a paltry field for enterprise.

MARMADUKE.

Ay, what shall we encounter next? This issue—
'Twas nothing more than darkness deepening darkness,
And weakness crowned with the impotence of death!—
Your pupil is, you see, an apt proficient. (*ironically*).
Start not!—Here is another face hard by;
Come, let us take a peep at both together,
And, with a voice at which the dead will quake,
Resound the praise of your morality—
Of this too much.

[*Drawing* OSWALD *towards the Cottage—stops short at the door.*

Men are there, millions, Oswald,
Who with bare hands would have plucked out thy heart
And flung it to the dogs: but I am raised
Above, or sunk below, all further sense
Of provocation. Leave me, with the weight
Of that old Man's forgiveness on thy heart,
Pressing as heavily as it doth on mine.
Coward I have been; know, there lies not now
Within the compass of a mortal thought,
A deed that I would shrink from;—but to endure,
That is my destiny. May it be thine:
Thy office, thy ambition, be henceforth
To feed remorse, to welcome every sting
Of penitential anguish, yea with tears.
When seas and continents shall lie between us—
The wider space the better—we may find
In such a course fit links of sympathy,
An incommunicable rivalship
Maintained, for peaceful ends beyond our view.

[*Confused voices—several of the band enter—rush upon* OSWALD *and seize him.*

ONE OF THE BAND

I would have followed him
Even to the jaws of hell.
[*They rush forwards to seize* Rivers.

RIVERS (*surrounded by them*)

Ha! is it so?

SEVERAL VOICES

Dispatch him—

RIVERS

If I pass beneath a rock [2282]
And shout, and with the echo of my voice
Bring down a heap of rubbish and it crushes me,
I die without dishonour.—Famished!
[*Smiles exultingly, his eyes fixed upon* Mortimer.
A fool and Coward blended to my wish. [2286]

A VOICE

Merciless traitor! [*They drag him off.*

Matilda *rushes out towards* Mortimer, *followed by* Robert.

MATILDA

It is a strong disease— Oh, save him, save him—

Enter several friars who crowd round Matilda *and conceal her from the audience.*

WALLACE

'Tis done.

ANOTHER OF THE BAND (*reentering*)

The merciless traitor!

WILFRED (*approaching* Mortimer)

My poor Master!

MORTIMER

Oh! my good Wilfred! [*He turns to* Lacy.
Lacy! on these borders
Many there are who will not want cause [2292]
To weep that I am gone.

---

261 Cf. *Macbeth*, V.vii.32: "Turn, hell-hound, turn!"

ONE OF THEM.

I would have dogged him to the jaws of hell—

OSWALD.

Ha! is it so!—That vagrant Hag!—this comes
Of having left a thing like her alive! [*Aside.*

SEVERAL VOICES.

Despatch him!

OSWALD.

If I pass beneath a rock
And shout, and, with the echo of my voice,
Bring down a heap of rubbish, and it crush me,
I die without dishonour. Famished, starved,
A Fool and Coward blended to my wish!
[*Smiles scornfully and exultingly at* MARMADUKE.

WALLACE.

'Tis done! (*stabs him.*)

ANOTHER OF THE BAND.

The ruthless Traitor!

MARMADUKE.

A rash deed!—
With that reproof I do resign a station
Of which I have been proud.

WILFRED (*approaching* MARMADUKE).

O my poor Master!

MARMADUKE.

Discerning Monitor, my faithful Wilfred,
Why art thou here? [*Turning to* WALLACE.
Wallace, upon these Borders,
Many there be whose eyes will not want cause
To weep that I am gone. Brothers in arms!

2287 Traitor] traitor *1849*

NORWOOD (*returning*)
The hell-hound—

LACY
Peace.

MORTIMER
Raise on this lonely Heath a monument [2294]
That may record my story for warning—

SEVERAL OF THE BAND (*eagerly*)
Captain!

MORTIMER
No prayers, no tears, but hear my doom in silence!
I will go forth a wanderer on the earth,
A shadowy thing, and as I wander on
No human ear shall ever hear my voice,
No human dwelling ever give me food [2315]
Or sleep or rest, and all the uncertain way
Shall be as darkness to me, as a waste
Unnamed by man! and I will wander on
Living by mere intensity of thought,
A thing by pain and thought compelled to live, [2319]
Yet loathing life, till heaven in mercy strike me
With blank forgetfulness—that I may die.

262–263 The idea of a monument may have been inspired by the Countess's Pillar on the Appleby road, or by William Gilpin's description of the memorial stone dedicated to Edward I: "The English borderers long revered the memory of a prince, who had so often chastised an enemy [the Scots], they hated: and in gratitude reared a pillar to his name; which still testifies the spot, on which he died. It stands rather on the edge of the marsh, and bears [a] simple inscription" (*Observations . . . on . . . Cumberland, and Westmoreland*, II, 113–114).

Raise on that dreary Waste a monument
That may record my story: nor let words—
Few must they be, and delicate in their touch
As light itself—be there withheld from Her
Who, through most wicked arts, was made an orphan
By One who would have died a thousand times,
To shield her from a moment's harm. To you,
Wallace and Wilfred, I commend the Lady,
By lowly nature reared, as if to make her
In all things worthier of that noble birth,
Whose long-suspended rights are now on the eve
Of restoration: with your tenderest care
Watch over her, I pray—sustain her——

SEVERAL OF THE BAND (*eagerly*).

Captain!

MARMADUKE.

No more of that; in silence hear my doom:
A hermitage has furnished fit relief
To some offenders; other penitents,
Less patient in their wretchedness, have fallen,
Like the old Roman, on their own sword's point.
They had their choice: a wanderer *must I* go,
The Spectre of that innocent Man, my guide.
No human ear shall ever hear me speak;
No human dwelling ever give me food,
Or sleep, or rest: but, over waste and wild,
In search of nothing, that this earth can give,
But expiation, will I wander on—
A Man by pain and thought compelled to live,
Yet loathing life—till anger is appeased
In Heaven, and Mercy gives me leave to die.

1795–6.

END OF FIFTH ACT.

Transcriptions

MS. 1, the Rough Notebook, With Facing Photographs

The Rough Notebook for *The Borderers*, DC MS. 12, has marbled cardboard covers, 8 by 6¼ inches, bound with a 2-inch strip of brown leather. The notebook comprises the remains of sixteen stitched gatherings of white laid paper folded in quarto and gathered in pairs to make gatherings of eight leaves. Each leaf is cut to 20.2 by 15.9 centimeters. Chain lines, of which there are eight to a leaf, are horizontal, 1 inch (2.5 centimeters) apart. The watermark consists of an encircled figure of Britannia surmounted by a large crown; the countermark consists of the initials G R surmounted by a less elaborate crown. Of the 124 leaves that originally constituted the notebook, all but 32 have been cut out, including the whole of the second half of the notebook (gatherings 9–16) and most of the first two gatherings. In numbering the leaves of the notebook, I have begun the sequence with the third leaf of the first gathering, as the first leaf of the first gathering and the last leaf of the last gathering were cut short (to 3.5 centimeters) in manufacture and glued to the boards, and the next leaf glued on top to form the "inside front cover" and "inside back cover" endpapers, respectively. As they survive, the first and second gatherings are not complete, but I have assumed that they were so originally, and have therefore allotted numbers to the postulated missing leaves.

Contents

(* denotes an entry postulated as belonging to the *Ur-Borderers* phase; see Introduction, pp. 7–15)

43^r–48^v	*Churchyard Scene
48^v–49^v	*Matilda at the Cottage Door Scene
49^v	*fragment connected with Ferdinand and Robert, Draft B
50^r–50^v	*Ferdinand and Robert, Draft A
51^r–51^v	*Ferdinand and Robert, Draft B (see also 49^v)
51^v	*Ferdinand soliloquy fragment, "These things," Draft B
52^r–52^v	*Ferdinand soliloquy draft
52^r	*Ferdinand soliloquy fragment, "These things," Draft A
53^r	*Ferdinand soliloquy fragment, "What after years"
	*Ferdinand soliloquy verse fragment, "Is there no hope"
53^r–54^v	*Margaret and Peasant Scene
55^r	bibliographical notes on Druids
55^v–57^v	*Edge of a Heath Scene
58–124	stubs (writing traces)
inside back cover	rough notes for *The Borderers*

Line numbers referring to the reading texts are placed in the left-hand margins of the transcriptions. When there is no reading text, act, scene, and line numbers referring to the early version are bracketed above the transcriptions.

[Inside front cover]

it is fit he should [?have ?recourse] to art
being so helpless:
   You shall have a will in you to haste the [?purpose]
[?hurdle] of your [?own ?going]

Irritat mulcet falsis terroribus implet

Calculations of various sorts visible in the photographs, such as "apples 2[d]—" here, are omitted from the transcriptions, as are penciled page numbers and line numbers, which are of recent origin. The Latin inscription, "He stirs up, he soothes, he fills with false fears," could be an epigraph summing up Rivers's behavior, especially in II.iii, to which the other lines here may refer. Facing the inside front cover, the first surviving leaf of the notebook, 14[r], contains lines that may also be connected with II.iii (Rivers's soliloquy, 220–241), thus suggesting that both entries may have been made after the intervening leaves were cut out. Seven stubs from the missing leaves survive. Nothing is visible on the first three; at the top of the fourth stub (9[r]) the beginning of one word, "Def," can be seen. On the fifth stub (10[r]) the beginnings of fifteen lines of prose in DW's hand are visible: "con / rela / of s / Ni / d / re / of / a / a / of / -ce / / a / la / ha / is"; on the verso eleven line endings can be seen: "ns / [?] / his / [?bro-] / of / im / int / / [?d] / [?any] / [?] / tion." The only other word partially visible on these stubs is at the bottom of 11[r]: "cotta"—presumably the beginning of "cottage" or "cottager."

Considerations better
Having once meditated upon doing it
The deed will thenceforward be putrefied

10

18.4
1..6
19..10

18-4
1 6

Memb: 4. Subs 1. Part 3. Sect 2. Them
young lasses are never better pleased, than
when as upon an Holiday after Evensong
they may meet their sweethearts, and dance
about a maypole, or in a town-green
under a shady elm. Nothing so familiar
in France as for citizens wives and maids
to dance a round in the streets, and often
too for want of better ~~music~~ instruments
to make good music of their own voices,
and dance after it. Yea many times this
love will make old men and women that
have more toes than teeth dance, —
"John come kiss me now", mask and mum;
For Comus and Hymen love masks,
and all such merriments above measure,
will allow men to put on Womens apparel,
in some cases, and promiscuously to dance
young and old rich and poor, generous
and base, of all sorts.—

[14^r]

Confident in Virtue
Having once meditated upon doing it
The deed will thenceforward be justified

[?]
Memb: 4.th Subs 1: part 3. Sect 2. The
young lasses are never better pleased, than
when as upon an Holiday after Even-song
they may meet their sweethearts, and dance
about a maypole, or in as town-greens
under a shady elm. Nothing so familiar
in {F france as for citizens wives and maids
to dance a round in the streets, and often
two for want of better ~~music~~ instruments
to make good music of their own voices
and dance after it. Yea many times this
love will make old men and women that
have more toes than teeth dance.——
"John come kiss me now", mask and mum;
For {C comus and Hymen love masks,
and all such merriments abo{ve ut measure,
will allow men to put on Women's apparel
in some cases, and promiscuously to dance
young and old, rich and poor, generous
and base, of all sorts.—

The lines at the top of the page may be connected with Rivers's soliloquy, II.iii.220–241. The bottom of the page contains an extract from a historical description in an unidentified hand.

3d act
heard at the inn where she had slept
Matilda having requested her con[ductor]
her father that he was gone to the convent
[illegible] had slept proceeds after him goes on
comes to a church yard — meets a pilgrim
whom she discovers to be her mother
Her joy at the thought of meeting
her father Danby meets Matilda
& her mother to whom as a friend
he relates the good fortune soon after
parting with her in this way he meets
with Ferdinand understands from him that
he has put Herbert to death he informs
him that he had discovered Matilda with
her mother. Ferdinand enraged. Danby to
drive Ferdinand to despair informs him that
he had invented these things. Ferdinand re-
solves to go back to see if Herbert
may yet be saved.

[14v]

3rd Act

heard at the inn where she had left
Matilda having executed her commission
her father that he was gone to the convent where
they had slept proceeds after him goes on
comes to a church yard—meets a pilgrim
whom she discovers to be her mother
Her joy at the thought of meeting
her father Danby meets Matilda
& her mother to whom as a friend
her
she relates [?she] } good fortune, soon after
parting with her in this way he meets
with Ferdinand understands from him that
he has put Herbert to death, then informs
him that he had discovered Matilda with
Danby
her mother. Ferdinand enraged. { [?hastes] to
drive Ferdinand to despair informs him that
he had invented these things. Ferdinand re-
solves to go back to see if Herbert [?]
may yet be saved.

The hand is DW's. Incidents equivalent to those sketched here occur in II.ii, III.i, and IV.ii of the finished play; leaves 43r–48v contain a draft for a scene in a churchyard in which the Pilgrim is an old man. See the reading texts, pp. 48 and 49–53.

Nothing is left of leaves 15–17 but stubs. No writing is visible on 15, but eight consecutive lowercase initial letters on 16r show that prose, not verse, was entered there. For the stub of 17, see note to 18r.

rushes in to prevent it at which time Danby
comes up who had suspected what Ferdinand
had done to Herbert intending to murder
him himself if he had found him.
Ferdinand's reason which had been
disordered restored by the sight of
Danby.

2nd act

[illegible]

[18r]

rushes in to prevent it at which time Danby comes up who had suspected what Ferdinand had done to Herbert intending to murder him himself if he had found him. Ferdinands reason which had been disordered restored by the sight of Danby!

2nd act

~~Mortimer and Rivers walking near the Inn~~ meet ~~with~~ beggar — — ~~Matilda and old Soldier~~ —
~~Scene a room~~ in the inn — ~~Mortimer~~ Rivers having stirred
him up to murder him they resolve — to lead him
to Mounteagle castle — Matilda and ould soldier —
Mounteagle castle, storm — Mortimer dialogue he goes
down to murder him — Rivers soliloqui[?ize] — Smugglers
seen on the top of the walls — Another part of the castle
Smugglers have overheard resolve to prevent scheme
Mortimer {goes / comes} up to Rivers — stirred up and
goes down a-gain — sees the light and hearing
vocies overcome with terrour and cannot do it
Rivers laughs at him a voice heard they discover
[?ther] a haunt of {b / [?B]}anditti—Mortimer tells rivers of
a plan—in which [? ? ?]—then
[?appears] to [?wait] [?] [?Rivers ?alone]

Above the line is a synopsis for part of the final act (see the reading text, p. 48), in the hand of DW, continued from 17, which is now a stub with the endings of nine lines visible on the verso; only the last three can be read: "[?] / [?dact] / tilda"—the last indicating that the person who "rushes in" is Matilda. Incidents described here are equivalent to those occurring in or near V.iii.220 of the finished play. Below the line is a revised synopsis of Act II which postdates the changing of names used in the earliest drafts (see Introduction, pp. 7–8). Incidents described are equivalent to those occurring in II.i (meeting the female Beggar), II.ii (Matilda and the Old Pilgrim), and II.iii.1–246. The reference to an "old Soldier" suggests that WW had in mind the male Pilgrim of the Churchyard Scene (43r–48v). The incidents at Mounteagle Castle derive from WW's earlier *Fragment of a Gothic Tale* (see Introduction, pp. 21–24, and Appendix I).

[18v] [I.iii. 77–90; V.ii. 30–35, 51–54]

waiting hence
old}
for whom — a blind [?]} [?man] well but look
Mark you me [?~~have~~] has done this
[?]
I'll point him out —— a maiden is his guide
Lovely as any rose. A little dog
Tied by a woollen cord moves on before
ith} {the /cur
W[?]} look as sad as he were dumb — {in ~~good~~
I owe him no ill will — but in Good sooth
He does his master credit — ~~then~~ ~~for herbert~~
Ay} {t
[?]} Gentlemen he{ is a ~~hypo~~crite feast to see him
Lank as a ghost & tall — his shoulders bent
And his beard white with age yet evermore
As if he were the only saint on earth
He turns his face to heavn
Well but softly
Who is it that has wrongd you

[?]
by the brink
a}
Of the} small pool of water he was laid
His face close to the water as it seemed
He had stooped down to drink and had remained
Without the strenght to rise
Mortimer
Well — well — he lives
[?but]
and how & where [?he] [?] his [?pain]
Oh God he lives — come — ~~take me to him~~ — ~~come~~ —
~~& what said he~~
~~Oh how shall I repay thee~~.
I believe
That there are beings for unknown ends permitted
To wear the shapes of men & thou art one of them
But human things have press'd so hard on me
I have no fear —
My flesh is like your own

[19r] [V.ii. 19–29]

[? ? ?]

but where was it where
[?lonely] on a ridge of rocks
A chapel stands — ~~it is~~ deserted now
— The bell remains which no one dares remove
And when the stormy wind blows oer the peak
It rings as if a human hand were there
To pull the cord — I fancy he ~~hear~~ had heard it
And towards the precipice had turned his steps
~~But poor~~
To climb up to the spot whence the sound came
Poor man — —
And {h / [?w]}e was very feeble —

The top half of the page has been cut away.

If the nights had been warmer it would
have been better to have made a bed
of the dry heath & wrapping ourselves
up in our cloaks have laid us down
on the ground together & thus divided
our journey by a necessary repose —
Indeed it was too much for me —

[19v]

if the nights had been warmer [?it ?would]
have been better to have made a bed
of the dry heath & wrapping ourselves
up in our cloaks have laid us down
on the ground together & thus divided
our journey by a necessary repose.——
Indeed it was too much for me.

The top half of the page has been cut away. What remains is part of a prose fragment for Act I (perhaps I.i.78–103); the first six lines are to be spoken by Matilda, the seventh by Herbert (see the reading text, p. 48). Following this leaf are six stubs on which scattered bits of writing can be seen but not read.

(20)

They come out

Mortimer and Rivers

228–53

Mortimer

This instant will we stop him — a father ~~too~~
A father too

Rivers.

By heavens he so incensed me
That I was half impelled to rush upon him
And force my sword into his heart at once.

Mort.

(Oh! to confound the miscreant (a victory
Worth fifty conquests o'er brute violence))
He shall behold my triumph — there is a spot
Where I can make him feel —

Rivers.

Nay be not hasty
For sometimes in despight of my conviction
He tempted me to think the story true
'Tis plain he loves the girl and what he said
That savoured of aversion to thy name
Appeared the genuine colour of his soul
Anxiety lest any harm should reach her

[26ʳ] [I.i. 197–204]

They come out
Mortimer and Rivers
Mortimer
a father too
This instant will we stop him —
A father too
Rivers
By heavens he so incensed me
mpell'd
That I was half incensed to rush upon him
And force my sword into his heart at once
Mort:
Oh! to confound the miscreant a victory
Worth fifty conquests oer brute violence
She shall behold my triump — there is a spot
Where I can make him feel —
Rivers
Nay be not hasty
For sometimes in despight of my conviction
He tempted me to think the story true
Tis plain he loves the girl and what he said
That savoured of aversion to thy name
Appeared the genuine colour of his soul
Anxiety lest any harm should reach her

After his death — for that was what he seemed
To fear the most

Mort

I tell thee he is a Tyrant
And most malignant in hypocrisy
After his death a cloak for selfishness
Hackney'd by every narrow soul on earth
And yet ~~that~~ she would not see it

Rivers

But sure he loves the girl and never love
Could find delight to nurse itself so strangely
And thus to plague her with inventions. ~~death~~ new
Tis not in man to do it
There must be truth in this

Mortimer

False — false as hell
Truth in the story — had the thing been true
He must have felt it then — known what it was
And ~~thus~~ to prey upon her heart had been
A tenfold cruelty.

Rivers

What strange pleasure

[26v] [I.i.205–213]

After his death — for that was what he seemd
To fear the most
Mort:
I tell thee he is a Tyrant
And most malignant in hypocrisy
After his death — a cloak for selfishness
Hackney'd by every narrow soul on earth
And yet
~~that~~ she could not see it
Rivers
But sure he loves the girl and never love
Could find delight to nurse itself so strangely
nay
And thus to plague her with inventions^ ~~death~~
Tis not in man to do it
There must be truth in this
Mortimer
False — false as hell
Truth in the story — had the thing been true
He must have felt it then — known what it was
so
And ~~thus~~ to prey upon her heart had been
A tenfold cruelty.
Rivers
What strange pleasures

So we poor mortals cater for ourselves

By heavens such monsters are not fit to live

A mind so warped infects the general air

I now am I half in doubt if ill report

Have wronged thee with him for he covers the

With which he taints her ear — ten times his hate
slanders
deems

Is deeply lodged and that

The price too high to seal he his own breath he'll hold her
So long as he has wrung out

To see him thus provoke her tenderness

With tales of symptoms and infirmities and yet

I'd wager on his life for twenty years.

Mortimer

Her mind is poison'd he has cut away

Her better soul — the villain has unnerved her

Oh Rivers —

Rivers:

From my heart I pity her —

Mortimer

For what? — thou scorn'st her tis her littleness

That moves thy pity faith compassion there

Has food enough — we will not waste
an hour

[27r] [I.i.214–218]

Do we poor mortals cater for ourselves
~~By heavens such monsters are not fit to live~~
~~A mind so warped infects the general air~~
I
~~I now am~~ { ~~half in doubt if ill report~~
~~Have wronged thee with him or he coins the~~
slanders
~~With which he taints her ear — tis plain his hate~~
~~Is deeply lodged and that~~ deems
seal {for
No price ~~too high to make her~~ {all his own
As long as he has breath he'll hold her
fast
wring out
To see him thus ~~provoke~~ her tenderness
With tales of symptoms and infirmities and yet
I'd wager on his life for twenty years.
Mortimer
Her mind is poison'd he has eat away
Her better soul — the villain has unnerved her
Oh Rivers ——
Rivers
From my heart I pity her —
Mortimer
For what? — thou scorn'st her tis her littleness
That moves thy pity 'faith compassion there
Has food enough — we will not waste
an hour

In such a cause — Six plundered families
But two days past came weeping to my tent
Where now they linger waiting from my sword
~~The little~~ that the sword can eer restore ~~to them~~
Lets to the border [illegible] dagger too is there
And I have [illegible] loved it
Why this is noble Rivers worthy of yourself
This is noble
~~Thou art thyself~~ a soul so feeble — she is not worthy of thee
But I hate her off at once and end the business
Mortimer
Matilda has a heart — it is her virtues
Of which he makes his instruments a man
That has so practised on the worlds cold sense
May well deceive his child What leave her thus
A prey to such a traitor no no no
Tis but a word and then — well to them instantly
Rivers
[illegible] I shall do better with the man alone
Let her depart — we soon may overtake her
~~Ha! what is here~~ (Goes)
[illegible]
[illegible]
[illegible]

[27v] [I.i.218–225]

In such a cause — Six plundered families
But two days past came weeping to my tent
till my sword shall give
Where now they linger waiting from my sword
~~The little~~ that the sword can eer restore ~~to them~~
Let's to the /bor/ders/da/nger/ too is there
And I have/ ev/er lo/ved it/ /
Rivers
Why this is noble worthy of yourself
This is noble
~~A soul so feeble~~
~~Thou art thyself — she is not worthy of~~ thee
Best shake her off at once and end the business
Mortimer
Matilda has a heart — it is her virtues
Of which he makes his instruments a man
That has so practised on the world's cold sense
May well deceive his child What leave her thus
A prey to such a traitor no no no
Tis but a word and then —— we'll to them instantly
Rivers
We shall do better with the man alone
{L ay}
{[?]et her depart — we soon m[?ay]} overtake
her
(Going —
~~Ha! what is here~~
Changes to the wood as before
Rivers and Mortimer Walking together
This is no common man — There is a mystery
About him which I have not skill to fathom

(25) 456–575

But tis all over now — the good old Lady
Has left a power of riches and I say it
If there's a lawyer in the land the rogue
Shall give me half — "

good ~~Lady~~ and woman

You have been insolent

Mortimer (eagerly)

But what's your business
With Herbert or his daughter

Beggar

Daughter truly
But how's the day — I fear my little boy
We've over slept ourselves — Sir, have you seen him

Mortimer

I must have more of this — you shall not stir
An inch till I am answered. Know you aught
That doth concern this Herbert?

Beggar! You are angry
And will misuse me Sir

Mortimer No trifling, woman

[31r] [I.iii.115–128]

But tis all over now — the good old Lady
Has left a power of riches and I say it
If theres a Lawyer in the land the rogue
Shall give me half —
[?]
Rivers and
fear woman
~~I doubt~~ good ~~Lady~~
You have been insolent
Mortimer (eagerly)
But what's your business
With Herbert or his daughter
Beggar
Daughter truly
But how's the day —— I fear my little boy
We've overslept ourselves — Sirs have you seen
him
offers to
go~~ing~~
Mortimer
have
I must ~~see~~ more of this — you shall not stir
An [?] inch till I am answered know you aught
That doth concern this Herbert
(surprized)
Beggar
You are angry
And will misuse me Sir
Mortimer
No trifling, woman

Rivers
You are as safe as in a sanctuary
Speak

Mortimer
Speak

Beggar
He is a most hard hearted man

Mortimer
Your life is at my mercy

Beggar
Do not harm me
And I will tell you all — you know not Sir
What strong temptations press upon the poor

Rivers
Speak out —

Beggar
Oh Sir I've ~~done a wicked thing~~ been a wicked woman
But the poor girl has fared the better for it
I was ~~[illegible]~~ flattered me and ~~told~~ said
What harvest it would bring ~~[illegible]~~ words.
I parted with the child

Mortimer
With whom you parted

[31v] [I.iii.129–137]

Rivers
You are as safe as in a sanctuary
Speak
Mortimer
Speak
Beggar
He is a most hard hearted man
Mortimer
Your life is at my mercy
Beggar
Do not harm me
o
And I will tell you all — you know n[?]}t Sir
What strong temptations press upon the poor
Rivers
Speak out —
Beggar
been a wicked woman
Oh Sir I've ~~done a wicked thing~~
But the poor girl has fared the better for it
~~hard~~ pressd said
I was he flattered me and ~~told~~
What harvest it would bring us both and so
I parted with the child
Mortimer
With whom you parted

Beggar
Matilda as he calls her but the child
Joanna
Mortimer
Your's woman — (a whore) Are you Herbert's wife
Beggar
Ay me and I was at the Christening of her
~~And he shall never rob me of the money~~ —
Mortimer
Death! are you Herbert's wife
Beggar. ~~[illegible]~~
~~his~~ wife sir not I
No ever was since I was born My husband
~~Mortimer~~
~~[illegible]~~. ~~[illegible]~~
Your husband
Beggar
~~[illegible]~~
~~[illegible] my husband [illegible]~~
~~He has been [illegible] in his grave~~
~~He~~ Was of [illegible] many snowy ~~winters~~
We have weathered out together — as poor Gilfred
He has been two years in his grave
Mortimer

[32r] [I.iii.138–143]

Beggar

girl
Matilda as he calls her but the child
Is mine

Mortimer

(a pause)
Your's woman—— Are you Herberts wif

Beggar

Ay mine and I was at the Christening of her
~~And he shall never rob me of the money~~ —

Mortimer

Death! are you Herberts wife

Beggar

(~~looking at Rivers~~
Sir
~~his~~ wife not I
My husband
Nor ever since I was born

~~Mortimer~~
~~Rivers~~

~~Enough~~
Your husband
~~again at Rivers~~

Beggar

[?]
~~John Gillfred is my husband's name — poor man~~
He was of fifeshire —
Hes not been two years in his grave ——
{W rkoswald
He {was of Ki~~lmarnock~~— many snowy winter
Gilfred
We have weather out together — ay poor ~~man~~
He has been two years in his grave

Mortimer

Mortimer

Do you good day I'll repair to
I'll meet you there
You shall have justice — Herbert is gone by
But— leave the rest to me —

Rivers

A lucky woman —
Depart and think that you have done good service—

Mortimer

this will help you (gives her money)

Rivers.

Here's for your little son and when you christen him
I'll be his good father.

Beggar Oh! sir you are merry with me —

[32ᵛ] [I.iii.143–152]

Mortimer
Enough
{~~W~~
{~~walking about in~~
~~agitation~~
~~— I have it now — infernal miscreant~~
This is most strange
~~then~~
~~Tis even as I conjectured — hellish miscreant~~
Rivcrs
We've solved the riddle — hellish miscreant
Mortimer Liddisdale
Emildon
good dame ~~Delavale~~
Do you ~~my friend~~ repair to ~~Ravensburgh~~
~~Within three days~~ Ill meet you there
And wait for my return
You shall have justice — Herbert is gone by
[?think ?further]
But — leave the rest to me —
Rivers
A lucky woman —
Depart and think that you have done good
service
~~Both to yourself and child~~
Mortimer (during this time walks
about the stage [?violently]
[?agitated]
At Ravensburgh
thither
And this will help you ~~on your way~~ (gives her
money)
Rivers
him
Here's for your little boy and when you christen
Ill be his good father.
Beggar
Oh! sir you are merry with
me——

Toward the top of the page, "This is most strange" is in pencil, as is "Emildon" two lines farther down.

In farm or grange this hundred scarcely owns

A dog that does not know me — these good

For love of God I must not pass their doors

But I will back with my best speed — as soon

As I can get away from them —

God bless and thank you Sir?

Emildor

Merlen

[33r] [I.iii.153–156]

~~people~~
~~There are a few good Christians in this neighbourhood~~
~~Whose doors for love of God I must not pass~~
hundred
~~Within~~ this ~~parish there is scarce a dog~~
~~In farm or grange; but knows me — these good~~
~~people~~
~~For love of God I must not pass their doors~~
In farm or grange this hundred scarcely owns
~~This parish scarcely owns in farm or grange~~
A dog that does not know me — these good
people
For love of God I must not pass their doors
But I will back with my best speed — as soon
for ever
As I can get away from them — ~~farewell~~
God bless and thank you Sirs
Rivers
Emildon
At [?]
[?] Ravensburgh
[? ?]
Let us begone
~~We shall have open field~~
Emildon [?Merl]
Merley
~~This is horrible~~
~~We must begone~~ — Let us begone

Toward the bottom of the page, the first "Emildon" is in pencil.

Host

sweet masters

You'll join the dance if there's a prettier maiden
Within three leagues she is here with her best looks

Herbert ~~grateful to you~~ ~~but~~
the convent on the ~~rock~~ ~~St Mary's convent~~
the good friars
~~This will not do for me~~ ~~for I must away~~
~~with whom~~ will
Will give me quiet lodging — You have a boy sir
And he must lead me back — Host

Rivers This is most lucky

Our journey lies that way — my friend and I
Will be ~~guides to you the~~ your guides

Herbert
Alas I creep so slowly

A wearisome companion

Rivers
Never fear
We'll not complain of that —

Herbert But for Matilda

A note must be left that she may know
What is become of me

Rivers Well thought

Host Good Herbert

[33v] [I.ii.59–64]

Host

sweet

masters

You'll join the dance if ther's a pretty Maiden

{'s

Within three leagues she{is here with her best looks

Herbert

~~our last nights bed~~

the convent on the heath

~~St Mary's Convent~~

~~This will not do for me~~ the good friars

~~With whom we yesternight~~

Will give me quiet lodging — You have a boy Sir

Host

And he must lead me back —

Rivers

This is most lucky

{ w

Our journey lies that {[?]ay — my friend and I

{y ~~guide you thither~~

Will be {gour guides

Herbert

Alas I creep so slowly

A wearisome companion

Rivers

Never fear

Well not complain of that ——

Herbert

But for Matilda

A notice must be left that she may know

What is become of me

Rivers

Well thought

Host

Good Masters

At the top of the page, "sweet" is in pencil.

Tis a surley place and

(28)

Rivers

Let it in the letter written well depart

Herbert

My limbs are stiff

I must repose a little — could you wait

An hour or less

Rivers

Oh certainly — the distance

Demands not haste and right above our heads

The sun shines hot — come let me lead you in

And while you take your rest my friend and I

Will stroll into the wood

Herbert. But for Matilda

A note must be left that she may know

What is become of me

Rivers. Well thought —

(Rivers conducts Herbert into the [Host] [the Mortimer]) Good Man —

The convent is a surley place —

Various villagers crowd in —

Rivers returns with Mortimer — they go out

together — Amongst the villagers a rustic

musician. ~~[illegible]~~ To him the Host.

Into the court my friend and perch yourself

~~Upon~~ Aloft before the chapel pretty maids

Garlands of flowers I culled and merry thoughts

[34r] [I.ii.64–71]

It is a surly place and
Rivers
Let's in the Letter written well depart
Herbert
My limbs are stiff
I must repose a little — could you wait
An hour or less
Rivers
ist
Oh certainly — the d{[?]ance
Demands not haste — and right above our heads
The sun shines hot — come let me lead you in
And while you take your rest my friend and I
Will stroll into the wood
Herbert. But for Matilda
A notice must be left that she may know
What is become of me.
Rivers.
Well thought — —
Rivers conducts Herbert into the house—) (to Mortimer)
Host
Good Master
~~I~~
~~That~~ The convent is a surly place—
Various villagers crowd in —
Rivers returns with Mortimer — they go out
together — — Amongst the villagers a rustic
musician. ~~crosses the~~ To him The Host
Into the court my friend and perch yourself
~~Upon~~ Aloft upon the elmtree pretty maids
Garlands & flowers & cakes and merry thought

Toward the bottom of the page, "I" and "That" are deleted by erasure.

Scene changes to ~~an~~ to the door of an Inn —

Herbert Matilda and Host

Herbert (seated)

As I am dear to you ~~you will~~ remember Child

This last request —

Matilda

You know me Sir farewell

(Kisses him)

Herbert (rising)

And are you going then come come Matilda

We must not part — I have measured many leagues

When these old limbs had need of rest — no no

I will not play the sluggard

Matilda

Nay sit down

Sir Host such tendance as you would expect

From your own children if yourself were sick

Let this old man find at your hands

poor boy

[34v] [I.ii.1–9]

Scene changes to ~~an In~~ the door
of an Inn —

{H
Herbert Matilda and {host
Herbert (seated)

r
As I am dear to you ~~you will~~ remember
Child
This last request —
Matilda
You know me Sir farewell
(Kisses him)
Herbert (rising)
And are you going then come come Matilda
We must not part — I have measured many
league
e}
When this } old limbs had need of rest — no no
I will not play the sluggard
Matilda

Nay sit down
Sir Host such tendence as you would expect
From your own children if yourself were sick
Let this old man find at your hands
poor tray

Toward the top of the page, "you will" is underlined in ink and deleted in pencil. Halfway down, when WW changed "this" to "these" he let the "i" serve as an "e."

We soon shall meet again – if thou neglects thy
Then ill befall thee ~~that wouldst thou ...~~ charge
The little fool is loth to stay behind
Sir Host by all the love you bear to courtesy
Take care of him and feed the truant well

Host

Fear not – I will obey you – but so young
And one so fair in sooth it is a pity
That you should travel unattended Lady
I have a palfrey and a groom and sir the lad I am bound to say ~~would it not be better sir~~
Shall squire you –   I would let him run
And ~~with~~ a less fee than I would let him run
For any lackey I have seen this twelvemonth

Matilda

You know sir I have been too long your guard
Not to have heart to laugh at little fears qualms
Why if a wolf should leap from out a thicket
A look of mine would send him
scouring back

[35r] [I.ii.10–25]

We soon shall meet again — if thou neglects thy
charge
Then ill befall thee ~~what wouldst thou [?be wandering]~~
The little fool is loth to stay behind
Sir Host by all the love you bear to courtesy
Take care of him and feed the truant well
Host
Fear not — I will obey you — but so young
And one so fair in sooth it is a pity
That you should travel unattended Lady
I have a palfrey and a groom the Lad
and sir I am proud to say it
Shall squire you — ~~would it not be better Sir~~
[?]
~~with~~ a
And ~~for~~ less fee than I would let him run
For any lady I have seen this twelvemonth
Matilda
You know Sir I have been too long your guard
Not to have heart to laugh at little fears
(gaily
Why if a wolf should leap from out a thicket
A look of mine would send him
scowring back

The inserted half line at the top of the page in is pencil.

Unless I differ from the thing I am
When you are by my side

Herbert

Matilda! wolves
Are not the enemies that move my fears

Matilda

Dear Sir no more of this — ~~four~~ three days at farthest
Will bring me back to you — farewell farewell
Exit Matilda

Host

Tis never drought with us — St Mary and her Pilgrims
Thanks to them are a stream of comfort to us
Pities the maiden did not wait a a little
She could not Sir have failed of company

Herbert

Now she is gone — I fain would call her back

Host

Holla!

Herbert

No No — the business must be done
But what is all this noise
a noise heard

Host

The villagers

[35v] [I.ii.26–37]

Unless I differ from the thing I am
When you are by my side
Herbert
Matilda! wolves
Are not the enemies that move my fears
Matilda
three
Dear Sir no more of this — ~~four~~ days at farthest
Will bring me back to you — fare well farewell
Exit Matilda
Host
Tis never drought with us — St Mary and her Pilgrims
to
Thanks to them are a stream of comfort } us
Pity the maiden did not wait a a little
She could not Sir have failed of company
They are passing to and fro [?at] [?] hour by hour
Herbert
Now she is gone — I fain would call her back
Host
Hola!
Herbert
No no —— the business must be done
a noise heard

But what is all this noise
Host
The villagers

Toward the bottom of the page, the inserted line is in pencil.

(30)

Are flocking in — a wedding-festival
That's all—a little merriment—

Enter ~~Rivers~~ and Mortimer

Host
God save you Sirs

Rivers
Ha! as I live the Baron Herbert

Marcy

Host
For God's sake Sir
Pray Sir step in I did not know your honour
Hold
~~poor~~ Tray my pretty dog — ill·

Rivers
So far into your journey on my life
You are a lusty traveller — but how fare you

Herbert
Well as an old man can expect — and you Sir

Rivers
I do not see Matilda

Herbert
The good creature
Is gone before to spare my weariness
But what has brought you hither

Rivers A little business
That will be soon dispatchd—

Herbert
But you have been at Dalewale

Rivers Ayes

[36r] [I.ii.38–48]

Are flocking in — a wedding-festival
That's all— a little merriment—

{Rivers
Enter {Mor and Mortimer
Host
God save you Sirs
Rivers
Ha! as I live the Baron Herbert
Host
Mercy
For God's Sake Sir
Pray Sir step in I did not know your honour
Step in hola!
~~Poor tray~~ my pretty dog — Ill
Rivers
So far into your journey on my life
You are a lusty traveller — but how fare you
Herbert
Well as an old man can expect — and you Sir
Rivers
I do not see Matilda
Herbert
The good creature
{before in pity to
Is gone {[?on][?] — to spare my weariness
th} this way
But what has brought you h}ither
Rivers
A little business
That will be soon dispatch'd —
Herbert
But you have been at Delavale
Rivers
O yes

The revisions and deletions in the fourth and fifth lines are in pencil.

Herbert
But ~~you have been at De~~ of the Letter
Rivers: 'Tis safe with him
And you have told him all good Rivers —
Rivers. All

Herbert
And how did he receive it
Rivers:
Be at peace
You'll hear no more of him
Herbert Well this is comfort
But then the silly girl — ay there's what galls me
She doats as much as ever — But I'll save her
As long as there is life in me my child
Will love me far too well Good Rivers
Ere to be ruined with her own consent
But say where is he now
Rivers:
Oh not far Halloo
There is no danger
Herbert
What a noise is this Cries again
I shall have neither sleep nor rest
Host

[36v] [I.ii.50, 58]

And
Herbert
of the letter
But ~~you have been at De~~
Rivers
It is safe with him
im
And you have told h[?] all good Rivers —
Rivers
All
Herbert
And how did he receive it
Rivers
Be at peace
You'll hear no more of him
Herbert
Well this is comfort
But then the silly girl — ay there's what galls
me
She doats as much as ever — But I'll save her
As long as there is life in me my child
G
Will love me far too well good Rivers
Ere to be ruined with her own consent
But say where is he now
Rivers
Oh not at Falkirk
There is no danger
Herbert
What a noise is this
(noise again
I shall have neither sleep nor rest
Host

At the top of the page, "And" is in pencil.

(31)

Hentzners.—Ithnerary
1598.— —

Next came the Queen in the
Sixty-fifth year of her age.
very majestic; her face oblong
fair but wrinkled, her eyes small yet
black and pleasant; her nose a little hooked,
her lips narrow and her teeth black, a
defect ye English seem subject to from their
too great use of sugar. she had in her ears
two pearls wth very rich drops, she wore false
hair & that red; upon her head she had
a small crown, reported to have been made
of some of ye gold of ye celebrated Luneburg
table: her bosom was uncovered, as all ye
English Ladies have it till they marry.
she had on a necklace of exceeding fine jewels

[37^r]

Hentzner's: — Itinerary
1598.—— —
Next came the Queen in the
sixty-fifth year of her age,
very majestic; her face oblong
fair but wrinkled, her eyes small yet
black and pleasant; her nose a little hooked,
her lips narrow and her teeth black, a
defect ye English seem subject to from their
two great use of sugar. she had in her ears
two pearls wh: very rich drops, she wore false
hair & that red; upon her head she had
a small crown, reported to have been made
of some of ye gold of ye celebrated Lunebourg
table: her bosom was uncovered, as all y^e
English Ladies have it till they marry.
she had on a necklace of exceeding fine jewels

After the title and opening three lines, the rest of this entry is in the hand of DW. The extracts are from Paul Hentzner's *Travels in England during the Reign of Queen Elizabeth*, trans. Horace Walpole (Strawberry Hill, date unknown). Walpole's translation was republished by Edward Jeffrey in a volume with Sir Robert Newton's *Fragmenta Regalia; or Observations on Queen Elizabeth's Times and Favourites; with Portraits and Views* (London, 1797). WW probably obtained a text of the rare Strawberry Hill edition, since the entry of the extracts appears to predate Jeffrey's reissue, though variations from the text of the Jeffrey volume are consistent with copyist error.

* Her father had been treated with ye same deference; James I suffered his courtiers to omit it

The ceremony of setting out her table is equally curious——

[37^{v}]

** Her father had been treated with ye same deference; James I suffered his courtiers to omit it*

The ceremony of setting out her table is equally curious — ——

The asterisk corresponds to an asterisk on 38^{r}, facing, and shows where the insertion was to be made.

(32)

her hands were small, her fingers long, & her stature neither tall nor low; her air was stately, her manner of speech mild and obleging. ——

—— —— —— —— ——

Wherever she turned her face as she was going along, every body fell down upon their knees.*

—— —— —— ——

As we were returning to our Inn (Windsor or Eton) we happened to meet some country people celebrating their harvest home; their last load of corn they crown with flowers, having besides an image richly drest by wch perhaps they wd signify Ceres. This they keep moving about while men and women, men & maid servants rid[g] thro' ye streets in ye Cart shout as loud as ye can till ye arrive at the barn. ——

—— —— —— —— ——

[38r]

her hands were small, her fingers long, & her stature neither tall nor low; her air was stately, her manner of speech mild and obliging.———

——— ——— ——— ———

*wherever she turned her face as she was going along, every body fell down upon their knees.**

——— ——— ——— ———

As we were returning to our Inn (Windsor or Eton) we happened to meet some country people celebrating their harvest home; their last load of corn they crown with flowers, having ~~be~~ besides an image richly drest by w^h. perhaps they w^d signify Ceres. This they keep moving about while men and women, men & maid servants rid^g. thro' ye streets in ye Cart shout as loud as y^y can till y^y arrive at the barn. ———

——— ——— ——— ——— ———

Extracts from Hentzner's *Itinerary* continue from 37r; the asterisk shows where the lines on 37v, facing, were to be inserted.

Lacey

I fear There is some thing here
More than we see — or whence this strong aversion
To one like thee ~~whose station qualities and bearing~~
~~Are envy's mark~~ — these tales have been most black —

Mortimer

Away — I tell thee they are his own coinage —
Fresh from the Baron's ~~heart~~ — tis plain his heart
Is deeply lodged — and that ~~the traitor~~ he deems
No price too high to seal ~~his~~ for his own

Rivers

But wherefore should his love exclude a rival
To one so helpless it would seem the safeguard
Of such a man as thee should be most welcome
I do not like this —

Mortimer

Like — for my part —
~~I do detest the scoundrel from my heart~~

Rivers

But there is some thing ~~Wretch~~ ~~What hast thou seen~~

Mortimer ~~These looks which mean~~
They

[38v] [I.i.225–234]

Rivers
I fear
There is something here
More than we see — or whence this strong aversion
like thee
To one ~~whose station qualities and bearing~~
~~Are envy's mark~~ — these tales have been most black ——
Mortimer
y
Away — I tell thee the } are his own coinage ——
m
Fresh from the Baron's {[?]int — tis plain his hate
he
Is deeply lodged — and that ~~the traitor~~ deems
No price too high to seal her for his own
Rivers
But wherefore should his love exclude a rival
To one so helpless it would seem the safeguard
Of such a man as thee should be most welcome
I do not like this —
Mortimer
it
Like — for my part —
~~I do detest the scoundrel from my heart~~ —
Rivers
t ~~which~~
But { here is something { ~~that~~
Mortimer
~~What hast thou seen~~
~~These looks what mean~~
~~they~~

Drafts for the Deception Scene begin here; they roughly correspond to I.i.225–234, running on to I.iii.157. WW had evidently not yet conceived of introducing the Beggar woman to corroborate Rivers's hints and lead to Mortimer's deception. The three sets of drafts are roughly continuous (though we lack a draft in which Rivers makes his hint specific, as in I.i.249–261). The first, beginning "There is something here," runs from 38v to 39v, 40r, and 40v. The short draft beginning "My tongue has uttered," at the bottom of 41r, appears to follow Rivers's hint that Matilda is being set up as a prostitute. The third draft, beginning "An atom at the centre," indicates that by this point Mortimer has been caught in Rivers's snare and begins to develop the imagery used in I.iii after the exit of the Beggar woman.

(33)

In our way to Dover wh was rough and dangerous
enough, the followg. accidt. happened to us, our
guide or postillion a youth was before, wth two
of our company about the dist. of a musket
shot, we by not followg. quick enough had lost
sight of our friends, we came afterwds to wre ye
road divided, on ye right it was downhill &
marshy on ye left was a small hill. Whilst
we stopped here in doubt, and consulted wch
of ye roads we should take, we saw all on a sudden
on our right hand some horsemen, their stature
dress and horses exactly resembling those of our
friends. glad of havg. found them again, we de-
termined to set on after ym but it happened
thro' God's mercy that tho' we called to them
ye did not answer us, to kept on down ye marshy
road at such a rate that their horses feet struck
fire at every stretch, wh made us wth reason
begin to suspect they were thieves, havg. had
warng. of such or rather ~~that~~ they were nocturnal
sprites who as we were afterwds told are frequently

[39r]

In our way to Dover w^h was rough and dangerous enough, the follow^g. accid^t. ha[?] p pened to us, our guide or postillion a youth was before, w^h two of our company about the dist. of a musket shot, we by not follow^g. quick enough had lost sight of our friends, we came afterw^ds to w^re ye road divided, on ye right it was downhill & Marshy on ye left was a small hill,. W whilst we stopped here in doubt, and consulted w^h. of ye roads we should take, we saw all on a sudden on our right hand some horsemen, their stature dress and horses exactly resembling those of our friends. glad of hav^g. found them again, we determined to set on aft[?] er y^m. but it happened thro' God's mercy that tho' we called to them y^y did not answer us, to kept on down ye marshy road at such a rate that their horses feet struck fire at every stretch, w^h made us w^h reason begin to suspect they were thieves, hav^g. had warn^g. of such or rather that they were nocturnal spectres who as we were afterw^ds. told are frequently

---

The extract from Hentzner's *Itinerary* continues from 38r.

Mortimer

I know thou lovest me

My patience here were else most foul and thou
A monster on this earth — ~~What hast thou seen~~

Rivers You do amaze me

~~Seen nothing~~ Mortimer

What hast thou seen

Rivers Seen! nothing

Mortimer
~~And~~ Which thou dost fear to look on thy breast
There is a brood of hellish thoughts
Which thou wouldst stifle there —
~~to what I feel~~

Rivers [illegible] error

Nay I will speak it if the knowledge cost
The friend that grasps thy hand — [illegible]
What shouldst thou mean
I am ashamed to see you thus disturbed
Nay I will
You force to give utterance to thoughts
Which now I would suppress as dangerous
[illegible] at another time I would move you [illegible] laughter

[39v]

Mortimer
I know thou lovest me

This[y] patience here were else most foul and thou
A monster on this earth — ~~What hast thou seen~~
Rivers
You do amaze me
~~Seen nothing~~
Mortimer
What hast thou seen
Rivers Seen! nothing —
Mortimer
[?thou] hast thought
~~And~~ Which thou dost fear to look on
In thy breast
There is a brood of hellish thoughts
Which thou wouldst stifle there — ~~the worst were~~
~~mercy~~
~~now endure~~
~~To what I feel~~
Rivers
This is most strange
~~A most strange error~~
Nay I will have it if the knowledge cost
[?skin] thou lovest me speak
The flesh that wraps thy heart —— ~~that something there~~
[?~~canst~~]
~~What [?dost] thou mean~~
I am ashamed to see you thus disturbed
Nay [?I will]
You force to give utterance to thought
Which now I would suppress as dangerous
But at another time twould move youre
Laughter

seen in those, there were likewise a great (34)
many Jack wth Lanthorns, so that we were
quite seised with horror and amazemt.
but fortunately for us our guide soon after
sounded his horn and we followd the noise
turn down ye left hand road and arrived safe
to our companions, who wn we asked them
if yy had not seen ye horsemen that had gone
by us, answered, not a soul. Our Opinions accd to
custom were various upon ye matter, but ye fr
ye thing was we were wtht doubt in immint
danger from wch that we escaped ye glory
is to be ascribed to God alone.

Flowers.
What should I speak — some small respects forcing me
These were with thee and would not [illegible]
[illegible]
If thou dost [illegible]
The flesh [illegible]

[40^r]

seen in those, there were likewise a great
many Jack w^h. Lanthorns, so that we were
quite seized with horror and amazem^t.
but fortunately for us our guide soon after
sounded his horn, and we follow^g. the noise
turn down y^e left hand road and arrived safe
to our companions, who w^n. we asked them
if y^y had not seen y^e horsemen that had gone
by us, answered, not a soul. Our opinions acc^g to
custom were various upon y^s. matter, but w$^{t.r}$
y^e thing was we were w$^{h.t}$ doubt in immin^t.
danger from w^h. that we escaped y^e glory
is to be ascribed to God alone.

Rivers
What should I speak — some small repute for wisdom
I have won with thee and would not wish to lose it
I am ashamed to see you thus disturbd
—~~If~~ {T thou dost know something if the knowledge [?cost]
The flesh that wraps thy heart Ill hunt it out

At the top, Hentzner's *Itinerary* continues from 39^r; at the bottom, the first draft for the Deception Scene continues from 39^v.

Well I was thinking
~~But~~ being an impostor known to nobody
It is too foolish - ~~[illegible]~~ no more of it

Mortimer

I'd rather be a soul in hell
Without a drop to wet this tongue of mine
Than what I am dost thou hear this

Rivers

~~You are [illegible] to see you [illegible] disturbed things~~
~~[illegible] now~~
You force me to give utterance to a ~~thought~~
Which now I would suppress as dangerous
But at another time twould move your laughter
In truth there's not a shadow to support it
But at the time it crost me and those whispers
I did not like them - that this [illegible]
We have not [illegible] the course how this story
Is what he makes it - and in truth those [illegible]
Mortimer
~~[illegible]~~ - sayst thou [illegible]

Tis even so - plain as the day - the Trooper
- It is not to be born - things terrible
Do hang upon it - if these seeming suspicion
Be slightly taken up - better thou wert
idiot [illegible]

[40v]

~~Well — I was thinking~~
{That
{But being an imposter known to nobody
s}
It is too foolish — p } haw no more of it
Mortimer
I'd rather be a soul in hell
Without a drop to wet this tongue of mine
Than what I am dost thou hear this
Rivers
~~u~~}
~~I am ashamed to see you thi}s disturbed~~ —
~~How now~~ ~~thing~~
You force me to give utterance to a ~~thought~~
Which now I would suppress as dangerous
But at another time 'twould move your Laughter
In
~~For~~ truth there's not a shadow to support it
But at the time it crost me^and those
kisses
I did not like them —
that this girl
We know not whence she comes her history
Is what he makes it — and in truth those
kisses
Mortimer
~~kisses~~ — sayst thou — ha
{T (a pause
{tis even so — plain as the day —— the thought
— It is not to be born — things terrible
Do hang upon it — if this same suspicion
Be slightly taken up — better thou wert
~~idly [?bred]~~
the

The first draft for the Deception Scene continues from 40r. The addition just preceding Mortimer's last speech was to go in at the caret above. The first line of Rivers's speech is deleted in pencil; four lines up from the bottom, "(a pause" is in pencil, as is the reinforcement of the capitalizing stroke on "Tis."

(35)

At his shew (Bartholomew fair) Tobias Salander Dr. of Ph. one of our company, had his pocket picked of his purse, wth 9 Crowns du Soleil, wch no doubt was so cleverly taken from him by an Englishman who always kept close to him that ye Doctor did not ye least perceive it.

— — — — —

At ye se spectacles (bull & bear baitg. &c) and every wh. else ye Engh are constly. smoakg tobacco and in this manner; they have pipes made of clay, into ye farthest end of wch. yy put ye herb &c. — &c. — . . .

I know not what [illegible] no matter how
The [illegible] was bred in thee tis here
'Tis [illegible] I thank thee for it
And when [illegible] Thou wilt forgive
[illegible] not [illegible] this — Thou hast done well
I know not what I say — I thank thee for it
'Tis what it ought to be — [illegible]
[illegible]

[41^r]

At this shew (Bartholomew fair) Tobias Lelander
D^r. of Ph. one of our company, had his pocket
picked of his purse, w^h. 9 Crowns de Soleil
w^h. no doubt was so cleverly taken from him
by an Englisman who always kept close to him
that ye Doctor did not ye least perceive it.

———— ———— ———— ———— ——

At y^se. Spectacles (bull & bear bait^g. &c) and
every w^re. else ye Eng^h. are const^y. smoak^g tobacco
and in this manner; they have pipes made
of clay, into ye farthest end of w^h. y^y put ye herb &
&c. — — &c. — . . .

My tongue has uttered
I know not what no matter how
The {[?thought] / [?thing]} was bred in thee t{is / [?]} here
Tis
~~And~~ where it ought to be I thank thee for it
Rivers Mortimer

I did not look for {[?for] / [?this]} this — Thou wilt forgive me
I know not what I say — thou hast done well
Tis where it ought to be — I thank thee for it
[?express ?an ?horrid]
[?]
~~No matter how tis here — and I am [?ruined]~~

At the top, the extract from Hentzner's *Itinerary* concludes; at the bottom is the second draft for the Deception Scene. Revision of the last line is in pencil, but the deleting lines are in ink.

An atom at the centre of the earth —
I did not look for this — Mt. Thou hast done well ~~Thou wouldst not look for this~~
'Tis where it ought to be — Mortimer: I thank thee for it
Why now let friendship cease ~~some liberty~~
~~To banished from the world~~ — ~~a meddling fool~~
~~What blessings have I heard~~ — since such return
Must wait on my good will — and one light thought
Shall cancel all the past

Mortimer

I am in hell.

~~Rivers~~

Why so — I am not used to rash conjecture
And — curse the stumbling chime by which so far
I differed from my self — ~~it is a thought~~ a silly fancy
Which should have died the moment of its birth
So long as she has dwelt with him ere now
She would have had some hint of it — in faith
We have too much of this —

Mortimer

I am undone
No living power can save me — sinking sinking

[41^{v}]

An atom at the centre of this earth —
Rivers
I did not look for this ^ —M Thou hast done well
~~Rivers~~
~~I did not look for this~~
Morti:
Tis where it ought to be — I thank thee for it
[?] Rivers
Why now let friendship cease ~~since Liberty~~
~~Is banished from the world~~ — ~~a meddling fool~~
~~What business have I here~~ — since such return
Must wait on my good will — and one light
thought
Shall cancel all the past
Mortimer
I am in hell
Rivers
Why so I am not used to rash conjectures
And — curse the stumbling chance by which so far
I differed from myself — ~~it is a thought~~
a silly fancy
Which should have died the moment of its birth
So long as she has dwelt with him ere now
She would have had some hint of it — in faith
We have too much of this ——
Mortimer
I am undone
No living power can save me — sinking ——
sinking

The third draft for the Deception Scene begins here, running over to 42^{r} and 42^{v}.

And feel that I am sinking — would this body
Were quietly given back unto the earth
From whence it came.

Rivers

How now my friend where is your fortitude
Or have you made divorce wi' the common reason
I cannot bear a touch of thought ere this
He would have paved the way — besides — he knows
That the more towering hint of the importune
Would blast his views and wither up at once
The filial love with which he cheers his age
Mere selfishness and old men have strange pleasures

Mortimer

What have I done that thou shouldst hate me thus.

Rivers.

Nay I will leave you

Mor:

[42r]

And feel that I am sinking — would this body
Were quietly given back unto the earth
{ From [? ?] with her and yet
{ [?] whence it came proof proof — I must have
has not it is [?not ?in] the [?Letter]
She would have mentioned it — I must have proof proof
[?shall] I must have proof
Rivers
How now my friend where is your fortitude
Or
And have you made divorce with common
reason
It cannot bear a touch of thought ere this
He would have paved the way — besides — he knows
Her heart is warm with the thoughts of manly beauty
{T most trivial {e
And {that the ^ slightest hint of th{is imposture
Would blast his views and wither up at once
The filial love with which he chears his age
Mere selfishness and old men have strange
pleasures
Mortimer
What have I done that thou shouldst hate
me thus.
Rivers
Nay I will leave you
Mor:
Stop

The third draft for the Deception Scene continues from 41v. All revisions around the third line are in pencil, as is the deletion of the line lower down, beginning "Mere selfishness."

[42v]

Rivers
Why should I stop
I never have been used to check my thoughts
And least of all with those I love but be it so
Since you will have it
Mortimer (stopping him
But to perish thus
~~In such a cause~~ — thou wilt forgive me Rivers
I did not wish to wrong thee but tis har
To have the firm foundation of my life
~~Thus to be overthrown~~ —
~~drop~~
Thus ~~sink~~ from under me —
drop
(cooly) this business
Rivers
by my r
Will ruin me
away
I must begone
Let us after [?this]
If you [?talk] thus
oh I am swept away
And like a drowning man when I would save
myself
Snatch at the foam of seas that overwhelm me
Let us be gone that I may be assured

The third draft for the Deception Scene runs over from 42r.

(37)

Act 3d

Scene a Churchyard

Peasants having just entombed a body

Peasant

That droning pipe heard from the wood below
Proclaims some pilgrim nigh

Old peasant. Of all that pass
I never till this afternoon beheld
One on whose brow Affliction's hand had left
So little of earthly: wrinkles that might seem
Wrinkles of sorrow rather than of years
Had traced his temples with religious touch
Acquainted though his eyes appear with weeping
~~Perpetual tears have not subdued their lustre~~
Nor tears nor sorrow have subdued their lustre
Bright lights break out at times about their orbs
That speak the wildness of great joy: perhaps
He is not in his true and perfect mind

[43^{r}]

Act 3^{d}
Scene a Churchyard
Peasants having just entombed a body

Peasant
1 That droning pipe heard from the wood below
2 Proclaims some pilgrim nigh
{O
Old peasant. {of all that pass
3 *I never till this afternoon beheld*
4 *One on whose brow Affliction's hand had*
left
5 *So little of earthly: wrinkles that might seem*
6 *Wrinkles of sorrow rather than of years*
7 *Had traced his temples with religious touch*
8 *Acquainted though his eyes appear with weeping*
~~*Perpetual tears have not subdued their lustre*~~
9 ~~*Per*~~ *Nor tears nor sorrow have subdued their lustre*
10 *Bright lights break out at times about their orbs*
11 That speak the wildness of great joy: perhaps
12 He is not in his true and perfect mind

Throughout the Churchyard Scene, which runs from 43^{r} on to the top of 48^{v}, marginal line numbers correspond to those of the reading text, pp. 49–53.

He begged an alms and lingering at my door
Talked much of those who at Jerusalem
Die in the Lord and from that very moment
And as he spoke he smiled with extreme joy
Are born to paradise and the ten thousand.
And sure he is a man beloved of heaven
For at the word a long slant evening beam
Such as in shower time dart between the hills
Shot from between two clouds upon his face
And added to his smile a fearful glory
I took it as a sign from him who hungth
The bow in heaven we are not all to sleep
But we shall all be changed —
For afterwards in milder mood he talked
Of man and of man's heart & things below
And human sufferings, chief of those that toil
After their friends are in the world of rest
Till the wild joy that lighted up his tears
Grown dim like dying lamps or suns that set
Gave one bright glance and seemed to pass for
ever

[43v]

He begged an alms and lingering at my door
Talked much of those who at Jerusalem
Die in the Lord and from that very moment
And as he spoke he smiled with extreme joy
Are born to paradise and the ten thousand
And sure he is a man beloved of heaven
For at the word a long slant evening beam
Such as in shower time dart between the hills
u
Shot from between two clouds {[?]*pon his face*
And added to his smile a fearful glory
I took it as a sign from him who hung ~~*the*~~
The bow in heaven we are not all to sleep
But we shall all be changed——
For afterwards in milder mood he talked
Of man and of man's heart & things below
And human sufferings, chief of those that toil
After their friends are in the world of rest
Till the wild joy that lighted up his tears
Grown dim like dying lamps or suns that set
Gave one bright glance and seemed to pass for
ever

---

22 Deletion by erasure.

(38)

But he approaches — tis the very same
Enter Pilgrim

I come not Brothers to disturb your rites
If Misery as we're told may give a claim
In heaven my prayers will sure be acceptable
Old Peasant

Thanks holy Pilgrim but the rites are
finished

Pilgrim

Hah! tis an infants grave — I once had
infants.
(a pause Pilgrims eyes fixed on the grave)
Old peasant
Then are they happy if the grave —
Pilgrim
The grave
May at the call of Nature, — one by one —
Receive the infant fruits of fondest love
And after a few throbs the heart be still

[44r]

32 But he appr$\left\{ {o \atop a} \right.$aches — tis the very same
Enter Pilgrim
33 I come not Brothers to disturb your rites
34 If Misery as we're told may give a claim
35 On heaven my prayers will sure be acceptable
Old Peasant
36 Thanks holy Pilgrim but the rites are
finished
Pilgrim
37 Hah! tis an infant's grave — I once had
infants
(a pause pilgrims eyes fixed on the grave)
Old peasant
38 Then are they happy if the grave ——
Pilgrim
The grave
39 May at the call of Nature,—one by one—
40 Receive the infant fruits of fondest love
41 And after a few throbs the heart be still

But Death has shapes so terrible (a pause)
— and yet
Heaven in his kindness surely took thee from me
— For it was at a ~~better~~ time — when fears
had just
Blanched my young hair and shattered my
: poor brain
We wandered much together through deep woods
And trackless wastes —— yes — yes — twas well —
I do demand your by (firmly) twas well
The very shewolf of the woods had been
a nurse less terrible than I
For he would mock at times with innocent mirth
My lifted hands and seem to tear his hair
Making a play thing of my bursting heart
At times my poor dear boy : he would
stare
And roll his (infant eyes in wildest motion
As if my face reflecting till I feared —
the sang froid boy no human face but mine
(Harvard)
To nurse him holy saints in idiotcy
(faints)

[44v]

42 But Death has shapes <u>so</u> terrible (a pause)
— and yet
43 Heaven in his kindness surely took thee from me
44 — For it was at a ~~bitter~~ time — when fear
had just
45 Blanched my young hair and shattered my
poor brain
46 We wandered much together through deep~~s~~ woods
47 And trackless wastes —— yes — yes — twas well —
I do demand your pity
(firmly) <u>twas</u> well
48 The very shewolf of the woods had been
49 a nurse less terrible than I
50 For he would mock at times with innocent mirth
51 My lifted hands and seem to tear his hair
52 Making a play thing of my bursting heart
53 At times my poor dear boy he would
stare
54 And roll his infant eyes in wildest motion
55 As if my face reflecting till I feared —
56 He saw poor boy no human face but mine
(Hurried)
57 To nurse him holy saints in ideotcy.
(faints)
[?] to make an ideot of him

---

46 Deletion by erasure.
The revision at the foot of the page is in pencil.

(39)

~~Margaret~~

Matilda

~~Help — help — fetch cooler water from the spring — go~~

Run Run — for Water from the spring oh God
How did her eyes shrink back into her head
— Ye saw the blackness pass across her face
At length thou shalt be quiet and lie still
Sorrow shall seek at morn & shall not find thee
Where are they? are they coming? ~~nay~~ crowd not so

Let the air breathe upon her — —
(after a pause pilgrim
recovering)
My good friends
Spare — Spare your needless pains that would undo
That shall work — for I feel I am myself.

Old Peasant

That cot below the waterfall — whose smoke
Curls from beneath the elms, is mine — two moons
Have lit our sheepwalks since I eat my meal

[45r]

~~Margaret~~
Matilda
~~cool~~
~~Help help fresh water from the spring ye~~
~~y~~}
~~saw~~}

{r
58 Run {Run— for Water from the spring oh God
59 How did her eyes shrink back into her head
{Y
60 —{ye saw the blackness pass across her face
61 At length thou shalt be quiet and lie still
62 Sorrow shall seek at morn & shall not find thee,
y}
63 Where are they? are thee} coming?
~~nay~~ crowd not so
64 Let the air breathe upon her— —
(after a pause pilgrim
recovering)
My good friends
65 Spare — spare your needless pains that would
undo
66 That spellwork — for I feel I am myself.
Old Peasant
67 That cot below the waterfall—whose smoke
68 Curls from beneath the elms, is mine—two
moons
69 Have lit our sheepwalks since I eat my
meal

59–66 The use of "her" in these lines probably indicates that WW was working from an earlier draft in which the Pilgrim, as in the synopsis on 14v, has been discovered to be Matilda's mother.

In solitude — since my son took the cross
Thoughts that a while could soften pangs
of parting
Have lost their influence and my heart is
void
That cot shall be your home — there shall you
dwell
And be to me in all things as a son.

Wily:

When you do not know me for sometimes
I am disturbed in mind ~~and~~

Old Peasant

A holy man
~~We know of~~
We know you are heaven-favoured. freshest
grass
Shall strew your chamber and a candlestick
And crucifix with picture of the virgin
Stand at the right hand of your humble bed
And you shall feed my sheep and the long day
Their quiet shall be yours

Wily.

Yes honest swain.
Give me a crook the simple flock to guide
The lost ones to recall — ah teach me first

[45v]

70 In solitude — since my son took the cross
71 Thoughts that a while could soften pangs
of parting
72 Have lost their influence and my heart is
void
73 That cot shall be your home — there shall you
go
~~dwell~~
74 And be to me in all things as a son.
Pilg:
75 Alas you do not know me for sometimes
76 I am disturbed in mind ~~and~~
Old Peasant
A holy man
{~~t~~
~~Be{hoved of~~
77 We know you are heaven-favoured freshest
grass
78 Shall strew your chamber and a candlestick
79 And crucifix with picture of the virgin
St}
80 H{and at the right hand of your humble bed
81 And you shall feed my sheep and the long day
82 Their quiet shall be yours —
Pilg.
Yes honest swain
83 Give me a crook the simple flock to guide
84 The lost one's to recall — ah teach me first

73 Revision is in pencil.
84 Deletion by erasure.

(40)

If not to bring back all I've loved at least
To rescue my poor thoughts which now and wa
Bleed helplessly in memory's piercing thorns,
A shepherd I — (smiling) I who have seen the lamb
Run from its milk to sport amid its fellows
Have seen it spring to meet its mothers call
Have seen and had no pleasure at the sight
No. No! ~~[illegible]~~ ~~my~~ heart ~~[illegible]~~
Answers not any purposes of being
And never will its uses be restored

Matilda

Yes trust me pilgrim long as thy red blood
Is warm this old man knows there is a power
Even in the common offices of love
And friendly ministration to revive
Nature within thee bid thee smile again
With those that smile and weep with them that weep.

Beggar

Look in my face — I have not yet forgotten

[46r]

If not to bring back all I've loved at least
To rescue my poor thoughts which now and ever
Bleed helplessly in Memory's piercing thorns
(smiling)
—A shepherd I—^ I who have seen the
lamb
Run from its milk to sport amid its fellows
Have seen it spring to meet its mothers call
Have seen and had no pleasure at the sight
~~Matilda~~ my }
No! No! a } heart ~~like mine~~
Answers not any purposes of being
And never will its uses be restored
{t
Ma{lilda
Yes trust me pilgrim long as thy red blood
Is warm this old man knows there is a power
Even in the common offices of love
And friendly ministration to revive
Nature within thee bid thee smile again
With those that smile and weep with
them that weep.
Pilg:
Look in my face — I have not yet forgotten

All functions of a man — I weep and laugh
But with no fond endearing unison
Of social smiles and sympathetic tears
No ties in dreadful contrariety
To all mankind as now I laugh that thou
Wert [illegible] damsel to the senseless dead
Matilda

But be persuaded —

Old Servant:

— do go home with me
Henceforth the seat beneath the elms is yours
And yours the corner chair when winds blow
Through the bare thorns — the sharp sound of the farm gate
At evening when you enter from the fields
Closing behind you shall be dear and welcome
The dog that barks at you shall be chastized
And my sons little-ones shall reverence you
And run with joy to lift the latch and meet you
And she their little sister had she not
Slept in that grave should have been
taught to love you — :

[46v]

102 All functions of a man— I weep and laugh
103 But with no fond endearing unison
104 Of social smiles and sympathetic tears
105 No tis in dreadful contrariety
106 To all mankind as now I laugh that thou
107 Givest Physic dansel to the senseless dead
Matilda
108 But be persuaded ——
Old Peasant
— do go home with me
109 Henceforth the seat beneath the elms is yours
110 And yours the corner chair when winds blow
sharp
111 Through the bare thorns— the sound of the farm
gate
112 At evening when you enter from the fields
113 Closing behind you shall be dear and welcome
114 The dog that barks at you shall be chastized
115 And my sons little-ones shall reverence you
116 And run with joy to lift the latch and meet
you
117 And she their little sister had she not
118 Slept in that grave should have been
taught to love you — —

(41)

Pilgrim

I am perplexed and can not think it true
That thus thou speak'st to me and where I am
I know not nor if this be the same air
And the same sun and we are fellow beings
For all is changed I am indeed perplexed
And poor old I understand thee not
And know not what it is that works within me

Matilda

Rest with this good old man a little while
And ~~he~~ soon shall he restore thee to thyself
Thy looks are changed already —

Pilg.

Tis most true
I never have been so beguiled before
But it is ~~[illegible]~~ past and I am once again
The thing I was. —

Old Servant

[47r]

Pilgrim

I am perplexed and can not think it true
That thus thou speake{st to me and where
I am
I know not nor if this be the same air
And the same sun and we are fellow beings
Or all is changed I am indeed perplexed
And poor old I understand thee not
And know not what it is that works within
me

Matilda

Rest with this good old man a little while
soon
An ~~he~~ shall he restore thee to thyself
Thy looks are changed already ——

Pilg:

Tis most true
I never have been so beguiled before
it
But it is ~~pass~~ {~~ed~~ past—and I am once again
The thing I was.—

Old Peasant

With patience you have
run
The race of duty — you have visited
The sepulchre — and now you ought to rest
Pilgrim

No good old man it cannot cannot be
A few days journey and these feet shall reach
My infant home the dwelling of my fathers
— That human pilgrimage performed and then —
a long leave
Yet old man I will thank thee — and my
ear
Though it be dull and cold shall vibrate
long
As if it heard thy voice — and I will pray
That he whose sun shines on the evil
and good
Who sends his rain upon the just and
unjust
That he will love to look upon thy sheepwalks
And chiefly be the shepherd of thyself
And family and this thy way scene
Old Peasant
Farewell — Exeunt Peasants

[47v]

131 With patience you have
run
132 The race of duty — you have visited
133 The sepulcre—and now you ought to rest
Pilgrim
134 No good old man it cannot cannot be
{these
135 A few days journey and {my feet shall reach
136 My infant home the dwelling of my fathers
137 — That <u>human</u> pilgrimage performed—and then—
a long pause
138 Yet old man I will thank thee—and my ~~ear~~
ear
139 Though it be dull and cold shall vibrate
long
140 As if it heard thy voice — and I will pray
141 That he whose sun Shines on the evil
and good
142 Who sends his rain upon the just and
unjust
143 That he will love to look upon thy sheepwalks
144 And chiefly be the shepherd of thyself
145 And family and i this thorny scene ——
Old Peasant.
146 Farewell— Exeunt Peasants

Manent (42)

Matilda and Pilgrim —

Matilda (aside)

With best success even to my father's wish
Thus far have I returned my errand sped.
And yet from such a service one short hour
I fain would spare for this sweet Pilgrim's sake
For I do feel in his sad story's spite
My heart has yet some cheerfulness behind
Which it would gladly lend him. —

Pilgrim

Know you maiden
How far tis called to Thuckland — —

Matilda

Thitherward
My journey lies - and fellowship in travel
May be endured when grief would otherwise
Covet to be alone : a few leagues hence
My father waits for me the good old man
Will clasp my hand and weep to hear you tell
And ever more at every piteous word
~~And he~~ will bid me listen.

Pily: ~~[illegible]~~ - the gay
On which the heart that owns it dare
not look

[48r]

Manent
Matilda and Pilgrim —
Matilda (aside)

{F
With best success even to my {father's wish
Thus far have I returned my errand sped.
And yet from such a service one short hour
I fain would spare for this sweet Pilgrims sake
For I do feel in his sad story's spite
My heart has yet some chearfulness behind
Which it would gladly lend him. —
Pilgrim
{en
Know you maid{s
How far tis called to Rhudland— —
Matilda
Thitherward
My journey lies — and fellowship in travel
May be endured when grief would otherwise
Covet to be alone a few leagues hence
My Father waits for me the good old man
Will clasp my hand and weep to hear you talk
And ever more at every piteous word
{s
~~And he~~ will bid me li{[?]ten.
Pilg:
~~Oh~~ — — the grief
On which the heart that owns it dare
not look

Doth ask no sympathy. But stay a moment
I have a little business yet that done
And we will on together
(Mortimer approaching the
grave which ~~she~~ requests stedfastly for some
time) ~~no the~~ No! the grave
Contains not all that perish though the dead
Be sacred and with darkness ought to dwell

Matilda at the cottage door

her cheek ~~with~~ her tongue in stupid grief—
protect.
Your Father whom last night I chanced to find
In those wild tracts which I am used to range
Your Father Lady .. from a wilful hand
Has met unkindness so indeed he told me
And you remember such was my report
From what has just befallen me I have cause
To fear he has been murdered.

Matilda

He is dead
Why comest thou to me with a tale like this

[48v] [V.iii.1–6]

162 Doth ask no sympathy, But stay a moment
163 I have a little business yet that done
164 And we will on together
(Pilgrim approaching the
{h
grave which [?]{ e regards stedfastly for some
time)— ~~no! the~~ No! the grave
dead
165 Contains not all that perish though the
166 Be sacred and with darkness ought to dwell

Matilda at the cottage door
her chee~~k upon her~~ hand in stupid grief—
Robert
1 Your Father whom last night I chanced to find
2 In those wild tracts which I am used to range
3 Your Father Lady
{h
from a wilful {[?m]and
4 Has met unkindess so indeed he told me
5 And you remember such was my report
6 From what has just befallen me I have
cause
7 To fear he has been murdered.
Matilda
He is dead
8 Why comest thou to me with a tale like this

In the Matilda at the Cottage Door Scene, which begins on the bottom portion of the page, equivalent to V.iii.1–6, the use of the name Robert for the Cottager indicates that the entry is later than those for the Edge of a Heath Scene (55vff.), where he is a "Cottager," or the Margaret and Peasant Scene (53v–54v), where he is a "Peasant."

(43)

~~I thought thou'dst other business.~~

Robert

It is fit

That a bad man should answer for his crimes.

Matilda

Thou seest me what I am

Robert

It was most heinous

And doth call out for vengeance

Matilda

Do not add

I prithee to the harm thou'st done already

~~Sit back upon thy ... [illegible]~~

Robert

~~Maid hereafter~~

Hereafter you will thank me

~~Thou'lt thank me~~ for this service

I met a man who from the plainest proofs

Of interfering heaven I have no doubt

Laid hands upon your father — fit it were

You should prepare to meet him he is coming

(Matilda continues silent taking no notice

of this)

[49r] [V.iii.7–15]

9 ~~I thought thou'dst other business~~

Robert

{I
{it is fit

10 That a bad man should answer for his crimes

Matilda

11 Thou seest me what I am

Robert

It was most heinous

12 And doth call out for vengeance

Matilda

Do not add

13 I prithee to the harm thou'st done already

14 ~~But back upon thy errand~~ —

Robert

~~Maid hereafter~~

Hereafter you will thank me

15 ~~Thou'lt thank m~~e for this service

[?In]

16 I met a man who from the plainest proofs
17 Of interfering heaven I have no doubt
18 Laid hands upon your father — fit it were
19 You should prepare to meet him he is coming

(Matilda continues silent taking no notice
of this)

The wounds were slight
But there are ways to end a man, that leave
Small trace of their effect
Matild: Ha! what say'st thou
I told your story of Robert. He did insist
To be conducted to you I suppose
That he may straight proclaim himself and so
Find all the ease he can expect on earth
The heavens have mercy on him (Matilda still silent)
I remember
I spied a mark upon your father's throat
Matilda
How! how! Robert But see him yonder guided by my wife
What must be done. Matilda looking that way
God of God
Speak — (Matilda Robert If your purpose
My wife but now has left her at my cottage
Tis scarce an arrow's flight — behind those trees
Shall I conduct you to her.
He might have died but to such a daughter
To tell the story thus : oh ye sweet heavens
Where was your mercies
Help me to my father — I have nothing
To do with him —

[49v] [V.iii.16–18]

20 The wounds were slight
21 But there are ways to end a man ^ that leave
22 Small trace of their effeit ——
thou
Matild: Ha! what sayst
Robert
I told your story &
He did insist
23 To be conducted to you I suppose
24 That he may straight proclaim himself and so
25 Find all the ease he can expect on earth
26 The heavens have mercy on him (Matilda still silent)
I remember
27 I spied a mark upon your fathers throat
Matilda
28 How! how!
Rober
wife
But see him yonder guided by my
29 What must be done.
Matilda looking that way
o
oh God {[?d]h God
{( )}
{Robert} your purpose
30a Speak — Matilda

cottage
My wife but now has left her at my {house
'Tis scarce an arrow's flight — behind
those trees
Shall I conduct you to her.

have
He might died but to such a aughter
th
To tell the story {[?]us oh ye sweet heavens
Where was your mercy

30b Help me to my father — I have nothing
To do with him —

The six lines set off toward the bottom are developed from drafts on 51r, and were entered before the other lines on the page; WW is jumping forward from the back of the notebook.

(44)

Ferdinand
dead dead dead

Robert

This business Sir seems to concern you nearly
I'll lead you to the maiden whom I left
With her dead fathers body at my heels
A few steps hence

Margaret

nay Robert tis not fit
Two wretched beings, each so miserable
Should come together — poor unhappy man

Robert

Thou dost forget thyself — I am convinced
And we must see (the bottom of it.
(turning to Ferdinand)
Sir
I wish that I could lead you to his daughter
In dignity [illegible] to [illegible] this dwellers [illegible]
Perhaps twere better
But it were fit that I go on before
and lead ne to her —
That she may be prepared —
Margaret
nay

Ferdinand

Thou hast said well
There will be need of preparation
Robert goes off —

[50r] [V.ii.75–88]

Ferdinand
dead dead dead
Robert
This business Sir seems to concern you nearly
I'll lead you to the maiden whom I left
With her dead fathers body at my hut
A few steps hencc
Margaret
nay Robert tis not fit
Two wretched beings, each so miserable
Should come together — poor unhappy man
Robert
Thou dost forget thyself — I am confirmed
And we must see the bottom of it.
(turning to Ferdinand)
Sir
I said that I would lead you to her {is} daughter
~~[?]~~
His daughter! Oh Yes ~~lead me to her~~
Ferd:
to his daughter lead me to her
Do!
Robert
Perhaps twere
~~But it~~ were fit that I go on before
~~o yes~~ lead me to her —
That she may be prepared —
Margaret
Nay
Ferdinand
Thou hast said well
There will be need of preparation
Robert goes off —

These lines are probably developed from a version that originally stood on the leaves following 58, now torn out: note that the Cottager has now been named Robert.

Margaret attempting to speak to Ferdinand
Sir

Ferdinand his eyes upon the ground.

Life is strong in the girl thou hast survived
Which will meet the
What is to come

Margaret

You seem most wretched Sir
Your limbs sink under you shall I support you

Ferdinand (leaning upon her)

This is an office of humanity —
Woman I've lent my body to the service
Which now thou takest upon thee — God forbid
That thou shouldst ever need a like occasion
With such a view as mine.

Withdrawing his hand in agitation

This must not be.
I can sustain my self let us advance

Margaret

Oh! why have I to do with things like these.

[50v] [V.ii.89–94]

Margaret a[?]tt}empt{s ing to speak to Ferdinand
— Sir —
Ferdinand his eyes upon the ground.
Life is strong in th{e is girl ~~thou hast survived~~
^a sight ~~Which would have ended me [?and] Yet~~
~~My sinews have been [?prouv'd]~~ well meet th[?]en} thus
What is to come
Margaret
You seem most wretched Sir
Your limbs sink under you shall I support you
Ferdinand (leaning upon her)
This is an office of humanity ——
Woman I've lent my body to the service
Which now thou takest upon thee — God forbid
That thou shouldst ever meet a like occasion
With such a view as mine.
Withdrawing his hand in agitation
This must not be.
I can sustain my self let us advance
Margaret
Oh! why have I to do with things like these.

(45)

And we must see the bottom of it flowing to Fer:

Sir

I said that I would lead you to his daughter

My wife but now has left her at my hut

Tis scarce an arrow's flight behind those trees

Shall I conduct you to her

Fer: Do, do, do,

Robert

Perhaps twere fit I should go on before

That she may be prepared —

Fer: Thou hast said well

There will be need of preparation (Robert goes off.)

(Margaret attempting to speak

To Ferdinand) Sir —

Ferdi

He might have died — but to

such a daughter

To tell the story thus — Oh ye sweet heavens

Where was your mercy?

Margaret looking after her husband

[51r] [V.ii.83–88]

And we must see the bottom of it (turning to Fer:
Sir
I said that I would lead you to his daughter
but
My wife ~~just~~ now has left her at my hut
Tis scarce an arrow's flight behind those
trees
Shall I conduct you to her
Fer:
Do, do, do,
Robert
Perhaps twere fit I should go on before
That she may be prepared —
Fer:
Thou hast said well
There will be need of preparation
(Robert goes off.
(Margaret attempting to speak
to ferdinand)
Sir —
Ferdi
i
He might have d{[?]ed — but to
such a daughter
To tell the story thus — Oh ye sweet heavens
Where was your mercy?
Margaret looking ~~after~~ her
husband

These lines are a later version of the drafts on 50r; a brief further development of some of them appears on 49v.

Would he had not gone.

Ferdinand his eyes fixed on the ground

Life is strong in the girl - well met then thus

What is to come

These things die of themselves - what it

was I know not but it did not belong to

this world - yet I think it has left me

more tranquil than before -

[51^v]

Would he had not gone.
Ferdinand his eyes fixed on the ground
Life is strong in the girl — well meet then thus
What is to come

These things die of themselves — what it
was I know not but it did not belong to
this world — yet I think it has left me
more tranquil than before —

The lines at the top of the page run on from the scene overleaf. The lines at the bottom are developed from drafts at the top of 52^r, facing.

these things of themselves what it was
I know not but I think it has left me more
tranquil than before
moving creature

How many hours have I wandered night
and day through every corner of this
dreary heath. My eyes have been strained
till they have lost their uses my voice
has called unceasing but in vain — I
shall never be able to travel half a mile
in the darkness of the night again. Not
a tree bush or solitary did I meet
of a moving creature
This morning the
huntsmen were abroad upon the moor I
halloed after them but they took no notice
of me. — There was something
most horrible in the cry of those
dogs — I think I shall hear it till
the hour of my death: And yet plaintively
the nights have not been cold. There is still
some hope — His food (with horror) I have taken
care of that — But what of food
the body does not ask it
There
hours

[52r]

These things die of themselves what it was
but it
I know not but ~~I think~~ it has left me more
tranquil than before

moving creature
How many hours have I wandered night
and day through every corner of this
dreary heath. My eyes have been strained
till they have lost their uses my voice
has called incessantly but in vain.—I
shall never be able to travel half a mile
in the darkness of the night again. Not
a ~~tree~~ bush or solitary tree did I meet
that ~~had not the~~ shape of a moving creature
did not take the moving ^
~~but my heart leaped~~. This morning the
huntsmen were abroad upon the moor I
halloed after them but they took no notice
of me. —— There was something
most horrible in the cry of those
dogs —— I think I shall hear it till
hour
the [?] of my death: And yet (plaintively)
h
the nights [?]ave not been cold. There is still
(with horror)
some hope—— His food —— I have taken
what of food
[?]
care of that. But ~~when the mind~~ is
~~troubled the body does not ask its~~
~~accustomed nourishment~~ —— I have

These lines and their continuation on 52v are developed from the Edge of a Heath Scene, which begins on 55v.

not eaten since I left ~~him~~ — and if I have no
need of ~~sustenance~~ — Die of hunger!
Never — A mortal thirst might seize
upon his vitals — Aye that is terrible —
The heath is full of deserted quarries
what if he is fallen into one of them and
is now lying at the bottom maimed and
unable to rise — Oh damned villain
if thou art within a thousand ~~miles~~ leagues
will drag thee to the spot — and I shall
see whether thou wilt find it an easy
death bed . . . Foolish old man in
the best of thy days most foolish. — What
was that child of thine but a piece of clay
warmed with the breath of ~~three~~ two summers.
There may be virtue in these things but
~~if~~ mine is not the eye that can find it.
What a fever have I about my heart
I could drink up whole rivers. Whither
shall betake me now (casting his eyes
about) Ha! here is one from something
may yet be learned.

[52v]

the
not eaten since I left ~~hi~~m — and I have not
need ~~of sustenance~~ — Die of hunger!
Never — A mortal thirst might seize
upon his vitals — Aye that is terrible ——
The heath is full of deserted quarries
What if he is fallen into one of them and
is now lying at the bottom maimed and
unable to rise — Oh danned villain
leagues
if thou art within a thousand ~~miles~~ I
we
will drag thee to the spot — and [?~~I~~] shall
see whether thou wilt find it an easy
death bed . . . Foolish old man in
the best of thy days most foolish. — What
was that child of thine but a piece of clay
two
warmed with the breath of ~~three~~ ^ summers
There may be virtue in these things but
mine is
~~I have~~ not the eye that can find it.
What a fever have I about my heart
I could drink up whole rivers. Whither
shall betake me now (casting his eyes
about) Ha! here is one from something
may yet be learned.

In the first line, the "t" of "not" was erased.

What after years of penury and pain of
darkness and solitude wert thou to come to
this at last and consume in an unextinguishable
fire that the blaze of a moment might not
stifle the breath of a puling infant

is there no hope
mercy mercy die of hunger – Never
mortal thirst might seize upon his entrails
ay that is terrible – foolish old man
I thy last days are spotted cast them out
full [illegible] & ripe in all thy faculties
and for a piece of clay warmed by human [illegible].
full grown [illegible] with a [illegible]

Scene Margaret and Peasant

Margaret

In what you say though strange I do not see
sufficient cause therein to justify
Your quick return and interpose delay
In these your errand affairs – you must do not hesitate
The inquest must be taken – never fear
His daughter will protect you

Peasant It may be
Bethink thee so that I shall soon be summoned
Elsewhere to give particular account
of all that has befallen me at this time

[53^{r}]

What after years of penury and pain of
k
dar[?]ness and solitude wert thou to come to
l
this at last and I consume in extinguishab[?e]e
fire that the blaze of a moment might not
stifle the breath of a puling infant
is there no hope
O mercy mercy — die of hunger — Never
A mortal thirst might seize upon his vitals
Ay that is terrible — foolish old man
In thy best days most foolish wert thou not
full grown & ripe in all thy facultes
And for a piece of clay warmed by two summers
risk a a body
Full grown & ripe in all its faculties

Scene

Margaret and Peasant

Margaret

1 In what you say though strange I do not see
2 Sufficient cause therein to justify
3 Your quick return and interpose delay
your errand do
4 In this^affair — ~~you mus~~t not hesitate
5 The inquest must be taken — never fear
6 His daughter will protect you

Peasant

It may be
7 Bethink thee so that I shall soon be summoned
8 Elsewhere to give particular account
O
9 of all that has befallen me at this time

The lines at the top of the page were presumably meant for insertion into the soliloquy on 52^{v}, facing, and the drafts in the center of the page (entered last) represent an effort to versify a portion of that soliloquy. At the bottom of the page the Margaret and Peasant Scene, roughly equivalent to V.i of the finished play, commences (line numbers correspond to those of the reading text, pp. 54–55); running on through 54^{v}, it was evidently intended to lead into Ferdinand's soliloquy on 52^{r} and 52^{v}.

Caution is needful & therefore hear no further

Margaret

You said a sudden turning of the road
Down in the neighbouring dingle to your eye
Did first present him —

Peasant   and at such short distance

That I could mark him well myself unseen
He leaned upon the bridge that spans the glen
And down into the bottom cast his eye
That fastened there as it would check the current
And so he stood for several minutes space
Then as it were from fearful interruption
Of things to me invisible he turned
And looked about him with an eye of fear that showed
As if it wished to miss the thing it sought

Margaret

But did he utter nothing that explained
The cause of these appearances.

Peasant   Anon

He smote his breast the motion of his eye
Settled upon the ground

[53^{v}] [V.i.1–13]

10 Caution is needful — therefore hear me further
[?]
Margaret
11 You said a sudden turning of the road
12 Down in the neighbouring dingle to ~~your~~ eye
13 Did first present him —
Peasant
distance
and at such short
14 That I could mark him well myself unseen
15 He leaned upon the bridge that spans the glen
~~a glance~~
16 And down into the bottom cast his eye
17 That fastened there as it would check the
l} current
18 And so he stood for severat} minutes space
Then as it were from fearful
19 ~~The~~ startin~~g up, it seemed from~~ intimation
turnd—
20 Of things to me invisible he ~~lookd~~
And looked about him with an eye
{[?]
21 ~~A {ll about him~~ with an eye ~~of fear~~ that showed
22 As if it wished to miss the thing it sought
Margaret
23 But did he utter nothing that explained
24 The cause of these appearances.
Peasant
Anon
25 He smote his breast the motion of his eye
26 Settled upon the ground

15–20 The even handwriting suggests that these lines were copied in separately from the surrounding entries, and may indeed have been entered first, though the sense is continuous.

I heard these words the whole of what he spoke
"The dust doth move and eddy at my feet"
This was most strange the air being dead
and still

Margaret

'Tis some poor wretch of a unsettled fancy
Broke from his keeper's servant

So at first I thought
And meant to pass him there forthwith
To meddle with a business that might lead
By interfering with my present errand
To dangerous issues

Margaret

Then you mark him further

That in this taint he spread out his arms as twice
To save him off from falling and our fears
In judgement may be made from such impressions
As I that never seen on human frame
That such convulsive starts of pointed limbs
As never seized before on mortal frame
I do believe some horrible phantom then
Did pass before him such as God will not

[54^r] [V.i.14–26]

27 I heard these words the whole of what he spoke
28 "The dust doth move and eddy at my feet"
{Most
29 This was {I strange the air being dead
and still
Margaret
n unsettled
30 Tis some poor wretch of a ~~disor~~dered fancy
~~disturbed~~
~~His minds disordered~~
31 Broken from his keepers
Peasant
So at first I thought
32 And meant to pass him there forthwith
unwilling
33 To meddle with a business that might lead
By interfering with my present ~~errand~~ object
~~view~~
34 To dangerous issues
Margaret
Then you mark him further
35 That instant he spread out his arms as twere
36 To save himself from falling and as far
37 As judgement may be made from such impression
I had never seen
38 As I ~~till then ne'er saw~~ on human face
39 And such co/nsulvi|se starts of j|oint /and limbs
40 As never se/ized be|fore on ~~hum~~| m/ortal frame
te}
41 I do belevie some ho{ rrible ~~impulse~~ phantom
then
{G
42 Did pass before him such as {god will not

31 The first half of the line was probably first omitted by mistake, then crowded in; deletion by erasure.

Permit to visit any but a man
Who has been guilty of a damning crime

Marg:

Alas poor man —

Peasant

dear wife when it is known
As soon it will be that I was the man
Last seen with him who perished yesterday night
Until the real murderer is found out
I never shall be safe I do believe
This stranger has some business with the
Of this my errand — and am now returned
To follow with the [illegible] it were best to do
But see him coming — I will watch further

[54^{v}] [V.i.21–22]

43 Permit to visit any but a man
44 Who has been guilty of a damning crime
Marg:
45 Alas poor man —
Peasant
when
dear wife {[?once] it is known
46 As soon it will be that I was the man
47 Last seen with him who perished yesternight
48 Untill the real murderer is found out
I
49 [?] {[?] never shall be safe I do believe
50 This stranger has some business with the
cause
51 Of this my errand — and am now returned
52 To plan with thee what it were best to do.
53 But see him coming — I will watch further

---

53 Evidently intended to lead into Ferdinand's soliloquy, 52^{r}–52^{v}.

49

Druids. —

C. Comment. Lib. 6.
Commentaries Lib. 6.
Plin. Nat. His: Lib. 16. c. 44. — Lib. 29. c. 3
Dray. Polyolbion. Ninth Song —
Mona. Antiqua 338
Dion Chrysostom. —
Tac. annals. L. 14th. c. 29. —
Luc. Phar. L. 3. —
Ammianus Marcellinus Lib. 15th
Procopius. Goth. Lib. 4. —

[55^{r}]

Druids.——

C. Comment. Lib. 6.~~———————~~
Commentaries Lib. 6. ~~———————~~ c. 3
Plin. Nat. His: Lib. 16.c.44.—Lib. 29.
Dray. PolyOlbion. Ninth. Song—
Mona. Antiqua 338
Dion Chrysostom. — — —
Tac. annals. L. 14th.c.29. — —
Luc. Phar. L. 3. — — — —
Ammianus Marcellinus Lib. 15th
B. Procopius. Goth. Lib. 4. —

The bibliography on Druids may have been drawn up as research on *Salisbury Plain*; see *SPP*, p. 35.

Scene the edge of a heath – Enter Ferdinand
his hair loose and deep disordered, his looks betraying
extreme horror.
How many hours have I wandered night and
day through every corner of this dreary heath –
My eyes have been strained, my voice has
called incessantly but in vain —— I shall
never be able to travel half a mile in the
darkness of the night again. Not a bush
or solitary tree did I meet but my heart
leaped. This morning the huntsmen were
abroad upon the moor – I halloed after them
but they took no notice of me – There was
something most horrible in the cry of those dogs –
– I think I shall hear it till the hour
of my death And yet (plaintively) The night was not cold &
~~have yet some~~ There is still some hope what a fever have I about
my heart – I could drink up whole rivers –
Whither shall I betake me now (casting his eyes abou

[55^{v}]

Scene the edge of a heath — Enter Ferdinand
dress
his hair loose and disordered, his looks betraying
extreme horror.

1 *How many hours have I wandered night and*
day through every corner of this dreary heath ——
2 *My eyes have been strained, my voice has*
called incessantly but in vain —— *I shall*
3 *never be able to travel half a mile in the*
4 *darkness of the night again. Not a bush*
or solitary tree did I meet but my heart
5 *leaped. This morning the huntsmen were*
abroad upon the moor. I halloed after them
6 *but they took no notice of me — There was*
7 *something most horrible in the cry of those dogs—*
— I think I shall hear it till the hour
{ely)
And yet (plaintiv{)
8 *of my death — The night was not cold I*
There is still some
9 ~~*have yet some*~~ ^ *hope what a fever have I about*
my heart—I could drink up whole rivers —
10 *Whither shall I betake me now (casting his eyes about)*

Line numbers correspond to those of the reading text of the Edge of a Heath Scene, pp. 56–58. A further development of this soliloquy may be found on 52^{r}–52^{v}, with additional fragments on 53^{r} and 51^{v}. The hand is DW's.

ha! here is one from whom something may be learnt
Enter Cottager

Have you seen
In any corner of this savage heath ~~a poor, forsaken~~
A feeble helpless miserable wretch
A poor forsaken famished blind old man?

Cottager

helpless old and blind
I heard— And such a one you heard

Oh [illegible]

Heard! — then I live again you heard?
When? when you heard him? where? ~~had you any food~~
~~Was any dwelling nigh?~~ He called you to him?
~~Oh what a night had~~ Cottager I
The search of a stray heifer yesternight
While yet the moon was up had led me far
Into the wildest part of this wild heath
When hearing as I thought a sudden voice
I stopped and listened not without such fear
Upon me as the time and place might breed
I looked but neither could I hear or see

[56r] [V.ii.1–12]

ha! here is one from whom something may be learnt —
Enter {C / [?]*ottager*}
Have you seen
In any corner of this savage heath ~~a poor, forsaken~~,
A feeble helpless miserable wretch
[?~~*fa*~~] *A poor forsaken famished blind old man?*
Cottager
helpless old and blind
I heard—— And such a one you heard
Ferd.
Oh God you heard him [?what ?when] where
Heard! —— then I live again you heard! {? / !}
him, where?
Where? when you heard him? ~~had you any food?~~
~~*Was any dwelling nigh?*~~ {~~*H*~~ / ~~*he called you to him?*~~}
~~Oh what a night had~~ ~~I~~
(Cottager)
The search of a stray heifer yesternight
While yet the moon was up had led me far
Into the wildest part of this wild hath
When hearing as I thought as sudden voice
I stopped and listened not without such fear
Upon me as the time and place might breed
I looked but neither could {*I*} *heard or see*

16,17 The deletion lines are in pencil.
21,24 Deletion by erasure.

Aught living, only silent as the ground
[Their horses of the mountains]
The cotters shaggy ponies pastured near
And geese ~~[illegible]~~ [from] far ~~[illegible]~~ sent ~~[illegible]~~ [forth] a dreary cry
So ~~thinking~~ that my fancy had deceived me
I turned away when straight a second sound
~~[illegible]~~ Woman voice distinct smote on my ear
Thus guided, distant a few steps I found
A ~~poor old~~ [aged] man and such as you describe

Ferd

Alive — alive did you not say alive —
~~And was he very feeble? of all men~~
I [illegible] that he was known
The best and kindest ~~now~~ shall I repay thee
[illegible] how looked he had [illegible] any food
~~[illegible]~~ [illegible] but how looked he? lead
~~[illegible]~~ what said he — oh [lead] me to him
That I may ask forgiveness what said he?
Quick, did he ~~speak~~ speak of me?

Cottager

He only spoke
Of a ~~[illegible]~~ dear daughter
Who, so he feared, would never see him more.

[56v] [V.ii.13–18, 29, 35–37]

{ *A*
25 {[?*a*]*ught living, only silent as the ground*
Three horses of the mountains
26 *The cotters shaggy ponies pastured near*
from *t*} *forth*
27 *And geese ~~were heard a~~far ~~to~~ send* {^*a dreary cry*
28 *So thinking that my fancy had deceived me*
29 *I turned away when straight a second sound*
{*A* {*human*
30 {*Smote* {*on voice distinct smote on my ear*
31 *Thus guided, distant a few steps I found*
{n aged
32 *A*{ *~~poor old~~ man and such as you describe*
Ferd
Alive — alive did you not say alive —
33 *~~And was he very feeble? of all men~~*
I said that he was living
34 *The best and kindest ~~how~~ shall I repay thee*
{you ~~had~~
But ~~speak~~ how looked he had {he any food
where
35 *~~My good Angel~~! but how looked he? lead*
me to ~~him~~
{*~~M~~* {T what said he — oh
36 {*~~me to him~~* {*that I may ask forgiveness what*
said he?
{*eak*
37 *Quick, did he sp*{*oke of me?*
Cottager
He only spoke
38 *of a ~~dear~~ dear daugh*
ter
39 *Who, so he feared, would never see him more,*

And of a stranger to him one by whom he
He had been sore misused — But you are troubled
Perhaps you are his son?

Ferd —

~~The~~ The Heaven knows

I did not think he had a living child
But ~~when~~ did he ~~[illegible]~~ soon ~~recovered~~?
And when they died of [illegible]

Cottager

He was torn
His head was bruised and there was blood about him

Ferd —

That was no work of mine

Cottager

Nor mine God knows

Ferd

~~He had strength~~
~~But had he~~ strength to walk? I could have borne him
A thousand miles.

Cottager

I am in poverty.

And I have felt the cruel gripe of power
[illegible]
And know how busy is Suspicion's eye
~~I did not wish his blood upon my head~~

[57r] [V.ii.38–49]

40 *And of a stranger to him one by whom ~~he h~~*
41 *He had been sore misused — But you are troubled*
42 *Perhaps you are his Son?*
Ferd.
~~no~~
{~~Son~~
{*~~No Son~~ Heaven knows*
43 *I did not think he had a living child*
did soon
44 *But ~~when he was recovered?~~*
And whither did you bear him
Cottager
He was torn
45 *His head was bruised and there was blood about him*
{Mor
{*Ferd.*
46 *That was no work of mine*
Cottager
Nor mine God knows
{din
Fer{.
w
~~He had strength~~
47 *~~But had he~~ strength to walk? I could have born him*
48 *A thousand miles.*
Cottager
I am in poverty
49 *And I have felt the cruel gripe of power*
My heart was willing sir, but I am one
Whose good needs will not stand by their own light
50 *And know how busy is Suspicion's eye*
51 *~~I did not wish his blood upon my head~~*

---

40 Deletion by erasure.

My wife and children came into my mind
And though it smote me—more than tongue can tell
I left him—

Ferdin. Left him—Robert ~~[illegible]~~ told me
Left him! oh! monster what to perish left him
There is no heart in man ~~inform and blind~~
~~Of all forsaken what~~ could nothing move thee?
What damning Fiend had poisoned thee with [illegible]
Oh monster, monster, there are three of us
~~In the flames~~ ~~[illegible]~~ in the flames for me I shall not lie alone
But we shall howl together. Where, Where was it
Let us to the spot and with the speed o' the wind
I've heard that men have. Lain whole weeks entranced
~~And to all [illegible]~~ and seeming dead
And life yet in them. If there is a spark
I'll find it

(dragging him along)

Cottager

'Tis needless spare your violence, his daughter

[57^{v}] [V.ii.50, 55–57, 60, 68]

52 *My wife and children came into my mind*
53 *And though it smote me — more than tongue can speak*
54 *I left him ——*

tis as I have said
Ferdin. Left him —
Robert ~~I have told~~ the truth

55 *Left him! oh! monster what to perish left him*
56 *There is no heart in man ~~infirm and blind~~*
57 *~~Of all forsaken what~~ could nothing move thee?*
58 *What damning Fiend has poisened thee in th'ear*
59 *Oh monster, monster, there are three of us*

R{eserved / [?]} *in the flames*
{*R* li}
60 *~~In the flames~~ {~~prepared~~ for me I shall not b{e alone*
Ther is no
61 *But we shall howl together — Where, where was* [?*it*]
62 *Let us to the spot and with the speed o'the wind*
63 *~~I've heard~~ that men have lain whole weeks entranced*
64 *~~And to all out~~ward seeming dead*
65 *And life yet in them; if there is a spark*
66 *Ill find it*
(dragging him along)
Cottager
67 *'Tis needless spare your violence, his daughter*

---

67 Here the scene breaks off, as only stubs of the rest of the notebook remain, up to the final leaf. The last part of the missing section of the scene is redrafted on 50^{r}–50^{v} and 51^{r}–51^{v}, with a further fragment on 49^{v}.

Most of the leaves were torn out efficiently, but two sequences of stubs, 96–99 and 101–105, retain scraps of the beginnings of lines, which seem to be in DW's hand and in the ink she was using on 57^{v}, the last surviving leaf. Each stub has enough small initial letters to show that the leaves contained only prose.

[Inside back cover]

Why
[?I ?perceive ?his] daughter [? ?knows] that the
[?monster ?murderd ?him. ?doth ?she ?live ?there]
for the [?monster ?should] be destroyed for
our [?]

Sent for a draught of water — [?nor ?one]
~~[?have ?we ?]~~
[?I ?have ? ?him]
We left him at a critical [?time]
[?In ?his] human disposition

All in pencil, these drafts may, like those on the inside front cover, be connected with II.iii.

Essay Prefaced to MS. 2, with Variants from DC MS. 27 in an *Apparatus Criticus*

The text is the version in Sara Hutchinson's hand which is prefaced to the fair copy of *The Borderers* in MS. 2 (DC MS. 23), a vellum-bound notebook that also contains fair copies of the two-part *Prelude* of 1798–99 and *The Beggar*. The notebook is fully described in the headnote to the facing transcriptions of MSS. 2 and 3, below. The *apparatus criticus* records all variants in the other manuscript of the essay, DC MS. 27, except those involving the ampersand and letters missing where MS. 27 is worn.

DC MS. 27 consists of three gatherings of white rolled paper folded in folio and gathered singly, with leaves machine-cut to 22.7 by 18.6 centimeters. The watermark reads I TAYLOR / 1795. Leaves 1^r–5^r contain a fair copy of the prefatory essay, untitled. The essay opens in what appears to be the hand of John Wordsworth, with much misspelling and no paragraph breaks; toward the bottom of 2^r the hand becomes that of Dorothy Wordsworth, and there are frequent paragraph breaks from that point onward. There are a few late revisions in pencil, possibly in Mary Wordsworth's hand. Leaves 5^v and 6^r are blank, and the epigraph for the play appears in Wordsworth's hand.

The stitching that held these gatherings together has been removed. On May 28–30, 1842, Mary Wordsworth wrote from London to pass on instructions for John Carter, at Rydal, "to have the goodness to send the MS. introduction to the Tragedy which he must detach from the Tragedy—I think it was left in the Sideboard drawer" (*The Letters of Mary Wordsworth: 1800–1855*, ed. Mary E. Burton [Oxford, 1958], p. 257). It is attractive to link this instruction with the removal of the stitching from DC MS. 27, and with the presence of penciled revisions in this manuscript (there are none to the text of the essay in MS. 2). The sideboard-drawer MS. was presumably one of the copies of the early version of the play referred to in letters of 1798–99, and it therefore predated DC MS. 23 (see Introduction, p. 6).

The two texts of the essay, in DC MSS. 23 and 27, are very similar, apart from the absence of paragraph breaks in the opening portion of MS. 27 (up to the point where Dorothy took over copying from John Wordsworth), and the relationship between the texts is not easy to establish. The spelling errors in MS. 27 imply that John, at least, found his original difficult to decipher: his rendering of "the Orlando of Ariosto, the Cardenio of Cervantes" as "the Orlando of aristo, the Candenio of carvantes" (ll. 55–56) appears to be the result of misreading, rather than mishearing or misspelling. The possibility that DC MS. 27 is a copy of DC MS. 23 can be ruled out, since the latter contains a haplographic error (l. 34) not reproduced in the former. The case for regarding DC MS. 23 as a copy of DC MS. 27 is stronger, especially as the change from one long paragraph to short paragraphs can then be attributed to a scribal change from John to Dorothy. Differences between the two texts are otherwise minor variants of the kind that a copyist working quickly often produces, with the exception, perhaps, of the references to Ariosto and Cervantes, which would require a knowledgeable or quick-witted copyist. The case is not proved, however; one can say with certainty only this: either the two texts have a common original or the text of MS. 23 was copied from MS. 27.

[1r]

*Let us suppose a young Man of great intellec-
tual powers, yet without any solid principles of
genuine benevolence. His master passions are pride
and the love of distinction— He has deeply imbibed a
spirit of enterprize in a tumultuous age. He goes
into the world and is betrayed into a great crime.—
That influence on which all his happiness is built
immediately deserts him. His talents are robbed of
their wei{g/dht—his exertions are unavailing, and he
quits the world in disgust, with strong misanthropic
feelings. In his retirement, he is impelled to exam
ine the reasonableness of established opinions &
the force of his mind exhausts itself in constant
efforts to separate the elements of virtue and vice.
It is h is pleasure & his consolation to hunt out
whatever is bad in actions usually esteemed virtu-
ous & to detect the good in actions which the
universal sense of mankind teaches us to repro-
bate. While the general exertion of his intellect
seduces him from the remembrance of his own
crime the particular conclusions to which he is
led have a tendency to reconcile him to himself.
His feelings are interested in making him a moral
sceptic & as his scepticism encreases he is raised
in his own esteem. After this process has been
continued some time his natural energy & restlessness
impel him again into the world. In this state pressed*

The hand, to l. 82, is JW's
3 master-passions
5 tumuluous
8 desirts talants
9 weight *no dash, no comma*
13 exausts
15 his
16 Vurtuous
19 exertions *with* s *del*
23 intrested
26 ristlesstness
27 world— state,

[1v]

by the recollection of his guilt he seeks relief from two sources, action & meditation. Of actions those are most attractive which best exhibit his own powers, partly from the original pride of his character and still more because the loss of Authority and influence which followed upon his crime & brought along with it those tormenting sensations by which he is assailed. The recovery of his original importance & the exhibition of his own powers are therefore in his mind almost identified with the extinction of those painful feelings which attend the recollection of his guilt. Perhaps there is no cause which has greater weight in preventing the return of bad men to virtue then that good actions being for the most part in their nature silent & regularly progressive, they do not present those sudden results which can afford a sufficient stimulus to a troubled mind. In processes of vice the effects are more frequently {i/ly}*mmediate, palpable and extensive. Power is much more easily magnif*{ested/ied} *in destroying than in creating. A child Rousseau has observed, will tear in pieces fifty toys before he will think of making one. From these causes assisted by disgust and misanthropic feeling the character we are now contemplating will have a strong tendency to vice. His energies are most impressively manifest in works of devastation. He is the Orlando of Ariosto ~~the~~ the Cardenio of Cervantes who lays waste the*

---

28 reccollection
29 of Actions
32 Character
33 folled
34 crime & brought] crime was the first circumstance which impressed him with the magnitude of that crime & brought
36 exibition
39 reccollection
45 sufficiant
46 immediate,
48 manifested
50 one.—
54 manifested
55 aristo
55–56 ~~the~~ the] the
56 Candenio of carvantes

[2r]

groves that should shelter him. He has rebelled against the world & the laws of the world & he regards them as tyrannical masters, convinced that he is right in some of his conclusions, he nourishes a contempt for mankind the more dangerous because he has been led to it by reflexion. Being in the habit of considering the world as a body which is in some sort at war with him, he has a feeling borrowed from that habit which gives an additional zest to his hatred of those members of society whom he hates & to his con– tempt of those whom he despises. Add to this, that a mind fond of nourishing sentiments of contempt will be prone to the admission of those feelings which are considered under any uncommon bond of relation (as must be the case with a man who has quarrelled with the world) the feelings will mutually strengthen each other. In this morbid state of mind he cannot exist without occupation, he requires constant provocatives, all his pleasures are prospective, he is perpetually ch[ ]sing a phanton, he commits new crimes to drive away the memory of the past. But the lenitives of his pain are twofold, meditation as well as action. Accordingly his reason is almost exclusively employed in justifying his past enormities & in enabling him to commit new ones. He is perpetually imposing upon himself, he has a sophism for every crime. The <u>mild</u> effusions of thought, the milk of human reason are unknown to him. His im{agi / mag}nation is powerful, ^being strengthened by the habit of picturing possible forms of soci- ety where his crimes would be no longer crimes, and he would enjoy that estimation to which from his intellectual attainments he deems himself entitled. The nicer shades of manners he disregards, but whenever upon looking back upon past ages, or in surveying the practices of different countries in the age in which he lives he finds such

59 *no comma*
62 reflection
67 scociety contempt
68 dispises *no comma*
70 feelings which are] feelings are
75 provocation *overwritten* provacatives prospective. he
76 chusing a phantom *no comma*
78 two folds, *with* s *del*
81 himself *no comma*
82 *DW's hand begins with* for *no comma*
83 imagination
84 powerful being strengthened by
88 *no comma* upon] in
89 *no comma*

[2v]

contrarieties {as / of} seem to affect the principles of morals, he exults o{ver / f} his discovery and applies it to his heart as the dearest of his consolations. Such a mind cannot but discover some truths, but he is unable to profit by them and in his hands they become instruments of evil

He presses truth and falshood into the same service He looks at society through an optical glass of a peculiar tint something of the forms of objects he takes from objects but their colour is exclusively what he gives them, it is one, and it is his own. Having indulged a habit, dangerous in a man who has fallen, of dallying with moral calculations he becomes an empiric and a da{r / ning} & unfeeling empiric. He disguises from himself his own malignity by assuming the character of a speculator in morals and one who has the hardihood to realize his speculations.

It will easily be perceived that to such a mind those enterprizes which are the most extraordinary will in time appear the most inviting. His appetite from being exhausted becomes unnatural. Accordingly he will struggle so to characterize & to exalt actions little and contemptible in themselves by a forced greatness of manner and will chequer & degrade enterprizes great in their atrocity by grotesque littleness of manner, and fantastic obli{quities / [?]}. He is like a worn out voluptuary—he finds his temptation in strangeness he is unable to suppress a low hankering after the double entendre in vice yet his thirst after the extraordinary buoys him up, and supported by a habit of constant reflexion he frequently breaks out into what has the appearance of greatness; and in sudden emergencies when he is called upon by surprize & thrown out of the path of his regular habits, or when dormant associations are awakened tracing the revolutions through which his character has passed in painting his former self he really is great

---

91 as *no comma*
92 over
94 *no comma*
95 evil.
96 service.
102 daring
107 be *written over* by
113 manner, checquer
115 obliquities.
116 strangeness—
118 entendre *altered in pencil to* entente (*1841*)
120 reflection
122 calld
123 regular *following* general *del* *no comma*
126 great.

[3r]

Benefits conferred on a man like this will be the seeds of a worse feeling than ingratitude. They will give birth to positive hatred. Let him be deprived of power, though by means which he despises, & he will never forgive. It will scarcely be denied that such a mind by very slight exter-nal motives may be led to the commission of the greatest enormities. Let its malignant feelings be fixed on a ~~a~~ particular object & the rest follows of itself.

Having shaken of{f/ } the obligations of religion & morality in a dark and tempestuous age, it is probable that such a character will be infected with a tinge of superstition. The period in which he lives teems with great events which he feels he cannot controul. That influence which his pride makes him unwilling to allow to his fellow-men he has no reluctance to ascribe to invisi-ble agents: his pride impels him to superstition and shapes out the nature of his belief: his creed is his own: it is made & not adopted.

A character like this, or some of its features at least, I have attempted to delienate in the following drama. I have introduced him deliberately prosecuting the destruction of an amiable young man by the most atrocious means & with a pertinacity as it should seem not to be accounted for but on the supposition of the most malignant injuries. No such injuries however appear to have been sustained. What are then his motives? First it must be observed that to make the nonexistence of a common motive itself a motive to action is a practice which we are never so prone to attribute exclusively to madmen as when we forget ourselves Our love of the ma{r/v}vellous is not confined to external things. There is no object on which it settles with more delight than on our own minds. This habit is in the very essence of the habit which we are de{li/lie}n{e/i}ating.

But there are particles of that poisonous mineral of which Iago speaks gnawing his inwards, his malevolent feelings are excited & he hates the more deeply because he feels he ought not to hate.

---

129 positive
134 ~~a~~ particular] particular
135 off
136 *no comma*
138 lives *superimposed on* teems
141 fellow-men
143 belief:] belief
146 delineate
152 are then] then are
153 non-existence
155 ourselves.
159 delineating.
160 *no paragraph*
162 excited,
163 more] more more

[3v]

We all know that the dissatisfaction accompanying the first impulses towards a criminal action where the mind is familiar with guilt acts as a stimulus to proceed in that action. Uneasiness must be driven away by fresh uneasiness, obstinacy, waywardness & wilful blindness are alternatives resorted to, till there is an universal insurrection of every depraved feeling of the heart.

Besides in a course of criminal conduct every fresh step that we make {*appears* / [?]} *a justification of the one that prece*{*de* / *ded*} *it, it seems to bring back again the moment of liberty and*^*choice*; *it banishes the idea of repentance and seems to set remorse at defiance. Every time we plan a fresh accum*{*ul* / [?]}*ation of our guilt we have restored to us something like that original state of mind that perturbed pleasure which first made the crime attractive*

If after these general remarks *what are Rivers's motives to the atrocity detailed in the drama? I answer they are founded chiefly in the very constitution of his character; in this pride which borders even upon madness, in his restless disposition in his disturbed mind, in his superstition, in irresistible propensities to embody in practical experiments his worst & most extravagant speculations in his thoughts & in his feelings in his general habits & his particular impulses in his perverted reason justifying his perverted instincts. The general moral intended to be impressed by the de*{*l* / *t*}*ineation of such a character is obvious, it is to shew the dangerous use which may be made of reason wh*{*e* / *a*}*n a man has committed a great crime.*

165–167 where . . . action *repeated (in 1841 del in pencil)*
169 blindness, till *following* still *del*
173 appears] seems
174 that precede] which preceded *no comma* *second* it *superimposed on* &
175 and choice;
177 accumulation of] to
179 attractive.
181 , I am asked *penciled into gap (1841)*
182 Rivers's *del in pencil to* Oswald's *(1841)*
183 drama. founded] found
186 disturbed *following* pro *del*
188 speculations,
190 impulses,
192 delineation
194 when

[4r]

There is a kind of superstition which makes us shudder when we find moral sentiments to which we attach a sacred importance applied to vicious purposes. In real life this is done every day and we do not feel the disgust. The difference is here. In works of imagination we see the motive and the end. In real life we rarely see either the one or the other and when the distress comes it prevents us from attending to the cause. This superstition of which I have spoken is not without its use; yet it appears to be one great source of our vices, it is our constant engine in seducing each other. We are lulled asleep by its agency and betrayed before we know that an attempt is made to betray us.

I have endeavoured to shake this prejudice persuaded that in so doing I was well employed. It has been a further object with me to shew that from abuses interwoven with the texture of society a bad man may be furnished with sophisms in support of his crimes which it would be difficult to answer.

One word more upon the subject of motives. In private life what is more common than when we hear of law-suits pro{*secu* / [?*su*]}*ted to the utter ruin of the parties, and the most deadly feuds in families to find them attributed to trifling and apparently inadequate sources. But when our malignant passions operate the original causes which called them forth are soon supplanted, yet when we account for the effect we forget the immediate impulse and the whole is attributed to the force from which*

---

198 vicious *following* virtuous *del*
215 *penciled* X *in margin* (*1841*)
217 prosecuted

[4v]

the first motion was received. The vessel keeps sailing on, and we attribute her progress {in / to} the voyage to the ropes which first towed her out of harbour.

To this must be added that we are too apt to apply our own mo{r / l}al sentiments as a measure of the conduct of others. We insensibly suppose that a criminal action assumes the same form to the agent as to ourselves. We forget that his feelings and his reason are equally busy in contracting its dimensions and pleading for its necessity.

---

a [?] Tragedy

Of human actions reason though you can,
It may be reason, but it is not man:
His principle of action once explore,
That instant tis his principle no more.
Pope. ——

---

225 Vessel
226 in
229 moral
233 feelings,
234–235 necessity.— — — — —
Epigraph *no title, no signature*
236 Of] On *no comma*
238 *no comma*
239 'tis *no period*

MS. 2: The Early Version (1799, Revised 1841–42)

facing

MS. 3: The Late Version (1841–42) with Variant Readings of MS. 4 (1842) in an *Apparatus Criticus*

followed by

MS. 2: Selected Photographs

Here are presented facing transcriptions of MSS. 2 and 3 of *The Borderers*. Beneath the MS. 2 text, on the left-hand pages, are cross-references to transcriptions of the entries in MS. 2A, a manuscript contemporary with the revisions entered in MS. 2 (1841–42). The *apparatus criticus* to MS. 3, on the right-hand pages, records variants to the revised text of MS. 3 found in MS. 4, the manuscript that served as printer's copy for the play in *Poems, Chiefly of Early and Late Years* (1842), as well as those found in MS. 4a; it also provides cross-references to MS. 3A, separately transcribed, and records variant readings in the surviving proof sheets, which cover the first ten pages of the printed text of the play (to l. 191 of MS. 3).

The transcriptions are keyed by two independent sets of line numbers: (*a*) The transcription of the MS. 2 text is accompanied by act, scene, and line numbers in the left margin. These numbers correspond with those of the reading text of the early version. Each line of verse has been numbered, but when the text changes to prose (as at II.iii.87), the numbers correspond with the prose lines as set out in the reading text rather than as set out in the manuscript. By this means it has been possible to keep the numbering in step with the reading text. These line numbers provide the key for the textual footnotes and the cross-references to MS. 2A. (*b*) The transcription of MS. 3 is accompanied by continuous, cumulative line numbers in the right-hand margin. These numbers correspond with those of the reading text of the late version, and provide a key for the textual footnotes and *apparatus* of variants in MS. 4, MS. 4a, and the proof sheets, as well as for cross-references to MS. 3A. When the play changes to prose, as at line 1903, the line numbers, like those of the reading text, have been kept in step with those of de Selincourt's text in *PW*, I.

MS. 2 of *The Borderers* is inscribed in a white vellum-bound notebook, DC MS. 23, containing six stitched gatherings of white laid paper folded in folio and gathered in eights to make gatherings of sixteen leaves, with leaves cut to 19.2 by 15.6 centimeters. There are eight horizontal chain lines per leaf, approximately 2.6 centimeters apart. The watermark consists of a large circle enclosing the image of Britannia and surmounted by a crown; the countermark is an elaborately ornamented "H" and the date, 1796. All gatherings are regular, but the manufacturer has glued the first two leaves of the first gathering and the last two leaves of the last gathering to the boards to form the inside front and back covers. The notebook therefore contains 184 pages, and I have disregarded the leaves stuck to the boards and have numbered from the first leaf of the notebook, 1^r.

Inside the front cover of MS. 2, Coleridge penciled "A letter [?] / What comes of it," perhaps referring to II.i.124–130, or V.iii.126–131. *The Borderers*, with its prefatory essay, occupies the first 72 leaves of the notebook, followed by MS. U of the two-part *Prelude* on 73^r–90^r and *The Beggar* on 90^v–92^v. All three works were entered as fair copies in 1799, the first five leaves of *The Borderers* and *The Beggar* in the hand of Sara Hutchinson, the rest of the play and the two-part *Prelude* in the hand of Mary Hutchinson. The original fair-copy text of *The Borderers* was overwritten late in 1841 with revisions, mostly in the hand of Mary Wordsworth (a few are in Wordsworth's own hand).

In the transcription of MS. 2, all underlinings may be understood to date from 1799 and all revisions from 1841, unless otherwise noted. Deletions by erasure made in 1799 are footnoted, but not those made in 1841. The overwriting of leading strokes that are part of the underlying 1799 fair copy is not noted.

MS. 2A, separately transcribed below, is a collection of drafts for *The Borderers* in DC MS. 151/8, formerly Verse 102(7), most of them versifying prose passages in the early version. The manuscript is made up of reused postal wrappers, one bearing the postmark December 4, 1841. Comparison suggests that the revisions in MS. 2 largely predate the equivalent text in MS. 2A, but it is also clear that the text of MS. 2A rarely derives directly from MS. 2. Either Wordsworth had worked from another manuscript (the "Sideboard-drawer" manuscript or the "other Copy" referred to on 26^v of MS. 2, perhaps) or from scrap sheets used for preliminary rough drafting of revisions to the play. The text of MS. 2A clearly predates its equivalent in MS. 3, which appears to derive directly from it.

MS. 3 of *The Borderers*, DC MS. 148, formerly Verse 16, originally consisted of at least eleven gatherings of rather poor-quality white rolled paper, with no watermark, folded in folio and gathered in sixes to make gatherings of twelve leaves, with leaves measuring 25.2 by 20.2 centimeters. Numerous pasteovers were stuck to parts of the original pages with sealing wax; they have now been lifted to allow recovery of the underlying text. As it survives, the manuscript consists largely of single leaves, with a few remaining part gatherings and stubs. They are insufficient to enable us to determine with any accuracy how many leaves were removed and their text recopied in the course of revision. One instance of such removal has survived in the form of a separate copy of pages 117–122 (Mary Wordsworth's numbering), which has been preserved at the Wordsworth Library in a separate binding but with the same DC MS. number as the main body of MS. 3, which contains recopied versions of these pages. Some instances of recopying are indicated by the survival of stubs, which occur as follows (Mary Wordsworth's numbering): one stub following page 100; four stubs following page 108; one stub following page 116; and two stubs following page 122. The first four pages of the text are missing, and the manuscript begins with the equivalent of I.i.89 in the early version. Thereafter, the text of the play is complete, and Mary Wordsworth's page numbering ignores stubs (except as noted above) and is continuous.

The base text of MS. 3 is a fair copy of a revised text of *The Borderers* in the hand of Mary Wordsworth. This fair copy appears to derive in part from MS. 2 directly, and in part from MS. 2A; in addition, as already observed, it may well derive from another early text revised, and from further scratch sheets. Since it clearly postdates MS. 2A, MS. 3 must have been copied out after December 4, 1841. The base text has been heavily revised, largely in Mary Wordsworth's hand but also in the hands of Wordsworth and John Carter. During this revision, MS. 2 was occasionally further revised to conform to the revised readings in MS. 3.

In the transcription, pasteovers (presented, like other revisions, in small type) are enclosed by horizontal rules. The recopied text of pages 117–122 has been presented in the same way as pasteovers, as have lines inscribed in the margin. When the handwriting is that of John Carter rather than Mary Wordsworth, this fact has been noted. It is sometimes hard to distinguish Wordsworth's hand from Mary's in revision; as the main bulk of revision was entered by Mary, the rule adopted here is to accept all revision as in her hand unless the orthographical evidence for Wordsworth's hand is very strong. There are also difficulties in distinguishing layers of revision of accidentals. Many corrections and reinforcements of letters and punctuation were made both in Mary's original copying and in revision. The stage of revision represented by these markings is often unclear; it is also frequently impossible to distinguish alterations from simple reinforcements. In the transcription, the simple reinforcement of letters has not been recorded except when it is accompanied by an alteration of spelling or wording; and all punctuation is shown on the line, not elevated (that is, treated as original or "base text" punctuation), *except* where different punctuation marks are clearly distinguishable, or where one mark has clearly been converted to another, or where clearly added punctuation is associated with substantive (that is, verbal) revision.

As I have observed, the opening four pages of MS. 3 are missing; in the transcription, the text facing MS. 2 has been supplied from MS. 4.

MS. 4 of *The Borderers* consists of the first sixty leaves of DC MS. 149, formerly Verse 17, a complete fair copy of the play drawn up in Dora's hand from MS. 3. The leaves are identical with those of MS. 3, and are largely single cut leaves, though they are occasionally folded in folio. The sixty-first and last leaf of DC MS. 149 repeats the last page of the play (from l. 2285) and is in the hand of Mary Wordsworth; it has therefore been designated MS. 4a. Revisions in MS. 4 are predominantly in Mary's hand, with a few emendations and reinforcements in the hands of Wordsworth and John Carter, as in MS. 3, and some comments by the printers, who set *The Borderers* from DC MS. 149.

The extant proof sheets (part of DC MS. 151, formerly Verse 102) consist of sheets listing the dramatis personae and covering the first ten pages of the play, with corrections and instructions in the hands of Mary Wordsworth, John Carter, and the printer.

The *apparatus* to MS. 3 provides a record of all variants from the revised text of MS. 3 in MSS. 4 and 4a and in the proof sheets. It does not record alterations in the form of speaker identification, or abbreviations used in stage directions, or variants involving the ampersand or the spelling of the name Idonea or the name change from Margaret to Eleanor. Hands appearing in the revisions to MS. 4 may be taken to be Mary's unless otherwise identified, although identification of single letters, even words, is often conjectural. Not recorded are single-letter miswritings corrected by the copyist, the erasure of false starts in the wrong position, or alterations of form that appear in the proof sheets (the use of uppercase letters for names, for example) as conventions imposed by the printer. The hand in the proof sheets is recorded only when it is clearly identifiable; base text and revisions in MS. 4a are in Mary's hand.

In addition to providing a record of variants in MSS. 4 and 4a and the proof sheets, the *apparatus* provides cross-references to MS. 3A in DC MS. 151/3, formerly 102(2), which has been transcribed in full—along with MS. 2A—following the transcriptions of MSS. 2 and 3.

The following abbreviations appear in the *apparatus criticus:*

alt	alternate
apos	apostrophe
cap	capital or capitalized
del	deleted
dir	direction
eras	erased or erasure
exclam	exclamation
ident	identification
illeg	illegible
parens	parentheses or parenthesis
P2	second-stage proof sheets in DC MS. 151, formerly Verse 102
punct	punctuation
rev	revised or revision

[MS. 2]

[5r]

Act 1.st

[I.i] *Scene, Road in a Wood.——*
Mortimer — Wilfred.

The base text on 5r is probably in SH's hand, but all deletions and revisions are late, in pencil, and in the hand of MW, unless otherwise noted. For a transcription of the epigraph on the facing verso, see p. 444, above.

[MS. 3]

I.

The Borderers:
A Tragedy.

Act 1st Scene, road in a Wood;}

Wallace and Lacy.

Lacy:

The Troop will be impatient; let us hie
Back to our post, and strip the Scottish Foray
Of their rich {S / spoil, *ere they recross the Border.*
—Pity that our young Chief will have no part
In this good service.

Wallace:

Rather let us grieve
th{e / is *undertaking which has caused*
That in ~~his~~ Enterprize ~~whate'er its aim~~,
His absence he hath sought,} *whate'er his aim*'}
~~*He should have sought Companionship with One*~~
Companionship with one of crooked ways,
From whose perverted soul can come no good
To our straight-forward, noble-minded, Leader.

Lacy:

True; and, remembering how the Band have proved

---

above Dramatis Personae on proof sheet: To the Printer / This page has an awkward appearance, / Mr W. thinks the notes would look / better placed below the Dramatis Personae / —as a Note *P2 (MW)*

below Dramatis Personae: Scene, Borders of England & Scotland / Time, the Reign of Henry 3.[d] / Readers &c *P2 (MW)*

1–10 *further developed in MS. 3A, 3*[r]
4 Young *lowercased P2*
6 *comma inserted following* That *P2*
7 *comma inserted following* absence *P2*
8 one *then capitalized P2*
10 Straight-forward] *so P2, but* confiding *in 1842*

The first four pages of MS. 3 are missing, and the opening pages of MS. 4 have here been transcribed in their place.

1 *Wil:* *Be cautious my dear Master!*
Mor: *(~~smiling~~) — — — — I perceive* [21]
2 *That fear is like a cloak which old men huddle*
3 *Around their love, as' t'were to keep it warm*
4 *Wil:* *— — — — — — Nay, but my heart is sad to part with you*
5 *~~To part with you~~ —— This ~~Rivers~~ — Stranger for such is he*
Mor: *— — — — — — — What of him?*
6 *Wil:* *You know that you have saved his life—*

---

1 Ink deletion of "smiling" may be early.
3 Deletion by erasure.

That Oswald finds small favour in our sight, 12

Wallace

Well may we wonder he has gained such power 13

Over our much-loved Captain.^ ~~*I have heard*~~ 14

I have heard

Of some dark deed to which in early life 15

His passion drove him—then a Voyager 16

Upon the midland Sea. *You knew his bearing?* 17

2.

~~*Wallace*~~*:*

^— — — — — — ~~*You knew his bearing*~~

In Palestine?

Lacy:

— — — — — —*Where he despised alike* 18

But enough 19

Mahomedan and Christian.—~~*We must be gone*~~*.*

The Band may else be foiled. Let us be gone. Exeunt 20

(~~*Exit Wallace & Lacy*~~

Enter Marmaduke and Wilfred.

Wilfred:

Be cautious, my dear Master!

Marmaduke:

— — — — — — — — *I perceive* 21

That fear is like a cloak which old men huddle 22

b t

Ar{ou{nd their love, as if to keep it warm. 23

Wilfred:

[?]

I grieve that we should part: This Stranger 24

Nay but ~~*my heart is sad to part with you*~~*.*

{F {is——

~~*This Stranger*~~*,* {*for such* ~~*is*~~ *he* {——

Marmaduke:

Your busy fancies, Wilfred, 25

Might tempt me to a smile, but {w

— — — — — — — — — {*What of him?* 26

Wilfred:

You know that you have saved his life.

---

12 *semicolon del to comma P2*

14–20 *further developed in MS. 3A, 4*[r]

19 enough, *then comma del to semicolon P2*

20 The Band may else be foiled. Let us begone. *then order of parts of line reversed with transposition mark and line rewritten:* Let us begone—the Band may else be foiled. *P2 (WW)*

26 *comma del to semicolon P2*

17b The caret points to a note at top of page: "To the Printer) omit the leading Strokes that run thro' this MS."

20 The word "Exeunt" is JC's.

Mor: — — — — — — — — *I know it* [27]
7 *Wil:* *And that he hates you! (~~seeing Mort: displeased~~)*
— — — — — — — — *Pardon me, perhaps*
8 *That word was hasty*
Mor: *Fie! no more of ~~this~~ it*
9 *Wil:* *Dear Master! Gratitude's a heavy burthen* [30]
10 *To a proud soul.— Nobody loves this ~~Rivers~~ Oswald*
11 *Yourself you do not love him*
Mor: — — — — — — — — — — *I do more*
12 {*Wil* / [?]} *I honor him.*
— — — — *O! Sir*
Mor: — — — — — *Peace my good Wilfred*
13 *Repair to Liddersdale, and tell the Band* [41]
14 *I shall be with them in two days, ~~at farthest~~. farew*
{*Wilfred* / *Wil: Fare*} *Farewell*

[5^{v}]

15 *Wilfred. ~~Farewell! and Heaven preserve you~~ —*
May He whose eye is over all protect you

Exit Wil.

Oswald
Enter ~~Rivers~~, with a bunch of plants in his hand

16 *Os* / *Riv*: *This wood is rich in plants and curious simples* [44]

The hand from 5^{v} onward is MH's, and the 1841 revisions (unless otherwise stated) are MW's.

12 Ink overwriting is SH's 1799 revision.

15 Portions of the revision below the line were evidently written in pencil before being inked; above the line are five words in pencil (erased): "May he whose eyes are."

16 Revisions of names here and throughout the scene are in pencil.

Marmaduke:

— — — — — — — — — I know it.

3

Wilfred:

And that he hates you!—Pardon me, perhaps
That word was hasty.

Marmaduke:

— — — — — — Fie, no more of it.

Wilfred:

Dear Master! gratitude's a heavy burden
To a proud Soul;—Nobody loves this Oswald—
Yourself, you do not love him.

Marmaduke:

— — — — — — — — I do more,
Strong feelings to his heart
I honour him.^ ~~What perils hath he shunned~~?
{;
Are natural { & from no one can be learnt
~~What difficulties hath he failed to conquer~~?
More of man's thoughts & ways than his experience
Has given him power to teach; & then, for courage
~~Answer these questions from our common knowledge~~,
And enterprize, }what perils hath he shunned?
*~~What difficulties hath he failed to conquer~~^*
~~And be at rest~~.
Answer these questions, from our common knowledge,
And be at rest.

^What obstacles hath he failed to overcome?

Wilfred:

— — — — — — — — Oh Sir!

Marmaduke:

— — — — — — — — — — Peace, my good Wilfred;
Repair to Liddisdale, and tell the Band
I shall be with them in two days, at farthest.

Wilfred:

May He whose eye is over all protect you!

(Exit.)

Enter Oswald (a bunch of plants in his hand)

Oswald:

This wood is rich in plants, and curious simples.

---

29 Fie *rev to* Fy! *P2*
33–37 *further developed in MS. 3A, 6*[v]
36 teach;] learn; *del to* teach: *P2 (JC)*

37/39 L. 38 is in the left margin.

m Oswald
Mor: *(looking at tho{se ~~in Rivers' hand~~)*
17 *The wild rose, and the poppy, and the night-shade*
18 *Which is your favourite, ~~Rivers~~? Oswald?*
Oswald}
~~Riv~~: —{— — — — *That which, while it is*
Os
19 *Strong to destroy, is also strong to heal.*
(looking forward as to a distance)
20 *Not yet in sight! we'll saunter here a while*
21 *They cannot mount this hill unseen by us.*
Mor: *(a letter in his hand)*
22 *It is no common thing when men like you*
23 *Perform these little services, and therefore,*
Oswald}
24 *I feel myself much bounden to you, Rivers{;*
25 *'Tis a strange letter this— You saw her write it?*
Os
26 ~~Riv~~: *And saw the tears with which she blotted it.*
27 Mor: *And nothing less would satisfy him?*
Os
~~Riv~~: — — — — — — — — — *No less.*
28 *For that another in his child's affection*
29 *Should hold a place, as if 'twere robbery,*
30 *He seemed to quarrel with the very thought.*
31 *Besides I know not what strange prejudice*
{B
32 *Seems rooted in his heart: this{band of ours*
33 *Which you've collected for the noblest ends,*

[6^r]

34 *Here on the ~~savage~~ confines of the Tweed & Esk*
s}
35 *To guard the innocent, he calls us outlaw[?]}*
36 *And for yourself in plain terms he asserts*
is g}
37 *Th[?at]{arb was taken up that Indolence*
{ty
38 *Might want no cover, and rapaci{ ou~~sness~~*
39 *Be better fed.*
Mor: — — — — — *Never may I own*
40 *The heart which cannot feel for one so helpless.*
41 ~~Riv~~. *Thou knowest me for a man not easily moved*
Os
42 *But death! it stirs my very soul to think*
43 *Of what I witness'd.*

16/17 Revision of "those" was made first in pencil.
26 Speaker identification altered first in pencil.
32 Overwriting in pencil.
34 Deletions in pencil, with "savage" also deleted in ink; revision in pencil, overwritten in ink.
35, 37 MH's 1799 corrections.
38 Deletion and revision in pencil, overwritten in ink.

4.

Marmaduke: (looking at them)
The wild rose, and the poppy, and the nightshade:
Which is your favorite, Oswald?

Oswald:
— — — — — — That which, while it is
Strong to destroy, is also strong to heal— (looking forward.)
Not yet in sight!—we'll saunter here awhile;
They cannot mount the hill, ~~unseen~~ by us. unseen.

Marmaduke: (a letter in his hand)
It is no common thing when One like you
Performs these delicate services, and therefore
I feel myself much bounden to you, Oswald;
Tis a strange letter this!—You saw her write it?

Oswald:
And saw the tears with which she blotted it.

Marmaduke:
And nothing less would satisfy him?

Oswald:
— — — — — — — No less;
For that another in his Child's affection
Should hold a place, as if 'twere robbery,
He seemed to quarrel with the very thought.
Besides, I know not what strange prejudice
Is rooted in his mind; this Band of ours,
Which you've collected for the noblest ends,
Along the confines of the Esk and Tweed
To guard the Innocent, —} *he calls us "Outlaws;"*

5

And, for yourself, in plain terms he asserts
This garb was taken up that Indolence
Might want no haven{*cover*}*, and rapacity*
Be better fed.

Marmaduke:
— — — — Ne'er may I own the heart
That cannot feel for one{'*—helpless as he is.*

Oswald:
Thou know'st me for a Man not easily moved,
Yet was I grievously provoked to think
Of what I witnessed.

---

46 favourite, *rev to* favorite, *P2*
65 Indolence *then lowercased P2*

---

66 The overwriting appears to be Dora's.

Mor: ——————— *Well! to day the truth*
Shall end her wrongs.
Os
~~Riv~~: ——————— *But if the blind man's tale*
Should yet be true.
Mor: ——————— *Would it were possible!*
Did not the soldier tell thee that himself,
And others who survived the wreck, beheld [75]
The Baron Herbert perish in the waves
Upon the coast of Cyprus?
Os
~~Riv~~: ————————— *True he did so;*
And something of the kind though where, I know not
It seemed that I had heard before: and verily
The tale of this his quondam Barony
Is cunningly devised: and on the back [80]

[6v]

Of his forlorn appearance could not fail
To make the proud and vain his tributaries
And stir the pulse of lazy charity.
The seignories of Herbert are in Cornwall
We neighbours of the Esk and Tweed: 'tis much [85]
The wily vagrant——
Mor: —————— *Nay be gentle with him*
Though I have never seen his face, methinks
There cannot be a time when I shall cease
To love him— I remember when a Boy [89]
Of six years growth or younger, by the thorn

Marmaduke:

— — — — — — — *This day will suffice*
To end her wrongs.

Oswald:

— — — — — — — *But if the blind Man's tale*
Should _yet_ *be true?*

Marmaduke:

— — — — — — — — — *Would it were possible!*
Did not the Soldier tell thee that himself,
And Others who survived the wreck, beheld
The Baron Herbert perish in the waves
Upon the Coast of Cyprus?

Oswald:

— — — — — — — — — *Yes, even so,*
And I had heard the like before: in sooth
The tale of this his qua{o / a}*nd*~~o~~*m Barony*
Is cunningly devised; and on the back
Of his forlorn appearance could not fail
To make the proud and vain his tributaries,
And stir the pulse of {*la* / [?*ch*]}*zy charity.*

6

The seignories of Herbert are in Wales; *Devon;*
We neighbours of the Esk and Tweed: tis much
The ~~*wily vagrant*~~ {A / arch-}{I / impostor} ——

Marmaduke:

Treat him gently, Oswald,
— — — — — — — ~~*Nay be gentle with him*~~*!*
Tho' I have never seen his face, methinks,
There cannot be a time when I shall cease

5

~~*To*~~ *To love him.—I remember when a Boy,*
Of ~~*six*~~ *scarcely seven years growth,* ~~*or younger, by the thorn*~~ ~~*less*~~*, beneath the* {*E* / *elm*}

77 Coast *then lowercased P2*
80 *comma inserted following* and *P2*
81 *comma inserted following* appearance *P2*
85 We] The *del to* We, *P2*
86 Arch Imposter, *then* I *lowercased, hyphen added, and period del to dash with instruction to printer:* Long break after / "Arch-Imposter"—not a period. Speech interrupted— *P2 (JC)* *final comma del to semi-colon P2*
88 be a time *rev to* come a day *P2 (JC)*
89 remember, *comma del after* Boy

79 The overwriting appears to be Dora's.
89 MS. 3 begins here.

out
64 *Which starts from*^*the ~~old~~ church-yard wall of Lorton,*
65 *It was my joy to sit and hear ~~Matilda~~* Idonia
66 *Repeat her father's terrible adventures,*
67 *Till all the band of play-mates wept together,*
m}
68 *And that was the beginning of y{y love*
69 *And afterwards, when we conversed together*
70 *This old man's image still was present: chiefly*
71 *When I had been most happy*
Os
~~*Riv*~~: *— — — — — — — — — Whence this paleness?*
72 *Two travellers* *(Mor: points)*
Mor: *— — — — The woman is Matilda*
73 *Riv:* *And leading Herbert*
Mor: *— — — — — We must let them pass*
74 *This thicket will conceal us.*
(They retire)
{t
En{der Matilda (leading Herbert blind)

[7r]

75 *Mat:* *Dear Father you sigh deeply: ever since*
76 *We left the willow shade, by the brook side,*
77 *Your natural breathing has been troubled.*
Her: *— — — — — — — — — — — Nay*
78 *'Tis not so bad with me, and yet I know not*
of} yesterday
79 *Our ~~last night's~~ march——}*
[?]

64 Revisions probably made first in pencil.
68 MH's 1799 revision.
74/75 MH's 1799 correction.
79a Deletion in pencil, revision in pencil overwritten in ink.

That casts̸ its shade over our village school,
~~*Which starts from out the church-yard wall of Lorton*~~,

~~It~~ {'T was my delight *~~joy~~ to sit & hear Idoni{e a*
Repeat her Father's terrible adventures,
Till all the band of play-mates wept together.
~~*if such a weakness may be told to thee*~~
~~*And that,^was the beginning of my love*~~
{And {at
{To th{ee was the beginning of my love.
~~*And afterwards when we conversed together*~~
And thro' all converse of our later years
~~This old Man's~~ [?] ~~ima~~ ~~ge~~ still was present, ~~chiefly~~
*An image of this old Man^*
When I had been most happy. Pardon me
If this be idly spoken.

See,
~~Yonder~~ they come,

Os: — — — — — — ~~*Whence this paleness*~~?

Two Travellers!
~~*Two Travellers*~~

Mar: — — — *The female ~~traveller~~*
(points) — — — ~~*The Woman*~~ *is Idon{e ia,*

Osw. *And {l teading Herbert—*

Mar — — — — — — — *We must let them pass*
(they step aside)
This thicket will conceal us.

Enter Idoni{e a, leading Herbert blind.

~~Idon~~{~~ea~~ ~~ia~~ *Idonea* *Dear Father, you sigh deeply; ever since*

6

We left the willow shade, by {the by brook-side,
Your natural breathing has been troubled.

— — — — — — — — — — *Nay,*
You are too fearful; yet must I confess,

Her: ~~*Tis not so bad with me*~~, *&* ~~*yet I know not*~~
Our march of yesterday— *had better suited*
A firmer step than mine.

---

91 casts
94 together.] together;
96 thro'] through *commas inserted after* And *and* years *P2*
100 *semicolon del to period after* Idonea
101 pass—
102 us.—

upon {*T*
Mat: *— — — — ~~Plague on~~* {*that dismal heath!*
In spite of all the larks that cheared our path [109]
I ne'er shall love it more. How chearfully
You paced along while the dim moonlight cloud
Mocked me with many a strange fantastic shape
I thought the convent never would appear
It seemed to move away from us: and yet
That you are thus the fault is mine: for truly
l} *y*}
The air was warm, no dew w{*as*{ *on the grass,*
had fallen
And midway on the heath, ere ~~the~~ night ~~fell~~, [117]
had fallen
covert walled & roofed with
I spied a ~~little hut built with green~~ sods,
A miniature it was: and as it seemed
Some shepherd's boy had raised it half in sport
shelter
To cheat the lazy time and half to ~~screen~~ him

79b Deletion in pencil and ink.
87 Revision in pencil.
88 Revision below line in pencil, above line in ink; deletion lines in pencil.
89 Deletions in pencil, except for "with"; revisions above line in pencil overwritten in ink.
92 Revision in pencil, overwritten in ink.

{t Ido:
Ma{r: — — — — — — — — — That dismal ~~heath~~ Moor— 108
In spite of all the Larks that cheered our path, 109
{ver more & {K how stedfastly 110
I ne{'er shall love it ~~more~~ {~~How cheerfully~~

{the
when{a bewildering { u
<u>You</u> paced along ~~while the dim~~ moonlight ~~clo~~{[?se]d 111
Mocked me with many a strange fantastic shape! 112
I thought the Convent never would appear; 113
It seemed to move away from us: & yet, 114
That you are thus the fault is mine; for truly 115
The air was warm, no dew lay on the grass, 116
moor
And midway on the ~~heath~~ ere night had fallen 117
I spied a ~~little~~ Covert ^walled & roofed with sods 118
Some Shepherd-boy, 119
A miniature it was; ~~& as it seemed~~

~~Belike he raised half in sport~~

~~Some Shepherd-boy had raised it half in s[?port]~~
{~~belike~~ {~~belike~~
Who ~~found~~ {~~a nothing~~ {[?] a nothing-doing hour
might have found
~~To cheat the lazy time, & half to shelter him~~
Heavier than work, raised it belike for shelter
~~From rain or [?] wind: in that small hut~~
Or in the pride of skill; in that small hut
could
We ~~might~~ have made a <u>cozie</u> bed of heath
And thankfully there rested side by side
~~And lying down together rested safely~~
Wrapped in our cloaks, & with recruited strength

Who might have found a nothing-doing-
hour 120
Heavier than work, raised it, belike for shelter 121a

---

108 Moor— *del to* Waste *then to* moor— moor *then capitalized P2*
110 I never more shall love it: and how stedfastly *then* Never can *alt del and line rev to* I never can forgive it: but how steadily *with* steadily (*JC*) Never can I forgive it: but how steadily *then transposed to* I never can forgive . . . *and* I never can *copied at foot of page P2 (WW)*
111 along,
112 shape!—
115 truly *del to* the air
116 The air was warm, *rev to* Was soft and warm,
117 moor *del to* Waste
118 sods: {—}
119 it was *del to* belike *and comma inserted after* miniature Some] some
120 *hyphen del before* hour
121a it,] it; *then semicolon del to comma P2* belike *del to* to serve *then del with last two words in line to* within that hut

or nipping
From rain and ~~the bleak~~ wind: in that small hut
cozee
We might have made a‸*bed of ~~the dry~~ heath*
And lying down together rested safely
Wrapped in our cloaks, and with recruited strength [124]
Have hailed the morning sun. But cheerly, Father
l
That staff of yours, I could af{most have heart
To fling't away from you; you make no use
Of me, or of my strength, come let me feel
That you do press upon me. There— Indeed [129]

[7^v]

Let us rest awhile
You are quite exhausted— ~~Here is a green bank~~
~~Let us repose a little~~. *(He sits down)*
On this green bank
Her: *(after some time) You are silent*
~~That is a silence which I know Matilda~~!
Idonia I understand your silence
S *why*
Mat: — — — — *~~Wherefore thus~~*‸*reproach me?*
why
When I behold the ruins of that face [135]
Those eye-balls dark—dark beyond hope of light
s
And think that they were bla{[?]ted for my sake
The name of Mortimer is blown away;

---

98 MH's 1799 correction.
93, 94, 102, 115, 120 Revisions in pencil, overwritten in ink.
103 Revision in pencil.
104 The revision, marked by a penciled X in left margin, is in pencil overwritten in ink, as is the "S."
105 Caret and correction above line are in pencil.
108 MH's 1799 correction.

Or in the pride of skill, [.] *{I} in that small hut* 121b
We might have made a kindly bed of heath 122
And thankfully there rested side by side
Wrapped in our cloaks, & with recruited
strength 124

7
Have hailed the morning sun. But cheerly Father,— 125
That staff of your's, I could almost have heart 126
To fling't away from you: you make no use 127
Of me, or of my strength;—come let me feel 128
That you do lean on me. There—indeed 129
You are quite exhausted. Let us rest awhile 130
On this green bank— (he sits down.)
Idoni{e/a}
Her (after some time) {y/You} are silent, 131
And I divine the cause. 132a
~~*Idonia, I understand your silence*~~

Ido: *Do not*
~~*Mat*~~*: — — — — — — — —* ~~*Why*~~ *reproach me*
patiently
I pondered [?~~*heedfully*~~*] your wish & will*
When I ~~*behold the ruins of that face*~~
gave way to your request, & now
When I behold the ruins of that face

Ido. — — — — — — — Do not reproach me: 132b
I pondered patiently your wish & will 133
When I gave way to your request, & now, 134
When I behold the ruins of that face, 135

Those eye-balls dark—dark {b/yeyond} hope of light, 136
And think that they were blasted for my sake, 137
~~*An*~~
[?]{~~*d ponder in my heart your wish & will*~~
Marma
The name of Mortimer} duke is blown away: 138

121b *del*
124 and, . . . strength,
125 cheerly *rev to* cheerily
126 yours
128 come,
129 lean *del to* press
131 bank.—

Father, I would not change this proud delight
For the best hopes of love.
Her: *— — — — — Nay be composed:*
Few minutes gone a faintness overspread [141]
My frame, and I bethought me of two things
I ne'er had heart to separate — my grave
And thee, my child!
honored e
Mat: *— — — — — — Believe me, Sir,*
'Tis weariness that breeds these gloomy fancies, [145]
And you mistake the cause: you hear the woods
Resound with music: could you see the sun,
And look upon the pleasant face of Nature——
comprehend
Her: *I ~~understand~~ thee: I should be as chearful*
As if we two were twins; two songsters bred [150]
In the same nest, my spring-time one with thine
Well, be it so—you have indulged me child!
In many an old man's humour. Sitting here
I feel myself recovered. The bequest

[8r]

Of thy kind patroness, which to receive [156]
We have thus far adventured, will suffice
To save thee from the extreme of penury
But when thy father must lie down and die
How wilt thou stand alone?
Mat. *(earnestly) — — Is he not strong?* [160]
Is he not valiant?
— — — — — — — — Am I then so soon
warnings
{warnings
Her: *Forgotten— Have my {[—?—] passed so*
quickly
Out of thy mind, My dear, My only Child?
This Mortimer—

A photograph of 8r is provided below, p. 716.

131–133 Space appears to have been left in 1799 for a line and two half lines; it was not filled until 1841, when penciled lines were inserted, beginning "Have my" and concluding with the third "My"; these lines were reinforced in ink, and the remaining material was added. Underneath "warnings," deletion of the original reading was in ink.

Father, I would not change this proud delight 139
For the best hopes of love.
Her: — — — — — — — — *Nay be composed:* 140
Few minutes gone a faintness overspread 141
My frame, & I bethought me of two things 142
I ne'er had heart to separate—my grave, 143
And thee, my Child!
Ido
~~*Mat*~~ — — — — — — *Believe me, honoured Sire!* 144

8

'Tis weariness that breeds these gloomy fancies, 145
And you mistake the cause; you hear the woods 146
Resound with music, could you see the sun; 147
And look upon the pleasant face of nature— 148
Her: *I comprehend thee—I should be as cheerful* 149
As if we two were twins; two songsters bred 150
In the same nest, my spring-time one with thine. 151
My fancies, fancies if they be, are such 152
~~*Well, be it so—you have indulged me Child*~~
As come dear Child! from a far deeper source 153
~~*In many an Old Man's humour. Sitting here*~~ .} {*W*
Than bodily *weariness,*} {*while here we sit* 154
~~*strength refreshed*~~
~~*recovered*~~} ~~*returning*~~.
~~*I feel myself*~~ *refreshed*}.—*The bequest* 155
I feel my strength returning.—
Of thy kind Patroness, which to receive 156
We have thus far adventured, will suffice 157
To save thee from the extreme of penury; 158
But when thy Father must lie down & die 159
How wilt thou stand alone?
Ido:
~~*Mat*~~ (~~*earnestly*~~) — — — *Is he not strong?* 160
Is he not valiant?
Herb: — — — — — — *Am I then so soon* 161
?} {*H*
Forgotten—} {*have my warnings passed so quickly* 162
Out of thy mind, my dear, my only Child; 163
Thou wouldst be leaning on a broken reed— 164
This Marmaduke——

139 proud *del to* dear this proud delight] the dear delight *del to* that sacred feeling *P2 (WW)*
140 the best hopes of love. *del to* all this world can give. *P2 (WW)* Nay,
144 honoured *rev to* honored *P2*
146 cause, :}
147 sun,
148 Nature— *final dash extended and note added:* longer break *P2 (JC)*
153 come,
162 have
163 mind: ?} only,

Mat: — — — — — *O could you hear his voice* [165]
Alas! you do not know him. He is one
(I guess not what bad tongue has wronged him with you)
All gentleness and love. His face bespeaks
A deep and simple meekness: and that soul
Which with the motion of a glorious act [170]
a look of terror upon guilt
Flashes ~~a terror-mingled look of sweetness~~
quiet
Is, after conflict, ~~silent~~ as the ocean
By a miraculous finger stilled at once [173]
Her: *Unhappy woman!*
Mat: — — — — *Nay it was my duty*
Thus much to speak. but think not I forget
~~But think not, think not father, I forget~~
Dear Father how could I forget & live
You & *~~The history~~ of that ~~lamentable~~ night,*
doleful
When Antioch, blazing to her topmost towers [178]
You rushed into the murderous flames, returned
Blind as the grave, but, as you oft have told me,

[8v]

You clasped your infant daughter to your heart.
Herb: *Thy mother too—scar[?]{c/e} had I gains{e/d} the door—*
I caught her voice, she threw herself upon me
I felt thy infant ~~arms~~ brother in her arms
She saw my blasted face—a tide of soldiers [185]
That instant rushed between us and I heard
Her last death-shriek distinct among a thousand.
Mat: *Nay father, stop not, let me hear it all*
'~~Twill do me good~~.
precious relic of that time
Herb: *Dear daughter, ~~dearest love~~*

150, 152 MH's 1799 corrections.

Ido:
~~Mat~~ ——— O could you hear his voice

9

Alas! you do not know him. He is one
{(I ~~guess~~ [know] not what ~~bad~~ [ill] tongue has wronged him with you)}
All gentleness & love. His face bespeaks
A deep~~ly~~ & simple meekness: & that soul,
Which with the motion of a glorious act
Flashes a look of terror upon guilt,
Is, after conflict, quiet as the ocean,
By a miraculous finger, stilled at once.
Herb: Unhappy woman!
Ido:
~~Mat~~ ———— Nay it was my duty
Thus much to speak; but think not I forget—
Dear Father! how could I forget & live—
You, & the Story of that doleful night
When, Antioch, blazing to her topmost Towers,
You rushed into the murderous flames, returned
Blind as the grave, but, as you oft have told me,
You clasped your infant Daughter to your heart.
Herb. Thy Mother too!—scarce had I gained the door;
I caught her voice; she threw herself upon me,
I felt thy infant brother in her arms—
She saw my blasted face—a tide of soldiers
That instant rushed between us & I heard
Her last death-shriek, distinct among a thousand.

10

Ido:
~~Mat~~: Nay Father, stop not, let me hear it all—
Herb: Dear daughter! precious relic of that time—

---

165 voice; *then semicolon del to colon P2*
167 know *del to* wot
169 Soul,
170 glorious *del to* virtuous
174 woman! *then capitalized P2*
177 *no comma* Story *then lowercased P2*
178 Towers, *then lowercased P2*
181 You clasped *del to* Clasping *P2 (WW)*
184 *dash del to semicolon P2*
185 soldiers,
187 thousand.—
188 all.—*then dash del*
189 daughter! *then capitalized P2*

---

167 Deletion and revision of "guess" in pencil reinforced in ink.

For my old age it doth remain with thee
To make it what thou wilt—Thou hast been told
That, when, on our return from Palestine
I found that my domains had been usurped.
I took thee in my arms, and we began
Our wanderings together. Providence
T
At length conducted us to Rossland there
Our melancholy story moved a stranger
To take thee to her home, and for myself
Soon after the good abbot of saint Cuthberts
Supplied my helplessness with food and raiment
humble cot
And as thou knowest gave me that ~~little cottage~~
we
Where now ~~I~~ dwell— For many years I bore
Thy absence, 'till old age and fresh infirmities,
~~*Now six months gone exacted thy return*~~
Exacted ~~thy return~~, & our reunion
stet

[9^r]

I did not think that during that long absence
My child forgetful of the name of Herbert
Had given her love to a base freebooter
Who here, upon the borders of the Tweed
Doth prey alike on two distracted countries
Traitor to both.
Mat: — — — — *Oh could you hear his voice*
I will not call on heaven to vouch for me
But let this kiss speak what is in my heart.

Enter a Peasant

Pea: *Good morrow to you, lady!*
I guess that you are strangers; if you need
One better skill'd—

---

164 MH's 1799 correction.
170 Revision in pencil.

For my old age it doth remain with thee
To make it what thou wilt. Thou hast been told,
That when, on our return from Palestine,
how
I found ~~that~~ my domains had been usurped,
I took thee in my arms, & we began
Our wanderings together. Providence
At length conducted us to Rossland,—there
Our melancholy story moved a Stranger
To take thee to her home—& for myself,
's
Soon after the good Abbot of St Cuthbert }
Supplied my helplessness with food & raiment,
'
And, as thou knowe}st, gave me that humble Cot
Where now we dwell. For many years I bore
Thy absence, till old age & fresh infirmities
Exacted thy return, & our reunion.
I did not think that, during that long absence,
My Child, forgetful of the name of Herbert,
Had given her love to a base Freebooter,
Who here, upon the borders of the Tweed,
Doth prey alike on two distracted Countries
Traitor to both.

II

Ido:
~~*Mat*~~: *— — — — — Oh could you hear his voice!—*
I will not call on heaven to vouch for me
But let this kiss speak what is in my heart—

Enter a Peasant

! } { I for you
Strangers, } { if ~~you~~ ^ ~~for~~ a Guide
Pea. *Good morrow ~~to you Lady!~~*
{ Be
{ [?We] waiting, let me serve you!
~~I guess that you are Strangers; if you need~~
Ido — — — — My Companion
~~One better skilled—~~
~~Ido~~

---

190 age,
191 *P2 ends with this line*
196 there,
206 child, *then capitalized*
207 base *del to* wild
209 Countries,
211 me,
214 waiting,] wanting,

---

213 The phrase "for you" is JC's.

{tell
hut or hos{pice
Mat: ——————— *The sight of ~~inn or cottage~~*
184 *Would be most welcome to us.*

’}
Pea: ——————————— *Yon white hawthorn}* [216]
gained
185 *You will look down into a dell, and there*
{ill
186 *W{e see an ash from which a sign-board hangs*
187 *The house is hidden by the shade—Old man*
188 *You seem worn out with travel—shall I support you* [220]
so}
189 *Herb: I thank you but our resting place ne} near*
190 *’Twere wrong to trouble you—*
Pea: ——————————— *God speed you both!*
191 *You cannot miss the place. (exit Peasant)——*

[9v]

192 *Herb: Matilda we must part!*
Mat:— Part!
Herb:— Be not alarmed
193 *’Tis but for a few days— a thought has struck me* [224]
{is {house
194 *Mat: That I should leave you at th{e {inn and thence*
195 *Proceed alone? It shall be so, I feel*
196 *You are quite exhausted—*
(Exit Herbert supported by M.)

Oswald
Re-enter Mortimer and ~~Rivers~~

197 *Mortimer— This instant will we stop him, ~~a father too!~~*
Be not hasty {B
198 *~~Rivers~~— ~~Nay, Mortimer, I prithee~~ {be not hasty*
Oswald
199 *For, sometimes in despite of my conviction*
200 *He tempted me to think the story true;* [230]
{maid
201 *’Tis plain he loves the {~~girl~~, and what he said*
202 *That savoured of aversion to thy name*

184/185 The “gained” was probably crowded in by MH in 1799 and the comma added in 1841.
186 Revision in pencil.
189 MH’s 1799 revision.
196/197, 198, 201 Revisions in pencil, rule added 1841.

~~*Hut or Hostel*~~
Hath need of rest; the sight of Hut or Hostel 215
~~*Ido*~~
~~*Mat*~~*:* — — — — — — — ~~*The sight of hut or*~~ {~~*H*~~ ~~*hostel*~~}
Would be most welcome } ~~*to us*~~

Pea — — — — — — — — *Yon white hawthorn gained*— ,} 216
You will look down into a dell, & there 217
Will see an ash from which a sign-board hangs 218
The house is hidden by the shade. Old man, 219
You seem worn out with travel, {— ,} *shall I support*
you? 220
a
Her: *I thank you, but,* ~~*our*~~ *resting place so near,* 221
T' were wrong to trouble you.
'{~~*T*~~ ~~*twere wrong to trouble you*~~}
Pea ~~*We cannot miss it now*~~
~~*Pea*~~ — — — — — — — — — *God speed you both.* 222
~~*You cannot miss the place*~~. *(exit Peasant)*
Idonea we must part
Her: — — — — — — — — ~~*Idonia, we must part*~~
Be not alarmed— 223
{~~*Idon*~~ *Mat*} ~~*Part! sa*~~*[?]* ~~*Part sa*~~{~~*id*~~ ~~*y you Father?*~~}
Tis but for a few days—a thought has struck me. 224
~~*Herb*~~ — — ~~*Be not alarmed—tis but for a few days*~~
~~*a thought has struck me*~~

12

Ido:
~~*Mat*~~*:* *That I should leave you at this house, & thence* 225
·} ;} *for strength* 226
Proceed alone?} *It shall be so,*} ~~*I feel*~~
Would fail you ere our journey's end be reached. 227
~~*That you are quite exhausted*~~
Herbert
(Exit ~~*H*~~ ^ *supported by* ~~*Mat*~~*)*
Idonea

Reenter Marmaduke & Oswald.

Mar *This instant will we stop him*—
Osw: — — — — — — — — *Be not hasty,* 228
For sometimes, in despite of my conviction, 229
He tempted me to think the Story true; 230
Tis plain he loves the Maid, & what he said 231
That savoured of aversion to thy {*n* *mame*} 232

---

218 hangs;
221 you;
222 *no apos*
223 part.
229 For,

203 *Appeared the genuine colour of his soul,*
204 *Anxiety lest any harm should reach her*
205 *After his death*
Mor: *— — — — — I have been much deceived.* [235]
maid
206 ~~*Riv*~~*:* *But sure he loves the* ~~*girl*~~*, and never love*
Osw
207 *Could find delight to nurse itself so strangely*
{*T* *torment*
208 ~~*And*~~ {*thus to* ~~*plague*~~ *her with* <u>*inventions*</u>*! death!*
209 *There must be truth in this*

[10r]

Mor: ~~*False! False as hell*~~
!}
210 <u>*Truth*</u> *in the story!*} ~~*had the thing been true*~~
211 *He must have felt it then, known what it was,* [240]
212 *And thus to prey upon her heart had been*
213 *A tenfold cruelty—*
Riv: *— — — — — What strange pleasures*
214 *Do we poor mortals cater for ourselves!*
215 *To see him thus provoke her tenderness*
weakness *y,*}
216 *With tales of* ~~*symptoms*~~ *and infirmities,*} ~~*and yet*~~
217 *I'd wager on his life for twenty years!* [246]
218 *Mor:* *We will not waste an hour in such a cause*
219 *Riv:* *Why this is noble! shake her off at once*
Idonia
220 *Mor:* ~~*Matilda has a heart— It is her virtues*~~
221 ~~*Of which he makes*~~ *his instruments—A man*
Her virtues are^ {*sense*
222 *Who has so practiced on the worlds cold* {[?] [250]
223 *May well deceive his child—what leave her thus*
designed for Clifford
224 *A prey to such a traitor——No—no—no—*
225 *'Tis but a word and then—*
Riv: *— — — — — — There must be something*
{*o*
226 *More than we see, or whence this str*{*ang*~~*e*~~ *aversion*
227 *Mortimer! I suspect unworthy tales* [255]
228 *Have reached his ear—you have had enemies*

206, 208 Revisions in pencil.
Deletions and revisions on 10r are in pencil.
210 Underlining added in pencil, 1841.
222 MH's 1799 revision.

Appeared the genuine colour of his soul— 233
mischief should befal ~~come to~~
Anxiety lest ~~any harm should reach~~ her 234
After his death.
Mar: *— — — — I have been much deceived.* 235
en,
Os *But sure he loves the Maid,^& never love* 236
Could find delight to nurse itself so strangely {! , 237
Thus to torment her with invet{n tions {! —death— 238
There must be truth in this.

13

his
Mar: *— — — — Truth in ~~the~~ story!* 239
He must have felt it then, known what it was, 240
~~in such wise~~ to^ rack
in suchwise ~~tender~~ gentle
And thus to ~~prey upon~~^her^heart, ~~had been~~ 241
Had been a
A^tenfold cruelty.~~+~~
Osw: *— — — — — ~~What~~ {S strange pleasures* 242
Do we poor mortals cater for ourselves! 243
To see him this provoke her tenderness 244
With tales of weakness & infirmity 245
twenty
I'd wager on his life for ~~fifty~~ years. 246
Mar. *We will not waste an hour in such a cause.* 247
Osw: *Why this is noble! shake her off at once.* 248
Mar: *Her virtues are his instruments.— A man,* 249
Who has so practiced on the world's cold sense, 250
May well deceive his {C child—what leave her th{us ere— 251
a deceiver
A prey to ~~such a traitor~~— No—no—no— 252
Tis but a word & then——
Something is here 253
Osw *— — — — — — ~~There must be something~~*
More *than we see, or whence this str{o ange aversion{?* 254
Marmaduke! I suspect unworthy tales 255
Have reached his ears{— [?]you have had enemies{. : 256

---

234 mischief should befal] harm should come to *del to* mischief should befall
239 *no underlining*
241 rack] prey upon *del to* rack *and* gentle *inserted (Dora)*
245 infirmity,{!
249 *no comma*
250 practised
251 there *rev to* thus *as MS. 3*
252 No] no

[10ᵛ]

Mor: *Away! I tell thee they are his own coinage*
Riv: *But wherefore should his love exclude a rival?*
The safeguard of a man like Thee it seems
~~*To one so helpless, it should seem, the safeguard*~~
Should be most welcome to his helplessness
ou}
~~*Of such a man as thee*~~{, ~~*should be most welcome*~~
I do not like this—
Mor: *— — — — — Like it! for my part—*
Riv: *But there is something here*
Mor: *— — — — — What hast thou seen?*
{*the*
in {*this thing stands clear of*
Riv: *No, no,*^ ~~*there is no mystery in this*~~
As you have said he coins himself the slander [262]
With which he taints her ear—For a plain reason
He dreads the presence of a virtuous man
Like you, he knows your eye would search his heart,
Your justice stamp upon his evil deeds [266]
The punishment they merit—All is plain
It cannot be—
Mor: *— — — — — — — What cannot be?*
Riv: *— — — — — — — — — Yet that a father*
Should torture thus the heart of his own child—
Mor: *Nay, you abuse my friendship!*

[11ʳ]

Riv: *— — — — — — — — Heaven forbid!* [271]
There was a trifling circumstance; indeed
Though at the time it struck me, I believe

Deletions and revisions on 10ᵛ are in pencil.

14

~~*Enemies*~~
~~*Of his own coinage*~~
~~*Aye & of his*~~
Mar: ~~*Away! I tell thee they are his own coining*~~
n
Enemies!—of his oww coinage.
Osw: That may be
Osw ~~*But wherefore should his love exclude a rival*~~.
But wherefore slight protection, such as you
~~*The safeguard of a Man like thee it seems*~~
? P
Have power to yield, perhaps he looks elsewhere.
~~*Should be most welcome to his helplessness*~~
I am perplexed.
~~*I do not like this*~~
~~*Mar:*~~ *— — — — —* ~~*What hast thou heard or seen?*~~
~~*Mar:*~~ *— — — — — —* ~~*Like it! for my part*~~
~~*Osw: But there is something here*~~
heard or
Mar: — — — — — — What hast thou^seen?
Osw— No—no—the thing stands clear of mystery
( )
As you have said, he coins himself the slander
With which he taints her ear.— For a plain reason,
He dreads the presence of a virtuous man
Like you; he knows your eye would search his heart,
Your justice stamp upon his evil deeds
:
The punishment they merit —All is plain:
It cannot be—
Mar: — — — What cannot be?
Osw. — — — — — — Yet that a Father
Should in his love admit no rivalship
~~*Should*~~ *torture thus the heart of his own Child——*
And

15

you
Mar: Nay, nay abuse my friendship!
Osw — — — — — — — — — Heaven forbid!—
, ,
There was a trifling circumstances^ indeed
Tho' at the time it struck me, I believe

257 be,
258 *comma del*
261 no] No *rev to* no *(JC)* mystery;
263 ear {, .— {f For *(JC)* reason,] reason;
269 rivalship,
272 circumstance—indeed;
273 Tho'] Tho *del to* For

259 The capital is JC's.

I never should have thought of it again
But for the scene which we just now have witnessed [275]
Mor: *What do you mean?*
Riv: *— — — — In truth I think I saw*
Tho'
'~~Twas~~ at a distance and he was disguised
Hovering round Herbert's door, a man whose figure
Resembled much that cold voluptuary
The villain Clifford—He hates you & he knows [280]
Where he can stab you deepest.
Mor: *— — — — — — — — Clifford never*
Would stoop to hover round a blind man's door—
It could not be—
Riv: *— — — — And yet I now remember*
That when your praise was warm upon my tongue, [284]
And I began to tell how you had rescued
A maiden from the ruffian violence
Of this same Clifford—Herbert grew impatient
And would not hear me—
Mor: *— — — — — No, it cannot be*
I dare not trust myself with such a thought [289]

[11ᵛ]

Yet whence this strong aversion? You are a
man
Not used to rash conjectures—
Riv: *If you deem it* [291]
A thing worth further notice, it befits us
To deal with caution, we must sift him artfully
(Exeunt Mortimer & Rivers)

---

248 MH's 1799 revision.
250 Revision in pencil.

I never should have thought of it again 274
But for the scene which we just now have
is your meaning *witnessed.* 275
Mar: *What ~~do you mean?~~*
gone —
Two days ∧ I saw, 276
Osw — — — — — — ~~*In truth I think I saw*~~
Tho' at a distance & he was disguised, 277
Hovering
~~*Hovering*~~ *round Herbert's door a man whose figure* 278
Resembled much that {*c* / } *old voluptuary* 279
The villain Clifford—{· / } *He hates you, & he knows* 280
Where he can stab you deepest.
Mar — — — — — — — — — — — *C*{*lif* / *hi*}*ford never* 281
a
Would stoop to hover round {~~*this*~~ / *a blind*} {M / *man's door—*} 282
It could not be—{· / }
Osw: — — — — — *And yet I now remember,* 283
That when your praise was warm upon my tongue, 284
the blind man had told how you had
And ~~I began to tell him how you~~ rescued 285
A m{*ai* / *ur*}*d*{*en* / *rer*} *from the ruffian violence* 286
became
Of this same Clifford, He~~rbert~~ grew impatient 287

16

And would not hear me.
Mar: — — — — — — — — *No—it cannot be—* 288
I dare not trust myself with such a thought— 289
Yet whence this strange aversion? You are a man 290
Not used to rash conjectures.—
Osw — — — — — — — — — — — — *If you deem it* 291
~~*act*~~
we must [?*do't*]} *act* 292
A thing worth further notice, ~~it befits us~~
{*W* *the matter*
~~*To deal*~~ {*with caution,* ~~/ *we must*~~ *sift* ~~*him*~~ *artfully.* 293
Exeunt Os. & Mar.

---

275 just now *del to* by chance
276 gone *inserted with caret*
282 hover round a blind man's *del to* sculk about a Cottage
284 That,
285 *as MS. 3 but* began] begun *then rev as MS. 3 but* had] was
287 *as MS. 3, rev as MS. 3*

[I.ii]

Hostel
Scene changes to the door of ~~an inn~~
Herbert, Matilda and Host

~~*Mat:*~~

Her: *(seated) As I am dear to you, remember child*
This last request—
Mat: *You know me, Sir! Farewell!*
Her: *And are you going then? Come, come Matilda*
We must not part— I have measured many a league
When these old limbs had need of rest—No, no,
I will not play the sluggard.
Mat: *— — — — — — Nay sit down (Turning to the Host)*
Good Host, such 'tendance as you would expect
From your own children, if yourself were sick
Let this old man find at your hands—poor Tray

[12r]

We soon shall meet again—If thou neglect ~~thy charge~~
~~*This charge, then*~~
~~*Th{y/en ill befal thee*~~
This Charge of thine then ill befal thee! Look
The little fool is loth to stay behind
Sir Host! by all the love you bear to courtesy
Take care of him—and feed the truant well.
Host *Fear not, I will obey you, but one so young*
it goes against my heart
And one so fair, ~~in truth it is a pity~~
That you should travel unattended, Lady!
I have a palfrey and a groom, The lad
Shall squire you (To Her:) would it not be better Sir?
And for less fee than I would let him run
For any lady I have seen this twelvemonth.

Revision of "an inn" in stage direction on 11v in pencil.
1 Deletion by erasure.
9 The name was evidently left blank in 1799, then supplied in 1841 in pencil and overwritten in ink.
10 Deletions in pencil and ink.

Scene, the door of the Hostel.

Herbert, Idoni{e/a}, & Host.

Her
(seated) As I am dear to you, remember, Child!
This last request.
Ido: — — — — — — — *You know me Si{re;/r, farewell!}*
Her: And are you going then? Come, come Idon{e/ia}
We must not part,—I have measured many a league
When these old limbs had need of rest,—No, no,
I will not play the sluggard.
Ido — — — — — — — — *Nay, sit down (turning to Host)*
Good Host, such tendance as you would ~~expect~~
expect

17

From your own Children, if yourself were sick,
Let this old man find at your hands; poor ~~Tray~~ Leader
(looking at the Dog)
We soon shall meet again. If thou neglect
This Charge of thine, then ill befal thee! Look
The little fool is loth to stay behind.
Sir Host! by all the love you bear to courtes{y,/ey}
Take care of him, & feed the truant well.
Host Fear not, I will obey you,—but {O/one} so young,
And {O/one} so fair, it goes against my heart
That you should travel unattended, Lady!
I have a palfrey and a groom: {t/The} lad
Shall squire you—(would it not be better Sir?)
And for less fee than I would let him run
For any Lady I have seen this twelvemonth.

---

296 come, Idonea,
298 No, no, *rev to* and now
299 sluggard *then capitalized (Dora)* Nay sit down.
302 leader, *then capitalized (Dora)*
304 thee!—Look,
310 Lady!—
312 you,

---

300 The "expect" at foot of page is JC's.

Mat: *You know, Sir, I have been too long your guard* [315]
little
Not to have learnt to laugh at ~~foolish~~ fears
little
Why if a wolf should leap from out a thicket
A look of mine would send him scouring back
Unless I differ from the thing I am
When you are by my side
Idonea
Her: *~~Matilda~~! Wolves* [320]
Are not the enemies that move my fears
I pray
Mat: *No more of this ^— Three days at farthest*
protect him heaven!
Will bring me back ~~to you~~ ^—Farewell! farewell
(Exit Matilda)

[12^v]

Cuthbert *is*
Host *'Tis never drought with us—St ~~Mary~~ & her} pilgrims*
Thanks to them! are a stream of comfort to us [325]
Pity the maiden did not wait a ~~little~~ while
She could not, Sir, have failed of company
Her: *Now she is gone I fain would call her back ~~again~~*
Host *(calling Matilda) Hola*
Her: *— — — — No, no the business must be done*
But what is all this noise? (a noise heard)
Host *— — — — — — The villagers*
Are flocking in—A wedding festival [331]
That's all —

Enter Mortimer & Rivers

(to them) God save you Sirs!
~~Oswald~~ *Oswald — — Ha! as I live*
~~Riv~~: *~~Ha! as I live the Baron Herbert~~*
The Baron Herbert
The Baron Herbert!
Host: *~~For Heaven's sake~~!—Mercy ^ ~~Sir I did not know your~~*
~~honour~~ *~~Lordship~~*
Os
~~Riv~~: *So far into your journey! on my life*
You are a lusty traveller—But how fare you? [335]
the wreck I am permits
Her: *Well, as ~~an old man can expect~~—And you Sir?*
Idonia
I do not see *~~Matilda~~*
Riv: *The good} cre*

---

23 Deletion and revisions are in pencil.
45 "The good cre" deleted by erasure and revised, 1799; "Matilda" revised to "Idonia" 1841.

Ido: *You know, Sir, I have been too long your ~~guide~~ guard*
Not to have learnt to laugh at little fears.
Why, if a wolf should leap from out a thicket
A look of mine would send him scouring back,
+*Unless I differ from the thing I am*
When you are by my side.
Her. — — — — — — — *Idonia, wolves*
Are not the enemies that move my fears.
Ido *No more I pray of this. Three days at farthest*
Saints,— } *. — }*
Will bring me back—protect him ~~heaven!~~ farewell!
(Exit Idonia)

18
Host *'Tis never drought with us—St Cuthbert & his Pilgrims,*
Thanks to them, are a stream of comfort to us.
Pity the Maiden did not wait a while,
She could not, Sir, have failed of company.
Her: *Now she is gone, I fain would call her back.*
Host
(calling) Holla!
Her — — — *No, no, the business must be done.—*
means riotous
What ~~is all~~ this‸noise?
Host — — — — — — — *The villagers*
Are flocking in—a wedding festival—
Thats all— *God Save you Sir~~s~~!* }
~~Marmaduke &~~
Enter ~~Idonia &~~ Oswald
Osw — — — — — — — — — — — *Ha! as I live,*
The Baron Herbert.
Host — — — — — — *Mercy, the Baron Herbert!*
Osw: *So far into your journey! on my life,*
You are a lusty Traveller. But how fare you!
Herb *Well, as the wreck I am permits. And you, Sir?*
{ *Osw* [?*River*] } *I do not see Idonia—*

---

323 Saints—
324 draught *rev to* drought *(Dora)*
325 to us. *del to colon at end of line and* to us *inserted after* are
336 Well,] Well

[13r]

{C
Her: *— — — — — — The good {creature*
Is gone before, to spare my weariness [338]
But what has brought you hither?
Riv: *— — — — — — — — A little business*
That will be soon dispatched
Her: *— — — — — — — — — There was a letter*
Which we entrusted to you?
(in)
Riv: *— — — — — — — — — ~~Be at peace~~*
Tis broken off {~~tis broken off~~
^You'll hear no more of him {——
This is true comfort—thanks
Her: *— — — — — — — — ~~Well this is comfort~~.*
a thousand times.
That noise! would I had gone with her as far [344]
As the Lord Clifford's mansion, I have heard
That in his milder moods he has express'd
{— {is
Compassion for me{ h{e ~~has great~~ influence is
great
With Henry our good King. ~~I might have restored~~
The Baron might
~~them~~
~~Perhaps he would have heard my suit—no matter~~
{~~he~~
~~Have {urged my suit & urged my p~~
~~I do not like the man (noise again) this noise alas~~
Have heard my suit & urged my plan at court
~~I shall have neither sleep nor rest—the convent~~
No matter ~~I dislike~~ he's a dangerous Man—that noise
~~Will give me quiet lodging—you have a boy, good~~
~~He~~ That noise is too disorderly for sleep or rest
~~Host~~
~~And he must lead me back~~.
Idonia would have fears for me the Convent
{ill
W{[?] give me quiet lodging— You have a boy, good host
~~Riv~~: *— — — — — — — — + ~~This is most lucky~~* [354]
And he must lead me back.
Os. *You are most lucky*
Our journey lies that way; my friend and I
Will be your guides.

A photograph of 13r is provided below, p. 717.
49 "The "(in)" is a direction to the copyist, 1841.

Dutiful Girl,
Her: — — — — — — — ~~*The good Creature*~~
She is
~~*Is*~~ *gone before, to spare my weariness.*
But what has brought you hither?

19

slight affair,
Osw — — — — — *A* ~~*little business*~~
That will be soon dispatched.
Did Marmaduke
Her — — — — — — — — — ~~*There was a letter*~~
R
[?] *eceive that letter?*—
~~*Which we entrusted*~~
tie
Osw — — — — — — — *Be at peace.—The* ~~*affair*~~
{~~*Is*~~ / *'Tis*} {*Is* / *broken*} ; ~~*off*~~ *will* *you'*~~*ll*~~ *hear no more of him.*
Her. *This is true comfort, thanks a thousand times*
That noise! would I had gone with her as far
As the Lord Clifford'{'/s} {*Castle:* / *Mansion.*} *I have heard*
That in his milder moods he has expressed
Compassion for me;{.} {H / *his influence is great*}
With Henry our good King,—{*t* / *The Baron might*}
Have heard my suit, & urged my plea at Court.
No matter—he's a dangerous Man.—{T / *that noise*} !
~~*That noise*~~ {*'T*} *is too disorderly for sleep or rest.*
Idonia would have fears for me,—The Convent
Will give me quiet lodging. You have a boy, good Host,
And he must lead me back.
Osw — — — — — — — — *You are most lucky;*
I have been waiting in the wood hard by
~~*I have*~~
~~*Our journey lies that way, my friend & I,*~~
For a Companion—here he comes; our journey *Enter Mar*
~~*Will be your guides*~~
Lies in your way, accept us as your Guides.

---

342 broken,
344 noise!—
346 That, . . . moods,
348 Henry, . . . King;—
349 *no comma*
350 noise!—
351 *no apos*
352 the
357 in *rev to* on way;

[13ᵛ]

Her: — — — — — — — *Alas! I creep so slowly,*
63 *A wearisome companion!*
Riv: — — — — — — — — — — — *Never fear*
64 *We'll not complain of that*
Her: — — — — — — — — — — *My limbs are stiff* [359]
And need *Could you but*
65 *~~I must~~ repose. ~~You cannot~~ wait an hour?*
Most willingly!
66 *Riv:* *~~O certainly!~~* ^ *come let me lead you in*
take your rest, think not of us
67 *And while you ~~rest yourseff, my friend & I~~*
68 *W{e'/ill stroll into the wood.*
(Rivers conducts Herbert into the house—various villagers croud in. Rivers returns to Mortimer, and they go out together. More villagers, and among them a rustic musician) to him)
69 *Host* *Into the court my friend! and perch yourself* [370]

Herb ——————— *Alas! I creep so slowly,* 358a
~~*A wearisome Companion*~~

20
Osw: ———————————— *Never fear,* 358b
We'll not complain of that.
Herb ————————— *My limbs are stiff* 359
And need repose. Could you but wait an hour [?] 360
Osw: Most willingly! Come let me lead you in, 361
And while you take your rest, think not of us 362

We'll stroll into the wood {*; lean on my arm*} *(Os: conducts Her: into the house—various villagers crowd in. Os: returns to Mar: they go out together—more villages, among them a Musician (to him)*

Host Into the co[?urt] {*urt*} *my friend! & perch yourself*
Aloft upon the Elm-tree— Pretty maids!
Garlands & flowers, & cakes, & merry thoughts
Are here to send the sun into the west.

We'll stroll into the wood; lean on my arm. (conducts Herbert. ~~*returning*~~ *into the house——* 363
(Oswald. *(Enter villagers)* *as he* ~~*Osw*~~ ~~*returni*~~{~~*s*~~ ~~*ng*~~} *to* ~~*himself*~~ *aside*
—I have prepared a most apt Instrument— ~~*while return ing towards*~~ *M*~~*armad*~~*.* 364
to himself
(coming ~~*The Arch-impostor*~~ *no doubt*
out ~~*wily vagrant*~~ *must* ^ *be hovering somewhere* 365
of the The ^ *Vagrant*
Hostel) About this ground; she hath a tongue well skilled 366
For mingling natural matter of her own 367
With all the daring fictions I have taught her 368
To win belief, such as my plot requires. *Ex: Mar & Os* 369

Enter more villagers, a Musician among them.

To the {*i*}*m* *Into the court, my friends* {*!*} *& perch yourself* 370
Host

358a slowly,{.}
361 willingly!—
362 And, . . . us;
363 Ex Mar. *added to stage dir (Dora)*
365 hovering *rev to* loitering
368 I] of *del to* I *(Dora)*
369 Marmaduke and *del from stage dir*
369/370 *stage dir, without comma, del, then rewritten, with comma after* Villagers *(Dora)* among] amongst *rev to* among
370 *stage dir* (to them) friends *with* s *del to exclam point, del, and comma inserted*

---

365 Revisions to the first two words above and below the line are JC's.

Aloft upon the elm-tree. Pretty maids!
Garlands, and flowers, and cakes & merry thoughts
Are here to send the sun into the west.——

[I.iii]

Scene changes to the wood adjoining
the Inn, Mortimer & Rivers {*e* / *intering*}

[14ʳ]

Mor: *I would fain hope that we deceive ourselves*
When I beheld him sitting there, alone,
It struck upon my heart—I know not how
~~*Riv*~~*:* ~~*Let us dismiss the business from our thoughts*~~
Os *To day will clear up all— You marked a cottage*
That ragged dwelling close beneath a rock
By the brook side; it is the abode of one
n{*innocent Maiden till ensnared* / *A* ~~*maid*~~, ~~*who fell a prey to the*~~} {*ę* / } *by* ~~*Lord*~~ *Clifford*
~~*And*~~ {*W* *o* / *he*} *soon* ^ *grew weary of her, but alas!*
turned her brain
What she had seen and suffered~~—*the poor wretch,*~~
Cast off by her Betrayer
~~*It turned her brain—and now*~~ *she* {*dwells* / *lives alone*}
Nor moves her hands to any needful work
She eats the food which every day the peasants
Bring to her hut. and so the wretch has lived
Ten years; and no one ever heard her voice
But every night at the first stroke of twelve
She quits her house, and in the neighbouring
church-yard
Upon the self same spot in rain or storm,

She paces out the hour 'twixt twelve and one
an Infants grave
She paces round and round, ~~*still round and round*~~
And in the church-yard sod her feet have worn
A hollow ring; they say it is knee-deep——
Ha! what is here?

(A female Beggar rises up
rubbing her eyes as if waking from sleep—
a child in her arms

Beggar — — — — — *Oh! Gentlemen I thank you*

Correction in the last line on 13ᵛ is from 1799.

Aloft upon the elm tree. Pretty Maids
Garlands & flowers & cakes, & merry thoughts
Are here to send the sun into the west.

Scene changes to the wood adjoining the

[?re] *and Oswald entering.*
Hostel—Marmaduke ~~*& Oswald entering*~~
~~*& Oswald sep*~~

Mar: *I would fain hope that we deceive ourselves:*
first I saw
When ~~*I beheld*~~ *him sitting there, alone,*
It struck upon my heart I know not how.
Osw *To day will clear up all—you marked a Cottage*
That ragged dwelling close beneath a rock
By the brook-side: it is the abode of one
t
An innocen{c~~*e*~~ *Maiden till ensnared by Clifford,*
Who soon grew weary of her, but alas!

21

What she had seen & suffered turned her brain.
Cast off by her Betrayer, she dwells alone
Nor moves her hands to any needful work:
She eats her food which every day the peasants
Bring to her hut, & so the wretch has lived
Ten years; & no one ever heard her voice;
But every night at the first stroke of twelve
She quits her house, &, in the neighbouring Church Yard
Upon the self-same spot in rain or storm,
hour
~~*ur*~~
She paces out the ~~*ho*~~*{use 'twixt twelve & one—*
She paces round & round, an Infant's grave,
And in the Church-yard sod her feet have worn
A hollow ring; they say it is knee-deep {—
Ha! what is here? *(a female Beggar rises up*
rubbing her eyes as if from sleep—a Child in her arms)
G
Beg — — — — *Oh! gentlemen, I thank you;*

---

372 *no comma*
373 *period del and line inserted:* More speedily ~~perhaps~~ than you perhaps would like
378 all.— you *then capitalized (JC)* Cottage,
379 raggèd dwelling, *then capitalized (JC)*
380 one,
381 Maiden,
382 her;
387 hut,] hut; wretch *then capitalized (JC)*
391 or] [?and] *del to* or (*Dora*)
395 knee deep—

[14[v]]

24 *I've had the saddest dream that ever troubled*
25 *The heart of living creature—My poor babe*
26 *Was crying as I thought, crying for bread*
27 *When I had none to give him, whereupon*
28 *I put a slip of foxglove in his hand*
29 *Which pleased him so that he was hushed at once*
30 *When into one of those same spotted bells*
31 *A Bee came darting, which the child with joy*
32 *Imprisoned there, and held it to his ear*
33 *And suddenly grew black as he would die*
34 Mor: *(to Riv:) We have no time for this (to the Beg:) my*
babbling gossip
35 *Here's what will comfort you*
(gives her money)
Beg: *(to Mortimer) —— The Saints reward you*
36 *For this good work— Well Sirs, this passed away*
37 *And afterwards I fancied a strange dog*
38 *Trotting alone, along a beaten road*
39 *Came to the child as by my side he slept*
40 *And fondling licked his face, then on a sudden*
41 *Snapped fierce to make a morsel of his head*
42 *But here he is! (kissing the child) It must have*
been a dream
43 Riv: *When next inclined to sleep take my advice*
44 *And put your head good Woman! under cover*

[15[r]]

45 Beg: *Oh Sir! you would not talk thus if you knew*
46 *What life is this of ours, how sleep will master*
47 *The weary-worn— You gentlefolks, have got*
48 *Warm chambers to your wish—I'd rather be*
49 *A Stone than what I am—but two nights gone*

I've had the saddest dream that ever troubled
The heart of living Creature—My poor Babe
Was c{ry / iring} as I thought, crying for bread
When I had none to give him; whereupon,
I put a slip of foxglove in his hand,
Which pleased {him / [?me]} so, that he was hushed at {once. / last}
When, into one of those same spotted bells,
A bee came darting, which the Child with joy
Imprisoned there, & held ~~it~~ [it] to his ear

21

And suddenly grew black, as he would die.
Mar *We have no time for this, my^[babbling] gossip;*
(~~to [?her:]~~)
Here's what will comfort you. (gives^[her] money)
Beg. *~~The~~ — — — — The Saints reward you*
For this good deed!— Well Sirs, this passed away
And afterwards I fancied a strange dog,
Trotting alone along the beaten road,
Came to my child as by my side he s{l / tept}
And fondling licked his face, then on a sudden
Snapped fierce to make a morsel of his head:
But here he is (Kissing the Child) It must have been a dream.
Osw *When next inclined to sleep take my advice*
And put your head, good Woman, under cover.
Beg *Oh Sir, you would not talk thus, if you knew*
What life is this of our's, how sleep will master
The weary-worn.— You gentlefolk have got
{W / Y}arm Chambers to your wish. I'd rather be
A ~~dog~~ [Stone] than what I am{. / —} {B / but} two nights' gone

399 crying, as
403 bells,] bells
405 ear,
407 gossip; *then capitalized*
409 Well, . . . away;
410 fancied,
411 Trotted *rev to* Trotting *(Dora)*
415 is, It] *del to* it *(JC)*
418 Oh,
419 *no apos*
422 than] that *rev to* than *(JC)* *no apos*

405 The undeleted "it" is JC's.
405/406 The page number was repeated by mistake.

50 *The darkness overtook me, wind and rain*
51 *Beat hard upon my head— and yet I saw*
52 *A glow-worm through the covert of the furze* [425]
calmly
53 *Shine as if nothing ailed the sky*
54 *At which I half-accused the God in heaven—*
55 *You must forgive me Sirs—*
Riv — — — — — — — *Well—well today*
56 *Has made amends*
Beg: — — — — — *Thanks to you—but oh! Sir!* [431]
57 *How would you like to travel on whole hours*
58 *As I have done, my eyes upon the ground*
59 *Expecting still I knew not how, to find*
f
60 *A piece on{ money glittering through the dust* [435]
61 *Mor: This woman is a prater—Pray good Lady*
62 *Do you tell fortunes?*
Beg: — — — — *Oh! Sir! you are like the rest*
63 *This little one— it cuts me to the heart*
64 *Well! they might turn a beggar from their door*
65 *But there are mothers who can see the babe* [440]

53 The "calmly" was written in 1841 above a space left blank in 1799.
60 MH's 1799 correction.

The darkness overtook me—wind & rain 423
Beat hard upon my head—& yet I saw 424
A glow-worm, thro' the covert of the furze, 425
Shin{e/ed} calmly as if nothing ailed the sky: 426
At which I half accused the God in heaven.— 427
You must forgive me{— / , ~~Sirs~~.
Oswald
Aye, and if you think 428

The Fairies are to blame, and you may chide 429
Your favorite Saint—no matter—this good 430

22

{[?~~think,~~] / ~~I~~ hope, ~~this lucky~~ day 430
Osw: — — — — — — — *Well~~, well~~*
Has {~~H~~
~~Today~~ {~~has~~ made amends.
Beg — — — — — — *Thanks to you both; but, O Si{r! / r~~s~~}* 431
How would you like to travel on whos{l / e hours 432
As I have done, my eyes {u / apon the ground, 433
Expecting still, I knew not how, to find 434
A piece of money glittering thro' the dust. 435
Mar *This {W / woman is a prater—{. / Pray, good Lady!* 436
Do you tell fortunes?
Beg — — — — — — *Oh ~~yes~~ Sir, you are like the rest.* 437
This little One—it cuts me to the heart— 438
Well! they might turn a beggar from their door, 439
But there are Mothers who can see the Babe 440

---

428 me,}
429 may *del to* should *(Dora)*
437 the *over illeg miswriting (Dora)*
439 door, *then* s *added*

Revision at foot of page 21[b], running over to p. 22, was developed on a loose sheet, now attached to the end of MS. 3:

You will forgive me
Oswald Aye {— / a and if you thought
The {Fairi / [?]es were to blame and roudly chid
Your favorite Saint—no matter—this good day
Hath made amends

431 The "Has" above the line is JC's.

[15^v]

{me
66 *Here at my breast and ask {if where I bought it*
67 *This they can do and look upon my face*
{you, Sir
68 *—But {Sir, you should be kinder*
Mor *— — — — — — — — — — — — Come hither Fathers*

{ither Come hither Fathers
~~Mor~~: ~~*Come he*~~*{re* ~~*ye fathers*~~
what Nature is from
69 *And learn^of this poor wretch*
70 Beg: *Aye, Sir there's nobody that feels for us* [445]
71 *Why now—but yesterday I overtook*
72 *A blind old grey-beard and accosted him*
73 *I'th' name of all the saints and by the mass*
74 *He should have used me better! Charity!*
75 *If you can melt a rock he is your man* [450]
76 *But I'll be even with him—here again*
77 *Have I been waiting for him*
Riv: *— — — — — — — — Well! but softly,*
78 *Who is it that has wronged you?*
Beg: *— — — — — — — — — — Mark you me*
79 *I'll point him out—a maiden is his guide* [454]
Spring's first
80 *Lovely as* ~~*any*~~ *rose, a little dog*
{len}
81 *Tied by a wool {en} cord moves on before*
82 *With look as sad as he were dumb, the cur*
83 *I owe him no ill will, but in good sooth*
84 *He does his master credit*

[16^r]

Mor: *— — — — — — — — — — As I live* [459]
85 *'Tis Herbert* ~~*and*~~ *no other*
'Tis}
86 Beg: ~~*Aye gentlemen it*~~ *is} a feast to see him*
87 *Lank as a ghost and tall—his shoulders bent*
{long
88 *And {his beard white with age—yet evermore*
89 *As if he were the only saint on earth*
90 *He turns his face to heaven*
Riv: *— — — — — — — — But why so violent* [464]
91 *Against this poor old gentleman?*
Beg: *— — — — — — — — I'll tell you*

---

66 MH's 1799 revision.
68 MH's 1799 revision to "you, Sir."

Here at my breast, & ask me where I bought it: 441
This they can do, & look upon my face— 442
But you, Sir, should be kinder
Mar *——————— Come hither, Fathers,* 443
And learn what Nature is from this poor Wretch. 444
Beg *Aye, Sir, there's nobody that feels for us.* 445
Why now—but yesterday I overtook 446
A blind old Greybeard & accosted him, 447

23

I'th name of all the Saints, & by the Mass 448
He should have used me better!—Charity! 449
If you can melt a rock, he is your Man; 450
But I'll be even with him—here again 451
Have I been waiting for him.
Osw *———————— Well but softly,* 452
Who is it that hath wronged you?
Beg *—————————— Mark you me;* 453
I'll point him out;—a maiden is his guide, 454
Lovely as Spring's first rose; a little dog, 455
Tied by a woollen cord, moves on before 456
With look as sad as he were dumb; the cur, 457
I owe him no ill will, but in good sooth 458
He does his Master credit.
Mar *————————— As I live* 459
{th
'Tis Herbert & no o{hter.
Beg *——————— 'Tis a feast to see him,* 460
Lank as a ghost & tall, his shoulders bent, 461
And long beard white with age—yet evermore, 462
As if he were the only Saint on earth, 463
He turns his face to heaven.

24

Osw *—————— But why so violent* 464
venerable Man?
Against this ~~poor old Gentleman?~~
Beg *—————————— I'll tell you:* 465

---

443 kinder.
446 but yesterday] *erased then reinstated with dash preceding (Dora)*
447 Grey[?] *rev to* Greybeard *(JC)*
455 spring's *then capitalized (Dora)*
460 *no comma*

92 *He has the very hardest heart on earth*
93 *I had as lief turn to the friars school*
94 *And knock for entrance in mid holiday*
95 Mor: *But to your story*
Beg: *— — — — — — ~~As~~ I was saying, Sir* [469]
spurned / *toad*
96 *Well—he has often ~~used~~ me like a {toad / dog}*
97 *But yesterday was worse than all—at last*
98 *~~And after trudging many a weary mile~~*
99 *I overtook him Sirs, my boy and I*
100 *'Twas on the middle of the heath, and so*
101 *I begged a little aid for charity*
102 *But he was s{n / happish} as a cottage cur*

[16ᵛ]

103 *Well then says I—I'll out with it, at wh{ich / itch}* [475]
104 *I cast a look upon the girl and felt*
105 *As if my heart would burst, and so I left him*
106 Riv: *I think good woman! you are the very person*
107 *Whom, but some few days past, I saw in {Eskdale / [?]}*
108 *At Herberts door*
Beg: *Aye, and if truth were known* [480]
109 *I have good business there*
110 Riv: *— — — I met you at the threshold ~~& it seemed~~*
And he seemed
111 *~~That he was~~* ^ *angry*
Beg: *— — — — Angry! well he might*
112 *And long as I can stir I'll dog him—yesterday*
113 *To serve me so, and knowing that he owes*
114 *The best of all he has to me and mine* [485]
115 *But 'tis all over now— Th{at / e} good old Lady*
116 *Has left a power of riches, and I say it*
~~knave~~
lawyer / *knave*
117 *If there's a {lawyer / ~~lawyer~~} in the land, the ~~rogue~~*
118 *Shall give me half*
What's this,
Riv: *— — — — — I fear good woman!*
119 *You have been insolent—{?}*
Beg: *— — — — Aye, Sir and there's a Lord*
120 *I spied him sculking in his peasant's dress* [491]
121 Riv: *How say you? In disguise?*

102, 103, 115 MH's 1799 corrections.

He has the very hardest heart on earth; 466
I had as lief turns to the Friar's School 467
And knock for entrance, in mid holiday. 468
Mar: *But to your Story.*
Beg *— — — — — I was saying Sir—* 469
l
Well!—he has often spurned me tike a toad, 470
But yesterday was worse than all, —at last 471
I overtook him Sirs, my babe & I, 472
~~*'Twas on the middle of the heath, & so*~~
And
~~*I*~~ *begged a little aid for charity:* 473
But he was snappish as a cottage Cur. 474
Well then, says I—I'll out with it, at which 475
I cast a look upon the Girl, & felt 476
As if my heart would burst; & so I left him. 477
Osw: *I think, good Woman, you are the very person* 478
Whom, but some few days past, I saw in Eskdale, 479
At Herbert's door.
Beg *— — — — — Aye; & if truth were known* 480
I have good business there.

25
Osw *— — — — — I met you at the threshold* 481
And he seemed angry.
Beg *— — — — — Angry, well he might;* 482
Y
And long as I can stir I'll dog him.—yesterday, 483
To serve me so, & knowing that he owes 484
&
The best of all he has to me or mine. 485
But 'tis all over now.— That good old Lady 486
Has left a power of riches; & I say it, 487
If there's a lawyer in the land, the knave 488
Shall give me half.
Osw *— — — — — What's this?—I fear, good woman,* 489
You have been insolent {. ?}
Aye And the Baron,
Beg *— — — — — — Yes,* ~~*Sir*~~*, & there's* ~~*a Lord*~~*,* 490
I spied him skulking in his Peasant's dress. 491
Osw *How say you? In disguise?—*

467 school
469 saying,
471 all;—
472 him,
474 Cottage
475 it, {;}
480 *no apos* &] and *over* if *(Dora)*
490 Aye, Sir, *del, as MS. 3* and *then capitalized*
491 peasant's

[17r]

But,
Mor: — — — — — — — *Whats your business*
122 *With Herbert or his daughter?*
Beg: — — — — — — — *Daughter! truly!—*
123 *But how's the day? I fear my little boy*
124 *We've overslept ourselves, Sir's have you seen him*
(offers to go)
125 *Mor: I must have more of this—you shall not stir*
126 *An inch till I am answered. Know you aught*
127 *That doth concern this Herbert?*
{provoked
Beg: — — — — — — — — *You are {angry*
128 *And will misuse me Sir!*
{~~Mor~~ Mor
{Riv: — — — — — — — *No trifling woman!*
129 *Riv: You are as safe as in a sanctuary*
130 *Speak.*
Mor: — — — *Speak.*
Beg: — — — — — — *He is a most hard-hearted man*
131 *Mor: Your life is at my mercy*
Beg: — — — — — — — *Do not harm me*
132 *And I will tell you all—you know not, Sir*
133 *What strong temptations press upon the poor*

[17v]

134 *Riv: Speak out*
Beg: — — — *Oh! Sir! I've been a wicked woman*
{S
135 *Mor: ~~Nay~~, {speak out, speak out—*
Beg: — — — — — — — *He flattered me and said*
136 *What harvest it would bring us both, and so*
137 *I parted with the child*
Mor: — — — — — — — *With whom you parted?*
Idonea
138 *Beg: ~~Matilda~~ as he calls her, but the girl*
139 *Is mine.*
Mor: Yours! Woman! are you Herberts wife?
140 *Beg: Wife Sir! his wife! not I, my husband, Sir,*

128 MH's 1799 overwriting.

Mar. — — — — — — — — — *But what's your business?* 492
With Herbert or his daughter?
Beg — — — — — — — — — *Daughter! truly!—* 493
But how's the day?—I fear, my little boy, 494
t
We've oversle~~pped~~ ourselves.—Sirs, have you seen him? 495

(offers to go)

26

Marmaduke I must have more of this;—you shall not stir 496
A
In inch, till I am answered. Know you aught 497
That doth concern this Herbert?
Beg — — — — — — — — — — *You are provoked,* 498
And will misuse me, Sir!
Mar: — — — — — — — *No trifling, woman!* 499
Osw *You are as safe as in a sanctuary;* 500
Speak.
Mar — — *Speak.*
Beg — — — — *He is a most hard-hearted Man.* 501
Mar: *Your life is at my mercy.*
Beg — — — — — — — *Do not harm me,* 502
Y
And I will tell you all!—you know not, Sir, 503
What strong temptations press upon the Poor. 504
Speak out.
Osw — — — + + + + + + + *~~Speak out~~.*
Beg — — *Oh Sir, I've been a wicked Woman.* 505
Nay—but
Osw *~~Speak~~, speak out!*
Beg — — — — *He flattered me, & said* 506
What harvest it would bring us both; & so, 507
I parted with the Child.
Mar — — — — — — — *With whom you parted?* 508
e
Beg *Idonia, as he calls her; but the Girl* 509
Is mine.

27

Mar: *Yours! Woman, are you Herbert's Wife?* 510
;
Beg *Wife Sir! his Wife—not I my husband, Sir,* 511

---

494 *first comma omitted*
499 woman!—
504 poor *then capitalized (Dora)*
506 Nay, but
510 Yours!! Woman! *with exclam points added*

---

495 "The "t" of the first correction was added by JC.

141 *Was of Kirkoswald—many a snowy winter*
My
142 *We've weathered out together—Aye poor Gilfrid!*
143 *He has been two years in his grave*
Mor: — — — — — — — — — — *Enough!* [514]
mis
144 *Riv:* *We've solved the riddle—* ~~*hellish*~~ *miscreant!*
Mor
Os — — — — — — — — — — — *Do you*
G ~~*straightway*~~
good dame repair
145 ~~*Mor*~~*:* ~~*Do you*~~, *repair good [?dame], to Liddisdale & wait*
F *be sure you shall have*
146 ~~*And wait*~~ *for my return,* ~~*I'll meet you there*~~ *justice*
147 ~~*You shall have justice—Herbert is gone by*~~

[18^r]

148 ~~*But leave the rest to me*~~
Riv: — — — — — — — — — ~~*A lucky woman*~~*!*
~~*Go you*~~
149 ~~*Depart and think that you have done good service*~~
A lucky Woman—go—you have done good service
150 *Mor:* *(to himself) Eternal praises to the power that saved her* [519]
151 *Riv:* *(gives the Beg: money) Here's for your little boy—and when you christen him*
152 *I'll be his God-father*
Beg: — — — — — — — *Oh Sir you are merry with me*
153 *In grange or farm this hundred scarcely owns*
154 *A dog that does not know me—These good people*
155 *For love of God I must not pass their doors*
156 *But I will be back with my best speed, for you* [525]
157 *God bless and thank you masters! (Exit Beggar*
Mor: *(after some time) Sinking, sinking*
158 *And feel that I am sinking—would this body*
159 *Were quitely given back unto the earth*
the burthen
^
160 *From whence* ~~*it*~~ *came*
Riv: *(aside)* — — — *Pierced to the heart!*
~~*Poor*~~ *forlorn*
Poor devoted Maid
~~*oh thou*~~
161 *Mor:* *(to himself) The cruel viper!—oh thou* ~~*poor Matilda*~~
162 *Now I do love thee*
Riv: — — — — — — ~~*Faith*~~*! I am thunderstruck*

---

145 Revision of "repair good [?dame]" was made in 1799, but "good" was capitalized in 1841.
160 MH's 1799 correction.

Was of Kirkoswald—many a snowy winter 512
We've weathered out together. My poor Gilfred! 513
He has been two years in his grave.
Mar — — — — — — — — — — — *Enough* 514
Os: *We've solved the riddle—Miscreant!*
Mar — — — — — — — — — — — — *Do you,* 515
Good Dame, repair to Leddlesdale & wait 516
For my return, be sure you shall have justice. 517
Osw. *A lucky Woman! go, you have done good service.* 518
(aside)
Mar:
(to himself) Eternal praises on the power that saved her! 519
Os: (gives
her money) Here's for your little boy—& when you christen him 520
I'll be his Godfather.
Beg — — — — — — — *Oh Sir, you are merry with me.* 521
is *H*
In grange or farm th{e {hundred scarcely owns 522
~~*k*~~ *know*
A dog that does not { ~~own~~ me.—These good ~~People~~ Folks, 523
For love of God, I must not pass their doors; 524
But I'll be back with my best speed:—~~+~~for you,— 525
both my gentle *B*
God bless & thank you^Masters! *(Exit {{beg)* 526
Mar:
(after a
pause) — — — — — — — — — ~~*Sinking, sinking*~~,

27

~~*And feel that I am sinking,—would this body*~~
ear
~~*Were quietly given back unto the*~~ [?~~*Deat*~~]{~~*th*~~
~~*From whence the burthen came*~~.
Os:
(aside)— — — — — — — ~~*Pierced to the heart*~~!
Mar: (to
himself) The cruel Viper!—poor devoted Maid, 527
Now I do love thee.
Osw — — — — — — — *I am thunderstruck.* 528

---

514 Enough.
516 Liddesdale, *then comma del*
517 return,] return;
519 her!—
522 Grange *then lowercased (Dora)*
526 both my gentle *inserted, as MS. 3* Masters!—
526/527 *lines del, as MS. 3*

---

522 The added capital is JC's.
526 The capital added in stage direction is JC's.
526/527 The page number was repeated by mistake.

[18v]

163 Mor: *Where is she? hola! (calling the beggar) she returns)*
looking at her stedfastly in the face)
— — — — — — — — You are Matildas mother?
164 *Nay be not terrified—it does me good* [530]
165 *To look upon you*
Riv: *(interposing) — — In a peasant's dress*
166 *You saw, who was it?*
Beg: *— — — — — Nay, I dare not speak*
167 *He is a man—if it should come to his ears*
168 *I never shall be heard of more*
Riv: *— — — — — — — — — Lord Clifford——*
169 Beg: *What can I do? Believe me gentle Sirs!* [535]
170 *I love her, though I dare not call her daughter*
rd
171 Riv: *Lo[?]} Clifford! did you see him talk with Herbert?*
Oak
172 Beg: *Yes to my sorrow—under the great ~~beech~~*
beside
173 *At Herbert's door, and when he stood ~~by the side~~*
{T *silent*
174 *~~Of~~ {the blind man, he looked at the ~~poor~~ girl*
175 *With such a look—it makes me tremble ~~Sir~~* [541]
176 *To think of it——*
~~Riv~~: *— — — — — Enough! you may depart*
Os

[19r]

177 Mor: *(to himself) Father! To God himself we cannot give*
178 *An holier name, and under such a mask*
179 *To lead a spirit spotless as the blessed* [545]
{ish
180 *To that abhorred den of brut{al vice!*
I feel
181 *The firm foundation of my life ~~appears~~*
Is gone ^ *Oswald*
182 *~~To sink~~ from under me. This business, ~~Rivers~~*
183 *Will be my ruin. ——*

171 MH's 1799 correction.

l}a! *who*

Mar: Where is she—hola}(calling to the Beg—^~~She~~ returns—looking

{e

at her stedfastly) You are Idon{ia's Mother?— 529

Nay be not terrified—it does me good 530

To look upon you.

Osw

(interrupting) ——— In a Peasant's dress 531

You saw, who was it?

Beg ————— Nay I dare not speak 532

t}

He is a Man, if is} should come to his ears 533

I never shall be heard of more.

Osw ————————— Lord Clifford? 534

Beg What can I do, believe me, gentle Sirs, 535

I love her, tho' I dare not call her daughter. 536

Osw. Lord Clifford—did you see him talk with Herbert? 537

28

Beg Yes, to my sorrow—under the great oak 538

[?]

At Herbert's door ~~/~~ & when he stood beside 539

Girl

The blind man—[he looked] at the silent ~~Maid~~ 540

With such a look—it makes me tremble, Sir, 541

To think of it.

Osw ———— Enough! you may depart. 542

Mar:

(to himself) Father!—to God himself we cannot give 543

A~~n~~ holier name; &, under such a mask, 544

To lead a Spirit, spotless as the blessed, 545

To that ahborrèd den of brutish vice!— 546

Oswald,

{t

{~~The~~ firm foundation of my life ~~I feel~~ 547

{ese

Th{is strange discoveries, 548

Is gone from under me. ~~This business, Oswald~~

Looked at from every point of fear or hope, 549

Duty, or love, involve, I feel, my ruin. 550

~~Will be my ruin~~.

End of first Act.

---

529 looking *rev to* he looks *in stage dir*
530 terrified *over illeg erasure (Dora)*
531 *no apos*
532 speak;
534 lord *then capitalized (Dora)*
539 door—
548 me. These *then period rev to colon and lowercased*

---

529 Except for change in spelling of Idonia, revisions are JC's.

[20r]

Act 2d.— Scene 1st

[II.i] *A Chamber in the* ~~*Inn*~~ *Hostel — Rivers alone, rising from a Table, as if he had been writing.*

They chose <u>*him*</u> *for their chief!* {! } — {Insult that / ~~*I had a*~~} {bred / gnawing}
More of contempt than hatred!—Shame on me
'Twas a dull spark—a most unnatural {fire / [?fire]}
{That / —*It died the moment the air breathed upon it.* [557]
—These fools of feeling are mere birds of winter
That haunt some barren island of the north
Where if a famishing man stretch forth his hand
They think it is to feed them—I have left him [561]
To solitary meditation; now
For a few swelling phrases; and a flash
Of truth enough to dazzle and to blind
And he is mine for ever. *—here he comes*

Enter Mortimer

Mor: *These ten years she has moved her lips all day* [566]
And never speaks
Riv: *— — — — — — Who is it?*
Mor: *— — — — — — — — — — I have seen her*
~~*Just now I have been standing at her door*~~
Riv: *Oh! the poor tenant of that ragged cottage*
She whom the ~~*villain*~~ *Monster Clifford drove to madness*

---

1 Underlining added 1841.
1–3 On 19v, facing, a revision was drafted, 1841:

{C / chief!—what covert part
The ~~modest Youth might in preference take~~
He in the ~~the~~ preference modest Youth might take
~~I care not — Twill~~
I neither know nor care, The

29

Act 2^d^. Scene 1st.

~~the~~
~~a~~
A Chamber in {an Hostel~~l~~—Oswald alone, rising from a
the
Table on which he had been writing.

what covert part 551
Os: *They chose <u>him</u> for their Chief! ~~Insult that bred~~*
He in the preference, modest Youth! might take 552
I neither know nor care. The insult bred 553
More of contempt than hatred. ~~Shame on me~~,
both are flown 554
That either e'er existed is my shame 555
'Twas a dull spark—a most unnatural fire, 556
That died the moment the air breathed upon it. 557
—These fools of feeling are mere birds of winter 558
That haunt some barren island of the north 559
Where, if a famishing Man stretch forth his hand, 560
They think it is to feed them. I have left him 561
To solitary meditation; now 562
For a few swelling
For a few swelling phrases & a flash 563
Of truth, enough to dazzle & to blind, 564
And he is mine for ever——here he comes. 565

Enter Marmaduke.

Mar: *These ten years she has moved her lips all day* 566
And never speaks!
Osw *— — — — Who is it?*
Mar *— — — — — — — — I have seen her.* 567
tenant
! ten
Osw. *Oh } the poor {[?peas]ant of that raggèd homestead,* 568
She whom the Monster Clifford drove to madness. 569

---

551 Chief!—
552 He, Youth,
554 *as MS. 3 but* hatred: *rev as MS. 3 but* flown;
555 *interlined as MS. 3* shame,
557 on it *del to* upon it.
558 —These
559 north,
562 meditation;—
563 phrases,
569 She *rev to* Her

In the top stage direction, "the" below the line is JC's.
562/563 The hand is JC's.
568 The "tenant" above the line is JC's.

[20^v^]

her home
18 *Mor:* *I met a peasant near ~~the spot~~, he told me* [570]
19 *These ten years she had sat all day alone*
20 *Within those empty walls*
Riv: *Yes— I have seen her*
21 *Chancing to pass this way some six months*
gone
22 *At midnight I betook me to the church-yard*
23 *(~~I do not think I ever told you of it~~)*
24 *'Twas a calm night as I remember well*
25 *The moon shone clear; the air was still—so still* [575]
26 *The trees were silent as the graves beneath them*
27 *The church-clock from within the steeple tower*
28 *Tick'd audibly—a full half hour did I*
29 *Prolong my watch; I saw her pacing round*
30 *Upon the self same spot, still round and round*
31 *Her lips for ever moving*
Mor — At her door
Rooted I stood for looking at the Woman
~~*Mor*~~: — — — — — — — — ~~*Poor Matilda*~~
32 ~~*Oh Rivers! when I looked upon that woman*~~
33 *I thought I saw a skeleton of* {*Idonia* / *Matilda*} [581]
34 *Riv:* *But the ~~old man~~? pretended Father?*
Mor: — — — — — — ~~*There is no*~~ {*E* / *earthly law*}
35 ~~*That*~~ {*M* / *measures*} ^*not* *crimes like his*
Riv: — — — — — — — *Would she were present!*
Idonea—to the end
36 ~~*Matilda fit it were*~~ *that we should hear*
37 *What she can urge in his defence—she loves him* [590]

20b Underlining added 1841.

30

Mar: *I met a Peasant near the spot; he told me*
These ten years she had sate all day alone
Within those empty walls.

too
Osw *— — — — — — ~~Yes~~, I^have seen her;*
is
Chancing to pass that{ way some six months gone,
At midnight, I betook me to the Church yard:
~~Twas a calm night, as I remember well~~
The moon shone clear, the air was still, so still
The trees were silent as the graves beneath them.
~~The Church Clock from within the Steeple Tower~~
{ably — a full half hour did I~~

Long did I &
~~Prolong my~~ watch, I{ saw her pacing round
Upon the self-same spot, still round & round,
Her lips for ever moving.

Mar *— — — — — — — At her door*
Rooted I stood; for, looking at the woman,
e
I thought I saw the skeleton of Idoni{a.

Osw *But the pretended Father——*

Mar *— — — — — — — — Earthly law*
Measures not crimes like his.

---

t {at Idonia
Osw *— — — — — — Would s{h{e ~~were present~~*
Were present might
~~Idonia,~~ to the end that we ~~should~~ hear
{is
What she can urge in h{er defence—she loves him

Osw *— — — — — We rank not happily*
With those ~~self~~ who take the spirit of their rule
From that soft class of Devotees who feel
Reverence for life so deeply that they spare
The verminous brood, & cherish what they spare
While feeding on their bodies. Would that Idonea
Were present, to the end that we might hear
What she can urge in his defence; She loves him.

---

570 me,
572 these *rev to* those
574 Yard
583b We rank not, happily,
588 *further developed in MS. 3A, 4*[v]
590 she loves

---

572 The insertion is by JC.
583a/583b On back of the pasteover is an address in MW's hand: "J. G. Lockhart Esq[re]/ Sussex Place / Regent's Park / London."

[21^r^]

38 *Mor:* *Yes loves him—'tis a truth that multiplies*
39 *His guilt a thousand fold*
Riv: — — — — — — — *'Tis most perplexing*
40 *What must be done?*
Mor: — — — — — — *We will conduct her hither*
41 *These walls shall witness it—from first to last* [594]
42 *He shall reveal himself* ~~*—his punishment*~~
43 *Shall be before her face*
Riv: — — — — — — — ~~*The thought is grand*~~
~~*Sublime resolve!*~~
{*B*
44 ~~*And worthy the occasion*~~ — {*but bethink you* *first*
45 ~~*Is it not possible that some may think*~~ *deem*
f} *t*} {*be*
46 *It*} *is*} {*unseemly in a man like you*
~~*that is*~~
47 *To take the life of* ~~*one*~~^ ~~*so helpless*~~
such a helpless Creature
Mor: — — — — — — — — — — — ~~*Oh*~~
48 *Would he were older! would he were more weak*
49 *A thousand times more helpless,* ~~*verily*~~
50 ~~*I do not think the tale will be believed*~~
51 ~~*Till I have shed his blood*~~
Riv: — — — — — — — — *Happy are we*
52 *Who live in these disputed tracts that own* [596]
53 *No law but what each man makes for himself*
54 *Here justice has indeed a field of triumph.*

[21^v^]

MM
{*b*
55 *Mor:* *Let us* {*ge gone and bring her hither; here* [599]
56 ~~*Shall he be stretched and after come what will*~~
The truth shall be laid open—his guilt proved
Before her face— The rest be left to me
The wretch must die thereafter come what will.
57 *Riv:* *That thought escaped me—This is an act of justice*

A photograph of 21^v^ is provided below, p. 718.
55 MH's 1799 correction; the "MM" above the line may have resulted from the testing of a pen.

31

Mar: Yes, loves him; 'tis a truth that multiplies 591
His guilt a thousand-fold.
Osw — — — — — — — Tis most perlexing: 592
What must be done?
Mar: — — — — — We will conduct her hither; 593
These walls shall witness it—from first to last 594
He shall reveal himself } ~~& his punishment~~ [&]
~~Receive~~
~~Shall be before her face~~
Osw — — — — — — — ~~Sublime~~ {~~resolve~~ thought
~~And worthy the occasion—but {B bethink you first~~
~~Is it not possible that some may deem~~
~~It {f} {it is} {be} unseemly in a Man like you~~
~~such a helpless Creature~~
~~To take the life of One that is so helpless~~
Mar: ~~Would he were older! would he were more weak~~ {~~er~~ /}
~~A thousand times more helpless~~
Osw — — — — — — — — — — Happy are we, 595
Who live in these disputed tracts that own 596
No law but what each man makes for himself; 597
Here justice has indeed a field of triumph. 598
Mar: Let us begone & bring her hither—here 599
The truth shall be laid open—his guilt proved 600
Before her face. The rest be left to me. 601
in ~~The Wretch must die—thereafter come what will~~
The wretch must ~~die, thereafter come what will.~~

Osw
You will be firm yet tho' we well may trust 602
32 ~~were unjust~~
The issue to the justice of the cause 603
~~Osw~~ ~~That thought escaped me—this is an act of justice~~
~~is^an act of Justice~~
Caution must not be flung aside; remember 604

---

592 *no hyphen* 'Tis
599 hither:—
600 open—{,}
601/602 *as MS. 3 but no comma, then del*
602–603 *inserted as MS. 3 but* firm; but
604 *inserted as MS. 3 but* remember,

601/602 The revision from "must" onward is JC's.

triu
And where's the {*h*[?]*mph if the delegate*
Must fall in the execution of his office?
Yours is no common life! Self-stationed here
C *you*
Upon these savage {*confines we have seen* {*you* [606]
Stand like an isthmus 'twixt two stormy seas
oft have
That^*checked their fury at your bidding—*
'Mid the deep holds of Solway's mossy waste
Your single virtue has transformed a band
Of fierce barbarians into ministers [611]
Of beauty and of order— The old man
Blesses their steps; the fatherless retires
For shelter to their banners. But it is
In darkness, and in tempest that we seek [616]
T *~~everlasting Justice~~*
{*The majesty of ~~the Almighty~~ — ~~Yes~~*
~~Majesty~~ of Him that rules the world
Benevolence that has not heart to use
The wholesome ministry of pain and evil [619]
Becomes at last weak *~~your virtues~~*
~~Is powerless~~ and contemptible: {*as yet*
~~Hitherto~~ Your ~~qualities~~ generous qualities have won due praise
~~Your virtues, the spontaneous growth of instinct~~
~~Have had their praise~~ {*~~& they deserved it well~~*
{*and* [?]
~~From vigorous souls can claim but little praise~~.
~~But in the eye of vigorous Souls to day~~
~~To day you will assume a character more awful~~
They
~~More awful and sublime — remember this~~
~~And think hereafter——~~
so
But vigorous Spirits look for [?*mo*]} *mething more*
Than Youths spontaneous products

[22^r]

And to day you will not disappoint them
And hereafter—
Annandale
~~Mort~~: — — — — — — *Talk not of hereafter*
This act has virtue for a thousand lives

58 MH's 1799 correction.

~~And where's the triumph if the del{igate~~ [st/e above]
her
~~Yes that resolve becomes you we must trust~~
~~Must fall in the execution of his office?~~
~~*Osw*~~ *~~The issue trust to the justice of the cause.~~*
Your's is no common life! Self-stationed here,
Upon these savage confines, we have seen you
h
Stand like an istmus 'twixt two stormy seas
That oft have checked their fury at your bidding:
Mid the deep holds of Solway's mossy Waste
Your single virtue has transformed a Band
Of fierce barbarians into Ministers
peace *Aged men with tears*
Of ~~beauty~~ & ~~of~~ Order. *~~The old Man~~*
Have blessed
~~Blesses~~ their steps, the Fatherless retires
For shelter to their banners. But it is
As you must needs have deeply felt, it
is
In darkness & in tempest that we seek
who
The majesty of Him ~~that~~ rules the world.
Benevolence, that has not heart to use
The wholesome ministry of pain & evil,
i
Becomes at last weak & contempt[?a]}ble.
Your generous qualities have won due praise,
But vigorous Spirits look for something more
and
Than Youth's spontaneous products, &^to-day
Y
~~And to-day~~ {~~you will~~ not disappoint them,
You will *& hereafter*——
~~And hereafter~~

33

You[?] have been
Mar: ——————— *~~Talk not of hereafter~~*
You have been wasting words, fixed is my purpose
~~This act has virtue for a thousand lives~~

604/605 *two lines del as MS. 3:*

Yes, that resolve becomes you, we may trust
The issue trust to the justice of the cause.

605 life.

608 bidding:} [. above :]

609 waste *then capitalized (Dora)*

612 *as MS. 3, rev as MS. 3 with* peace *in Dora's hand*

613 *as MS. 3, rev as MS. 3*

614 shelters *then* s *del*

617 *as MS. 3, rev as MS. 3*

623 products; to day

607, 623 Revisions are JC's.

624 The phrase "You will" is JC's.

81 *Riv:* *But 'tis an act ~~act~~ of reason and bethink you*
82 *Should any rashness—*
Hear me once for all
{*Anan* / *Mor:*} *— — — — — — ~~Hark'ee Rivers Oswald~~*
83 *You are a man—and if compassion's milk*
84 *Be known unto you, you will love this woman* [628]
85 *Even as I do, but I should loath the light* —}
86 *If I could think one weak or partial feeling* }
87 *Riv:* *You quite mistake me—*
Mor: *— — — — — — If I ever knew*
88 *My heart, and naked saw the man within me*
89 *'Tis at this moment— Rivers! I have loved* [633]
90 *To be the friend and father of the helpless*
91 *A comforter of sorrow—there is something*
92 *Which looks like a* <u>*transition*</u> *in my soul* [636]
{*i* {*hither*
93 *And yet it is not— Let us lead ~~th~~* {*em* {*in*
Stoop for *~~from this height & [?stoop]~~*
94 *Riv:* ^ *A moments ~~pause~~— ~~To benefit their fellows~~*
{*to*
95 *~~Great souls must stoop— Let~~* {*us survey the case*
96 *Just as it is—the deed is done—performed*
97 *Here where we stand—a tribe of vulgar wretches* [642]
98 *Rush in—the villains seize us—*
Mor: *— — — — — — — — — — Seize!*

[22v]

Osw *~~Yes they will be~~* *Yes they*
Will be more prompt than we have been, their hands

81 MH's 1799 correction.
93 The "them" corrected to "him" 1799, with the "t" erased.

Osw: *But tis an act of reason, & bethink you*
Should any rashness
You are wasting words— hea me then
Mar ——————— *~~Hear me~~*‸*once for all ~~Oswald~~*
ar} then ~~for~~}
You are wasting words, he[?re]} me‸*once [?ere]} for all:* 625
You are a Man—~~& if compassion's milk~~
Was and therefore, if compassion, 626
~~Be known unto you you will love this woman~~
Which to our kind is natural as life, 627
Be known unto you, you will love this woman, 628
Even as I do; but I should ~~lothe~~ the light, 629
loathe ——
If I could think one weak or partial feeling— 630
will forgive me——
Osw *You ~~quite mistake me~~*——
Mar: ———————— *If I ever knew* 631
could penetrate its inmost core, 632
My heart, ~~& naked saw the Man within me~~
Tis at this moment.— Oswald I have loved 633
oppressed, 634
To be the friend & father of the ~~helpless~~
A comforter of sorrow;—there is something 635
Which looks like a transition in my soul, 636
And yet it is not.— Let us lead him hither. 637
tis an act of justice, 638
Osw *Stoop for a moment; ~~to survey the case~~*
And where's the triumph if the delegate 639
~~Just as it is—the deed is done—performed~~
Must fall in the execution of his office. 640
The deed is done—if you will have it so— 641
{th t}
Here where we stand—{ a } tribe of vulgar wretches 642
You saw them gathering for a festival 643
Rush in—the villains seize us—— 644a
Mar: ——————————— *Seize!*

34
Osw: ———————— *Yes, they* 644b
Men who are little given to sift & weigh 645
~~been~~—
~~Will be more prompt than we have,‸their hands~~

---

625 words;
633 Oswald,
638 Stop *rev to* Stoop *(JC)* justice;
640 office?
643 *interlined, within parens*
644b Yes, they—
645 *as MS. 3 but comma after* been *rev to dash; entire line rev as MS. 3 but* weigh—

---

625 The last "for" was entered by JC.
626 "Was" in pencil reinforced in ink; the "and" is JC's.
629 The "loathe" is JC's.

Will execute on us ~~the instant~~ judgment
Riv: — — — — — — — — — — *The eye*
immediate
~~*Of vulgar men knows not the majesty*~~
~~*With which the mind can clothe the shapes of things*~~
~~*They look but through the spectacles of forms*~~
~~*And from success alone they judge of actions*~~
{T *farewell*
Mor: ~~*Fear not*~~, {*the cloud will soon disperse*—~~*but stay*~~
But stay
^ ~~*Th*~~*ou wilt relate the story*—~~*farewell*~~ —
Riv: — — — — — — — — — — — *Am I then*
~~*Of such light value*~~*?*
Mor: — — — — — — — *I had many hopes*
That were most dear to me—I mention it
That I may live in thee
Riv: — — — — — — — *What* !} *after I am dishonored?*
Mor: I would preserve thee; how may it be done? [652]
look beyond the instant
Riv: By shewing that you ~~*calculate, and look*~~
~~*Beyond the present object of the sense*~~—
A few leagues hence we shall have open field [655]
And tread on ground as free as the first earth
Which nature gave to man. Before we enter
The barren heath, just half way to the convent
We pass the beetling rock from which there hangs
A ruined castle you have heard of it
It is a noted spot where Clifford oft

99–102 A penciled X in margin marks these lines for deletion.
107 The added exclamation point is in pencil.
115 MH's 1799 correction.

Would wreak on us the passion of the moment 646
~~Will execute on us immediate judgement~~.

The cloud
Mar: *~~Fear not~~, {~~I~~ ~~the cloud~~ will soon disperse{— farewell— but stay,* 647
~~but stay~~
Thou wilt relate the story. ~~/farewell~~
Am I neither 648
Osw: ——————————*~~Am~~* [?] } { *~~I~~* [?] } { *~~then~~* [?]
To [?*~~no~~*]
~~Neither to~~ bear a part in this ~~just deed~~ man's punishment 649
~~Of such small value~~
~~So soon forgotten~~
Nor be its witness?
Mar —————— *I had many hopes* 650
& some will bear 651
That were most dear to me, ~~/I mention it~~
To be transferre{,d to thee.
~~That I may live in thee~~
When I'm ?}
Osw —————— *~~What! after I am~~ dishonored!{?* 652
Mar *I would preserve thee ;{H how may th{is at be done?* 653
Osw *By shewing that you look beyond the instant.* 654
A few leagues hence we shall have open
~~field~~ ground, 655
~~And on the Earth is n~~
~~And tread on ground as free as the first Earth~~
And nowhere upon Earth is place so fit 656
To ~~witness such~~ a deed.
~~Which Nature gave to Man~~. Before we enter 657
To look upon the deed
{M moor, ~~there hangs, as you well know~~,
The barren heath ~~just half way to the Convent~~
~~there~~ hangs from a beetling rock 658
~~We pass the beetling rock from which there hangs~~
~~A ruined Castle—You have heard of it~~
The s{h [?]attered Castle in
~~It is a noted spot~~ wh{ich ere Clifford ~~of~~ [?~~t~~]{oft 659

---

646 *as MS. 3, rev as MS. 3 but* moment.
648 Am I, then, *with* then *del to* neither *as MS. 3*
649 *as MS. 3 except* deed, *then rev as MS. 3 but* man's *capitalized*
652 transferred *question mark rev to exclam point*
657 look upon the] witness such a *del to* look upon the

646/647 "The cloud" is JC's.
648 "Am" above the overwritten line is JC's.
659 The final "oft" is JC's.

[23^r]

118 *Has held most h{ellish / orrid} orgies with the gloom*
119 *And very superstition of the place*
120 *Seasoning his* ~~*lusts*~~ [*wickedness*]*. The* ~~*savage*~~ *debauchee*
121 *Would there perhaps have gathered the first fruits*
122 *Of this foul monster's guilt.*

Ente{r / [?]} Host conducting Herbert

Host — — — — — — — — *The Baron Herbert*
123 *Attends your pleasure*
Riv: *(to the Host) We are ready—(to Herbert) Sir!*
124 *I hope you are refreshed—I have just written*
125 *A notice for your daughter that she may know*
126 *What is become of you—you'll sit down & sign*
it
127 *'Twill glad her heart to see her father's signature*
(gives him a letter which was lying upon the table)
128 Her: *Thanks for your care (he sits down & writes) Exit Host*
Riv:) *aside to Mor:) — — Perhaps it would be useful*
129 *That you too should subscribe your name*
(Mortimer looks over Herbert, then writes
examines the letter eagerly — —
Mor: — — — — — — — — *It shall not be*
130 *I cannot leave this paper (he puts it up in*
great agitation
Riv: *(aside) — — — The Blockhead! Come*

[23^v]

(Mortimer goes towards Her: and supports him—
Mor: trembles much and beckons Rivers to take
his place

118, 122/123 MH's 1799 corrections.

35

infernal
Has held ~~most hellish~~ orgies, with the gloom, 660
And very superstition of the place, 661
wickedness {*D*
Seasoning his ~~wretchedness~~. The {*debauchee* 662
Would there perhaps have gathered the first fruits 663
mock Father
{*~~M~~*
Of this ~~foul~~ {*~~monster~~'s guilt.*

Enter Host conducting Herbert.

{*T*
Host — — — — — — — — {*the Baron Herbert* 664
Attends your pleasure.
Osw
(to Host) — — — — *We are ready—~~Sir~~!*
~~Mar:~~ *(to Herbert) Sir!* 665
I hope you are refreshed.— I have just written 666
A notice for your daughter, that she may know 667
What is become of you,—You'll sit down & sign it; 668
'Twill glad her heart to see her Father's signature. 669
(gives the letter, he had written)
Her *Thanks for your care.*
(sits down & writes—Ex Host)
Osw:
(aside to — — — — — *Perhaps it would be useful* 670
Mar:)
That you too should subscribe your name 671
(Mar: overlooks Her—then writes—)
—examines the letter eagerly)
{*d*
Mar: *I cannot leave this paper. (He puts it up, agitate*{[?]*)*

Osw. *Dastard!*
(aside) — — — — — *The ~~Blockhead!~~ Come.* 672
(Mar: goes towards Her: & supports him—Mar: trembles}
ing}
&} *ng*
—}*beckons Oswald to take his place)*

---

660 orgies, —}
664a *as MS. 3, rev as MS. 3 but* Father's
672 The] *omitted*
672/673 tremblingly *in stage direction*

---

662 The capital is JC's.
672/673 To clarify messy revision, "ng" was added to the overwriting.

Mor: (as he leaves Her:)
There is a palsy in his limbs — he shakes
Exeunt Rivers & Herbert together—Mortimer follows

[II.ii] *Scene changes to a Wood—A group of Pilgrims & Matilda amongst them*

1st Pil: A grove of darker, and more lofty shade
I never saw
2d Pil: — — — The music of the Birds
Drops deadened from a roof so thick with leaves
This news
an old Pil: (~~to~~ Mat:)^It made my heart leap up with joy
Mat: — — — — — — — — ~~This news~~
I scarcely can believe it
3d Pil: — — — — — — — Myself I heard
The sheriff read in open court a letter
Which purported it was the Royal pleasure
The Baron Herbert who, as was supposed
Had taken refuge in this neighbourhood
Should be forthwith restored

[24r]

Pil: — — — — — — — — The hearing, Lady
[?]
~~Brought tears into mine eyes~~
{F
~~It~~ {~~filled my eyes with tears.~~ When I returned
Filled my dim eyes with tears
From Palestine, and brought with me a heart
Though rich in heavenly, poor in earthly comfort
I met your Father, then a wandering outcast.
but grieved
He had a guide a Shepherd's boy, ~~his heart~~
He Was ~~grieved~~ that one so young should pass his youth
In such sad service, and he parted from him.
We joined our tales of wretchedness together
And begged our daily bread from door to door.
I talk familiarly to you, sweet Lady
For once you loved me.

36

Mar: There is a palsy in his limbs—he shakes.⌿ 673

(as he quits Her: *Ex Os: & Her—Mar following)*

Scene changes to a Wood—a Group~~e~~ of Pilgrims

and Idon{e / ia with them.

1.st *Pil.* *A grove of darker, & more lofty shade* 674
I never saw.

2^d^ *Pil* *— — — The music of the Birds* 675
Drops deadened from a roof so thick with leaves. 676

An old Pil: *This news! It made my heart leap up with joy.* 677

Ido *I scarcely can believe it.*

3^d^ *Pil:* *— — — — — — — Myself I heard* 678
The Sheriff read, in open Court, a letter, 679
Which purported it was the royal pleasure 680
The Baron Herbert, who, as was supposed, 681
Had taken refuge in this neighbourhood, 682
Should be forthwith restored. {T / the hearing,
Lady, 683
Filled my dim eyes with tears. When I returned 684
From Palestine, & brought with me a heart 685
Tho' rich in heavenly, poor in earthly, comfort, 686
I met your Father, then a wandering Outcast {: / ,} 687

37

He had a Guide, a Shepherd's boy, but grieved 688
He }
[?]} *was, that One so young should pass his youth* 689
In such sad service; & he parted ~~from~~ *with* *him.* 690
We joined our tales of wretchedness together, 691
And begged our daily bread from door to door. 692
I talk familiarly to you, sweet Lady! 693
For once you loved me.

---

673 shakes.—
673/674 group *then capitalized in stage direction (Dora)*
674 *comma del*
678 can] could *del to* can Myself,
679 *final comma omitted*
685 heart,
686 *final comma omitted*
688 boy;
689 *no comma*

---

690 Deletion and revision in pencil overwritten in ink.

Mat: — — — — — — — *You shall back with me*
And see your friend again. The good old man
{W be rejoiced
'~~T~~ {will ~~glad his heart~~ to greet you.
old Pil: — — — — — — — — — *It seems but yesterday*
—That cavern—does he ever ~~talk of it~~
No doubt you've h~~eard the~~ tale a thousand times
~~It was a dreary~~ afternoon—and we
That a fierce storm oertook us, worn with travel
~~Were worn with travel when a storm oertook us~~
{—
In a dep wood remote *from any town {*
A cave that opened to the road presented
A friendly shelter and we entered in
Mat: *And I was with you.*

[24[v]]

Old Pil: — — — — — — *If indeed 'twas you*
But you were then a tottering little one
We sate us down. The sky grew dark & darker
I struck my flint, and built up a small fire
With rotten boughs and leaves such as the winds
Autumns
Of many ~~winters~~ in the cave had piled
Meanwhile the storm fell heavy on the woods
Our little fire sent forth a cheering warmth
And we were comforted, and talked of comfort.
But 'twas an angry night and o'er our heads
The thunder rolled in peals that would have made
A sleeping man uneasy in his bed
Oh Lady! you have need to love your father
His countenance, methinks I see it now
When after a broad flash that filled the cave
He said to me that he had seen his child
— A face — and a confused gleam of human flesh
And it was you, dear Lady
Mat — — — — — — — *Heaven be praised*
That I have lived to be a comfort to him!

---

28 MH corrected "remote" but not her miswriting of "deep" in 1799.
35 MH's 1799 correction.

Ido — — — — — *You shall back with me*
And see your friend again. The good old Man
Will be rejoiced to s{gr/ee} {t/} you.
Old Pil — — — — — — — *It seems but yesterday*
That a fierce storm o'ertook us, worn with travel,
In a deep wood remote from any town.+
A cave that opened to the road prev {s/}ented
A friendly shelter, & we entered in.
Ido *And I was with you.*
Old Pil — — — — *If indeed 'twas you—*
But you were then a tottering Little-one—
We sate us down. The sky grew dark & darker:
I struck my flint, & ~~stru~~ built up a small fire
With rotten boughs & leaves, such as the winds

38

Of many autumns in the cave had piled.
Meanwhile the Storm fell heavy on the woods:
Our little fire sent forth a cheering warmth
And we were comforted, & talked of comfort;
But 'twas an angry night, & o'er our heads
The {t/T}hunder rolled in peals that would have made
A sleeping Man uneasy in his bed.
O Lady, you have need to love your Father.
His ~~*countenance*~~ *voice, methinks I* ~~*see*~~ *hear it now; his voice*
When, after a broad flash that filled the c{ave,/[?]}
He said to me that he had seen his Child,
no cherub's face more ~~*so*~~ *beautiful!*
+*A face,* ~~*& a confus{s/ed} gleam, of human flesh*~~
Revealed by lustre brought with it from Heaven;
And it was you, dear Lady!
Ido — — — — — — — ~~*Heaven*~~ *God be praised*
That I have ~~*lived to be a comfort to him!*~~ *been his Comforter!* ~~*so long*~~ *till now,*

---

694 You shall back with me *over* It seems but yesterday *anticipating l. 696, erased (Dora)*
701 you.] you?
707 storm . . . woods;
714 *as MS. 3, rev as MS. 3 but comma del to dash, and* now,
715/716 a gla *del*
716 me,
717 *comma del and parens enclosing last five words*
719 praised,
720 *exclam point del, comma rev to exclam point*

will end our journey
Let us be gone ~~it is not~~ two leagues, ~~hence~~
And we shall greet him with these happy tidings
This is a day of thankfulness and joy ——
Exeunt Matilda & Pilgrims

[25r]

[II.iii] *Scene—The area of a ruined Castle—on one side the entrance of a dungeon— Mortimer and Rivers*
pacing bac{*kw* / [?]}*ards and forwards ——*
Mor: *'Tis a wild night*
Riv: *I'd give my cloak and bonnet* [725]
For sight of a warm fire
Mor: *— — — — — The wind blows keen;*
My hands are numb.
Riv: *(blowing his fingers) Hu! hu! 'tis nipping cold*
I long for news of our brave comrades; Lacy
Would drive those Scottish rovers to their dens
If once they blew a horn this side the Tweed [730]
~~*He is a stripling of great promise*~~
Mor: *I think I see a second range of towers*
This castle has another area—come
Let us examine it
Riv: *— — — — — In truth 'tis cold*
I hope Matilda is well housed—Th{*at* / *e*}* horseman*
Who ~~passed us~~ at full speed{*swept by us* / *,*}* wh*{*ere* / *ile*}* the ~~dark~~ wood*
Roared in the tempest was within an ace [736]
Of sending the old ~~fellow~~ Traitor to his grave—
That would have been ^a vile^ mischance
Mor: *— — — — — — — — — It would.*

[25v]

Riv: *Justice would have been most cruelly defrauded.*
Mor: *Most cruelly——*

In the setting on 25r, correction of "backwards" was made in 1799.
15 Probably a 1799 insertion.

And will be so thro' every change of fortune 721
And every sacrifice his peace requires.—— 722
Let us be gone~~—two leagues will end our journey~~
(~~& he will hear~~)
~~Let us be gone~~ with speed, that he may hear 723
~~And we shall greet him with these happy tidings~~
These joyful tidings, from no lips but mine. 724
~~This is a day of thankfulness & joy~~.
(Exeunt Ido & Pilgrims).

half-
Scene, the Area of a^{-ruined Castle—on one side the
entrance to a dungeon— Osw. & Mar: pacing backwards
& forwards)

39

Mar: 'Tis a wild night.
Osw ————— I'd give my cloak & bonnet 725
For sight of a warm fire.
Mar: —————— The wind blows keen, 726
My hands are numb.
Osw (~~blowing his fingers~~) Ha! ha! 'tis nipping cold. (blowing his fingers)
I long for news of our brave Comrades; Lacy 728
Would drive those Scottish {R / [?]overs to their dens 729
If once they blew a horn this side the Tweed. 730
Mar: I think I see a second range of Towers, 731
This Castle has another Area—come 732
Let us examine it.
Tis a bitter night; 733
Osw ————— In truth tis cold
I hope Idoni{e / a} is well housed. That horseman, 734
Who at full speed swept by us where the wood 735
Roared in the tempest, was within an ace 736
{O / If} sending the old Traitor to his grave. 737
That would have been a vile mischance.
Mar: ———————— It {would. / wood} 738
had
Justice ~~would have~~ been most cruelly defrauded. 739
Mar: Most cruelly.

---

724 *comma del*
731 *comma rev to semicolon*
732 come,
733 'Tis
737 the old Traitor *del and* our precious charge *added to line*

---

729 Revision is JC's.

~~you not hear me~~ ~~[?]~~
Riv: ———— *~~Did I not mention to you~~*
as
~~That as we mounted~~ up the ~~open~~ steep
he d}
I led him oer the torrent his voice blesst } me
I saw a distant fire in the north-east?
I took it for the blaze of Cheviot Beacon
With proper speed our quarters may be gained [743]
Early tomorrow evening (looks restlessly towards the mouth of ~~the~~ dungeon ——)
a
~~While~~ across the plank
Mor: ————— *~~When I conducted him across that plank~~*
I led him his voice d}
~~Hung~~ o'er the torrent ~~did you hear him~~ bless } me
When he had gained the other side? I think
You could not hear ~~— you were behind — 'twas windy~~
And the foam beat the rocks with deafening noise
Those words were most delicious to me
Riv: ———————————— *A feast*
{w
For t{henty years — How was it?
Mor: ————————— *And you think*
This is the fittest place?
Plague
Riv: *(aside)* ————— *~~Zounds~~! he's turning soft*
Mor: *(listening) What an odd moaning that is!*
Riv: —————————— *Mighty odd* [751]
The wind should pipe a little while we stand

[26^r]

{ el }
Cooling our he{[?ad]}s in this way — I'll begin
And count the stars

---

18 The "bl" of "blesst" began as "he," which was then used without alteration before a new "he" was added above the line.
29,33 MH's 1799 corrections.

40

Osw —— ~~*D*~~[?]{ $\overset{\text{~~i~~}}{}$ } ~~*d*~~ { *you* ~~*hear me say*~~ / ~~*I not mention to you*~~

~~*That as we mounted*~~^ *As* *up the* ~~*open*~~ *steep we clomb,* 740
I saw a distant fire in the north-east; 741
I took it for the blaze of Chi{*e*} *viot Beacow*{*n*} *:* 742
With proper speed our quarters may be gained 743
~~*Early*~~ {*T*} *tomorrow evening* (*looks restlessly towards the mouth of the dungeon*)

~~*While As when across the plank*~~ 744
Mar: ————— ~~*While I conducted him*~~
When, across{*upon*} *the plank,* ~~*bless'd*~~ {*'d*
~~*I led him oer the torrent his voice bles*~~{~~*t me*~~
I had led him oer the torrent his voice bless'd me: 745
~~*belike*~~
~~*When he had gained the other side—I think*~~
for the foam beat the rocks 746
You could not hear, ~~*/ you were behind—'twas windy*~~
With deaf'ning noise,—the benediction fell 747
~~*And the foam beat the rocks with deaf'ning noise*~~
Back on himself, but changed into a curse. 748
~~*Those words were most delicious to me*~~
~~*No wonder*~~ ~~*how was it?*~~
~~*Os*~~*:* ~~*A feast*~~
~~*And well it might indeed it might*~~
~~*For twenty years—How was it?*~~
Osw *As well indeed it might.*
Mar: ——————————— *And*^ *this* *you think* 749
~~*This is*~~ {*T*} *the fittest place*
———— *He is growing pitiful* 750
Osw (aside) ————— ~~*Plague, he's turning soft*~~
Mar *What an odd moaning that is!*
(listening)
Os: ———————— *Mighty odd* 751
The wind should pipe a little, while we stand 752
Cooling our heels in this way,—I'll begin 753
And count the stars.

---

744 evening.
745 o'er belike *at end of line del*
746 *caret or comma del following* foam
747 deaf{e / 'ning
750 place. pitiful.
751 is!—

---

740 The insertion is JC's.

Mor: *(still listening) You are sure that dog of his*
35 *Could not come after us—he must have perished—*
36 *The torrent would have dashed an oak to splinters—*
37 *You said you did not like his looks—that he*
38 *Would trouble us; if he were here again*
39 *I swear the sight of him would quail me more*
40 *Than twenty armies*
Riv: *— — — — — — How?*
Mor: *— — — — — — — The old blind man*
41 *Wept when you told him the mischance, and hung*
42 *Listening above the precipice*
Riv: *— — — — — — — — — — — In faith*
43 *He has a tender heart!*
Mor: *— — — — — — — You should not, Rivers*
44 X *Have hurled the innocent animal from the precipice*
45 *You should not—there was no occasion for it—*
(Riv: offers to go down into the dungeon)
46 *How now? what mean you?*
Riv: *— — — — — — — Truly I was going*
Imposter
47 *To waken the old ~~fellow~~ —were there not*
48 *A farm or dwelling-house within five leagues*

[26ᵛ]

49 *We should deserve to wear a cap and bells*
50 *Three good round years for playing the fool here*
51 *In such a night as this*
Mor: *— — — — — — — Stop! stop,*
Riv: *— — — — — — — — — — Perhaps*
52 *You'd better like we should descend together*
53 *And lie down by his side, what say you to it?*

44–45 A penciled X is entered in left margin, and "the precipice" and "occasion" are underlined in pencil.

41

Mar: (still listening) *x You are sure that dog of his*
x You &c 754
Could not come after us—he <u>*must*</u> *have perished—* 755
The torrent would have dashed an oak to splinters. 756
You said you did not like his looks—that he 757
Would trouble us; if he were here again 758
I swear the sight of him would quail me more 759
Than twenty armies.
Osw — — — — — — *How?*
blind ,~~hung~~
Mar: — — — — — — — — — *The old ~~blind~~ Man* 760
~~Was troubled~~ troubled
{W had , was troubled 761
~~Wept~~ {when you^told him the mischance, ~~& hung~~
Even to the shedding of some natural tears ~~into torrent~~ 762
~~stream~~
~~Listening above the precipice~~
[?~~Onto~~] Into the torrent over which he hung, 763
Listening in vain.
Osw — — — — — — — — — *~~In faith~~ ~~truth~~*
~~His heart is tender!~~
— — — — — — — — *He has a tender heart!* 764
~~He has a tender heart~~
~~Mar~~: — — — — — — — — *~~You should not, Oswald~~*
~~You should not, there was no occasion for it~~
(Os offers to go down into the dungeon)
Mar: How now, what mean you?
Osw — — — — — — — *Truly I was going* 765
our stray Baron. {W
To waken ~~the old Imposter~~, {were there not 766
A farm or dwelling house within five leagues, 767
to wear
We should deserve^a cap & bells, 768
Three good round years, for playing the fool here 769
In such a night as this. 770a

42
Mar: — — — — — — — — *Stop, Stop,*
Osw — — — — — — — — — *Perhaps,* 770b
You'd better like we should descend together, 771
And lie down by his side—what say you to it? 772

---

754 That dog of his you are sure
755 *final dash del to colon*
758 again,
760 was troubled *miscopied at end of line, del*
767 farm—or dwelling-house

---

754 The insertion is JC's.

Three of us—we should keep each other warn^{m} }
I'll answer for it that our four-legged friend
Shall not disturb us, further I'll not engage [775]
Come, come for heavens sake
Mor: — — — — — — — *These drowsy shiverings,*
This mortal stupor which is creeping over me
What do they mean? Is not the depth
Of this man's crimes beyond the reach of thought? [781]
And yet in plumbing the abyss { *for judgment* / *of vengeance* }
Something I strike upon which turns my thoughts
Back on myself— I think again —my breast
Concenters all the terrors of the universe
I look at him and tremble like a child— [786]
Riv: Is it possible
Mor: — — — — *One thing you noticed not*
Just as we left the glen a clap of thunder

[27r]

Burst on the mountain with hell-rousing force
"This is ~~the~~ ^{a} *time" said he; "when guilt may shudder* [790]
But there's a providence for them who walk
In helplessness when innocence is with them"
At this infernal blasphemy I thought
The spirit of vengeance seemed to ride the air
Yet nothing came of it—I listened but
The echoes of the thunder died away
Along the distant hills
~~*what then*~~

54 MH's 1799 correction.
"See other Copy" is written vertically in the left margin of 26v in MH's hand, alongside ll. 57–61.
69 Revision in pencil reinforced in ink.
76/77 The "what then" attached to Mortimer's speech is a (1799) copyist's error.

Three of us, ⎫ *we should keep each other warm:* 773
I'll answer for it that our four-legged friend 774
Shall not disturb us; further I'll not engage. 775
Manhood's
Come, come for ~~Heavens~~ sake.
Mar: — — — — — — — — *These drowsy shiverings,* 776
This mortal stupor which is creeping over me, 777
: ⎫ ⎧ *ing*
What do they mean; ⎭ *were this my single body (collect* ⎩ *g himself.)* 778
Armies
Opposed to ~~thousands~~ not a nerve would tremble: 779
Why do they tremble now?— Is not the depth 780
reach
Of this man's crimes beyond the ~~power~~ of thought? 781
And yet, in plumbing the abyss for judgement, 782
⎧ *upon*
Something I strike ⎩ *[?which] which turns my mind* 783
her
Back on ~~my~~self I think again—my breast 784
Concenters all the terrors of the universe: 785
I look at him & tremble like a child.~~/~~ 786
Osw: *Is it possible.*
Mar — — — — *One thing you noticed not:* 787
Just as we left the glen a clap of thunder 788

43

Burst on the mountains with hell-rousing force. 789
This is a time, said he, when guilt may shudder; 790
⎧ *P*
But there's a ⎩ *providence for them who walk* 791
In helplessness, when innocence is with them. 792
audacious
At this ~~infernal~~ blasphemy I thought 793
The spirit of vengeance seemed to ride the air. 794
~~*Yet nothing came of it. I listened, but*~~
~~*The echoes of the thunder died away*~~
~~*Along the distant hills*~~ — —

775 engage;
776 sake!
778 *colon del to question mark, stage dir del*
779 *colon del to dash*
781 *as MS. 3, rev as MS. 3*
782 judgement,
784 *as MS. 3, rev as MS. 3 but* self, I think,
785 Concentres
787 possible?
790 *first comma omitted*
793 *as MS. 3, rev as MS. 3, but* blasphemy,

791 The capital is JC's.

Os.— — — — *Why are you not*
The Man you were ~~Po—po~~ that moment? Great Soul
~~*Riv:*~~ ~~*What then! Great souls*~~
~~Pooh!~~ ~~great souls~~
77 *Look to the world within*~~*—I mark'd you then*~~
78 ~~*Why are you not the man you were that moment*~~ [795]
(He draws {*M* / *mortimer near the dungeon)*
79 *Mor: You say he was asleep—look at this arm*
80 *And tell me if 'tis fit for such a work*
(Rivers draws him near Mortimer leans upon him)
81 *Mor: Rivers! Rivers!*
Riv: — — — — *This is some sudden seizure*
82 *Mor: A most strange faintness—will you hunt me* {*out* / [?]
83 *A draught of water?*
Riv: — — — — — *Nay to see you thus* [800]
84 *Moves me beyond my bearing I will try*
85 *To gain the torrents brink—*
Exit Rivers
Mor: (after a pause) — — — *It seems an age of life*
86 *Since that man left me — No I am not lost*

[27v]

(Herbert is seen at the mouth of the Dungeon)
87 *Her:* ~~*Give me your hand—where are you my friends? & tell me*~~
~~*Where are*~~ *give* ~~*me your hand, where are you*~~
88 *Mor:* ~~*This is lucky—I wanted company*~~
Give me your hand—where are you friends, & tell me
89 ~~*Her*~~*: How goes the night?*
Tis hard to measure time
90 *Mor:* '~~*Tis hard to say—we are not within the sound of*~~
~~*Any clock In such a time & such a place*~~
In such a night & such a place
91 *Herb: I do not hear the voice of my friend, Rivers* [807]
A minute past he went for we were thirsty
92 *Mor:* ~~*We were thirsty—he is gone to seek for a draught*~~
To fetch a draft of water—'Tis you'll say
~~*of water—'tis a chearless beverage*~~.
A chearless beverage—go
94 *Her.* ~~*How*~~ {*G* / *good it was in you* ~~*to stay behind! I was beginning*~~
To stay behind *hearing at first no answer*
~~*To be afraid when I heard no answer*~~
I was [?~~beginning~~] alarmed

78/79 MH's 1799 correction.
A photograph of 27v is provided below, p. 719.
87–297 Further developed in MS. 2A, 1r–4r.

Osw — — — — — — — ~~*Why are you not*~~
Why are you not the Man you ~~*were*~~ *were that moment?* 795
[?~~*great*~~]
~~*The Man you were that moment—Great*~~ *Souls*
~~*Look to the world within*~~. *(He draws Mar: to the Dun:)*
Mar: You say he was asleep;—look at this arm, 796
And tell me if 'tis fit for such a work. 797
(leans upon Osw)
Oswald, Oswald!
Osw — — — — *This is some sudden seizure?* 798
Mar: A most strange faintness,—will you hunt me out 799
A draught of water?
Osw. — — — — — — *Nay, to see you thus* 800
Moves me beyond my bearing—I will try 801
To gain the torrent's brink.
(Exit Osw.)
Mar: — — — — — *It seems an age* ~~*of life*~~ 802
(after a pause)

44
Since that Man left me.— No, I am not lost—— 803
(Herbt—at the mouth of the dungeon)
Her: Give me your hand; where are you Friends?
& tell me 804
How goes the night.
Mar — — — — — — *'Tis hard to measure time,* 805
weary ,
In such a^night } *+& such a place.* 806
Herb: I do not hear the voice of my friend Oswald. 807
Mar: A minute past, he went, for we were thirsty, 808
To fetch a draught of water. + 'Tis, you'll say, 809
A cheerless beverage.
Herb: — — — — *How Good it was in you* 810
h at first
To stay behind: { *Hearing^no answer* 811
I was alarmed.

---

798 *question mark rev to exclam point*
803 *final dash del to period*
804 you,
810 Good *then lowercased*
811 behind { !— / : } Hearing

---

811 Revision to lowercase "h" is by JC.

96 *Mor:* ~~*Why, yes,*~~ ~~*this is a place to make one fearful without*~~
No wonder this is a place
~~*knowing why*~~
To make One fearful without knowing why
a roofless rock had been a
~~*even*~~
97 *Her:* *Well* ~~*any shelter was*~~ *a comfort,* ~~*bewildered as we were*~~
Storm-beaten & bewildered as we were
~~*and such a storm bursting over our heads, and in a*~~
And in a
^*night like this to lend your cloaks* ~~*to make bed for me*~~
~~*It was so kind—my poor girl will weep when she hears*~~
{*To make a bed for me it was so kind!*
{*of it—*
My Girl will weep to hear it. ~~*This daughter*~~
Is } *This daughter*
101 *Mor:* ~~*This daughter of yours*~~ { *is very dear to you*
102 *Her:* *Oh Sir! (laying his hand upon him) but you are young; forty years must roll over your head 'ere you can know how much a father may love his child*
105 *Mor:* *(aside) I thank you old man for this*
106 *Her:* *I am a poor and useless man — with a kind hand you have protected me this evening—I have no return to make but my prayers—may the God*

[28r]

of Heaven bless your old age with such a daughter— When I was an outcast, even as you see me—a miserable outcast—but I am going to talk fondly.
111 *Mor:* *Oh let me have it by all means, 'tis pleasant to me to hear you.*
112 *Her:* *You will forgive me but my heart runs over—when my poor dog perished in the waters what a piercing cry you sent after him! I have loved you ever since (starts) where are we?*

Mar — — — — *No wonder; this is a place* 812
That may well put some fears into your heart 813
~~*To make one fearful, without knowing why.*~~
?}
Why so :}
Herb. ~~*Well!*~~ *a roofless rock had been a comfort* 814
Storm-beaten & bewildered as we were; 815
And, in a night like this, to lend your cloaks 816
{my
{My Girl will weep 817
To make a bed for me!~~*—it,was so kind!*~~
When she is told of it.
~~*My Girl will weep to hear of it*~~
Mar: — — — — — — — — — *This Daughter of yours* 818
Is very dear to you.
Herb[t]. *O* ~~*Sir!*~~ *but you are young;* 819

45

Over your head twice twenty years must roll, 820
With all their natural weight of sorrow & pain, 821
Ere can be known to you how much a Father 822
May love his Child. *is}*
Mar: — — — — — *Thank you, old Man, for that} (aside)* 823
Herb. *Fallen am I, & worn out, a useless Man,* 824
Kindly have you protected me tonight, 825
And no return have I to make but prayers; 826
{.—
May you in age be blest with such a daughter{— 827
from the Holy Land I had returned— 828
When ~~*I became an Outcast as you see me*~~
Sightless, & from my Heritage was driven, 829
A wretched Outcast—but this strain of thought 830
Would lead me to talk fondly.
Mar: — — — — — — — — *Do not fear;* 831
Your words are precious to my ears; go on. 832
Her *You will forgive me, but my heart runs over.* 833
{ped
When my old Leader slip{t into the flood 834
And perished, what a piercing outcry you 835
Sent after him. I have loved you ever since. 836
You start—where are we? 837a

---

813 *as MS. 3, rev as MS. 3, but* heart.
?}
814 so;}
816 *first comma omitted*
823 this!
825 to night
826 to make *over illeg eras (Dora)*
{!—
827 daughter{.
834 *as MS. 3, rev as MS. 3*
837a we *over* you *eras (Dora)*

---

817 The added "my" and the "weep" are JC's.

115 *Mor:* *Oh! there is no danger—'Tis a cold night*
116 *Her:* *'Twas a foolish question—but I never shall forget*
the shuddering that seized you when you led me
over the torrent but for you there had not been
a hair betwixt my death and me
119 *Mor:* *But when you were an outcast—The heavens are*
just—piety like yours could not go unrewarded
The little orphan would be of service to you I suppose
122 *Her:* *I turned away from the dwellings of my Fathers*
when I was remembered only by those who had
trampled me underfoot— I bore her in my arms—
her looks won pity from the world—when I had none
to help me she brought me food, she was a raven
sent to me in the wilderness—Have I not cause to
love her?
127 *Mor:* *— — — — — — — — Oh! yes!*

[28ᵛ]

128 *Her:* *More than ever parent loved a child?* [849]
129 *Mor:* *Yes! yes!*
130 *Her:* *Merciful God! thou hast po{ured}{red} out the phials*
of thy wrath upon my head — but I will not murmur
—blasted as I am thou hast left me both ears to hear
the voice of my daughter and arms to fold her to
my hea{rt}{t} — I will adore thee and tremble!
(Enter Rivers with water in a hunting horn)
134 *Riv:* *(aside) Herbert! Perdition (to Mor: presenting the horn*
Well here it is —.
135 *A charming beverage to carouse upon*
136 *This bitter night.*
Her: *— — — — — — Ha! Rivers! ten bright crosses* [857]
137 *I would have given not many minutes gone*
138 *To have heard your voice*

130, 130/134 MH's 1799 overwritings.
130/134 A letter "s" at the end of "thou" was erased in 1799, to correct a copyist's error.

Mar: — — — — — — — *O, there is no danger*
The cold blast struck me.

46
Herbert — — — *Twas a foolish question.*
{M
{Aar: *But when you were an Outcast?—Heaven is just;*
Your piety would not miss its due reward;
The little Orphan then would be your succour,
And do good service, tho' she knew it not.
Herb^t. *I turned me from the dwellings of my Fathers,*
Where none, but those who trampled on my rights,
To the wide world
Seemed to remember me. ~~*Within my arms*~~
in my arms;
I bore her, ~~*from the world*~~*. her looks won pity;*
She was my Raven in the wilderness,
{H
And brought me food. ~~*/*~~ *{have I not cause to love her?*
{.
Mar: *Yes,* ~~*yes*~~*.*
Herb^t. — — *More than ever Parent loved a Child?*
Mar *Yes, yes.*
Her — — *I will not murmur, merciful God!*
I will not murmur; blasted as I have been,
Thou hast left me ears to hear my daughter's voice,
And arms to fold her to my heart. Submissively
Thee I adore & find my rest in faith.

Enter Oswald

Confusion
Osw *Herbert!* ~~*Perdition!*~~ *Here it is, my friend, (presenting the Horn)*
A charming beverage for you to carouse {,
This bitter night.

47
Herbert — — — — — *Ha! Oswald! ten bright crosses*
I would have given, not many minutes gone,
To have heard your voice.

837b danger;
838b 'Twas
844 *no commas*
848 her.
849 Yes, Yes.
854 adore,
854/855 presents the Horn *del from stage dir*
855 *as MS. 3, rev as MS. 3 but* presents *in stage dir*

Riv: — — — — — — — My good friend I am sorry
& yet
{[?]
139 Your rest has been disturbed— ~~And~~ {~~yet~~ that place
140 When the tempestuous wind first drove us thither [861]
You'd better turn
141 Felt warm as a wrens nest— ~~My good old brother~~
And rest within the covert till day breaks
{A [?] ~~or till the~~ stor
142 ~~You had better stop in~~ {~~again beneath the covert & lie down~~
Or till the storm abate ~~afresh~~ ~~till the~~
143 ~~The storm is gather~~ing (He leads Her: to the entrance of the dungeon)
(To Mortimer) He has restored you ?} ~~then~~?
144 No doubt you have been nobly entertained?
{came {forth
145 But soft, how {comes he {here? The night-mare, conscience
146 Has driven him out of harbour?
Mor: — — — — — — — — — — — I believe [867]
147 You have guessed right

[29r]

Riv: (walks about with satisfaction) turning back to Mortimer and looking at Herbert)
[?to] looking at
But
— — — We must cure these wanderings
148 I know a sovereign remedy— at times
149 The tooth-ache twinges me, and luckily
150 I have a phial
Mor: — — — — — — Poison! Poison!
Riv: — — — — — — — — — — — — — — Think you
I would defraud that sword of yours so vilely?
152 Humanity's the word with me— I wish
153 That since all hope~~s~~ of penitence is vain
154 The little time which he has left, should be
155 A time of peace
{the thought
Mor: — — — — — Hold! hold! {it is a thought
156 ~~Conceived in hell~~
{I
~~The thought~~ {is devilish!
~~Devilish!~~
Riv: — — — — — ~~Hell! say you~~? ~~Poor old man~~!
157 Os While he is human, like ourselves, all night
158 Must those cold arches drip on his grey head!
159 His blood is thin, his bones can ill sustain
160 The rigours of a night like this—'Tis mercy

---

153 Deletion in pencil.

Osw ———— *I am sorry, my good friend,*
Your rest has been disturbed, & yet that place, 860
When the tempestuous wind first drove us thither, 861
Felt warm as a wren's nest. You'd better turn 862
And rest within the covert till day breaks, 863
Or till the storm abate. ~~/~~ *(~~Leads Herb to the~~ entrance ~~of the dungeon~~*

(To Mar) ———— *He has restored you* {.? ~~then?~~} 864
No doubt you have been nobly entertained? 865
aside
But soft! how came he forth? The {N night-mare *Conscience* 866
Had driven him out of harbour? }
Mar: ——————————— {I [?]} *believe* 867
You have guessed right. 868a
Osw. ——————— *We must cure these wanderings*
I know a sovereign remedy—at times
The tooth-ache twinges me, & luckily
I have a phial
Mar: ———— *Poison, poison*
Osw ————————— *Think you*
I would defraud that sword of yours so vilely.

48

Humanity's the word with me—I wish
That since all hope of penitence is vain
The little time that he has left should be
A time of peace
Mar: ———— *Hold, hold the thought* is devilish
~~*Is develish*~~.
Osw *While he is human like ourselves, all night*
Must those cold arches drip on his grey head!
His blood is thin, his bones can ill sustain
The rigour of a night like this. 'Tis mercy

---

860 disturbed,{;}
861 *as MS. 3, rev as MS. 3*
864 you.
866 soft!—
867 harbour?

'Tis very mercy (~~*He bursts away from Mortimer and stops suddenly rummaging his Pockets*~~
aside
— — — — — Plague I have mislaid it!
{*No* / *It matters* {*for* / *not— the main end will be answered*)}
(~~*to himself*~~))} *'Tis a*{*dark* / *n odd thought*~~*—I like the*~~ *& better for its* *color* ~~*of it*~~
To have an old man drugged that he may kill him
(goes up to Her: and presents the horn gaily)

[29v]

Here is some cool refreshment—you will pledge us
If it were ~~*only for a traveller's pleasure*~~ *but to tell*
~~*To tell by your fire side*~~ *what hearty cheer*
You met with at the castle
Her: *— — — — — — — — You are gay*
And you are wise—I think for a short while
I could be merry too (he drinks)
(Mor: who had approached, turns from him)
Riv: *(following Mortimer) A gentle dose!*
That will compose him to a child-like sleep
There is no justice when we do not feel
For man as man.
Her: *— — — — The trees begin to murmur*
The big drops scatter round us. Come my friends
And let us house together
(Riv: conducts him into the dungeon)

Riv: *(returns)* ~~*I must deal plainly with you*~~, {*H* / *had I not*
Esteemed you worthy to conduct th{*e* / *is* ~~*business*~~ *affair*
To its most just conclusion do you think
I would so long have struggled with my nature
And smothered all that's man in me? away!
(looking towards the dungeon)
He is the property of him who best
Can feel his crimes—I have resigned a privilege
It now becomes my duty to resume it.

[30r]

Mor: *Touch but a finger—*
Riv: *— — — — — — What then must be done?*
Mor: *Which way soe'er I turn me I am curst*
Riv: *Now on my soul I grieve for you. The misery*

'Tis very mercy— (aside) Plague I have mislaid it)
No matter, for the main end will be answered)
Aside
'Tis a dark thought & better for its colour
To have an Old Man drugged that he may kill him
(goes up to Her: & presents the horn gaily)
Here is some cool refreshment, you will pledge us
If it were but to tell what hearty cheer
You met with at the Convent
Her *— — — — — — — — You are gay*
And you are wise. I think for a short while
I could be merry too— (He drinks) Mar: who had approached turns from him Osw following him)

49

Osw *— — — — — — — A gentle dose!*
That will compose him to a child-like sleep
There is no justice when we do not feel
For man as man
~~You have a~~
renew their
Herb *— — — — — The trees ~~begin to~~ murmur:*
~~The big drops scatter round us. Come my friends~~
Come,
~~And~~ let us house together.
(Os: conducts him to the dun.)
Os: (returns) — — — — — — Had I not
Esteemed you worthy to conduct the affair
To its most just conclusion, do you think
I would so long have struggled with my Nature
And smothered all that's Man in me? away!—
This Man *(looking towards the dungeon)*
~~He~~ is the property of him who best
{C
{Aan feel his crimes.—I have resigned a privilege;
It now becomes my duty to resume it.
Mar: Touch not a finger——
Osw: — — — — — — What then must be done?
Mar: Which way so'e'er I turn ~~me~~ I am ~~curst~~ perplexed.
Osw Now, on my soul, I grieve for you. The misery

869 Come,] Come
871 just *del to* fit
873 me?—
874 He *rev to* His *then* is *del and* This Man's *inserted with carets*
878 *last letter of* soe'er *over illeg eras (Dora)* turn,

Of doubt is insupportable. Pity the facts [880]
honest men
Did not admit of stronger evidence. Twelve ~~neighbours~~
Their
Plain ~~honest~~ men might set us right. ~~Their~~ verdict
Would ~~fortify your spirit—end this weakness~~—
abolish these weak scruples
Weak
Mor: ^*I am weak—~~There is my hell~~*
{*V*
{*verily*
Riv: — — — — — — — — ~~*True*~~ *when he said*
How his old heart would leap to hear her steps [886]
You thought his voice the echo of ~~Matilda's~~ Idonia's
Mor: *And never heard a sound so terrible*
Riv: *Perchance you think so now?*
Mor: — — — — — — — — *I cannot do it*
Twice did I spring to grasp his withered throat [890]
When such a sudden weakness fell upon me
I could have dropped asleep upon his breast
Riv: *Justice! Is there not thunder in the word?*
Shall it be law to stab the petty robber
Who aims at one poor life, and shall this monster—
But you are fallen!——

189 Underlining added 1841.

Of doubt is unsupportable. Pity the facts
Did not admit of stronger evidence. ~~*Twelve honest men*~~

50

Twelve honest men, *plain men, would set us right;*
~~would~~
~~*Plain men might set us right: their verdict*~~
Their verdict
{W
^{*Would abolish these weak scruples.*
!
Weak ~~,~~ I am weak—there does my torment lie,
Mar — — — — — — — — ~~*Weak, I am weak*~~
Feeding itself.
~~*There is my torment*~~
Feeding itself.
Osw — — — — — *Verily, when he said*
How his old heart would leap to hear her steps,
e}
You thought his voice the echo of Idoni{*a's.*
Mar *And never heard a sound so terrible.*
Osw. *Perchance you think so now?*
Mar — — — — — — — — *I cannot do it:*
Twice did I spring to grasp his withered throat,
When such a sudden weakness fell upon me,
I could have dropped asleep upon his breast.
Osw *Justice—is there not thunder in the word;*
Shall it be law to stab the petty robber
Parricide
Who aims at one poor life, & shall this *monster*——
~~*For such he is*~~

[in margin]
ish}
He is far worse if foul det {*onour*
Be worse than death) to that confiding creature
Whom he to more than filial love & duty
Hath falsely trained—shall he fulfill his purpose
—But you are fallen

—But you are fallen!

---

880 insupportable.
893 *semicolon del to question mark*
895 *as MS. 3, rev as MS. 3 but* Monster *underlined*
895–899 *further developed in Additions to MS. 3A, 11*[r]
900a —But you are fallen! *del to*

For such he is, to the confiding Creature
Whom in the sanctities of filial duty
He hath falsely trained *interlined then del*

in margin: Worse is he far, far worse (if foul dishonour *etc., as in margin of MS. 3, but* Creature . . . purpose? . . . fallen.

---

885 The lower "Feeding itself" is JC's.

[30v]

should I be
Mor: — — — — — — — — *Fallen^indeed!*
203 *Murder! asleep! blind! old! alone! betray'd!*
204 *Drugg'd and in darkness! Here to strike the blow*
205 *Visible only to the eye of God! (flings away his sword)*
206 *Away! away!*
Riv: — — — *Nay I have done with you*
207 *Let's lead him to the convent—He shall live*
208 *And she shall love him. With unquestioned title*
209 *He shall be seated in his Barony.*
210 *And we two bless ourselves for his good deeds*
211 *I now perceive we do mistake our masters*
212 *And most despise the men who best can teach us*
213 *Henceforth it shall be said that bad men only*
214 *Are brave—Clifford is brave, and that old man*
215 *Is brave (taking up Mortimer's sword and giving it him)*
He would have lead his daughter hither
216 *In to this dungeon, to this house of victims*
Mor: *(advancing to the dungeon)*
217 *It must be ended*
Riv: — — — — — *For heaven's sake do not rouze him*
218 *He will deny it to the last. He lies*
219 *Within the vault—a spears length to the left*
(Mor: descends into the dungeon)

---

216 MH's 1799 revision.

Mar: — — — — — — — *Fallen should I be indeed—* 900b

perhaps *d*
Murder—^*asleep, bling*{, *old, alone,* ~~*betrayed*~~ 901
Betrayed,
~~*Drugged*~~ ^ *& in darkness! Here to strike the blow—* 902
~~*Visible only to the eye of God*~~ *(flings away his sword)*
Away! away! 903a

51

Osw. — — *Nay, I have done with you;* 903b
We'll lead him to the Convent. He shall live, 904
And she shall love him. With unquestioned title 905
He shall be seated in his Barony, 906
chaunt the praise of
And we two, ~~*bless ourselves for*~~ *his good deeds.* 907
now
I {[?*do*] *perceive we do mistake our masters* 908
And most despite the men who best can teach us: 909
e
H{[?]*nceforth it shall be said that bad men only* 910
:
Are brave{ ~~*,*~~ *Clifford is brave, & that old Man* 911
Is brave: (taking Marmaduke's sword & giving it to him)
To Clifford's arms he would have led 912
~~*He would have led his daughter hither into*~~
desolate
His Victim—haply to this ~~*very*~~ *house.* 913
~~*Into this dungeon, to this house of Victims*~~
Mar: *(advancing to the dungeon)*
It must be ended!—
Softly;
Osw — — — — — — ~~*For heaven's sake*~~ *do not rouse him;* 914
He will deny it to the last. He lies 915
Within the Vault, a spear's length to the left. 916
(Mar descends to the Dungeon)

903a away!—
903b *no comma* you:
907 two] too
911 is brave;
912 Is brave; *then semicolon overwritten with comma, and draft following stage dir:*

To Cliffords arms he would have led

~~led~~{t
~~Who would have~~ {~~To Clifford's arms he would have led~~
~~led to~~
~~Who would have led to Clifford's arm~~ {s [?~~ies~~]

bottom line of draft is JC's
916 spears-length

[31^r]

Os:
Riv: *(alone) The villains rose in mutiny to destroy me*
I could have quelled the cowards—but this stripling
Must needs step in, and save my life—the look
With which he gave the boon—I see it now—
~~*What if he did the deed in love—so be it—*~~
~~*I hate him not—now I begin to love him*~~
For this old venerable grey-beard—faith
'~~Tis his own~~ fault if he hath got a face
{th
Which do { play tricks with them that look upon it
'Twas he that put it in my thought—his countenance—
'}
His step, his figure— Murder! what} of whom?
{W worn out horse a
~~Of whom—or what~~? {we kill a^toad, a newt
A rat—I do believe if they who first
Baptised the deed had called it murder, we

224–225 A vertical line in the margin marks these lines for deletion.
228 MH's 1799 insertion.

Osw (a {l / tone) The Villains rose in mutiny to destroy me; 917
I could have quelled the {Cowards / crowds, ≁ but this Stripling 918
Must needs step in, & save my life {·} ≁ {T / the look 919
With which he gave the boon—I see it now! 920
———*The same that tempted me to loath the givf.*—— 921
For ^this old venerable {G / grey-beard—faith 922

52
Tis his own fault if ~~t~~he hath got a ~~f[?aic]~~ face 923
thereon; 924
Which doth play tricks with them that look ~~upon it~~
'Twas {t / h{is / e that put it in my thought—that countenance— 925
His staff—his figure.—Murder! what, of whom? 926
-out horse, 927a
We kill a wor{n- / m, a toad, a newt,
A rat. I do believe if they, who first
Ba{p / [?]tized the deed, had called it murder, we

---

921 gift.—
923 'Tis
924 thereon— *del to* on it: *(JC)*
925 thoughts—
926 *no period*
927–935 *further developed in MS. 3A, 13v*
927a–935b a toad, a newt, *del to* & who but women *and next five lines, through 935b, as MS. 3, then all del to:*

Sigh for the deed, {?} {H / hew down a withered tree
And {none / who looks grave but dotards [?He] He may live
To thank me for this service. Rainbow arches,
High ways of dreamy passion, have too long,
Youth tho' he is, diverted wish & hope

then continued in right margin:

From the unpretending ground we
mortals tread
Then shatter the delusion set it up *all del and fresh continuation*

started in left margin:

wish & hope
From the unpretending ground we Mortals tread—
Then shatter the delusion, break it up
And let him free. What follows? I have learned
That things &c

919, 922 The capitals are JC's.

Had quaked to think of it. How many fools
shudder I
Would ~~laugh if I~~ should } say this youth may live
To thank me for this service! I have learned
o'th'
That things will work to ends the slaves ~~of the~~ world [936]
Do never dream of. I have been what he
This boy when he comes forth with his bloody hands
Might envy and am now— but he shall know
What I am now (goes and listens at the dungeon)
Praying or parleying? Tut [940]
Is he not eyeless? he has been half dead
These fifteen years——
(Enter the female Beggar with two or three of her companions

[31v]

thing
Rivers (turning round abruptly) Ha! speak what art thou?
(recognizes her) Havens my good friend! (to her companions
Beg — — — — — Forgive me gracious Sirs

Begone, ye slaves! or I will raise a whirlwind
And send you dancing to the clouds like leaves [945]
(They retire affrighted)
Beg: Indeed we meant no harm—we lodge sometimes
In this deserted castle——I repent me
(Rivers goes towards the dungeon & listens he returns to the Beggar
Riv: Thou hast a little helpless babe. Depart
Beg: I do repent me, Sir, I fear the curses [951]
Of that Blind man—'Twas not your money, Sir,
Riv: Depart
Beg: (going) — There is some wicked deed in hand—
Would I could find the old man or his daughter! [954]
(Exit Beggar

250 Underlining added 1841.

Had quaked to think of it. How many fools
Would shudder should I say, this {Y youth may live 929b
To thank me for this service!—I have learned, 930a, 935b
That things will work to ends the Slaves o'th' world 936
Do never dream of. I <u>*have*</u> *been what he—* 937
This boy—when he comes forth with ~~his~~ bloody hands— 938
Might envy, & am now—but he shall know 939
What I am now—(goes & listens at the dungeon)
Praying or par {l teying?—tut! 940
Is he not eyeless? He has been half-dead 941
These fifteen years——

(Enter female Beggar with two
or three of her Companions)

Osw: turning abruptly) Ha! speak, {— what Thing art thou? 942
(recognizes
her) Heavens! my good friend! (to her)} ~~compan~~
gracious
Beg — — — — — — — — — Forgive me ^ Sir!— 943
Os: (to her Companions) Begone, ye slaves, or I will raise a whirlwind 944
And send ye dancing to the clouds, like leaves. (They
retire affrighted) 945

53

Beg: Indeed we meant no harm; we lodge sometimes 946
In this deserted Castle——<u>*I repent me*</u> 947
(Os: goes to the dungeon—listens—
returns to the Beggar)

Woman, helpless Infant—keep 948
Osw ^ {t Thou hast a ~~little helpless Babe. Depart~~
Thy secret for its sake, or verily 949
That wretched life of thine shall be the forfie {ei t. 950
Beg. I do repent me, Sir; I fear the curses 951
Of that blind Man. 'Twas not your money, Sir— 952
Osw: ~~Depart~~ Begone. *(~~Exit Beggar~~*
~~Mar~~:
Beg (going) There is some wicked deed in hand. (aside) 953
&
Would I could find the old Man {& ~~or~~ his daughter.— 954
(Exit Beg

---

936 o'the world
939 now,—
942 thing *then capitalized (Dora)*
953 hand:

929b The capital is JC's.

(Mor: re-enters from the dungeon)

254 Riv: *Well! 'tis all over then—don't you laugh at*
your foolish fears? you have done it cleverly—
sent him into the other world without a groan
never trouble your head about burying him—

[32r]

we'll shove him into a corner—In the torrent
away
hard by there is water enough to wash‸all the blood
in the universe (examining him) Death! I don't see
a stain about you. That was dexterously managed
indeed (looks at his sword) Zounds!——did you
strangle him?

261 Mor: *What made you come down and lay your hand*
upon my shoulder? when I spoke to you, why did
not you answer? you were afraid of waking him
I suppose—He must have been in a deep sleep,
for I whispered to him twice—There are damned
echoes in that place—

265 Riv: *Tut! let them gabble to all eternity! 'Twas an*
excellent method— You would have the grast of a
dæmon—you are sure you finished him?

268 Mor: *Scarcely had I found the place where he was lying*
when I felt as if there were a string round my
wrist and the blind man's dog pulling at it

271 Riv: *Well! but after? Let me have it*

272 Mor: *There was something in his face the very counter-*
part of Matilda

273 Riv *Let that alone—never will my life afford me such*
another opportunity— why did not you allow me
a share in your triumph— Oh how I envy you—

276 Mor: *Her very looks smiling in sleep——*

[32v]

277 Riv: *Hell! have you been playing the coward?*

278 Mor: *'Twas only for a single moment—but it sent me*
to my prayers

279 Riv: *Plague! is he alive*

280 Mor: *— — — — — Alive! who alive?*

281 Riv: *Herbert! the Baron Herbert! since you will have*
it, he who will be the Baron Herbert when Matilda
is Clifford's Harlot—Is he living

254/261 Caret and revision in pencil.

~~(O (~~ *Mar:* ~~(~~*re-enters from the dungeon*~~)~~

Osw. ' ~~*Well*~~ ~~*Tis*~~ ^*It is* *all over then;*— {*y* / *Your foolish fears*
Are hushed to sleep, by your own act & deed
Made quiet as he is.——
Mar —————— *Why came you down?*
And when I felt your hand upon my arm
And spake to you, why did you give no answer?
Feared you to waken him? he must have been
In a deep sleep. I whispered to him thrice.
There are the strangest echoes in that place!—
Osw *Tut! let them gabble till the day of doom.*
Mar: *Scarcely, by groping, had I reached the Spot*
When round my wrist I felt a cord drawn tight
As if the blind Man's dog were pulling at it.

54
Osw *But after that?*
Mar ———— *The features of Idon* {*e* / *ia*
Lurked in his face——
Osw: —————— *Psha,* {*!* } {*Never* / *heaven to* ~~*my*~~^*th* {*es* / *ine eyes* ~~*life*~~
Will retribution shew itself again
With aspect so inviting ~~/~~ {*.* } {*W* / *why forbid me*
To share your triumph?
Mar ———————— *Yes her very look,*
Smiling in sleep——
———— {A / [?A] pretty feat of Fancy!
Osw ———— ~~*You have been playing the Coward*~~ ~~*Again you have played*~~*?*
{*M* / *Aar* *Tho' but a glimpse, it sent me to my prayers.*
Osw *Is he alive?*
Mar ——— *What mean you, who alive?*
Osw *Herbert,* {*!* } *since you will have it, Baron Herbert;*
He who ~~*will*~~ *will*^*gain* ~~*have*~~^~~*gain*~~^ *his Seig* {*'* } *n* {*'* *o* / *iry when Idon* {*e* / *ia*
Hath become Clifford' {*'* } *s harlot*— ~~*Is*~~ *he*^*is* *living?*

964 spot *then capitalized (Dora)*
968 these] thine *rev to* these
976 seignory

976 The first "gain" is JC's.
977 The "is" above line is JC's.

283 *Mor:* *The blind man lying in that dungeon is alive* [978]
284 *Riv:* *Then curse me, if ever in camp or field I obey*
an order of yours again—I will proclaim you,
and before the whole body—they shall hear it all—
You a protector of humanity! an avenger of
innocence!
287 *Mor:* *'Twas dark, dark as hell—yet I saw him—I tell thee*
I saw him, his face towards me—the very looks of
Matilda sent there by some fiend to baffle me— It
put me to my prayers—I cast my eyes upwards, &
through a crevice in the roof I beheld a star twinkling
over my head, and by the living God, I could not do it—
—
(sinks against the scene exhausted) }
292 *Riv:* *(after some time) Now may I perish if this be not joy to me.*
293 *A meaner spirit would be overwhelmed (turns to him)*

[33r]

294 *— — — — — — — My dear Mortimer*
295 *Those words were rashly spoken—I would recall them* [993]
296 *I feel my error— Shedding human blood*
297 *It is a serious thing—*
Mor: *— — — — — — — Not I alone—*
298 *Thou too, art deep in guilt* X
Riv: *— — — — — — — — — We have indeed* [996]
299 *Been most presumptuous— There is guilt in this*
300 *Else could so strong a mind have ever known*
301 *These strange infirmities? 'Tis plain that heaven*
302 *Has marked out this foul wretch as one whose crimes*
303 *Must never come before a mortal judgement seat* [1001]
304 *Or be chastized by mortal instruments—*

---

298 An X was added in the margin; its purpose is unclear.

Mar: *The Old Man in that dungeon* <u>*is*</u> *alive.* 978

H
Osw: *Th{enceforth then, will I never in Camp or field* 979
Obey you more. Your weakness, to the Band, 980
: *all*
Shall be proclaimed,/{ brave men, they^*shall hear it* all. 981
~~*all!*~~
You a protecter of humanity! 982
you!
Avenger^*of outraged innocence!* 983

55

d
Mar: *'Twas dark— {[?]ark as the grave, yet did I see,* 984
Saw him—his face turned toward me; & I tell thee 985
e
Idonia's filial countenance was there 986
To baffle me—it put me to my prayers. 987
Upwards I cast my eyes, & thro' a crevice 988
Beheld a star twinkling above my head, 989
And, by the living God, I could not do it. 990
Osw (sinks exhausted)
(To himself) Now may I perish if this turn doth more 991
Than make me change my course.
(To Mar) — — — — — — — Dear Marmaduke, 992
My words were rashly spoken; I recal them: 993
I feel my error; shedding human blood
Is a most serious thing.
Mar: *— — — — — — — Not I alone,* 995
Thou too art deep in guilt.
Osw *— — — — — — We have indeed* 996
Been most presumptuous. There <u>*is*</u> *guilt in this,* 997
Else could so strong a mind have ever known 998
{H
These strange infirmities? 'Tis plain that {heaven 999
{W
Has marked out this foul {wretch as one whose crimes 1000
-seat, 1001
Must never come before a mortal judgement-~~seat~~
Or be chastised by mortal Instruments. 1002

---

978 Old *then lowercased (Dora)*
981 they shall hear it all. *then* all *del and inserted with caret, as MS. 3*
983 *first exclam point del*
988 and, crevice,
990 *first comma omitted*
1002 instruments.

999–1001 The revisions are JC's.

305 Mor: *A thought~~s~~ that's worth a thousand worlds! '~~Tis past~~*
306 *~~And I am saved from tortures~~*
307 *~~To which the agonies of hell are mercy~~*
(goes towards the dungeon

?
308 Riv: *~~Nay, whither~~ } ~~now~~? Nay whither?*
Mor: *— — — — — It ~~must be — I must see~~*
I must behold that face of his again
309 *~~That face of his again — I must behold it~~*
310 *'Twere joy enough to end me (~~Rivers appears downcast~~*
~~But~~
~~Nay what ails you~~?
311 Riv: *~~I am dejected~~ I am grieved*
312 *To think I ever caused you so much pain*

[33v]

313 Mor: *Fie! 'tis all over now, and we are safe* [1005]
Riv: *(as if to himself—yet speaking aloud)*
—The truth is hideous but
314 *~~It must come to his ears at last~~, how stifle it*
315 *(turning to him) Give me your sword—nay here are stones & fragments*
M.
316 *The least of which would beat out a man's brains*
And yo
317 *~~—That wall if you should drive your head against it—~~*
Or you might drive your head against that wall
the tale
318 *No! this is not a place to hear { it,*
319 *It should be told you pinioned to your bed,* [1011]
320 *Or on some vast and solitary plain*
321 *Blown to you from a trumpet*
Mor Whateer the monster Why talk thus
322 Mor: *~~What monster you have~~ brooding in your breast*
I care Fear I have none & cannot fear
323 *~~I know~~ not. ~~This I know I have no fear~~*
324 *~~And cannot fear~~ (The sound of a bugle horn is heard)*
325 *That horn again! 'tis some one of our troop* [1016]
326 *What do they here? Listen!*
Riv: *— — — — — — — — Dogg'd then like thieves*

Enter Lacy and Wallace

~~Be~~
You are found at last thanks to the Vagrant troop
~~here you are~~
327 Lacy *~~Ha~~! ~~you are found at last — thanks to the~~*
For not misleading us.
Riv: *(looking at Wallace)— — That wily grey-beard*
328 *I'd rather see my father's ghost*

---

305 Deletion of "s" by erasure, 1799.
324–325 Long parens extended into horizontal line 1841.

56

Mar: *A thought that's worth a thousand worlds.* 1003a

(~~goes towards the Dun~~).

Osw ——————— *Nay whither?*

Mar: *I must behold that face of his again,*

'Twere joy enough to end me.

Osw ————————— *I am grieved* 1003b

To think I ever caused you so much pain. 1004

~~No more~~. Think not of that tis over

Mar: *~~Fie~~,* +} *'~~tis all over now~~, & we are safe.* 1005

Osw *(as if to himself yet speaking aloud)*

The truth is hideous, but how stifle it.)} *(turning to M)* 1006

Give me your sword—nay here are stones & fragments, 1007

The least of which would beat out a man's brains; 1008

Or you might drive your head against that wall. 1009

No! this is not the place to hear the tale: 1010

It should be told you pinioned on your bed, 1011

Or on some vast & solitary Plain 1012

Blown to you from a trumpet.

Mar: ———————— *Why talk thus—* ?} 1013

What'eer the monster brooding in your breast 1014

I care not: fear I have none, & cannot fear—— 1015

(The sound of a horn is heard)

That horn again—'Tis some one of our Troop; 1016

What do they here? List {*en!* / *!*}

What *thives*

Osw: ^*Dogged ~~then~~ like Slaves* 1017

57

Enter Wallace & Lacy &—

Lacy. *You are found at last, thanks to the Vagrant Troop* 1018

For not misleading us.

subtile

Osw (looking at Wallace) — That ~~wily~~ ^ {*Grey-beard—* / *Vagrant*} 1019

I'd rather see my Father's ghost.

1003a (goes toward the dungeon) *stage dir, not del*
1005 *as MS. 3, rev as MS. 3 but* No more *omitted and* that! tis over—
1006 it?
1011 on] in
1014 Whate'er
1017 List! *del to* Listen! Dogged like Thieves! *then* What, *inserted, as MS. 3*
1017/1018 and Lacy &c. *in stage dir*
1019 wily *del to* subtle

1017 The "thives" above line is in pencil.

Lacy (to Mor:) — — — — — — — My Captain
329 *We come by order of the band. Belike*
330 *You have not heard that Henry has at last*

[34r]

331 *Dissolved the Baron's League and sent abroad*
332 *His sheriffs with fit force to reinstate*
333 *The genuine owners of such Lands and Baronies*
334 *As in these long commotions have been seized*
335 *His power is this way tending. It befits us*
336 *To stand upon our guard and with our swords*
337 *Defend the innocent*
Mor: — — — — — — — — — Lacy! we look
338 *But at the surfaces of things, we hear*
339 *Of towns in flames, fields ravaged, young and old*
340 *Driven out in flocks to want and nakedness*
341 *Then grasp our swords and rush upon a cure*
342 *That flatters us because it asks not thought*
343 *The deeper malady is better hid*
344 *The world is poisoned at the heart*
Lacy — — — — — — — — — — What mean you?
345 *Wal: (whose eye has been fixed suspiciously upon Rivers)*
Aye what is it you mean?
Mor: — — — — — — — — Hark'ee my Friends
(with an appearance of relaxed gaiety)
346 *Were there a man who being weak and helpless*
a m
347 *And most forlorn should bribe an {other pressed*
348 *By penury to yield him up her daughter*
349 *A little infant, and instruct the babe*
350 *Prattling upon his knee to call him, Father*

[34v]

351 *Lacy Why if his heart be tender that offence*
352 *I could forgive him*

---

347 MH's 1799 revision.

Lacy (to
Mar) — — — — — — — — — — *My Captain,* 1020
We come by order of the Band. Belike 1021
{h
You have not heard that Henry {was at last 1022
Dissolved the Baron's League, & sent abroad 1023
His Sheriffs with fit force to reinstate 1024
The genuine Owners of such Lands & Baronies 1025
ei}
As, in these long commotions, have been sie{zed. 1026
His Power is this way tending. It befits us 1027
To stand upon our guard, & with our swords 1028
Defend the innocent.
Mar: — — — — — *Lacy! we look* 1029
But at the surfaces of things; we hear 1030
g }
Of towns in flames, fields ravaged, youn[?d]} & old 1031
troops
Driven out in ~~flocks~~ to want & nakedness, 1032
Then grasp our swords & rush upon a cure 1033
That flatters us, because it asks not thought: 1034
The deeper malady is better hid, 1035
The world is poisoned at the heart. 1036a

58
Lacy — — — — — — — — — — *What mean you?* 1036b
Wall (whose {*A* {*is it you mean?*
eye has been {*Yye, what* {~~*mean you?*~~
fixed suspiciously
upon Osw)
F
Mar: — — — — — — — — — — — — *Hark'ee, my friends;*— 1037
(appearing gay)
Were there a Man who, being weak & helpless 1038
And most forlorn, should bribe another, pressed 1039
{D
By penury, to yield him up her {daughter— 1040
A little Infant, & instruct the Babe, 1041
Prattling upon his knee, to call him Father—— 1042
Lacy *Why, if his heart be tender, that offence* 1043
I could forgive him.

1022 *as MS. 3, rev as MS. 3 (Dora)*
1025 owners *then capitalized (Dora)*
1032 *as MS. 3, rev as MS. 3 (MW) and* troops *repeated (JC)* nakedness;
1035 hid;

1037, 1040 The capitals are JC's.

Mor: *(going on in the same way) And should he make the child*
An instrument of falshood; should he teach it
To stretch its little arms and dim the light
Of infant innocence with piteous looks
Of misery that was not
Lacy *— — — — — — Faith 'tis hard*
But in a world—
Mor *— — — Ay, ay (assuming a serious tone)*
This self same man
Even while he printed kisses on {t/h}he cheek
Of this poor babe, and taught its innocent mouth
To lisp the name of father, could he look
To the unnatural harvest of that time
When he should give her up, a woman grown
To him who bid the highest in the market
Of foul pollution
— — — — — — — The whole visible world
Lacy *— — — — — — — — ~~Hell itself~~*
Contains not such a monster
Mor: *— — — — — — — — For this purpose*
Should he resolve to taint her soul by means
Which bathe {the/my} limbs in sweat to think of them
Should he by tales which would draw tears from iron
Work on her nature and so turn compassion

[35^r]

And gratitude to ministers of ~~treason~~ vice
And make the spotless spirit of filial love

358 MH's 1799 correction.

{C
Mar (going on) *And should he make the* {*child* 1044
An instrument of falshood, should he teach her 1045
arms, and dim the gladsome light 1046
~~*natural*~~
her ~~gladsome~~
To stretch ~~*its little arms, & dim the*~~^~~*light*~~
~~*gladsome* [?] *innocence piteous*~~
Of infant ~~*innocence with infant*~~^~~*looks*~~
innocence,^*with piteous looks* 1047
Of misery that was not——

Troth, ~~*Troth*~~
Lacy — — — — — — —^~~*Faith,*~~} *'tis hard*— 1048
~~*our*~~ {~~*a*~~ ~~*w*~~
a

^}
But in a} *world* ~~*like this*~~— like ~~ours~~ *ours*——
{M
Mar (assuming a serious tone) This self-same {*man*— 1049
Even while he printed kisses on the cheek 1050
{B
Of this poor {*babe, & taught its innocent tongue* 1051
To lisp the name of Father—could he look 1052

59

To the unnatural harvest of that time 1053
{W
When he should give her up, a {*woman grown,* 1054
To him who bid the highest in the market 1055
Of foul pollution——
Lacy—— — — — — *The whole visible world* 1056
Contains not such a Monster!
Mar: — — — — — — — — *For this purpose* 1057
Should he resolve to taint her Soul, by means, 1058
Which bathe the limbs in sweat to think of them; 1059
Should he, by tales which would draw tears from iron, 1060
Work on her nature, & so turn compassion 1061
And gratitude to ministers of vice, 1062
And make the spotless spirit of filial love 1063

1045 falsehood,
1047 *comma del*
1048 *no comma*

1044, 1049, 1051, 1054 The capitals are JC's.
1046 In the revision, "arms, and dim" and the phrase "gladsome light" are JC's.
1047 Revision below the line is JC's.
1048 The undeleted "Troth" is JC's.
1049 The undeleted "a" and the final "ours" are JC's.

372 *Prime mover in a plo[?]{t} to damn his victim*
373 *Both soul and body—*
Wal: *— — — — — — — ’Tis too horrible*
374 *Rivers what say you to it?*
Lacy *— — — — — — — — Hew him down*
375 *And fling him to the ravens*

Mor: *— — — — — — — — But his ass{s}pect*
376 *It is so meek his countenance so venerable*
Wal: *(with an appearance of mistrust)*
377 *But how what say you Captain?*
Lacy *(at the same moment) Stab him then,*
378 *Before the alt[?]{ar}*
Mor: *— — — — — — What if he be sick*
379 *Tottering* ~~*almost*~~ *upon the very verge of* ~~*nature*~~, *life*
380 *And old, and blind*
Lacy *— — — — — — Blind say you!*
Riv: *(coming forward) — — — — Are we men,*
381 *Or own we baby spirits? Genuine courage*
382 *Is not an accidental quality*
383 *A thing depend[?]{en}t for its casual birth*
384 *On opposition and impediment*

[35ᵛ]

385 *Wisdom, if justice speak*~~*s*~~ *the word, beats down*
386 *The Giant’s strength, and at the voice of Justice*
387 *Spares not the worm— The Giant and the worm*
388 *She weighs them in one scale. The wiles of Women*
389 *And craft of age, seducing reason first*
390 *Made weakness a protection, and obs[?]{cur}ed*

372, 375, 378, 383 MH’s 1799 revisions.
385 Deletion by erasure, 1799.
390 MH’s 1799 revision.

Prime mover in a plot to damn his ~~V~~*ictim* [v above] 1064

Both^ ~~S~~*oul &*^ ~~B~~*ody*—— [s, b above]

Wall ——————'*Tis too horrible;* 1065

Oswald, what say you to it?

Lacy ————————*Hew him down,* 1066

And fling him to the ravens.

Mar: ———————*But his aspect,* 1067

It is so meek, his countenance so venerable. 1068

Wal (with an appearance of mistrust) *But how, what say you,* ~~*Captain*~~*?* [*Oswald?* above] 1069a

60

Lacy *(at the same moment) Stab him,* , were it [~~it~~ *it* above] 1069b

Before the Altar.

Mar: ————*What, if he were sick,* 1070

Tottering upon the verge of life, [~~very~~ above] 1071

And old & blind—— [*very* above]

Lacy ——————*Blind say you?*

Osw *(coming forward)* ————*Are we men,* 1072

Or own we baby spirits? Genuine courage 1073

Is not an accidental quality, 1074

A thing dependent for its {~~*casual*~~ / *natural birth*} [*casual* above] 1075

On opposition & impediment. 1076

Wisdom, if justice spea{*k* / *k*~~*s*~~} *the word, beats down* 1077

The giant's strength; &, at the voice of {*J* / *justice,*} 1078

Spares not the worm. The Giant & the worm— 1079

She weighs them in one scale. The wiles of women, 1080

And craft of age, seducing reason first,/ 1081

Made weakness a protection, & obscured 1082

1064 victim,
1067 *no comma*
1069a *second comma omitted and* you *underlined*
1073 Spirits{?/!}
1080 women,] Woman,
1081 craft *over the* eras *(Dora); recopied above line* reas on,
1082 *comma del at end of line*

1064–1065 The revisions are JC's.
1069b Revision above the line is JC's.
1071 Revision below the line is JC's.

The moral shapes of things. His tender cries
And helpless innocence, do they protect ~~the~~
The infant lamb? and shall the infirmities
Which have enabled this enormous culprit
hi
To perpetrate { *[?th]s crimes serve as a sanctuary*
To cover him from punishment? Fie—Justice,
Admitting no resistance, binds alike
needs
The feeble and the strong— She ~~wants~~ not here
Her bonds and chains which make the Mighty feeble
—We recognize in this old man a victim
Prepared already for the sacrifice——
Lacy *By Heavens! his words are reason—*
Riv: *— — — — — — — — — Yes my friends*
His countenance is meek and venerable
And by the mass, to see him at his prayers——
—I am of flesh and blood, and may I perish
When my heart does not ache to think of it!
Poor victim! Not a virtue under heaven
But what was made an engine to ensnare thee
But yet I trust, Matilda, thou art safe
Lacy *Matilda!*

[36r]

Wal: *— — — How! what! your Matilda?*
Mor: *— — — — — — — — — — Know you Clifford?*
Lacy *Clifford! who ever heard of this wild castle*
And doth not know him

---

392 Deletion by erasure, 1799.
395 MH's 1799 revision.

The moral shapes of things. His tender cries 1083
And helpless innocence—do they protect 1084

? ? }
The infant lamb! } *& shall the infirmities,* 1085

C
Which have enabled this enormous ^ *culprit* 1086
To perpetrate his crimes, serve as a sanctuary 1087

61

shame!
To cover him from punishment?—~~Fie~~—Justice, 1088
Shame!
Admitting no resistance, binds alike 1089
The feeble & the strong. She needs not here 1090
Her bonds & chains; which make the mighty feeble. 1091
—We recognize, in this old Man, a victim 1092
Prepared already for the sacrifice. 1093
Lacy *By heaven, his words are reason.*
Osw *— — — — — — — — Yes, my friends,* 1094
His countenance is meek & venerable; 1095
And by the Mass to see him at his prayers!— 1096
—I am of flesh & blood, & may I perish 1097
When my heart does not ache to think of it!— 1098
Poor Victim!—not a virtue under heaven 1099
But what was made an engine to ensnare thee; 1100

{ e
But yet I trust, Idon { *ia, thou art safe.* 1101

{ e
Lacy *Idon* { *ia!*

Wall: — — How, what! your Idonia? *to Mar* [ ]
Mine
But now no longer mine { *Y*
Mar *— — — — — — — — Know* { *you Cliff* [ ]
He is the man to whom the Maiden, pure
~~*Lacy*~~ ~~*Clifford! whoever heard of this wild Castle*~~
{ ~~*nd*~~
~~*As beautiful a*~~ { ~~*s pure & was to be yielded up*~~
~~*And doth not know him*~~

1087 Sanctuary
1088 punishment? Shame!—
1089 binds] bends
1091 chains,
1092 *no commas*
1099 *dash inserted*

1086 The capital is JC's.
1088 Revision below the line is JC's.

threescore
413 *Wal:* *I have lived ~~little short of seventy~~ years*
414 *And by the head of my own child this man*
415 *Must die. This wrinkled hand shall mat itself*
416 *In his grey hairs*
Mor: *(to Wallace) —— I love the father in thee*
417 *—You know me, friends I have a heart to feel*
418 *But Justice! justice*
Lacy *— — — — — — We will have ample justice*
419 *Who are we friends? Do we not live on ground*
420 *Where souls are self-defended, free to grow*
421 *Like mountain Oaks, rocked by the stormy wind*
422 *Mark the almighty wisdom which decreed*

obedient and benign meek gentle &
As beautiful, ~~& beautiful as pure~~ benign
And in her wide deep heart loving even me
~~Wal~~: — — — — — — I have lived threescore years
{up.
Was to be yielded {[?]
~~And by the head of my own child this Man~~

---

e}
Wallace — — — How, what! your Idoni{a? (to Mar:)
Mar: — — — — — — — — — — — — Mine, 1102
~~Lord~~
Lord
But now no longer mine. You know ^ Clifford; 1103
He is the Man to whom the Maiden, pure 1104
and
As beautiful, ~~meek~~, gentle & benign,
ample heart 1105
And in her ~~wide deep heart~~/ loving even me, 1106
Was to be yielded up. 1107a

Lacy — — — — — — — — — Now, by the head 1107b
62
~~Must die. This wrinkled hand shall mat itself~~
Of my own Child, this Man must die; my hand, 1108
~~In his grey hairs~~
A worthier wanting, shall itself entwine 1109
In his grey hairs.
Mar La} { y ~~I love the father in thee~~
(to [?La]}c}[?y]) — — — — I love the father in thee. 1110
{F
You know me, {friends; I have a heart to feel, 1111
And I have felt, more than perhaps becomes me, 1112
~~But Justice! Justice~~
Or duty sanctions.
Lacy — — — — — — We will have ample justice. 1113
{F
Who are we, {friends? Do we not live on ground 1114
Where Souls are self-defended, free to grow 1115
Like mountain Oaks rocked by the stormy wind. 1116
Mark the Almighty Wisdom, which decreed 1117

1102 Mine;
1104 Maiden{—
{,
1106 me{—
{,
1110 hairs!— Father
1111 *first comma omitted*
1116 oaks

1103 Revision above the caret is JC's.
1110b The hand is JC's, as is revision in the next line.

This monstrous crime should be laid open—here
Where Reason has an eye that she can use
And men alone are umpires. To the camp
He shall be led and there the country round
All gathered to the spot, in open day
He shall be sacrificed
Riv: *— — — — — — — — 'Tis nobly thought*
His death will be a monument to ages

[36v]

Mor: *— — — — — — — — — Lacy*
I thank you for this hint. He shall be brought
Before the camp, and would the good and just
Of every age might there be present— There
His crimes shall be proclaimed—and for the rest
It shall be done as wisdom shall decide—
Mean while do you two hasten back and see
That all is well prepared
Wal: *— — — — — — — — We will obey you*
Mor: *Tell where you found us. At some future time*
I will explain the cause.

[37r]

Act 3d.

[III.i] *Scene The door of the Inn; a group of Pilgrims*
as before, Matilda and the Host amongst them

Host: *You'll find your father, Lady at the convent*

{op
This monstrous crime to be laid {[?]en,—here, 1118
Where Reason has an eye that she can use, 1119
And men alone are umpires. To the camp 1120
He shall be led, & there, the Country round 1121
All gathered to the Spot, in open day 1122
Shall Nature be avenged.
~~He shall be sacrificed~~.
Osw — — — — — — — *'Tis nobly thought;* 1123
{for
His death will be a monument {to ages. 1124
Mar: — — — — — — — — — — — *~~Lacy!~~*
{H
I thank you for that hint. {Te shall be brought 1125
{at best & wisest 1126
Before the camp, & would th{e ~~good & just~~

63

~~And wisest~~
country be
Of every ~~age~~ ^ might ~~there be~~ present. There, 1127
His crime shall be proclaimed; + & for the rest, 1128
It shall be done as Wisdom shall decide: 1129
Meanwhile do you two hasten back & see 1130
That all is well prepared.
Wal. — — — — — — — *We will obey you.* 1131
Mar: *Tell where you found us. At some future time* × 1133
I will explain the cause. 1134
End 2^d Act

64 *Act 3*

(Scene; the door of the Hostel, a group of Pilgrims
as before; Idonia & the Host among them)

Lady,
Host *^ You'll find your Father at the Convent* 1135

1120 Umpires. Camp
{S
1122 {spot *(Dora)*
ll}
1123 Sha[?]} *(Dora)*
1124 *stage dir* (to Lacy) *added and* Lacy! *del*
1126 Camp,
1127 *no comma*
1128 *no comma*
softly! {nearer
1131/1133 aside. But ^ we must look a little {further ~~aside~~
nearer
{T
Act {third, *parens enclosing stage dir del and period added*

1127 The "be" above line is JC's.
1135 The revision is JC's.

As I have told you. He left us yesterday
With two companions: one of them I judged
Was his familiar friend (going) There was a letter
Of which I heard them speak—but I ~~suppose~~ fancy
It was forgotten—
Mat: (to the Host) — — — Farewell!
Host: (— — — — — — — — — — Gentle Pilgrims
Cuth
Saint ~~Mary~~ speed you on your holy errand!
(Exeunt Mat: and Pilgrims

[III.ii] *Scene a Heath*

Rivers (alone) Carry him to the camp! Yes to the camp
O Wisdom! a most wise resolve— and then
That half a word should blow it to the winds!
This last device <u>must</u> end my work—methinks
It were a pleasant pastime to construct
A scale and table of belief — as thus—
Two columns, one for passion, one for proof,
Each rising as the other falls: and first
Passion a unit and against us—proof!

[37^{v}]

Nay we must travel in another path
Or we're stuck fast for ever—passion then
Shall be a unit for us — proof oh no
We'll not insult her majesty by time
And place— The where the when, the how and all

In l. 7 of III.ii, a concluding comma replaces erased exclamation point, 1799.

As I have told you/ :} {h *He left us yesterday*
With two Companions, ;} *one of them I judged*
Was his familiar friend. (going) There was a letter
Of which I heard them speak, but∧ *that* *I fancy*
{*Has* {*been*
{*It* {*was forgotten.*

Ido (to Host) — — — — *Farewell!*
Host — — — — — — — — *Gentle Pilgrims*
St Cuthbert speed you on your holy errand.
(Ex: Ido & Pil:)

Scene — a ~~*Heath*~~ desolate {*M* *moor.*

Osw (alone) *Carry him to the Camp! Yes, the Camp.*
O Wisdom! a most wise resolve! & then,
That half a word should blow it to the winds!
This last device must end {*my* *it* *work.—*{*M* *methinks*
It were a pleasant pastime to construct
A scale & table of belief—as thus—

65

Two columns, one for passion, one for proof,
Each rises as the other falls: & first,
Passion a unit/ {+ *& against us, proof—*
Nay we must travel in another path
Or we're stuck fast for ever;—passion, then,
Shall be a unit for us; ~~+~~*proof—*{*O* *o no,*
We'll not insult {*t* *he*/ *majesty by*∧ *time* ~~*time*~~ ~~*time*~~ ~~*thought*~~

~~time~~} ~~Of and~~} ~~and~~
Person ~~*And*~~ *place. The where, the when, the how,* ~~*& all*~~

1136 He
1137 {C companions; One of them, *(Dora)* I judged *del to* as seemed,
1138 Was his *rev to* His most
1141/1142 Exit *rev to* Exeunt *in stage dir*
1142 Yes ∧ to the Camp. *(Dora)*
1148 proof;
1150 against *underlined* us— *then dash del*
1153 for *underlined* O *del and* —passion! *added to line*
1154 the] her *rev to* thy

The dull particulars ~~whose~~ that intrusi{de / on} {to} mars
The dignity of demonstration. Well
A whipping to the moralists who preach
That misery is a sacred thing! For me [1160]
I know no cheaper engine to degrade a man
Nor any half so sure. This stripling's mind
It hath been rudely shaken, and the dregs
Float on the surface—yea the very dregs—
And in the storms and anguish of his spirit [1164]
This wretch, unutterably miserable
{Ha / Doth dream} {'t} that he is happy—We d{e / i}ssect
The senseless body and why not the mind?

---

25 Miscorrection of "dissect" probably 1799.

dull brains require ~~[ ] [?] She~~
And all brains
~~The dull~~ *particulars that*^~~*intrude to mar*~~
~~Is~~ {*J* / [?]~~udge~~ To constitute the spiritless {s / Shape of Fact—
~~*The dignity of demonstration. Well*~~
They idolize, calling it demonstration.
—A whipping to the Moralists who preach

Person & place. The where, the when, the how,
that
And all particulars^*dull brains require*
t{less}
To constitute the spiri^*{t&} shape of Fact,*
They bow to, calling the idol, Demonstration—
{a
A whipping to the Moralists, who pre{ech

That misery is a sacred thing!—For me,
{~~*eaper*~~
I know no ~~*ch*~~ {~~[?]~~ *cheaper engine to degrade a man,*
{*S*
Nor any half so sure. This {*stripling's mind*
till the dregs float on the
[?~~I~~] Is {r
~~*It hath been rudely*~~ *shaken,* ~~*& the dregs*~~ su{ffFace
Is shaken till the dregs float on the surface;
~~*Float on the surface Yea the very dregs*~~
{t {e
And, in the storm & anguish of { *h*{*is* ~~*spirit*~~ heart
{~~*W*~~ *Has talked*
~~*This* {*wretch, unutterably miserable*~~,
~~Must talk~~ of a transition in his Soul,
{~~An~~ {~~ssect~~
{~~*hath dreamt*~~ *that he is happy. We* ~~*de*~~{~~*sect*~~ dissect
D
~~And~~ dreaming
The senseless body & why not the mind?—

1155 place.—} {t The *(JC)*
1158 Demonstration.—
1159 *comma del*
1160 thing.:—} {f For *(JC)*
1164 the] his *del to* the *as MS. 3*
1164/1165 This Wretch unutterably miserable, *del as MS. 3*
1165 Has talked] Must talk *del to* Has talked *rev to* He talks
1166 Dreaming] And dream *del to* Dreaming

1162 The capital is JC's.
1163 In JC's hand.

27 *These are strange sights—the mind of man upturned*
28 *Is a strange spectacle—Hem! shall I stop*
29 *No. Thoughts and feelings will sink deep but then* [1171]
30 *They have no shape— Let a few minutes pass*
31 *And something shall be done which memory*
32 *May touch when she looks back upon it—he—*
(Enter Mortimer from behind)

Riv: *(turning to meet him) (earnestly)*
33 *'Tis for my peace of mind*
Mor: *— — — — — — — — Why I believe you man*

[38^r]

34 *Riv:* *But hear the proofs*
[?]
35 *Mor:* *Aye—~~for the proofs~~—prove ~~to me~~ when two peas*
36 *Lie snugly in a pod ~~that then~~ the pod must then* [1177]
{*Be*
37 {*Is larger than the peas—prove this—'twere matter*
38 *Worthy the hearing*
Fool that I was to dream
39 *It ever could be otherwise!*
Riv: *— — — — — — — — Last night* [1180]
40 *When I returned with water from the torrent*
41 *I overheard the villain~~s~~— Every word*
42 *Like red hot iron burnt into my heart*

These are strange sights—the mind of man upturned, 1168
~~hideous~~ ~~Hem!~~ *there*
~~*Is a strange spectacle Hem! shall I stop*~~
Is in all natures a strange spectacle—
~~eous~~
~~In some a hid[?]~~ ~~one Hem! Shall I stop~~

66

Is in all natures a str nge spectacle, 1169
In some a hideous one—hem! shall I stop— 1170
No.—Thoughts & feelings will sink deep, but then 1171
substance. Pass but ~~but~~
They have no ~~shape Let~~ ^ a few minutes ~~pass~~ 1172
And something shall be done which memory 1173
c *e'er her Vassals are at work* ~~Ey!~~ 1174
May tou{gh, when ~~she looks back upon it he!~~ —

Enter Marmaduke, from behind)

Osw. *(turning to meet him),* ~~*earnestly*~~*)*
But listen, for my peace—
~~*Tis for my peace of mind*~~

Mar: — — — — — — — *Why I believe you.* ~~*Man*~~
Osw *But hear the proofs—*
, that
Mar — — — — — *Aye, prove ^ when two peas* 1176
Lie snugly in a pod, the pod must then 1177
Be larger than the peas—prove this—'twere matter 1178
Worthy the hearing.

~~*Osw*~~ ~~/ / / / /~~ *Fool!* ~~*that I*~~ *was* I *to dream* 1179
It ever could be otherwise!—
Osw:
~~*Mar:*~~ — — — — — — — — *Last night,* 1180
brook
When I returned with water from the ~~torrent~~ 1181
s
I overheard the Villain—Every word 1182
e
Like red hot iron burnt into my ~~very~~ heart. 1183

1169 strange spectacle;
1170 stop {? / ?—
1172 minutes,
1174 . . . when she looks back upon it.— *then* ever *inserted after* when *then all after* when *del to* e'er her Vassals are at work.
1175 *no comma, dash apparently del*
1176 *no comma*
1179 *no exclam point* to *over illeg false start*
1180 *no comma*
1182 Every
1183 red-hot heart.] soul *overwritten* heart. *(Dora)*

Said one "It is agreed on—The blind man
"Shall feign a sudden illness—and the girl
"Who on her journey must proceed alone
"Under pretence of violence be seized—
"She is"—continued the detested slave,
"She is right willing—~~A~~ fool if she were not
"They say Lord Clifford is a savage man
"But faith! to see him in his silken tunic
"Fitting his low voice to the minstrel's harp
"There's witchery in't. I never knew a maid
"That could withstand it. True" continued he
"When we arrang'd the affair she wept a little
"(Not less the welcome to my Lord for that)
"And said "my Father he will have it so"
Mor: *I am your hearer*
Riv: ——————— *This much I caught, and more*
That may not be retold to any ear.

[38[v]]

The obstinate bolt of a small iron door
Detained them near the gateway. I could see
dim
By a ~~small~~ lantern which the stouter held
That they were carrying to some inner room
a
Materi[?]ls for a banquet. They themselves

63 MH's 1799 revision

{M
Said one, "It is agreed on. The blind {*man*
"Shall feign a sudden illness & the Girl,
"Who on her journey must proceed alone,

67

"Under pretence of violence be seized.
"She is", continued the detested Slave,
strange
"She is right willing—~~fool~~, if she were not!—
strange^
"They say, Lord Clifford is a savage man;
"But, faith, to see him in his silken tunic,
"Fitting his low voice to the Minstrel's harp,
"There's witchery in't. I never knew a ~~M~~aid
m
"That could withstand it. True", continued he,
"When we arranged the affair she wept a little
"(Not less the welcome to my Lord for that)
"And said, {' *my Father he will have it so* '"} *.*
Mar: I am your hearer.
Osw: — — — — This ~~much~~ I caught, & more
That may not be retold to any ear.
The obstinate bolt of a small iron door

---

of the castle
~~I~~}
Detained them ne[ ] the gateway } *~~could I~~ see*
~~I could see that they~~
~~their~~
~~By a^dim lantern which the stouter held~~
a
{*~~W~~* *~~charged with preparations for a banquet~~*
~~That they~~ {*~~were carrying to some inner room~~*
By a dim lantern's light I saw that ~~flowers~~ wreathes
~~Which~~
~~for a banquet. They themselves~~

1185 illness, *dash at end of line del to comma*
1186 *comma and dash at end of line del to comma*
1187 *dash after* violence *del to comma; exclam point at end of line del to period*
1193 in't] in it *rev to* in't *(Dora)*
1194 That *over illeg eras (Dora)*
1199 ear. *reinforced and recopied above line (JC)*

1189 Revision below the line is JC's.
1193 The revision is JC's.

Must share it with their master, if 'twas true
What I distinctly heard the villains say
{ne
With dam{md laughter, and most foul allusion
Mor: *Oh misery!*
Riv: *— — — I knew it would disturb you*
And therefore chose this solitary heath [1209]
Here to impart the tale, of which, last night,
I strove to ease my heart when our two comrades
Commissioned by the band, burst in upon us
Avengers
Mor: *Last night when I would play the ~~murderer~~'s part*

---

66 MH's 1799 revision.

Of [ ]*wers* *as if designed*
∧ [ ]*ere in their hands* ~~*for festive decoration*~~
~~*Must share it with their Master, if 'twas true*~~
~~*heard*~~
~~*And them say*~~
ha
For festive decordtion but they would s[?] *re the banquet*
~~*What I distinctly heard the villains say*~~
W[ ]*h their Master & the Lady,* ~~*& heard them say*~~
W[ ]*h brutal laughter, & most foul illusion.*
see loose step

Mar: Oh misery!

Detained them near the gateway of the Castle } / 1201
By a dim lantern's light I saw that wreaths 1202
Of flowers were in their hands, as if designed 1203
For festive decoration; & they said, 1204
~~*allusion foul*~~
With brutal laughter & ~~*most foul allusion*~~
most foul allusion, 1205
foul
That they should share the banquet with their
Lord 1206
And his new Favorite.
Mar — — — — — — — *Misery!* 1207a

---

68 — — — — — — — — — — — *I knew* 1207b
this
How you would be disturbed by ~~*this*~~ *dire news,* 1208
Osw — — — ~~*I knew it would disturb you*~~
~~*woul*~~
And there chose this solitary ~~*heath*~~ *Moor* 1209
fore
Here to impart the tale, of which, last night, 1210
mind,
I strove to erase my ~~*heart*~~, *when our two comrades,* 1211
Commissioned by the Band, burst in upon us. 1212

~~*e*~~ {A
~~*Moved as I was to act tha*~~ ~~*avenger's part*~~
~~*Mar: Last night, when I would play the Avenger's part*~~
do work { ~~work I believed~~
Last night when moved to act } the Avengers ∧ ~~part~~

1207a {F favorite. *(Dora) with cap* F *repeated (JC)* Misery!—
1209 Moor,
1211 comrades,] {C comrades

1200/1201 The loose slip alluded to at the end of this passage (with "slip" miswritten "step") was apparently pasted on later.
1205/1206 The bottommost "foul" is JC's.

I did believe all things were shadows, yea, [1214]
Living and dead all things were bodiless;
Till that same star summoned me back again
Now could I laugh till my ribs ached, Oh! fool!
To let a creed built in the heart of things [1219]
Dissolve before a twinkling atom{*s eye* / ,}
Philosophy! I will go forth a teacher
And you shall see how deeply I will reason [1224]

~~*Then*~~
{~~*then*~~
~~*I*~~ {[?~~*had*~~] *believe~~d~~ all things were shadows, yea*
I did ^
{L
~~*Yea*~~, {*living & dead all things were bodiless;*
~~Or but the mutual mockeries of body~~
~~Or only various Forms of the same Nature~~
~~*Till that same Star summoned me back again*~~
Or but the mutual mockeries of body
Till that same star summoned me back again.
Now could I laugh till my ribs ached. Oh fool!
To let a creed built in the heart of things
s} *Oswald* {~~*Now*~~
Di {*solve before a twinkling atom~~s eye~~.*{
~~*Will I go forth.*~~ *Oft have I chidden you for daring talk*
~~*Philosophy. I will go forth a Teacher*~~
Could I go forth a teacher in philosophy
ou} *d*} *could*
And you shal{*l* {*see how deeply I* ~~*will*~~ *reason*
Of love in all its shapes, & spinnings, ends
~~*Of qualities*~~ *& substances & laws*
diverse
Of moral qualities, in their ~~*various*~~ *aspects*
~~*Of actions, & their ends & differences*~~

Marmaduke
lift the avenging steel 1213
Last night, when moved to ~~*do the Avenger's work*~~,
shadows, yea, 1214
I did believe all things were ~~*bodiless*~~*;*
Living or dead all things were bodiless, 1215
Or but the mutual mockeries of body, 1216
Till that same star summoned me back again. 1217
Now I could laugh till my ribs ache~~d~~. O fool! 1218
To let a creed, built in the heart of things, 1219
Dissolve before a twinkling atom!—Oswald, 1220
~~*Young as I am I oft have chidden you*~~
~~*Oft have I chidden you*~~
I could fetch lessons out of wiser schools 1221
~~*For daring talk, now I am better schooled*~~
Than you have entered, were it worth the ~~*pains*~~ *pains.* 1222
~~*I might go forth a teacher in philosophy*~~
Young as I am, I might go forth a teacher, 1223
And you should see how deeply I could reason 1224

1213 *as MS. 3, rev as MS. 3*
1218 ache.] ached.
1224–1227 *further developed in MS. 3A, 10^v^*

1213–1226 On the back of this pasteover, in an unknown hand, is written: "Note! / See—'Stanzas / composed in the Simplon Pass / Vol. iv. P. 164." The reference is to WW's 1836 edition.
1222 The final "pains" is JC's.

{O
81 ~~Of laws~~, {of qualities and substances & laws
82 Of actions, and their ends and difference~~s~~}
83 Riv: You take it as it merits

[39r]

Mor: One a King
84 General or Cham, Sultan or Emperor [1229]
85 Strews twenty acres of good meadow ground
86 With carcases, in lineament and shape
87 And substance nothing differing from his own
{of
88 But that they cannot stand up {for themselves
ith'
89 Another sits ~~in the~~ sun and by the hour [1234]
rivulet— Of this Pair
90 Floats king-cups in the ~~brook— They are wise men~~
91 ~~Both are wise men~~
but Times
Other }
One we call Hero—the [?Times] {~~is~~ ^—Spendthrift
~~Riv~~: — — — — — — ~~Faith! I begin to think so~~
But both are fools or, if you chuse, it wise
Each in his way
Osw — — — — — — –Troth, I begin to think so
{or:
92 M{or: Now for the corner stone of my plilosoply [1240]
93 I would not give a denier for the man
Who on such provocation as this world
{Yields
94 {Who could not chuck his babe beneath the chin
95 And send it with a fillip to its grave.
96 Riv: Nay you leave me behind—
Mor: — — — — — — — That such a one! [1245]
97 So pious in demeanour! in her look
98 So saintly and so pure!—Hark'ee my friend
99 ~~I have a scheme of pleasure— on my life~~
I'll plant my self before
100 ~~There's promise in't. I'll go to the~~ Lord Clifford's
castle
101 ~~Plant myself full before his castle wall~~
102 A surly mastiff kennels at the gate
103 And he shall howl, and I will laugh, a medley [1250]
104 Most tunable— ~~What say you to it?~~

---

82 Underwriting deleted by erasure.
88 MH's 1799 correction.

Of love in all its shapes, [*,* over deleted mark] *beginnings, ends;*
Of moral qualities in their diverse aspects;

Of Actions, & their laws, & tendencies.
Osw: *You take it as it merits——*
Mar — — — — — — — — *One a King,*
General or Cham, Sultan or Emperor,
Strews twenty acres of good meadow ground
With carcases, & [*in* over] *lineament & shape*

69

And substance, nothing differing from his own,
But that they cannot sit up of themselves:
Another sits i'th'sun, & by the hour
Floats kingcups in the^ *brook* *brook* ~~*rivulet of this Pair*~~ a Hero~~/~~, one
We call, & scorn the other as Time's spendthrift;
~~*One we call Hero—the Other but* T/*time's spendthrift*~~
~~But verily they stand on common ground~~
~~Yet~~
~~*But both are fools each in his way*~~
But stand they not on common ground? both Fools~~/~~—
Each in his way
Osw: — — — — — — — — *Troth, I begin to think so.*
Mar: *Now for the corner-stone of my phy*[*i* over]*losophy:*
I would not give a denier for the man
Who, on such/ *provocation*/ *as this world*
Yields, could not chuck his babe beneath the chin,
And send it with a fillip to its grave.
Osw *Nay, you leave me behind.*~~/~~
Mar ~~*Mar*~~ — — — — — — — *That such a One,*
So pious in demeanor! in his look
So saintly & so pure!— Hark'ee, my friend,
I'll plant myself before Lord Clifford's Castle,
A surly mastiff kennels at the gate
And he shall howl & I will laugh, a medley
Most tun~~e~~*able.*

1227 *second comma omitted*
1235 *no comma*
1239 way.
1249 gate,

1235 The undeleted "brook" is JC's.

In faith a pleasant scheme
Riv: — — — — — — — — — — — ~~*Faith!*~~—
But take your sword along with you, for that
~~*ea*~~ } {~~*B*~~
105 ~~*A pl*[?]{ *sant scheme* — {*but first what must be done with*~~ ——
106 ~~*How shall we wash our hands of* —— *eh*~~*?*
Might in such neighbourhed find seemly use——

[39^v]

But first {*h* / {*How wash our hands of th*{*is* / *e Old Man?*
Mor: — — — — — — — — — — — — — ~~*Oh! truly*~~
{*path*
Oh yes *viper in the* {*sun* ~~*Yes*~~
107 ~~*That*~~ *mole, that* ^~~*weazle, that old water-rat*~~ —
Him
108 *Plague on my memory! I had forgot* ~~*him*~~— [1256]
ten
109 *Riv:* *You know we left him sitting—see him yonder*
110 *Mor:* — — — — — — — — — — — — —*Ha, ha!*
Riv: *As you will make short work of it*
you follow as may suit you
111 *I* ~~*will*~~ *stroll on,* ~~*and take the way of the Inn*~~—

[III.iii] (*Scene changes to another part of the heath, at a small distance Herbert is discovered, seated on a stone*

1 *Her:* *A sound of laughter too!—'tis well—I feared* [1260]
2 *The stranger had some grief which pressed upon him.*
3 *Hush! 'tis the feeble and earth-loving wind*
{*er*
4 *That creeps along the bells of the crisp heath*{ ~~*plant*~~.
5 *Alas! 'tis cold—I shiver in the sunshine*— [1265]
6 ~~*My limbs are cold — I could believe the air*~~
The air portends a storm—
7 ~~*Portended storm*~~ — ~~*in truth*~~^*they tarry long*
8 *What can this mean?—There is a psalm that speaks*
God's parental mercies, with Idonea
9 *Of* ~~*the tender*~~ *mercies* ~~*of God, which with Matilda*~~
it *ere*{
10 *I used to sing — Listen*~~*en*~~*—what foot is that*}

---

105 The first correction was made in 1799.

Osw *In faith a pleasant scheme;*
But take your sword along with you, for that
Might in such neighbourhood find seemly use.

70

But first how wash our hands of this old Man.
Mar: *Oh yes, that Mole, that viper in the path;*
Plague on my memory, him I had forgotten:
Osw: *You know we left him sitting—see him yonder.*
Ha! ha!
Mar: — — — — — — — — — ~~*Ha*~~, ~~*ha*~~*!*
As 'twill be but a moment's work,
Osw: ~~*As you will make short work of it*~~
~~*as you will*~~
I will *when 'tis done.*
~~*I'll*~~ ^ *stroll on, you follow* ^ ~~*as may suit you*~~*.*

Moor ~~*Moor*~~
(Scene changes to another part of the ^ ~~*heath*~~*/ at*
a short distance {. / *Herbert is discovered seated* {*on* [?]} *a stone)*

Herb: *A sound of laughter too! 'tis well—I feared*
pitiable sorrow ~~*pressing upon*~~
The Stranger had some ~~*grief which pressed upon him*~~
Pressing upon his solitary heart *him—*
Hush!—'tis the feeble & earth-loving wind
That creeps along the bells of the crisp ~~*heath*~~{~~*er*~~, ~~*plant*~~
heather.
Alas! tis cold—I shiver in the sunshine—
~~*The air portends a storm, they tarry long*~~
What can this mean? There's a psalm that speaks
Of God's parental mercies—with Idon{*e* / *ia*
I used to sing it. Listen!—what foot is there?

1251 faith,
1253 use.—
1256 forgotten.
1258 ha!—
1259/1260 *parens enclosing stage dir del* distance— stone.
1260 too!— feared,
1261 *as MS. 3 but* {S / stranger *(Dora) then rev as MS. 3*
1262 *interlined, as MS. 3, with comma at end del to period*
1266 There's *rev to* There is
1268 it.—

1259 The "I will" is JC's, as is the first "Moor" in the scene description, below.

11 ~~*Which creeps along the grass*~~*?*
~~*Stealing*~~
En{t/der Mortimer

Mor: *(looks at Herbert) aside*
12 *And I have* <u>*loved*</u> *this man? and* <u>*she*</u> *hath loved him*
13 *And I loved her, and she loved the Lord Clifford*
14 *And there it ends— if this be not enough*

[40ʳ]

15 *To make mankind merry for evermore*
16 *Then plain it is as day—that eyes were made*
17 *For a wise purpose — verily to weep with! (looking round)*
18 *A pretty prospect this, a master-piece*
19 *Of nature— finished with most curious skill:*
Good Baron *(to Her:*
20 ~~*My an{tient*~~ *{e* *have you ever practiced {tillage/farming?*
21 *Pray tell me what this land is worth by the acre?*
Her: 22 *How glad I am to hear your voice—I know not*
23 *Wherein I have offended you— last night*
24 *I found in you the kindest of protectors*
This morning when I spoke
25 ~~*When I complained*~~ *of weariness,* ~~*this morning*~~
from my shoulders took my scrip & threw it
26 *You* ~~*took my scrip of food from off my shoulders*~~
About
27 ~~*And threw it round*~~ *your own—but for these two hours*
Once only have you spoken *past*
28 ~~*You have only spoken to me once*~~*—when the lark*
29 *Whirred from among the fern beneath our feet*
I no coward in my better days
30 *And* ~~*then you half terrified me.*~~
Was almost terrified
Mor: *— — — — — — — — — That's excellent!*
31 *So you bethought you of the many ways*
32 *In which a man may come to his end, whose crimes*
33 *Have roused all nature up against him—pshaw!*
34 ~~*'Twas very idle*~~
Her: *— — — — — —* ~~*Cast your eyes about*~~
35 *For mercy's sake is nobody in sight?*
36 *No traveller, peasant, herdsman?*

11/12 Correction of "Enter" was made in 1799.
12 Underlining of "she" added 1841.

Enter ~~Oswald~~ Marmaduke

Mar: *(aside, looks at Her)*
And I have loved this Man? & <u>she</u> hath loved him,
And I loved her, & she loved the Lord Clifford;

71

And there it ends;—if this be not enough
To make manking}d merry for evermore,
Tha{e}n plain it is as day,—that eyes were made
For a wise purpose—verily to weep with! (looking round)
A pretty prospect this, a master piece
Of Nature,—finished with most curious skill.
To Her) *Good Baron, have you ever practised tillage?*
Pray tell me what this land is worth by the a^cre}?
Her: *How glad I am to hear your voice—I know not*
Wherein I have offended you;—last night
I found in you the kindest of Protectors,
This morning, when I spoke of weariness,
You from my shoulder took my scrip & threw it
About your/own; but for these two hours past
Once only have you spoken, when the lark
Whirred from among the fern beneath our feet,
And I, n{o}ow coward in my better days,
Was almost terrified.
Mar: *— — — — — — — That's excellent!—*
So, you bethought you of the many ways
In which a man may come to his end, whose crimes

72

Have roused all Nature up against him—pshaw!—
Her *For mercy's sake, is nobody in sight?*
No traveller, peasant, herdsman?

1268/1269 *comma del to dash and* looks *rev to* looking *in stage dir*
1269 *question marks following* Man *and* him *rev to exclam points*
1270 she loved] *rev to* she loves Clifford?}!
1274 wise *over illeg eras (Dora)* with!—
1275 master-piece
1276 skill.}!
1278 acre?
1279 *dash del to comma*
1281 the *inserted with caret (JC)*
1282 *over same line, miswritten (with* morning *omitted), then erased (Dora)*
1286 our] your *rev to* our *(Dora)*

Mor: ——————————*Not a soul!*
Here is a tree ragged, and bent and bare
Which turns its goatsbeard flakes of pea-green moss [1295]

[40^v^]

From the stern breathing of the rough sea wind—
We have no other company my friend!
Commend me to this place. If a man should die
And leave his body here, it were all one
As he were twenty fathom underground [1300]
{mon friend
Her: Where is your com{rade?
Mor: ——————*Do you believe*
In ghosts?— the spirit of a murder'd man
Might have fine room to ramble about here
A grand domain to squeak and gibber in
Her: Poor wretch! if thou hast any close-pent guilt
Pressing upon thy heart, and this the hour [1306]
Of visitation
Mor: ————*No that will not do—*
Her: Restore him heaven!
{desperate
{cruel
Mor: —————*Oh villain!* ~~*damned villain!*~~
wretch!
She smell'd most sweet and she was fair—and now
They have snapped her from the stem—Poh! let her lie
Besoil'd with ~~*the*~~ *mire, and let the houseless snail* [1311]
Feed on her leaves—you knew her well—ay there
Old man! you were a very lynx, you knew

Mar: ——————————— *Not a soul:* 1293
Here is a tree, ragged,/& bent & bare, 1294
That
~~Which~~ turns its goats-beard flakes of pea-green moss 1295
From the stern breathing of the rough sea-wind; 1296
We have no other company, my friend!— 1297
Commend me to this place. If a man should die 1298
And leave his body here, it were all one 1299
As he were twenty fathoms underground.
Her: *Where is our common friend?* 1300
Mar ———————— *~~Do you believe~~*
A ghost, methinks, 1301
{T
~~In ghosts~~? {the Spirit of a murdered man, for ~~instance~~
instance, 1302
Might have fine room to ramble about here, 1303
A grand domain to squeak & gibber in. 1304
Lost Man! *have*
Her: *~~Poor wretch~~! if thou ~~hast~~ any close-pent guilt* 1305
Pressing upon thy heart, & this the hour 1306
Of visitation——
A bold word from you!— 1307
Mar —————— *~~No that will not do~~*
Her *Restore him Heaven!* 1308a

73
{Mar: *The* *{wretch!—*
{~~Oh villain~~ ————— ~~Oh villain~~,/desperate {villain
{A
~~A flower among~~ *{a flower,* 1308b
~~She smelle{d most sweet, & she was fair — & now~~
Fairest of all flowers, was she once, but now 1309
They have snapped her from the stem—Poh! let her lie, 1310
Besoiled with mire, & let the houseless snail 1311
.} {Y *e}*
Feed on her leaves/—} {you knew her well—ay} there, 1312
{L
Old man! you were a very {lynx, you knew 1313

1294 raggèd
1295 *as MS. 3 but* goat's-beard *rev as MS. 3 (WW)*
F
1297 friend *(JC)*
1307 *final dash del*
1308 Heaven!—
1310 *no comma*
1311 mire *over illeg del (JC)*
1313 Man! Lynx, *not underlined*

1035 The "have" is JC's.
1312–1313 The capitals are JC's.

The worm was in her
Her: *— — — — — — Mercy! {S / sir what mean you?*

[41r]

Mor: *You have a daughter*
Her: *— — — — — — Oh that she were here!* [1315]
She hath an eye that sinks into all hearts
And if I have in aught offended you
Soon would her gentle voice make peace between us
Mor: *I do believe he weeps—I could weep too*
There is a vein of her voice that runs through h {is / [?ers] [1320]
Even such a man my fancy bodied forth
From the first moment that I loved the maid
And he was still a brother in my love—
These tears—I did not think that aught was left in me
Of what I have been— Yes I thank thee heaven [1325]
One happy thought has passed across my mind—
—It may not be—I am cut off from man
No more shall I be man, no more shall I
Have human feelings!—now for a little more
About your daughter
Troops of
Her: *— — — — — — — Armed men*
Met in the roads would bless us—little children [1331]
Rushing along in the full tide of play
Were silent as we passed them I have heard
The boisterous carman in the miry road
Check his loud whip and hail us with mild voice
And speak with milder voice to his poor beasts [1336]
Mor: *And whither were you going?*
Her: *— — — — — — — — Learn young man*
To fear the virtuous, and reverence misery.
Whether too much for patience, or like mine

57, 63 MH's 1799 corrections.
78 MH's 1799 revision.

The worm was in her——
Her: *— — — — — — Mercy! Sir, what mean you?* 1314
Mar: *You have a* {*D* / *daughter!*}
Her *— — — — — — Oh that she were here!* 1315
She hath an eye that sinks into all hearts, 1316
And, if I have in aught offended you, 1317
Soon would her {*gentle* / *quiet*} *voice make peace between us.* 1318
Mar: *I do believe he weeps—I could weep too—* 1319
There is a vein of her voice that runs thro' his: 1320
Even such a man my fancy bodied forth 1321
From the first moment that I loved the {*M* / *maid,*} 1322
And ~~*he was still a brother in my love*~~ / *for his sake I loved her more: these tears—* 1323
~~*These tears*~~ */I did not think that aught was left in me* 1324
Of what I have been—{*Y* / *Yes, I thank thee,*}{*H* / *heaven!*} 1325
One happy thought has passed across my mind. 1326
—It may not be—I am cut off from man— 1327

74

No more shall I be man—no more shall I 1328
Have human feelings!—{*N* / *now, for a little more*} 1329
About your {*D* / *daughter.*}
Herb: *— — — — — — Troops of armed men,* 1330
Met in the roads, would bless us;/little children, 1331
Rushing along in the full tide of play, 1332
~~*Were*~~ ~~*Grew*~~ *Stood silent as we pass*{*e* / [?]*d them! I have heard*} 1333
The boisterous Carm[?]{*an*}*, in the miry road,* 1334
Check his loud whip & hail us with mild voice, 1335
And speak with milder voice to his poor beasts. 1336
Mar *And whither were you going?*
Her *— — — — — — — — — Learn, young* {*M* / *man,*} 1337
To fear the virtuous, & reverence misery 1338
Whether too much for patience, or, like mine, 1339

1315 *question mark following* Daughter *rev to exclam point* here!—
1322 Maid;
1325 *first comma omitted*
1327 *final dash del to semicolon*
1330 *period rev to exclam point*
1338 misery,

1315, 1322, 1325, 1329–1330, 1337 The capitals are JC's.

[41^v]

Softened—till it becomes a gift of mercy
82 Mor: *Now this is as it should be!* ~~*on my soul*~~
83 ~~*I do admire you for it*~~
Her: *— — — — — — — I am weak!*
84 *My daughter does not know how weak I am,* [1342]
85 *And as thou seest, beneath the arch of heaven*
86 *Here do I stand alone in helplessness*
87 *W{ith / [?hich]} w{hic / [?it]}h the God of heaven has visited me!*
88 *But I had once a spirit and an arm——* [1346]
89 Mor: *Now for a word about your Barony,*
90 *I fancy when you left the Holy land*
91 *And came to— what's your title— eh? your claims*
92 *Were* ~~*little heeded*~~*? undisputed!*
Her: *— — — — — — Like a Mendicant*
93 *Whom no one comes to meet I stood alone* [1351]
94 *I murmured, but remembering him who feeds*
95 *The pelican and ostrich of the Des{e / s}rt,*
96 *From my own threshold I looked up to heaven,*
97 *And did not want glimmerings of quiet hope,* [1355]
98 *So from the court I passed and down the brook*
99 *Led by its murmur, to the ancient oak*
100 *I came, and when I felt {its / the} cooling shade,*
101 *I sat me down and cannot but believe*
102 *While in my lap I held my little babe* [1360]
103 *And clasped her to my heart—my heart that ached*
104 *More with delight than grief—I heard a voice*

---

87 MH's 1799 corrections; writing under the second deleted by erasure.
95 MH's 1799 correction.
100 MH's 1799 revision.

Softened/ till it becomes a gift of mercy. 1340
Mar *Now, this is as it should be!*
Her *— — — — — — — — I am weak!* 1341
My daughter does not know how weak I am, 1342
under
And, as thou see'st, ~~beneath~~ the arch of heaven 1343
{to
Here do I stand, alone, {in helplessness, 1344
By the good God our common Father, doomed! 1345
~~With which the God in heaven Hath visited~~
{n ~~me!~~
But I had once a spirit & a{rm arm— 1346

75

{:
Mar: *Now, for a word about your Barony,{* 1347
I fancy when you left the holy land, 1348
And came to—what's your title—eh? your claims 1349
Were undisputed!
Her: *— — — — Like a mendicant,* 1350
Whom no one comes to meet, I stood alone/— 1351
{H
I murmured/—but, remembering {him who feeds 1352
{of {the {Desert,
The pelican & the Ostrich {in {the {wilderness 1353
From my own threshold I looked up to heaven, 1354
And did not want glimmerings of quiet hope. 1355
So, from the court I passed & down the brook 1356
Led by its murmur to the ancient oak 1357
I came, & when I felt its cooling shade/ 1358
I sate me down, & cannot but believe— 1359
While in my lap I held my little Babe 1360
And clasped her to my heart,/—my heart that ached 1361
heard
More with delight than grief—I ~~had~~ a voice, 1362

1341 be!— weak!—
;}
1342 am,}
1343 *as MS. 3, rev as MS. 3*
1344 *as MS. 3, rev as MS. 3*
1345 God, doomed!—
{H
1348 {holy Land
1350 undisputed!—
1351 alone;—
1353 Desart,
1354 *no comma*
1356 passed, brook,
1357 murmur,
1361 *as MS. 3, rev as MS. 3*
1362 *no comma*

Such as by Cherith on Elijah called,
It said "I will be with thee"
A little boy

[42^r]

A Shepherd's lad, e're yet my trance was gone
Hailed us—as if he had been sent from heaven
And said with tears, that he would be our guide;
I had a better guide—that innocent babe
Who to this hour hath saved me from all ~~evil~~, harm
hunger
From cold, from ~~death~~, ~~from~~ penury and ~~hunger~~, death
Therefore I bless her: when I think of man
I bless her with sad spirit; when of God
I bless her in the fulness of my joy!
Mor: — — — — — — — ~~*Look there! he prays*~~*!*
The name of daughter in his mouth, he prays!
With nerves so steady, that the very flies
Sit undisturbed upon his staff—innocent!
If he were innocent—then he would tremble
may
And be disturbed as I am—It ~~might~~ be proved,
~~*our*~~
~~*My eyes are weak—there is a judge above—*~~

121 Revision in pencil, deleted in ink.

Such as by Cherith on Elijah called; 1363
It said, "I will be with thee".

A little {b / Boy}, 1364

A {s / Shepherd's lad, ere yet my trance was gone, 1365
Hailed us, as if he had been sent from heaven, 1366

And said, with tears, that he would be our guide, }; 1367

I had a better guide—that innocent {B / babe, 1368
Her who hath saved / *from*
Who ~~to~~ this hour ~~hath saved me from all~~ harm, 1369

76 *2 Good I have or wish for upon earth* 1372
From cold, from hunger, penury, & death: 1370
1 *Her to whom I owe the best of all* 1371
Therefore I bless her: when I think of man, 1374
I bless her with sad spirit; when of God, 1375
I bless her in the fullness of my joy! 1376
Mar: *The name of daughter in his mouth, he prays!* 1377
With nerves so steady, that the very flies 1378
unmolested
Sit ~~undisturbed up~~on his staff.—{I / innocent! 1379
If he were innocent—then he would tremble 1380
I have read 1381
turning aside *And be disturbed as I am. ~~/ It may be proved~~*
In story, what men now alive have witnessed, 1382
How, when the People's mind was racked with doubt, 1383
Appeal was made to the great Judge: ~~that~~ the Accused 1384

1364 (no paragraph) *in margin*
1365 shepherd's lad's *then apos and* s *del to hyphen*
1366 *first comma omitted*

Her, who to this hour,
1369 ~~Who to this hour~~ hath saved me,^from ~~all~~ harm,
1370 *colon rev to semicolon*
1370/1374 Her, unto whom I owe the best of all
The good I have, or wish for, upon earth *interlined, then* & more *added, then all del and restarted in right margin with* The good I have *then rewritten in left margin:*

and death—
To whom I owe the best of all the good
I have, or wish for, upon earth—& more
And higher far than lies within earth's bounds;
Therefore I bless her

1371–1372 *further developed in MS. 3A, 12r*
1374 Man,
1375 spirit,—
1379 Innocent!—
1381 disturbed, *stage dir within parens inserted with caret after period*
1382 {S / story *(Dora)*

1364, 1368 The revisions are JC's.

It dawns on me—I see the end for which
hand
~~An~~^~~arm~~^invisi~~b~~le^~~hath~~ le~~d~~ me^~~hither~~ — to^this Waste
~~He heard a voice—a shepherd's lad came to him~~
~~And was his guide—if once—why not again?~~ [1395]
~~the whole~~
~~And in this des[?]rt? if never then is he damned~~
note *~~Is but one damning falsehood~~*
~~Beyond a madmans dream!—here will I leave him~~
~~Here where no foot of man is found, no ear~~
~~Can hear his cries—it is a fearful~~ {Ø / ordeal!
~~But God is everywhere~~
~~Here (looking round) cold and hunger~~! Pain is of the heart [1399]
And what are a few throes of bodily suffering
If they can waken one pang of remorse? ({G / g}oes up to Herbert)
Old man! my wrath is in a flame burnt out [1402]
It cannot be rekindled— Here is a sword (draws his sword)
Nay I can point it to thy heart with pulse
Calm as a sleeping child—I have led thee hither
To save thy spirit from perdition ——

---

123 The carets mark the place for insertion of a late revision of ll. 123–131 copied on the verso of a slip of paper pasted over ll. 117–132:

is   to this Waste
~~Fit Subject he for a blindfold walk~~
Bare is it, without house or track & destitute
~~Oer burning plowshares but that Ordeal~~
[ ] obvious shelter as a Ship at sea
[?] [?]
~~It were too terrible~~—All-seeing God,
Here will I leave him, here^
{Such as he is, / [? ? ?]} to thee do I commit ~~him~~
dreary
His trial in this ~~pathless~~ solitude
He heard a voice—a Shepherds lad came to him
And was his guide—if once, why not again
And in this desert?—if never—then the whole
Of what he says, & look~~e~~s, & does, & is
~~but~~
Makes up one damning falsehood. Leave him
here
To cold & hunger—Pain is of the heart

Related drafts appear in MS. 2A, 8[r], and 8[v].
126, 133 MH's 1799 revisions.
126/127 The marginal "note" probably points to the draft revisions quoted above, l. 123.
129 Underlining added 1841.

n } *~~end~~*

~~*It dawns o[?]} me—I see the {[?] for which*~~

With naked feet walked over burning plowshares. 1385

Here is a man by Nature's hand prepared 1386

~~*A hand invisible led me to this Waste*~~

For a like trial, but more merciful. {*W* 1387

Why else have I been led to this bleak {*waste?* 1388

Bare is it, without house, or track, & destitute 1389

less}

Of obvious shelter, as a Ship at } *sea.* 1390

—here—

Here will I leave him^*—All-seeing God,* 1391

& sore perplexed as I am— 1392

Such as he is, ~~*to thee do I commit*~~

I will commit him to this ~~*fearful*~~ *Ordeal!—* 1393

~~*His trial in this dreary solitude*~~

final

{*s*

He heard a voice—a {*Shepherd lad came to him* 1394

And was his Guide;—if once, why not again, 1395

And in this desert? If never, then the whole 1396

{*o*

Of what he says, & looks, & d{*ies, & is,* 1397

Makes up one damning falsehood. Leave him here, 1398

To cold & hunger!—Pain is of the heart, 1399

And what are a few throes of bodily suffering 1400

If they can waken one pang of remorse? (goes up to Her) 1401

{*as*

Old Man! my wrath is {*in a flame, burnt out,* 1402

77

It cannot be rekindled. ~~*Here is a sword (draws his sword*~~ 1403a

~~*Nay I can point it to thy heart with pulse*~~

~~*Calm as a sleeping Child—I have led thee hither*~~

Thou art here, 1403b

~~*To save thy spirit*~~ *from perdition;*

1386 {M / man *(JC)*

1388 {W / waste *as MS. 3 (Dora)*

1390 {s / Shipless *(Dora)*

1391 *comma del to exclam point*

1392 *dash del to comma*

1394 {V / voice shepherd-lad

1395 {G / guide

1396 desert?] desart? *comma del to dash*

1402 *as MS. 3, rev as MS. 3*

1403b *no comma*

1388 The capital is JC's.

1390 The revision is JC's.

[42ᵛ]

Her: — — — — — — — — *Mercy!*
kill me
What *<u>me</u>! would you ~~destroy~~ me? ~~drink the blood~~*
~~Of such a wretch as I am~~!
Nay,
Mor: — — — — — — — — *~~That~~ is past*
Her: *Oh! mercy! mercy!*
Mor: — — — — — *I will be merciful*
I know the need which all men have of mercy,
by life or death
And therefore do I this— ~~three days old Man~~
~~Will be the limit of thy mortal course~~.
A righteous judgement speedily must come
Her: *My child! my ~~child~~! blessed Child!*
Mor: — — — — — *No more of that*
Thou wilt have many guides if thou art innocent
Yea from the utmost corners of the world
That woman will come o'er this heath to save thee
(He pauses & looks stedfastly at Herbert's staff)
is} &} own
Ha! what's} here!} carved by her^hands (reads upon the staff)
"I am Eyes to the blind saith the Lord
"He that puts his trust in me shall not fail"
Yes be it so—repent and be forgiven—
God and that staff are now thy only guides
(He leaves him on the heath)

[III.iv] *Scene an eminence—a Beacon on it. top of it*
Lacy, Wallace, Lennox, ~~Norwood~~ & c & c

several of the Band confusedly — *But patience ~~patience~~*

[43ʳ]

One of the band — — *Curses on th{at/e} Traitor! Oswald*
Our {C/L}aptain made a prey to {f/c}oul device.

---

143 The revision phrase "old Man" is in pencil.
146 MH's 1799 revision.
149 Deletion by erasure.
150 MH's 1799 correction.

Let by my hand to save thee^ ~~*thou will have*~~ 1404

t}
Thou will} *have time to breathe & think—*

O!}
Her — — — — — — — — — — — — — —} *Mercy!* 1405

~~*What me? would you kill me*~~

~~*Mar*~~ — — — — — — — — — — ~~*Nay, that is past*~~

~~*Her:*~~ ~~*Mercy! oh! mercy!*~~

~~*Mar*~~ — — — — — — — ~~*I will be merciful*~~

{ *that*
Mar *I know the need* {*which all men have of mercy,* 1406

And therefore leave thee to a righteous judgement. 1407

~~*A righteous judgement. speedily must come*~~

Her: *My Child! my blessed Child!—*

Mar — — — — — — — — — — *No more of that;* 1408

Thou wilt have many guides if thou art innocent; 1409

Yea, from the utmost corners of the earth, 1410

{*W*
{*waste*
That Woman will come oer this ~~*heath*~~ *to save thee.* 1411

)}
(He pauses & looks at Herberts staff—} ~~*ha! what is here & carved*~~

Ha! what is here! & carved by her own hand (reads upon the 1412
staff

"I am eyes to the blind, saith the Lord. 1413

He that puts his trust in me shall not fail." 1414

Yes, be it so;—repent & be forgiven— 1415

God & that staff are now thy only guides. 1416

{*M*
(He leaves Her: on the ~~*Heath*~~ {*moor)*

78

Scene, an eminence—a Beacon on the top

Lacy, Wallace, Lennox, &c &c

Several of the *But*
Band (confusedly) *Patience* ~~*but patience*~~

One of the Band — — — *Curses on that Traitor Oswald!* 1417

Our Captain made a prey to foul device! 1418

1405 *dash after* Mercy! *del*
1407 judgment.
1408 blessèd that] this *rev to* that
1411 come *over* o'er *miswritten (Dora)* o'er
!}
1412 hand:}
1414 fail!"
1416/1417 *parens added then del around stage dir, and* Moor—
Scene, an Eminence, a Beacon on the summit *inserted*
1417 Patience! Traitor, Oswald!—
1418 device!—

1411 The capital in the revision was added by JC, as was the capital in stage direction at foot of page.

Len: (to Wal:) I would have spoken out some three months gone
But that I'd rather have a nest of vipers [1423]
Between my breast-plate and my skin than know
This ~~Rivers~~ was my enemy
Oswald
Lacy: — — — — — — — We have been fooled
~~Wal: (To Len~~:) But for the motive—
Wal
~~Len~~: — — — — — — — — Natures such as his
Spin motives out of their own bowels ~~Wallace~~ Lacy
I learnt this when I was a Confessor—— [1429]
I know him well, there needs no other motive
Than that most strange incontinence in crime
Oswald
Which haunts this ~~Rivers~~—Power is life to him
And breath and being; where he cannot govern [1433]
He will destroy—you know he hates us all
Confusion
Lacy To have been trapped like moles! ~~Damnation~~!
Wal: — — — — — — — — — — Peace!
{~~Len~~
{Nor: He is a guilty man—I have often heard
Len
Dark rumours of some strange and heinous crime
Which he committed in his youth.

His Tool the Wandering Beggar ~~told me all~~

having first

Len to
Wal: *~~I would have spoken out some three months gone~~*

Bespoken my protection, told me all

But that I'd rather have a nest of vipers
Between my breast-plate & my skin, than know
This Oswald was my enemy.

Lacy — — — — — — We have been fooled

But for the motive

Wal: *— — — — — — Nature's such as his*
Spin motives out of their own bowels, Lacy
I learnt this when I was a Confessor—
I know him well, there needs no other motive
Than that most strange incontinence in crime
Which haunts this Oswald. Power is life to him
And breath & being, where he cannot govern
He will destroy— ~~You know he hates us all~~

[ ] [?]

~~*Lacy* *To have been trapped like* [*?moles*]*! confusion!*~~

~~He wrecks not~~

~~*Wal*~~ — — — — — — — — — — — — — — — ~~*Peace*~~

~~often~~

~~*Len:* *He is a guilty Man—I have*~~ ^ ~~*heard*~~
~~*Dark rumours of some strange & heinous crime*~~

~~which he~~

~~*Which he committed in his youth*~~ *~~early days~~*

~~[ ]~~ *~~(to Len)~~* — — — — — — ~~*You knew him*~~

Len (to
Wallace) *His Tool, the wandering Beggar, made last night* 1419
A plain confession, such as leaves no doubt, 1420
Knowing what otherwise we know too well, 1421
That she revealed the truth. Stand by me now; 1422
For, Friends, I'd rather have a nest of {*v* / *Vipers*} 1423
Between my breast-plate & my skin, than make 1424
Oswald my special enemy, if you ~~deny me~~ 1425
Deny me your support.

Lacy *— — — — — — We have been fooled* } ⁄ 1426
But for the motive?
Wal *— — — — — Natures such as his* 1427
Spin motives out of their own bowels; Lacy, 1428
I {*'d* / *learnt*} *this when I was a Confessor.* ⁄ 1429
I know him well; there needs no other motive 1430
Than that most strange incontinence in crime 1431
Which haunts this Oswald. Power is life to him 1432
And breath & being; where he cannot govern, 1433
He will destroy. 1434a

1428 *semicolon del to comma* Lacy!

1419–1423, 1426–1427 See notes to ll. 1859–1866 and to ll. 2137–2140.

~~Osw~~ *You knew him*
Wal: *(to Len:) ~~You knew this Rivers, as you say, in Syria~~?*
In Siria . . ~~h~~
Yes, ~~& wh~~ e ~~dispis~~
where he dispised alike
Len: *~~I knew him there — he did despise alike~~*
Mohammedon and christian—

[43^v]

L{acy / en} *I have noticed*
~~Nor~~: *— — — — — ~~I have noticed~~*
~~That when the name of God is spoken of~~ [1438]
in *sudden*
~~A most strange blankness overspreads his face~~
one of the Band *(in another part of the stage)*
Plague on your tongues! I have a dagger here
Sharp as an adder's tooth
Len: *(~~to Nor:~~) — — — — ~~Aye, there you have it~~*
~~Yet~~
~~Yet reasoner as he is~~, his pride has built [1440]
Yet reasoner as he is *his*
Some uncouth superstition of its own
Wal: *I do not understand you*
Len: *— — — — — — — Once he headed*
A band of pirates in the Norway seas
And when the King of Denmark summoned him
To the oath of fealty, I well remember [1445]
'Twas a strange answer that he made, he said
"I hold of spirits, and the sun in heaven"

20b In the revision, the "e" in "noticed" was added late.
21/22 The "in" in the margin is a direction to the (1841) copyist.

79

In ~~Syria~~? Palestine?

{T
Len *— — — ~~Yes~~, {where he ~~was~~ despised alike*

{ om
Mah{[?a]mmedon & Christian

Lacy To have been trapped like moles
There is no crime from which this Man would shrink
Lacy *— — — — — — — — ~~I have noticed~~*
He wrecks not human law, & ~~I have~~ noticed
often
That ^ when the name of God is ~~m[ ]tioned~~ uttered

Lacy *— — — To have been trapped like moles!—* 1434b
Yes, you are right, we need not hunt for motives: 1435
There is no crime from which this Man would shrink; 1436
He wrecks not human law; & I have noticed 1437
That often, when the name of God is uttered, 1438

A sudden blankness overspreads his face. 1439
{P his pride
Len: *Yet, reasoner as he is, {~~pride~~ has built* 1440
Some uncouth superstition of its own. 1441
have seen traces of it 1442a
Wal: *I ~~do not understand you~~*
Lennox
~~Lacy~~ *— — — — — — — Once he headed* 1442b
{N
A band of Pirates in the {[?]orway seas; 1443
And, when the King of Denmark summoned him 1444
{O
To the {oath of fealty, I well remember, 1445
'Twas a strange answer that he made; he said 1446
{S
"I hold of Spirits, & the {sun in heaven." 1447

1434b *dash del*
1435 for *miswritten, recopied above (Dora) and below line (JC)*
1437 wrecks *then* w *del as MS. 3*
1438 *first comma omitted*
1442a *as MS. 3, rev as MS. 3 but* it.
1444 *no comma*
1445 oath
1446 *no apos* said,

Lacy
~~*Wal*~~*: He is no mad-man*
Wal ——————A most subtile Doctor
Were that man who could draw the line that parts
Pride & her daughter cruelty from madness
F Fit to be scourged not [?pitied]—
~~*Wal*~~ *Lacy*
~~*Len*~~*: —————— ~~Wallace~~! restless minds*
Such minds as find amid their fellow men [1452]
No heart that loves them, none that they can love
Will turn, perforce, and seek for sympathys
In dim relations to imagined beings

[44^r]

One of the Band } *What if he mean to offer up our Captain* [1456]
An expiation, and a sacrifice
To those infernal fiends?
——————————I call on you
Wal: My friends I call on you to swear, that if
The event should be as Lennox has ~~foretold~~ declared
That heart of his shall have as many wounds [1460]
As there are daggers here
Lacy ——————————What need of swearing!
One of the Band } *Let us away*
Another ————Away!
a Third ——————Hark how the horns

33–34 "Lacy" in the revision is a correction of "Wallace" in l. 33b. On the recto of a slip of paper pasted onto 42^r is a revision:

He is no madman a most subtile doctor
Were that Man who could draw the line that parts
Pride & her daughter cruelty from madness
That should {—
Fit to be scourged {& not pitied

Lacy He
~~[———]~~ [? ~~It~~]‸*is no madman.*

Lacy. *He is no madman.*
Wall *A most subtle doctor* 1448
Were that man, who could draw the line
that parts 1449
Pride and her daughter, Cruelty, from Madness 1450
That should be scourged, not pitied. Restless minds, 1451

{*R*
Wal — — — — — ~~*Lacy*~~/ {*restless minds,*
Such minds as find amid their fellow-men 1452
No heart that loves them, none that they can love, 1453
Will turn perforce & seek for sympathy 1454
In dim relation to imagined Beings. 1455
One of the
Band *What if he mean to offer up our Captain* 1456
An expiation & a sacrifice 1457
To those infernal fiends? 1458a

80
Wal — — — — — — — — ~~*I call on you*~~
~~*Now swear my friends*~~
~~*My friends, I call on you to swear that if*~~
Now if the event 1458b
~~*The event should be as Lennox has declared*~~
Should be as Lennox has fortold, then swear, 1459
~~*That heart of his shall have as many wounds*~~
My friends, his heart shall have as many wounds 1460
As there are daggers here.
Lacy — — — — — — — — *What need of swearing?* 1461
One of
the band *Let us away!*
Another — — — — *Away!*
a Third — — — — — — *Hark! how the horns,* 1462

1450 Madness *over illeg eras (Dora)*
{M
1451 {minds,
{M
1452 {minds
1459 foretold,
1461 swearing!—
1462 away!— . . . Away!— horns,] Horns

1448–1451a The entire pasteover is in JC's hand.
1451b The capital is JC's.

46 *Of those scotch rovers echo through the vale*
47 *Lacy* *Stay you behind and when the sun is down*
48 *Light up this beacon*
One of the Band — — — — — *You shall be obeyed* [1465]

(They go out together)

[III.v] *Scene the Wood on the edge of the heath*
1 *Mor (alone) Deep, deep and vast, vast beyond human thought*
2 *Yet calm—I could believe that there was here*
3 *The only quiet heart on earth— In terror*

[44ᵛ]

4 *Remembered terror there is love and peace* [1469]

(Enter Rivers)

5 *Riv:* *Ha! my dear ~~friend~~ [Captain] !*
Mor: *(with a faint smile) — — ~~Rivers~~ [Oswald]! I am happy*
6 *to meet with you again*
Riv: — — — — — — — *Alone I see*
7 *~~We may be merry now~~*
~~Mor~~: — — — — — *~~We may be happy~~*
8 *~~Riv~~:* *You have done your duty*
I had hopes which now [1472]
9 *I feel that you will justify*
Mor: — — — — — — — — *I had fears*
10 *Which now I feel are vain—but 'tis my wish*
11 *To be alone and therefore we must part*
12 *Riv:* *Nay then—I am mistaken—There's a weakness* [1476]
13 *About your ~~heart~~ [Still]— you talk of solitude*
14 *Ask yourself if you fear a human face*

Of those Scotch Rovers, echoe thro' the {v Vale. 1463

Lacy *Stay you behind;{, & when the sun is down* 1464
Light up this beacon.
One of Band *—————— You shall be obeyed.* 1465
(They go out together)

Scene the Wood on the edge of the heath.

Mar: (alone) *Deep, deep & vast, vast beyond human thought,* 1466
Yet calm—I could believe, that there ~~were~~ as here 1467
The only, quiet heart on earth. In terror, 1468
Remembered, terror, there is ~~love &~~ peace & rest. 1469

Enter Oswald.

~~*Enter Oswald*~~

Osw *Ha! my dear Captain.*

Mar: *—————— Oswald, I {' am ~~happy~~ not prepared* 1470a
F} r} T} o} meet ~~with~~ ing you ~~again~~ soon.

81

Osw *————————— Alone, I see;* 1471b
You have done your duty. I had hopes, which now 1472
I feel that you will justify.
Mar: *————————— I had fears,* 1473
From which I have freed myself—, 1474a
~~*Which now I feel are vain—*~~*but 'tis my wish* 1474b
To be alone, & therefore we must part. 1475
Osw *Nay then—I am mistaken. There's a weakness* 1476
About you still; you talk of solitude,— 1477
~~*Ask yourself if you fear a human face—*~~

1463 those] these *rev to* those
1467 calm.— was] were *rev to* was *as MS. 3*
1470a/1471b

A later meeting, ~~not prepared~~
Oswald, ~~I am happy~~
{F {r ~~ing~~ ~~so soon~~
{~~To~~ { ~~meet with~~ you ~~again.~~
Would have been better timed.

1474a have] had *rev to* have
1477 *comma del as MS. 3*
1477/1478a *line del as MS. 3*

1469/1470 The uncanceled stage direction is by JC.

I am your friend—
Mor: *— — — — — — Why say'st thou this to me?*
Riv: *(with an appearance of openness)*
Because you are my master, and have taught me
What there is not another living man [1481]
Had strength to teach (altering the tone of his voice)
Therefore I'll cleave to you

[45^r]

In ~~the~~ camp~~s~~ and citie~~s~~ in the wood and mountain
In evil, and in solitary pain
You still shall find that I will cleave to you
Mor: *Wherefore press this on me?*
Riv: *(resuming his former tone of openness) Because I feel* [1484]
That I am bound to you by links of adamant
rule
You have taught mankind to seek the ~~measure~~ of justice
By diving for it into their own bosoms
To day you have thrown off a tyranny
That lives but by the torpid acquiescence [1489]
Of our emasculated souls, the tyranny
Of moralists and saints and lawgivers ·}
You have obeyed the only law that ~~wisdom~~ sense
And wisdom
~~Can ever~~ recognize the immediate law
{F clear
~~Flashed~~ {from the^light of circumstances flashed
Upon an independent intellect [1496]
{r path
Henceforth new prospects ~~ought to~~ open on you {
Your faculties should grow with the ~~occasion~~ demand
(altering the tone of his voice as before)
I still will be your friend, will cleave to you [1499]

---

19 Deletion of "the" by erasure in 1799.

I am your friend. 1478a

[?]

Mar: — — — — — *Why say'st thou this* {? ~~*to me*~~*?*
Oswald — — — — — — — — *Because* 1479b

Os: (~~*with Because*~~ {~~*I*~~ ~~*you are*~~ ^~~*now in truth my*~~ ~~*my Master & have taught me*~~
[?~~*ap*~~] *You are now in truth my Master; you have taught* 1480
What there is not another living Man me 1481
& therefore gratitude 1482
Had strength to teach;— ~~*Therefore I'll cleave to you*~~
Is bold, & would relieve itself by praise. 1483
~~*In Camps & Cities, in the Wood & Mountain*~~
~~*In evil, & in solitary pain*~~
~~*You still shall find that I will cleave to you*~~
Mar *Wherefore press this on me?*
Osw — — — — — — — *Because I feel* 1484
That I am bound to you by links of adamant:
You have taught {*m* *Mankind to seek the rule of justice*
for it
By diving ~~*first*~~ *into their own bosoms.* 1487
To {- *day you have thrown off a tyranny* 1488
That lives but in the torpid acquiescence 1489
Of our emasculated {*s* *Souls, the tyranny* 1490
the worlds masters & the abstract rules 1491
Of ~~*moralists, & Saints & lawgivers, & Saints;*~~

82 *By which they hold their craft*
~~*As they uphold their craft*~~ *from age to age:* 1492
You have obeyed the only law that sense 1493
Submits to
~~*And wisdom*~~ *recognize, the immediate law* 1494
From the clear light of circumstances flashed 1495
Upon an independant Intellect. 1496
on
Henceforth new prospects open [?*to*]} *your path;* 1497
Your faculties should grow with the demand;~~*+*~~ 1498
I still will be your friend, will cleave to you 1499

1478a/1479b Why say'st thou this? *del to* What need of this assurance / At any time? & why given now?

1480 {M master; *(Dora)*

1481 another living *over illeg eras (Dora)*

1488 To day

1491 Of Moralists, and lawgivers and Saints, *del to* Of the World's Masters with the abstract rules

1492 *as MS. 3, rev as MS. 3 but* which] with *del to* which

1494 law,

1495 flashed,

1496 independa{e nt {I intellect:/.}

Through good and evil, through scorn and infamy
Mor: *I would be left alone*
Riv: *(exultingly) — — — I know your motives*
I am not of the worlds presumptuous judges
Who damn where they can neither see nor feel [1504]
In the hard-hearted pride of ignorance
I saw the matter as it was I knew——
Mor: *Wherefore this repetition?*

[45v]

Riv: *— — — — — — — — — It may be*
That some there are, squeamish, half-thinking cowards
r
Who will turn pale upon you, ~~and~~ call you murdered
And you will walk in solitude among them [1510]
A mighty evil! Bodies are like ropes

45 MH's 1799 overwriting.

{ob {o
{[?]l {iquy &

Thro' good & evil, ~~thro'~~^ scorn ~~& infamy~~, 1500
{O {t as ~~should~~ dare
{If { they ~~presume~~ to follow in your steps 1501
Mar I would be left alone.
Os — — — — I know your motives: 1502
(exultingly)
I am not of the world's presumptuous judges, 1503
Who d——, where they can neither see nor feel, 1504
In the hard-hearted pride of ignorance.
I saw the matter as it was; I knew——
{e
Mar: Wherefore this rep{itition?
Osw — — — — — — — — It may be, 1507b
That some there are, squeamish half-thinking cowards, 1508
Who will turn pale upon you, call you murderer, 1509
And you will walk in Solitude among them; 1510
~~Bodies are~~ Not with mind it fares
ct}
are}
A mighty evil!—^ Bodies^ like ropes 1511a
As with the body

1500 scorn. *then period del to comma*
1501 If they should dare to follow on your steps. *interlined as MS. 3, then first three words del to* Oft as they
1504 d——, *rev to* damn
1504/1507b *dash following* knew *del or shortened*
1509 murderer] murderers *then* s *del*
1510 solitude
1511a–1513 Not with [?] mind it fares
not with {ct
A mighty evil!—Bodies a {re like ropes
As with the body; bodies act like ropes
When interwoven, stronger by mutual strength;
By neighbourhood protected, so it is
Thanks to our Nature! 'tis not so with minds.
With minds, but Nature has her own exceptions;
Join twenty tapers of unequal height,
Yet join ten
And light them joined, and you will see the less,
Nor with brute matter absolute is the rule

then mostly del and revised versions entered in left margin:

With minds in some degree, but Nature makes
In both
Her own exceptions, makes them for our honour;
With minds but Nature makes in both exceptions,
For her own honour, among [?Ment]
makes them, among Men:
Join

then all del and clean version entered in right margin, running over to top of next page:

A mighty evil! Bodies act like ropes
When interwoven, stronger by mutual strenght
Thanks to our nature 'tis not so with minds;
Nor even with matter, absolute is the rule
Join twenty tapers of unequal height
And light them joined, & you will see the less

When interwoven, stronger by mutual strength
Thanks to our nature! tis not so with minds.
Join twenty tapers of unequal height
And light them joined and you will see the less
How 'twill burn down the taller and they all
Shall prey upon the tallest— Solitude! [1515]
The eagle lives in solitude
Mor: — — — — — — — — *Forgive me*
If I should smile at this
Riv: — — — — — — — *You will perceive it*
Fortitude is the child of enterprize [1535]
Great actions move our admiration, chiefly

When interwoven, stronger by mutual strength.
Thanks to our Nature! 'tis not so with minds.
Nor with brute matter ~~always~~ absolute is the rule
Join twenty tapers of unequal ~~length~~ height, 1512
And light them joined, & you will see the less, 1513
r ; and they all 1514
How 'twill burn down the talle~~st / Solitude~~

83

Shall prey upon the tallest. Solitude! 1515
The Eagle lives in Solitude!— 1516a
Mar — — — — — — — — *Forgive me,*
If I should smile at this.
Soon will you learn, ~~that~~ 1534b
Osw — — — — — — — — *~~You will perceive it~~*
That Fortitude is the child of {E enterprize; 1535
Great actions move our admiration, chiefly 1536

1515 Solitude!—
1516–1535 *further developed in MS. 3A, 12ᵛ and 13ʳ*
1516a/1534b *row of carets between half lines leads to note in margin:* To the Printer See the last Page of this act—Even so &c *On that page is the following revised version:*

Page 80. The Eagle lives in Solitude

Marmaduke
~~Mar~~ — — — — — — — — — Even so,
The Sparrow so on the house-top, & I
The weakest of God's creatures stand resolved
To abide the issue of my Act, alone.
~~Osw~~ Oswald
Now would you? and for ever? My young {F friend,
As time advances either we become
The prey or masters of our own past deeds.
Fellowship we must have, willing or no;
And if good Angels fail, slack in their duty
Substitutes, turn our faces where we may,
Are still forth-coming; {s Some which ^though they bear
Ill names can render no ill services,
In recompense for what themselves required.
So meet extremes in this mysterious world,
And opposites thus melt into each other.
Marmaduke
Time, since Man first drew breath, has never moved
With such a weight upon his wings as now,
~~Nor will it quickly be~~ {~~flung~~ ~~cast off~~. But they will soon be lightened—
Oswald
Aye, } Look up—
~~And~~ {C cast round you your mind's eye, & you will learn
Fortitude is the child of Enterprize

1535 That *del*

Because they carry in themselves an earnest
That we can suffer greatly
Mor: *— — — — — — — — Very true*
Riv: *Action is transitory a step a blow—*
The motion of a muscle—this way or that [1540]
'Tis done—and in the after vacancy
We wonder at ourselves like men betray'd.
Suffering is permanent, obscure and dark
And has the nature of infinity
Your drift I know not
Mor: *~~I do not understand you~~*

[46^r]

Riv: *— — — — — — — — — What if you have bid*
Eternal farewell to unmingled joy [1546]
And the light dancing of the thoughtless heart
toy
It is the ~~passion~~ of fools and little fit
For such a world as this. The wise abjure
All thoughts whose idle composition lives [1550]
In the entire forgetfulness of pain—
—I see I have disturbed you
Mor: *— — — — — — — — — — By no means*
Riv: *Compassion! pity! pride can do without them*
And what if you should never know them more.
He is a puny soul who, feeling pain [1555]
Finds ease because another feels it too.
If e'er I open out this heart of mine
It shall be for a nobler end, to teach
And not to purchase puling sympathy
——Nay you are pale
Mor: *— — — — — — It may be so.*

Because they carry in themselves an earnest
That we can suffer greatly.
[?] {*V*
Mar: ——————— {[*?*]*ery true.*
{—
Osw: *Action is transitory*{, *a step, a blow,*⌿
The motion of a muscle—this way or that—
'Tis done;⌿*&* *in the after vacancy*
{ *men*
We wonder at ourselves like {[*?one*] *betrayed:*
Suffering is permanent, obscure & dark,
{*s* {*res*
And { *ha*{*s the nature of infinity.*
Mar —*Your drift I know not.*
Osw —————— *What, if you had bid*
Eternal farewell to unmingled joy
And the light dancing of the thoughtless heart,
It is the toy of fools, & little fit
For such a world as this. The wise abjure
All thoughts, whose idle composition lives
In the entire forgetfulness of pain.
——*I see I have distrubed you.*
Mar: —————————— *By no means.*

84
Osw— *Compassion!—pity!—pride can do without them;*
And what if you should never know them more.
He is a puny soul who, feeling pain,
Finds ease because another feels it too.
If e'er I open out this heart of mine
a *end,*
a} *s* }
It shall be for {*nobler end,* {*to teach*
And not to purchase, puling sympathy.
——*Nay you are pale.*
Mar: —————— *It may be so.*

1539 *first comma omitted*
1541 'Tis done, and *over illeg eras (Dora)*
1545 *first half line as MS. 3, del to* Truth—& I feel it. What{! ,
1547 heart;
1550 *comma del*
1553 Compassion,{!—
1554 more!—
1558 end,—
1559 *no comma*

1538 The capital is JC's.
1558 The final revisions are JC's.

Riv: *— — — — — — — — — Remorse,* [1560]
It cannot live with thought, think on, think on
And it will die— What? in this universe
Where the least things controul the greatest where
The faintest breath that breathes can move a world
What feel remorse where if a cat had sneezed [1565]
A leaf had fallen the thing had never been
Whose very shadow gnaws us to the vitals
Now whither are you wanding
Mor: *~~Why what is it that ails you~~? That a man*
So used to suit his language to the time
Should thus so widely differ from himself [1570]
It is most strange

[46v]

Riv: *— — — — Murder! what's in the word?*
I have no cases by me ready made
deeds
To fit all crimes. Carry him to the camp!
A foolish shallow project—you have seen
~~You have seen deeper~~—taught us that the institutes
More deeply
Of nature by a cunning usurpation [1576]
exist
Banished from human intercourse, ~~exist~~ ~~survive~~
Only in our relations to the beasts
That make the field their dwelling. If a viper snake
Crawl from beneath our feet we do not ask
A licence to destroy him, our good governors [1581]
Wise thinkers! have by forms and ceremonies
Hedged in the life of every pest and plague
~~end~~
That bears the shape of man, and for what ~~purpose~~
purpose
But to protect themselves from extirpation [1584]
~~You have burst through this flimsy superstition~~
This flimsy barrier you have overleap'd
Mor: *~~He is delivered to the judge of all things—~~*
My office is fulfilled the Man is now
Delivered to the judge of all things
— — — — — — — — — — — Dead
Riv: *~~Dead~~?*

Osw — — — — — — — — — — — — *Remorse,*
It cannot live with thought; think on, think on,
And it will die.—What? {! *in this universe,*
Where the least things controul the greatest, where
The faintest breath that breathes can move a world;
What! feel remorse, where, if a cat had sneezed,
A leaf had fallen, the think{g *had never been?*
Whose very shadow gnaws us to the vitals.
Mar: Now, whither, are you wandering? That a man,
So used to suit his language to the time,
Should thus so widely differ from himself—
It is most strange.
Osw: — — — — — — *Murder! ~~what's in the~~* [an abused] *word* {?/!
I have no cases by me ready made
To fit all deeds. Carry him to the Camp!
A foolish shallow project;—you have seen

85

More deeply, taught us that the institutes
Of Nature, by a cunning usurpation
Banished from human intercourse, exist
Only in our relations to the beasts
That make ~~their~~ field their dwelling. If a snake
Crawl from beneath our feet, we do not ask
A licence to destroy him— {: *our good governors*
Hedged in the life of every pest & plague
That bear, the shape of man; & for what purpose,
But to protect themselves from extirpation {?— / —
This flimsy barrier you have overleaped.
Mar *My Office is fulfilled—the* {M / m *an is now*
Delivered to the Judge of all things.
Osw — — — — — — — — — — — *Dead!—*

1560 *comma del to dash*
1564 breath *over illeg eras (Dora)*
1565 feel remorse *over illeg eras (Dora)*
1571 *as MS. 3 but* Murder!— . . . word!— *rev as MS. 3 but* word!—
1573 Camp!—
1574 foolish *del and* of late *inserted after* you
1576 usurpation,
1578 beasts] *del to* brutes
1580 *no comma*
1581 licence] license
1583 bear *rev to* bears
1587 *no dash*

Mor: — — *I have borne my burden to its destin* {*ed end* / *y*}
Riv: *This instant we'll return to our companions* [1589]
Oh! how I long to see their faces again.
(*Enter Matilda along with the Pilgrims*)
Marmaduke, recovered Marmaduke
Mat: *What ~~Mortimer~~! (throws herself upon his neck)*
(*The pilgrims retire*) (*after some time*)
Now thou art mine for ever—Rivers too!
You shall relate the news to my good father
Yourself shall tell it—it will be thrice welcome

[47^r]

Riv: *I fear I interrupt you* {?}
Ido — — — — — — — — *Think not so*
Mor: — — — — — — — ~~*Oh! Matilda*~~ *Idonea*
ever
That I should‸*live to see this ~~hour~~ moment—*
Mat: *Forgive me—Rivers knows it all—he knows*
Each word of that unhappy letter fell [1600]
A blood-drop {*s*} *from my heart*
Riv: — — — — — — — — *'Twas even so*
ave
Mor: *I ~~had~~ much to say but for whose ear—not thine*

---

108 MH's 1799 revision.
116 MH's 1799 insertion above caret.

Mar *I have borne my burthen to its destined end.* 1588
Osw: *This instant we'll return to our Companions!—* 1589
Oh how I long to see their faces again! 1590

Enter Idonea with Pilgrims, who {c / [?]} *ontinue their journey.*

now thou art mine for ever. 1591

Ido: *What, Marmaduke—* {! / ~~*recovered Marmaduke*~~}
And Oswald too! (to Mar) ~~*Together we will*~~ *will we go*
Now will we to my Father 1592
after ~~*Now thou art mine for ever!*~~ *(*~~*throw herself upon his neck*~~*)*
some time ~~*With these glad*~~
~~*the Pilgrims*~~ {~~*retire*~~ / [*?return*]}
~~*And*~~ ~~*Oswald too!*~~ ~~*together will we go*~~
~~*You shall relate the news to my good Father*~~
With these glad~~*some*~~ *tidings—& such proofs received* 1593a, 1594b
~~*Yourself shall tell it—it will be thrice welcome—*~~
Of his own rights restored—wh {*hi* / *s*} *gratitude* 1595b

86

To God above will make him feel for our's 1596
Osw. ~~*I fear*~~ *I interrupt you?*
Ido: — — — — — — — *Think not so.*
Mar — — — — — — — — — — — — *Idonia,* 1597
That I should ever live to see this moment!— 1598
Ido *Forgive me—Oswald knows it all—he knows* 1599
Each word of that unhappy letter fell 1600
As blood-drop~~*s*~~ *a from my heart.*
Osw: — — — — — — — — — *'Twas even so.* 1601
Mar: *I have much to say but for whose ear?—not thine.* 1602

1589 we'll] will we *rev to* we'll *(Dora)*
1590 again!—
1592 too!— Now *del to* On
1592/1593a We'll go together & such proof *del*
1593a these *rev to* the
1594b —and such proofs received *then* s *on* proofs *del*, *then all del to* , which this day hath brought;
1594b/1595b And such a proof received by my dear Father *rev to* We'll go together, &, such proof received
1595b *dash del to comma*
1596 our's] ours.
1597 *no comma*
1599 me.— he knows,
1601 blood drop
1602 say,

1592b In JC's hand.

121 *~~Of grave and serious of sublime and peaceful~~*
122 *~~—— Rivers speak to her~~*
all things
123 Riv: *A trifle ~~you~~ may soon set ~~all things~~ even*
124 Mat: *Aye, plead for me good Rivers! plead for me*
125 *You are my father's friend*
(to Mortimer) — — — Alas! you know not
126 *And never can you know how much he loved me* [1605]
127 *Twice had he been to me a father, twice*
128 *Had given me breath, and was I not to be*
129 *His daughter, once his daughter*
Mor: *— — — — — — — — Gracious heaven!*
130 Riv: *'Twas virtue 'twas a noble sacrifice*
131 Mat: *Could I behold his face, could I behold*
132 *The terrible pleading of that face of his*

[47v]

133 *And could I feel his arms and hear him pray*
134 *That I would not forsake him nor permit*
135 *My heart to abandon him in his old age (hides her face)*
136 Riv: *Indeed she could not do it*
Mor: *— — — — — — — God of justice!*
137 *She weeps, she weeps—my brain shall burn for hours* [1612]
138 *Ere I can shed a tear*

122 MH's 1799 correction.

p
Ido: *Ill can I bear that look—{Plead for me, Oswald!* 1603
plead
~~*Osw: A trifle—all things you may soon set even*~~
~~*Mar: Aye, plead for me good Oswald! plead for me*~~
Ido: ~~*Plead for me No wonder you look grave*~~
F
You are my{father's friend.
(to Mar) Alas you know not, 1604
And never <u>can</u> you know, how much he loved me. 1605
Twice had he been to me a father, twice 1606
Had given me breath, & ~~I~~ was I not to be 1607
?
His daughter, once his daughter—{could I withstand 1608

~~*Mar:*~~ *— — — — — — — — — — — ~~Gracious heaven~~ [~~?God~~]*
~~*Osw*~~ ~~*'Twas virtue, 'twas a noble sacrifice*~~
withstand
Mat ~~*Could I behold his face*~~*, could I ~~behold~~*
pleading of his face & feel his arms
The ~~terrible plead[ ]of that face of his~~
And hear his prayer that I would not forsake him
~~*And could I feel his arms & hear him pray*~~
In his old age

---

p *clasping*
His{[?]leading face, & feel his^arms, 1609
And hear his prayer that I would not forsake
him 1610
In his old age—— 1611a

~~*That I would not forsake him nor permit*~~

87
~~*My heart to abandon him in his old age*~~ *(hides her face)*
~~*Osw: Indeed she could not do it*~~
Mar *— — — — — — — — — ~~God of Justice~~*
Patience—heaven grant me patience!— 1611b
She weeps, she weeps—<u>my</u> brain shall burn for hours 1612
Ere <u>I</u> can shed a tear. 1613a

1603 Plead
1604 father's
1613a *underlining del*

1603 Revision below the line ("plead") is JC's, as is the capital in l. 1604.
1609–1611a On back of the pasteover, in MW's hand, are ll. 2226–2227:

Proof after proof pressed on me, guilt
Made evident, as seemed, by blacker guilt

Mat: *(rising) — — — — I was a woman*
139 *Shut out from every noble enterprize (breaking off*
140 *Oh! let me be forgiven!*
Mor: *— — — — — — — I do forgive thee—*
141 Mat: *But take me to your arms—this breast alas!* [1619]
142 *It throbs, and you have a heart that does not feel it*
143 Mor: *(exultingly) She is innocent (he embraces her)*
aside {W
Riv: *— — — — — — — ~~Now if I~~ {were a moralist*
144 *I should make wonderous revolutions here*
145 *It were a quaint experiment to shew*
146 *The beauty of truth (addressing himself to them)*
I see I interrupt you
147 *I shall have business with you Mortimer* [1625]
{*Hostel*
148 *Follow me to the* {*Inn*
Exit Rivers

[48r]

Mat: *— — — — — — — — — ~~Oh~~ Mortimer*
149 *This is a happy day. My father soon*
150 *Shall sun himself before his native doors*
151 *The lame, the hungry ~~shall~~ be welcome there*
will
152 Mor: *Now is this possible*
Mat: *— — — — — — — What joy for us*
153 *No more shall he complain of wasted strength* [1630]
fail
154 *Of thoughts that ~~leave him~~ and a decaying heart*
wi }
155 *His good works sha{ll be balm and life to him*
156 Mor: *This is most strange I know not what it was*
157 *But there was something which most plainly said*
158 *That thou wert innocent*

Ido:
~~Mat:~~ — — — — — — — I was a woman
rising) And balancing the hopes that are the dearest
To Womankind with duty to my father
I yielded up those ~~hopes~~, precious hopes ~~if erring~~ which ~~else~~ nought
~~Shut out from every noble enterprize.~~
On earth ~~have~~ could else have wrested from me if erring
Oh let me be forgiven.
Mar: — — — — — — — I do forgive thee.
~~Mat:~~ But take me to your arms—this breast, alas!
Ido
It throbs, & you have a heart that does not feet}l it/.
Mar (exultingly) ~~Sh~~
She is innocent. (he embraces her)
Osw (aside) — — — Were I a Moralist,
I should make wonderous rev{e ol{a utions here;
It were a quaint experiment to shew
The beauty of truth—(addressing them)
I see I interrupt you;
I shall have business with you, Marmaduke;
Follow me to the Hostel. (Exit Oswald)
Ido:
~~Mat:~~ — — — — — — — — — Marmaduke,
This is a happy day. My Father soon
Shall sun himself before his native doors;
The lame, the hungry, will be welcome there.

88
~~Mar: Now is this possible~~
~~Ido:~~
~~Mat~~: — — — — — — ~~What joy for us~~
No more shall he complain of wasted strength
Of thoughts that fail & a decaying heart;
His good works will be balm & life to him.
Mar This is most strange!—I know not what it was,
But there was something which most plainly said,
That thou wert innocent.

1613b *stage dir del* woman;
1613–1616 *further developed in MS. 3A. 12ʳ*
1614–1617 *inserted, as MS. 3, and* Shut out from every noble enterprize— *del as MS. 3*
1614 And,
1615 Father,
1616 precious hopes,
1617 me;—if erring,
1622 wondrous revelation *rev to* revolution *(Dora)*
1626 Hostel,}
1628 sun *over illeg miswriting (Dora), then rewritten (JC)*
1630 strength,
1631 fail,

Mat: — — — — — — — *How! innocent!*
159 *Oh heavens! you've been deceived*
Mor: — — — — — — — — — — *Thou art a woman*
perdition
160 *To bring ~~damnation~~ on the universe*
161 *Mat:* *Already I've been punished to the height*
162 *Of my offence (smiling affectionately)*
I see you love me still
163 *The labours of my hand are still your joy*
164 *Bethink you of that hour when on your shoulder*
(pointing to the belt on which was suspend{e/dd the)
scrip of Herbert
165 *I hung this belt*

[48v]

Mor: — — — — — — — — *Mercy of Heaven!*
(sinks against the scene
Mat: — *What ails you? (looks round in a distracted manner)*
166 *Mor:* *Oh! misery! the scrip which held his food!*
167 *And I forgot to give it back again* — }
168 *Mat:* *(returns to Mor:) How feel you now?*
Mor: — — — — — — — — *'Tis but a shooting pang—*
may
169 *I know not what I said— all ~~will~~ be well*
170 *'Tis a dull pain— I was disturbed to see you*

164/165 MH's 1799 correction.

Ido:
~~*Mat:*~~ — — — — — — — *How innocent!—* 1635
Oh heavens! you've been deceived.

Mar — — — — — — — — — — — *Thou art a* {*W* / *woman*} 1636
To bring perdition on the universe. 1637
~~*Mat:*~~ *Ido* *Already I've been punished to the height* 1638
Of my offence. (smiling affectionately)
I see you love me still, 1639
The labours of my hand are still your joy; 1640
Bethink you of the hour when on your shoulder 1641
I hung this belt. (pointing to the belt on which was suspended Herbert's scrip)

Mar: — — — — — — *Mercy of Heaven! (sinks* {)} {~~*)*~~}
Ido — — — — — — *What ails you (distractedly)* 1642

Mar *The* [*scrip* ?] *that held his food, & I forgot* 1643
To give it back again. 644a
— — — — — — — — — ~~*What ails*~~
~~*Mat:*~~ ~~*What ails you*~~*!*
~~*What ails you?*~~ ~~*looks round in the distan*~~{~~*ra*~~ / ~~*c*~~} {~~*tedly*~~ / *e*}
Ido — — — — — — *What mean your words?* 1644b
Mar *I know not what I said—all may be well;* 1645
Ido: *That smile hath life in it!*
Mar — — — — — — *This road is perilous;* 1646
I will attend you to a Cot that stands 1647
Near the wood's edge—rest there to night, I pray you: 1648
For me, I have business, as you heard, with Oswald, 1649
But will return to you by break of day. 1650
End of ~~*3rd*~~ *Act 3*

89

Ido:
~~*Mat:*~~ — — — — — — *What ails you (distractedly)*
Mor: ~~*Oh heavens!*~~ {*T* / *the scrip which held his food, & I forgot*}
~~*And I forget*~~ {*T* / *to give it back again*——}
Ido: — — — — — — *What mean your words?*
~~*Mat (to Mor) How feel you now?*~~
Mor: — — — — — — — '~~*Tis but a shooting pang*~~
I know not what I said,—all may be well—
~~*I know not what I said—all may be well*~~
'~~*T*~~{~~*was*~~ / ~~*is a dull pain—I was disturbed to see you*~~}

1636 Woman,
1641 your *over* this

1636 The capital is JC's.
At foot of page 88, the "3" following "Act" is in pencil.

Mat: ~~*Oh*~~*! you* ~~*can*~~ *smile again—* {*T* / *that*} *smile has lift*{*e*} *in it!—*

Mor: {~~*This*~~ *This* / *'Tis*} ~~*a bleak*~~ *road* ~~*across the heath*~~ [*is perilous*] *at even* {*tide* / *ing*}

[*stands*] [*not far off*]

There ~~*is*~~ *a cottage* ~~*on its skirts*~~*—I pray you*
Rest there to night, my dearest innocent!

[*dire*] [*s*]

We shall do well—I had ~~*a*~~ *thought*{*s*} *indeed—*

[*woodlands edge*]

I will attend you to the ~~*edge of the heath*~~
You'll see the cottage there—for me—I have business
With my friend Rivers——

Mat: — — — — — — — — *On the morrow early*
I shall expect you—Will you look again
As you were wont to do—The Heavens preserve you!

Exeunt together

[49r]

Act 4th

[IV.i] *Scene 1st A desolate prospect—a ridge of rocks rises at the bottom of the stage, an old chapel on the summit of one of them;—the moon behind the rocks—the night stormy—the irregular sound of a bell is heard— Herbert enters in the depth of the stage much exhausted; he crosses the stage with difficulty——*

[*it is not rung by human hand*]

Her: *That bell*—~~*if I ha*~~{~~*ve*~~ / ~~*d strength—to reach it—oh*~~}*!*

~~*But by*~~ {~~*me*~~ / ~~*w*~~[?]} [*But by the wind— in Mercy guided me*]

(Stretching out his hand)

[*Oh but that I had strength to reach the place*]

This wall of rocks—and the sound never nearer—
Hear me ye men upon the cliffs that pray

[*Daily before that Chapel's Altar*]

~~*To God the father of all mercy,*~~ ^ *—hear me—*
My child—my child—dark—dark—I faint—this wind [1657]

---

171 Capitalization of "that" was done in 1799.
1 MH's 1799 overwriting.

~~is~~
~~Mat:~~ ~~You smile again~~ ~~That smile hath life in it!~~
Ido That smile hath life in it!
~~Mar:~~ ~~This road is perilous at eventide~~
This road is perilous
~~There stands a Cottage not far off—I pray you~~
I will attend you to a Cot that stands
~~Rest there tonight my dearest Innocent!~~
Near the wood's edge—rest there tonight I pray you
~~We shall do well. I had dire thoughts indeed~~
For me I have business as you heard, with Oswald.
~~—I will attend you to the woods edge~~
by
~~Farewell my dear~~ But will return to you at } break
~~You'll see the Cottage there—for me I have business~~
of day.
~~With my friend Oswald—~~
Ido:
~~Mat:~~ — — — — — — — ~~On the morrow early~~
~~I shall expect you. Well you look again~~
~~As you were wont to do. The Heavens preserve you.~~
Ex together.

90

Act 4.th

Scene—A d {esol / [?]} ate prospect—a ridge of rocks ~~rises~~ a/
Chapel on the summit of one—Moon behind the rocks—
Night stormy—irregular sound of a bell—Her: enters
exhausted—

{C
{chapel bell in mercy seemed to guide me, 1651
Her: That ~~bell! it is not rung by human hand~~
But now it mocks my steps; its fitful stroke 1652
~~But by the wind—in mercy guided me~~
{carce} be
Can ~~Is~~ s { ure } ly ~~not~~ the work of human hands. 1653
~~Oh but that I had strength to reach the place!~~
Hear me, Ye Men, upon the Cliffs, if such 1654
~~This wall of rocks, & the sound never ne~~arer
There be who pray nightly before the Altar. 1655
~~Hear me, ye men upon the cliffs that pray~~
but
Oh, that I had ^ strength to reach the place! 1656
~~Daily before that Chapels Altar—hear me~~
My Child—my child—dark, dark—I faint/—this wind/— 1657

---

in scene setting: of rocks. A
1651 Chapel-bell
1653 Is surely not *del to* Doth [*del to* Can] scarcely be
1655 pray *over illeg del (Dora)*
1656 the place! *del and repeated above line*
1657 dark— dark—

This / *These* *stifling* *wind* / *blasts* *(~~he sinks down in a corner of the stage~~*
God help— (he sinks down)

Enter Robert at another part of the stage

Rob: ~~*Better this*~~
Better this
fence
Than ~~have~~ a case of dungeon walls to ~~screen~~ a man
From the rough visitation of the sky
These aching fingers (a mourning voice is heard)
Ha! what sound is that
Trees creaking in the wind send forth such noises,
&— *k* / *fitful*
But all is naked here— That ~~tin~~ ~~gling~~ bell
~~*Is it rung by ev*~~
~~*It half confounds a man perchance these rocks*~~—
Who rings it? 'twould confuse a saint in prayer
Again — I never heard a sound so like
~~*lying*~~ —
A human groan— Ha! what is ^ here— / *Poor Man*
~~*Poor man! what has befallen you? speak my friend*~~

[49ᵛ]

Murdered! alas! speak, speak, I am your friend—
lost
No answer: hush, ~~poor~~ wretch he lifts his head [1669]
And lays it to his heart (kneels by him) I pray you speak
In very sorrow of my heart I pray you,
I know not what has harm'd you— hush—again
O heaven——
Her: *(in a feeble voice) A stranger has done this to me*
And in the arms of a stranger I must die, [1672]

---

15 MH's 1799 correction.

These stifling blasts—God help me! 1658a

Enter ~~Robt~~ Eldred

{*Eldred*
{*Robt* — — — — — — — — — — — *Better this* 1658b
{*T* *for shelter.—* 1660
{*than a case of dungeon walls ~~to fence a Man~~*
~~From the rough visitation of the sky~~
These aching fingers—(a moaning voice is heard)
Ha! what sound is that? 1661b
(but none are here) 1662
Trees creaking in the wind send ~~forth such noises~~,
Send forth such noises—& that weary 1663
~~here~~ */* } { *~~T~~* *~~Chapel~~*
~~But all is naked here~~ — } *~~&~~* { *~~that fitfull~~ bell—*
Surely some evil Spirit abroad to night 1664
ing ? } { *~~in~~*
~~Who~~ rings it, } *'~~twould confuse a Saint~~* {*~~it~~* [?] *~~prayer~~.* 1665
Is *stop*
~~Again—I never heard a sound so like~~
And that! what is it never was sound so like 1666
A human groan. / Ha! what is here? Poor Man 1667

91
Murdered!—alas! speak, speak, I am your friend.— 1668
{*an*
No answer—hush—lost wretch, he lifts his h{*ead* 1669

And lays it to his heart—(kneels to him) I pray you speak ;}? 1670
What has befallen you? 1671a
~~In very sorrow of my heart I pray you,~~
~~I know not what has harmed you hush again~~
~~O heaven~~

Her: *(feebly) A stranger has done this* ,} *~~to me~~* 1671b

And in the arms of a stranger I must die, .} 1672

1658b bare rock, *added at end of line*
1658b/1660 Tho' it were tottering over a man's head,
1660 tight *inserted before* case *comma del after* walls shelter— *then dash del*
[1661a] *first half line del to* From such rough dealing
1662 *as MS. 3 but no comma, rev as MS. 3 but* wind—
1663 *interlined as MS. 3 but* bell!

1664 *interlined:* Some evil spirit is abroad {to / [?]night *then* Surely *prefixed and* is *del*

1665 Who rings it? 'twould conf {ound / use a Saint in prayer. *then first phrase del to* Who rings it *then* Is ringing it *entered in margin, then all del to* Is ringing it—'twould stop a Saint in prayer,
1666 *as MS. 3, rev as MS. 3 but* that—what is it?
1667 groans. *with* s *del* Man—

1668 Murdered! alas! speak—speak, I am your friend— :}

1663/1664 The capital "T" is JC's.

God be praised!—Rob: Cheerly, cheerly, are you wounded?
Her:—*I have a daughter—carry a blessing to her*
Tell her that she will never see me more
Rob: *Come let me raise you up, indeed, indeed*
This is a dismal place—well—that is well—
We shall do well—I feel you are quite stout
hut
I was afraid—my ~~cottage~~—(draws him gently off the stage
is not far off

[IV.ii] *Scene a room in the {Hostel / Inn}*
Mortimer and Rivers

Mor: *But for Matilda I have cause to think* [1677]
That she is innocent—
Leave that awhile
Riv: *(collecting himself) ~~I shall be able~~*

~~God be praised!~~ *so:* 1673a
Eldred Nay, think not

~~*Robt.*~~ — — — — — {*~~e~~* / *~~Cheerily,~~*} { — *~~you~~* *~~cheerily, are you wounded~~* ?} *!*

Her: *Come, let me raise you up,* {; *indeed, indeed,* 1673b

[?] {rais / es}
This is a dismal place—well—that is well— him) 1674
~~We shall do well—I feel you are quite stout~~

too fearful—~~but~~ —} *—take me for your guide,* 1675

I was afraid { — *my hut, is not far off, (draws him gently* 1676
And your support *off the stage)*

~~a room~~
Scene, ~~Mar~~ in the Hostel—Mar & Os:)
a room

Mar *But for Idon*{e / ia}*!—I have cause to think* 1677
That she is innocent. 1678a
~~*Osw*~~ — — — — — *What stronger cause*
For stifling feeling as the foe to truth
~~*Os*~~ — — — — — — — *~~Leave~~ that ~~to me awhile~~* 1678b

---

1673 Nay, think not so: cheerily—are you wounded? *then last phrase del to* nay think not so *then all following first* so *del to* come, let me raise you up:
1673b Come, . . . indeed, *as MS. 3 without first comma, then all del*
1675 *no comma*
in scene setting: room *blotted and rewritten (JC)*
1678b–1685 *full transcription of MS. 4 may be helpful (the passage is further developed in MS. 3A, 13^v):*

Oswald
Leave that thought awhile,
To keep the place which in your heart it took
What stronger cause
As one of those beliefs lovers lock up
For stifling feeling as the foe to truth
oft times nothing better
As precious pearls though they perhaps be nought
Has ere existed since the world began
Than feathers hung upon their points of passion.
Than you within these two days past have had.
This day's event has laid on me the duty
Innocent! leave that treacherous thought awhile,
Of opening out my story; you must hear it,
And listen to my story.— In my youth
And without further preface.— In my Youth, *then all del*

and revised in margin:

Leave that thought awhile,
As one of those beliefs ~~Lovers lock up~~ which in their hearts
Lovers lock up as ~~precious pearls~~, tho' oft no better
Than feathers clinging to their points of passion.
This day's event has laid on me the duty
Of opening out my story. &c—

1676/1677 In the stage direction, "a room" below line is JC's.

~~To throw [?] some light on this part~~ of my history
And listen to my story
~~r~~
~~You are unacquainted with — I am a murdered~~
~~(seeing his astonishment~~)
~~Ay just as I expected~~ — In my youth

[50[r]]

s
I was the pleasure of all heart[?] —the darling [1687]
Of every tongue—as you are now—you've heard
That I embarked for Syria—on our voyage
Was hatched
A
~~I was convinced~~ a foul conspiracy ~~was hatched against~~
A & I believed
~~Was laid~~ against my honour that the captain
its lay
Was ~~the~~ prime agent—well—we ~~were~~ becalmed—
Until— Ship had failed
The water of the ~~vessel was exhausted~~— [1694]
vei
I felt a double fever in my [?brai]ns
Yet
My rage suppressed itself—to a deep stillness
Did my Pride tame my pride—for many days
Beneath the burning sky on the dead sea
I brooded o'er my injuries—deserted [1699]
By man and nature—if a breeze had blown
It might have found its way into my heart
And I had been—no matter—do you mark me?

---

3 Deletion of illegible word by erasure.
4 The "murdered" was corrected in 1799.
6, 13 MH's 1799 corrections.

Has ere existed since the world began
~~*And listen to my story*~~
-*Th*{*a* / *en*} *you, within these two days past, ha*{*ve* / [?]} *had.*
-*Innocent,* {*!* / —}{*L* / *leave*} *that treacherous thought awhile,*
In my youth,
-*And listen to my story.* 1684b
-*Except for that abatement which is paid* 1685
~~*I was the pleasure of all hearts—the darling*~~
-*By envy as a tribute to desert,* 1686
-*I was the pleasure of all hearts—the darling* 1687
Of every tongue—as you are now.+You've heard+ 1688
That I embarked for Syria—on our voyage 1689

92 *Was hatched*
~~*among the Crew w*~~
Among the Crew was hatched against my honour 1690
~~*Was hatched a foul conspiracy, as I believed*~~
A foul conspiracy in which plot
~~*Against my honour, & that*~~ *the Captain* 1691
Was {, *I believed* / ~~*the*~~} *prime*{*A* / *agent*}— *The wind fell* ~~*Well—we lay becalmed*~~ 1692
We lay becalmed week after week—until 1693
~~*Until*~~ {*T* / *the*} *water of the* ~~*Ship*~~ *vessel* {*was* / *had*} ~~*failed*~~ *exhausted* 1694
I felt a double fever in my {*veins* / *brain*} 1695
Yet rage suppressed itself;—to a deep stillness 1696
Did my Pride tame my pride—for many days 1697
On a dead sea beneath the burning Sky 1698
~~*Beneath the burning sky on the dead sea*~~
I brooded o'er my injuries—deserted 1699
By man & nature—if a breeze had blown 1700
It might have found its way into my heart 1701
And I had been—no matter—do you mark me? 1702

1686 desert{, / —}
1687 *dash del to comma*
1689 Syria{. / —}{O / on}
1690 Among the Crew was hatched against my honour *del to* Was hatched among the Crew a foul Conspiracy
1691 *del to* Against my honour, in the which our Captain
1692 believed, {A / agent} *dash del to period* fell;
1693 *dash del to comma*
1694 exhausted;
1695 veins,
1697 pride;—
1698 beneath the *del to* under a sky
1699 *dash del to comma*
1700 nature;—

1678b/1684b The "ve had" of "have had" is JC's.

Quick
~~What crime~~ ~~On~~ to the point—surely some untold
Mor: *~~Your crime? what was your~~ crime?*
Doth haunt your memory
Patiene further
Riv: — — — — — — — *Hear me ~~further~~ ~~patiently~~*
in silence did
One day ~~at noon~~ we drift~~ed silently~~ at noon
By a bare rock, narrow and white and bare [1706]
There was no food, no drink, no grass, no shade
No tree nor jutting eminence, nor form
ni
Ina{[?]mate, large as the body of man
Nor any living thing whose span of life
Might stretch beyond the measure of one moon, [1711]
To dig for water ~~we landed~~ there—the captain landed
With troop
~~And~~ a small ~~party~~ of which myself was one
e
The}re I reproach'd him with his treachery
rose
His temper ~~was imperious, and he struck me~~—
Imperious at all times^

[50v]

He struck me on the spot
~~A blow~~!^I would have killed him, ~~but my comrades~~
And put an end to his insolence, but my comrades
Rush'd in between us—~~They all hated him~~—
then did I insist
~~And they insisted~~—I was stung to madness
They all hated him &^
That we should leave him there, alive—we did so [1720]
Mor: *And he was famished?*
Naked {the
Riv: — — — — — — *'~~T~~was {a spot*
Methinks I see it now—how in the sun
Its stony surface glittered like a shield:
It swarmed with shapes of life scarce visible;

26 MH's 1799 correction.

if any
Mar: *Quick—to the point—~~surely some~~ untold crime* 1703
Doth haunt your memory
Osw: *— — — — — — — Patience, hear me further* 1704
One day in silence did we drift at noon 1705
By a bare rock, narrow & white & bare 1706
No food was there, no drink, no grass, no shade 1707
No tree nor jutting eminence, nor form 1708
Inanimate, large as the body of man 1709
lot
Nor any living thing whose ~~span~~ of life 1710
Might stretch beyond the measure of one moon; 1711
on the spot
To dig for water ~~there~~ ,} {t *.* } {*The Captain ~~landed~~* 1712

Landed *93*
{*w* {*being*
^{*With a small troop ~~of which~~, myself* {*was one:* 1713
There I reproached him with this treachery. 1714
Imperious at all times his temper rose; 1715
& that instant had I
He struck me; ~~on the spot, I would have~~ killed him, 1716
And put an end to his insolence, but my comrades 1717
Rushed in between us—then did I insist/ 1718
{(*A*
~~They~~ {*all hated him & I was stung to madness* } 1719
That we should leave him there, alive—we did so. 1720
Mar: *And he was famished?*
Osw *— — — — — — Naked was the spot;* 1721
Methinks I see it now—how in the sun 1722
Its stony surface glittered like a shield. 1723
It swarmed with shapes of life scarce visible;

1704 memory. further!
1706 narrow, and white, and bare;
1707 shade,
1708 tree,
1709 *comma eras* man,
1711 moon.
1712 *no punct*
1715 times,
1718 *dash del to colon following* us
1720 alive;—
1725 beings *del to* creatures *(?WW)*
1727 Or] Nor
1723–1727 *rewritten in margin (WW):*

Yet swarming with ephemeral life, enough
To testify lifes miserable power:
Th}
Al}ere was he left, alone but for Companions
Not one of which while breath remained could help [?] him
Or
~~Nor~~ mourn him dead—

41 *And in that miserable place we left him—* [1724]
42 *A giant body mid a world of beings*
help while alive
43 *Not one of which could ~~give~~ him ~~any aid~~*
44 *~~Living or dead.~~ Or mourn him dead*
Mor: *— — — — A man by men ~~deserted~~ cast off*
45 *Not buried in the sand—not dead nor dying*
46 *But standing, walking—stretching forth his arms*
47 *In all things like yourselves but in the agony* [1730]
48 *With which he called for mercy— and even so*
49 *He was forsaken*
Riv: *— — — — — There is a power in sounds*
50 *The groans he uttered might have stopped the boat* [1733]
51 *That bore us through the water*
Say, you returned
Mor: *— — — — — — — — — ~~Rivers~~ — ~~Rivers~~*
52 *I ought to tear you piece-meal*

[51r]

53 Riv: *Some scoffed at him with hellish mockery* [1736]
54 *And laugh'd so loud it seem'd that the smooth sea*
55 *Did from some distant region echo us*
56 Mor: *We are all of one blood our veins are filled*
57 *At the same poisonous fountain*
Riv: *— — — — — — — — 'Twas an island*
Only sufferance
58 *~~But~~ by ~~permission~~ of the winds and waves,*
Which with their foam could bury it at will
59 *I know not how he perish'd, but the calm* [1742]
60 *The same dead calm continued many days*
61 Mor: *But then he was a traitor— these expedients*

miserable
And in that ~~visible~~ place we left him—
A giant body—mid a world of beings
Not one of which could help him while alive,
Or mourn him dead.
Mar: — — — — — *A man by men cast off,*
Left without burial! nay, not dead nor dying,
~~Not buried in the—sand—not dead nor dying~~
But standing, walking, stretching forth his arms,
ourselves but in
In all things like ~~ourselves~~, ~~but in~~ the agony
for mercy; and, even so
With which he called ~~for mercy—& even so~~
?
He was forsaken!
?

94

Osw — — — — *There is a power* {*in* / *of sounds:*
cries
The ~~groans~~ he uttered might have stopped the boat
u
That bore i{*s thro' the water*——
{*Y*
Mar — — — — — — — — ~~*Say*~~ {*you returned*
Upon that dismal hearing—did you not?
~~I ought to tear you piece-meal~~
Osw *Some scoffed at him with hellish mockery,*
And laughed so loud it seemed that the smooth sea
re
Did from some distant {[*?gr*]*gion echo us.*
Mar: *We all are of one blood, our veins are filled*
At the same poisonous fountain!
Osw: — — — — — — — — — *'Twas an island*
Only by sufference of the winds & waves,
Which with their foam could bury it at will.
I know not how he perished; but the calm,
The same dead calm, continued many days:
{*him*}
{~~*is*~~ *own crimes had brought* {[?] *his*} *to this doom*
Mar: *But ~~then h~~*{*~~e was a traitor—these expedients~~*
His wickedness prepared it these expedients

1730 ourselves,
1731 for *inserted with caret (JC)* and—even so—
1741 sufferance
1744 days.
1745 But then he was a traitor: these expedients *then all but first two words del to* his crime had brought on him this doom *then* his *del and* But then *del to* But his own
1746 His wickedness prepared it; these expedients *interlined, with* prepared it *del and rewritten*

1730–1731 Revisions are in JC's hand.
1734 The capital is JC's.

{Yet ours is not
Are terrible— {*But* ^ *the fault* ~~*is not ours*~~
Riv: *The man was famished and* ~~*he*~~ *was innocent* [1748]
Impossible ~~*it* [?*could*] *not* [?*be*]~~
Mor: ~~*False, false by all the fiends in hell*~~ —
The man had never wronged me
Riv: — — — — — — — — — — — ~~*The man*~~
~~*Had never wronged me*~~.
~~*Banish the thought & let your*~~
Banish the thought & {*l* {*your* ~~*mind have*~~
Mor: — — — — — {*Let* {*not* ~~*the thought trouble you*~~
mind have peace
His guilt was marked—these things could never be [1751]
Were we not instruments in ~~*the hands of*~~ *heaven* {*s*} —
own hand
For some good purpose
Riv: *I had been deceived*
from that hour
Mor: *And the miserable* ~~*victim was heard of*~~ *no more*
man no more was heard of

[51ᵛ]

Riv: *I had been betrayed*
{*Death*
Mor: *O* {*hell! and he found no deliverance*
Riv: *The crew received me gladly, 'twas a plot*
lo} {*hed*
To rid them of a master whom they h{*at*{*ed*
So *but*
~~*Well*~~ *—we pursued our voyage—and when we landed* [1760]
~~*departed*~~
The tale was spread abroad—my power ~~*shrunk from*~~
& schemes *at once* ~~*me*~~
Shrunk from me plans &}
~~*My plans of heroism*~~, *my* { *lofty hopes*
All vanished—I could not support the change,
I sunk into despair; Do you attend?
Mor: *(with a hurried manner, as if recovering from*
a fit of deep ~~*ab*~~*sence*

Are terrible. Yet our's is not the fault. 1747
Osw: The man was famished, & was innocent! 1748
Mar: Impossible!
Osw: ——— The man had never wronged me. 1749
~~unwarrantable thought; in heaven~~
Mar: Banish the ~~thought, & let your mind have peace~~
thought, crush it! & be at peace. 1750
~~In heaven~~ and
His guilt was marked—these things could never be 1751
~~Were there not eyes that see of higher Powers~~
~~Were we not instruments in heavens own hand~~
~~of higher Powers~~
~~For some good purpose~~. [~~?~~]

95 ends
Were there not eyes that see & for good ~~purpose~~ 1752
Where ours baffled.
are
Osw: —————— I had been deceived. 1753
miserable
Mar: And from that hour the^man ~~no more was heard of?~~ 1754
No more was heard of?
Os: —————— I had been betrayed. 1755
Mar: And he found no deliverance? 1756a

Osw ————————— The Crew
{G
{gave me a hearty welcome they were rid
~~they Instantly were glad~~
~~were [?pl]~~
Of a tyrannic Master whom they
[~~?~~]
~~Gave me a hearty welcome~~ ~~twas a plot~~
~~they~~ were rid of a ~~tyrant~~
~~To rid them of a Master whom~~
~~They [?loathed]~~ loathed
~~The tale was spread abroad—my power at once~~
So we pursued our voyage—when we landed
The tale was spread abroad my power at once
Shrunk from me, plans & schemes, & lofty hopes
gave way
All vanished. I ~~could not support the change~~
I ~~sunk into despair~~; Do you attend!
Mar: (~~hurried in manner~~—after a fit of absence)

1747 terrible.} {y Yet *apos del*
1750 crush *over illeg eras (Dora)*
1752 see, purpose *del to* ends,
1756a deliver{a ence! ? *(Dora)*

?}
79 *The crew received you* }
Riv: ——————— *The unhappy man*
80 *He had a daughter*
Mor: *(turning away)* —— *Enough, enough*
81 *Riv:* *His only child—she did not long survive it*
82 *She was a lovely maid—she had conjured me*
83 *At parting never to forsake her father*
84 *To stand by him in all extremities*
85 *The tidings reached her; from that very time*
86 *She neither saw nor heard as others do*

[52r]

87 *But in a fearful world of her own making*
88 *She lived—cut off from the society*
89 *Of every rational thing—her father's skeleton*
90 *Mor:* *She shall not die—no I will have her curse*
91 *Here at my heart*
Riv: ———— *You do not listen to me*
Nay command yourself
92 *Mor:* *It is a dismal night—how the wind howls!* [1765]
93 *Go on*
hid my head with
Riv: —— ~~*Well*~~ *I* ~~*betook me to*~~ *a convent*
94 *And dozed away the time—how long I know not*
was no life
95 *This* ~~*would not do*~~ *for me—I was o'erthrown*
96 *But not destroyed*
You ought to have seen
Mor: —————— *The proofs,* ~~*the proofs,*~~
The guilt & touched it to the quick
97 ~~*You ought to have seen to have touch'd the guilt*~~ *the heavens*
more {*l*
98 ~~*Have*~~ *kindly dea*{*lt with me, let me be thankful*
99 *Riv:* *You have good cause*
A fresh tide of crusaders

The Crew 1756b
Gave me a hearty welcome; they had laid 1757
The plot to rid themselves, at any cost, 1758
Of a tyrannic Master whom they loathed. 1759
So we pursued our voyage: when we landed, 1760
The tale was spread abroad; my power at once 1761
Shrunk from plans & schemes & lofty hopes; 1762
?
All vanished. I gave way——Do you attend ~~*!*~~ 1763
?

Mar: *The Crew deceived you?*
Osw — — — — — — *Nay command yourself.* 1764
—
Mar: *It is a dismal night* {[?]*how the wind howls!—* 1765
~~*Go on*~~
Osw *I hid my head within a Convent,* *there* 1766
{*Lay* {*w*
{*Th*[?] *passive as a Dormouse in mid* {*Winter.* 1767
~~*And dozed away the time—how long, I know not*~~
Lay passive
at}
This} *was no life for me—I was o'erthrown,* 1768
But not destroyed. 1769a

Mar: — — — — — *The proofs, you ought to have seen*
~~*Have touched the guilt*~~ *more kindly Providend*
~~*The guilt & touched it to the quick, the elements*~~
~~*Hath*~~} *have*}
[?][?]} [?][?]} *touched*
~~*More kindly*~~ *dealt with me—let me be thankful*
Hath *(Osw) Yes*
Osw *You have goo*[ ]*ause*
A fresh tide of Cr[ ]*aders*

Mar: — — — — — *The proofs you ought to have seen* 1769b
The guilt—have touched it—felt it at your heart— 1770
As I have done.
Osw — — — — *A fresh tide of Crusaders* 1771

1759 {M / master *(Dora)*
1762 me, *inserted after* from *semicolon del to dash*
1763 Do] to *overwritten* do *(Dora)* attend!
1767 {d / Dormouse *(JC)*
1769b proofs— seen—

1767/1768 "Lay passive" is in JC's hand.

100 *Drove past the place of my retreat—three nights* [1772]
101 *Did constant meditation dry my blood*
102 *Three sleepless nights I past in sounding on*
103 *Through words and things, a dim and perilous way;*
104 *And wheresoe'er I turned me I beheld* [1776]
105 *A slavery, compared to which the dungeon*
106 *And clanking chain are perfect liberty*

[52^v]

I was *ed*
107 *You understand me,* ~~*with an awful*~~ *comfort*
108 *I saw that every possible shape of action*
109 *Might lead to good—I saw it and burst forth* [1781]
of those *s* *that fill*
110 *Thirsting for some exploit* ~~*of power and terror*~~
(marking the expression of Mortimers countenance)
earth
F *d*
This *for sure re* *[?]emption* *lost peace*
111 ~~*Nay*~~ *you have had the worst—* ~~*The victory*~~
112 ~~*Already was accomplished—my*~~ *ferocity*
.
113 *Subsided like a storm that dies at once*
~~*d*~~
114 ~~*I felt I ha*~~*[?]* ~~*been fettered by a straw,*~~
115 ~~*I stood astonished at myself—my brain*~~
116 ~~*Was light and giddy, and it teemed with projects*~~
117 ~~*Which seemed to have no limit*~~
~~*Mor:*~~ *— — — — — — — —* ~~*Unhappy man*~~*!*
118 ~~*Yet I will take thee to my heart*~~
And yet
~~*Riv:*~~ *(*~~*smiles*~~*) — — — —* *I had within me evermore*
s
119 *A* *lalient spring of energy, a fire*
120 *Of inextinguishable thought—I mounted*
121 *From action up to action with a mind* [1789]
122 *That never rested—without meat or drink*
123 *I have lived many days— my sleep was linked*
124 *To purposes of reason— my very dreams*
125 *Assumed a substance and a character*

114, 119 MH's 1799 corrections.

96

by
Drove ~~past~~ the place of my retreat ; + {: / three nights 1772
Did constant meditation dry my blood, 1773
ssed
Three sleepless nights I pa{st in sounding on 1774
Thro' words & things, a dim & perilous way, 1775
And, wheresoe'er I turned me, I beheld 1776
A slavery, compared to which the dungeon 1777
And clanking chains are perfect liberty. 1778
You
~~You~~ understand me—I was comforted; 1779
I saw that every possible shape of action 1780
Might lead to good—I saw it, & burst forth, 1781
Thirsting for some of those ~~occasions~~ Exploits that fill 1782
e
Th{is earth
^ *for sure redemption of lost peace. (marking Marmaduke's countenance)* 1783
Nay, you have had the worst. Ferocity 1784
in a moment, like a wind 1785
Subsided ~~like a storm that dies at once~~.—
That drops down dead out of a sky it vexed. 1786
And yet I had within me evermore 1787
.
A salient spring of energy{ , ~~a fire~~ I mounted 1788
~~Of inextinguishable thought. I mounted~~
From action up to action with a mind 1789
That never rested—without meat or drink 1790
bound 1791
I have lived many days,—my sleep was ~~linked~~
—not a dream 1792
To purposes of reason— ~~My very dreams~~
But had its continuity and a character 1793a
&
~~Assumed~~ {a substance ~~& a character~~ 1793b

1773 blood;
1774 on,
1775 way;
1777 *no comma*
1780 shape] state *rev to* shape *(Dora)*
1781 *no comma*
1782 exploits
1783/1784 *in stage dir* countenance.
1788 energy;
1791 *no comma*
1793a But had a substance and a character *then* substance *del to* continuity *and* a character *del to* substance

---

1774, 1779 Revisions are JC's.
1788 The added phrase is in JC's hand.
1793a The phrase "and a character" is in JC's hand.

s} *yet from out their Reasons depth*
Mor: *The traitor* *}! ~~and no meaner prey would satisfy him~~!*
Rises thy expiation like a cloud
Riv: *We drove to Syria— Oft I left the camp*
When all that multitude of hearts was still [1803]

[53ʳ]

And followed on through woods of gloomy cedar
Into deep chasms troubled by roaring streams
Or from the top of Lebanon surveyed
The moonlight desart and the moonlight sea;
In these my lonely wanderings I perceived [1808]
What mighty objects do impress their forms
elevate
~~To build up this~~ our intellectual being,
s}
And felt if aught on earth deserved} a curse,
'Twas that worst principle of ill that dooms
A thing so great to perish self-consumed [1813]
——So much for my remorse
Unhappy Man
Mor: *— — — — — — ~~Oh my poor friend~~!*
~~By all that thou hast suffered doubly dear~~ ——
Riv: *When from these forms I turned to contemplate*
The opinions and the uses of the world,
I seemed a being who had passed alone [1817]
{~~mind~~
~~Beyond the visible barriers of the~~ {world
~~And travelled into~~ things to come
Into a world of

~~*As vivid as belongs to waking thought.*~~ 1794
{~~ely~~
That waking life life hath scar~~ce~~{*[?~~their ?perfection ?ere~~] ~~long~~*
Mar: The traitors!—~~Yet from out of their treason's depth~~
~~risen~~ ~~Has risen~~ power to keep
~~Has~~ {~~r n~~}
{~~Rises~~} ~~thy expiation like a cloud~~

97

~~Uprose thy expiation~~
~~Osw~~ ~~So it was~~
~~Osw~~ ~~Yet their perfidy brought unto me abundant recompense~~
~~*Osw*~~*: ~~We drove to Syria—oft I left the Camp~~*
Osw: Give them not a thought. From Palestine 1801
;}
We marched to Syria: oft I left the camp~~—~~} 1802
When all that multitude of hearts was still, 1803
{C
And followed on, thro' woods of gloomy {cedar, 1804
Into deep chasms troubled by roaring streams; 1805
{s
Or from the top of Lebanon {Surveyed 1806
:}
The moonlight desert, & the moonlight sea;} 1807
In these my lonely wanderings I perceived 1808
What mighty objects do impress their forms 1809
To elevate our intellectual being, 1810
And felt, if aught on earth deserves a curse, 1811
'Tis
~~'Twas~~ that worst principle of ill that dooms 1812
A thing so great to perish self-consumed.~~—~~ 1813
—So much for my remorse!—
Mar: — — — — — — — Unhappy Man! 1814
Osw. When from these forms, I turned to contemplate 1815
The opinions & the uses of the world, 1816
I seemed a Being who had passed alone 1817
region of ~~fu~~ futurity, 1818
Into a ~~world of things to come~~
Where freedom was a natural element. 1819a

1794 As vivid as belongs to waking thought. *del to* That waking life has rarely power to give.
1802 Camp,
{c
1804 {Cedar, *(Dora)*
1807 desert,] dessart, *then* s *del*
1810 being;
1811 if *over illeg eras (Dora)*
1812 that] the *rev to* that that *del to* which
1814 remorse!
1819a *del and rev to* Whose natural element was freedom. *and new half line given to Marmaduke:* Stop, *with comma del to dash*

No more
Mor: — — — — — — — — — — ~~*Poor wretch*~~*!*
I cannot follow
146 ~~*My heart aches for*~~ *thee*
Os — — — — — — *You must;* ~~*you sh*~~
Riv: — — — — — — — — ~~*Is not shame I said*~~
~~*ment*~~
147 ~~*A mean acknowledg*~~ *ement* ~~*of a tribunal*~~
148 ~~*Blind in its essence, a most base surrender*~~
149 ~~*Of our own knowledge to the worlds ignorance*~~
150 *I had been nourished by the sickly food*
151 *Of popular applause. I now perceived* [1822]
W *as* *in us*
152 ~~*That*~~ *we are praised* ~~*by*~~ *men* ~~*because*~~^ ~~*they see in us*~~
do recognize

[53^v]

An *of what they are*
153 ~~*The*~~ *image of themselves;* ~~*that a great mind*~~
thing that
Or the empty^ ~~*that*~~ *they would wish to be*
154 ~~*Outruns its age and is pursued with obliquy*~~
155 ~~*Because its movements are not understood*~~
merit has no surer test ~~*than obliquy*~~
156 *Than obliquy* *I felt that* ~~*to be truly the worlds friend*~~
That if we wished to serve ~~*the world*~~
157 *We must become the object of its* ~~*hate*~~ *fear*
The world in substance not deceived by shew
We must become obnoxious to its hate
158 *Mor:* ~~*I can forgive you but the merciless traitors*~~*!*
Or fear disguised in simulated scorn
I pity—can forgive you—but those traitors
Those merciless Traitors
159 *Riv:* ~~*Having no fear at once I found myself*~~
Nay keep down your wrath
160 ~~*The master of the better half of wisdom*~~.
False shame discarded spurious fame dispised
161 ~~*I saw unveiled the general shapes of things*~~,
Twin sister both of Ignorance I found
162 ~~*I saw the feeble props of them that stood*~~
Life stretched before me ~~*like*~~ *smooth as some broad way*

147 MH's 1799 correction.
A photograph of 53^v is provided below, p. 720.

Mar: — — — — — — — — — ~~*No more*~~
{~~*Stop*~~ *, for*
~~*No*~~ {[~~*?more*~~] *Stop,*^*I cannot follow thee.*
[~~*?Mar*~~] ~~*I cannot follow thee*~~
Os — — — — — — ~~*You must, you must*~~ *You must.* 1820
I had been nourished by the sickly food 1821
Of popular applause. I now perceived 1822

98

That only in us
We are praised,^*as men*^~~*do recognize*~~*,* 1823
{*Do recognize some* 1824a
{[*?That*] [?]
~~*An*~~ *image of themselves*—~~*of what they are*~~*,* 1824b
An abject counterpart of what they are 1825
Or the empty thing that they would wish to be. 1826
I felt that merit has no surer test 1827
an} *o*}
That{ *obli*{*quy;* ~~/~~*that, if we would wish to serve* 1828
~~*We must become the object*~~
The world in substance, not deceive~~*d*~~ *by shew,* 1829
We must become obnoxious to its hate, 1830
Or fear disguised in simulated scorn. 1831
,} *,*} *wretches* 1832
Mar: *I pity*—{ *can forgive*{ *you; but those* ~~*traitors*~~*,*
~~*Those*~~ {*M*
{*merciless* ~~*traitors*~~. *perfidy*
{*K*
Osw: — — — — — — — ~~*Nay*~~, {*keep down your wrath:* 1833
False shame/ *discarded, spurious fame despised,* 1834
Twin sisters both of Ignorance, I found 1835
Life stretched before me smooth as some broad way 1836

1820 *further developed in MS. 3A, 11*[v]
1820 Stop for I *del to* I may not, *and comma inserted after* cannot
1823 We are praised, as men in us do recognize *del to* That we are praised only as men in us
1824b An image of themselves—of what they are *del to* Do recogniz{s/e} {some/an image of themselves,
1825 *interlined, as MS. 3 but* are,
1828 would *del*
1829 shew] show
1831 fear,
1832 traitors, *with comma del to dash then all del to* wretches—
1833 *as MS. 3, rev as MS. 3, but* perfidy! keep *capitalized (JC)*
1834 shame *and* fame *capitalized (JC)*

1820 The uncanceled "You must" is JC's.

163 *~~And was astonished at the stupefaction~~*
Cleared for a Monarch's progress
164 *~~Of them who had fallen~~ — And ~~now~~ the ~~very~~ men*
{T so much
165 *~~The men~~ {to whom I owe this ~~triumph, they~~*
166 *~~Who made me what I am~~, you would destroy ~~them~~*
t} {ank} their blind services
167 *Join me in {h {eap {ing ~~blessings on their heads~~*
~~Os~~: in
Mor: (looking ~~up & gnashing his teeth~~)
Tis a strange aching that when we would curse
168 *~~May he who made us — (breaking off) but I have not heard aright~~*
And cannot
169 *~~In truth I have been strangely troubled lately~~*
170 *~~What did you say~~?*
[?]
Riv: — — — — — — You know wherein I differ
171 *From common minds—and in a wiser hour*
172 *You have been proud to call me friend—one man*
173 *Was famished and ten thousand have been saved*
at O
looking ^ & gnashing teeth
174 *Mor: It is a strange aching that—when we would curse* [1845]
{Y
175 *And cannot— ~~Monster~~ {you have betrayed me*
I have done—

[54r]

Riv: What! for saving a poor man perchance
176 *From a ten years visitation of the stone*
177 *Or the more gentle mercies of the palsy?*
178 *Mor: Thou poor old man and I had heart for this*
{ed'st
179 *Because thou lov{'d the infant that had fed thee*

167/168 The "in" is a direction to the 1841 copyist.
175–182 Further developed in MS. 2A, 4v.
177, 179 MH's 1799 corrections.

see scrap sheets
Cleared for a monarch's progress,‸‸And the men, 1837a

[*in margin*] *I had been* 1839b
And in that dream had left my native land 1840
One of Love's boyish bondsmen— Twas a chain 1841
~~Broken~~ for ever & the very men 1842
Was off

To whom I owe so much, you would destroy. 1843b

Join me in than{ks for / king} their blind services! 1844

Mar: *~~It~~ {'T} is a strange aching that, when we would curse* 1845

And cannot— {y / You} have betrayed me—I have done— 1846

I am content, } I know that he is guiltless.—{ 1847

Thou poor old {m / Man!}—& I had heart for this, 1849b, 1850a

Because thou lov'dst the{~~y~~ / e}‸daughter that had fed thee, 1850b

---

1837–1842 *further developed in MS. 3A, 15r*
1837a And the men *del to* I had been
1837a–1844 *after l. 1837a MS. 4 continues:*

To whom I owe so much, you would destroy.
Join me in thanks for their blind services. *all del to*
(And in that dream had left my native land)
One of Love's boyish hostages—twas a cloud
Dispersed for {very / [?ever]} men ever, & the very men,
To whom I owe so much you would destory:
Join me in thanks for their blind services. *then all but last line del to revised passage in margin:*

Cleared for a monarch's progress. Priests might spin
Their veil but not for me—'twas in fit place
Among its kindred cobwebs. I had been,
And in that dream had left my native land,
One of Love's ~~boyish~~ simple bondsmen {— / &} the‸soft chain
Was off for ever; & the Men from whom
~~Came this deliverance~~—
This liberation came you would destroy;

1837–1842 *further developed in MS. 3A, 13v and 15r*
1847 guiltless—
1847/1849b That both are guiltless, without spot, or stain, *interlined*
1849b {M / man} *(JC)*
1850b {D / daughter} *(JC)*

1837a The scrap sheets appear not to have survived.
1844 The "for" in revision is JC's.

180 *Thy daughter—she that was the light of thy path*
181 *The very blood that moved in thee—O! fool——*
182 *(to Rivers) Monster you have betray'd me*
Riv: — — — — — — — — — — — ~~*I have done*~~
183 *in* ~~*What you perhaps may live to thank me*~~ *for*
Mor: *(laying his hand tranquilly on his breast)*
184 *I am content— I ^ know ^ that ^ he is ^ guiltless (walks about)*
185 ~~*Peace—Peace—*~~ *patience—peace*
~~*Together we propped up his*~~ *steps, he leand*
186 ~~*He leaned*~~ {*U* / *upon us both*}
We are coupled *I there youve hit the truth*
187 *Riv:* ~~*I've join'd us*~~ *by a chain of adamant,*
let us be *from this hour*
188 *Henceforth* ~~*we are*~~ *fellow-labourers——*~~*to enlarge*~~ [1855]
To enlarge
189 *^ The intellectual empire* ~~*of mankind*~~ *All*
I *downright*
190 *'~~T~~i's slavery——*~~*all is*~~ *slavery, we receive*
191 *Laws, and we ask not whence those laws have come*
192 *We need an inward sting to goad us on* [1859]
193 ~~*—Heavens—where's the harm of ridding an old wretch*~~
194 *Mor:* *'Twas in his face— I saw it in his face*
195 *I've crushed the foulest crime*

[54v]

Riv: — — — — — — *Away with that—*
196 *More noble triumphs are prepared ~~for~~ you*

---

183 The "in" is a direction to the 1841 copyist.
186/187 Taking dictation, MW wrote "I" for "Aye."

{She
{Her, who, from very infancy, had been 1851
Light to thy path, ~~/~~ warmth to thy blood; ~~—patience~~ 1852
—together ~~patience~~

99

~~O fool~~ [—?—] *{W {we propped his steps, {, he leaned upon us both.* 1853
~~Together we propp'd up his steps, he leaned~~
~~Upon us both.~~
Osw — — — *~~Ay, there you've hit the truth~~*
{w
Aye, {We are coupled by a chain of adamant; 1854
[?~~the~~] *~~We are~~ Let us be then, to enlarge* 1855
~~Henceforth let us be~~ follow-labourers, ~~/ from this hour~~
~~to enlarge~~
~~To enlarge~~ {T {~~the intellectual empire—All is~~
.} {W
Man's intellectual empire,} {we subsist 1856
n} all is
Is} slavery, ~~downright~~ slavery, we receive 1857
but t}
Laws, & we ask nor} whence those laws have come; 1858

We need an inward sting to goad us on.
~~Mar 'Twas in his face! I saw it in his face~~
~~I've crushed the foulest crime~~
{st th}
Mar Ha{ve y}ou betrayed me man speak, speak to that
thou
~~Osw~~ — — — — — — — — — *~~Away with that~~*
speak to that
~~The penalty be mine—your's the reward~~
~~Osw~~ I would have made you equal with myself

We need an inward sting to goad us on. 1859
inward
Mar: Have you betrayed me? Speak to that.
Osw — — — — — — — — *The mask,* 1860
Which for a season I have stooped to wear, 1861

1851 Her who, from very infancy, had been *del to* ~~The Creature~~ who from ^very^ infancy, had ~~given~~ ^Her^ been

1852 blood!— {T {together *added stage dir* (turning to Oswald

1854 *no comma*

1857 *semicolons for both commas* receive *del to* recieve

1859–1866 On back of the pasteover in MW's hand are ll. 1426–1427, with no punctuation after "support" and "fooled."

1859 The "inward" below the line is JC's.

And nobler ~~sympathies~~—of this hereafter—
That ~~silly~~ girl—I felt for your ~~delusion~~ ~~reward~~
The penalty be mine—yours the reward
I would have made you equal with myself
But that was a vain hope—you have struck home [1867]
With a few drops of blood cut short the business
Therein for ever [you] must yield to me
Enough is done to save you fro{n/m} the curse
Of living without knowledge that you live. [1871]
~~*You will be taught to think—and step by step*~~
~~*Led on from truth to truth, you soon will link*~~
~~*Pleasure with greatness, and may thus become*~~
~~*The most magnificent of characters*~~
~~*Something*~~ *{Y/youve} {r} suffer{ing now but/ed} for the future ~~hour~~ {Day/[?]}*
'Tis his who will command it. Think of my story— [1873]
Herbert is innocent.

Mor: *(in a faint voice) That ~~blind~~ [sightless] man*
I've spoken very lightly—if you do but
Echo my words

---

203 MH's 1799 insertion.
204 MH's 1799 correction.

Must be cast off.—{K / know then that I was urged
For other impulse let it pass was driven
To seek for Sympathy, because I saw
mirror
In you ~~an image~~ of my youthful self;
I would have made us equal once again,

But that was a vain hope} ⁄, {Y / you have struck home;
With a few drops of blood cut short the business;
Therein for ever you must yield to me.
But what will {~~blank~~
~~Enough~~ is done ~~to~~ save you from the {~~curse~~
blank
Of living without knowledge that you live:
Now you are suffering—
~~Youre suffering now, but~~ for the future day,

Tis his who will command it. Think of my Story—
~~Herbert—the penalty be mine—~~
~~Herbert is innocent~~
Herbert is innocent

Mar: in a faint voice M[ ]r [ ]ubt
~~That sightless Man~~
~~I've spoken very lightly—if you do but echo my words~~
You do but echo
~~Echo my words~~
My own wild words?

Osw — — — — *Young Man, the seed must be*

Tis his who will command it.—Think of my Story—
Herbert is innocent
Mar: in a faint voice & doubtingly — — — — *You do but echo*
My own wild words?

1862 urged,
1863 *interlined, as MS. 3, but* pass, *and* driven] urged *del to* driven
1865 *as MS. 3, rev as MS. 3*
1867 home,
1873 'Tis

1862, 1867 The capitals are JC's.
1870 The uncanceled "blank" below line is JC's.

Young Man
Riv: — — — — — *The seed must be*
Hid in the earth or there can be no harvest
'Tis nature's law. What I have done in darkness [1877]
I will avow before the face of day
Herbert is innocent

[55r]

action
Mor: What fiend could prompt ~~thee~~ to this ~~damning~~
~~deed~~ innocent
breaking
~~Innocent~~! Oh ~~my~~ heart! Alive or dead
I'll find him— (rushes out)
perdition
Riv: — — — — — — — — *Alive?* — — *~~damnation~~!*
(Exit Rivers)

[IV.iii] *(Scene 3d The inside of a poor cottage)*
Matilda & Margaret seated.

for poor or rich
Mat: The storm beats hard—A mercy ~~to the wretches~~
{eads {are
Who h{ave ~~no~~ {roof to shelter ~~their poor heads~~
less in such a night
Such nights as these
who have you there within
{~~h v~~}
A voice from without} ~~What~~ Hola! ~~you~~{ ar}~~e merry there~~
Marg't — — — — — — — — — *Oh Heavens!*
can this
?}
Mat: What^means} ~~this~~?

100

Osw: — — — — — — — *Young Man, the seed must b* {~~li~~ / ~~i~~ lie} 1875b
Hid in the earth, or there can be no harvest; 1876
'Tis Nature's law. What I have done in darkness 1877
I will avow before the face of day. 1878
Herbert <u>*is*</u> *innocent.* 1879a

~~*In shape of Man*~~
What fiend could
Mar: ~~*What fiend could prompt to this action*~~ {~~*Innocent*~~ / *O*[?]} ~~*innocent!*~~ ~~*prompt*~~ ~~*heart*~~ *prompt*

innocent [ ]
This action ^ *Oh breaking heart!* ~~*alive*~~,
~~*Oh! breaking heart! Alive or dead, I'll find him*~~
~~*exit Mar*~~

Alive or dead I'll find him
~~*Osw Alive? perdition! Ex.[t] Osw sever*[?]~~
Oswald — — — *Alive, perdition!*

Mar. — — — — — — — — *What fiend could prompt* 1879b
This action. Innocent!—Oh breaking heart!— 1880
Alive or dead, I'll find him.
Osw. — — — — — — — — — — *Alive—perdition!* 1881

(Exeunt)

Scene, the inside of a poor Cottage

Margaret & Idon{*e* / *ia*} *seated.*

Ido *The storm beats hard—Mercy for poor* ~~&~~ *or rich,* 1882
Whose heads are shelterless in such a night. 1883

A voice Hol{*la* / *a*}*! who have you there, within?*
without *Holla!*
Marg[t] — — — — — — — — — — — — — *O save us!* 1884
Ido
~~*Mat*~~ *What can this mean?*

1876 *no comma*
1881 *stage dir* (Exit) *added after first half line and* (Exeunt) *below (Dora) rev to* (Exit) *(JC)*
1881/1882 *in scene setting:* Cottage.
1883 in] on *rev to* in *(Dora)*

1879b–1881 The entire pasteover is in the hand of JC.
1884 Revisions are JC's.

Alas {for poor
Marg^t^. — — — — {Oh! my^ husband!
~~Voice from~~ (~~with tumult~~ — — ~~In good faith~~
~~without~~
Voice [?]
6 *We'll have a counting of our flocks tomorrow* [1886]
7 *The wolf keeps festival these stormy nights*
(~~confused noises are heard that~~ die away at a distance)
the voices
they are ~~rude~~
8 *Marg^t^. Be calm sweet Lady—'~~tis some~~ wass e llers*
~~Are~~
9 *in ~~Returning~~ from the wake—my heart beats so—*

[55^v^]

10 *A noise at midnight does so frighten me——* [1890]
11 *Mat: (listening) Hush!*
on my husband
Marg^t^. — — They are gone—'~~twas~~ such a night ~~as this~~
{~~M~~ ~~Once was dragged out~~ of
12 *~~They dragged~~ {~~my husband from~~ his bed*
Dragged from his bed was
13 *~~And~~ cast ~~him deep~~ into a dungeon—~~Lady~~*
Where hid from me he counted many years
14 *~~—The place I never saw—and he was innocent~~*
~~A criminal in no ones eyes~~ [~~?living~~] [~~?creatures~~]
15 *~~Innocent of all crimes and now you see~~*
A criminal in no ones eyes but theirs
16 *~~That this wretched cottage cannot save us~~*
Not even in there's whose brutal violence
17 *~~From cruelty and insult~~*
Thus dealt with him
noble
Mat: — — — — — — I have a^ friend
{Who
18 *{He lives but to protect the injured ~~(listening) there again~~*
There again (listening Good
19 *Marg^t^. It is my husband's foot—~~Poor~~ Robert! ~~Lady~~,*
imprisonment
20 *Has a kind heart, but his ~~confinement~~* [1900]
21 *Has made him fearful, and he'll never be*
22 *The man he was*
Mat: — — — — I will retire—good night
(Matilda goes into an inner room of the cottage)
Enter Robert (while he speaks goes and sits down
in a dark part of the room

---

8 MH's 1799 correction to "wassellers."
9 The "in" is a direction to the 1841 copyist.

Marg.ᵗ — — — — — — *Alas for my poor husband* {*!—* / *:*}
We'll have a counting of our flocks tomorrow;
~~*Voices*~~ *The wolf keeps festival these stormy nights:*
(~~*without*~~)
They die away *Be calm,* ~~*my good*~~ [*sweet*] *Lady, they are wass*{*a* / *ellers*}
in the distance
Returning from the [*ir*] ~~*Wake*~~ [*Feast*]*—my heart beats so—*
A noise at midnight does *so* *frighten me—*

{*Ido* / *Ma*} *Hush!—(listening)*

Margᵗ — — *They are gone* {*·*} *+* {*O*} *on such a night, my husband,*
Dragged [~~*out*~~] *from his bed, was cast into a dungeon*
Where {*,*} *hid from me* [*[?]*] {*,*} *he counted many years,*
A criminal in no‸[*ones*]*eyes but theirs—*

101

Not even in their's—whose brutal violence
~~*Thus*~~ [*So*] *dealt with him.*

Ido: — — — — — *I have a* ~~*friend*~~ *noble friend*
Who lives but to protect the‸[*weak or*]*injured.*
There again!—(listening)

Margᵗ — — — ~~*It*~~ {*'T*} *is my husband's foot. Good* ~~*Robert*~~ *Eldred*
Has a kind heart; but his imprisonment
Has made him fearful, & he'll never be
The man he was.

Ido — — — — *I will retire—good night!—*
(She goes within)
Enter ~~*Robert*~~ *Eldred (hides a bundle)*

1888 wassaillers
1889 *as MS. 3, rev as MS. 3*
1890 me.— *then dash del*
1893 *comma after* years *only*
1894 one's eyes *over* eyes but *eras (Dora)*
1895 *no apos*
1896a *as MS. 3, rev as MS. 3*
1898 weak or *inserted as MS. 3*
1902 retire;—

23 *Rob:* — — — — — — — — — *'Tis very late—*
Not yet in bed Margaret? (he rises up & hides a bundle
There are stains in that frock which must be
washed out—

[56^r]

25 *Marg^t. What has befallen you?* [1905]
26 *Rob: (draws near) I have been detained to night, and you*
must know the cause (speaking low) that is the blood of an
unhappy man
28 *Marg^t. Oh we are undone for ever* [1908]
29 *Rob: Heaven forbid that I should lift my hand against*
any man (he pauses) Margaret I have shed tears
to night, and it comforts me to think of it
32 *Marg^t. Where, where is he?* [1912]
33 *Rob: I have done him no harm* {*b* / *(ut* } *(hesitating) Heaven*
will forgive me, it would not have been so once
35 *Marg^t. You have not <u>buried</u> any thing? you are no richer than*
when you left me?
37 *Rob: Be at peace I am innocent* [1917]
38 *Marg^t. (fervently) Oh! God I thank thee—(a pause in*
which she looks at him, her countenance mantling
with pleasure) Robert I am
Happy to see you (a short pause—she falls upon his neck
40 *Rob: To night I met with an old man lying stretched upon*
the ground— a piteous spectacle
42 *Marg^t. (as if ready to run) Where is he? (Robert looks grave*

[56^v]

You were not able to bring him <u>all</u> the way with you
Let us return—I am quite stout
(Robert shakes his head)

---

33 MH's 1799 correction.

Eldred
~~*Rob.t*~~ *— — — — —* ~~*Tis very late*~~ {*N* / *not yet in bed Margaret?*}

~~*Not yet in bed Margaret*~~*?* {*T* / *there are stains in that*}
{*frock* / [*?shirt*] *which must be washed out.*

Marg[t] *What has befallen you?* 1905

Eld: ~~*I*~~ *I am belated*
~~*Rob*[t]~~ ~~*I have been detained to night*~~, *& you must know the cause—(speaking low) that is the blood of an unhappy man.*

Marg[t] *O we are undone for ever.* 1908

Eld:
~~*Rob*[t]~~ *Heaven forbid that I should lift my hand against any man—Marg*[t]*. I have shed tears tonight, & it comforts me to think of it.*

Marg[t]*. Where, where is he?* 1912

Eld:
~~*Rob*[t]~~ *I have done him no harm, but——it will be forgiven me; it would not have been so once.*

Marg[t]*. You have not* <u>*buried*</u> *any thing? You are no richer than* 1915

102

{*w* / *When you left me?* 1916

Eld:
~~*Rob*[t]~~ *Be at peace; I am innocent.* 1917

Marg[t] ~~*O God I thank thee*~~ {~~*Eldred*~~ / ~~*Rob*[t]~~*.* ~~*I am thankful*~~ ~~*happy*~~ 1918
Then God be thanked—
~~*to see you*~~ *(a short pause, she falls upon his neck)*

Eld
~~*Rob*[t]~~ *To night I met with an old man lying stretched*
sad
upon the ground—a ~~*piteous*~~ *spectacle : I raised him up with a hope that we might shelter & restore him.*
~~*as I was struggling on*~~ [*?h*]

were
Marg[t] *Where is he? You were not able to bring him*
(as if ready to run) <u>*all*</u> *the way with you; let us return, I* {*c* / *am*} *help* ~~*quite*~~
you *Eld*
~~*stout*~~ *(*~~*Rob*[t]~~*. shakes his head)*

1902/1905 *Eldred's speech began:* — — — — — Not yet in bed Margaret? *then half line erased and line rewritten:* Not yet in bed, Eleanor?—there are stains in that *(Dora) and in next line* Frock *rev to* frock *by JC*

[1907] {c / Cause *(JC)* Man.
1908 O!
[1910] {m / Man *(JC)* Marg.[t]] Eleanor,
[1911] {me / Me *(JC)*
[1924] you. *before stage dir in next to last line*

Marg^t^. *(alarmed)*
44 *But what was it that would not have been so once?*
45 *Rob*: *He did not seem to wish for life; when I had raised*
him up in my arms, by the light of the moon I
saw the stains of blood upon my clo{*ath*/*the*}*s—he waved*
his hand, as if it were all useless & I let him sink
again to the ground
49 *Marg*^t^. *(sighing deeply) Oh! that I had been by your side* [1929]
50 *Rob*: *(with some impatience) I tell you his hands and*
body were cold—how could I disturb his last
moments? he strove to turn from me as if he
wished to compose himself to sleep
53 *Marg*^t^. *But his wounds?*
54 *Rob*: *I looked at them—he had fallen—and his*
face was bruised—but I think his malady
was cold and hunger
56 *Marg*^t^. *Oh! Robert I shall never be able to look up*
at this roof in dry or storm but I shall tremble

[57^r^]

58 *Rob*: *It is not enough that I have been so unfortunate*
as to have been abroad to night till this hour, I came
home, and this is my comfort
60 *Marg*^t^. *But did he say nothing which might have* [1940]
set you at ease?
61 *Robt* *I thought he grasped my hand while he* ^*was* *mutter*{*ing*/*ed*}
something about his child—his daughter—what
is that? (starting as if he heard a noise)
63 *Marg*^t^. *Robert you are a father* [1945]

45/49 MH's 1799 correction.
61 MH's 1799 correction.

Eld. He

(Marg[t] *{did*

alarmed) ~~Did~~ {he not seem to wish for life, :} *as I was* *~~when I had~~* 1925

struggling on

~~up~~

~~raised him~~ [?]} *~~in my arms~~, by the light of the*
moon I saw the stains of blood upon my clothes—he
waved his hand, as if it were all useless; & I let
him sink again to the ground.

Marg[t] (sighing) *Oh that I had been by your side.* 1929

Eld:

~~Rob[t]~~ *I tell you his hands & his body were cold—how* 1930
could I disturb his last moments? he strove to
turn from me as if he wished to compose himself to
sleep.

for the

Marg[t] *~~But his wounds?~~* 1933

Eld: *must have*

~~Rob.[t]~~ *I looked at them; he ~~had~~ ^ fallen; & his face was ~~bruised,~~*
but I think his malady ^ was cold & hunger.

Eldred,

Marg[t] *Oh ~~Rob.[t]~~ I shall never be able to look up at this roof* 1936

or fair

in ~~dry or~~ storm ^ but I shall tremble.

Eldred

103

s} t} *my ill stars have kept me*

~~Rob[t]~~ *It} is} not enough that ~~I have been so unfortunate as to have~~*

?} *{o*

~~been~~ abroad to night till this hour—} I c{ame home & this is
my comfort!

Marg[t] *But did he say nothing which might have set you at* 1940
ease? 1941

Eld

~~Rob[t]~~ *I thought he grasped my hand while he was muttering* 1942
something about his Child—his daughter— (starting as 1943
if he heard a noise) what is that? 1944

Eldred,

Marg[t]: *~~Rob[t]~~ ^ you are a Father.* 1945

1929 side!
[1932] compose himself to sleep. *del to* settle into sleep.
1933 But, his wounds? *then last two words del to* for the stains of blood—
[1934] I looked at them; he must have fallen; and his face was bruised; *del to* He must have fallen I fancy, for his face was cut; *then* face *del to* head
first line of p. 103 as MS. 3, rev as MS. 3 and been *del as MS. 3 in next line*
1944 What

1925 The "Eld" as speaker identification is JC's.

64 Rob: *(with a faultering voice) God knows what was in my*
heart & will not curse my son for my sake
66 Margt. *But you prayed by him? you waited the hour*
of his release
67 Rob: *It was far from home—the night was wasting fast*
I have no friend—I am spited by the world—if I had
brought him along with me & he had died in my
arms——Hush! I am sure I heard something breathing
and this chair?
71 Margt. *Oh! Robert you will die alone—you will have*
nobody to close your eyes—no hand to grasp
your dying hands—I shall be in my grave—
A curse will attend us all—

[57v]

74 Rob: *(sternly) Have you forgot the bed on which you*
lay when I was in dungeon [1959]
75 Margt. *And you left him alive?*
76 Rob: *Alive! the damps of death were upon him, he*
could not have survived an hour
78 Margt. *(weeps(In the cold, cold night* [1962]
79 Rob: *(in a savage manner) Aye & his head was bare,—*
I suppose you would have had me leave my
bonnet to cover him (checking himself)
You will never rest till I meet with a felon's end

Eldred *in*
~~*Rob*~~[t]. *(with faultering voice) God knows what was my heart, and*
will not curse my son for my sake.
Marg *But you prayed by him? you waited the hour of his* 1948
Eld: *release?* 1949
~~*Rob*~~[t] ~~*It was far from home*~~ *; the night was wasting fast; I have*
; his wounds terrified me
no friend—} I am spited by the world—if I had brought
him along with me, & he had died in my arms!—Hush!—
in
I am sure I heard something breathing &} this chair?
Eldred,
Marg[t] *Oh!* ~~*Robert,*~~ *you will die alone—you will have nobody to* 1954
close your eyes—no hand to grasp your dying hands—I shall
be in my grave—A curse will attend us all. 1956
Eldred *your own troubles,*
~~*Rob*~~[t] *Have you forgot* ~~*the bed on which you lay*~~ *when I was in*
(steadily)
the dungeon? 1958

Marg *And you left him alive?* 1959
Eld:
~~*Rob*~~[t] *Alive!—the damps of Death were upon him—he could* 1960
not have survived an hour.

104
Marg[t] *In the cold, cold night.* 1962
(weeps)
Eldred
~~*Rob.*~~[t] *(in a savage tone) Aye, & his head was bare; I suppose*
nd
you would ~~*me*~~ *have had me l*~~*eave*~~ *my bonnet to*
it. *lend* *am brought*
cover ~~*him*~~*——you will never rest till I* ~~*have a*~~
to a
o *end.*
^fell}n's {grave

[1946] faltering *in stage dir*
[1950] *as MS. 3, rev as MS. 3 but* {T / the
[1951] his wound terrified me— *inserted with caret before* if
[1952] hush!— *del*
[1953] breathing— in *del to* & *del to*—and chair?} / !
1954 *no exclam point, dash del to period*
1956 *dash del to semicolon*
[1957] *no comma*
1962 *second* cold *over* night *erased*

[1964] The "lend" below the line is JC's.

Marg^{t}. (~~*with feeling*~~)
82 *Is there nothing to be done cannot we go to the*
Convent?
83 *Rob: Certainly! & say at once that I have murdered him* [1967]
84 *Marg^{t}. Robert I know that ours is the only house upon*
the heath—~~*in my dreams a thousand times have*~~
~~*I heard the cracking of your joints upon that*~~
~~*dreadful engine (affecting chearfulness) but*~~ *let*
us take heart—this man may be rich—And
could he be saved by our means, his gratitude {—
89 *Rob:* (~~*in a softer tone*~~) *'Tis all in vain* [1971]

[58^{r}]

90 *Marg^{t}.* (~~*more eagerly*~~) *But let us make the attempt—This*
old man may have a wife—and he may have
children—let us return to the spot, we may
restore him & his eyes may yet open upon those
that love him
93 *Rob: He will never open them more—even when he*
spoke to me, he kept them firmly sealed as if
he had been blind
95 *Mat: (rushes out) —— It is, it is my father* [1978]
Rob: (after his first surprize looking sternly at his wife)
96 *We are betrayed*
Marg^{t}. (turning to Mat: who is sunk senseless on the floor)
97 *His daughter! God of mercy!*
98 *Mat: He is dead— Oh lift me up—carry me to the place*
You are safe
The whole world shall not harm you
100 *Marg^{t}. Robert this Lady is his daughter*
101 *Rob: (much moved) I'll lead her to the spot* [1983]
Mat: (springing up with wild agitation)
102 *Alive! you heard him breath?—quick—quick—*
Exeunt Mat: Rob: & Marg^{t}.

Marg[t] *Is there nothing to be done, cannot we go to the Convent?*

Eld: Forsooth we may,

Rob[t] *~~Certainly!~~ & say at once that I ~~have~~ murdered him,* 1967

Eldred,

Marg[t] *~~Robert~~ I know that our's is the only house upon the* 1968

{W

{waste—let us take heart—this man may be rich—

a

And could he be saved by our means, his gratitude

Eld *may reward us.*

~~Rob~~[t] *^'Tis all in vain.* 1971

~~Marg~~ *Mar* *But let us make the attempt. This old Man may have a wife, & he may have Children—let us return to the spot; we may restore him, & his eyes may yet open upon those that love him.*

Eld:

~~Rob~~[t] *He will never open them more; even when he spoke to me, he kept them firmly sealed as if he had been blind.* 1976

Ido: *(rushes out)* *It is, it is, my Father——* *(~~She sinks senseless~~)*

(~~rushes out~~)

~~Marg~~[t] *~~His daughter~~*

Eld:

~~Rob~~[t] *We are betrayed. (looking at Ido)* *~~turning~~*

His daughter!—God have mercy! *(turning to Idonia)* 1979

Marg[t] *~~Robert that Lady is his daughter~~*

~~Rob~~[t] *~~I'll lead her to the spot~~*

105

Ido: *~~He is dead~~ Oh! lift me up/ & carry me to the place. ~~You are~~*

{~~Safe~~

{You You are safe ; *the whole*

~~The whole~~ world shall not harm you. 1981

Marg.[t] *This Lady is his daughter.* 1982

Eldred

~~Rob~~[t] *(moved) I'll lead you to the spot.* 1983

Ido (springing up agitated) *Alive!—you heard him breathe? quick, quick——*

(Exeunt)

[1966] done, ?}

1967 Forsooth we may, *del to* Aye, & him.

1968 *no apos*

[1969] *dashes del to semicolons*

[1973] children

in first line of p. 105 stage dir added, in pencil: (sinking down) *(JC)*

[1984] *in stage dir* agitated. End of fourth Act. *below line*

[1969–1970] The capital "W" and the lowercase "a" were added by JC.
The lines at foot of p. 104 were probably deleted before transcription of p. 105 was begun.

[59r]

[V.i] *Act 5th Scene a wood on the edge of the heath*
Enter Rivers and ~~two woodmen~~. a Forrester

~~1st Wood~~: For *He leaned upon the bridge that spans the glen* [1985]
And down into the bottom cast his eye
That fastened there as it would check the current
Riv: *He listened too? did you not say he listened?* [1988]
~~2d Wood~~: For ~~*Aye Sir he listened*~~
As if he had heard such moaning in the water
As ~~we~~ {is heard / fear} often after stormy nights
~~1st Wood~~: *Then as it seemed from ~~some~~ strange ~~intimation~~* intimation [?]
Of things to {me / us} invisible, he turned
And looked around him with an eye that shewed
As if it wished to miss the thing it sought
Riv: *But did he utter nothing which explained*
The cause of these appearances
~~2d Wood~~: For ~~*Look there*~~ Look there*! (Mortimer appears crossing the stage at some distance—an expression of vacancy in his eye which at last settles upon the ground)*
Mor: *The dust doth move and eddy at my feet*
~~2d Wood~~: ~~*This is most strange*~~; ~~*the air is dead & still*~~
~~1st Wood~~: For ~~*Look there how he spreads out*~~ His senses play him false & see his arms ~~*as 'twere*~~

[59v]

Outspread, as if
^To save himse{l / ff} from falling! ~~such impression~~
~~I~~ {N / ~~never saw before on human face~~}
I ~~do~~ believe some terrible phantom now is
~~Doth~~ Is pass before him such as God will not
Permit to visit any but a man ing [1998]
Who has been guilty of a damning crime
(Mortimer disappears)

---

17 The "himself" was corrected in 1799.

106

Act 5th

Scene, a wood on the edge of the Waste.
Enter Oswald & a Forester.

For: *He leaned upon the bridge that spans the glen,* 1985
And down into the bottom cast his eye 1986
{te} That fas{hio}ned there, as it would check the current. 1987
{Osw: / Mor:} *He listened, too; did you not say he listened?* 1988
For: *As if {t / he} {re / ~~had heard~~} came such moaning {from / in the} ~~water~~ ~~river~~ flood* 1989
As is heard {o n / after} after stormy nights. 1990
~~Then a~~{~~nd~~ / s} {~~no~~ / ~~it~~} {~~doubt~~ / ~~seemed from intimation strange~~}
~~Of things to me invisible, he turned~~
~~And looked around him with an eye that shewed~~
~~As if it wished to miss the thing it sought~~.
Osw: *~~But did he utter nothing~~ {?} ~~which explained~~*
The cause of these appearances {?}
See him there! 1991b
For: *(Mar: appear[?]ing~~s) at a distance~~) ~~Look there!~~*
Mar: *Buzz: buzz! ye black & wingèd Freebooters,* 1992
~~Mar~~: *~~The dust doth move & eddy at my feet~~*
That is no substance ~~that~~ which ye settle on. 1993
For: *His senses play him false, & see, his arms* 1994
Outspread, as if to save himself from falling!— 1995
Some terrible phantom I ~~do~~ believe {is / now} 1996

107

~~Is~~{P / passing} before him, such as God will not 1997
Permit to visit any ~~man~~ but a man 1998
Who has been guilty of some horrid crime. 1999
(Mar: disappears)

Forrester *in top stage dir*
1988 *no comma*
1990/1991b But did he utter nothing? *then* that explained the cause, *added and del* / The cause of these appearances? *del*
1991b See, him there! *then* him *del and rewritten without underlining*
1992 Buzz, buzz,
1993 *as MS. 3, rev as MS. 3*
1994 false;

1990 The "no doubt" in the following line is JC's.

Riv: *The game is up*

For

~~*2^d Wood*~~*:* — — — — *If it is needful, Sir,*

I

~~*We*~~ *will assist you to lay hands on him*

Riv: *No, no my friends you may pursue your business* [2002]

'Tis a poor wretch of an unsettled ~~*fancy*~~ *mind*

Who has a trick of straying from his keepers;

We must be gentle with ~~*him*~~, *leave him to my*

For *care* [2005]

(Exeunt ~~*Woodmen*~~*)*

Riv: (alone)

the young man

What have ~~*him*~~ *whipped and howling? No,* ~~*no, no*~~,

~~*That will be needless I will tame these freaks*~~

~~*I have an eye that will take care of him*~~,

These freaks of troubled fancy shall be tamed

~~*And tame these freaks and curvetings of fancy*~~

By my own eye— My master shall become

~~*Into a sober fire. Henceforth I'll have him*~~

A shadow of myself, made by myself. [2009]

[60^r]

[V.ii] *Scene the edge of the Heath*

Enter at opposite sides of the stage Mortimer & Robert Mortimer raises his eyes from the ground and perceiving Robert——

Mor: — — — — — — — ~~*Have you seen*~~

In any corner of this savage ~~*heath*~~ *waste*

~~*A feeble, helpless miserable wretch*~~

Have you, good {*pea* / [?]*sant seen*}

~~*A poor, forsaken, famished*~~, *blind old man?*

Rob: *I heard*—

Mor: — — — ~~*O Heavens*~~*! you heard him, where, where*

Rob: — — — — — — — — — *As you know*

Osw: *The game is up!—*

For: *— — — — If it* {*be* / *is*} *needful, Sir,*

I will assist you to lay hands upon him? {*.*}

Osw: *No, no, my* {*F* / *friend*}*, you may pursue your business—*
'Tis a poor wretch of an unsettled mind,

Who has a trick of straying from his Keeper {*s;* / *s*}

We must be gentle—/. {*L* / *leave*} *him to my care.*

(ex. Forester.)

Osw: ~~*What! have the young man whipped & yelling—no*~~*.* (above: ~~*him shackled as a Maniac*~~)
If his own eyes play false with him, these freaks
~~*These freaks of troubled fancy shall be tamed*~~
Of ~~*troubled*~~ *fancy shall be tamed by mine;* (above: *quickly*)
~~*By my own eye.*~~ *My Master shall become*
The goal is reached^
A shadow of myself—made by myself.

Scene, the edge of the ~~*heath*~~ *Moor.*

{*Marmaduke* / *Oswald*} *&* ~~*Rob*~~[t] *enter, from opposite sides.* (above Rob[t]: *Eldred*)

Mar: *(raising his eyes, & perceiving* ~~*Rob*~~[t] *El:)*
In any corner of this savage waste,
Have you, good Peasant, seen a blind old Man?—

~~*Rob*~~[t] *Eldred* *I heard——*

Mar: *— — — You heard him, where—* {*?*} {*when* / *where?*} *heard him?*

~~*Rob*~~[t] *Eldred* *— — — — — — — — — — — — As you know,*

2003 {W / wretch
2005/2006 Forrester *in stage dir*
2007 *as MS. 3, rev as MS. 3*
2008 reached.
2010 *no comma in stage dir above line*
2011/2012 You heard him, where? {when / where / [?]} {heard / [?]}? him? *(Dora)*

2002 The revision is JC's.
2004 The first "s" added to "Keeper" is in pencil.

The first {*h* / [?*T*]}*ours of last night were rough* *with* ~~&~~ *stormy* [2013]
I was abroad—the search of a stray heifer
While yet the moon was up had led me far
Into the wildest part of this wild ~~*heath*~~ *waste*
When hearing, as I thought, a sudden voice
I stopped and listened, not without such fear
Upon me as the time and place might breed
But thinking that my fancy had deceived me [2016]
I turned away, when streight a second sound
A human voice distinct smote on my ear
Thus guided, distant a few steps I found
An aged man and such as you describe [2020]
~~*Mor*~~*:* ~~*Alive? alive? did you not say alive*~~*?*

[60ᵛ]

Rob: ~~*I said that he was living*~~
Mor: — — — — — — — — ~~*But where? how*~~*?*
You heard— he called you to him? Of all men
The best and kindest lead me to the spot
This instant lead me
Rob: — — — — — *On a ridge of rocks*
A lonesome Chapel stands, deserted now [2024]
The bell remains, which no one dares remove
And when the stormy wind blows o'er the {*st* / *p*}*e*{*ep* / *ak*}
It rings as if a human hand were there
To pull the cord.— I fancy he had heard it
And it had led him towards the precipice [2029]
To climb up to the spot whence the sound came
Poor man!
~~*Mor*~~*:* — — — ~~*And*~~ *he was* *too* ~~*very*~~ *feeble for such effort*

6 MH's 1799 overwriting.

108

The first hours of last night were rough with storm.
I had been out in
~~I was abroad; the~~ search of a stray heifer;
{~~had~~
~~While yet the moon was up,~~ {it ~~led me far~~
~~Into the wildest part of this wild Waste~~.
{~~d~~ ~~g~~}
~~starti~~{ng ~~by a moanind~~} ~~sound I stopped~~
[~~?man's~~]}
[?]}
~~When hearing as I thought a human voice~~
~~I stopped & listened not without such fear~~
Returning late, I heard a moaning sound;
~~Upon me as the time & place might breed~~
Then,
~~But~~ thinking that my fancy had deceived me,
I hurried on, moan~~s~~,
~~I turned away,~~ when straight a second ~~sound~~
struck }
[?smote]}
A human voice distinct, ~~fell~~ on my ear.
So
~~Thus~~ guided, distant a few steps, I found
An aged Man, & such as you describe.
Mar: You heard!—he called you to him? Of all men
but where is he, guide me,
The best and kindest!~~—lead me to the spot~~
~~Lead me this instant~~ —
~~This instant lead me~~—
That I may see him.
Eldred
~~Robt~~ — — — — — — On a ridge of rocks
A lonesome Chapel stands, deserted now,
is left,
The bell ~~remains~~, which no one dares remove;
And when the stormy wind blows oer the peak
It rings, as if a human hand were there
guess must have
To pull the cord. I ~~fancy~~ he ~~had~~ heard it;
And it had led him towards the precipice,
;}
To climb up to the spot whence the sound came,}
But he had failed thro' weakness; From his hand
~~Poor man, he was too feeble for such effort~~

2013 storm:
2024 now:
2026 o'er
2028 *as MS. 3, rev as MS. 3*

2014/2015 The revision of "starting" is in pencil, as is the correction of "moaning."

Rob: — — — — — — — — ~~*His head was bare*~~
lay
His staff ~~was~~ by his side; and near the brink
Of a small pool of water he was laid [2033]
might
His face close to the water. As ~~it~~ seem~~ed~~
He had stooped down to drink and had remained
Without the strength to rise
Mor: — — — — — — — — — *Well, well, he lives* [2035]
Oh God! he lives! What said he?

[61ʳ]

But few words
Rob: He only spake to me of a dear daughter
Who, so he feared, would never see him more [2038]
And of a stranger to him, one by whom
He had been sore misused— But you are troubled
Perhaps you are his son?
The Allseeing
Mor: — — — — — — — ~~*Heaven*~~ *knows*
I did not think he had a living child
——And whither did you carry him?
Rob: — — — — — — — — — *He was torn,*
His head was bruised, and there was blood about him [2045]
Mor: That was no work of mine
was it
Rob: — — — — — — — — *Nor*‸*mine,* ~~*God knows*~~
Mor: But had he strength to walk? I could have born him
A thousand miles
Rob: — — — — — — *I am in poverty*
And know how busy are the tongues of men

109

~~was~~ had dropped ~~&~~ & close upon
His staff ~~lay by his side~~; ~~&~~ ^ ~~near~~ ^ the brink 2032
he ^ was laid, 2033
Of a small pool of water ~~as might seem~~
~~His face close to the water. As might seem~~
~~Like one who having stooped to drink~~,
~~He had stooped down to drink & had remained~~
As if he had stooped to drink, & so remained 2034
Without the strength to rise.
Mar. — — — — — — — Well, well, he lives (impatiently) 2035
~~Well, well~~
~~O God, ^ he lives! What said he?~~
^ And all is safe; what said he?
Eldred
~~Robt.~~ — — — — — — — — But few words: 2036
{a
He only sp{oke to me of a dear daughter, 2037
Who, so he feared, would never see him more; 2038
And of a Stranger to him, one by whom 2039
he forgave ~~the wrong~~ 2040
He had been sore misused. But ~~you are troubled~~;
The wrong
And the wrong-doer —You are troubled 2041
Perhaps you are his Son?
Mar — — — — — — — The Allseeing knows, 2042
I did not think he had a living Child.— 2043
But
~~/ And~~ whither did you carry him?
Eldred
~~Robt.~~ — — — — — — — — — — — He was torn, 2044
—}
His head was bruised, & there was blood about him, } 2045
Mar: That was no work of mine.
Eldred
~~Robt~~ — — — — — — — Nor was it mine. 2046
Mar: But had he strength to walk? I could have borne him 2047
A thousand miles.
Eldred
Robt. — — — — I am in poverty, 2048
; } ;
And know how busy are the tongues of men. } 2049

2035 *speaker ident over illeg eras (Dora)* lives,
2036 safe, words.
2040–2041 *as MS. 3, rev as MS. 3 but* wrong-doer. You are troubled—
2042 *speaker ident over illeg eras (Dora)*
2046a *speaker ident over* Eldred *erased (Dora)*
2047 *speaker ident over illeg eras (Dora)*

2032 Revision above the line appears to be JC's.

48 *My heart was wi{l tling, Sir, but I am one* [2050]
good
49 *Whose deeds will not stand by their own light*
50 *And though it smote me more than tongue can speak*
51 *I left him*
Mor: *(looks at him for some time)*
I believe that there are beings
52 *For unknown ends permitted to put on*
53 *The shape of man, and thou art one of them*

[61v]

54 *But human things have pressed so hard on me* — —}
55 Rob: *My wife and children came into my mind* [2058]
56 Mor: *Oh monster! monster! there are three of us*
57 *And we shall howl together (after a pause in a feeble voice)*
I am deserted ~~at~~
58 *At my worst need: my crimes have brought a judgement*
59 *(pointing to Rob:) On this innocent man—where was it? where?*
(dragging him along)
60 Rob: *'Tis needless, spare your violence. His daughter* [2063]
n word a thousand curses lodge
61 Mor: *Aye, is} there ~~not damnation in the word~~?*
62 *This old man had a daughter*
Rob: *— — — — — — — — To the spot*
63 *I hurried back with her—oh save me, Sir,* [2066]
64 *From such a journey—there was a black tree*
65 *A single tree—she thought it was her father*
66 *Oh Sir! I would not see that hour again*
67 *For twenty lives. The day-light dawned and now* {—
~~Mor: (as if waking from a dream)~~
68 ~~*What damning fiend has poisoned the i'th' ear?*~~

48 MH's 1799 correction.
57/58 Deletion in 1799 by erasure.

110

My heart was willing, Sir, but I am One 2050
Whose good deeds will not stand by their own light; 2051
words can tell, ~~I can~~ 2052
And, though it smote me more than ^ ~~*tongue can speak*~~
I left him. ~~/~~ ^ Phantoms
for some time {*B*
Mar: *(looks at him) I believe that there are* {~~*beings*~~ 2053
That in the shape of Man do cross our path 2054
~~*For unknown ends permitted to put on*~~
On evil instigation to make sport ~~*of our di*~~ 2055
On our distress *t*}
~~*The shape of Man*~~, *& thou are*} *one of them!—* 2056
~~*Of our dstress—but things substanti*~~[*?al*]
~~*But human things on me*~~ *have pressed so hard*—— 2057
But things substanti[*?al*]
Eldred
~~*Rob*^t^~~. *My wife & children came into my* ~~*head*~~ *mind.* 2058
Mar: *Oh Monster! Monster! there are three of us* 2059
And we shall howl together. *(after a pause, & in a feeble voice)*
I am deserted 2060
in a net 2061
At my worst need; my crimes have ~~*brought a judgement*~~
~~*Upon*~~ *Entangled this* ~~*good*~~ *poor*
pointing
~~*On* ^ *this innocent*~~ ^ *Man—where was it*—*?*} *where?—* 2062
to ~~*Rob*^t^~~ *Eld:* *(dragging him along)*
Eld:
~~*Rob*^t^~~. *'Tis needless; spare your violence. His daughter—* 2063
scorpions
Mar: *Aye, in the word a thousand* ~~*curses*~~ *lodge;* 2064
This old man <u>*had*</u> *a daughter.* ^
Eldred
~~*Rob*^t^~~. *— — — — — — — — To the spot* 2065
{*O*
I hurried back with her {*o save me, Sir,* 2066
!—} {*T*
From such a journey— } {*there was a black tree,* 2067
;} *.—*}
A single tree—} *She thought it was her Father—* } 2068
Oh Sir, I would not see that hour again 2069
For twenty lives. The day-light dawned, & now— 2070

2051 light:
2053 *stage dir del* Beings, *del to* Phantoms
2054 *as MS. 3 but* ends, *rev as MS. 3 but* man
2055 *interlined as MS. 3, but with dash before* to *del to comma*
2056 The shape of Man, *del to* Of our distress,
2057 *del to* But things substantial have so pressed on me— *with false start* B *in margin*
2059/2060 voice. *in stage dir*
2064 lodge:
2065 Man
2067 there

[62ʳ]

Rob: *Nay, hear my tale, 'tis fit that you should hear it* [2071]
As we approached a solitary crow
Rose from the spot—the daughter clapped her hands
And then I heard a shriek so terrible
(Mortimer shrinks back against the scene)
~~frighted~~ startled
The ~~very~~ bird quivered upon the wing [2075]
~~And had an earthquake followed instantly~~
~~It could not more have moved me~~
Dead Dead ~~Dead~~
Mor: — — — — — — — — — *~~Dead, dead, dead~~*
A
~~It is~~ a dismal matter is it Sir
Rob: *(after a pause) ~~matter Sir disturbs you~~*
[?~~in~~]
This ~~business Sir seems to concern you nearly~~
To me, & seemeth [?in]
I'll lead you to the maiden whom I left
With her dead Father's body at my hut
A few steps hence
(Margaret who had been standing for some time at a distance, comes forward)
Margᵗ. — — — — — *Nay Robert, 'tis not fit*
Two wretched beings, each so miserable,
Should come together. ~~Poor unhappy man~~!
~~Silence~~ Thou dost forget thyself
Rob: *~~Thou dost forget thyself—I am confirmed~~*
~~Thou dost forget thyself~~
W *gentle*
~~And~~ we must see the bottom of it (~~to Mortimer~~) Sir,
I said that I would lead you to his daughter
~~Mor: His daughter— Yes lead me to his daughter~~

[62ᵛ]

Rob: *Perhaps 'twere fit I should go on before*
That she may be prepared
Mor: — — — — — — *Thou hast said well*
There will be need of preparation
(Rob: goes off)
(Margᵗ. makes an effort as if to check Rob:—then turns to Mortimer
Master
Margᵗ. — — — — — — — — — *~~Sir~~!* [2080]
Your limbs sink under you; shall I support you?

---

76 The uncertain readings above and below line may be directions to the (1841) copyist.

III

Eldred
~~*Robt*~~. *Nay, hear my tale, 'tis fit that you should hear it.* 2071
As we approached, a solitary crow 2072
Rose from the spot;—the {*D* / *daughter*} *clapped her hands,* 2073
And then I heard a shriek so terrible, 2074
(Mar. shrinks {*b* *ck* / [?]*a*[?]}
The startled bird quivered upon the wing. 2075
Mar: Dead, dead!—
Eldred
~~*Robt*~~ *(after a pause) A dismal matter* ~~*is it*~~ {*S* / *sir*}, *for me,* 2076
~~*For*~~
{*F* / ~~*To me*~~}, {*And* / *&* *seem*} {*s the like* / ~~*eth to be so*~~}, {*fr* / *to*} *you; if 'tis your wish,* 2077
I'll lead you to ~~*the Lady*~~ *his Daughter*{*;* / ~~*—*~~} *but 't* {*were* / *is*} *best* 2078
~~*—Perhaps 'twere fit I should go on before*~~
That she {*should* / *may*} *be prepared; I'll go before?* 2079
Mar: — — — — — — ~~*Thou hast said well*~~—
There ha{*wi* / }*ll be need of preparation*{*.* / *—*} *(*{*El* / *R.*} *goes off)*
~~*(Margaret checks Robt—then turns to Marmaduke)*~~
(Enters ~~*enter*~~*)*
Margt — — — — — — — — — *Master!* 2080
Your limbs sink under you, shall I support you? 2081

2071/2072 *speaker ident* Eldred *del*
2072 As *over eras (Dora)*
2074 *no comma*

2073 The capital is JC's.

Mor: *(taking hold of her arm)*
Woman! I've lent my body to the service
Which now thou tak'st upon thee—God forbid
That thou should'st ever meet a like occasion
purpose in thine heart
With such a[?] ~~view~~‸as mine! ——
was
Marg[t]*. Oh! why have I to do with things like these?*
(Exeunt)

[V.iii] *Scene changes to the door of Robert's cottage*
Matilda seated at the door in stupid grief— to her
enter Robert.

Rob: *Your father, Lady from a wilful hand*
Has met unkindness, so indeed he told me

[63[r]]

And you remember such was my report
From what has just befallen me I have cause
To fear ~~he has been murdered~~ the very worst
My father
Mat: *— — — — — — — — ~~He~~ is dead*
dost come e e
Why ~~comest~~ thou to me with ~~a tale~~ like thi}s}?
words
Rob: *A wicked man should answer for his crimes*
Mat: *Thou see'st me what I am—*
Rob: *— — — — — — It was most heinous*
And doth call out for vengeance
Mat: *— — — — — — — — — Do not add*
I prithee, to the harm thou'st done already
Rob: *Hereafter you will thank me for this service*
I met a man, who, from the plainest proofs
Of interfering Heaven, I have no doubt
Laid hands upon your Father—fit it were
You should prepare to meet him—
~~But see the murderer guided by my wife~~
I have nothing to do with Others— ~~help me~~
Mat: *~~Oh help me to my father I have nothing~~*

93 Deletion of doubtful reading in 1799 by erasure.

Mar (taking her arm) *Woman I've lent my body to the service* 2082
Which now thou tak'st upon thee. God forbid 2083
That thou should ever meet a like occasion 2084
With such a purpose in thine heart as mine was. 2085
Marg^t. *O, why have I to do with things like these?* 2086
(exeunt)

112

Eldred's
Scene, (changes to the door of ~~Robt.~~ ^ts Cottage
Idon{e/ia seated}. ~~in stupid grief)~~

Enter ~~Robt.~~ {Eldred/Robt} *Your {F/father, Lady, from a willful hand* 2087
Has met unkindness; so indeed he told me, 2088
And you remember such was my report: 2089
From what has just befallen me I have cause 2090
To fear the very worst.
Ido ~~Mat~~ *——————— My Father is dead,* 2091
Why dost thou come to me with words like these? 2092
Eldred ~~Robt.~~ *A wicked man should answer for his crimes.* 2093
Ido: *Thou see'st me what I am.*
Eldred ~~Robt~~ *——————— It was most heinous,* 2094
And doth call out for vengeance.
Ido *————————— Do not add,* 2095
I prithee, to the harm thou'st done already— 2096
Eldred ~~Robt~~ *Hereafter thou wilt thank me for this service.* 2097
Hard by ~~I [?had]~~ a man I met who, from plain proofs 2098
~~I met a man who from the plainest proofs~~
Of interfering heaven, no {I} have no doubt, 2099
Laid hands upon your Father. Fit it were 2100
You should prepare to meet him.
Ido *~~I have nothing to do w~~ I have nothing* 2101

2084 should *rev to* shouldst *(Dora)*
2087 *second comma omitted*
2091 very *blotted, recopied above line*
2093 Man
2097 thou wilt *del to* you will
2098 by, met,

2087 The capital is JC's.

18 *~~To do with him~~*
Help me to my father
~~*Rob:*~~ *— — — — ~~You must speak to him~~*

[63^v]

Matilda turns her head & sees Mortimer who enters leaning upon Margaret— Matilda throws herself upon his neck——after some time
19 *Mat:* *In joy I met thee: '~~tis~~ but a few hours back*
{ thus one human stay
20 *And {now we meet again^— ~~Nay shake not so~~*
Better than all earths sympathy could give
21 *—~~In such a wilderness~~——*
Is left me still in thee—Nay shake not so
In such a wilderness thing
Mor: *— — — — — — To see no ~~thing friend~~*
22 *No not the moon in heaven*
Mat: *— — — — — — — And perish so* [2107]
~~mourn~~
23 *Mor:* *Without a dog to ~~howl~~ for him—*
{T
Mat: *— — — — — — — ~~Oh~~ {think not of it*
24 *But enter there and see him how he sleeps*
25 *Tranquil as he had died in his own bed—* [2110]
in
26 *Mor:* *Tranquil— why not?*
Mat: *— — — — — — Oh Peace! in*
Mor: *— — — — — — — — He is ~~at~~ peace*
27 *His body is at rest— there was a plot* [2112]
hideous
28 *A ~~damned~~ plot against the soul of man*
29 *'~~Tis baffled—I have baffled it~~*
*'I took effect & yet I baffled^it^*
In some degree
Mat: *— — — — — — — — — — ~~Alas~~!*
Beloved Marmaduke
30 *~~You too have need of comfort~~*

[64^r]

Mor: *— — — — — — — — ~~I remember~~*
31 *'~~Twas the first riddle that employed my fancy~~*
Give me a
32 *~~To hunt out~~ reason~~s~~ why the wisest thing*
33 *That the earth owns should never chuse to die* [2120]

---

26 Above and below line are directions to the (1841) copyist. The deleting line is in pencil; underlining was added in 1841.
29 The stroke at end of line may indicate end of text on this page.
29–30 Further developed in MS. 2A, 4^v.

To do with others; help me to my Father——
(She turns & sees Marmaduke)
leaning on Marg[t]*- throws*
herself upon his neck
& after some time)

113

In joy I met thee, but a few hours back;
And thus we meet again; one human stay
~~*Better than all earthly sympathy could give*~~
Is left me still in thee—} *Nay, shake not so.*
Mar: *In such a wilderness—to see no thing,*
pitying
No—not the ^ *Moon* ~~*in heaven.*~~
Ido — — — — — — — — *And perish so.*
Mar: *Without a dog to moan for him.*
Ido — — — — — — — — *Think not of it,*
But enter there & see him how he sleeps,
Tranquil as he had died in his own bed.
Mar: *Tranquil,* —} *why not?*
Ido: — — — — — — *Oh, peace!*
Mar — — — — — — — — — — *He* *is* *at peace;*
His body is at rest, :} *there was a plot,*
A hideous plot, against the soul of man:
It took effect—& yet I baffled it,
In *some* *degree.*
Ido: — — — — — *Between us stood, I thought,*
A cup of consolation, filled from heaven
For both our needs; must I, & in thy presence,
Alone partake of it?—Beloved Marmaduke!
Mar: *Give me a reason why the wisest thing*
That the earth owns shall never chuse to die

---

in final stage dir on p. 112 neck,
2107 *as MS. 3, rev as MS. 3 but* Moon!

34 *But some one must be near to count his groans—*
35 *The wounded deer retires to solitude—*
36 *And dies in solitude— all things but man*
37 *All die in solitude— ~~an awful lesson~~*
38 *~~There is much wisdom in it~~—*
(~~Mor: leaves Mat: and goes towards~~
~~the cottage~~
Mysterious God

~~turns towards the Cottage~~
~~Mor:~~ (in going) — — — ~~The fault's not mine~~—
39 *If she had never lived I had not done it*
Mat: — — — — — — — — Alas the thought
40 *Of such a cruel death has overwhelmed him*
(as Mortimer enters the cottage
~~But will pass away~~
41 *I will go too*
I will go too, Lady
~~will~~
Rob: — — — — ~~Lady, you^do well~~ unjust suspicion
You will do well—~~if you should hear a groan~~
42 *~~He has been dead and silent many hours~~*
Or from his side
43 *~~If you should hear a groan or from his side~~*
~~Or~~
44 *He should uplift his hand—that would be evident*
Shame , Shame
45 *Marg^t. ~~Fie~~, Robert fie!*
Mor: (coming from the cottage) to himself)
The dead have but one face
(goes up to Matilda)

[64^v]

meek
46 *And such a man—so ~~mild~~ and unoffending*
Helpless & harmless as a babe. A Man
47 *~~A Man~~ By obvious signal, to the world's protection*
48 *Solemnly dedicated— to decoy him——*
(Robert comes forward, ~~listening eagerly~~)
49 *Mat: Oh! had you seen him living!—~~he had a face~~—*
Mar. ~~This world of ours~~
50 *in ~~There's not a soul~~ — ~~I am~~ T ~~to thee~~ am I*

41 MH's 1799 insertion of "will."
41–44 Further developed in MS. 2A, 4^v.
50 The "in" is a direction to the 1841 copyist.

114

But some one must be near to count his groans. 2121
The wounded deer retires to solitude, 2122
{*a*
And dies in solitude: {*All things but man,* 2123
(Moving *towards the*
All die in solitude. (~~*He moves apart*~~)
cottage door)
Mysterious God, 2124
If she had never lived I had not done it!— 2125
Ido *Alas the thought of such a cruel death* 2126
must follow— {~~*Mar*~~
Has overwhelmed him~~—*I will go too*~~ (~~*As*~~ {[?] ~~*enters the Cottage*~~)

Eldred
~~*Rob*^t^~~ — — — — — — — — — — — — — *Lady!* 2127
{*u*
You will do well; (she goes) {*Unjust suspicions may* 2128
:}
Cleave to this Stranger; } *if, upon his entering,* 2129
The dead man heave a groan, or from his side 2130
—}
Uplift his hand, } *that would be evidence.* 2131
Eldred, Shame!
Marg^t^ *Shame,* ~~*Rob*^t^*. shame!*~~
both
(*returning*— — *dead*
Mar — — — — *The* ~~*dead*~~ *have but one face.* (*to himself* 2132
(~~*coming from the Cottage*~~) [?]
~~*to himself*~~
{( )}
{~~*to Ido*~~} *And such a man—so meek & unoffending—* 2133
:} *a*
Helpless & harmless as a babe. } ~~*A*~~ *man* 2134
By obvious signal to the world's protection 2135
Solemnly dedicated—to decoy him! 2136

~~*Aye, so filled*~~
Ido ~~*Oh had you seen him living! Oh! had you*~~
{[?~~*So*~~]
ar} *I,* {*Aye so filled*
M[?*or*]} — — — — — — — — — [~~? *To*~~] ~~*thee am I*~~,

2126 Alas,
2127 follow—}
2131 hand,— *with comma del*
2131–2133 *further developed in MS. 3A, 9*^r^
2132 Shame! Eldred shame! both *prefixed to stage dir*
2136 him!—

2132 The "dead" above the line is JC's.
2134 The "a" above the line is JC's.

So filled with horror is this ~~world of ours~~ wretched world
Mor: — — — — — — *~~Now mark this world of ours~~*
~~Am~~ the most precious thing it now con[?]~~ns~~

~~A man may be a mur~~ {~~d~~ [?] ~~erer and his hand~~
~~Shall tell no tales nay the first brook he meets~~
~~Shall wash it clean~~
~~A man may be the father's murderer~~
~~And to the daughter the most precious thing~~
The world contains—Matilda at this moment
I feel a most unusual fondness for thee
Therefore {b my me the truth must be revealed
Thou must be wise as I am thou must know
By whom thy Parent
{~~T~~ ~~What human nature is decoyed~~, betrayed— Idonea
I have the proofs {!
Mat: — — — — — — *Oh! miserable father!*
Thou did'st command ^me to, bless all mankind
Nor to this moment have I ever wished
Evil to any living thing— but hear me
Hear me ye Heavens! (kneeling) may vengeance haunt the fiend
For this most cruel murder—let him live
And move in terror of the {el leements.—

[65r]

The thunder send him on his knees to prayer
In the open streets, and let him think he sees
If e'er he entereth the house of prayer
The roof self-moved, unsettl{e ing o'er his head

51, 66 MH's 1799 corrections.

With horror is this world, am unto thee
~~So filled with horror is this wretched world~~,
thing ~~a~~ that
The^most precious ~~th~~{~~ing~~ it now contains,

---

had
Ido *Oh ~~had~~^you seen him living!——*
Mar *— — — — I, so filled* 2137
With horror is this world, am unto thee 2138
The thing most precious that it now contains: 2139
through me alone
Therefore ~~by me the truth~~ must be revealed 2140

~~Therefore by me the truth must be re[ ]aled~~
~~Thou must be wise as I am, thou must know~~

115

~~The proofs~~ *destroyed,*
~~s~~ e
By whom thy Parent was ~~dec~~{~~oyed~~, Idoni{a! 2141
I have the proofs!—
Ido: *— — — — — Oh miserable Father!* 2142
Thou didst command me to bless all mankind; 2143
Nor, to this moment, have I ever wished 2144
Evil to any living thing; but hear me, 2145
Hear me, ye Heavens! (kneeling) may vengeance haunt the fiend 2146
For this most cruel murder; let him live 2147
s ;
And move in terror of the element{,{~~+~~ 2148
The thunder send him on his knees to prayer 2149
In the open streets, & let him think he sees, 2150
If e'er he entereth the house of ~~Prayer~~ God, 2151
The roof self-moved, unsettling oer his head; 2152

2137–2138 *commas del to parens*
2139 precious,
2141 *comma del to period*
2144 *first comma omitted*
2146 Heavens!—
2152 roof,

2137 The revision is JC's.
2137–2140 On the back of this pasteover is:

His Tool the Wandering Beggar made last night
A plain confession such as leaves no doubt
Knowing what otherwise we know too well
That she revealed the truth. Stand by me now
[ ] nest of vipers

See ll. 1419–1423.

And let him stepping into bed at nights
Point to his wife the blood-drops on his pillow [2154]
Mor: *Heaven is my witness that my heart has joined*
thee
Mat: *(leaning on Mortimer)*
Left to the mercy of that savage man
How could he call on his beloved child!
Mor: *Aye come to me and weep (he kisses her)*
(to Robert) Yes look my friend
do
The devils at such sights clap their hands [2160]
(Robert retires into the cottage alarmed
Mat: *Thy limbs are torn, thy face is pale and hagard*
Hast thou pursued the monster?
Mor: *— — — — — — — — Aye and found him*
And he must perish
Mat: *— — — — — Leave him to the pangs*
Of his own breast

[65ᵛ]

Mor: *— — — — He must be put to death,*
And for thy sake for he will haunt thy bed

A photograph of 65ᵛ is provided below, p. 721.
81b Comma deleted by erasure, 1799.

when he would lie down at night,
And let him, ~~stepping into bed at nights~~ 2153
Point to his wife the blood-drops on his pillow. 2154
My voice was silent, but
Mar: ~~In deep sincerity~~^my heart hath joined thee. 2155
Ido: (leaning
on Mar) Left to the mercy of that savage Man!/ 2156
{w upon
How {could he call ~~on~~^ his ~~beloved~~ Child! (turns to Mar.). 2157
O Friend! 2158
My faithful, true & only Comforter.
Mar: Aye, come to me & weep. (he kisses her)
maduke Eldred ~~Varlet~~
(to ~~Robt~~) ~~Yes, look my friend~~
Eldred) Yes, Varlet, look, 2159
{p
The devils at such sights do cla{sp their hands. 2160
Eldred
(~~Robt.~~ retires, alarmed)
vest is
Ido: Thy ~~limbs are~~^ torn, thy face is pale & haggard; 2161
Hast thou pursued the Monster? 2162a

11[ ]

Mar — — — — — — — — — I have
~~Aye—~~
And he must perish & found hi[ ]
Ido — — — — Leave him to the pangs
Of his own breast.
Mar: — — — — — — — — He must be put to [ ]

Mar: — — — — — — — — — I have found him.— 2162b
~~And he must perish~~
Ido: — — — — — ~~Leave him to the pangs~~
~~Of his own breast~~
Mar: — — — — — ~~He must be put to death.~~

~~And for thy sake, for he w{ill {ou d} haunt thy bed~~

2154 pillow.} !
2157 would] could
2159a *no comma*
2160/2161 *no comma in stage dir*
2161 face is pale and haggard; *del and rev to* cheek is deadly pale;

2162b On the back of the pasteover is:

— — — — — — — — I have found him
he must perish
Leave him to the pangs

See ll. 2162b ff.

83 *Thy prayers, thy waking and thy sleeping thoughts*
84 *—Oh would—that thou had'st perished in the flames*
85 Mat: *Art thou not here the friend of all the helpless*
There was a time when this protecting hand
86 Mor: ~~*The feeble sought me once and my protection*~~
87 *Availed against the mighty never more* [2166]
upon a
88 *Shall ~~any~~ blessings wait ~~on~~ deed of mine*
Love would in me have power ~~in me~~ to play with words
89 Mat: ~~*Those words, I could make mockery of them*~~*, but*
~~*Love would have power in me to*~~
That seem
{*I*
90 ~~*Your voice*~~ {~~*is dreadful*~~ ~~*—Oh my only friend*~~
Safeguard
91 ~~*What thoughts are these*~~*? (taking hold of his arm)*
~~*Are these*~~ {*T*
~~*What mean*~~ {*these desperate thoughts*
~~*Are these*~~ *Here is no malady*
92 Mor: *Here is a malady (striking his breast & forehead)*
And here, and here
93 *A mortal malady*
That seem so void of meaning but your voice
~~*Mat*~~: *— — — —* ~~*Heavens*~~*!*
Is dreadful— Safeguard of my Soul ~~be calm~~ what thoughts
Are these be calm.—Here is no malady
{*H*
{*here is*
ac
Mor: *— — — — — — — I am^curst*
94 *All nature curses me and in my heart* [2175]
95 *Thy curse is fixed*
That seem so void of meaning but your voice
Is dreadful. Safeguard of my Soul ~~what thoughts~~
what mean

[66r]

Mat: *(forcing a smile) — — Come, come this desperate effort*
96 *To rid my spirit of its present sorrow*
97 *Indeed it is ill-judged*
— — — — — — ~~*Too long the truth*~~
Mor: *— — — — — — —* ~~*Look on my face*~~ *L*
~~*Has lingered*~~ *Look on my face*
98 ~~*Mat*~~: ~~*Oh! when has this affliction visited thee*~~*?*

92, 95 Underlinings probably added in 1841.
A photograph of 66r is provided below, p. 722.

~~*Thy prayers, thy waking & thy sleeping thoughts—*~~

l *st*
~~/~~*Oh! wou* {*d'* ~~*st*~~ *that thou had* {*perished in the flames!* 2163

I *to* ~~*succour the bereft*~~
M{*do :* ~~*Art thou not here—the friend of all the helpless?*~~

t
Here are{ *thou, then can I be desolate?—* 2164

Mar : There was a time, when this protecting ~~*arm*~~ *hand* 2165
Availed against the mighty; never more 2166
Shall blessings wait upon a deed of mine. 2167

Idon: Wild words for me to hear, for me an Orphan, 2168
~~*Ido : Love would in me have power to play with words*~~

ua
Committed to thy gau{*rdianship by Heaven;* 2169
~~*That seem so void of meaning, but your voice*~~

st
And, if Thou has{ *forgiven me, let me hope,* 2170
~~*Is dreadful. Safeguard of my Soul, what thoughts*~~
In this—deep sorrow trust, that I am thine, 2171
~~*Are these—be calm— (taking hold of his arm)*~~
For closer care;——
here is no malady (taking his arm) 2172

{*Th*
Mar : {*there is a malady.*
And here, & here, 2173
(striking his heart & forehead)
A mortal malady—I am accurst: 2174

me
All nature curse ~~*s me*~~, *& in my heart* 2175
s

;—the truth must be laid bare. 2176
Thy curse is fixed

{~~*C*~~
~~*Ido (forcing a smile)*~~ {~~*come, come, this desperate effort*~~
~~*turn*~~ ~~*from*~~
~~*To rid my spirit of its present sorrow*~~
~~*Indeed it is ill-judged*~~
~~*Mar :*~~ *——————* ~~*Look on my face*~~

bare
~~*'Twill help my speech to lay bare the truth^at once*~~
~~*Ido : Oh! When hath this affliction visited thee?*~~

2170 thou
2171 *dash del* sorrow, *final comma del*
2172 here, malady.
2173 There, *period del to dash* {a / And}
2176–2183 *further developed in MS. 3A, 9*[r]
2176 *no dash*

2175 Revision above the line is JC's.

[?reason]
'Twill help my speech to lay ~~bare the truth~~^at once.
~~Thy Father perished by~~
e
~~Mor:~~ ~~I am thy~~}~~father's murderer~~ ~~of thy father~~
(Matilda runs ~~off~~ into the cottage)
Mor: (alone)
Three words have such a power!—This mighty burden
All off at once! 'Tis done, and so done too
~~must~~ That
~~That~~^I^have cased her heart in adamant
~~As is my own this scrip that would not cause~~
~~This little scrip when first I found it here~~
~~The little finger of a Child to ache~~
~~I sunk ten thousand fathoms into hell~~
t
{[? ~~Yes~~}] {~~Lie~~ ~~Up~~}
{[?]}{[?] [?~~like~~] ~~a mountain~~ u{~~pon my bosom with a load~~^
I was a coward then—but now am schooled
Coward I was but now
~~To firmer purposes~~, there doth not lie
l
Within the compass of a mortat}thought
but to endure
A deed that I would shrink from—~~and I can endure~~
That is my destiny——the only end
~~If I had done it with a mind resolved~~
~~The only end & purp~~[?] for which henceforward I on
~~There had been something in the deed~~ earth must
[?live]
~~To give me strength to bear the recollection~~
~~I on earth~~
~~But as it is this scrip which would not cause~~
~~The little finger of a child to ache~~
~~Doth lie upon my bosom with a load~~
*~~A mountain could not equal~~^*

[66v]

(Enter Matilda from the cottage dragging Robert)
en
X *Rob: Already I've be[?] forced, an innocent man*
For many moons to make my bed with toads
But it is come at last and I must die
Mat: (repeating Robert's former words)
"Your father has been murdered" (turning to Robert
By thy hands——

---

99 Revised in 1799 from "I am thy father's murderer" to "I am the murderer of thy father," probably in DW's hand.
107 MH's 1799 correction.
116 MH's 1799 correction. The meaning of the X here and at l. 123 is unclear.

117

~~'Twill help my speech to lay truth bare at once~~
the truth must be laid bare.

~~Mar:~~ *It must be told, & borne—I am the Man*
(Abused, betrayed, but how it matters not)
Presumptuous above all that ever {breathed / [?lived]}
Who casting, as I thought, a guilty Person
Upon heaven's righteous judgement, did become
An Instrument of Fiends.— ~~By~~ Thro' me, ~~by~~ thro me
Thy Father ~~was abandoned—thro me he perished!~~ perished. Thro
(Ido: ~~runs into the Cottage)~~
Would fail to tea{c / [?]}h me that those words are true— / Perished thro thee! a miracle
~~Three words have such a power! This mighty burden~~
Beloved! {So / I would call thee} if I dared
~~All {O me / off}~~ ^ ~~at once—! 'Tis done, & so done too~~
& in {t / h}{y / er} frozen heart,
~~That in her frozen heart~~ {C / conflict} must {~~end~~ / [?ease]}
~~That I have cased her heart in adamant—~~ cease
absolute
The extremes of suffering ~~will~~ meet in ^ peace.
Coward I was, but now there doth not lie
Within the compass of a mortal thought
A deed that I would shrink from — but to endure—
That is my destiny—the only end
For which ^ on earth henceforward I ^ ~~on earth~~ must live.
Enter Idonia, dragging Eldred

Eld: *Already I've been forced, an innocent Man*
For many moons to make my bed with toads
But it is come at last, & I must die
Ido: (repeating Eld's former words) *"Your father has been murdered" (turning to Eldred*
—by thy hands

At this point in the manuscript (p. 117), the original pp. 117–120 were lifted out as a bifolium; the original leaf now numbered 121–122 was cut away, as was a preceding leaf (now missing). Two bifolia replaced pp. 117–120; the first replacement leaf was then torn out, but the text is not affected and continues on replacement pp. 117a–122a. Surviving original pages have been reintegrated into the base text, while the pages containing revisions (117a–122a) have been treated as though they were pasteovers.

120 *Rob:* *And would you use me thus?*
Marg[t]. — — — — — — — *You fear too much*
121 *He is a man too wretched far*
122 *To be your enemy*
Eldred
Mat: *(to Robert)* — — *Thou hast prevailed*
123 *Upon his gentle nature*
Mor: *(to Robert) stepping forward) If the dregs*
124 *Of such a life as thine be worth these tears*
125 *Go dry them up—thou shalt not die for this*
(Turns to Matilda—presents her a letter)

---

123 See note to l. 116, above.

118

Eldred And would you use me thus?

Marg^t^. {— / Y} *— — — — — — You fear too much*
He is a man too wretched far, to be, ~~*your enemy*~~
Your enemy
Ido: (to Eldred) Thou has prevailed
Upon his gentle nature
Mar (stepping forward to El) — If the dregs
Of such a life as thine be worth these tears
Go dry them up—thou shalt not die for this
(~~*Turns to Idonia*~~*—* {& / } *gives a letter)*
Ido
(reads) Be not surprized if you hear that some signal
judgement has befallen {th / me} *Man who calls himself*
Your Father, he is now with me, as his signature
will shew—~~*suspend*~~ [*abstain from*] *conjecture till you see me*
Herbert
Marmaduke
The writing your's the signature my Father's
You have then seen my father?
Mar — — — — — — — — — He has leaned
Upon this arm

117[a]

laid bare—
It must be told, & borne. ~~/~~ *I am the Man,* 2177
(Abused, betrayed, but how it matters not) 2178
Presumptuous above all that ever breathed, 2179
Who, casting, as I thought, a guilty Person 2180
Upon {H / heaven'} {' / s} *righteous judgement, did* {become / [?perceive]} 2181
An Instrument of Fiends. ~~/~~ *Thro* {' / ugh} *me, thro* {' / ugh} *me,* 2182
Thy Father perished.
—by what mischance? 2183
what
Ido: — — — — — — Perished ~~*thro thee — a miracle*~~
~~*Would fail to teach me that those words are true*~~
Mar: Belovèd:—if I dared, so ~~*I*~~ *would* {I} *call thee—* 2184
Conflict must cease, &, in thy frozen heart, 2185
The extremes of suffering meet in absolute peace. 2186
(He gives a letter)

2180 {P / person}
2183–2186 *further developed in MS. 3A, 16^r^*

2183 The "what" below the line is JC's.

Mat: *(reads) "Be not surprized if you hear that some*
signal judgment has befallen the man who calls
himself your father he is now with me as his

[67r]

signature will shew—suspend your judgement
till you see me — *Herbert*
Mortimer
(Mor: points)
Mat: *The writing yours—that signature my father's* [2193]
~~*be it so*~~
You have then seen my father ~~*—what of that*~~*?*
~~*how & where?*~~
~~*It was not kind! you should have told me of it*~~
~~*he has leaned*~~
~~*Mor: (his hand pointing to his heart)*~~
~~*O that, that eye of thine were present here!*~~
~~*Now will I tell thee how I dealt with him*~~ —
~~*Into a foaming torrent*~~
Mat: — — — — — — — ~~*He was found*~~
~~*My father he was found upon the heath*~~
Mor: *If a man have a tongue to tell these things*
A heart that cannot suffer and a soul
That cannot fear—what has he lost? These charms
These horrid charms of thought
~~*Mor:*~~ ~~*He has leaned upon me as I*~~ *He has leaned*
~~*Upon this arm his guide*~~
Upon this arm, {T
{towards {t ?}
~~*Mat:*~~ — — — — — — — — *{The convent }* ~~*Mor*~~*{*~~*maduke*~~
{timer
Ido——— You led him

A photograph of 67r is provided below, p. 723.

Ido: *(reads) "Be not surprized if you hear that some signal*
"judgment has befallen the Man who calls himself
{~~y~~ "your
{~~Your~~
"~~Idonias~~ Father; he is now with me, as his sig{nature
{—
"will shew ~~/~~: abstain from conjecture till you see
"me.
"Herbert.
"Marmaduke."
Oswald's m}
The writing ~~yours~~, the signature th{y Father's:
And here is yours or do my eyes deceive me
You have then seen my Father?
{— —
Mar: *{He h — — — — — He has leaned*
Upon this arm.

Ido *— — — You led him towards the Convent?*

9}
117}

d}
Peng{ ragin}
That Convent was } Castle. Thither
We were his guides. I that night resolved
That he should wait thy coming till the day
Of resurrection— Oswald
Ido: *— — — — — — — — — Name him not*

(Enter female Beggar)

Beg *And he is dead! that Waste how shall I cross it*
By night, by day—never shall be able
To travel half a mile alone—Good Lady!
!}
Forgive me!—Saints forgive me,{ had I thought
It would have come to this!
Ido: *— — — — — — What mean ye—speak!*
T} *sweet*
Beg (pointing I{his innocent Gentleman,—[?]} heavens! I told him
at Mar:
Such tales of your dead Father—God is my judge
I thought there was no harm—but that bad man
He bribed me with his gold & looked so fierce
Mercy! I said I know not what—Oh pity me
I said, sweet Lady, you were not his daughter—
—Pity me—I am haunted—thrice this day
My conscience made me wish to be struck blind
And then I would have prayed—& had no voice

2187/2191 *no comma in third line of letter*
2193 yours, *del to* Oswald's;
2194 *interlined, as MS. 3 but* yours— . . . me? *and stage dir added:* looks steadily at the paper *del and rewritten in margin*

~~Bord Oswald~~
Mor: *That convent was ~~Mounteagle~~ Castle—Thither* [2197]
{we {ere
~~Thither~~ {he wa {s his guides ~~that~~ & I that night
~~I led him on that very night resolved~~ resolvd
That he should wait thy coming till the day
Of resurrection.—~~Rivers~~ Oswald

[67ᵛ]

Oswald
Mat: — — — — — — *~~Rivers~~! ~~oh!~~*
~~The name has terror in it~~ Name him not

(Enter female beggar)

Beg: — — — — — — — — *~~Mercy——mercy~~*
{at
And he is dead! th{is heath how shall I cross it
By night by day—never shall be able [2207]
To travel half a mile alone—Good Lady
~~The~~ Sants
Forgive me—~~Heaven~~ forgive me—had I thought
?}
It would have come to this—}

118[a]

Ido: — — — — *You led him towards the Convent?*
Mar: *That Convent was Castle. Thither*
on
We were his guides. I ^ that night resolved
s}
That he w{hould wait thy coming till the day
Of resurrection—— Oswald——
Ido — — — — — — — — *Name him not.*

Enter Female
Beggar. {*W*
Beggar —And he is dead!—that {*waste, how shall I cross*
?} *I* *it,*
By night, by day—{*never shall ^ be able*
To travel half a mile alone.—Good Lady!
me. {*H*
Forgive me!—Saints forgive ^ ! {*had I thought* *?}*
It would have come to this!— *brings you hither!*}
hither

2197 Stone Arthur *written into blank*
2200a–2205b Oswald—— *and Idonea's* Name him not. *del to:*

Idonea
Miserable woman
{Too quickly moved—}
{Too easily giving way} too easily giving way
pain }
Yet under stress of [?]} which oft the might
Of duty was too feeble to contend with
I put denial on thy suit & hence
With the disastrous issue of last night
Thy perturbation & these frantic words
Be calm I prithee
pray ^
Marmaduke
Oswald—
Idonea
Name him not

then recopied in margin:

Idonea
Miserable woman
Too quickly moved too easily giving way
~~Yet under stress of pain which oft the might~~
~~Of duty was too feeble to contend with~~
I put denial on thy suit & hence,
With the ~~issue of~~ disastrous issue of last night
{e
Thy p{urturbation & these frantic words
Be calm I ~~prithee!~~
pray Thee
Marmaduke.
Oswald—

2200–2205 *further developed in MS. 3A, 1r*
2206 *first dash omitted; first comma del to dash, second to question mark*
2207 *punct del*

2206 "Beggar" above the line and the added capital are JC's.
2207 The inserted "I" is JC's.
2209 The capital is JC's.

Ido
Mat: — — — — — — — ~~*This is most s{t/frange*~~
What mean ye—speak!
Beg: *(to Matilda & pointing to Mor:)*
This innocent gentleman—Sweet Heavens! [2211]
I told him
S{u/hch tales of your dead father—God is my judge
I thought there was no harm, but that bad man
He bribed me with his gold & looked so ~~*terrible*~~ *fierce*
Mercy I said I know not what—oh! pity me
I said sweet lady! you were not his daughter [2216]
~~*Rob: Peace! woman peace!*~~
Pity me
~~*Beg: (to Robert)*~~ — — ~~*I tell you*~~ *I am haunted*
thrice this day
~~*Three times today I wished I were*~~ *struck blind*
My conscience made {m/we wish to be
And then I would have prayed—and had no voice

151b, 153 MH's 1799 corrections.

Ido: — — — — — — — — — *What ~~mean you, speak!~~*
brings you hither?

Beg (pointing to Marmad) This innocent Gentleman. ≁} *Sweet heavens! I told him*
Such tales of your dead Father!—God is my judge,
I thought there was no harm; but that bad man,
He bribed me with his gold, & looked so fierce.
Mercy! I said I know not what—oh pity me—
I said, sweet Lady, you were not his daughter—
—Pity me, I am haunted;—thrice this day
My {c Conscience made me wish to be struck blind;
And then I would have prayed—& had no voice.

---

o} 122}

Ido: Was it my Father—no, no, no, for he
Was meek & patient, feeble, old & blind
Helpless & loved me dearer than his life
—I have a heart
—But hear me. For one question ^ ~~a heart~~
That will sustain me. Did you murder him?
—But hear the process
Mar: No, no, not murder him. ~~But knowest thou this?~~
(showing the scrip
~~*Ido Know it! that belt—the first gift of my love*~~

~~And here's~~ the Scrip that held my father's food!
Mar Proof after proof was pressed upon me guilt
[ ]~~*ar*~~ ~~*We led him to the middle of th*~~{*e* ~~*is Waste*~~
~~*Guilt after guilt*~~ {*M made evident as seemed by blacker guilt*
Whose impious folds enwrapped even thee: but still
~~*withou*~~[ ] ~~*food*~~
~~*I left him there & so he died*~~
~~*He to the middle of the Heath was led*~~
wou} {d
Pity sti}l {l crossed the path of my resolve
And strewed it with perplexity & doubt
Bewilderied I looked up to heaven, & cast

Ido: sinks senseless

Marg[t] & Beggar crowd round
~~(Eldred Marg[t] & Beg: crowd round~~ & bear her into the
Idonia, thy {blind Father Father on the Ordeal
Cottage)

2210 hither? speak!—
2213 harm:
2217 *no opening dash*
2219 *dash del to comma*

2210 The "hither" above the line and the phrase below are JC's.

[68r]

Mat: *Was it my father no, no, no for he* [2220]
Was meek and patient, feeble, old ~~and blind~~ [above: *~~dark~~ & blind*]
Helpless, and loved me dearer far than life [above: *~~& sightless~~*]
—But hear me—For one question I have a {*bove all* / *voice*}
That will sustain me—Did you murder him? [2224]
{*Mar* / *Mor:*} *No, no, not murder him—But knowest thou this*

left [ ]d
Of the bleak Waste—so [ ] died.—
(~~Meanwhile~~)
Mar: Why may we speak these things and do no more

---

here's the Scrip that held my father's food!
Mar: Proof after proof was pressed upon me, guilt
Made evident, as seemed, by blacker guilt
Whose impious folds en~~w~~rapped [?] even thee, but still
Pity would cross the path of my resolve
And strew it with perplexity & doubt;
Bewildered, I looked up to heaven & cast—
Eldred Marg[t] Beg: croud round—
Idonia, thy blind Father on the Ordeal
Of the {b / wleak Waste—left him—& so he died.—
Ido: sinks senseless
Why may we speak these things & do no more
born off
is [~~? ?~~]

Why should a thrust of the arm have such a power—
And words that tell these things be heard in vain
She is not dead. Why if I loved this Woman
I would take care she never woke again
But she will wake & she will weep for me
And say no blame was mine—& so poor fool
Will waste her curses on another name
(He walks about ~~distracted~~)
~~I'll prove it that I murdered him—I'll prove it~~
~~Before the dullest court in Christendom.~~

119[a]

Ido: Was it my Father—no, no, no, for he
(to Marmaduke)
Was meek & patient, feeble, old & blind,
Helpless, & loved me dearer than his life.
—But hear me. For one question, I have a heart
That will sustain me. Did you murder him?

by stroke of arm. {learn :
Mar. No ~~no~~, not ~~murder him~~. But {hear the process,
was {up
Proofs after proof pressed { on me; guilt
Made evident, as seemed, by blacker guilt,

2220 *question mark inserted before dash*
2224 him *over* me *(Dora)*

2223 The underlining under "have" is canceled.
2226–2227 See note to ll. 1609–1611a. Ll. 2226–2236 are developed in MS. 3A, 10[v]

Know it
Mat: ^*That belt—the first gift of my love*
—~~It is~~ the scrip that held my father's food
And here's
Mor: *I led him to the middle of this ~~heath~~ waste*
I left him without food and so he died

Eldred
Matilda sinks senseless on the ground—~~Robert~~
Margaret & the Beggar crowd round her and
during the course of the of the following speech
they bear her into the cottage

Mor: *Why may we speak these things and do no more*
Why should a thrust of the arm have such a power
words that tell these things
And ~~things like these~~ be heard in vain
—She is not dead—Why if I loved this woman
I would take care she never woke again
—But she will wake and she will weep for me
And say no blame was mine—and so poor fool
Will waste her curses on another name
~~And this will be when I am in my grave~~
(He walks about with a quick step)
I'll prove it that I murdered him—I'll prove it
Before the dullest court in Christendom

[68v]

(Enter Robert from the cottage)

Rob: *Do Sir come in and see what may be done*
To bring her to herself—If she should die
What will become of us?

169–170 Revised on 72v in 1841 as follows (a photograph of this page is provided below, p. 725):

proof ~~were~~ pressed upon me
~~Proof after had [?]~~
~~was multiplied of guilt~~
Proof after proof ~~were pressed upon me~~
Guilt made evident as seemed by blaker gult
{heath
He to the middle of the{waste was led—
{P
Yet {pity crossed the path of my resolve
~~[?]~~ still
And strewed it with perplexity & doubt
~~He to the middle of the Waste was led~~
{~~M~~
~~A thought And still~~ {~~my was~~ checked
Bewildered I looked up to heaven & cast
the
Idonia, thy blind Father on that ordeal
left him
Of the bleak Waste^& so he died—

;
Whose impious folds enrapped even thee. } *& truth*
, embodied ;
And innocence, ~~that pleaded~~ in his looks,
rve
His words, & tones, & gestures, did but se { *em*
serve
With me to aggravate his crimes, & heaped
Ruin
Ruin upon the cause for which they pleaded.
of my
Then pity crossed the path { *then resolve;*
Confounded, I looked up to heaven, & cast,
e
Idoni { *a! thy blind Father, on the Ordeal*
Of the bleak Waste—left him—& so he died!—
(Ido: sinks senseless—Beg. Marg^t. &c crowd round & bear her off.)
Why may we speak these things, & do no more;
Why should a thrust of the arm have such a power,
And words that tell these things be heard in vain?
She is not dead. Why!—if I loved this woman—
I would take care she never woke again.
But she will wake, & she will weep for me,

120[a]

no blame
And say, { *poor fool was mine—& so, poor fool,*
Will waste her curses on another name.
(He walks about distractedly—Enter Oswald)

1
125

~~And flung it to the dogs. But I forgive thee~~
Strong to destroy—
[ ]*ter Os:*— — — — — — *~~This is well~~*
[ ]*himself* *Strong also to build up*—
[ ]*w: The starts & sallies of our last encounter*
I trust
Were natural enough—but that's ~~gone by~~
Is all gone by—you have cast off the chains
~~You have outrun my hopes~~. ~~The chains are broken~~
~~I perceive~~

2229 *final comma del*
2230 *first comma omitted, second del*
2234 { H / heaven *(JC)*
2240 *second dash omitted*
2241 *period del to semicolon*
2244 Enter Oswald *del from stage dir, then reinstated (JC)*

2230 Revision below the line is JC's.
2232 The revision is JC's.
The deleted line at the top of p. 125 (revised to 121) runs over from one of the leaves now removed. The missing letters in the left margin are visible on the stub left when this leaf was cut out.

	Mor:	*— — — — — — — Hark'ee my friend,*
185		*That woman was to have been my wife*
		(laughs hysterically) ha! ha!
		(laying his hand on Robert)
186		*Not yet, not yet;——Thy coming is well timed*
187		~~*There is a service to be done for me*~~
188		*Thou must conduct me hence. The executioner*
189		*Must do the business*
	Rob:	*— — — — — — The old man died of cold—*
190		*You are not master of the elements*
191		*It was a bitter night—I was half-frozen*
	Mor:	*(in a commanding tone)*
192		*Did'st hear me, man? The Baron of St Clair*
193		*Lives in this district—lead me to his court*
194	*Rob:*	*Good Master! there was not a wound about him*
195		*That would have killed a mouse*
	Mor:	*— — — — — — — — What's {t/h}{at/e} to me?*
		(drags Robert along)

[69^r]

196	*Rob:*	*Good Sir! be merciful—If I do this*
197		*I ne'er shall sleep in quiet*
	Mor:	*— — — — — — — — — There is something*
198		*That must be cleared away*
	Rob:	*— — — — — — — — How Sir?*
	Mor:	*— — — — — — — — — — That staff*
199		*Which bars the road before me there—'Tis there*
200		*'Tis there breast-high and will not let me pass*
201	*Rob:*	*Good Sir! be calm*
	Mor:	*— — — — — — ~~Bestir thee~~— {L/let's} begone*
202		*She will be waking soon—Dost hear me, man?*
		(dragging him along)
203		~~*Howl, howl poor dog! Thou'lt never find him*~~ more
204		~~*Draggled with storm and wet, howl, howl amain*~~
205		~~*But not in my ears—I was not the death of thee*~~
206		~~*What dost thou there friend? get thee out of the way*~~
207		~~*We must not trouble it*~~—
	~~*Rob*~~*:*	*— — — — — — —* ~~*Be patient, Sir*~~
208	~~*Mor:*~~	~~*What art thou made of man? I would cleave a stone*~~
209	*Rob:*	*Good Sir! The body must be borne to Church*
210		*This is a lonely place—but from the convent*
211		*The ~~Holy~~ friars will bring us needful aid*

The vertical deleting stroke on 69^r is in pencil.

That fettered your nobility of M *mind—*
De{l *tivered heart & head——*
~~And sooner than I prophesied~~. Let us to Syria
This is a paltry field for enterprize
[ ]*ar* *Aye what shall we ~~do next~~ — ~~Infirm & blind~~*
encounter next—this issue—
~~But what of that! If I sent him to his grave~~
Twas nothing more than darkness deepening darkness
And crowning all with the impotence of Death!
(ironically
I am, you see, tho' young, an apt Proficient!—
(Os: confused)
Start not. Here is another face hard by
Come
^*Let us take a peep at both together*
And with a voice at which the dead will quake
Resound the praise of your morality!
(drawing Os: towards the Cottage door
~~(Confused noises with uproar~~ *stops short ~~at the door~~*
But of this strain too much—Men are there Oswald
[ ]*~~oices Hola—there! huzza! (enter Lacy, Wallace &c &c with the Beggar & Wilfred~~*
Who with bare hands wiuld have plucked out thy heart
And flung it to the dogs: but I am raised

2
126

Above, or sunk below all further sense
Of provocation. Leave me with the weight ~~[?]~~
~~One of the Band~~ — — — — ~~I would have dogged~~ [ ]
Of that old man's forgiveness on thy heart
Pressing as heavily as it does on mine
~~To the jaws of Hell! (They rush forward to seize Osw~~[ ]
(confused noises wi[ ]
But for some peaceful end beyond our view
~~I would have dogged him to the jaws of hell~~
Several of the Band enter— { *&* / *(They rush forward & sieze Osw*[ ]
One of them *I would have dogged him to the jaws of Hell—*
vagrant
Osw: *Ha! is it so!* {*That* / *Vile*^*Hag, this ~~issue~~ comes*
From having left a thing like {*her* / *thee alive, (aside*
(Several Despatch him!
voices)
Oswald — — — If I pass beneath a rock
And shout; & with the echo of my voice
Bring down a heap of rubbish & it crushe~~s~~ } *me*

[69v]

212 *Mor:* *~~Right fellow~~! Thou sayest well*
213 *We never shall get thither*
Beg. *(who had entered a little before from the cottage)*
He is crazed
214 *Poor Gentleman! and I have wrought this evil*
215 *The little children from the cottages*
216 *Will be his friends—he will be blessed and pitied*
217 *——What will become of me?—*
Mor: *(to Robert)* *Take heed good angels*
~~angels~~ {*T*
218 *~~Take heed good friend~~,* {*that she recover~~s~~ not & could*
~~Help them fellow~~ thou help them
219 *~~Thou wilt redeem~~ the worst of all the crimes*
And [?coulds] [?turn] help them fellow
220 *Thou hast to answer for*
(Enter Rivers— he looks at Mortimer unobserved by him)
Buzz, buzz ye fools!
221 *That is no substance that ye settle on*
222 *Away! away!*
{*n*
Rob: *(to himself)——Would that some help were* {*high*
Riv: *(to himself*
223 *Strong to destroy—strong also to build up* [2245]
224 *Beg:* *(observing Rivers) Look there!—oh save me from him*

[70r]

(Mortimer & Rivers mutually fasten their eyes on each other for some time
There are men
Mor: *—————— I am a man again*
Who with bare hands would have plucked
out ~~thy~~ heart
225 *~~Riv~~:* *~~Nay something more (pointing to Roberts cottage~~*
And flung it to the dogs
~~Dead~~?
Mor: *———————— ~~Quiet~~*
Riv: *————— ~~As his best friends could wish~~*
~~The~~ starts & sallies of our last encounter
{*~~And~~*
226 {*A~~[?] you~~ Were natural enough but that's gone by*
You have outrun my hopes—the chains
~~Mor~~: *——— ~~Almost as quiet~~*

---

222 MH's 1799 revision.
226 MH's 1799 correction to "And you."

starved
I die without dishonour—Famished^*(smiles exulting*[ ]
scornfully
at Marmadu[ ]
A Fool & coward blended to my wish.
~~*from within*~~
~~*A voice*~~ ~~*(Idonia rushes out towards Marmaduke followed*~~
~~*by Eldred*~~*)*
~~*mind is labouring under*~~
~~*Ido*~~*:* ~~*His is a*~~^~~*strong disease*~~*—O* ~~*save him save him.*~~
~~*Deal with him kindly it will pass away!*~~
~~*round*~~
~~*round*~~
(~~*Enter several Friars, who crowd*~~ *together*
~~*Idonia & conceal her*~~*)*
Wal: Tis done! (Stabs him
Another of the Band— The merciless Traitor!
(~~*reentering*~~*)*
~~*& speaking together*~~
Mar — — — — — — — — A rash deed!
With that reproof do I resign a Station
Of which I have been proud.
Wilfred (approaching Mar:) — — — — ~~*My poor Master!*~~
O my poor Master!

120[a]
Os. (to himself)
o'erturn,
Strong to ~~*destroy*~~*, strong also to build up.—*

2245 *speaker ident del, then reinstated (JC)*

That fettered your nobility of mind
And sooner than
~~Riv~~: ~~(with great pride)~~ — — ~~So~~ I prophesied
This is a paltry field for enterprize
227 ~~We are then friends~~
Mor: — — — — — I am the friend of all men
228 Riv: Of me especially
Mor: — — — — Why yes!
Riv: — — — — — — — A pledge—
229 Mor: Here is my hand— The hue of a pure lily
230 A Lady hand—none of your crimson spots
?
231 Not the less welcome—eh!

[70v]

— — — — — — — — — — — — Most noble
232 The starts and sallies of our last encounter [2246]
233 Mor: Mere foolish freaks!——
Riv: — — — Bravo!—The vessel's cleared —
234 That pestilential weight of heaven knows what
235 Those bundles packed some thousand years ago
236 All plunged into the sea
Mor: — — — — — — — Even so
Riv: — — — — — — — — — And you are happy?
237 Mor: Never so happy
Riv: — — — — Hum! — Stay what's your age?
238 Mor: Just three and twenty summers
Riv: — — — — — — — And his? (pointing to the cottage
An
Mor: — — — — — — — — — — Sixty
r
239 A few moons more ol less
prophesied
Riv: — — — — — — — Let us to Syria
240 This is a paltry field for enterprize— [2251]

[71r]

241 Mor: Aye—what shall we do next? To him
Infirm &
~~Riv~~: — — — — — — — ~~Sickly and~~ blind ~~& infirm~~
~~deserted~~
242 Mor: ~~Drugged, betrayed and starved~~!

231, 239 MH's 1799 corrections.
A photograph of 17r is provided below, p. 724

encounter
{~~enco~~
to Mar: The starts & sallies of our last {~~adventure~~
Were natural enough—but that I trust
Is all gone by.⌿ You have cast off the chains
That fettered your nobility of mind—
Delivered heart & head!
Let~~s~~ us to Syria;
This is a paltry field for enterprize.
Mar: Aye, what shall we encounter next—this issue—

2246–2262 *further developed in MS. 3A, 10*r

2247 *dash following* were *del*

2252 next {? —{T / this

But what of that! If I sent him to his grave
243 ~~*Riv*~~: ~~*Devils*~~*! 'Twas nothing more than darkness deepening darkness*
And crouning all with the impotence of death
I am
Mor: —— You see ~~*I am*~~ *an apt proficient*
Starts
244 *Riv:* ~~*Hell*~~
Starts not—
Mor: —— Nay here is another face hard by [2256]
245 *Let's in and take a peep at both together*
~~*And with one voice that*~~
246 ~~*'Twill be a comment of your morality*~~
and with a voice at which the dead will quake
~~*Resound the praise*~~
Leads *(*~~*Rivers*~~ *towards the cottage)*
Resond the praise of your morality
when he comes to the door stops short
247 ~~*Riv*~~: ~~*Beyond my expectation*~~
Mor: (when he comes to the door stops short) There are men
248 *Who with bare hand would have plucked out thy heart* [2261]
am humbled
249 *And flung it to the dogs — But*^*I forgive thee*
{Yet
{And humbled as I am I can forgive thee

243, 244 The 1841 revisions leave Rivers silent, add a stage direction, and give "Start not" (miswritten) to Mortimer.

249, 249/250 WW's revisions are in pencil, as is the caret.

Twas nothing more than darkness deepening
darkness

weakness crowned
And ~~crowning all~~ with the impotence of death!—
Your Pupil is,
~~I am~~, you see, an apt proficient. (ironically—
Oswald confused)
Start not!—Here is another face hard by;
Come—let us take a peep at both together,
And, with a voice at which the dead will quake,
Resound the praise of your morality!—(drawing Os.
towards the
~~/~~But of this strain too much. Cott:—stops
millions, short at the
Men there are, Oswald, door
Who with bare hands would have plucked
out thy heart,
And flung it to the dogs: but I am raised
Above, or sunk below, all further sense
Of provocation. Leave me with the weight

121[a]

Of that old Man's forgiveness, on thy heart
Pressing as heavily as it doth on mine.

[121a]

have been,
Coward I ~~was—but~~ know, there lies not now
Within the compass of a mortal thought,
[?]
A deed that I would shrink from;—but to endure,
.} May it
That is my destiny,} ~~& will~~ be thine: ~~I trust~~
(Turn to the other side of the page)
~~And~~ {f
{~~For a peaceful end beyond our view~~.——
Thy office &c. beyond our view ⁙

2253 'Twas deepening darkness,
{P
2255 {pupil *(Dora)* Oswald confused *del from stage dir*
2257 Come,
2260 strain *del* *as MS. 3, rev. as MS. 3 but* 2 *inscribed under* there *with comma added and* 1 *under* are *to show reversal*
2261 *no comma*
2264 me,
2265 *no comma*
2267 *first comma rev to semicolon, third omitted*
2269 but *underlined*
2270–2278 *further developed in MS. 3A, 16*[r]

2270/2271 The direction and the symbol point to ten lines developed on the bottom half of p. 122a. The top portion of p. 122a repeats lines from the original transcription on the page now numbered 123. Two stubs stand between p. 122a and p. 123.

(Confused {v noi {c ses are heard with uproar)

250 ~~*Voices —Hola— There! there! Huzza*~~*!*

(Lacy, Lennox, Wallace ~~Norwood~~ &c &c &c.
rush in the Beggar & Wilfred with them

one of the Band — — — — — — — — *I would have {dragged} ~~followed~~ him*

251 ~~*Even*~~ *to the jaws of hell*

(They rush forwards to sieze Rivers)

[71ᵛ]

Riv: (surrounded by them) — *{Hah} ~~And~~ ~~Ha~~! is it so? (Turng to the Beg*
Vile hag this issue come
From having left a thing like thee alive

Several Voices)
252 *Dispatch him* —

Riv: — — — — — — *If I pass beneath a rock* [2282]

253 *And shout; and with the echo of my voice*
254 *Bring down a heap of rubbish & it crushes me*
255 *I die without dishonour — Famished! (smiles exul-*
(tingly his eyes fixed upon Mortimer)
256 *A fool and Coward blended to my wish.* [2286]

A Voice — — *Merciless traitor! (they drag him off)*

(Matilda rushes out towards Mortimer followed
by ~~Robert~~ Eldred

257 *Mat: It is a strong disease Oh save him save him*

(Enter several friars who crowd round Matilda
and conceal her from the audience

258 *Wal: Tis done*

another of the band reen{t dering} — — *The merc{i yless traitor!*

---

251 Underlining added 1841.
258/259 MH's 1799 correction.

[122a]

May it be thine, {;
Thy Office, thy Ambition, be henceforth 2271
To feed Remorse, to welcome every sting 2272
Of pene {i *tential Anguish, yea, with tears.* 2273
When seas & continents shall lie between us,— 2274
The wider space the better,—we may find 2275
In such a course fit links of sympathy, 2276
An [?] *incommunicable rivalship* 2277
Maintained, for a peaceful end {s *beyond* {our / the *view.* 2278

Confused noises Band enter—

[121a]

(Confused noises, & *—several of the Band enter,)*
rush upon Os:, & sieze him

One of them
I would have dogged him to the jaws of hell— 2279

Os.— *Ha! is it so!—That Vagrant Had* {g *!—this comes* 2280
Of having left a Thing h {li *ke her, alive! (aside)* 2281

Several voices *Despatch him!—*
Osw *— — — — — If I pass beneath a rock* 2282
And shout; &, with the echo of my voice, 2283
Bring down a heap of rubbish, & it crush me, 2284
I die without dishonour. Famished, starved— *smiles scornfully & exultingly at Marmaduke* 2285
A Fool, & Coward blended to my wish! 2286

Wallace *Tis done!— (Stabs him)*

Another of the Band *The merci* {less / ful *{T / traitor!*

Mar {r *maduke — — — — — — — — — — A rash deed!—* 2287
With that reproof I do {I *resign a station* 2288
Of which I have been proud. 2289a

2271 {a / Ambition
2273 *second comma omitted*
2278 *comma del*
2278/2279 {C / confused noises—several of the Band Enter—rush upon Oswald and seize him.

2280–2281 *further developed in MS. 3A, 9*[v]
2281 *no comma* aside *rev from* alive *in stage dir (Dora)*
2283 shout,
2286 wish!— *so MS. 4a*
2287 'Tis *so MS, 4a* merciless] *del to* ruthless *MS. 4a*

Wilfred (approaching Mortimer) My poor Master!
Mor: Oh! my good Wilfred! (he turns to Lacy

[72^r]

Wallace ~~Lacy~~! on these borders
{T ~~[?] many~~ se eyes
~~Many~~ {there are^who^will not want cause [2292]
To weep that I am gone
~~Norwood~~)returning) — — — ~~The hell-hound~~
~~Wilfred~~

~~Lacy~~ — — — — — — — — — — — — ~~Peace~~
Brothers in Arms
{~~F~~
~~Brothers &~~ {~~friends Brothers~~
Mor: Raise on this lonely Heath a monument
~~tale~~ story to your care
That may record my ~~story for warning~~

122[*a*]
Wil (approaching Mar) — — — O my poor Master!—

---

127 3

~~My faithful Wilfred,~~
~~Mar:~~ ~~Oh my good Wilfred~~! (~~turns to W~~ {~~al~~ / [?]}~~lace~~
~~Discerning Monitor, my faithful Wilfred~~
~~Why art thou here?~~ ~~(turning to Wallace~~
~~Wallace~~ {, / }! {~~up~~ / ~~on these borders~~}
Many
{t / There} {be / are} whose eyes will not want cause—/—

122[*a*]

Mar: Descerning Monitor, f{m / }y faithful Wilfred,
Why art thou here? (turning to Wallace)
Wallace, upon these {B / borders}
Many there be {w / those} eyes will not want cause/

[127 3]

To weep that I am gone./ {— / } Brothers in Arms,
Raise, on this lonely ~~Heath~~ Moor, a monument
That my record my Story. To your care,

2290 Discerning *MS. 4, but MS. 4a as MS. 3*
2292 be *rev from* are *MS. 4a*
2293 {A / arms,} *MS. 4a*
2294 *first comma omitted, so MS. 4a* this lonely Moor, *del to* that dreary Waste, *the reading of MS. 4a*
2294–2304 *further developed in MS. 3A, 14ʳ and 15ʳ*
2295a Your care, *del to* you *following line del to:*

> For present care—that lovely work of nature
> In all things worthy of her noble blood
> Now on the Eve of rights recovered. *then* And *prefixed to last line*

caret after Story *points to insertion inscribed in left margin:*

> That may record my story: and let words
> Few must they be & delicate in their touch
> As light itself, be not withheld from her
> Who, through most wicked arts, was made an Orphan
> By One who would have died a thousand times
> To [?] shield her from a moment's harm. To you
> Wallace & Wilfred I commend the Lady
> By lowly Nature reared to make hers. *line runs on to top margin*
> In all things worthy of her noble birth.
> Whose long-suspended are now on the eve *continued on p. 713*

Wallace & Wilfred I commend the Maid
Now on the eve of rights recovered
eagerly)
several of { ~~*eagerly*~~
the band ([?]) — — — *Captain!*
No more of that — in silence
Mor: ~~*No*~~∧~~*prayers*~~,∧~~*no*~~∧~~*tears*~~∧, ~~*but*~~∧*hear*∧*my doom* ~~*in silence*~~*!*
my case
I will go forth a wanderer on the earth,
~~*A shadowy thing and as I wander on*~~,

263/264 In stage direction, the overwriting and repetition of "eagerly" were done in 1799.
266a "A shadowy thing" was deleted in pencil, then in ink.

Wallace & Wilfred, I commend the Maid 2301
The
Now on the Eve of rights recovered.
{(eagerly)
Several of the Band {— — — — Captain!
Mar: No more of that; in silence hear my doom:— 2307
fit relief 2308
A Hermitage has furnished ~~a retreat~~
{e
To some Offenders; other Penit{ants, 2309
Less patient, in their wretchedness, have fallen, 2310
, on own ~~edge~~
Like the Old Roman, ~~by~~ their sword's ~~point~~ edge 2311
point;
They had their choice: A wanderer must I go— 2312
A lonely ~~Wanderer will I go forth~~
~~I will go forth a Wanderer on the earth~~
/—The Spectre of that innocent Man ~~points out my course~~
my guide./ 2313

Continued from p. 711
Of restoration. With your tenderest care ~~watch her &~~
&} ~~pray~~
Watch her—{ pray sustain her *these lines incorporated into base text of MS. 4a:*

nor
That may record my Story: & let words,
Few must they be, & delicate in their touch
there
As light itself, be ~~not~~ withheld from her
Who, through most wicked arts, was made an Orphan
By One who would have died a thousand times
To shield her from a moment's harm. To you,
I commend the Lady
{~~such~~
Wallace & Wilfred, ~~for such care as~~ {[—?—]
~~The place and time~~
~~with~~
~~Is needed.~~ ~~I venture to commend~~
By lowly nature reared, as if to make her
~~at~~}
~~This~~{ ~~loveliest Flower that ever lowly Nature~~
In all things worthy of that noble birth
Whose long-suspended rights are now on the Eve
Of restoration:—with your tenderest care
~~Reared for her own delight & yet a Lady~~
~~Watch her, I pray sustain~~
~~In all things worthy of her noble birth~~
Watch over her, I pray—sustain her—.
~~And~~
~~And now on the Eve of rights recovered~~

2301 Maid *del to* Lady
2308–2321 *further developed in MS. 3A, 9^v*
2311 point, *MS. 4* point *MS. 4a*
2312 choice *over illeg eras MS 4a* *underlining del under* must *and added under* I *MS. 4, but both words underlined MS. 4a* go,
2313 Man, Guide. *so MS. 4a*

e speak
No human ear shall ever hear my voice
No human dwelling ever give me food [2315]
.
Or sleep or rest, and all the uncertain way
Shall be as darkness to me, as a waste
Unnamed by man! ~~and I will wander on~~
~~Living by mere intensity of thought~~
Man
~~A thing by pain and thought compelled to live~~ [2319]
[?]
Yet loathing life till heaven in mercy strike me
With blank forgetfulness——that I may die.

[?And ?travelling] that we may live

By pain & mere intensity [?of] thought
Such lot be mine so may I live & breathe

271b–273 Horizontal cancellation is in pencil, as is WW's draft revision at the foot of the page. In l. 273 "thing" is also deleted in ink.

No human ear shall ever hear me speak;
No human dwelling ^ever^ me food,
Or sleep, or rest: but, over waste & wild,
In search of nothing, that this earth can give,

4}
128}

But expiation, will I wander on;—
A Man by pain & thought compelled to live,
Yet loathing life—till anger is appeased
In Heaven, & Mercy gives me leave to die.
O be [?it] with humble hope in my last breath

1795–6

2319 A *over* By *MS. 4a*

2321 die, } . *MS. 4a*
final line added, as MS. 3, but breath! *(Dora); so MS. 4a, but del*
End of Act 5th *inscribed below date (Dora); so MS. 4a, but* 5.th

Of thy kind patroness, which to receive
We have thus far adventured, will suffice
To save thee from the extreme of penury
But when thy father must lie down and die
How wilt thou stand alone?

Mat. (earnestly) - - - Is he not strong?
Is he not valiant? Am I then so soon

Her:– Forgotten – Have my warnings ~~[illegible]~~
~~[illegible] of thy mother, my dear~~ My only child.
Miss Marton

Mat: - - - - - - O could you hear his voice
Alas! you do not know him. He is one
(I guess not what bad tongue has wronged him with you)
All gentleness and love. His face bespeaks
A deep and simple meekness: and that soul
Which with the motion of a glorious act
Flashes ~~a terror~~ a look of terror upon guilt ~~[illegible] look of [illegible]~~
Is, after conflict, ~~silent~~ quiet as the ocean
By a miraculous finger stilled at once

Her: Unhappy woman!

Mat: - - - - - Nay it was my duty
Thus much to speak. ~~but think not I forget~~
~~but think not thou art [illegible] father I forget~~
Dear Father how could I forget & live
You & The ~~mem~~ory of that ~~[illegible]~~ dreadful night
When Antioch, blazing to her topmost towers
You rushed into the murderous flames, returned
Blind as the grave, but as you oft have told me

Her: - - - - - - - - - - The good creature
Is gone before, to spare my weariness
But what has brought you hither?

Riv: - - - - - - - - - - - - A little business
That will be soon dispatched

Her: - - - - - - - - - - - There was a letter
Which we entrusted to you?

Riv: - - - - - - - - - - (Ony) [illegible] -
^ you'll hear no more of him [illegible]

Her: This is true comfort -- thanks [illegible]
That noise! would I had gone with her as far
As the Lord Clifford's mansion, I have heard
That in his milder moods he has express'd
Compassion for me -- his [illegible] influence is
With Henry our good King; [illegible]
[illegible]
Our journey lies that way; you are most lucky my friend and I
Will be your guides.

M

Mor: Let us be gone and bring her hither; here
[illegible] the wretched and after [illegible]
The truth shall be laid open— his guilt proved [illegible]
Before our face— They rest by left to the
[illegible] must die [illegible] come afterwards
Riv: That proud [illegible] escaped me— This is an act of justice
And where's the triumph if the delegate
Must fall in the execution of his office?
Yours is no common life! Self stationed here
Upon these savage confines we have seen you
Stand like an isthmus 'twixt two stormy seas
That oft have checked their fury at your bidding
'Mid the deep holds of Solway's mossy waste
Your single virtue has transformed a band
Of fierce barbarians into ministers
Of beauty and of order— The old man
Blesses their steps, the fatherless retires
For shelter to their banners. But it is
In darkness, and in tempest that we seek
The majesty of [illegible] rules the world
Benevolence that has not heart to use
The wholesome ministry of pain and evil
Becomes at last weak and contemptible: [illegible]
[illegible] generous qualities have won due praise
[illegible]
[illegible]
[illegible]
[illegible] character [illegible]
[illegible] and sublime— [illegible]
[illegible] hereafter
But vigorous spirits look for something more
Than Youth's spontaneous products

(Herbert is seen at the mouth of the dungeon)

[illegible]

Mor: This daughter of yours is very dear to you

Herb: Oh Sir! (laying his hand upon him) but you are young, forty years must roll over your head ere you can know how much a father may love his child.

Mor: (aside) I thank you old man for this

Her: I am a poor and useless man — with a kind hand you have protected me this evening — I have no return to make but my prayers — may the

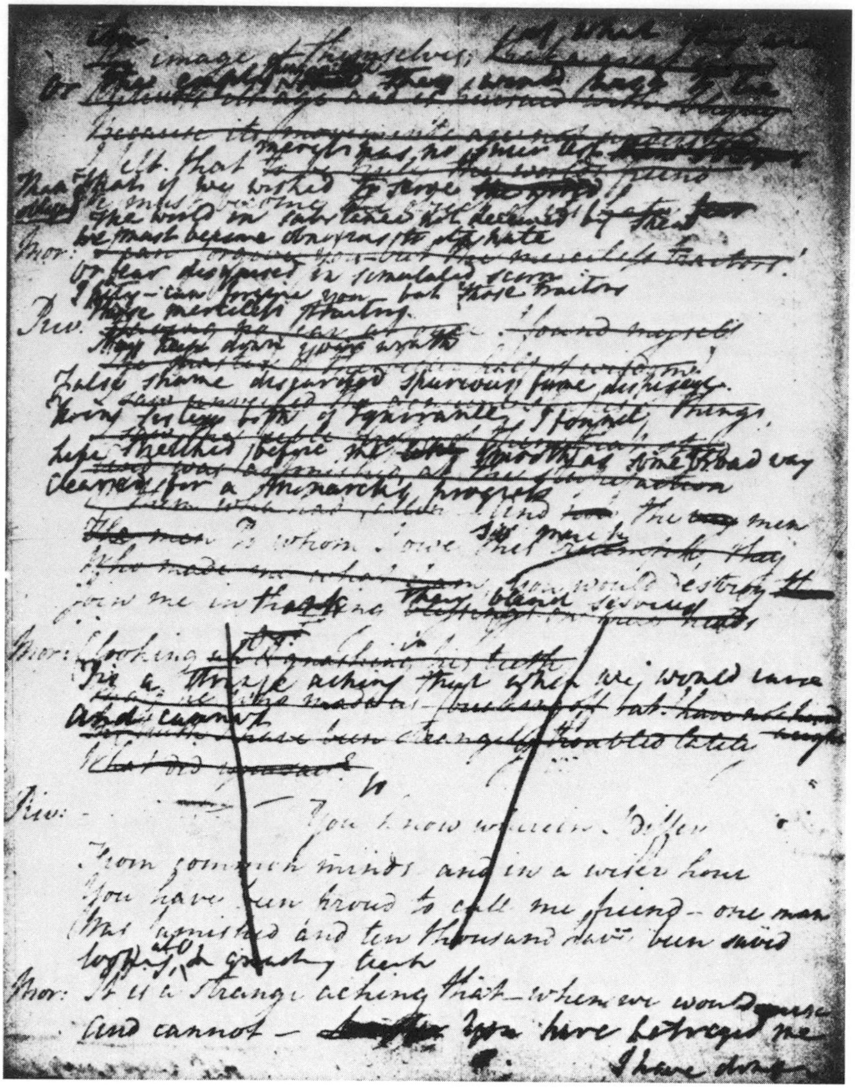
image of themselves;
I felt that mercy was no longer
That if we wished to serve the world
We must become
Mor: I can forgive you—but the merciless traitors!
Or fear disguised in simulated scorn
I pity—can forgive you but those traitors
Those merciless traitors
Riv: found myself
False shame disgraced spurious fame despised
I found things
Hope stretched before me smooth as some broad way
Cleared for a monarch's progress
Mor: Looking gnashing his teeth
'Tis a strange aching that when we would curse
And cannot
Riv: You know wherein I differ
From common minds and in a wiser hour
You have been proud to call me friend—one man
Was punished and ten thousand have been saved
Mor: It is a strange aching that—when we would curse
And cannot— you have betrayed me
I have done

Mor: - - - - - - - - - He must be put to death,
And for thy sake for he will haunt thy bed
Thy prayers, thy waking and thy sleeping thoughts
—Oh would—[illegible] thou hadst perished in the flames

Mat: Art thou not here the friend of all the helpless

Mor: There was a time when thy protecting hand
[illegible]
Availed against the mighty never more
Shall [illegible] blessings wait upon deed of mine

Mat: Love would in me have power to [illegible]
[illegible]
[illegible]
[illegible] dreadful [illegible] friend
Safeguard [illegible] What thoughts are these? (taking hold of his arm)
[illegible] What mean these desperate thoughts
Here is no malady

Mor: Here is a malady (striking his breast & forehead
And here, and here
A mortal malady

That seem to [illegible] of meaning but your words
Is dreadful — Safeguard of my soul [illegible] thoughts
Like these be calm. — Here is no malady

Mor: Here is
- - - - - - - - - - I am cursed
All nature curses me and in my heart
Thy curse is fixed

That seem to [illegible] of meaning but your words
Is dreadful. Safeguard of [illegible]

Mat: (forcing a smile) — Come, come this desperate effort
To rid my spirit of its present sorrow
Indeed 'tis ill judged

Mor: Look on my face

Mat: Twill help my spirit to lay ... at once

Mor: ... of thy father

(Matilda runs off into the cottage)

Mor: (alone)
Three words have such a power! This mighty burden
All off at once! 'Tis done, and so done too
That I have cased her heart in adamant

Was a coward then — but now am schooled
Coward I was, but now there doth not lie
Within the compass of a mortal thought
A deed that I would shrink from — but to endure

To give my strength to bear the recollection

The finger of a child to ache
Doth lie upon my bosom with a load

signature ~~will~~ shew — suspend your judgement
till you see ~~me~~ — Herbert
Mortimer

(Mor: points)

Mat: The writing yours — that signature my father's
You have then seen my father — ~~[illegible]~~ ?
~~It was not kind! you should [illegible]~~

~~Mor: (his hand pointing to his heart)~~
~~O that that word were written here!~~
~~Now will I tell thee how I dealt with him~~
~~Into a [illegible]~~

Mat: . . . . ~~He was found~~
~~My father — he was found upon the heath~~

Mor: If a man have a tongue to tell these things
A heart that cannot suffer and a soul
That cannot fear — what has he lost? These chains
These woven chains of thought
He has leaned

Mat: — upon this arm — toward the convent ~~[illegible]~~
9 do — ~~You led him~~

Mor: That convent was ~~[illegible]~~ castle — Thither
~~[illegible]~~ his [illegible] ~~[illegible]~~ } That [illegible]
That he should wait thy coming till the day
Of resurrection ~~[illegible]~~ Oswald

Mor: Aye—what shall we do next?

Riv: - - - - - - - - - - - [illegible] to him [illegible] Dungeon

Mor: Dungeon betrayed deserted and starved!

Blast what [illegible] If I sent him to his grave

Riv: Doubt! [illegible] nothing more than darkness deepening darkness

And covering all with the impotence of death

Mor: - - Sure you [illegible] an apt proficient

of Stoic

Riv: Hell Stoics note - - -

Mor: - - - Nay there is another [illegible] hard by

Let's in and take a keepsake! Both together

[illegible]

[illegible] and with a voice ah whither [illegible]

[illegible] towards the cottage

[illegible] when he comes to the door stops

Riv: Beyond any [illegible]

short

Mor: (when he comes to the door stops short) There are men

Who with bare hand would have plucked out thy heart

And flung it to the dogs—But I forgive thee

[illegible] (confused voices are heard with uproar)

Voices—Stole—Thee! Thee! Beggar!

Lacy, Lennox, Wallace [illegible] &c &c &c.

rush in the Beggar & [illegible] with them

one of the Band - - - - - - - - - - - I would have dogged him

[illegible] to the jaws of hell

(They rush forward to seize Rivers)

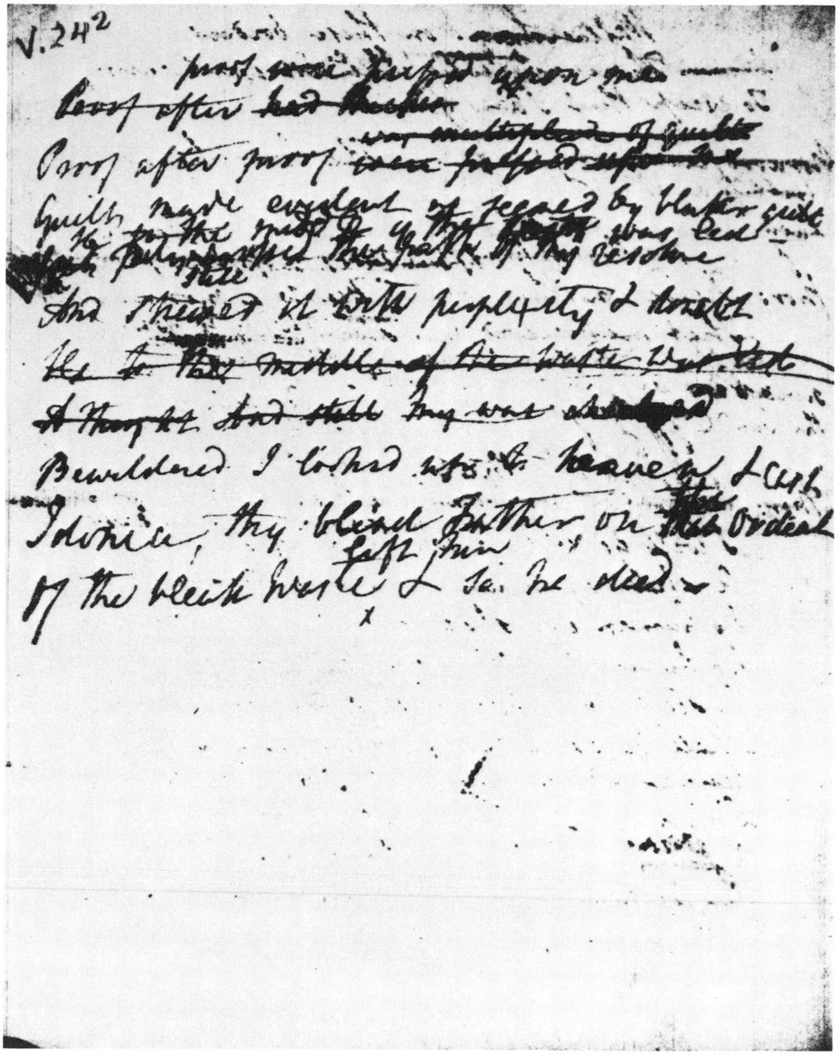
V.24²
Proof after proof
Bewildered I looked up to heaven & earth
Idonea, thy blind Father on the Ordeal
Of the bleak waste

MSS. 2A and 3A

MSS. 2A and 3A are the remains of two homemade notebooks put together from scraps rescued from postal wrappers addressed to Rydal Mount. The sheets comprising MS. 2A—DC MS. 151/8, formerly Verse 102(7)—are folded in folio and trimmed to form leaves measuring approximately 20.2 by 16.4 centimeters, sewn to form a single gathering. This stitching has been removed. Seven leaves and the stub of an eighth survive. Postmarks visible on 6^{r} indicate a letter posted November 25, 1841, received at Ambleside on December 4, and on 7^{r} a letter posted in Brighton on December 3, 1841. Entries consist of fair-copy passages and draft revisions in Mary Wordsworth's hand, most of them versifying prose passages in MS. 2 (see p. 12, above), as follows:

1^{r}–2^{v}	verse equivalent to the prose of II.iii.87–137
3^{r}–4^{r}	verse equivalent to the prose of II.iii.254–297
4^{v}:	three verse fragments equivalent to IV.ii.175–182, V.iii.29–30, and V.iii.41–44
5–7	blank
8^{r} (reversed)	verse fragment equivalent to the paste-in revision of III.iii.123–131
8^{v} (reversed)	verse fragment related to the entry on 8^{r}, equivalent to III.iii.123–131

In these MS. 2A drafts the name Mortimer has been replaced by Annandale, as in MS. 2, on 22^{r} and 70^{v}.

MS. 3A—DC MS. 151/3, formerly Verse 102(2)—consists of drafts for *The Borderers*, for a few other poems, and for the *PELY* prose notes. The handwriting is that of William or Mary Wordsworth, as distinguished in the transcriptions. No postmarks are visible on the reused postal wrappers. The contents appear to be work toward the revised text of MS. 3 and to predate MS. 4, though some of the material (such as the abortive drafts toward revision of the opening twenty lines of the play) appears neither in the revised text of MS. 3 nor in *PELY*. The manuscript consists of sheets folded in folio and trimmed to give leaves measuring approximately 22.2 by 14.3 centimeters, sewn to form a single gathering (the stitching has since been removed). Fifteen leaves and the stub of a sixteenth survive. The manuscript has no clear beginning or end, top or bottom, but the sequence of some of the leaves may be determined by the entries, or by ink blots that have marked the facing leaf.

I have assembled the leaves, and assigned numbers to them, so that the contents of the manuscript are ordered as follows:

1^{r}	*Borderers*, ll. 2200–2205
1^{v}	blank
2	stub
3^{r}	*Borderers*, ll. 1–10
3^{v}	draft for "When Severn's sweeping flood" (*PW*, III, 413)
4^{r}	*Borderers*, ll. 14–20
4^{v}	*Borderers*, c. l. 588
5^{r}–6^{r}	blank
6^{v} (top)	prose note on *Musings near Aquapendente* (*PW*, III, 202)
(bottom, reversed)	*Borderers*, ll. 33–37
7^{r}	blank
7^{v}–8^{r}	drafts for Sonnet xiii, *Ecclesiastical Sonnets*, III (*PW*, III, 390–391)
8^{v} (reversed)	*Borderers*, ll. 2262–2266, 2278
9^{r}	*Borderers*, ll. 2131–2133, 2174–2183
9^{v}	*Borderers*, ll. 2280–2281, 2308–2321
10^{r}	*Borderers*, ll. 2260–2262, 2246–2259
10^{v}	*Borderers*, ll. 1224–1227, 2226–2236
11^{r} (top)	prose note for *Guilt and Sorrow*, stanza IX, l. 9
(bottom)	*Borderers*, ll. 895–899
11^{v}	*Borderers*, c. l. 1820
12^{r} (top)	draft for Sonnet xiv, *Ecclesiastical Sonnets*, III (*PW*, III, 391)
(bottom)	*Borderers*, ll. 1371–1372, 1613–1616
12^{v}	*Borderers*, ll. 1516–1527
13^{r}	*Borderers*, ll. 1528–1535, 1678–1683
13^{v}	*Borderers*, ll. 1839–1842, 927–935
14^{r}	*Borderers*, ll. 2294–2304
14^{v} (reversed)	*Borderers*, ll. 1678–1684
15^{r}	*Borderers*, ll. 2295–2300, 1837–1842
15^{v}	draft for Sonnet xxvii, *Miscellaneous Sonnets*, III (*PW*, III, 52)
16^{r}	*Borderers*, ll. 2183–2186, 2270–2278
16^{v}	prose note on Sonnet iv, *Miscellaneous Sonnets*, I (*PW*, III, 3)

In transcriptions of MS. 2A drafts, cross-references are given to the early version of *The Borderers;* for the MS. 3A drafts, cross-references are given to the late version.

MS. 2A

[1r] [II.iii.87–101]

(Herbert from the mouth of the cave)

Give me your hand—Where are ye friends? {*tell* / *how* / *me*

of

How goes the night

Ann. ~~*'Tis hard to measure*~~ {~~*'Tis hard to measure time*~~ / ~~*time in such a weary*~~} ~~*night*~~
In such a weary night & such a place!
Her *I do not hear the voice of my friend Oswald*
Ann: *A minute past he went for we were thirsty*
To fetch a draft of water from the brook
Her: {*H*
A cheerless beverage— {*how good it was in you*
To stay behind; hearing at first no
answer
I was alarmed
{*No wonder*}
Ann ~~*No wonder!*~~ {*this is* } *this is a place*
To make one fearful without knowing why
Her *Even a roofless rock had be a comfort*
Storm-beaten & bewildered as we were
And on a night like this to lend your cloaks
To make a bed for me. My Girl will weep
When she is told of it.
Annandale —— *This daughter of yours*

[1v] [II.iii.101–114]

Is very dear to you
Herb ——— *O but you are young*
Over your head twice twenty years must roll
With all their natural weight of sorrow & pain
Ere can be known to you how much a Father
May love his Child
Ann: ——— *Thank you old Man for this*
Herb. *Fallen am I & worn out a useless Man*
Kindly have you protected me to night
And no return have I to make but prayers

May you in age be blest with such a daughter.
When I became an Outcast as you see me
A wretched Outcast—but this strain of thought
Would lead me to talk fondly
Ann: *— — — — — — Do not fear*
Your words are precious to my ears, go on—
Herb. *You will forgive me but my heart runs over*
When my {old / [?] Leader ~~perished~~ slipped in the flood
And perished, what a piercing outcry you
Sent after him—I have loved you ever since
You start— where are {we? / ?

[2[r]] [II.iii.115–133]

Ann: *— — — — O there is no danger*
T{he / his cold blast ~~made me shiver~~ struck me.
Herb *— — — — — — — — Twas a foolish question*
Ann. *But when you were an Outcast? Heaven is just*
Your piety would not miss its {due / just reward
The little Orphan then, would bring you succour
And do ~~you~~ good service tho' she knew it not—
Herb *I turned me from the dwellings of my {F / fathers*
Where none but those who had trambled on my rights
Seemed to remember me. Within my arms
I bore ~~my child~~ her—from the world her looks won pity
She was my haven in the Wilderness
And brought me food, have I not cause to love her?
Ann: *Yes, {Yes / O you!*
Herb *More than ever Parent loved a Child*
Ann *{Yes yes / [?]*
Herb. *— — I will not murmur merciful God*
I will not murmur, blasted as I have been
Thou hast left me ears to hear my daughters voice
And arms to fold her to my heart. Submissively

[2^v] [II.iii.133–137]

find my rest in faith
Thee I adore & ~~tremble~~

Enter Oswald

Os: *Herbert! Perdition!—Here it is (presenting*
aside *my friend the Horn*
to An)

~~A charming beverage this~~

to
A charming beverage for you carouse this
~~bitter night~~

This bitter night
Herb: *— — — — Ten bright crosses*
I would have given not many minutes
gone

[3^r] [II.iii.254–272]

Annandale reenters from
the dungeon
Oswald Tis all over then—your foolish fears
Are hushed to sleep; by your own act & deed
Made quiet as he is
Ann *— — — — Why came you down*
And when I felt your hand upon my arm
why did
And spake to you ~~you answered not~~
Feared you why did you give no answer
~~Were you afraid~~ to waken him? he must
have been
In a deep sleep. I whispered to him twice,—
the st} {~~place~~
There are^ strange } echoes in that {dungeon
place!
Tut
Oswald ~~Tut, tut~~ let them gabble ~~on to all eternity~~
till the day of doom
Ann: *~~Scarce had I groped my way to his resting-place~~*
Scarcely by groping had I reached the spot
When round my wrist I felt a cord drawn tight
As if the blindman's dog were pulling at it.
Osw *But after that?*
Ann— *The features of Idonia*
Lurked in his face

[3v] [II.iii.273–283]

Osw — — — *Psha! ~~psha~~ Never ~~shall~~ W my life*
~~Will such occasions~~
Will retribution shew itself again
With aspect so inviting—Why forbid me
To share your triumph.?
Ann: — — — — *Yes her very look*
Smiling in sleep
Osw. — — — — *You have been playing the Coward?*
Ann *~~'Twas only for a moment, but it sent me To~~* *~~but the vision~~*
Though but a glimpse, it sent me to my prayers
Osw *Is he alive?*
Ann: *What mean you* {? / —*who alive?*
{*O* / *Osw*} *Herbert, since you will have it* Baron *Herbert*
Seignory
He who will ~~hold his Lordship when~~ have his Seignory when Idonia ~~Idonia~~
Hath become
Is ~~Is~~ Cliffords harlot. Is he *living?*
{*Annan* / *M*} *The bling* {*d*} *Man in that dun* {*geon* / *eon*} *is alive*

[4r] [II.iii.284–297]

Osw. *The* {*He*} *nceforth then ~~never will~~ will I never in I Camp & field*
Obey you *more* {*Y* / *Iour*} *weakness to the Band*
Shall be proclaimed, brave men, they shall hear it all!
You a protector of humanity!
Avenger you of outraged innocence?
did I see ~~[?]~~
Ann: *'Twas dark, dark as the grave yet ~~I saw~~ him*
{*See* / *Saw*} *him ~~I tell thee~~, his face* ^*turned* *toward me*
& I tell thee
Idonias filial countenance was there
To baffle me—it put me to my prayers

Upwards I cast my eyes & thro' a crevice
Beheld a star twinkling above my head
And by the living God I could not do it
~~*this joy to me a meaner Spirit*~~
Os: ~~*Now may I perish if there be not joy*~~
to himself {~~*S*~~
~~*A meaner*~~ {~~*spirit would be over whelmed*~~
[?~~*who*~~]
{~~*Not*~~
{*But* ~~*so with me*~~ {*check*
Now may I perish if this turn doth {*more*
~~*Than*~~ *Doth more than make my course*
to An ~~*My gallant Annandale*~~
My *Dear Mortimer*
~~*Those*~~ *words were rashly spoken, I recal them*
{*I feel*
{[?~~*Fee*~~] *my error, shedding human blood*
Is a most serious thing
Not I alone
~~*Not I alone*~~
Ann
Thou too art

[4v] [IV.ii.175–182]

Ann

{~~*n*~~
~~*Mo*~~ {[?] ~~*ster*~~ *you have*
betrayed me
I have done
{~~*ati*~~
~~*Peace p*~~ {[?]~~*ence peace*~~
~~*Thou poor old Man*~~
patience peace
Thou poor old Man & I had heart for this
Because thou lovdst the daughter that had fed thee
Her who from very infancy had been
Light to thy path Warmth to thy blood
O fool (turning to
Together —

[V.iii.29–30]

Between us stood *I thought*
A cup of consolation filled from heaven
For both our needs must I, & in thy presence
Alone partake of it Beloved Marmaduke
Mar *she goes*

[V.iii.41–44]

You will do well *Unjust suspicion may*
R *~~fall cleave to~~*
~~Unjust suspicion~~ may ~~rest upon this Stranger~~
Cleave to this Stranger if upon his entering
~~If upon his entering your father heave a groan~~
his *or*
~~Your father~~
The dead man heave a groan or
from his
side

[8r] [III.iii.123–131]

to this Waste
is it
Bare without house or track & destitute
Of visible succour as a Shipless Sea
Here will I leave him here allseeing God
Such as he is to thee do I commit
His trial in this dreary solitude
This be his Ordeal Thou his only judge
He heard a voice A Shepherds

[8v] [III.iii.123–131]

to this Waste
Fit subject is he
~~He is prepared tis true~~ for a blindfold walk
Oer burning plowshares but that Ordeal
It were too terrible ~~for one so weak~~
~~So helpless so infirm Eternal~~
All-seeing God
Such as he is
To thee do I commit ~~his trial in this~~
His trial in this pathless solitude
~~Here will I give him up to earth & heaven~~
~~Here cold & hunger~~
~~For an acquittal~~
~~For judgment~~
He heard a voice a Shepherd's lad came to him
And was his guide—if once why not again
~~If never [?]~~
And in this desert—if never, then the whole
Of what he says {*& looks* / *of* [?] } *& does & is*
Makes up one damning falsehood—leave him here
To cold & hunger, pain is of the heart

MS. 3A

[1r] [ll. 2200–2205]

Miserable Woman
Too quickly moved too easily giving way
oft
Yet under stress of pain ~~which~~ {[?] the might *~~Of duty was [?off] too~~*
~~Did~~ I put denial on thy suit & hence
~~This~~ With the disastrous issue of last night
is
Thy} perturbation & these frantic words—
Be calm I prithee
M *Oswald——*
M *Name*
~~Which oft the might~~
of duty was too feeble
too feeble to contend
with

[3r] [ll. 1–10]

the Band
Lacy *Too long ~~already~~ have we been absent from ~~our~~*
{Who need our ~~help & guidance~~ *~~Comrades~~*
{[?] *~~&~~}*
~~The Band have urgent business~~ *{~~they require~~ ~~need~~*
~~guidance help for~~ help to [~~?~~] strip the Scottish
~~Our help for promt recovery of the Spirit~~ *Foray*
Of the rich the spoil wherewith it
~~With which the Scottish Foray~~ will be laden
it
Ere ~~the~~ recross the Border Pity '~~tis~~ it is
in this service we *{s*
~~That they~~ should not be headed ~~in this~~ {Service
By our Commander
Wal: *More may we regret*
sole
That he has chosen for his ^ Companion
~~That the Companion~~
~~In this untoward absence~~
~~to towards~~
Oswald ~~who in our noble-minded Leader~~
in whose warped Nature can subsist
~~Can~~
No feelings towards our noble-minded Leader

[?]
~~That do not verge on jealousy~~
But jealousy—or {*hatred* / [?]} {*~~dislike~~* / [?] *or*}

[4^r] [ll. 14–20]

Lacy — — — — — — — — — — *He is one*
Given up to crooked ways I have often heard
~~inhuman deed to which~~
Of some ~~dark deed in which he bore~~
~~inhuman impulses~~ {*~~that~~* / the} { *in* / [?]} *Youth*
~~[? ?] *midland Sea gave way*~~
dark deed to which he was impelled
~~In~~ Upon the midland sea
Wall — — — — — *Did you not know him*
In Palestine.
Wh
Lacy — — — *~~Aye~~, th* {*ere he despised alike*
Mahommedan & Christian —— *We must be gone*

Enter Mar & Wilfred

[4^v] [c.l. 588]

haply you prefer
That we like eastern Devotees should show
Our reverence for ~~the principle of~~ life
~~They [?] cherish as you know the vermin~~
~~That prey on their own bodies—~~
Her very look
show
That we should ~~[?prove] our reverence for life~~
~~By [?]~~ haply you prefer
After ~~the [?guize]~~
{[?] eastern
That we should {[?] like Devotees
Before the principle of life—~~they cherish~~ spare
~~You know~~
And Cherish even the verminous brood that prey
Upon their own bodies—
Yes her very look

[6v] [ll. 33–37]

Strong feelings to his heart
Are natural ~~more of man's heart & ways~~
& from no one can be learnt
~~Than his experience~~
More of Man's heart & ways than his experience
Has given him power to teach, & then for
courage
And enterprize what perils hath he shunned

[8v] [ll. 2262–2266, 2278]

Take heed good Angels
That she recover not, & couldst thou {h / [?]elp
them
That would redeem the worst of all the crimes
Thou hast to answer for.
Enter Oswald looking at M
unobserved
~~*Osw*~~ *— — — — — — Buzz buzz ye fools*
That is no substance which ye settle on
~~Away away~~ away—

~~to the dogs~~
& flung it to the dogs
But I am raised| {A / above or sunk below
sense of provocation
All further ~~provocation~~| leave me with the
weight
Of that old Man's forgiveness on thy heart
Pressing as heavily as it doth {on / [?] mine.
But for some peaceful end beyond
our view

[9r] [ll. 2131–2133, 2176–2183]

Uplift his hand that would be evidence
*Marg*t *Shame Robert Shame*
[?*returning*]

Mar: *The dead have but one face*
[?from] Cottage
to himself
turn to Ido *And such*

hath
~~*Thee, that long*~~
~~*Too long Has lingered*~~
Look on my face
{T
& '{twill help my speech to lay ^truth bare
at once
~~*To*~~ *It must be told & borne,* ~~*hear it & own*~~*:*
I am the Man—
{(A
~~*How*~~ *{abused, betrayed but how it matters not*
)}
not}
~~*Who*~~ *Presumptuous above all that ever breathed*
Who ~~*a guilty Person*~~ *a guilty person*
Cast~~*ing thy Father*~~ *as I thought,* ~~*upon*~~ [~~ ? ~~]
did {o
Upon heaven's righteous judgment, ~~*I*~~ *bec{ame*
~~*Thy Father's*~~
~~*All but his Murdered thro' me he perished*~~
{A {i
{an {Instrument of Fiends— ~~*thro' me thro' me*~~
by me, by me,
Thy Father was abandoned thro' me he perished
adamant

[9v] [ll. 2280–2281, 2308–2321]

Ha! is it so! ~~*I am reaping my deserts*~~
{ ~~*m*~~
~~*this co*~~ *{[?]*~~*es*~~
{Hag This
Vile {Vile issue comes
From having left a thing like thee
alive

{A {H
{~~*The*~~ *{hermitage has furnished a retreat*
~~*to some Offenders*~~
~~*Others Penitents*~~
To some Offendes, other Penitents
Less patient in their wretchedness
have fallen
Like the Old Roman on their own swords
point

~~Neither example fits my woeful case~~
I will go forth a wanderer in the earth

No human ear shall ever hear m~~y~~e s speak
No human dwelling ever give me food
But over wates & wild
Or sleep or rest~~—& I will wander on~~
In search of nothing that this earth can give
But expiation will I wander on
A Man by pain & thought compelled to live
anger
Yet loathing life till [~~?~~] ~~is~~ is appeased
In heaven, & Mercy gives me leave to die.

[10r] [ll. 2260–2262, 2246–2259]

save thee from [?][ ]
M & O — They recognise [?]
[*?would*]
Men are ~~There are men~~
Who with bare hands wuld have
plucked out thy heart~~—& flung it to~~
And
~~the dogs~~ [?] *flung it to the dogs—But I*
am raised [*?~~forgive~~*] *~~thee~~*

starts
Os *The ~~freaks~~ & sallies of our last encounter*
Were naturlar enough butt that's gone by—
~~And~~ the
You have outrun my hopes—~~Your~~ chains
are broken
More~~ And sooner than I prophesied~~
That fettered your nobility of Mind
And sooner than I prophesied. Let us to
Syria
This is a paltry field for enterprize
Mar *Aye what shall we do next?—Infirm & blind*
But what of that!—if I sent him to his grave
~~at once~~
'Twas nothing more than darkness deeping
darkness
And crowning all with the impotence of death—
~~The young I am~~ I am you see the yound
~~You see I am~~∧ *an apt proficient ~~in~~ [~~?yr~~]*
~~Young am I~~ as you see school
~~And~~
~~Here is another face~~
Start not—here is another face hard by
at both
Lets in & take a peep together

And with a voice at which the dead will
quake
Resound the praise of your morality

[10v] [ll. 1224–1227, 2226–2236]

Thou are calm
Could reason
Of love in all its shapes beginnings ends
Of moral qualities in their various
aspects
Of actions, & their laws & tendencies

Proof after proof pressed on me, guilt
as
Made evident {~~by~~ seemed by blacker guilt
Whose impious folds enwrapped even thee & truth
And innocence that pleaded in his looks
His words & tones & gestures did serve
crimes
With me to aggravate his ~~guilt~~ & heaped
Then pity crossed the path of my resolve
Ruin upon the cause for which they pleaded
Confounded I looked up to heaven & cast
Idonea thy blind Father on the Ordeal
Of the bleak Waste left him—& so he died

[11r] [ll. 895–899]

And shall this Parricide
For such he is to the confiding creature
in
Whom ~~he has trained~~ to the sanctities of filial duty
to
He ~~was~~ hath falsely trained shall he

~~For such he is and worse if foul dishonour~~
Worse is he far far worse if foul dishonour
Be worse than death to that confiding Creature
Whom he to more than filial love and duty
Hath falsely traind shall he fulfil his purpose?
But you are fallen,

[11^{v}] [c. l. 1820]

there all
Powers are about us my Young Friend
{I More than we think of ~~—some that bear ill names~~
{ill names and though some do bear
But { render no ill services
{[?]
welcome
they render one day services
In due return for what themselves recevd
Who wills, may win their favor—

when the [? ? ?]
With that unscrupulous Leaders hope to hear
selfish { at
Their purposes {[?] length have wrought
Upon a patient people till they [?find]
[~~?~~]
Whose natural element was freedom—
Mar ~~stop~~
Stop
[~~?~~]
I cannot follow thee— You must—you ~~must~~

[12^{r}] ll. 1371–1372, 1613–1616]

Her unto whom I owe the best of all
The good I have or wish for upon earth

I was woman
And balancing the hopes that are the dearest
To ~~man kin~~ woman kind with duty to my
hopes
I yielding up those pretious to me

[12^{v}] [ll. 1516–1527]

The Eagle lives in Solitude
Mr *Even so*
The Sparrow so on the house top & I ~~the weakest of G~~
The weakest of Gods creatures stand resolved
To abide the issue of my act alone
Os *Now would you? ~~Then~~ & for ever? My Young friend*
As time advances either we become
The prey or masters of our own past deeds
Fellowship we must have willing or no
And if good Angels fail slack in their duty

Substitutes turn our faces where we may
Are still forth-coming Some which tho they bear
Ill names can render no ill services

[13r] [ll. 1528–1535, 1678–1683]

In recompence for what themselves required
So meet extremes in this mysterious world
and ~~&~~ opposites thus melt into each other
Man first drew breath has
Mar Time since ~~the worlds creation~~ never moved
With such a weight upon his wings as now
~~As he has moved since Yesterday~~
~~Nor~~ will ~~it quickly be cast off~~
ll
But they wi [?] soon be lightened
Osw Aye Look up
r minds eye
Cast ~~your eyes~~ round you & you ~~soon~~ ^ will learn
F the
~~That~~ fortitude is ~~the~~ child of enterprize

And without further preface In my youth
Os Leave that thought awhile
heart
To keep the place which in your ~~mind~~ it took
As one of those beliefs lovers lock up
nought
As precious pearls tho they perhaps be not
Than feathers hung up on their points of passion
This days event has laid on me the duty
Of opening out my Story You must hear it

[13v] [ll. 1839–1842, 927–935]

I had been
dream
And in that state had left my native land
One of Love's boyish dotards 'twas a cloud
Dispersed for ever & the very men

We kill a worn-out horse & who but Women
Sigh for the deed hew down a witherd tree
H
And who look grave but dotards. he may live
To thank me for this service. Rainbow bow arches
High-ways of dreaming passion have too long

Youth tho' he is diverted wish & hope
From the unpretending ground we mortals tread
Then shatter the delusion break it up ~~& set him free~~
And set him free. What follows I have

[14^r] [ll. 2294–2304]

d}
Who by most wickel} arts was made an
Orphan
To a man
~~The part, the [?]~~ ~~One~~ to destroy ^ who would have
And let words
~~Record my story few they must be~~
Few they must be & delicate in their touch
not withheld from ~~the Murder~~
As light itself be ~~given to~~ her ~~the innocent [?]~~
most wicked arts one to destroy
Who ~~by~~ was made an engine
~~Of these of Whose filial piety that wicked art~~
[?She] to destroy ~~who had revered its object~~
~~Was made an object engine to destroy its~~
object
~~thro~~ m ~~welcomed death~~
w} ~~Thro' me, who would have died for her~~
One W} ho
A thousand times,—for her dear sake to you
{[?]
{[?] your best care W & W
W & W I commend the Lady ~~for your best care~~
{For {t lovely
{To present {That beautiful work of nature ~~in all things~~
~~for y best care~~
In all things worthy of her noble blood
And now on the eve
Capt

[14^v] [ll. 1678–1684]

4 Act
Oswald
—leave that thought awhile
As one of those beliefs which in their hearts
Lovers lock up as pearls tho' oft~~times~~ no~~thing~~ better
Than feathers hung upon their points of passion.
This days event has laid on me the duty
Of opening out my Story: you must hear it
And without further preface—In my Youth

[15r] [ll. 2295–2300, 1837–1842]

And let words
Few must they be & delicate in their touch
As light itself be not withheld from her
Thro'
Who by most wicked arts was made an Orphan
By One who would have died a thousand ~~deaths~~ times
To shield her from a moments harm. To you

progress. ~~Oft was flung~~
~~The solemn veil of cobwebs spun by Priests~~

Priests might spin
~~solemn~~ [?] ~~eyes~~
Their veil ~~for others eyes for whom they hoped to blind~~
but not for me 'twas no fit place
Among its kindred cobwebs— I had been
And in that dream had left my native land
One of Loves simple Bondsmen the soft chain
Was off for ever

[16r] [ll. 2183–2186, 2270–2278]

Thy Father perished
Ido Perished thro thee a miracle
~~not suffice~~
Would ~~fail~~ to fix in me that faith
fail
~~Conflict~~ ~~Conflict must cease~~
~~And in thy frozen heart~~ the
Conflict must cease & in thy frozen heart
The extremes of suffering must meet in peace

~~Is now my destiny & duty—be it thine~~
Thy Office thy ambition be henceforth
To feed remorse to welcome every story
yea with tears
Of penitential Anguish ~~When Seas~~
When seas & continents shall lie between
may us
The wider space the better we [?] find
In such a course fit links of sympathy
An incommunicable ~~fellowship~~ rivalship
a
Maintained for peaceful ends beyond
our view

Appendixes

Appendix I

Fragment of the *Gothic Tale* (1796)

Reading Text
Transcriptions, with Facing Photographs

I

Drafts for the fragment of the *Gothic Tale* are scattered through DC MS. 2, a brown leather-bound notebook that Wordsworth first used in the late 1780s, and to which he returned in 1795–96 to fill up blank spaces with drafts including *The Convict*, the fragments published in *SPP* (pp. 289–292), and the *Gothic Tale* (see *Chronology: EY*, pp. 344–345). The notebook contains thirteen full gatherings of azure laid paper cut to leaves of 23.2 by 20.2 centimeters and gathered in eights. The chain lines are vertical, spaced 2.6 centimeters apart. The watermark is the "Garden of Holland" design: the inscription PRO PATRIA at the top left of the design is faced by a man wearing a hat seated on a low fence holding a pole with another hat on the end of it, while within the fence, beneath the inscription, struts a small lion rampant, with a coronet on its head, clutching arrows and a sword in left and right forepaws respectively. The countermark consists of the letters I NIND. As Carol Landon observed in her London University dissertation, and kindly reported to me, the page number "5" on the first extant leaf indicates that leaves were removed after the notebook had been put into use. I have included the missing leaves in my leaf count, which also includes stubs omitted in Stephen Gill's leaf count for *SPP* (Appendix I, pp. 293–303), but since recovered in the recent restoration of the notebook.

Entries for the *Gothic Tale* are for the most part grouped in a series of runs. As a general rule, entries toward the front of the notebook represent the most developed versions: Wordsworth here, as in DC MS. 12, evidently worked forward through the notebook in filling up blank pages left between his earlier entries. Entries presented in the transcriptions and notes below appear in the notebook as follows (those marked with an asterisk are the most developed version of each stanza, and form the basis of the reading text):

6^{v}	drafts for VI	38^{v}	drafts for *XII, *XIII
9^{v}	drafts for *V, VI	39^{r}	drafts for *XIV, *XV
38^{r}	drafts for *X, *XI	39^{v}	drafts for *XVI, *XVII

40^{v} drafts for *XVIII, *XIX
41^{r} drafts for XVIII
42^{r} drafts for *XX, *XXI
42^{v} drafts for *XXII, *XXIII
43^{r} drafts for *XXIV, *XXV
60^{v} draft for *I
79^{v} fragment of XI
80^{v} drafts for XVII
81^{v} drafts for XIV, XV
82^{r} drafts for XV, XVI
82^{v} fragment of XVII
85^{r} fragment of XIV
86^{r} draft for IX
87^{v} drafts for VI, IX
88^{r} drafts for *II, IX
88^{v} drafts for *VII, *VIII, IX
89^{r} drafts for *IX, X
89^{v} draft for VIII
90^{r} fragment combining VIII, IX, and X
90^{v} drafts for VIII
96^{r} drafts for *VI, VII
96^{v} drafts for VIII
100^{v}–101^{r} drafts for *IV
102^{v} draft for *III
107^{r} fragment of XI

Differences between the versions of each stanza suggest that successive entries may sometimes be developed from a common original text.

In my reading text, I have arranged these stanzas according to the logic of the narrative, and have supplied an editorial summary, based on the evidence of the extant stanzas, to indicate the probable content of missing portions of the *Tale*. Readers familiar with de Selincourt's text (*PW*, I, 287–292) will see that I have altered the sequence in which he arranged the opening stanzas. De Selincourt begins his text with the travelers crossing the bridge (Stanza II), then pressing on "along the sable avenue" where the horseman appears (Stanza III), and only then viewing the castle (Stanza I). In Stanza I, however, the castle is viewed from the top of the other side of the ravine, which must be crossed by means of the loose plank; moreover, the reference to "that antient pile" in the "sable avenue" stanza is unlikely to precede what is obviously the description of the first sight of the castle, a "dim-discovered form! / Like some grim eagle." The other major deviation here from de Selincourt's text is in presenting Stanzas IX–XII as a sequence of complete stanzas, with no missing lines.

The text adopted for the reading text is based on the latest uncanceled readings in ink. Pencil revisions have been ignored, except where noted, as they represent later impulses that are often tentative. When an alternative reading existed, later canceled in pencil, the canceled alternative has been recorded in the footnotes, as have uncanceled alternative readings. Text supplied from readings canceled in ink is given in brackets, which are also used to supply missing letters editorially and (when left empty) to indicate a blank in the manuscript text. In lines 79 and 146 the reading in brackets has been supplied from a penciled-in entry. The text of Stanza IV is a composite derived from 100^{v} and 101^{r}, as these two pages were worked on simultaneously.

In the reading text, obvious misspellings have been silently corrected, but capitals and variant spellings have been preserved; ampersands have been expanded and editorial punctuation has been introduced without comment. In the transcriptions, faced with photographs, only the entries for the *Gothic Tale* have been presented, and the nature of the omitted materials is identified in footnotes.

II

The *Gothic Tale* reveals various literary debts, not least to earlier writings of Wordsworth himself. There is one entry that demonstrates a relationship between the 1780s material in the notebook and the text of the *Gothic Tale*. On 86^r the notebook contains a draft of an early description of a castle in a night storm (c. 1788), which is echoed in Stanza I of the *Gothic Tale*:

                                                  high
Now gleam'd the Moon; and on a rock he view'd
A Castle perch'd—on either side a wood
Wavd solemn to the hollow wind, —it seem'd
Like some grim Eagle on a naked rock
Clapping it's wings and wailing to the storm.

A longer draft version of this description appears in DC MS. 6, a 16-leaf notebook containing late 1780s materials, on 12^v, with the fair copy transcribed below on leaf 5^v:

                                    And on a rock sublime
By glimpse of moonshine thro the clouds he viewd
A Castle perch'd; on either side a wood
Wav'd solemn to the hollow wind; it seem'd
{L
{Bike some grim Eagle on a naked rock
Clapping its wings and wailing to the storm.
                                                          dreary
Now all was dark—what means that deadly cry
Was it the wailing wind that nightly glides
                                                    dl} shriek
Piping thro' these cleft rocks, or dea[?]{y call
                                             {'
Of Spirit moaning from you haunt{ed towers

For discussion of these entries in DC MS. 2 and in DC MS. 6, and a more general discussion of the earliest materials in DC MS. 2, see *Chronology: EY*, Appendixes V and VI (pp. 307–314). For discussion of the later entries in DC MS. 2, see *Chronology: EY*, Appendix XVI (pp. 344–345), and Carol Landon, "Wordsworth's Racedown Period: Some Uncertainties Resolved," *BNYPL*, 68 (1964), 100–109, and "Some Sidelights on *The Prelude*," *Bicentenary Wordsworth Studies*, ed. Jonathan Wordsworth (Ithaca, 1970), pp. 359–376.

The combination of ruined castle dungeons, a phantom (which has, in the *Gothic Tale*, a rational explanation), and trees tossing in the night wind had previously appeared in Wordsworth's *Vale of Esthwaite* (c. 1788) (see *PW*, I,

270–283, especially ll. 39–42, 46–47, and 210–267). In *Vale of Esthwaite*, the speaker is merely indulging "the pleasures of imagination"; in the *Gothic Tale* the protagonist is no longer the poet, but the "stripling" who has determined to murder the blind and aged sailor in his charge, and is hypersensitive to what is taking place around him at the castle. The psychology of perception in an abnormal state of mind had been a theme of *Adventures on Salisbury Plain*, and was also a theme of *The Convict* (1795–96). For discussion of other psychological backgrounds of the *Gothic Tale*, see my Introduction, pp. 19–24.

[Fragment of the *Gothic Tale*]

[*A blind sailor with a dog is being guided by a young man. They are overtaken by nightfall. The night is stormy, and the young man looks for a place to shelter.*

I

And looking round [   ] on cliff he view[ed]
(The moon forth-darting then the darkness brok[e])
A castle hung; on either side a wood
Waved in the roaring wind's tempestuous shoc[k.]
It seemed thus perch[ed] a dim-discovered form!
Like some grim eagle on a naked rock
Clapping its wings and wailing to the storm.
Forthwith our Travellers to that Castle high
Reared their laborious steps, no better mansion nigh.

II

Along a precipice they wound their way,
And as the path conducted they must go
Where a loose plank across a torrent lay,
Whose waves sent deafness from the chasm below.
His hand on th'other's shoulder close applied,
O'er the rude bridge the blind man tottered slow,
And when his fear was ended blessed his guide.
That passage thus accomplished, soon they gained
The platform of the cliff, for little space remained.

[*At this point Wordsworth probably intended to place a stanza or stanzas describing how a fragment of rock broke off under the stress of the storm, only just missing the blind sailor, and how the sailor's dog fell or was kicked into the ravine. The two travelers then decided to continue toward the castle.*]

III

So, pressing on to reach that antient pile,
Forsaken now, and subject to the sky,
[Along] the [sable] avenue they toil,

1, 2, 4, 5 Missing letters are editorially supplied.
21 Bracketed words were deleted in ink.

The wind still eddying round them fierce and high.
When, all unlooked for in that lonely place,
With furious steed a horseman galloped by,
Come from a quarter which

[Here the stanza breaks off]

[The blind sailor was fortunate to escape being trampled to death by the horseman. The travelers approached the castle, the young man in the lead.]

IV

[Advancing] on he saw a sullen light
Red as a star, but star it could not be;
Its station scarcely seemed to reach the hight
Of oak full-grown, or any forest tree.
The bright moon sever[ed] the black clouds in twain,
And gave him o'er the gateway's ridge to see
A man who stepped along a tower to gain;
Where, but the key-stone seen to link the arch
Else broken, crept [he on], in high an[d] perilous march.

V

When he had reached a tower on th'other side
He turned and cast a short survey around
(And as he turned the youth a cutlass spied)
As if to staunch the blood of recent wound.
The blind [man] now impatiently inquired
If better covert might not there be found;
So, leading him along, the youth retired
Behind a wall with trees secure and dark,
And stood, of that strange sight the sequent thence to mark.

VI

By entrance through a broken window made
He saw that daring traveller disappear,
Nor single word of this discovery said
To his forlorn dependant standing near.
A full half hour the youth prolonged his watch;

---

28 The first word was deleted in ink.

32 The texts read "severing," but revisions make "severed" necessary for grammatical sense.

36 The bracketed words were deleted in ink, as was an alternate, "along"; the bracketed letter is editorially supplied.

41 The bracketed word is editorially supplied.

But whether deed it were whose after-Fear
Must sleep upon the proof of sure dispatch,
Or that the lantern gave him to explore
Some other passage out, that man appeared no more.

VII

"Troth," cried the boy, "well need some favourite girl
"Were looked for this attendance to requite!
"Poor service 'tis while winds around us whirl
"Thus scantly roofed to weather out the night.
"My legs with standing ache to th'very bone,
"And many hours must pass ere morning light.
"Be cheerful, comrade, think thou'rt not alone;
"'Tis time to search, if here we must sojourn,
"Some more commodious spot, where we may sleep till morn."

VIII

So saying, by the hand he led his charge
Through the dark passage of the pond'rous keep,
That opened to a court of circuit large,
Whose walls had scattered many a stony heap.
The unimaginable touch of time,
Or shouldering winds, had split with ruin deep
The towers that stately stood as in their prime,
Though shattered, stood of undiminished height,
And plumed their heads with trees that shook before the night.

IX

Beyond a spatious gap in distance seen
A second court its battlements upreared,
And 'cross this ample area's midway green
The youth with his attendant thither steered.
The chasm scarce passed he cast his eyes around,

---

51 The "deed" was left as an alternate to "work."

The chasm scarce traversed, on a rugged mound
Beneath a corner tower two men appeared,
Who 'mid the wreck that strewed th'encumbered ground
A long white burthen in their arms conveyed—
—A third behind them brought an iron bar and spade.

And underneath a corner tower appeared
[(Amid the wreck that strewed th'encumbered ground)]
Two armed men who 'cross the stones conveyed
A burthen of such weight as ask'd their mutual aid.

X

"'Tis not for me this business to gainsay,"
Thus inly to himself the stripling spoke,
"To some close covert hence we must away,
"For work is here which none may overlook."
So towards the shadow of the eastern wall
His backward course incontinent he took,
When all at once, as at a demon's call,
The pile was troubled by a fiercer blast,
And with impervious clouds the moon was overcast.

XI

Nor stayed the tempest here. The thunder-stroke
Burst on the mountains with hell-rousing force;
And as the sulphurous bolt of terror broke
The blind man shuddered to life's inmost source,
For through the darkness of his brain the flash
With sudden apparition melts its course.
Again the fleecy clouds together clash,
Revealing to the guide a short descent
That promised safe retreat, and thither down they went.

XII

It was a spot where once a length of stairs
Led to a dungeon far from any sound,
A den where feudal Lords of antient years
The vassals of their will in durance bound;
But now, filled up with earth, with grass o'ergrown,
Smooth was the passage to the vault profound.
"What change!" [the] blind man, gently guided down,
Exclaimed, "How still! Here, comrade, will we stay,
"Nor better can betide till Morning bring the day.

---

79 Supplied from penciled insertion.
89 The "fiercer" is in pencil, replacing "deeper," canceled in ink and pencil.
100 The "length" was left as an alternate to "depth."
106 The bracketed word is editorially supplied.

XIII

"Methinks I could almost be happy now,
"To find us safe and warmly lodged at last;
"And yet my soul within, I know not how,
"Is sad to think upon the perils past
"Tonight, and many other nights and days.
"I owe thee much, and wish thee better placed.
"Good youth, my debt thy earning ill repays,
"For twice this very evening but for thee
"There had not been a hair betwixt my death and me.

XIV

"On the loose plank which spanned that roaring flood,
"How had we fared alone, my dog and I;
"Or 'mid the darkness of the deafning wood,
"When at full speed the horseman galloped by?
"In truth, from thee it comes that now I live.
"My recompence should with thy service vie,
"But little recompense have I to give;
"Yet something have I stored to meet the hour
"When crippling Age shall bring the wanderer to his door.

XV

"Broken I am in health, and child have none;
"And, couldst thou be content our lot to share,
"Ere to the grave my wife and I be gone
"That store for thee might grow by thrifty care.
"But on a stranded vessel thou wilt seem
"To waste thy pains—forlorn of inward chear.
"So oft I fancy, and myself I deem
"A Burthen to the earth whereon I tread,
"A Poor and useless man, and better with the dead."

XVI

His hopes the youth to fatal dreams had lent,
And from that hour had laboured with the curse

131–132 An uncanceled alternate was inscribed at the foot of the page:

But on a stranded vessel thou wilt dost seem
To waste thy pain, for I can scarce forbear.

136 An uncanceled alternate line reads: "Since to those fatal dreams the youth had lent."

Of evil thoughts; nor had the least event
Not owned a meaning monstrous and perverse.
And now these latter words were words of blood,
And all the man had said but served to nurse
Purpose most foul with most unnatural food;
And every kindred object which had braced
His mind that dismal night he busily retraced.

XVII

For as they came the precipice's ridge
[Lessons of death] [at every step] had given,
And at the crossing of the pendent bridge
With impulse horrible his heart had striven;
And now with black regret he cursed agen
The fragment which the winds had idly riven,
But chief that place and those mysterious men
There seen did for his bloody purpose plead,
Of every human fear disburthening the deed.

XVIII

At length confirmed, and to the work addressed,
The youth broke silence; but the summons found
No answer, for betaken to his rest
The blind man sleeping lay upon the ground.
So towards his throat the other, groping, drew,
When in that ample [dungeon's] farthest bound
Red sparks revealed a hand of fleshly hue;
And such the import which that phantom bore
That had it long endure[d] his heart had beat no more.

XIX

But that grim shape, as if it ne'er had been,
Soon vanished. [ ] and anon
In place of those dull sparks a light was seen
That from the cavern's depth came gliding on.

---

146 The first bracketed phrase was deleted in ink; the second is supplied from a penciled addition.

159 The bracketed word was deleted in ink, as was an alternate word, "cavern's."

160 The first word and an alternate, "Dim," were deleted in pencil.

162 The bracketed letter is editorially supplied; the "ad" of the second "had" is a pencil overwriting of illegible letters. The phrase "the man had lived no more" was left standing as an alternate to "his heart had beat no more" until selection was made by pencil cancelation.

And now the legs, as of a human frame,
Appeared; and with that light which dimly shone
Forth-with a gloomy figure nearer came,
And, stopping short, replaced a kerchief bound
About his arm that bled as from a recent wound.

XX

Glad respite did that black Appearance give,
When every inward vessel 'gan dispart
With ghostly terrors never sent to live
Amid the weakness of a mortal heart.
The pendent cutlass and the belt, descried
By what faint glare the lantern could impart,
Marked out the shape which he before had spied.
His work arranged, the man at distance short
Passed through the deep recess and sought the upper court.

XXI

And gone he left the stripling light of soul,
Nor doubting but the hand that vault had shown
Was earthly, 'mid lamp-smothering vapours foul,
So fashioned to his eye by sparkles thrown
On the thick air from fire-detaining wood
Or flint whose sound the wind had made its own.
[*Here the stanza breaks off*]

XXII

His ear, though startled oft, recovering felt
No sound but of the moaning wind; his eye
Though rolling, inly busy, only dealt
With darkness or the shapes of Phantasy.
At length he rose, by irksome thought impelled,
And, looking up in restless walk, on high
Above the dungeon's roof a star beheld,
Whose sparkling lustre through [the] crevice shed
Sent to his fluttering heart a momentary dread.

---

173 "For" was left as an alternate to "When" until canceled in pencil.

197 The bracketed word was deleted in ink. "Whose twinkling lustre through the crevice shed" stood as an alternate to "Whose sparkling light through smallest crevice shed" until selection was made by pencil cancelation.

XXIII

At length, the open area to explore
(For in that vault no second foot appeared),
Up to the dungeon's mouth his course he bore.
The winds were past away, the sky was cleared,
Nor did the court or silent walls present
Object or shape whose motion might be feared;
Only the crimson moon, her lustre spent,
With orb half-visible was seen to sink,
Leading the storm's remains along th'horizon's brink.

XXIV

So back he slunk, and to the corner came
Where lay his friend devoted to the grave;
But as he 'gan to lift his murderous aim
A rumbling noise along the hollow cave
Was heard remote, succeeded by a sound
Of uncouth horror, to which echo gave
Such rending peal as made the vault rebound.
Nor whelming crash it seemed, or shriek or groan,
But painful outcry strange to living ear unknown.

XXV

"Whence comes that uproar?" starting from his sleep
The Sailor cried, nor could the other make
Reply, o'ercome with shock of horror deep.
And when returning thought began to wake
In bare remembrance of that [uproar] dwelt
Such power as made his joints with terror quake,
And all which he that night had seen or felt
Showed like the shapes delusion loves to teem,
Sights that obey the dead, or phantom[s] of a dream.

---

209 The phrase "the man" was left as an alternate to "his friend" until canceled in pencil.

210 The phrase "in the lifting of" was left as an alternate to "as he 'gan to lift" until canceled in pencil.

218 The manuscript reads "others."

221 The words "larum" and "uproar" stood as alternates to "sound there" until all three readings were canceled, "sound there" and "larum" in pencil.

225 The bracketed letter is editorially supplied.

Whose each soft affection of the soul
By passing through a broken window [illegible]
[illegible], he saw her disappear
Nor [illegible] said
To him his blind companion standing near
But when it was [illegible] where [illegible] dispatch
Must [illegible] from [illegible] till after [illegible]
Of half [illegible]

And oft these eyes have seen it rest
Oft on her bosom, [illegible]

Of such appearance not a word he said
To [illegible] his blind companion standing [illegible]
[illegible] to the blind man leaning by
A [illegible] he stood upon the watch
Of that appearance [illegible]
But whether [illegible] dispatch
[illegible] of time
Tis dead – and flits in lonely flight wings
A dismal journey – black as night –

[6^{v}]

By passage through a broken window made
~~The~~~~[? n]~~ into to that tower, he saw him disappear
[?eager] [?with] [?respect]
Nor ~~word~~ of ~~that sight a single~~ said
To him his blind companion standing near
But where it wer work whose sure dispatch
be [?secure] from every
Must ~~exclude~~ all after fear
Of [?thalf] perform

Of ~~this a~~ such appearance not a word he said
To h{im / is} his {b / clind} companion standing near
{~~A~~ / ~~L~~}~~nd when~~ Nor to the blind man leaning by
[?there] [?paused]
A ~~long half hour he stood~~ upon the watch
Of that appearance any mention
But whether work it were whose sure dispatch
Ask{s / ed} ~~time~~ length of time

These versions of Stanza VI lead to the fullest version on 96^{r}. The lines visible in the photograph but not transcribed appear to be drafts of *The Death of a Starling* (*PW*, I, 263), overleaf in the notebook.

And toward [illegible] a wall with trees secure and dark
With his blind comrade straight twas he retired
And stood the issue of that sight to mark
Nor to his friend who better [illegible] desired
Of such appearance any mention made
But whether would it were where end required
His hasty hands or by the Lanterns aid

When he had reached a tower on th' other side
He turned and cast a short survey around
And as he turned the youth with [illegible]
As if to stanch the blood of recent wound

The blind man impatiently required
If better covert might not there be found
So leading him along the youth retired
Behind a wall with trees secure and dark
And stood, of that strange sight the sequel there to mark

To the blind standing by
Of such any mention was there made upon the water
But stood

must exclude all after-fear

of ill purpose
The youth saw his [illegible]
[illegible] through a broken window near
[illegible] or

[9^v]

And toward ~~a [?w ?ivied]~~
a wall with trees secure and dark
~~With his blind comrade straigh~~tway he retired
And stood the issue of that sight to mark
Nor to his friend who better roof ~~requ~~ desired
such d
Of ~~that~~ appearance any mention mak} e
But whether work it were whose end required
No hasty hand or by the lanterns aid
[?S]

When he had reached a tower on th' other side
He turned and cast a short survey around
And as he turned the youth a cutlass spied
Hung to a belt with which
As if to staunch the blood of recent wound

The blind now impatiently required
b covert
If [?]etter ~~shelter~~ might not there be found
So leading him along the youth retired
~~Into~~ Behind a wall with trees secure and dark
{t
And stood, of that strange sight the sequen {l thence to mark

To the blind standing by
Of such any mention mention made
But stood upon the watch
must exclude all after-fear
Of half perform
The youth saw him disappear
by
~~His~~ passage through a broken window made
O[?] [?ou]

At the top and bottom is further work on Stanza VI, moving toward the fullest version on 96^r. In the middle is the only version of Stanza V in the notebook; the revision between ll. 3 and 4, had it been completed, would presumably have made better sense of the stanza.

36.

'Tis not for me this business to gainsay
Thus inly to himself the stripling spoke
To some close covert hence we must away
For work is here which none may overlook
So towards the shadow of the eastern wall
His backward course incontinent he took
[illegible]
The pile was troubled by a fiercer blast
And with impervious clouds the moon was overcast

Shouted the [illegible] the thunder stroke
Nor stunned the tempest [illegible] with bolt-riving force
Burst on the mountain [illegible]
[illegible] the sulphurous bolt [illegible] to lifeless [illegible]
The blind man [illegible] dead [illegible] the flash
For through the darkness of his brain [illegible]
With sudden apparition rolls its course
Again the clouds [illegible] shafts descent
That provided [illegible] retreat and thither down they [illegible]

[38r]

Tis not for me this business to gainsay
Thus inly to himself the stripling spoke
To some close covert hence we must away
For work is here which none may overlook
o
So tw wards the shadow of the eastern wall
His backward course incontinent he took
~~Ere~~ When all at once as ~~with~~ at a demons call
~~But in a moment light was not at all~~
fiercer
The pile was troubled by a ~~deeper~~ blast
clouds
And with impervious^the moon was overcast

~~watry~~
[?Spouted] the [?~~waters~~]
Nor stayed the tempest here the thunder strooke
[?~~rampart~~]
mountains
Burst on the [?~~mountains~~] with hell-rousing force
W
~~And with fiercest gleam the forky lightning broke~~
And as the sulphurous bolt of terror broke
The blind man shuddered to lifes inmost source
For
['As] through the darkness of his brain the flash
With sudden apparition melts its course
Again the ~~el~~ fleecy clouds together clash
~~the guide revealed~~
~~And to the stripling showed~~ a short descent
Revealing to the guide
s
That promi ded safe retreat and thither down they went

Between ll. 7 and 8 of the first stanza, the word "fiercer" is in pencil, as is the deleting stroke on "deeper." This stanza, Stanza X, is developed from the version on 89r; the next, Stanza XI, develops the single line that appears on 79v—"with sudden apparition melts its way"—and two fragments on 107r:

every searching
At ~~every each~~ terrific flash the blind man felt
The lightning pierce the darkness of his brain
disburthen though
earths
That night the [?tower] deepest forth forests shook
Throug throug all its roots so potent was the blast

It was a spot where once a depth of stairs
Led to a dungeon far from any sound,
~~In which the~~ [illegible] feudal Lords of antient years
The vassals of their will in durance bound
But now filled up with earth with grass o'ergrown
Smooth was the passage to the vault profound
What but ~~[illegible]~~ strange ... the blind man gently ... down
~~Have [illegible]~~ [illegible] still; here comrade will we stay
Nor better can betide, till Morning bring the day

Methinks I could almost be happy now
To find us safe and warmly lodged at last
And yet my soul within ~~I~~ know not how
Is sad to think upon the perils past
~~And~~ To night and many other nights and days
I owe thee much and wish thee better placed
Good youth my debt thus earning ill repays
For twice this very evening but for thee
There had not been a hair betwixt my death
And me

[38v]

length
It was a spot where once a depth of stairs
Led to a dungeon far from any sound,
A den where s}
~~In which~~ the feudal Lord }of antient years
{their
The vassals of {his will in durance bound
But now filled-up with earth with grass oergrown
Smooth was the passage to the vault profound
{ ch change blind man gently
What {~~joy~~ ex~~claimed the sailor~~ guided down
Exclaimed how !}
~~How warm and~~ still } here comrade will we stay,
,}
Nor better can betide} till Morning bring the day.

Methinks I could almost be happy now
To find us safe and warmly lodged at last
And yet my soul within I know not how
Is sad to think upon the perils past
~~And~~ Tonight and many other nights and days
I owe thee much and wish thee better placed
Good youth my debt thy earning ill repays
For twice this very evening but for thee
There had not been a hair betwixt my death
and me

On the five stubs that precede leaf 38, only traces of writing are visible; 36r contains the following beginnings of lines: [?] / [?] / / [?] / [?] / [?] / An / [?] / W / B / Is / [?] / A / Th / M / W / Va / W / M / To.

The only surviving versions of Stanzas XII and XIII.

[39^{r}]

On the loose plank which spanned that roaring flood
How had we fared, alone, my dogs and I
Or mid the darkness of the deafning wood
When at full speed the horseman galloped by
In truth from thee it comes that now I live:
My recompence should with thy service vie
But little recompense have I to give
Yet some thing have I stored ~~against~~ to meet the hour
{A
When crippling {age shall bring the wanderer to his
door

Broken I am in health and child have none
And could'st thou be content our lot to share
~~One~~
Ere to the grave my wife and I be gone
for thee
That ~~little~~ store^might grow by thrifty care.
~~For thee and thine, but this is all a dream~~
But on a stranded vessel thou wilt seem
~~Nor scarce a moment past could I forbear~~
To waste thy pains; forlorn of inward chear
~~For loss of inward chear myself to deem~~
So oft I fancy and myselft I deem
A Burthen to the earth whereon I tread
A Poor and useless man & better with the dead
But on a stranded vessel thou wilt dost seem
To waste thy pain, for I can scarce forbear

Stanza XIV, at the top, is developed from versions on 85^{r} and 81^{v}. The deletion in l. 2 is by erasure. Stanza XV, at the bottom, is developed from versions on 81^{v} and 82^{r}; in the second line WW crossed the "l" in "lot."

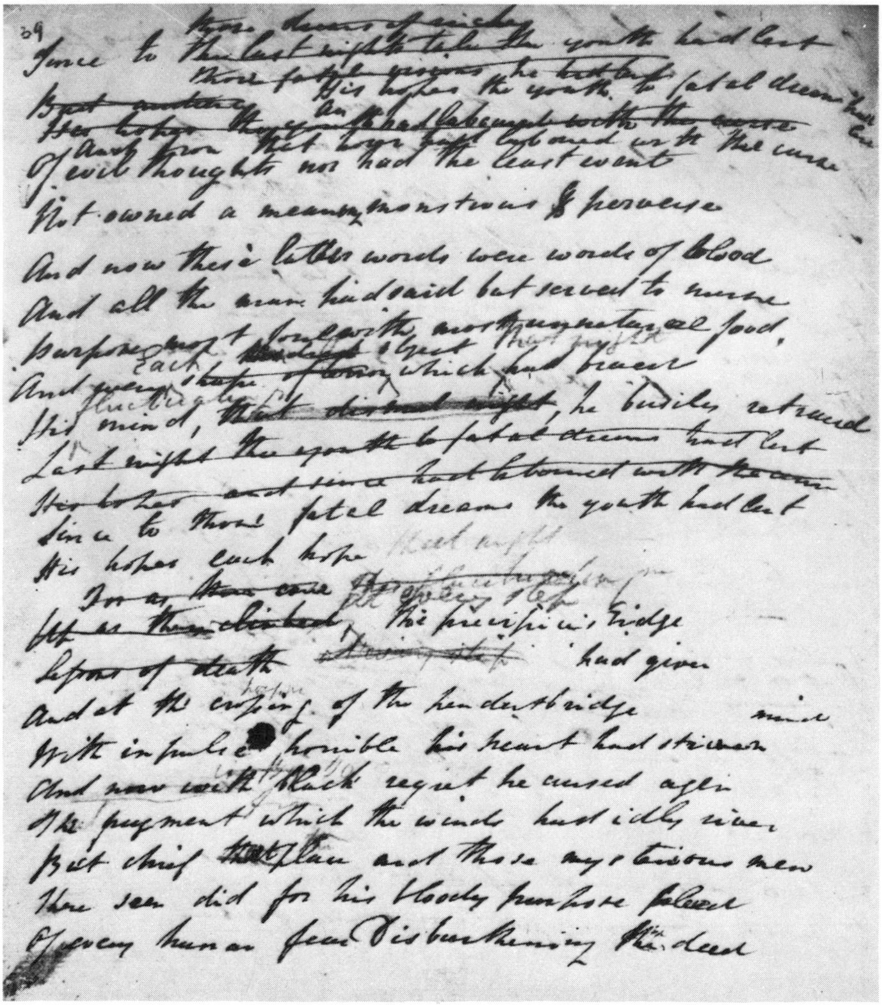

[39v]

those ~~dreams of riches~~
Since to ~~the last nights tale the~~ youth had lent
~~those fatal visions he had lent~~
His hopes the youth to fatal dreams had lent
~~Bad audience~~
An
~~His hopes the youth had laboured with the curse~~
And from that hour had laboured with the curse
Of evil thoughts nor had the least event
Not owned a mean{ing monstrous p{& perverse
And now these lat{ter er words were words of blood
And all the man had said but served to nurse
Purpose most foul with most unnatur{a el food{,
Each {[?] kindred object that night
And every ~~shape of terror~~ ^ which ^ had braced
fluctuating
His ^ mind, ~~that dismal night~~, he busily retraced
~~Last night the youth to fatal dreams had lent~~
~~His hopes and since had laboured with the curse~~
Since to those fatal dreams the youth had lent
His hopes each hope

that night
~~For as they came~~ [?~~this] fluctuat~~ing
at every step
~~Up as they climbed~~ ^ the precipice's ridge
~~Lessons of death~~ ~~at every step~~ had given
passing
And at the crossing of the pendent bridge
mind
With impulse horrible his heart had striven
~~in By~~ [?To]
And ~~now with~~ black regret he cursed agen
Th{at e fragment from which the winds had idly riven
But chief th{e at e} [?the] place and those myster{i ous men
There seen did for his bloody purpose b{p le{a ed
Of every human fear disburthening th{[?] e deed

The first stanza, Stanza XVI, is developed from the version on 82r; except for the phrase "kindred object," all revisions and deletions affecting the last two lines are in pencil, as is the added comma after "food." Between the stanzas are lines revising the opening of the first stanza. The second stanza, Stanza XVII, is developed from versions on 80v and 82v. Revisions and deletions are in pencil except for the deleting lines on "Up as they" and "Lessons of death," the readings "For as they came" and "mind," the first overwriting and the added "i" in l. 7, and the revision in l. 8. One penciled phrase on 40r, facing, "on looking high," may be related.

"At length the stripling [illegible] the work adelayed
The youth
Broke silence; but the [illegible] the summons forbade
"No answer: [illegible] for taken to his rest
The blind man sleeps
[illegible] lay upon the ground
"To groping, towards his throat the other drew
When in that ample cavern farthest bound
Dull sparks revealed a band of flashing hue
And such the import which that phantom bore
That had it long endured his heart had beat no more
No nearer to his bed the stripling drew
But that grim shape as if it fear had been
Soon vanished and anon
In place of those dull sparks a light was seen
That from the cavern's depth came gliding on
And now the legs as of a human form
Appeared; and with that light which dimly shone
Forth-with a glaring figure nearer came
And stopping short upward a [illegible] chief found
About his arm that bled as from a recent wound

[40v]

^} confirmed and to
At length,} ~~the stripling, to~~ the work addressed,
The youth the summons found
Broke silence; but ~~the blind man to the sound~~
;} for
No answer} ~~made~~ betaken to his rest
The blind man sleeping
^~~And fast asleep he~~^lay upon the ground
{, groping,
So, ~~groping~~, towards his throat the other{^ drew
~~cavern's~~
When in that ample ~~dungeons~~ farthest bound
~~Dim~~
~~Red~~^sparks revealed a hand of flesh{ly / y} hue
And such the import which that phantom bore
lived
That had it long endure ~~the man had been~~ ~~no more~~
ad}
his heart h[?]} beat
So nearer to his bed the stripling drew

But that grim shape as if it h ne'er had been
Soon vanished ~~and~~ and anon
In place of those dull sparks a light was seen
That from the cavern's depth came gliding on
And now the legs as of a human frame
{at which
Appeared; and with th{e light ~~that~~ dimly shone
Forth-with a gloomy figure nearer came
And stopping short replaced a kerchief bound
About his arm that bled as from a recent wound

In the first stanza, Stanza XVIII, revisions to "Red" in l. 6, the deletion in l. 9, and the overwriting "had" are in pencil, as is the revision of l. 4 written between stanzas. On 41r, facing, are four lines that incorporate revisions here and represent the only other version of Stanza XVIII in the notebook:

k}
At length confirmed and to the word} addressd
The Youth broke silence but the summons found
No answer for betaken to his rest
[?asleep]
o}
The blind man sleeping [?laup}n] the ground

The second stanza here, Stanza XIX, is the only version in the notebook. The deletions in the first two lines are by erasure.

[42ʳ]

{A
Glad respite did that black {appearance give
When
~~For~~ every inward ~~Ves~~ vessel gan dispart
With ghostly terrors never sent to live
Amid the weakness of a mortal heart
The pendent cutlass and the belt descried
By what faint glare the lantern could impart
Marked out the shape which he before had spied.
His work arranged the man at distance short
deep recess
Passed through the ~~gloomy~~ vault and sought the
upper court.

And gone he left the stripling light of soul
Nor doubting but the hand that vault had shown
Was earthly mid lamp smothering vapours foul
{ion
So fash{[?]ed to his eye by sparkles thrown
{from
On the thick air {by fire-detaining wood
Or ~~sound~~ flint whose sound the wind had made its own

The only surviving versions of Stanzas XX and XXI. The deletion of "For" in Stanza XX is in pencil. The lines visible in the photograph but not transcribed are from WW's 1788 prose fragment, *A Tale*.

[illegible]

With darkness or the shapes of [illegible]

At length he [illegible]

[illegible] with [illegible] eye

Above the [illegible] beheld

Which [illegible] through the crevice shed

Sent to his fluttering heart a momentary dread

At length the open area to explore

For in that vault no second foot appeared

Up to the dungeon's mouth his course he bore.

–The winds were past away, the sky was cleared

Nor did the court or silent walls present

Object or shape whose motion might be feared

Only the crimson moon her lustre shot

With orb half-visible was seen to sink

Leading the storm remains along th' horizon's brink

[42ᵛ]

His ear though startled oft recovering felt
No sound but of the moaning ~~startled~~ wind; his eye
Though rolling inly busy only dealt
~~His ear though often troubled only felt~~
~~cavern~~
~~The low vault to the moaning gust reply~~
~~often~~
~~His sight though inly busy only dealt~~
With darkness or the shapes of Phantasy
At length he rose by irksome thought impelled
~~looking~~ up in restless walk on high
~~And pacing restless~~, with uplifted eye
Above the dungeons roof a star beheld
sparkling ~~light through smallest crevice shed~~
Whose ~~twinkling~~ lustre through ~~the~~ crevice shed
Sent to his fluttering heart a momentary dread

At length the open area to explore
For in that vault no second foot appeared
Up to the dungeon's mouth his course he bore.
—The winds were past away, the sky was cleared
Nor did the court or silent walls present
Object or shape whose motion might be feared
Only the crimson moon her lustre spent
With ~~h~~ orb half-visible was seen to sink
Leading the storms remains along th'horizons brink

The only surviving versions of Stanzas XXII and XXIII. In Stanza XXII the following deletions are in pencil: the second stroke in l. 2, the first stroke in l. 6 and the stroke through "looking" just above, the stroke through the 7/8 interline, and the first stroke in l. 8. In Stanza XXIII the deletion in l. 8 is by erasure.

So back he slunk and to the corner came
Where lay ~~the man~~ his friend devoted to the grave
But in ~~the lifting~~ at his pang to life of his murderous arm
A rumbling noise along the hollow cave
Was heard remote, succeeded by a sound
Of uncouth horror to which echo gave
Such rending peal as made the vault rebound
Nor whelming crash it seemed or shriek or groan
But painful outcry strange to living ear unknown.

~~What groans~~ When came that upon starting from his sleep
The ~~[illegible]~~ Sailor voice, nor could the other make
Reply overcome with shocks of horror deep
And when returning thought began to wake
In sore remembrance of that ~~[illegible]~~ storm dwelt
Such powers as made his youth with terror quake
And all which he that night had seen or felt
~~[illegible]~~ Should like the shapes ~~[illegible]~~ delusion [illegible]
[illegible] that obey the dead or phantom of a dream

That clamorous cry the sailor from his sleep
And to his guide alone at his [illegible]
Who answered not as

[43r]

So back he slunk and to the corner came
his friend
Where lay ~~the man~~ devoted to the grave
{g
as he {ban to lift
But ~~in the lifting~~ of his murderous aim
A rumbling noise along the hollow cave
e}
Was heard remote, succea{ded by a sound
Of uncouth horror to which echo gave
Such rending peal as made the vault rebound
{gr
Nor whelming crash it seemed or shriek or {moan
But painful outcry strange to living ear unknown.

Whence comes
~~What means~~ that uproar starting from his sleep
Sailor
The ~~blind man~~[?] cried, nor could the others make
Reply oercome with shocks of horror deep
And when returning thought began to wake
~~uproar~~
In bare remembrance of that ~~sound there~~ dwelt
~~larum~~
Such power as made his joints with terror quake
And all which he that night had seen or felt
to teem
~~App~~ Showed like the shapes ~~that from~~ delusion loves
Sights that obey the dead or phantom of a dream

e
Th~~at~~ clamour roused the sailor from his sleep
And to his guide alarmed he spake
Who answered not one

The only surviving versions of Stanzas XXIV and XXV. In the first stanza the deletions are in pencil; in the second, the vertical line in the left margin is in pencil, as are the deletion strokes in ll. 5 and 5/6 and the revision of "that" at the foot of the page. The illegible letter in l. 2 and the "s" in l. 3 are deleted by erasure.

More dark and desolate though I had been
Worse storm, no stranger to such nights as these
Yet had I fears from which a life like mine
Might long have rested, and remember well
That as I floundered on disheartened sore
With the rough element and pelting shower
I safe sheltered by the viewless furze
~~the lowliest child of earth~~
~~And~~ saw the lowliest child of earth
~~The tiny glow-worm~~ by the viewless furze
~~The glow-worm sheltered~~
~~Thron his green lodge~~
~~Shine through the rain~~ with undiminished light
Shine through the rain, and strange comparison
Of Envy linked with pity touched my heart
And such reproach of heavenly ordonnance
As shall not need forgiveness

And looking round and on cliff & river
~~[illegible]~~ The moon forth-darting from the darkest [illegible]
A castle ~~[illegible]~~ on either side a wood
Waved in the roaring winds [illegible]
It seemed [illegible] discontented form!
Like some [illegible] on a naked rock
Flapping its wings and [illegible] to the storm
[illegible]
Named [illegible] no [illegible]

[60^{v}]

And looking round ~~and~~ on cliff he view
~~Forth~~ The moon forth-darting then the darkness [?brok]
hung {on
A castle ~~perche~~ {& either side a wood
Waved in the roaring winds tempestuous shoc
{ I
{[?]t seemed thus perch a dim discovered form!
Like some grim eagle on a naked rock
Clapping its wings and wailing to the storm.
Forthwith our {C
~~Our~~ Travellers to that {castle high
Reared their laborious steps, no better mansion nigh

The only version of Stanza I, though it is probably developed from material on 62^{r}, where the stub shows the following beginnings of lines: A / Of / Wav / So / Lik / Clap / For / Rear / / And / Of / ~~Ere~~ / As / Tha / [?She] / I ~~am~~ / Whe / An. Above this stanza are lines from "The road extended o'er the heath," the passage transcribed in *SPP*, p. 296.

[80^v]

~~Dire wishes on th~~h[?]
The hazard
the precipices ridge
~~with~~ wishes dire
{d
Lessons of {[?]eath ~~and~~ had given
passage of [?the ?penden]
u}
Along the perilo[?]}s [~~?br~~] Along the bridge
hazard
With impulse horrible his heart had striven
from {h
~~With~~ black regret his Soul~~d~~ {[?]ad cursed with in
That fragment which the winds had idly riven
had [?work]
And those mysterious men ~~whose hope~~s akin
thought, ~~urge to [?]~~
To his ~~foul dark wish~~ and ~~prompted~~ [?kindre] deed

safe ascending
The plunder ~~his that~~ perchance ~~that cliffs mounting~~ ridge
Lessons of ~~de~~ had not vainly given
~~the~~ trembling
Nor vainly on ~~th~~ unstedfast bridge
the
With impulse horrible his heart had striven
{b
With {[?]lack [?regret] his soul now [?] again
The fragment which the winds had idly riven
The [?th] figures of those dark misterious m
{ed to view
~~R~~eturn{ing ~~and [?urge ?pressd] the~~ return to the [?d]
[?]

Drafts of Stanza XVII here lead toward the version on 39^v. In l. 3 of the first draft, the "d" is deleted by erasure. On 82^v are further drafts toward the most developed version:

And now with black regret he cursed ag~~ain~~
The fragment which the winds had idly riven
This hollow dungeon men
~~But chief the shapes~~ of [?place] and those mysterious
~~In thought still present urged him to the deed~~
And [?] [~~?shal~~] ~~of all~~

On the bare plank ~~that~~ which spanned that roaring flood
How had we fared alone my dog and I
Or mid the darkness of the deafening wood
When at full speed the horseman galloped by
In truth from thee it comes that now I live
My recompence should with this service vie
[illegible]
But little recompense have I to give
Yet something have I stored to meet the hour
When crippling age shall bring the wanderer to his door.
But I am ~~of broken~~ [illegible]
[illegible] content our life [?] to thee
Ere to the grave [illegible]
Our little store may grow by thrifty care
For thee and thine [illegible]
~~Small pittance have I [illegible]~~

And helpless as I am myself and blind
A brother to the earth when or

[81ᵛ]

{O which
{In the loose plank ~~that~~ spanned that roaring flood
How had we fared alone my dog and I
Or mid the darkness of the deafening wood
When at full speed the horseman galloped by

{l
In truth from thee it comes that now I {give
My recompence should with thy service vie
{ ~~B~~
{~~[?]ut I have little but vain thanks to give~~
{so saved
Yet {[?]mething have I ~~kept~~ small
~~Something I have preserves a pittance from little store~~
But little recompense have I to give
Yet something have I stored to meet the hour
{n
When crippling age shall bri { gn the wanderer
to his door.

But I am broken [?deep]
[~~?ch~~]
~~and child~~ ~~we~~ have
I Broken I a in health
And could
~~And if thou art~~ content our ~~life~~ lot to share
my wife & I be
Ere to the grave s ~~we be~~ gone
{ store
Our little {[?] may grow by thrifty care
[?] I see deem
For thee and thine, ~~alas I fondly dream~~
but speak in [?this]
~~Small faculty have I [?spare]~~

and
And helpless as I am myself I deem
A burthen to the earth whereon

Drafts of Stanzas XIV and XV lead to the versions on 39ʳ; a further draft of XV is on 82ʳ, facing. On 85ᵛ are five lines of draft for XIV:

On the loose plank that span'd that roaring flood
How had we fared alone my dog and I
a
Or mid the darkness of ~~that~~ straining wood
by
When at full speed the horseman galloped
~~g~~{
~~If recompense sufficient I coud [?]~~ }~~ive~~
fit recompense & now I cannot [? give]

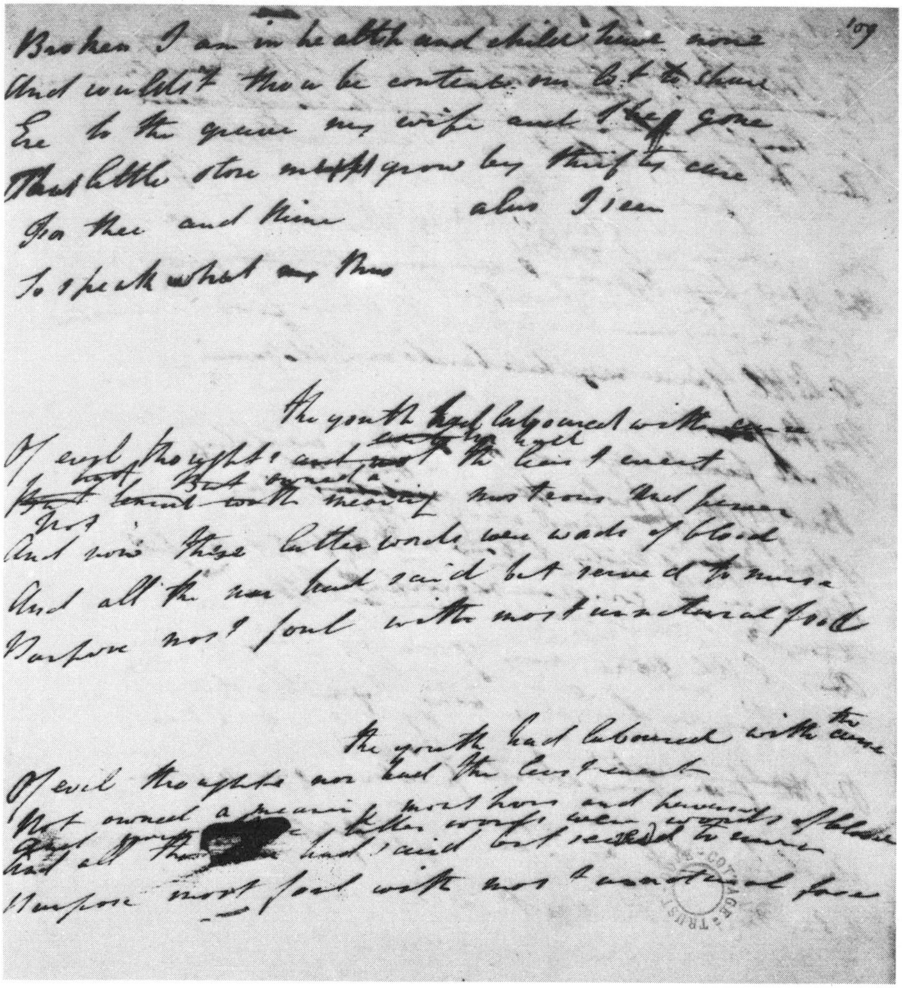
107

Broken I am in health and child have none
And wouldst thou be content on bit to share
Ere to the grave my wife and I be gone
That little store might grow by thrifty care
For thee and thine   alas I can
To speak what my thus

The youth had laboured with care
Of evil thoughts and not the least event
Nor owned But owned a meaning most harsh and perverse
And now these bitter words were words of blood
And all the man had said but served to nurse
Purpose most foul with most unnatural food

The youth had laboured with the care
Of evil thoughts nor had the least event
Not owned a meaning most harsh and perverse
And now these bitter words were words of blood
And all the man had said but served to nurse
Purpose most foul with most unnatural food

[82r]

Broken I am in health and child have none
And coulds't thou be content our lot to share
Ere to the grave my wife and I be gone
{That {ight
{[?Our] little store m{ay grow by thrifty care
For thee and thine alas I seem
To speak what ~~my~~ thus

{h
the youth {[?]ad laboured with curse
~~each~~ nor had
Of evil thoughts ~~and not~~ the least event
~~had~~ ~~But~~ owned a
~~But temed with~~ meaning monstrous and perverse
Not
And now these latter words were words of blood
And all the man had said but served to nurse
Purpose most foul with most unnatural food

the
the youth had laboured with curse
Of evil thoughts nor had the least event
Not owned a meaning monstrous and perverse
And now these latter words were words of blood
{rved
And all the man had said but se{emed to nurse
Purpose most foul with most unnatural [?fare]

Drafts for Stanzas XV and XVI. Stanza XV is developed from 81v, facing; Stanza XVI works toward the version on 39v.

Now gleam'd the Moon; and on a rock [higher] rear'd
A Castle perch'd—on either side a wood
Wav'd solemn to the hollow wind. it seem'd
Like some grim Eagle on a naked rock
Clapping its wings and wailing to the storm

Beyond a spacious [illegible] in distance obscurely seen
A second ridge of wall. its height appeared
[illegible]
The youth with his companion [illegible]
[illegible]
[illegible]
Amid the [illegible]
[illegible]
A burthen of such weight [illegible]

[86^r]

in distance
Beyond a spatious gap obscurely seen
wall ~~whose~~ [~~?~~]
A second ~~ridge of~~ wall its height upreared
And cross this ample areas midway green
The youth with his companion thither steered
The chasm scarce passed he cast his eyes around
a corner tower
And underneath a ~~turret there~~ appeared
wreck strewd
Amid ~~the stone~~ that ~~pile~~ [?th encumbered] green
whose towards [?this] stairs conveyed
[?]
Two armed men ~~who bore with mutual~~ aid
A burthen of such weight as asked their mutual aid

A draft of Stanza IX; other versions are on 87^v, 88^r, 88^v, and 89^r, together with a single line on 90^r: "And other battlements appeared behind." Revisions of l. 1 are in pencil, as are the entire last line and all revisions in ll. 7–8 except "strewd" and the illegible alternate for "mutual." Deletions in ll. 7–8 are in pencil except for those of "pile" and "mutual." Above this stanza is the 1788 description of a castle in a night storm, transcribed above, p. 748.

[87^{v}]

By passage through a broken window made
And to his blind companion standing near
~~Of that appearance mention made~~
One word of such appearance said

Seen thr{e} chasms and fractures there appeared
~~A range of t~~ a second range of battlements behind

~~Which to~~
And towards th a spacious gap his steps inclined

~~A second range of battle~~ment appeared ~~by~~
Of battlement a second range appeared
Across this ample areas midway green
Across this ample areas midway green
The youth his steps undaunted steer
{For [?]
{Or through the chasms and yawning fractures
A second range of battlements [?]

Drafts for Stanza VI leading (like those on 6^{v} and 9^{v}) to the version on 96^{r}, followed by drafts for Stanza IX, of which the most developed versions are on 88^{v} and 89^{r}. In the bottom draft "by" is deleted by erasure.

Dire was the shouting of his voice above his breath
His clashing arms his heart — before him tears
Moved like a shower — as some huge Giant wave
Stalks on with shipwreck covered like a robe
Breaks in his wrath the tall cliffs [illegible]
And covers all the vales with driven spray

along a precipice they wound their way
And as the path conducted they must go
Where a loose plank across a torrent lay
Whose waves sent [illegible]
His hand on the others shoulder close applied
O'er the rude bridge the blind man ~~tottered~~ slow
And when his fear was ended blessed his guide
That passage thus accomplished till they gain
The platform of the cliff [illegible] little space

[illegible]

[88r]

Along a prece{i pice they wound their way
And as the path conducted they must go
Where ~~a~~ a loose plank across a torrent lay
Whose waves sent deafness from the chasm below
His hand on th'others shoulder close applied
O'er the rude bridge the blin[?]{d man tottered slow
And when his fear was ended blessed his guide
That passage thus accomplished ~~till~~ soon they gaind
The platform of {the a cliff {for but little space remained

a spatious [?]
Beyond these chasms and [?fractures] dimly seen
wall its height
A second range of battlements appeared
[?~~thrusting~~] cross
And ~~cross this~~ ample area midway
~~Thither with youth with~~
The youth ~~with~~ his companion thither steers
[?height]
That ~~wall~~ scarce past he looks around
And underneath a turret high [?upreared]
amid the stones [?that] [?piled] [?the]
~~Whose [?heaping]~~ [?fragment ?strewed] th encumber

At the top is work on the heroic poem (no. 2 in *Chronology: EY*), followed by the only surviving version of Stanza II, in the hand of DW, then by additional work on Stanza IX (see note to 86r).

Troth cried the boy well need some favourite girl
Were looked for thus attendance to requite
Poor service 'tis while winds around us whirl
Thus scantily [illegible] to weather out the night
My legs with standing ache to th' very bone
And many hours must pass ere morning light
Be cheerful comrade think thought not alone
[illegible]
[illegible] if here we must sojourn
'Tis time to search
Some more commodious spot where we may sleep till morn

So saying by the hand he led his charge
Through the dark passage of the ponderous keep
That opened to a court of circuit large
Whose walls had scattered many a stony heap
The unimaginable touch of time
Or [illegible] hid with ruin deep
The towers that stately stood, as in their prime,
Though shattered stood of undiminished height
And [illegible] their heads with trees that shook before the [illegible]
Beyond a [illegible] spacious gap in distance seen
A second row of [illegible] battlements appeared
And cross this ample area's midway green
The youth with his attendant thither steered
The [illegible] stair traversed, on a [illegible] around
Beneath a corner tower two men appeared
Who with the wreath that strewed the encumbered ground
A [illegible] in their arms conveyed
— A third behind them brought [illegible]

[88^{v}]

Troth cried the boy well need some favourite girl
Were looked for this attendance to requite
Poor service 'tis while winds around us whirl
roofed
Thus scantly ~~lodged~~ to weather out the night
My legs with standing ache toth' very bone
~~Be chearful~~
And many hours must pass ere morning light
Be cheerful comrade think thou'rt not
~~Come cheerly think thou are not here~~ ^ alone
~~Let's on~~ [?seek] ~~and search~~
~~And let us try~~ if here we must sojourn
Tis time to search
Some more commodious spot where we may sleep till
morn

So saying by the hand he led his charge
Through the dark passage of the pondrous keep
That opened to a court of circuit large
Whose walls had scattered many a stony heap
The unimaginable touch of time
shouldering winds
Or ^ ~~tempests shock~~ had split with ruin deep
{ t
The {[?]owers that stately stood, as in their prime,
Though shattered, stood
(~~For so it seemed~~) of undiminished height
And plumed their heads with trees that shook before the night

Beyond a g spatious gap in distance seen
~~Be chearful~~ [~~?comrade~~]
A second court its battlements upreared
And cross this ample area's midway green
The youth with his attendant thither steered
on a rugged mound
The chasm scarce traversed, ~~as he looked around~~
Beneath a corner tower two men appeared
{c
Who mid the wre{ak that strewed thencumbered ground
A long white burthen in their arms conveyed——
—A third behind them brought and iron bar & spade

Three stanzas are here: Stanza VII, developed from the version on 96^{r}; Stanza VIII, developed from drafts on 89^{v}, 90^{r}, 90^{v}, and 96^{v}; and a version of Stanza IX in which the last five lines differ substantially from those on 89^{r}, facing—the most finished version.

123

Beyond a spatious gap in distance seen
A second wall its battlements upreared
And cross this ample area midway green
The youth with his ~~companion~~ Mortimer thither steered
The chasm scarce passed he cast his eyes around
And underneath a corner tower, appeared,
Two armed men who cross the stones conveyed
A burthen of such weight as asked their mutual aid

'Tis not for me this business to gainsay
A work is doing here which none but they
~~Who [illegible]~~
[illegible]
To some close covert hence we must away
[illegible]
Thus inly to himself the stripling spoke
And by the shadow of the eastern wall
His backward course in cautious silence took
~~[illegible]~~
~~[illegible]~~
Soon had he turned [illegible]
But in a [illegible] shall
[illegible] on a rugged [illegible]

[89r]

Beyond a spatious gap in distance seen
court
A second ~~wall~~ its battlements upreared
And cross this ample area's midway green
attendant
The youth with his ~~companion~~ thither steered
The chasm scarce passed he cast his eyes around
'
And underneath a corner tower appeared
Amid the wreck that strewed th'encumbered ground
Two armed men who cross the stones conveyed
A burthen of such weight as askd their mutual aid

Tis not for me this business to gainsay
A work is doing here which none but they
~~Who dip the hand therein must overlook~~
Thus inly to himself the stripling [?]
To some close covert hence we must away
For work is here which none must overlook
Thus inly to himself the stripling spoke
And by the shadow of the eastern wall
n
His backward course incontine ttly took
~~But in a moment courts & turrets all~~
~~Were In search~~ of i
h
Scarce [?]ad he turned when strait as at the call
But in a moment light was none at all
on a rugged mound

The most developed version of Stanza IX, followed by Stanza X in a version that leads to the one on 38r; on 90r is a line of draft for X:

course
And towards the eastern wall his ~~steps~~ inclined
that

In IX, revisions in ll. 2 and 6 and all of l. 7 are in pencil.

Had sunk asleep each tenant of or haunts the thicket

The nightingale

Was hush'd, and immelodious were the passing breeze

All nature slept & not a sound was heard

To break the solemn midnight calm —. The raven

Mov'd thro the silent waters —

So saying by the hand he led his charge

On through the passage of the gloomy keep

Which opened to a court of circuit large

Flanked with huge towers which at the tempest's sweep

Or unimaginable touch of time

yet stood as in their prime

For so it seemed of undiminished height

[89v]

So saying by the hand he led his charge
On through the passage of the gloomy keep
W} {ich
T{h}at opened to a court of circuit large
Flanked with huge towers which at the tempests sweep
Or unimaginable touch of time

yet stood as in their prime
For so it seemed of undiminished height

A draft of Stanza VIII, leading toward the version on 88v. Above it is work on a heroic poem (no. 2 in *Chronology: EY*). Leaf 90r, facing, contains a further related fragment of draft: "High was the court and large."

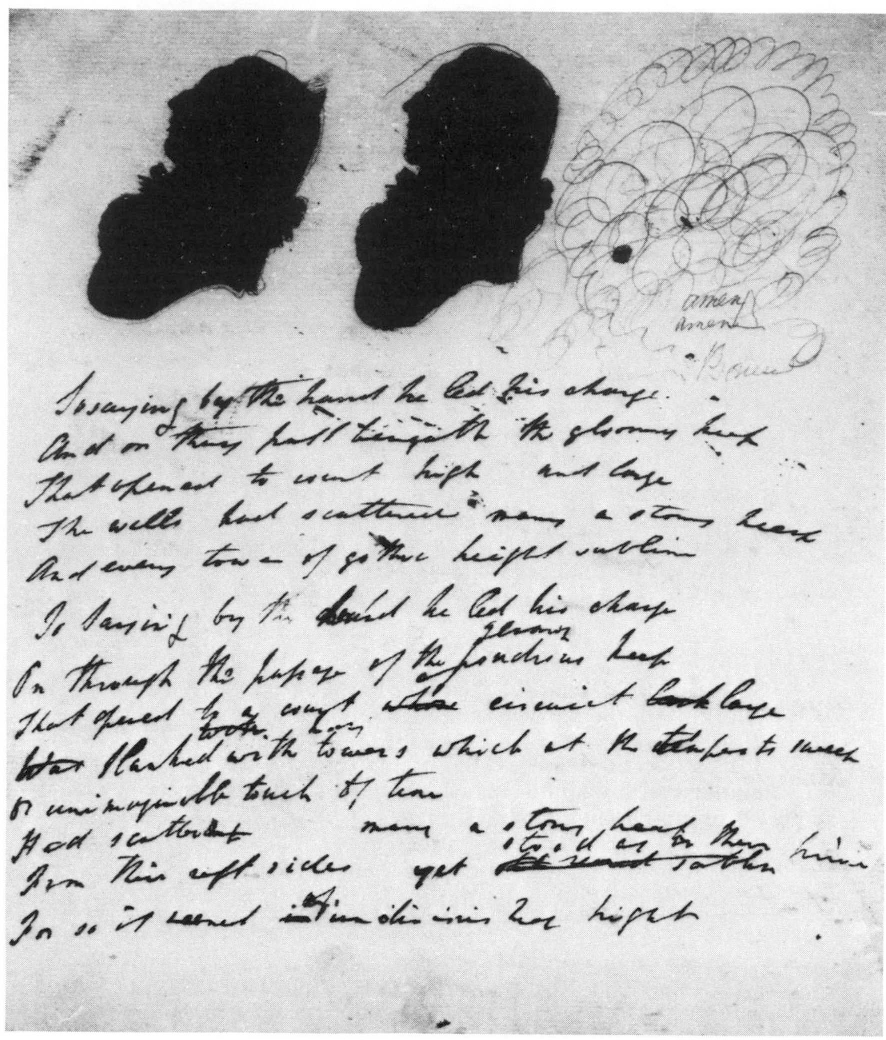

[90[v]]

So saying b {y / u~~t~~} the hand he led his charge
And on they past beneath the gloomy keep
That opened to court high and large
The walls had scattered many a stony heap
And every tower of gothic height sublime

So Saying by the {hand / [?arm]} he led his charge
On through the passage of the [gloomy] pondrous keep
That opened to a court ~~whose~~ [of] circuit ~~lark~~ large
~~Was~~ [~~with~~ [?hoary]] flanked with towers which at the {te / [?wi]} mpests sweep
Or unimaginable touch of time
Had scatter {ed / ~~ing~~} many a stony heap
From their reft sides yet [stood as in their prime] ~~all reared sublime~~
For so it seemed ~~in~~ [of] undiminished hight

Drafts for Stanza VIII, leading toward the version on 88[v]. The "t" in l. 1 was deleted by erasure.

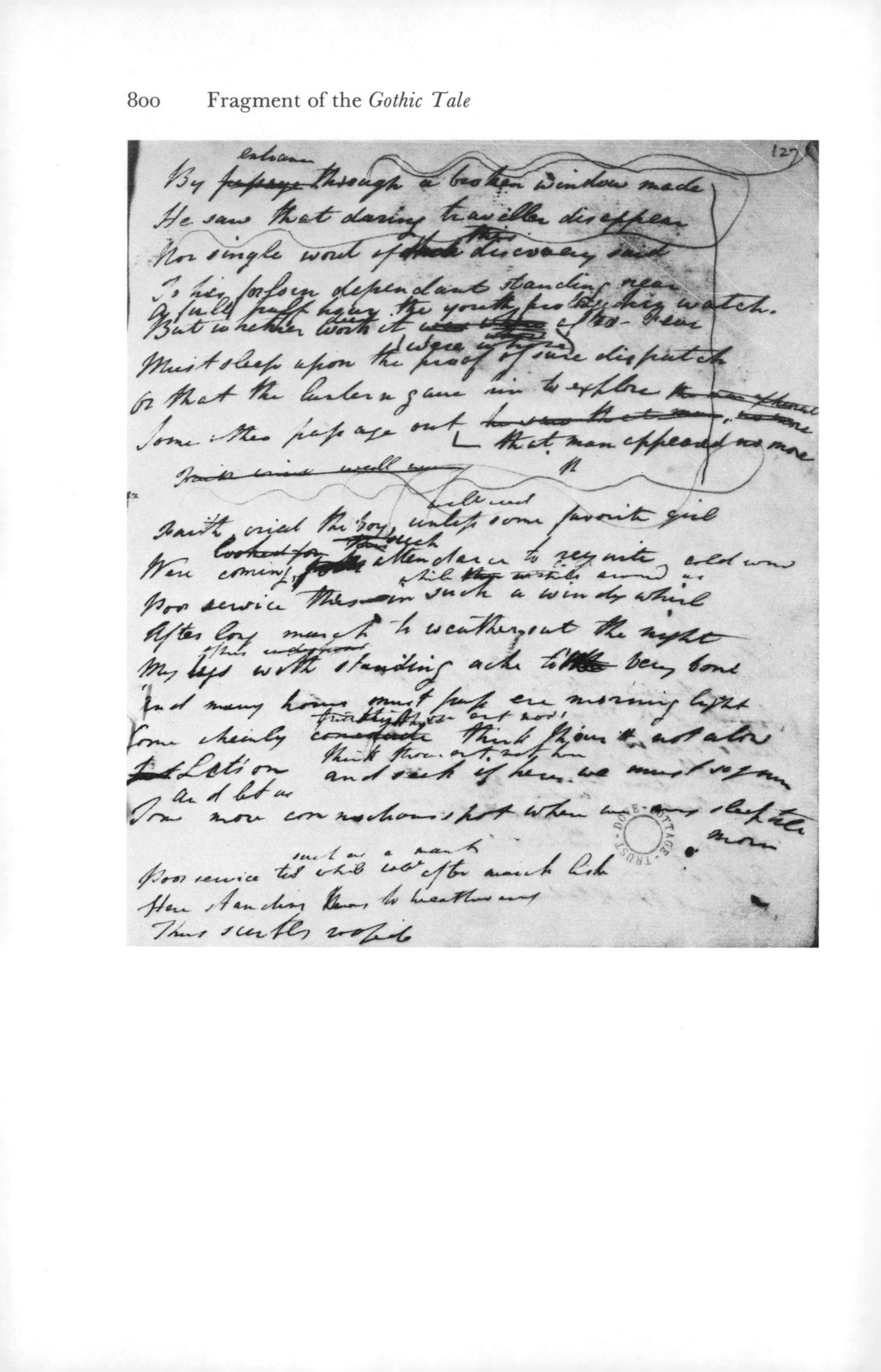

[96r]

entrance
By ~~passage~~ through a broken window made
He saw that daring traveller disappear
{~~such~~ this
Nor single word of {~~the~~ discovery said
To his forlorn dependant standing near
A full half hour the youth prolonged his watch.
{t deed
But whe{hher work it ~~was where~~ after-Fear
~~whose~~
were whose
Must sleep upon the proof of sure dispatch
Or that the lantern gave him to explore ~~the man appeared~~
Some other passage out ~~he saw that man, no more~~
that man appeared no more

Faith cried well ne th
well need
Faith cried the boy, unless some ~~favori~~te girl
such
~~looked for~~ rth} this
Were coming, ~~fo~~[?]} attendance to requite
cold cold wind
while [?~~these~~ ?~~winds~~] around us
Poor service this—in such a windy whirl
After long march to weather-out the night
Thus [?~~indesposed~~] {'th
My legs with standing ache to {~~the~~ very bone
And many hours must pass ere morning light
ou art not
[?friend] ~~think thou~~
Come cheerily ~~comrade~~ think th'our't not alone
think thou art not here
~~Let~~ Let's on and seek if here we must sojourn
And let us
Some more commodious spot where we may sleep till morn
such as a man [?]
Poor service tis while cold
{ [?thus] after march [?like]
Here standing{[?] to weather out
Thus scantly roofed

The most finished version of Stanza VI (drafts are on 6v, 9v, and 87v), followed by a version of Stanza VII which leads to the fuller version on 88v. The wavy horizontal lines are in pencil.

He howled and through his shaggy hair
His green swollen eyes did glimmer glare
Like tapers when the death bells sound
Expiring on the grass-green ground
a deadly glare
giant
And through his [illegible] that stream
That stream'd all wild round his head
Like black clouds wandering in a storm
[illegible] eyes that long blazes
Like meteors in the stormy storm

his black eyebrows were
like a cloud of smoke [illegible]
by the [illegible] round
[illegible] on the [illegible] grass
So saying by the hand he led his charge
[illegible] they pass'd beneath the gloomy keep
That opened to a vault [illegible] large
The walls had scattered many a stony heap
[illegible]
[illegible]
[illegible]
[illegible]

[96^{v}]

So saying by the hand he led his charge
~~So say~~ And on they pass'd beneath the gloomy keep
            to }   { a
That opened [?a] } a court   high {[?a]nd large:
The walls had scattered many a stony heap
        And every tower of gothic height
~~Each tower~~ of ~~undiminished~~ height sublime
                          [~~? ?~~]
[?~~Recorded~~] on its side. The [?whirlwind]
And the [?rent]
~~Showed With cloven sides~~ [?~~carried~~] ~~the whirl~~

Below drafts for the heroic poem (no. 2 in *Chronology: EY*) is a version of Stanza VIII, less finished than the one on 88^{v} (see note to 88^{v}).

sable shadow cast
Death like a Rock his shade has cast
Black o'er the sad vale of my days
I view his giant form aghast
As cold I tread the shadowy maze.
[illegible] on he saw a sullen light
Red as a star but star it could not be
Its station scarcely seemed to reach the height
Of [illegible] full grown or any forest tree
The moon [illegible] that cleft the clouds in twain
Did to the wanderer give a man to see
Who [illegible] the gateway [illegible]
Where but the key-stone seem to link the arch
Else broken, [illegible] in high and perilous march
When the moon [illegible] the black clouds in [illegible]
And o'er the gateway gave the [illegible] to see
A man who [illegible] a tower to [illegible]
And gave him o'er the gateway's ridge to see
A man

[100ᵛ]

And soon, the guid
~~Advancing~~ on he saw a sullen light
Reds as a star but star it could not be
It station scarcely seemed to reach the hight
Of ~~all f~~ oak full-grown or any forest tree
The moon that cleft the cloud in twain
g
Did to the [?m uider] other give a man to see

~~Who crossed~~

walls
[?~~passed~~] a tower
Who [?~~bove~~] the gateway [?~~as] a tower to gain~~
Where but the key-stone ~~linked~~ seen to link the arch
~~on h~~ ~~he on~~ [?]
Else broken, crept ~~along~~ in high an perilous march
severing
When the moon ~~parting~~ the black Clouds in [?]
~~boy~~
And ~~oer~~ the gateway ~~and~~ gave the ~~guide~~ to see
[~~?~~]
A man who onward marched a tower to gain
~~The moon~~
And gave him oer the gateways ridge to see
A man

Below work on the heroic poem (no. 2 in *Chronology: EY*) is a version of Stanza IV, developed in conjunction with that on 101ʳ, facing.

The other powers of the mind ran to wake Reason
sleeping on the Deck. He stood up and like Ch[rist]
stilld the storm. —— He stood before
him on a sudden like what has been
at the altar of a Convent when the moon
looks through the window.

amusing
one Zephyr's breath has wak'd

the rose smiling in sleep.—

Dim in the watry glare

a sullen light
Shed as a star but star it could not be
Tho stationd scarcely seemed to reach the hight
Of full oak full-grown or any forest tree
The bright moon severing the black clouds in twain
The moon shone full & shining deep those sleepy bubbles
And gave another him on the gateways side to see
A man who stretched along a town to gain
The moon shone full ...
Or on the gateway ... could see
A man who towards ... the gentle ... sea

[101r]

a sullen light
Red as a star but star it could not be
s} station
It} scarcely seemed to reach the hight
{tr
Of ~~any full~~ oak full-grown or any forest {[?st]ee
The bright moon severing the black clouds in twain
shind did
The ~~moon shone~~ forth ~~and did~~ those [?dark] [?brighten]
And gave ~~on the~~ him on the gateways ridge to see
stepped along
~~wal~~}
A man who ~~onward~~ [?]} ~~ked~~ a tower to gain
The moon shone forth [?discovering] [?whence] it came
could
As on the gateway ~~top the~~ [?~~guid] to see~~ see
gave
A man who towards gave the guide to see

Below work on the heroic poem (no. 2 in *Chronology: EY*), is a version of Stanza IV, developed in conjunction with that on 100v, facing.

Where were ye nymphs when the remorseless
Closed o'er your little favourites hapless head
For neither did ye mark with solemn dread
In Derwent's shallows the white [illegible]
Pace like a [illegible] through the [illegible]
Of Derwent

So pressing on to reach that antient pile
Forsaken now and subject to the sky
Up through the [illegible] avenue they toil
The [illegible] winds echoing round them fierce and high
When all unlooked for in that lonely place
With furious steed a horseman gallop'd by
[illegible] the [illegible]
Came from the quarter which
and when he saw the day sink down
Into the boundless waters of the sea

[102^{v}]

So pressing on to reach that antient pile
Forsaken now and subject to the sky
~~Up~~ through the [?darkness] [?woods] ~~[—?—]~~ toil
~~Along~~ the ~~sable~~ avenue they toil
~~[?fast]~~ still
The ~~loud~~ wind eddying round them fierce and high
all
When ~~sight~~-unlooked for in that lonely place
With furious steed a horseman galloped by
[—?—]
~~Leaving the quarter~~
Come from the quarter which

Below work on *The Dog: An Idyllium* (*PW*, I, 264) is the only surviving version of Stanza III, left incomplete. The last two lines appear to be contemporary, but do not belong to the *Gothic Tale*.

Appendix II

Argument for Suicide (1797)

Transcription

Argument for Suicide is neatly written in Wordsworth's hand on the recto of the second leaf of a reconstructed folio notebook, DC MS. 13, described in *RC & Pedlar*, pp. 7–8, 79. It is entered at the top of the leaf, below a faint red line.

De Selincourt published the text as XXXI in his Appendix of Juvenilia in *PW*, I, 316. As he observes in his note (p. 375), the "mood and style in which these lines are written recall that of *The Borderers*." On several occasions Rivers inveighs against those who overstress the sanctity of human life (see Introduction, above, pp. 28–29), and in Act IV, Scene ii, he speaks of murder

> saving a poor man, perchance,
> From a ten years' visitation of the stone,
> Or the more gentle mercies of the palsy?
> [IV.ii.176–178]

This thought is echoed in the *Argument for Suicide:*

> Has misery then no friend?—if you would die
> By licence, call the dropsy and the stone
> And let them end you—
> [ll. 9–11]

Argument for Suicide, like the other early materials in DC MS. 13, dates from between late 1796 and the summer of 1797 (see *Chronology: EY*, p. 346).

The repetition of the final line below the poem is in pencil.

Argument for Suicide —}

Send this man to the mine this to the battle
Famish a n} ~~n~~a{g ked beggar at your gates
And let him die by inches—but for worlds
Lift not your hand against him— Live Live on
As if this earth owned neither steel nor arsenic
A rope a river or a standing pool
Live as if you dread the pains of hell, or think
Your corpse would quarrel with a stake—alas
Has misery then no friend?—if you would die
By licence, call the dropsy and the stone
And let them end you—strange it is
And most fantastic are the magic circles
Drawn round the thing called life—till we have learned
To prize it less we ne'er shall learn to prize
The things worth living for.—

The things worth living for

Appendix III

Wordsworth's Notes to *The Borderers*

In *PELY*, in which Wordsworth misdated *The Borderers* a year early, the first of the following notes appears. A manuscript copy of it may be found in DC MS. 151/4, formerly MS. Verse 102(3), comprising a single sheet of white rolled paper, 32.2 by 19.7 centimeters. On one side of the paper, which bears no watermark, is the text of the note in the hand of Mary Wordsworth; on the other side, John Carter has entered a partial list of the contents of *PELY*. The text given below, drawn from *PELY*, is accompanied by an *apparatus* that records all manuscript variants except Mary's miswriting of single letters and her use of ampersands. No variants appear in the later lifetime printings of the note (1845, 1846, 1847, and 1849).

The Fenwick note is reproduced from Edward Quillinan's transcription, the only surviving manuscript, DC MS. 153.

[The 1842 Note]

This Dramatic Piece, as noted in its title-page, was composed in 1795–6. It lay nearly from that time till within the last two or three months unregarded among my papers, without being mentioned even to my most intimate friends. Having, however, impressions upon my mind which made me unwilling to destroy the MS., I determined to undertake the responsibility of publishing it during my own life, rather than impose upon my successors the task of deciding its fate. Accordingly it has been revised with some care; but, as it was at first written, and is now published, without any view to its exhibition upon the stage, not the slightest alteration has been made in the conduct of the story, or the composition of the characters; above all, in respect to the two leading Persons of the Drama, I felt no inducement to make any change. The study of human nature suggests this awful truth, that, as in the trials to which life subjects us, sin and crime are apt to start from their very opposite qualities, so are there no limits to the hardening of the heart, and the perversion of the understanding to which they may carry their slaves. During my long residence in France, while the Revolution was rapidly advancing to its extreme of wickedness, I had frequent opportunities of being an eye-witness of this process, and it was while that knowledge was fresh upon my memory, that the Tragedy of "The Borderers" was composed.

---

sheet headed (To the Printer, the following to be added to the Notes already sent)

1 This] The *rev to* This   title *inserted with no hyphen*   Page,

4 Friends.   *no commas*

5 M.S.,

8 revised *over* res[?] *erased*   care;

8–9 but . . . not *inserted with caret replacing* without

10 has been made *inserted with caret*

11 Characters;

12 Persons *over* ones *erased*

13 *following* change *the word* especially *inserted, then del*   The study of *del, then rewritten*

14 this *rev from* the   truths *with* s *del*   as *inserted with caret*

15–16 from . . . no] from qualities that [that *inserted with caret*] are their very opposites, there are *then rev to 1842*

17 may *inserted with caret*

20 process;

21–22 *no comma, no quotes*

[The Fenwick Note (1843)]

The Borderers a Trajedy. Of this dramatic Work I have little to say in addition to the short printed note which will be found attached to it. It was composed at Race Down in Dorset:re during the latter part of the year 95 & in the course of the following year. Had it been the work of a later period of life it would have been different in some respects from what it is now. The plot would have been something more complex & a greater variety of characters introduced to relieve the mind from the pressure of incidents so mournful. The manners also wd have been more attended to— my care was almost exclusively given to the passions & the characters, & the position in which the persons in the Drama stood relatively to each other, that the reader (for I ~~never~~ had then no thought of the Stage) might be moved & to a degree instructed by lights penetrating somewhat into the depths of our Nature. In this endeavour I cannot think upon a very late review that I have failed. As to the scene & period of action little more was required for my purpose than the absence of established Law & Government —so that the Agents might be at liberty to act on their own impulses. Nevertheless I do remember that having a wish to colour the manners in some degree from local history more than my knowledge enabled me to do I read Redpath's history of the Borders but found there nothing to my purpose. I once made an observation to Sir Walter Scott in which he concurred that it was difficult to conceive how so dull a book could be written on such a subject. Much about the same time, but a little after, Coleridge was employed in writing his Trajedy of Remorse, & it happened that soon after thro' one of the Mr Pooles Mr Knight the actor heard that we had been engaged in writing Plays & upon his suggestion mine was curtailed, & I believe Coleridge's also was offered to Mr Harris Manager of Covent Garden. For myself I had no hope nor even a wish (tho' a successful Play would in the then state of my finances have been a most welcome piece of good fortune) that he should accept my performance so that I incurred no disappointment when the piece was *judiciously* returned as not calculated for the stage. In this judgement I entirely concurred, & had it been otherwise it was so natural for me to shrink from public notice that any hope I might have had of success would not have reconciled me altogether to such an exhibition. Mr C—s play was as is well known brought forward several years after thro' the kindness of Mr. Sheridan. In conclusion I may observe that while I was composing this play I wrote a short ~~essay~~ essay illustrative of that constitution & those tendencies of human nature which make the apparently *motiveless* actions of bad men intelligible to careful observers. This was partly done with reference to the character of Oswald & his persevering endeavour to lead the man he disliked into so heinous a crime, but still more to preserve in my distinct remembrance what I had observed of transition in character & the reflections I had been led to make during the time I was a witness of the changes through which the French Revolution passed.